Futures of
Dance Studies

Futures

Dance St

DANCE

The Danc
dance sch
and incre
intellectua
inclusive,
research,
arts, hum
American
well as sp
Dance Res
the Studie
groups an
States an
and leade

DSA Pr

DSA Ed

CHAIR:

Sanja An

Melissa B

Clare Cr

Hannah

SanSan K

Royona

Linda To

Futures of
Dance Studies

Edited by
SUSAN MANNING, JANICE ROSS,
and REBECCA SCHNEIDER

THE UNIVERSITY OF WISCONSIN PRESS

Publication of this book has been made possible, in part,
through support from the Andrew W. Mellon Foundation

The University of Wisconsin Press
728 State Street, Suite 443
Madison, Wisconsin 53706
uwpress.wisc.edu

Gray's Inn House, 127 Clerkenwell Road
London ECIR 5DB, United Kingdom
eurospanbookstore.com

Printed in the United States of America
This book may be available in a digital edition.

Library of Congress Cataloging-in-Publication Data
Names: Manning, Susan, editor. | Ross, Janice, editor. |
Schneider, Rebecca, editor.
Title: Futures of dance studies / edited by Susan Manning,
Janice Ross, and Rebecca Schneider.
Other titles: Studies in dance history (Unnumbered)
Description: Madison, Wisconsin : The University of Wisconsin Press, [2020] |
Series: Studies in dance history | Includes bibliographical references and index.
Identifiers: LCCN 2019008305 | ISBN 9780299322403 (cloth)
Subjects: LCSH: Dance—Study and teaching. | Dance—Social aspects.
Classification: LCC GV1589 .F88 2020 | DDC 793.307—dc23
LC record available at https://lccn.loc.gov/2019008305

Contents

Illustrations

Acknowledgments

This volume results from a very fortuitous combination of events. The coeditors were at the right career stage at the right institutions to gain the support of the Andrew W. Mellon Foundation for a six-year (2012–18) initiative called "Dance Studies in/and the Humanities." The authors were part of the early-career cohort targeted by the initiative. Coming together for intensive summer seminars (2012–15) and for a publication workshop (2016), the authors learned as much from each other as from the coeditors, and the coeditors learned as much from the authors as from their own peers in the field.

This doesn't mean that we did not benefit from the guest faculty who contributed their insights to the summer seminars: at Northwestern (2012 and 2015) Ann Cooper Albright, Ananya Chatterjea, Susan Cook, Anita Gonzalez, Anthea Kraut, Carrie Lambert-Beatty, Gerald Siegmund, and Priya Srinivasan; at Brown (2013) Mark Franko, Nadine George-Graves, and André Lepecki; at Stanford (2014) Thomas F. DeFrantz, Sherril Dodds, Susan Foster, and Carrie Noland. Norm Hirschy, senior editor at Oxford University Press, returned summer after summer to talk about the process of transforming a dissertation into a book; Suzanna Tamminen, director of Wesleyan University Press, and Mike Levine, former acquisitions editor at Northwestern University Press, also contributed their insights. We heartily thank Jennifer Britton, project assistant for Mellon Dance at Northwestern, who kept all the paperwork flowing.

At the Andrew W. Mellon Foundation we thank Mariët Westermann, Harriet Zuckerman, and Joseph Meisel for their crucial investment in the field. At Northwestern Adrian Randolph, Sarah Mangelsdorf, Holly Clayson, and Wendy Wall provided administrative endorsement, while faculty from several departments—Dance (Susan Lee and Joel Valentin-Martinez), Art History (Jesús Escobar), History (Tessie Liu), Performance Studies (E. Patrick Johnson and Ramón Rivera-Servera), and Theatre (Harvey Young)—contributed in varied ways to the project. At Brown administrative endorsement was provided by Erik Ehn and Patricia Ybarra, while the dance faculty Julie Strandberg, Michelle Bach-Coulibaly, Sydney Skybetter, and Shura Baryshnikov, as well as affiliates in other departments, especially Michelle Clayton (Hispanic Studies and Comparative Literature) and Kiri Miller (Music), supported the postdoctoral fellows and enhanced dance programming on campus. At Stanford Patrice O'Dwyer provided administrative expertise, Martha Langill oversaw compliance, Dean Richard Saller contributed much-appreciated material support, and Theatre and Performance Studies faculty—Peggy Phelan, Jennifer Brody, Harry Elam, and Branislav Jakovljević—contributed to the summer seminar and postdoctoral fellows in residence.

We thank the editorial board for Studies in Dance Studies, a book series initiated by the Society of Dance History Scholars that now continues under the aegis of the Dance Studies Association, especially its former chair Rebecca Rossen. At the University of Wisconsin Press, we thank Raphael Kadushin, Amber Rose, Adam Mehring, Mary Hill, Paul Grant, Casey LaVela, and Katilin Svabek. Huge thanks to Lizzie Leopold, one of our authors who also served as editorial assistant for this volume.

We dedicate this anthology to all those committed to the futures of dance studies.

Futures of
Dance Studies

Introduction

SUSAN MANNING, JANICE ROSS,

and REBECCA SCHNEIDER

Futures of Dance Studies is an outrageously arrogant title. In fact, one editor refused to consider a volume so named because he believed that the title would become meaningless as soon as the volume appeared in print. But we understand the word "futures" differently, because for us, it indicates not only time to come but a very present and even persistent investment, trajectory, dream. We are, in fact, excited about the future of/as dance studies and have used the word "futures" for several reasons that are worth plotting in greater depth at the start.

One sense of "future" that we beckon in the title is literally emergence. At the time of publication all the scholars in this book are early career. These scholars carry the future—indeed, the multiple *futures*, as each essay is different—of dance studies outward into their careers, across their multiple fields. In brief, we have looked for the most rigorous and exciting work by scholars for whom "dance" (in all the ways that word might be conceived) is a focus of study, means of study, method of study, or motivator of study.

A second sense of "futures" is also at play in our title. In financial terms, "futures" are contracts toward future exchange, albeit economic rather than strictly choreographic (though one might make an interesting argument about how choreography and training both "trade in futures" for dance). Of course, trading in futures can be risky, and if risk inheres in this meaning of the term, then we hope that readers and writers in nondance disciplines will risk further engagement in dance just as we hope, simultaneously, that early-career scholars in dance will risk continued congress across disciplines. We fostered an idea of sharing that risk into our futures.

Another dictionary meaning of "future" relates to kinship in the sense of the "not yet" that is betrothal. This might remind us of recent debates in queer theory around utopian futurities that do not rely on either heteronormative or overdetermined reproduction of the capital relation but *gesture* to otherwheres and otherwise. In this sense, *Futures of Dance Studies* can never be over the minute the book hits print! Rather, futures multiply, bend, and even reach back to review the past. Our title thus signifies a good-faith effort toward what we hope will be a fertile multiplication of futures upon futures for the field. Our hope, of course, is that futures will continue to unfold as open, virtual, and full of unexpected possibility.

"Dance Studies in/and the Humanities"

Futures of Dance Studies marks two recent initiatives in the field: the six-year project funded by the Andrew W. Mellon Foundation titled "Dance Studies in/and the Humanities" (2012–18), which directly led to the compilation of this volume, and the 2017 merger of two preexisting dance studies organizations into the Dance Studies Association (DSA), under whose aegis this volume appears. Indeed, we believe that the conjunction of unprecedented support from the Mellon Foundation and the decade-long effort to bring together the Congress on Research in Dance (CORD) and Society of Dance History Scholars (SDHS) are not unrelated developments but reflect the vibrancy of English-language dance studies in the twenty-first century. The essays published here build on the research of several generations of scholars in the field, augmenting, complicating, and amplifying previous research as they question rather than break in radical ways from previous scholarship. *Futures of Dance Studies* heralds the flourishing of the field.

For many years, the Mellon Foundation had funded dance presenters and dance preservation, but dance studies did not come to the foundation's attention until the first decade of the twenty-first century, when program officers recognized the dynamism of performance as a research topic and invited a few selected scholars to their New York headquarters to discuss the state of the field. Thus, Susan Manning found herself seated across the table from Harriet Zuckerman and Joseph Meisel in the summer of 2008, just a few weeks after the annual conference of SDHS, where she had delivered the keynote address at the conclusion of her four-year term as president, tracing the development of dance studies in the United States since the mid-twentieth century. Marking the thirtieth anniversary of SDHS, the program paired her address, "Looking Back," with a plenary panel of advanced graduate students titled "Moving Forward," and their impressive comments on how they envisioned the future of the field were still on her mind during the meeting at the Mellon Foundation.[1] Thus, when Zuckerman and Meisel asked her to submit a proposal for funding, she immediately decided that a field-building initiative should invest in the rising generation of scholars.

This focus on a distinctive career stage suited the funding preferences of the foundation, and so too did the focus on the humanities. Although the foundation has shifted its priorities since then, at the time proposals were divided between the arts and the humanities.[2] Thus, Manning devised a proposal advocating for dance studies within the humanities, a position that accorded with her own career trajectory as a professor triply appointed in English, theater, and performance studies. At her home institution, Northwestern University, the Program in Dance had never enjoyed the level of support accorded the Departments of Theatre and Performance Studies, and she reached out to colleagues at research universities with similar profiles where dance had less institutional recognition than theater and performance. Thus Janice Ross at Stanford and Rebecca Schneider at Brown joined Manning as codirectors, and the three drafted a proposal with two aims: first, to strengthen dance studies at their home institutions by appointing postdoctoral fellows on each campus and, second, to embolden early-career scholars by staging intensive summer seminars where they could share research and strategies for building the field.

The focus on the humanities was intended not only to fulfill the Mellon mandate but also to rethink the place of dance studies within the U.S. academy. Dance studies entered the academy in the mid-twentieth century as a supplement to training in modern dance, and the dance department continues to serve as an essential site for scholarship; even while modern dance remains a central research topic, the field has broadened as the range of techniques taught in U.S. dance departments expanded to include West African dance, jazz and tap, Indian classical dance, salsa, tango, and hip hop, among other forms. Yet scholars pursue research outside dance departments as well. Among the authors published in this volume, less than 30 percent received their graduate training in a dance department, while more than 40 percent received their training in theater and performance studies, and the remaining 30 percent in a range of fields—African diaspora studies, anthropology, English, history, musicology, religion, and visual culture.[3] As the authors' careers developed, nearly half took tenure-stream positions in dance departments, while others found permanent employment outside dance departments—in arts policy and community engagement, Asian studies, musicology, theater, and performance studies.

Indeed, the project's title, "Dance Studies in/and the Humanities," was meant to query the shifting parameters of the field. Seminar participants and guest faculty debated a range of issues: Does the inclusion of dance studies within performance studies undermine the distinctiveness of the field—or open up the possibility of viewing culture as dance? Is it imperative to follow established protocols for research and writing when developing dance as a subfield within adjacent disciplines such as musicology or philosophy? Or is it feasible to alter existing protocols and hence reshape established disciplines? After several decades of research on the body across the humanities, is it possible for dance studies to become an interdiscipline that originates and disseminates this thinking? How should dance studies and studio dance be integrated in the same course, and what are best practices for teaching dance studies to students without intensive dance training? What role might the museum play as a site for scholarship? How can we take advantage of institutional interest in public out-reach and community engagement in order to advocate for dance studies? How can we pursue activism for social justice inside and outside the profession?[4]

Futures of Dance Studies publishes essays from almost all the postdoctoral fellows and around 20 percent of participants from the summer seminars. Not that the editors draw a distinction between the two groups, for all attended together at least two summer seminars, including one devoted to intensive peer review of essays for this volume. In fact, there are many other participants—and applicants—whose research is equally exciting, not to mention their early-career peers who were too advanced or too junior to apply to the project. We believe that the essays published here are just a snapshot of the current land-scape and cannot capture the full panorama. The essays suggest but do not exhaust the dynamism and vitality of the field.

In many ways, the authors published here draw on approaches pioneered by earlier generations of scholars, yet at the same time their research moves in urgent new directions. In contrast to a number of earlier anthologies that emphasized the rupture brought about by the field's embrace of critical the-ory,[5] *Futures of Dance Studies* emphasizes how current research amplifies and complicates earlier research. To the extent that earlier anthologies still drew a distinction between "ethnographic" and "historical" approaches, the essays here seamlessly integrate these methodologies. To the extent that earlier antholo-gies argued for the value of critical theory for dance studies, the essays here assume that value and boldly assert what dance studies contributes to knowl-edge production in adjacent disciplines. Early-career scholars no longer assume the centrality of Paris or St. Petersburg or New York City—the metropoles that largely shaped the canons of what was once called "Western theatre dance." Challenging the nation-state as a stable category for analysis, the essays here trace the impact of globalization—across the Americas, the African dias-pora, the Global South—and the force of the local—in Washington, DC, New Orleans, Vancouver, Québec, Havana, Buenos Aires, Mexico City.

There are many ways to read the essays published here, and the keywords titling the seven sections provide only one possible approach to *Futures of Dance Studies*. Editorial introductions to each section suggest thematic and theoretical links among the essays gathered under "Archives," "Desires," "Sites," "Politics," "Economics," "Virtuosities," and "Circulations." Reading any one section will reveal a rich dialogue around the keyword, and readers may start with the section that interests them most. Yet each essay resonates not only with its near neighbors on the table of contents but also with distant relations in other sections. To assist readers in finding connections not spelled out in the table of contents, what follows is an alternate account of interconnections between the twenty-eight essays that is organized around questions of method and topic. This alternate account further demonstrates the extent to which the current flourishing of the field builds on the insights of previous scholarship, even while the writers published here push beyond the parameters of earlier inquiries.[6]

Extending a method for rich and thick description developed by their predecessors, the writers published here deploy descriptive movement analysis wherever possible.[7] To cite just a few of many examples, Gillian Lipton analyzes a film of Arthur Mitchell's *Rhythmetron* (1971) to recover its critical edge in the era of the Black Arts Movement, while Rachel Carrico works from live performance and video recordings to interpret how choreography by Camille Brown, Jawole Zollar, and Latanya d. Tigner stages second lining in the wake of Hurricane Katrina in New Orleans. Victoria Fortuna analyzes film documentaries on Argentinian choreographers Silvia Vladimivsky and Silvia Hodgers to uncover how their use of tango responds to the national trauma of dictatorship and disappearance. Autoethnography also blends with movement description, as Adanna Kai Jones recalls winin' at the annual West Indian American Day Carnival in Brooklyn, and Alana Gerecke recalls how attending a site-specific work in Vancouver made her attentive to her own movement qualities. Whereas earlier writers at times scripted primers for movement analysis, early-career writers today assume its value for inquiries into the myriad meanings and broadly political resonances of movement.

Yet dance research does not always involve movement that can be experienced directly or viewed onstage or on-screen, and writers here amplify methods for performance reconstruction and performance remains developed by Susan Manning, Rebecca Schneider, and Priya Srinivasan. In fact, Hannah Kosstrin addresses the issue directly of how the scholar's own embodied knowledge inflects her interpretation of archival documents like photographs or reviews, a method she terms "kinesthetic seeing" and proposes is as foundational to the field as descriptive movement analysis. Other writers take up the challenges of analyzing and interpreting dance that leaves scant archival trace. Kathryn Dickason reads medieval manuscripts on King David to trace how changing conceptions of dance over several centuries served political agendas of the era. Joanna Dee Das questions how the scholar might read against the "colonialist archive" of the 1893 World's Columbian Exposition to discern how the "Dahomean dancers," performers hired from the area of present-day Benin, potentially resisted their framing as "primitive." Melissa Templeton pieces together an early work by Les Ballets Jazz, *Jérémie* (1973), and argues that its racial politics paralleled the liberation movement of Québec of the time, when French-speaking Canadians identified with blackness as a way of resisting the dominance of English-speaking Canadians. Elizabeth Schwall too questions how to read sparse archival evidence for dances staged by the Conjunto Nacional de Danza Moderna in Cuba in the early 1970s, arguing for speculation as a method to recover possible political meanings in works by Eduardo Rivero, Gerardo Lastra, and Víctor Cuéllar.

Among earlier scholars, descriptive movement analysis supported a sharp focus on the choreographic work as the object for study. More recently, scholars have challenged conventional definitions of choreography,[8] and authors published here extend their challenge in varied directions. First is a call to take seriously the intermedial dimensions of theatrical dance, as Daniel Callahan does in analyzing how Agnes de Mille and Justin Peck differently interpret the gender and sexual dissidence of Aaron Copland's *Rodeo* and as Royona Mitra does in analyzing how Sonia Sabri's and Aakash Odedra's costuming choices inform their staging of British brownnesses. Directing attention away from the choreographer, Anusha Kedhar calls for heightened attention to the dancers' experience, especially of physical injury and economic precarity, in a profession governed by neoliberal economics. Ariel Osterweis also focuses on the dancers' experience in probing how and why Yve Laris Cohen, Narcissister, and John Jasperse eschew virtuosity in performance. And Laura Karreman focuses on breath as an underexamined dimension of dance and choreography.

Other writers use movement analysis to illuminate the dynamics of political protest and economic infrastructure, turning their focus away from the theatrical stage. Clare Croft demonstrates how Jill Johnston used language and physical action to disrupt a 1971 gathering of writers and activists, including Norman Mailer and Germaine Greer, and to embody lesbian "as not just an identity, but a strategy." Natalie Zervou analyzes how dancers in Athens joined hands and walked backward to protest cuts in arts funding brought about by the Greek financial crisis. Sarah Wilbur looks at how a single institution, Dance Place in Washington, DC, is sustained through the embodied infrastructure of its staff, students, and supporters. Lizzie Leopold probes how the "choreographic commodity," works licensed by an elite tier of choreographers to companies globally, reinforces "the raced and classed implications" of the category of high art.

The turn away from the theatrical stage also has resulted in heightened attention to the museum, the exhibition, and the choreographic object, as evidenced in a spate of recent performances and exhibitions on dance in museums.[9] Challenging the assumption that dance entered the museum only in the late twentieth and early twenty-first centuries, Amanda Jane Graham recovers an earlier moment in the late 1930s, when Grant Hyde Code established the Dance Center at the Brooklyn Museum. Giulia Vittori examines how Virgilio Sieni's *Vangelo secondo Matteo* (2014) composes gestures and poses in tableaux that are neither dance nor painting but somehow both. And VK Preston interprets a wooden sculpture, *Turning Tables* (2010), by First Nations artist Jordan Bennett as a response to the "imagined dances" of seventeenth-century French travel writer Marc Lescarbot.

That so many of the authors published here address questions of racialization points to another conversation instigated by earlier scholars that the current generation complicates and continues. Richard Long, Brenda Dixon Gottschild, John Perpener, Jacqui Malone, Nadine George-Graves, and Thomas F. DeFrantz all highlighted the complexities of black dance in the United States, while Susan Manning and Anthea Kraut followed their lead and drew attention to how US dance staged whiteness in relation to blackness. Other scholars in turn moved away from the binary of blackness and whiteness, exploring the racialization of Asian and Asian American bodies (Srinivasan, Chatterjea, O'Shea, Kwan, Wong), Latin American and Latinx bodies (Savigliano, Rivera-Servera, Garcia, Blanco Borelli), and Indigenous and Native bodies (Shea Murphy) in a global era. At issue in this literature is how the racialized dynamics of dance differ from one nation to another.

In *Futures of Dance Studies* authors take previous inquiries in new directions. Rebecca Chaleff proposes a radical rereading of how *Giselle* constructed the whiteness of ballet in an era of imperialism. Jasmine Johnson proposes that the objectification of black female sexuality in hip hop lyrics coexists with "the potential for pleasure" and "subversive power." Heather Rastovac-Akbarzadeh examines how Western spectators see themselves as saviors of Iranian émigré dancers like Afshin Ghaffarian even while overlooking the West's complicity in creating the conditions that push dancers into exile. Hentyle Yapp documents the differing ways Asian and Western audiences perceive contemporary global dance by Tao Ye and in so doing proposes a new way to conceptualize the racialized body in dance. Emily Wilcox recovers the transnational career of Choe Seung-hui, a Korean-born dancer who developed dance modernism first in relation to Japanese models and then solidified her approach in North Korea and the People's Republic of China, a career that points toward the significance of circulation within the Global South. Jose Reynoso calls for the global turn in Anglophone dance studies to engage dance studies in the Global South, highlighting the work of the Centro Nacional de Investigación, Documentación e Información de la Danza José Limón in Mexico City.

In many ways, this volume marks the longing for a home for dance studies that, like an imagined future, no longer or has never existed as a stable site. Whether approached via the keywords in the table of contents and read in the order noted above or in another sequence, the essays here reveal a matrix of theory, method, and topic that demonstrates the dynamism of the field. We invite you to read these essays in an order of your own choosing and thus join us as a collaborator in helping to shape a prospective view of dance studies. The fluid sequencing is a way of making sense that, like the essays themselves, creatively rethinks newness while calling into question the pasts of dance studies and disciplinary structures. This new generation of scholars challenges these pasts—the traditions, histories, and longing for continuities—that marked so much earlier dance scholarship. In so doing, they offer a multitude of potentialities for how to narrate relationships between pasts, present, and, always, futures in the field.

Notes

1. Randy Martin introduced panelists Harmony Bench, Lauren Erin Brown, Kate Elswit, P. Kimberleigh Jordan, Katherine Profeta, and Christina Fernandes Rosa. See Manning's (2008) keynote and Martin's (2008) introduction and compilation of the panelists' remarks.

2. Another initiative that emerged from conversations the Mellon Foundation held with scholars in the field is the Mellon School of Theater and Performance Research at Harvard, directed by Martin Puchner since 2010. An example of Mellon's more recent approach to integrating arts and humanities funding is the Center for Ballet and the Arts at New York University, founded in 2014 and directed by Jennifer Homans.

3. These percentages are roughly comparable to the disciplinary training for accepted participants in "Dance Studies in/and the Humanities": of the 101 participants, 10 of whom were postdoctoral fellows, 28 percent did graduate training in dance-specific programs (Ohio State, Temple, UCLA, UC-Riverside), while 36 percent did graduate training in theater and performance studies (Berkeley, New York University, Northwestern, Stanford, the University of Texas at Austin, plus programs in Great Britain and Europe). The remaining 36 percent trained in a diverse range of fields. See the project website at www.mellondancestudies.org for brief bios of all participants.

4. For an edited version of one conversation, see Bernier-Solomon (2013).

5. Fourteen anthologies published over a fourteen-year period from 1993 to 2007 demonstrate the rhetoric of rupture. See Thomas (1993, 1997), Foster (1995, 1996), Morris (1996), Goellner and Shea Murphy (1995), Desmond (1997, 2001), Buckland (1999, 2006), Doolittle and Flynn (2000), Thomas and Ahmed (2004), Lepecki (2004), Franco and Nordera (2007). More recently, Oxford University Press has published a series of

handbooks that present the best new research in a range of subfields, commissioned by Norm Hirschy.

6. This volume includes more case studies of theatrical dance than of social and popular dance. For research on social and popular dance see Dodds (2011). Dodds (2019) provides a balanced overview of the many subfields within dance studies.

7. Predecessors include Susan Foster (1986), Lynn Garafola (1989), Cynthia Novack (1990), Ann Cooper Albright (1997), Sally Banes (1998), Linda Tomko (1999), and Janice Ross (2007).

8. The essays collected in Foster (2009) show how scholars have unsettled conventional understandings of "choreography."

9. Two edited volumes, Lepecki (2012) and Franko (2017), suggest the overlap between visual culture and dance over the last decade.

Works Cited

Albright, Ann Cooper. 1997. *Choreographing Difference: The Body and Identity in Contemporary Dance.* Middletown, CT: Wesleyan University Press.

Banes, Sally. 1998. *Dancing Women: Female Bodies on Stage.* London: Routledge.

Bernier-Solomon, Noémie, ed. 2013. "Inside/Beside Dance Studies: 2013 Mellon Summer Seminar Roundtable." *Dance Research Journal* 45, no. 3: 5–28.

Blanco Borelli, Melissa. 2016. *She Is Cuba: A Genealogy of the Mulatta Body.* New York: Oxford University Press.

Buckland, Theresa J., ed. 1999. *Dance in the Field.* New York: St. Martin's Press.

———, ed. 2006. *Dancing from Past to Present: Nation, Culture, Identities.* Madison: University of Wisconsin Press.

Chatterjea, Ananya. 2004. *Butting Out: Reading Resistive Choreographies through Works by Jawole Willa Jo Zollar and Chandralekha.* Middletown, CT: Wesleyan University Press.

DeFrantz, Thomas F., ed. 2002. *Dancing Many Drums: Excavations in African American Dance.* Madison: University of Wisconsin Press.

DeFrantz, Thomas F., and Anita Gonzalez, eds. 2014. *Black Performance Theory.* Durham, NC: Duke University Press.

Desmond, Jane, ed. 1997. *Meaning in Motion: New Cultural Studies of Dance.* Durham, NC: Duke University Press.

———, ed. 2001. *Dancing Desires: Choreographing Sexualities on & off Stage.* Madison: University of Wisconsin Press.

Dodds, Sherril. 2011. *Dancing on the Canon: Embodiments of Value in Popular Dance.* New York: Palgrave Macmillan.

———, ed. 2019. *Bloomsbury Companion to Dance Studies.* London: Bloomsbury Academic.

Doolittle, Lisa, and Anne Flynn, eds. 2000. *Dancing Bodies, Living Histories: New Writings about Dance and Culture.* Banff, Alberta: Banff Centre Press.

Foster, Susan Leigh. 1986. *Reading Dancing: Bodies and Subjects in Contemporary American Dance.* Berkeley: University of California Press.

————, ed. 1995. *Choreographing History*. Bloomington: Indiana University Press.

————, ed. 1996. *Corporealities: Dancing Knowledge, Culture and Power*. Bloomington: Indiana University Press.

————, ed. 2009. *Worlding Dance*. New York: Palgrave Macmillan.

Franco, Susanne, and Marina Nordera, eds. 2007. *Dance Discourses: Keywords in Dance Research*. London: Routledge.

Franko, Mark, ed. 2017. *The Oxford Handbook of Dance and Reenactment*. New York: Oxford University Press.

Garafola, Lynn. 1989. *Diaghilev's Ballets Russes*. New York: Oxford University Press.

Garcia, Cindy. 2013. *Salsa Crossings: Dancing Latinidad in Los Angeles*. Durham, NC: Duke University Press.

George-Graves, Nadine. 2010. *Urban Bush Women: Twenty Years of African American Dance Theater, Community Engagement, and Working It Out*. Madison: University of Wisconsin Press.

Goellner, Ellen W., and Jacqueline Shea Murphy, eds. 1995. *Bodies of the Text: Dance as Literature, Literature as Dance*. New Brunswick, NJ: Rutgers University Press.

Gottschild, Brenda Dixon. 1996. *Digging the Africanist Presence in American Performance: Dance and Other Contexts*. Westport, CT: Greenwood Press.

Kraut, Anthea. 2008. *Choreographing the Folk: The Dance Stagings of Zora Neale Hurston*. Minneapolis: University of Minnesota Press.

————. 2016. *Choreographing Copyright: Race, Gender, and Intellectual Property Rights in American Dance*. New York: Oxford University Press.

Kwan, SanSan. 2013. *Kinesthetic City: Dance & Movement in Chinese Urban Spaces*. New York: Oxford University Press.

Lepecki, André, ed. 2004. *Of the Presence of the Body: Essays on Dance and Performance Theory*. Middletown, CT: Wesleyan University Press.

————, ed. 2012. *Dance: Documents of Contemporary Art*. Cambridge, MA: MIT Press.

Long, Richard. 1989. *The Black Tradition in American Dance*. New York: Rizzoli.

Malone, Jacqui. 1998. *Steppin' on the Blues: The Visible Rhythms of African American Dance*. Urbana: University of Illinois Press.

Manning, Susan. (1993) 2006. *Ecstasy and the Demon: The Dances of Mary Wigman*. Minneapolis: University of Minnesota Press.

————. 2004. *Modern Dance, Negro Dance: Race in Motion*. Minneapolis: University of Minnesota Press.

————. 2008. "Looking Back." In *Proceedings of the Society of Dance History Scholars*, 1–9.

Martin, Randy. 2008. "Moving Forward." In *Proceedings of the Society of Dance History Scholars*, 10–25.

Morris, Gay, ed. 1996. *Moving Words: Re-writing Dance*. London: Routledge.

Novack, Cynthia. 1990. *Sharing the Dance: Contact Improvisation and American Culture*. Madison: University of Wisconsin Press.

O'Shea, Janet. 2007. *At Home in the World: Bharata Natyam on the Global Stage*. Middletown, CT: Wesleyan University Press.

Perpener, John. 2001. *African-American Concert Dance: The Harlem Renaissance and Beyond*. Urbana: University of Illinois Press.

Rivera-Servera, Ramón H. 2012. *Performing Queer Latinidad: Dance, Sexuality, Politics*. Ann Arbor: University of Michigan Press.

Ross, Janice. 2007. *Anna Halprin: Experience as Dance*. Berkeley: University of California Press.

Savigliano, Marta. 1995. *Tango and the Political Economy of Passion*. Boulder, CO: Westview Press.

Schneider, Rebecca. 2011. *Performing Remains: Art and War in Times of Theatrical Reenactment*. London: Routledge.

Shea Murphy, Jacqueline. 2007. *The People Have Never Stopped Dancing: Native American Modern Dance Histories*. Minneapolis: University of Minnesota Press.

Srinivasan, Priya. 2012. *Sweating Saris: Indian Dance as Transnational Labor*. Philadelphia: Temple University Press.

Thomas, Helen, ed. 1993. *Dance, Gender and Culture*. New York: St. Martin's Press.

———, ed. 1997. *Dance in the City*. New York: St. Martin's Press.

Thomas, Helen, and Jamilah Ahmed, eds. 2004. *Cultural Bodies: Ethnography and Theory*. Oxford: Blackwell Publishing.

Tomko, Linda. 1999. *Dancing Class: Gender, Ethnicity, and Social Divides in American Dance, 1890–1920*. Bloomington: Indiana University Press.

Wong, Yutian. 2010. *Choreographing Asian America*. Middletown, CT: Wesleyan University Press.

———, ed. 2016. *Contemporary Directions in Asian American Dance*. Madison: University of Wisconsin Press.

Archives

In one way or another, all the essays in this section reflect on the relations between archives and embodiment. How is it possible for scholars to research the embodied dimensions of dance within archives? Are tools specific to dance studies required, or simply an attention to details in archival sources that other scholars have overlooked? How might archives constructed by spectators from dominant cultures reveal the embodiment of dancers from subordinated cultures? How does the twenty-first-century turn toward the digital reconfigure our understanding of both archives and embodiment?

In "Kinesthetic Seeing: A Model for Practice-in-Research" Hannah Kosstrin proposes a dance-specific methodology for archival research, what she calls "kinesthetic seeing" and what others have called the "bodily archive" (Srinivasan 2012, 71) or "theories in practice" (Rivera-Servera 2012, 18). Kosstrin demonstrates how she used her own dance training—both in Graham technique and in Laban Movement Analysis—to recover the choreographic signature of Anna Sokolow, even and especially for works not documented on film. Well aware of recent critiques of Laban—his and his disciples' claims of universality and his own support of National Socialism—Kosstrin argues nonetheless that his concepts offer invaluable tools for understanding works created in the wake of midcentury modernism. Offering a step-by-step analysis of the male duet from Ohad Naharin's *Decadance* (2000), Kosstrin layers Laban's concepts with sociopolitical insights to read the dance in context. While recognizing the temporal and cultural limits of Laban's systems, she proposes "kinesthetic seeing" as a research methodology broadly applicable across the humanities.

Kathryn Dickason's research method for "King David in the Medieval Archives: Toward an Archaic Future for Dance Studies" is in contrast to Kosstrin's dance-specific methodology. Quite simply, Dickason asks new questions about the surviving manuscripts and illustrations of King David, the

Old Testament monarch who celebrated his army's recovery of the Ark of the Covenant with a festive dance. Tracing medieval imagery of King David's dance from the fourth through the fourteenth century, Dickason demonstrates the changing political functions of medieval dance. First, early Christian leaders "depaganized the dance of David" in order to distance his devotion from Roman spectacle and entertainment. Then theologians created a typology between David's holy dance and Christ's passion, an association that reinforced prejudice against Jews. Finally, during the years of the Crusades, images of David's dance cast Muslims as subordinate peoples, even while crusaders in Jerusalem enjoyed entertainments by Islamic dancers. In the end, Dickason's attention to dance in the medieval archives challenges the standard historiography that locates the origins of Western theater dance in the Renaissance. On the contrary, Dickason suggests, the dynamics of inclusion and exclusion, "politics and pleasure, appropriation and assimilation" have marked dancing bodies centuries earlier than scholars have recognized.

Like Dickason, Joanna Dee Das examines overlooked sources in the archives. In "Dancing Dahomey at the World's Fair: Revising the Archive of African Dance," Das reassesses the evidence of reviews, photographs, and publicity for the 1893 World's Columbian Exposition in Chicago and the 1894 California Midwinter International Exposition (known as the Midwinter Fair) in San Francisco for "embodied traces" of the dancers hired to perform at the Dahomey Village, featured at both fairs. Contrasting, even contradictory views of the performers emerge from what Das terms a "colonialist archive" and point toward the dancers' agency in resisting their commodification as "primitive peoples." Equally consequential are the ways that subsequent artists—notably, Bert Williams and George Walker in their 1902 musical *In Dahomey* and choreographer Sammy Lee in Jerome Kern and Oscar Hammerstein's 1927 musical *Show Boat*—made reference to the Dahomean dancers, vivifying the convergence and divergence between African and African American dance styles. Thus, Das suggests, the Dahomean dancers embodied an African diasporic presence in American performance at a time when colonialist assumptions dominated US culture.

Whereas both Dickason and Das draw new conclusions from existing archival sources, Gillian Lipton helped create the archive that she mines in "Critical Memory: Arthur Mitchell, Dance Theatre of Harlem, and the Rise of the Invisible Dancers." Lipton assisted Mitchell in organizing his archive; thus, oral history with the artist is one of many sources for her reappraisal of the early years of Dance Theatre of Harlem. Interestingly, Lipton deploys the Foucaultian concept of the archive as "the system of rules that control the discourse" in her analysis, positing the whiteness of ballet as part of its discourse before

Mitchell proved the association wrong in his ascent as a dancer at the New York City Ballet. After the assassination of Martin Luther King Jr., Mitchell became tired of his status as an exception and so resolved to found a company for "my own people." Reading early publicity for the company and Mitchell's choreography for *Rhythmetron* (1971), Lipton shows how Dance Theatre of Harlem shifted the terms of ballet's discourse. In so doing, she adapts Houston Baker's concept of "critical memory" and Jacques Rancière's notion of the "distribution of the sensible" to illuminate Mitchell's new assemblage of ballet and blackness.

Like Lipton, Laura Karreman looks to French philosophy as a research method for dance studies. For Karreman, the philosopher most relevant for her inquiry into "breathing matters" in her chapter, "Breathing Matters: Breath as Dance Knowledge," is Luce Irigaray. Irigaray's writings about breath "as an ethical gesture that offers a fundamental possibility for compassion and understanding" provides a starting point for Karreman's analysis of the centrality of breath in performance and in motion-capture technology. Describing a duet between Anne Teresa De Keersmaeker and flutist Chryssi Dimitriou, *My Breathing Is My Dancing* (2015), Karreman relies on her own embodied presence as a spectator, while she relies on the internet for access to experimental digital works, such as Thecla Schiphorst and Susan Kozel's work designed for wearable technology, titled *exhale* (2007). In Karreman's essay, the archive in both conventional and Foucaultian senses disappears in an era when digital technology prioritizes embodiment.

In one sense, Karreman's essay circles back to Kosstrin's, for she notes the absence of an analytical variable for breath in Laban's systems and, in fact, argues that computer animations of human movement that rely on Laban's systems must add a facsimile for breath in order to appear truly lifelike. If Kosstrin suggests that a dance-specific methodology potentially contributes to inquiries across the humanities, Karreman suggests that contemporary digital culture already relies on dance-specific conceptions to archive human movement. Taken together, the essays in this section point toward the wide range of approaches to archives and embodiment in *Futures of Dance Studies*.

Kinesthetic Seeing

A Model for Practice-in-Research

HANNAH KOSSTRIN

Flipping through an album in the archives of the Sokolow Dance Foundation, I notice a photograph of Anna Sokolow dancing. I feel her Martha Graham–trained spiraling torso with my back muscles immediately. Sokolow danced in Graham's company in the 1930s, and this picture evidences Graham's kinesthetic imprint on Sokolow's bodily practices. Sokolow dips her right shoulder down as tension between her scapulae pulls her left elbow skyward; she looks beyond her raised elbow, and her neck rotation completes the spiral. Having practiced this movement combination in Graham technique classes, I fit my physique to match hers. I realize the softness in Sokolow's hands results from her upper back's and abdominals' concentrated efforts, confirming the opposing tensions that mark Graham's style. Based on my knowledge of how Sokolow used Graham's codified vocabulary in her choreography, I deduce what movements might precede or follow the arrest in this photograph. My visual-kinesthetic identification of Sokolow's spiral results from participating in a shared history of practicing Graham technique that allows me to read the photograph in this manner. I describe Sokolow's physicality in this archival image through what I am calling "kinesthetic seeing," a modality in which researchers recognize movement in other people's bodies that they have practiced in their own. When I see kinesthetically, I tap my vocabularies of practice to mobilize my empathetic relationship to a dance and describe how it unfolds (Foster 2011b, 174–75), taking care to acknowledge how dancers' subjectivities differ from mine (Hartman 1997; Croft 2015, 30).

I focus this essay on using kinesthetic seeing for archival research and argue that kinesthetic seeing is a modality that dance studies contributes to humanities research protocols. Although widely utilized (Srinivasan 2012, 67; Elswit 2014, xxiii), kinesthetic seeing has not yet been generalized and distinguished as a key research approach in dance studies within an academy that often lacks language to analyze bodies and views embodied knowledge with suspicion.[1] By employing kinesthetic seeing, I undertake what I call practice-in-research, or PiR, a dynamic research modality integrating somatic knowledge with primary-source evidence in dance scholarship. With PiR I name a long-exercised research practice in which dance scholars use kinesthetic analytical tools to insert themselves into their inquiries by training in a form under investigation or rendering dances from archival evidence (Novack 1990; Sklar [1991] 2001a, 2001b; Ness 1992; Albright 2007, 2010; Hahn 2007; George-Graves 2010; McCarren 2013).

Kinesthetic seeing in dance is akin to close reading in literature: it is a foundational method for the discipline, and everyone does it their own way based on their training. It prepares researchers to parse subtle changes that code movement patterns within genres, geographical locations, and historical contexts and clarify characteristics of dance forms as they circulate. In an interdisciplinary field where scholars employ multiple modalities, naming this dance-based research tool establishes dance studies as a discipline with transferable research methods. Dance studies' analytical focus on embodied knowledges as quarries for evidence about the human condition distinguishes it from adjacent fields (Blanco Borelli 2016, 423, 438n6). PiR reinforces dance studies' disciplinary investments.

PiR engenders nuanced language for critical analysis by making practice part of the evidence gathering instead of part of the outcome. It is inspired by, but distinct from, practice-as-research, or PaR, in which researchers ask and answer questions through their studio practices (Nelson 2013). PaR produces an art product as the nexus of knowledge production instead of or alongside a written document. PaR practitioner Robin Nelson asserts that performance-based PaR processes rely on transferring knowledge through kinesthetic, not verbal, execution (2006, 107). PiR is a scholarly corollary to PaR or to practice-led research: in PiR the scholarly inquiry leads the research, resulting in written scholarship, and the practice informs the analysis but is neither the inquiry's driving force nor the outcome. PiR retains PaR's reflexive inquiry (Nelson 2006, 112). PaR asks: How do my research practice's component parts interact and manifest (Midgelow 2017)? PiR in general and kinesthetic seeing in particular similarly lead researchers to think through a dance practice's kinesthetic logics to produce written analysis.

In dialogue with cultural studies analyses of gender, race, class, geopolitics, and spectatorship, kinesthetic seeing engenders an ethnographic approach to the archive, that is, a manner of attending to evidence that examines positionality and power to center dancing in historical investigations (Dirks 2002; Burton 2005; Stoler 2009; Srinivasan 2012). Historian Joan Wallach Scott (1992) argues that considering experience as evidence opens spaces in the historical record for subordinate subject positions; kinesthetic seeing similarly reveals historical practitioners' subjectivities and implicates researchers' bodies in corporeal assumptions during the interpretive processes of archival research. PiR's embodied research-writing practices enable scholars to reproduce movements' sensuality when analyzing choreography (Stoller 1997; Foster 2011a). When archival evidence lacks moving images, PiR generates material options. My experience writing about live performances and my Laban training, which disciplined me to visually identify taxonomies in other people's bodies as I understand them in my own (without replacing their subjectivities with mine), enable me to build dances from photographs, reviews, and concert programs. My use of PiR enlivens the past to generate performance discourse (Taylor 2003). As dance theorist Randy Martin asserted, "People make history, but the history they make cannot be evaluated simply by noting the presence of the people. . . . [T]he relation of formal and informal, represented and unregistered, is materialized in the tension between performers and audiences that enables performance to produce itself as historicity" (1998, 44). In this way, rendering historical dances through PiR goes beyond accounting for them to empowering them as mobilizing forces.

PiR's kinesthetic seeing affirms and illuminates how bodies circulate cultural discourses. By mining their shared kinesthetic experiences with the practices they examine, scholars identify constitutive dance moments to articulate how dance events produce culture. Dance theorist Priya Srinivasan terms the kinesthetic seeing relationship the "bodily archive," through which, she argues, corporeality is a discourse in which people's physicalities circulate values through the kinesthetic markings of their bodily practices (2012, 67–73). In Srinivasan's bodily archive, the body is a repository of its learned techniques. When, for example, Srinivasan recognized white dancer Ruth St. Denis performing a *hamsasya* mudra in a 1941 film, Srinivasan knew from mastering this hand gesture's intricacies of forefinger touching thumb with the other fingers fanned out that St. Denis learned it from other practitioners and not from static library sources, as St. Denis's biographers typically asserted. By bringing her practice into her research, Srinivasan uncovered the labor of the invisibilized migrant Indian men and women in New York who taught St. Denis South Asian dances. Since the researcher's kinesthesia indexes discrete somatic source material, Srinivasan argues, the body is one way through which we understand archival sources and the politics of their circulation to unveil colonialist workings in concert dance (2012, 67–71, 83–97, 186n10). Srinivasan's moment of recognition, when she felt the mudra in her own hand as she watched St. Denis perform it onscreen, was kinesthetic seeing in action.

Kinesthetic seeing operates in both ethnographic inquiries and archival ones. Dance theorist Ramón Rivera-Servera employs kinesthetic recognition to show how performance events produce culture through shared participation. Embodied experiences and cerebral reasoning generate theory, he argues, and his term "theories in practice" defines the knowledge that performance practices and embodied events produce (2012, 18). Rivera-Servera's kinesthetic participation identifies bodily citations of queer *latinidad* and *communitas* on the concert stage, in the club, and on the street. He identifies how these conduits of knowledge operate when, for example, responding to young Latinos' taunts of his queerly signifying corporeality as he walked in his neighborhood and in the way Latinx gay men and lesbians dancing in a club reclaim movements for their own pleasure that mark their bodies as Other outside the club (137–41, 152–56). Rivera-Servera's kinesthetic seeing comes from his queer *latinidad* embodiment and shows how movement practices circulate corporeal discourses.

My argument for PiR grows from my experience researching and writing *Honest Bodies: Revolutionary Modernism in the Dances of Anna Sokolow* (2017), in which I argue that Sokolow's choreography from the 1930s through the 1960s circulated American modernism among Jewish and communist channels of the international Left in the United States, Mexico, and Israel. My evidence included concert reviews, programs, and photographs; Labanotation scores; film and live performance; and my kinesthetic experiences with Sokolow's choreography and Graham technique. Bringing together these sources of evidence, I developed an analytical matrix that built on earlier approaches, drawing from (1) Srinivasan's bodily archive; (2) dance historian Susan Manning's methods for reconstructing dance production and reception from archival evidence ([1993] 2006, 2004); (3) the concept of the "bodymind" articulated by PaR advocate Vida Midgelow as critically embodied engagement during movement processes (2015, 14); (4) Laban-informed movement description skills that approach dance visually and somatically; and (5) dance critic Marcia Siegel's concept of lexicon, a catalog of movements informed by Laban Movement Analysis that constitute a dance's specific vocabulary (2001, 205–6). Siegel's lexicon, which I have learned from her workshops, employs descriptive verbs to encapsulate dances' progressions (208). Siegel's nuanced manner of attending to movement details, which dance theorist André Lepecki has called her "close attention" (quoted in Solomon 2013, 26), benefit kinesthetic seeing interactions. Employing embodied knowledge to analyze dances' properties and their circulation through people's bodies, my methodological mix enabled me to distinguish the features of Sokolow's movement vocabularies. My research process manifested in a writing practice of analytical movement description, in which my discussion balances directing readers to see dances in terms of my argument with presenting the archival evidence in a way that allows for the possibility of alternate arguments (Manning [1993] 2006, 12–13). Departing from PaR, which answers practical questions with practices, PiR draws answers from embodied experiences alongside other evidential sources to answer scholarly questions.

Using PiR's somatic interpretive processes in modern dance archives prompts further questions: How does translating my contemporary embodiment into my best inference of the historical embodiment cause slippages in my critical inquiry? How do we understand the implications of historical bodies' corporealities within their time (Foster 1995; Albright 2010)? To answer these queries, this essay probes research methods for midcentury modern dance and its myriad legacies, addressing the place of Laban analytical systems in dance studies past and present.

What Is the Outside Surface of My Elbow Doing?
Using PiR to Flesh Out the Archive

Laban modalities generate my conception of PiR, since Laban Movement Analysis (LMA) and notation (Labanotation / Kinetography Laban) trained me to see kinesthetically and hence inform how I engage practice in my scholarship. Moreover, Laban ideologies were prominent in midcentury concert dance practices, so their logics partially compose the modern dance archive. My attention to movement intricacies stems from engaging Laban frameworks and tools to write analytical movement description. Labanotation defines actions for body parts, directions, and levels in space, whereas LMA delineates dynamic qualities of movement (effort) and the relationship of the body to space, known as choreutics or space harmony (Guest [1954] 2005; Bartenieff and Lewis 1980; Maletic 2005). By ascertaining the relationship of dance studies to what is sometimes called Laban studies,[2] a field with a complicated inheritance, I acknowledge that Laban frameworks inform my embodied research foundations and how I bring practice into my research. Since PiR is a dynamic research process relating to the researcher's own mixed methods, Laban-based tools are central to my PiR, kinesthetic seeing, and the way I conceive practice in research, but they will not factor into all researchers' PiR modes.

The kinesthetic seeing germane to this discussion utilizes Laban training to generate fine-grained, somatic-informed, movement-descriptive evidence for analysis. Laban systems are predicated on a high level of detail so that you can ascertain, for example, how the outside surface of your elbow leads your body through space by carving a specific design. Get out of your reading position and try that with me (adapt the instruction as necessary for your physicality). Now carve the same pathway, but lead it with the inside surface of your forearm.

What words differentiate moving the same body part with discrete initiations? Describing dances entails parsing any number of elements: What body parts are doing what, and with what kind of energy? What is the overall and specific shape or intention of the movement? Where does a movement originate? Is it more important to record movement as it appears to viewers or as performers experience it, if those are two different things? Researchers' choices for translating movements into written form determine how dances circulate for others to analyze that event. While LMA can be reductive in assigning a movement quality without explaining it (e.g., it was strong and direct), training scholars to identify these elements deepens their written nuance. I am reminded here of how anthropologist Sally Ann Ness (1992) incorporates LMA concepts while keeping LMA assumptions in check to describe aspects of the Filipino *sinulog*. Ness adapts LMA vocabulary, including trace forms (1, 9, 139), resilient phrasing (53, 222–23), and core and distal initiation (120) to transmit movements' temporality and shapes to her reader. Her descriptive words identify patterns in the way *sinulog* practitioners enact the form in different contexts. Laban-based vocabularies introduce one way to cultivate a descriptive engagement and to articulate the work dance movements do within their historical and cultural contexts.

That Laban-based taxonomies demand embodied analysis drives my conception of PiR. Notation theorist Victoria Watts (2013) argues that in order for a dance notation score to manifest, a researcher must physically read (perform) it through the body. Dance notation scores document changes in embodied subjectivity, she says, because they record how individual dancers execute movements in a given rehearsal; researchers reading scores can thus ascertain elements of practitioners' historical embodiments. Similarly, dance ethnographer Deidre Sklar explains that Laban-based qualitative movement analysis relies on "translating from the sight of a movement to the sensation of doing it" (2001b, 3). Likewise, what I am calling kinesthetic seeing simultaneously mobilizes embodied knowledge to analyze dances. For example, the ability to physically demonstrate the difference between movement that floats (a combination of light weight, sustained time, and an indirect relationship to space, like a feather meandering on a breeze) and punches (a combination of strong weight, sudden time, and a direct relationship to space, like a sucker punch) makes it easier to kinesthetically/visually identify these elements when watching other people move and engenders more evocative movement description than cerebral reasoning alone (for more, see Brooks 1993).

Laban concepts train practitioners to look for certain things, and like all analytical systems, are culturally bound. It is not efficacious for all dance researchers to speak in the specialized terms of Laban Movement Analysis or to be able to read Labanotation scores, because the underlying concepts are not equally applicable to all movement systems. What is transferable is the epistemic concept of kinesthetic analysis. PiR contributes to the academy a close attention to movement and an investment in somatic analysis and interpretation.

The Laban systems have drawn suspicion over the past twenty years, for good reason: Rudolf Laban upheld Nazism (Karina and Kant [1996] 2003), and Laban practitioners have forwarded colonialist claims that the systems are universal. The poststructural turn of the 1980s made suspect the claim, widespread earlier, that any one system could account for nearly all cultural phenomena. The postcolonial turn of the 1990s then rendered suspect the practice, widespread earlier, of examining one cultural phenomenon through another culture's analytical tools, especially when looking through Western lenses that subjugate non-Western aesthetics. The Laban systems, fraught with Eurocentric biases, are among many research modalities with colonialist impulses in their genetic makeups. In consequence, Laban-based analysis nearly disappeared from dance studies scholarship after the 1990s. Yet at the same time, Laban systems have played an influential role in robotics and computer engineering over the last decade as scientists employed systematic ways to quantify movement (Truong, Boujut, and Zaharia 2006; Bernstein et al. 2015; Choensawat, Nakamura, and Hachimura 2015). The Laban codifications afford nuance that enables linking descriptive evidence into analytical and theoretical inquiries, which is likely why they have attracted scientific fields.

However, despite the decline in Laban-inflected scholarship in the arts and humanities, many of the underlying concepts have persisted in dance studies, albeit not named as such. In an important sense, due to the widespread influence of German expressive dance in the early and mid-twentieth century and the global spread of Laban analysis and notation practices in the late twentieth and early twenty-first centuries, Laban tenets are foundational to but unacknowledged in the way concert dance practitioners and researchers make and write about dances. Descriptive language widespread in rehearsal studios and dance studies classrooms in modern and contemporary dance draws on concepts of space, weight, time, and flow—concepts that Laban and his students like Irmgard Bartenieff codified to train practitioners to see movement at an unrivaled granular level of detail for description and analysis.

By recuperating Laban systems' usable parts, I reintroduce them as dance studies tools while acknowledging the residue of their discriminatory histories and eschewing a false sense of objectivity. The postcolonial and poststructural turns demonstrated how all analytical lenses have bias. As Ness argues, claims for objectivity do a disservice to research modes. Her phrase "the evidence fail" pinpoints cross-cultural research slippages: "What I am calling 'cultural difference' occurs at that moment when a conceptual object—in this case the dance-object—however preconceived, *fails* to represent the researcher's understanding of the very practices they seek to identify by it and to study" (1996, 246). When researchers examine objects through culturally specific assumptions they believe to be objective and then claim significant discoveries, Ness says, they limit instead of expand their analyses. New approaches to old modalities—exploiting Laban frameworks for their PiR and kinesthetic seeing potential while redressing how to responsibly use them—is part of the futures of dance studies. In the modern dance archive, researchers negotiate biases when rendering subjects' movement characteristics.

Kinesthetic seeing in archival dance research requires attention to dances' historical and contemporary resonances because people carry traces of their practices in their physicalities, and their kinesthetic sense of their world marks their corporealities as bound by time and history. Dancers traveling to teach or learn dance forms in geographic locales outside their point of origin, moreover, circulate communal principles through the bodies of the dancers who learn them. As dance theorist Susan Foster asserts, a researcher's somaticization of historical kinesthesia is a mode of empathetically approaching historical cultural contexts (1995, 7). When I researched my Sokolow book, Laban-informed close-attention skills helped me mobilize kinesthetic evidence of her work. Despite the 1930s New York leftist press having the best movement description in print, I relied on scant traces of dances to piece together Sokolow's choreography to understand why it was revered across leftist, Jewish, African American, and mainstream constituencies. Although no film of Sokolow's 1930s dances exist, her celebrity as a leading Graham and revolutionary dancer affords her substantial archival traces that generate a kinesthetic picture of her work. By getting a sense of Sokolow's and her dancers' physicalities from photographs, watching films of dances or restagings from that time, drawing upon my kinesthetic knowledge of Graham technique, and reading critics' dance descriptions from their social positions, I looked for elements to generate a movement lexicon or signal a dance's through line. I rendered Sokolow's dances by collating this evidence in a similar way to how I decipher my notes from performances in darkened theaters. There are gaps, but there is fleshy immediacy. Randy Martin argued that analyzing dances is a political process based in understanding the labor of the dancer, the labor of the spectator, and the charged space between them that makes meaning. His analytical tool "overreading" relies on dances' choreographic structures to unveil their political workings (1998, 55–106). Overreading a dance by applying its cultural context to its movement, he claimed, shows a dance's full political impact. My kinesthetic inferences from archival sources clarified Sokolow's dances' logics.

The stakes for researchers inferring aspects of historical embodiment to flesh out a dance within its time necessitate discernment in word choice and conclusions. Kinesthetic seeing cannot justify a researcher evacuating a research subject's personhood when engaging kinesthetic empathy (Hartman 1997); similarly, when embodying from the archive, a researcher must recognize how movement practices, even if codified, change over time. Performing dances from score, rendering dances from archival sources, and analyzing dances from video or live contexts all rely on sensitive interpretive processes to pursue responsible discussion. What follows is a PiR toolkit for Laban and non-Laban practitioners alike to cultivate kinesthetic seeing, write analytical movement description, and bring dance scholars' embodied knowledges into archival research. As with any research practice, we must consider how inheritances implicate the way researchers implement analytical models by addressing the ethics of training in vocabularies with discriminatory pasts and think twice before applying them to forms outside their primary cultural context.

A Toolkit for Kinesthetic Seeing

Honing a Laban-based kinesthetic-seeing close attention requires discerning actions of body parts and their surfaces, their relationships with other bodies' parts and surfaces, qualitative phrasing properties with which they engage interactions, and their relationship to gravity (weight). Pinpoint, for example, each metacarpal joint and finger surface without losing sight of the whole hand or its reaction to weight. The center of weight is the conceptual center of the Laban systems. It resides within the pelvis as if it is a piece of fruit suspended in a bowl of gelatin but with the density of a shot-put ball. Is the weight suspended, falling, or still? Is it resisting or yielding to gravity? Finally, identify movements' phrasing properties. Some choices include phrasing that ends abruptly, like one fist smashing into an open palm (impact); phrasing that initiates from a distinct body part and then dissolves into something else (impulse); and phrasing that quivers like an electric toothbrush (vibratory).

Buttressing these tools are inquiries that somatically estimate dances in preparation for analyzing choreography. One Laban process called "motif description" identifies the overall shape of a series of movements. The researcher ascertains a dance's "aboutness," its through line (Guest and Curran 2008), by relying on a descriptive catalog of bodily actions. Motif scoring includes mobility and stability (defined by the center of weight's motion), tracking the prominence or absence of movements that turn or occur on the floor or in the air, and whether movements foreground actions like flexion or joining multiple body parts in space. Siegel's and Foster's LMA-informed strategies, moreover, mobilize verbal description as evidence for scholarly analysis. Siegel's lexicon identifies specific vocabulary that distinguishes dances' assets and signifies multiple interpretations. During the lexicon process a viewer identifies whether or not a dance is "about" any one thing—gendered relationships, or alienation, or worship (Siegel [1995] 2010, 191–92; 2001, 206–7). Foster's conceptualization of style, a dance's "individual identity" (1986, 59), is undergirded by LMA motion factors of space, weight, time, and flow. Style, as Foster explains, "results from three related sets of choreographic conventions: the quality with which the movement is performed, the characteristic use of parts of the body, and the dancer's orientation in the performance space" (77). Laban-inflected kinesthetic seeing tucks into these processes, identifying movements' "aboutness" (lexicon, style). These close-attention scoring skills generate descriptive prose to use in systems-level analyses (Foster 1998, 2003) to link into cultural and theoretical investigations. Bringing kinesthetic seeing together with a host of other factors—researchers' social positions from which they view the work, their understanding of cultural and historical context, their ability to recognize genre markers, the depth of their vocabularies—generates evocative analytical description that can be used for evidence to make claims about a dance. Kinesthetic seeing can be further employed as the basis for performative writing and as a rendering mechanism for sifting through archival materials to identify what a dance was in its time and how it resonates now.

To get evocative movement description from archival fragments, we need to practice with extant dances. Consider the example of a men's duet from Israeli choreographer Ohad Naharin's compendium work *Decadance* ([2000] 2013) for Batsheva Dance Company.[3] Laban techniques are imprinted in Israeli contemporary dance's DNA because German expressive dancers fostered Jewish theatrical dance in 1920s and 1930s British Mandate Palestine (Spiegel 2013, 97–131), so Laban-informed modes of kinesthetic seeing track effectively for this example. My case study demonstrates how to describe the dance, articulate the work's through line, and broaden the analysis to incorporate cultural context and historical specificity.

The duet, from Naharin's *Shalosh* (Three) (2005), highlights the relationship between homosexuality and the Israeli state through a popular Bollywood love song. Rajesh Roshan and Ibrahim Ashq's "Kyun chalti hai pawan" (Why does the wind blow?) (also "Na tum jaano ha num" [Neither do you know nor do I]) is a yearning love song about how some questions cannot be answered from Rakesh Roshan's 2000 film *Kaho naa . . . pyaar hai* (Say You Love Me). During this song's sequence, the character Raj entertains sublime fantasies about Sonia, the woman he desires, across New Zealand's diverse landscapes.[4] When the song occurs in the film, Raj has learned that Sonia is interested but does not know he is the doppelgänger of Rohit, the lover Sonia lost in India. Cultural theorist Jayashree Kamble explains this common Bollywood plot twist in terms of the wealthy cosmopolitan masculinity Raj displays as opposed to Rohit's localized poverty-inflected physique, which pits Indian nationalism against diaspora cosmopolitanism (2012, 99). The song's intertext brings romantic yearning into Naharin's duet and resonates with a nationalism-infused experience of lovers lost and recovered through time.

Israeli societal relationships with Indian cultural products give a sense for how "Kyun chalti hai pawan" signifies the men's love in Naharin's duet. Since the 1992 establishment of diplomatic relations between India and Israel, India has been a popular tourist destination for young Israelis after completing their army service (Parciack 2008, 230), and some contemporary Israeli folk dances appropriate Bollywood-inspired movement sequences. According to cultural theorist Ronie Parciack (2008), moreover, the Israeli telecommunications company Bezeq used the Hindi-language song "Mera naam chin-chin-chu" in a 1996 television advertisement campaign targeting Israeli Jews to signify harmonious unity despite cultural and regional conflicts. The commercials featured opposing Israeli political figures coming together, and, Parciack argues, since Bezeq did not use subtitles, the song became an allegory for incomprehensibility, which the state-run utility metaphorically solved through its communication technologies.

Naharin's men's duet similarly engages Bollywood's love songs to entwine communication with the state. In rehearsal, Naharin coached one pair of dancers to sink into each other's gazes instead of assuming machismo's impenetrable edges, teasing, "[The] last thing I expected of you guys [was] to be macho" (quoted in Heymann 2015). Onstage, the dancers' comfortable intimacy unfolds through their fingertips delicately skimming along the floor and each other and playful tosses, spins, shimmies, and sneaking parts of their limbs into the negative spaces of each other's body. They match the rhythm in each other's hips as they cha-cha back and forth before spasming and slipping away in quiet shame, exposed by the stares of a lined-up group of people who appear partway through the song. Israel decriminalized homosexuality in 1988 and has prohibited discrimination in the military since 1993, but state-sanctioned marriages are governed by the Orthodox Jewish Rabbinate, which opposes homosexuality (Hadar 2005, 16, 19–21, 32–33). Moreover, a persistent cultural model of heteronormative gender roles, upheld by state-level religious Judaism and a pervasive tough masculinity in Israeli society resulting from required conscription, prevails (Herzog 2005). The men's love in Naharin's duet is not forbidden, but their postures react sharply to the bystanders' scrutiny as normative, even nationalist, stances eclipse their cozy playfulness.

My words direct how to see the men's intimacy. In Laban terms, the performers' fingertips move with light weight and a direct relationship to space as they retain a sliding contact with the floor. What body parts? Their fingertips (the fingertip-end surface of their fingers). What action? Skim (light and direct sliding contact). How? Delicately (light, sliding). I reproduce this movement combination in my own hand against my desk and my arm over and over again. The fingertips retain the same movement quality as they traverse the bodies and the floor. Strong weight (the opposite of light) would not allow easily sliding contact, and an indirect relationship to space (the opposite of direct) would not produce the clear traces that one dancer leaves on the other. I have to feel the shifting weight in my own physicality to figure out how to describe what I see, and I run through the Laban indices to explicate my words for it. "Skimming" reinforces delicate strength in the shadow of vulnerability. By saying that the dancers' fingertips skim across the floor and each other, I intone an intimacy that accompanies such skimming.

After the song ends, I stop the video and write one, two, or three separate words in response to this question: "What is this dance About?" By spelling "About" with a capital *A*, I signal that I am not interested in chronological narratives. Instead, "About" intends to get at the dance's inner workings. I take this concept from the "aboutness" Laban movement analysts use to identify dances' characteristics. Once I have words on the page, I write description from my viewing to support each of my About words, then ask myself: "What did you see that made you say that?" (Visual Thinking Strategies 1995). This About process enables reciprocal interpretation with description. It connects Laban-level movement specificity to analytical frames, including race, class, gender, and spectatorship. For me, this segment is About vulnerability: intimate vulnerability, defiant vulnerability, defeated vulnerability. The vulnerability comes first from a trusting, gentle, playful familiarity among the two men and then from each bystander's ensuing insolent baring of the ventral edge of their ribcages by peeling up their own shirts. Some do this fast and showy, others slow and susceptible, still others matter-of-fact. The last man steps forward, examines his palms, and offers them to the audience. Suddenly, his surrender becomes the segment's most revelatory moment.

Practice is part of this interaction, even though I sit in front of a screen: first, from my shared kinesthetic history taking Gaga classes (Naharin's movement practice in which Batsheva dancers train) and my research in Israeli concert dance; and second, because employing Laban taxonomies as part of describing movement implies embodying them. Explaining what I saw that provokes vulnerability led to employing Martin's overreading by considering the ramifications of two men dancing tenderly to a love song in a cultural environment

that foregrounds masculinity and toughness and a political atmosphere where
the state does not perform same-sex marriages but recognizes those conducted
elsewhere. In this way, the movement becomes evidence to bolster my arguments about this work. Researchers' analyses vary based on their evidence and
positionalities, and diverse points of viewing generate multiple meanings for
dances, so our assertions about the same dance will differ. This is significant
for the spectatorial properties of how PiR produces analytical movement description for critical analyses of dances.

I apply PiR in the archive by using source materials similarly to how I use
my performance notes to discern a dance's aboutness. For example, in Sokolow's
Case History No.— (1937), a solo about urban poverty, critics described how
Sokolow's nervous energy in her performance reflected the precarious plight
of impoverished youth in Manhattan's poorest neighborhoods. Photographs
of this dance evidence how strong weight (in Laban terms) drove Sokolow's
performance; that is, her pelvis motored her choreography, and her movement
retained a downward pull and a sense of weight circling through undercurves
like a marble rolling around a run—smoothly, but with timing that alters between suspension and falling. These movement qualities gave Sokolow's social
justice dance gravitas in her portrayal of New York's dismissal of the working
poor. To complete the exercise: What is this dance About? Alienation. What
do I see that makes me say that? In one photograph Sokolow painfully peels
her body off the floor; one critic described Sokolow as trudging ever onward
through city streets; and a dancer from Sokolow's company at the time recalled
the estrangement she felt watching Sokolow perform (Kosstrin 2017, 46–51).

The dance's musical score, by Wallingford Riegger, which I hired a musician
to play, provided temporal and aural evidence of alienation that supported the
archival materials. Sokolow had assisted Louis Horst, a musician who defined
American modern dance composition in the first half of the twentieth century.
By applying my knowledge of his composition practices, which have clear rules
for combining music with movement, and from Sokolow's interviews asserting how Horst's methods influenced the way she used music, the music score
further aided my historical kinesthesia for estimating what the dance may have
looked like. The PiR modality materialized how effectively Sokolow transmitted social-political concerns through her solo dancing body and changed how
I understood her as a leading revolutionary artist. She was piercing yet plain-
tive. If we only know her later work or stories about her temperament, we lose
this core, embodied aspect, which determines her place in history.

PiR manifests when scholarship contains these elements: analytical movement description that critically centers people's dancing bodies and their corporeal lived experiences as sources of evidence; kinesthetic seeing from a researcher's

shared history of a practice that engenders embodied empathetic examinations of primary-source materials; and the researcher's statement of positionality for how these components constitute a research project. PiR works interstitially with archival, ethnographic, theoretical, and discursive analytical methodologies to undergird humanities inquiries. Poststructuralist frameworks allow for multiple interpretations of cultural objects to exist alongside each other within their networks of meaning, and PiR affords concrete access to dances in scholarship for practitioners and nonspecialists. PiR offers a critical research paradigm grounded in kinesthetic inquiry, which is an unstated hallmark of dance studies, and opens this methodological approach to all humanities disciplines concerned with what it means to write from the body.

Notes

1. A 1988 issue of the *Drama Review* brought together movement analysis systems with those of gender, culture, and nation. In it, dance historian Ann Daly addressed the semiotic implications of the ways movement evokes meanings in order to ascertain how movement analysis could become a performance studies methodology and provide movement studies' entrance into the humanities (1988, 48). My argument diverges from Daly's, but my interest in reinforcing embodied knowledge in the academy builds on what she started in that volume.

2. This includes Labanotation, Laban Movement Analysis (LMA), and the work of Rudolf Laban's students, including Irmgard Bartenieff, Ann Hutchinson Guest, Warren Lamb, Vera Maletic, and Lisa Ullmann.

3. https://www.youtube.com/watch?v=D2jmN-AoD4c (accessed April 11, 2019). Duet begins at 1:00:30.

4. https://www.youtube.com/watch?v=VorYgCrs_jg (accessed November 7, 2017). Thanks to Kaustavi Sarkar for this connection and to Ila Nagar for translation assistance.

Works Cited

Albright, Ann Cooper. 2007. *Traces of Light: Absence and Presence in the Work of Loïe Fuller.* Middletown, CT: Wesleyan University Press.

———. 2010. "Tracing the Past: Writing History through the Body." In *The Routledge Dance Studies Reader*, 2nd ed., edited by Alexandra Carter and Janet O'Shea, 101–10. London: Routledge.

Bartenieff, Irmgard, and Dori Lewis. 1980. *Body Movement: Coping with the Environment.* Langhorne, PA: Gordon & Breach.

Bernstein, Ran, Tal Shafir, Rachelle Tsachor, Karen Studd, and Assaf Schuster. 2015. "Laban Movement Analysis Using Kinect." *International Journal of Computer, Electrical, Automation, Control and Information Engineering* 9 (6): 1574–78.

Blanco Borelli, Melissa. 2016. "Gadgets, Bodies, and Screens: Dance in Advertisements for New Technologies." In *The Oxford Handbook of Screendance Studies*, edited by Douglas Rosenberg, 421–38. New York: Oxford University Press.

Brooks, Lynn Matluck. 1993. "Harmony in Space: A Perspective on the Work of Rudolf Laban." *Journal of Aesthetic Education* 27 (2): 29–41.

Burton, Antoinette, ed. 2005. *Archive Stories: Facts, Fictions, and the Writing of History.* Durham, NC: Duke University Press.

Choensawat, Worawat, Minako Nakamura, and Kozaburo Hachimura. 2015. "Gen-Laban: A Tool for Generating Labanotation from Motion Capture Data." *Multimedia Tools and Applications: An International Journal* 74 (23): 10823–46.

Croft, Clare. 2015. *Dancers as Diplomats: American Choreography in Cultural Exchange.* New York: Oxford University Press.

Daly, Ann. 1988. "Movement Analysis: Piecing Together the Puzzle." *TDR/The Drama Review* 32 (4): 40–52.

Dirks, Nicholas B. 2002. "Annals of the Archive: Ethnographic Notes on the Sources of History." In *From the Margins: Historical Anthropology and Its Futures*, edited by Brian Keith Axel, 47–65. Durham, NC: Duke University Press.

Elswit, Kate. 2014. *Watching Weimar Dance.* New York: Oxford University Press.

Foster, Susan Leigh. 1986. *Reading Dancing: Bodies and Subjects in Contemporary American Dance.* Berkeley: University of California Press.

———. 1995. "Choreographing History." In *Choreographing History*, edited by Susan Leigh Foster, 3–21. Bloomington: Indiana University Press.

———. 1998. "Choreographies of Gender." *Signs: Journal of Women in Culture and Society* 24 (1): 1–33.

———. 2003. "Choreographies of Protest." *Theatre Journal* 55 (3): 395–412.

———. 2011a. "Choreographies of Writing." Lecture, the Pew Center for Arts and Heritage, Bryn Mawr College, Bryn Mawr, PA. Accessed March 22, 2016. http://danceworkbook.pcah.us/susan-foster/choreographies-of-writing.html.

———. 2011b. *Choreographing Empathy: Kinesthesia in Performance.* London: Routledge.

George-Graves, Nadine. 2010. *Urban Bush Women: Twenty Years of African American Dance Theater, Community Engagement, and Working It Out.* Madison: University of Wisconsin Press.

Guest, Ann Hutchinson. (1954) 2005. *Labanotation: The System of Analyzing and Recording Movement.* New York: Routledge.

Guest, Ann Hutchinson, and Tina Curran. 2008. *Your Move: The Language of Dance Approach to the Study of Movement and Dance.* New York: Routledge.

Hadar, Ira. 2005. "Lesbians in Israel: A Legal Perspective." In *Sappho in the Holy Land: Lesbian Existence and Dilemmas in Contemporary Israel*, edited by Chava Frankfort-Nachmias and Erella Shadmi, 15–38. Albany: State University of New York Press.

Hahn, Tomie. 2007. *Sensational Knowledge: Embodying Culture through Japanese Dance.* Middletown, CT: Wesleyan University Press.

Hartman, Saidiya. 1997. *Scenes of Subjection: Terror, Slavery, and Self-Making in Nineteenth-Century America.* New York: Oxford University Press.

Herzog, Hanna. 2005. "Homefront and Battlefront: The Status of Jewish and Palestinian Women in Israel." In *Israeli Women's Studies: A Reader*, edited by Esther Fuchs, 208–28. New Brunswick, NJ: Rutgers University Press.

Heymann, Tomer, dir. 2015. *Mr. Gaga: A True Story of Love and Dance*. Tel Aviv: Heymann Brothers Films.

Kamble, Jayashree. 2012. "The Globalized Avatar of the Hindi Cinema Hero: Hrithik Roshan's 'Double Role' in *Kaho Naa . . . Pyaar Hai* (2000)." *Film International* 10 (4–5): 92–100.

Karina, Lillian, and Marion Kant. (1996) 2003. *Hitler's Dancers: German Modern Dance and the Third Reich*. Translated by Jonathan Steinberg. New York: Berghahn Books.

Kosstrin, Hannah. 2017. *Honest Bodies: Revolutionary Modernism in the Dances of Anna Sokolow*. New York: Oxford University Press.

Maletic, Vera. 2005. *Dance Dynamics: Effort and Phrasing*. Columbus, OH: Grade A Notes.

Manning, Susan. (1993) 2006. *Ecstasy and the Demon: The Dances of Mary Wigman*. Minneapolis: University of Minnesota Press.

———. 2004. *Modern Dance, Negro Dance: Race in Motion*. Minneapolis: University of Minnesota Press.

Martin, Randy. 1998. *Critical Moves: Dance Studies in Theory and Politics*. Durham, NC: Duke University Press.

McCarren, Felicia. 2013. *French Moves: The Cultural Politics of Le Hip Hop*. New York: Oxford University Press.

Midgelow, Vida. 2015. "Some Fleshy Thinking: Improvisation, Experience, Perception." In *The Oxford Handbook of Dance and Theater*, edited by Nadine George-Graves, 109–22. New York: Oxford University Press.

———. 2017. "Questioning Research Salon." Lecture, Ohio State University, October 24.

Nelson, Robin. 2006. "Practice-as-Research and the Problem of Knowledge." *Performance Research* 11 (4): 105–16.

———. 2013. *Practice as Research in the Arts: Principles, Protocols, Pedagogies, Resistances*. London: Palgrave Macmillan.

Ness, Sally Ann. 1992. *Body, Movement, and Culture: Kinesthetic and Visual Symbolism in a Philippine Community*. Philadelphia: University of Pennsylvania Press.

———. 1996. "Observing the Evidence Fail: Difference Arising from Objectification in Cross-Cultural Studies of Dance." In *Moving Words: Re-writing Dance*, edited by Gay Morris, 215–35. London: Routledge.

Novack, Cynthia. 1990. *Sharing the Dance: Contact Improvisation and American Culture*. Madison: University of Wisconsin Press.

Parciack, Ronie. 2008. "Appropriating the Uncodable: Hindi Song and Dance Sequences in Israeli State Promotional Commercials." In *Global Bollywood: Travels of Hindi Song and Dance*, edited by Sangita Gopal and Sujata Moorti, 221–39. Minneapolis: University of Minnesota Press.

Rivera-Servera, Ramón. 2012. *Performing Queer Latinidad: Dance, Sexuality, Politics*. Ann Arbor: University of Michigan Press.

Scott, Joan Wallach. 1992. "Experience." In *Feminists Theorize the Political*, edited by Judith Butler and Joan Wallach Scott, 22–40. New York: Routledge.

Siegel, Marcia B. (1995) 2010. "Bridging the Critical Distance." In *The Routledge Dance Studies Reader*, 2nd ed., edited by Alexandra Carter and Janet O'Shea, 188–96. London: Routledge.

———. 2001. "Using Lexicons for Performance Research: Three Duets." In *New Approaches to Theatre Studies and Performance Analysis*, edited by Günter Berghaus, 205–16. Tübingen: Max Niemeyer Verlag.

Sklar, Deidre. (1991) 2001a. "Five Premises for a Culturally Sensitive Approach to Dance." In *Moving History / Dancing Cultures: A Dance History Reader*, edited by Ann Dils and Ann Cooper Albright, 30–32. Middletown, CT: Wesleyan University Press.

———. 2001b. *Dancing with the Virgin: Body and Faith in the Fiesta of Tortugas, New Mexico*. Berkeley: University of California Press.

Solomon, Noémie, ed. 2013. "Inside/Beside Dance Studies: A Conversation." *Dance Research Journal* 45 (3): 3–28.

Spiegel, Nina S. 2013. *Embodying Hebrew Culture: Aesthetics, Athletics, and Dance in the Jewish Community of Mandate Palestine*. Detroit: Wayne State University Press.

Srinivasan, Priya. 2012. *Sweating Saris: Indian Dance as Transnational Labor*. Philadelphia: Temple University Press.

Stoler, Ann Laura. 2009. *Along the Archival Grain: Epistemic Anxieties and Colonial Common Sense*. Princeton, NJ: Princeton University Press.

Stoller, Paul. 1997. *Sensuous Scholarship*. Philadelphia: University of Pennsylvania Press.

Taylor, Diana. 2003. *The Archive and the Repertoire: Performing Cultural Memory in the Americas*. Durham, NC: Duke University Press.

Truong, Arthur, Hugo Boujut, and Titus Zaharia. 2006. "Laban Descriptors for Gesture Recognition and Emotional Analysis." *Visual Computer: International Journal of Computer Graphics* 32 (1): 83–98.

Visual Thinking Strategies. 1995. Accessed July 25, 2017. http://www.vtshome.org.

Watts, Victoria. 2013. "Archives of Embodiment: Visual Culture and the Practice of Score Reading." In *Dance on Its Own Terms: Histories and Methodologies*, edited by Melanie Bales and Karen Eliot, 363–88. New York: Oxford University Press.

King David in the
Medieval Archives

Toward an Archaic Future for Dance Studies

KATHRYN DICKASON

Over the past twenty-five years, dance studies has generated productive scholarship exploring the complex relationship between dance and religion. Several
of these studies, focusing on the Euro-American tradition, have analyzed the
ways that twentieth-century dance pioneers appropriated ancient and Eastern
religions to empower women, modernize aesthetics, and/or mythologize their
craft (Desmond 1991; Manning [1993] 2006; Franko 1995; LaMothe 2006;
Scolieri 2012). Scholars have also explored how luminaries of the African and
Jewish diasporas envisioned emancipation, collective memory, and resistance
by integrating innovative movement with religious motifs (DeFrantz 2004; Ross
2014; Rossen 2014).

These avenues of inquiry have enriched the discipline, yet they are shaped
by the twentieth- and twenty-first-century contexts that they engage. To date,
dance studies remains a modern and contemporary-centric field. Diverging
from mainstream scholarship, this essay examines dance and religion in medieval Western Europe. Given its historical framing, this project demands an
examination of medieval archival materials. Here I do not deploy "the archival" in a critical, theoretical, or Derridean way. More conventionally and as a
medievalist, my archival base constitutes unpublished manuscripts, manuscript
illustrations, and primary texts produced in premodernity and preserved in
collections. Through my examination of these medieval materials—including
biblical commentaries, religious iconography, and crusader chronicles—I show
how, from the fourth to fourteenth century, ecclesiastical authorities, theologians, and artists of France, Italy, and beyond repurposed sacred dance to address
contemporary concerns.

There are three sections in this chapter, and each revolves around approaches
to biblical dancing. Throughout the Middle Ages in Europe, the Bible was the

foundational narrative by which ecclesiastical authorities legitimated Christian dance. Accordingly, I discuss texts and images that reimagined the dance of King David, a monarch from the Old Testament. The first section explores how, beginning in late antiquity, early Christians fashioned David as the prototype for holy dance. In doing so, they effectively distanced him from pagan performers in their midst. The second section turns to medieval treatments of the dance of David. Medieval theologians and artists formed a typological relationship between David and Christ, aligning David's dance with Christ's Passion, as well as with unique Christian virtues. David's Christianization, however, shaped and reinforced discrimination against medieval Jews. The third section studies the relationship between dance and violence. Specifically, I analyze how, during the Crusades, biblical dance reemerged to influence military propaganda and attitudes toward Muslims. The archives communicate that whether at court, on the battlefield, or in church, religious dance functioned as a tool of political ideology. Put differently, the archives reveal a darker side of medieval dance. Under the banner of Christendom, dance was equally complicit in the degradation, demonization, and even destruction of religious "Others."

The Bible in Late Antiquity: Depaganizing Dance

The Vulgate, or Bible translated into Latin (ca. late fourth or early fifth century AD), comprised the most copied, read, and analyzed text of the Middle Ages. Of interest to dance scholars are the Vulgate's dance references. The Old and New Testaments associated dancing with praise, thanksgiving, joy, and prophecy. Both Testaments also contain counterexamples in which dance enacted desecration, idolatry, and sin. Perhaps the performance that has left the strongest impression across the ages was that of King David (Zimmermann 2007, 60–65; Manor 1992). For medieval commentators, David created the functional paradigm of dance as religious worship.[1] As this section demonstrates, early Christian exegetes (or biblical interpreters) employed hermeneutical strategies to reconcile the exuberance of David's dancing with the solemnity of the Christian rite. In other words, late antique religious authorities depaganized the dance of David, differentiating him from licentious performers and Roman spectacle. The reformed David set a precedent for Christian devotion and exerted lasting effects on medieval performance.

Readers first encounter the dance of David in 2 Samuel 6 (2 Regum 6, Vulgate) amid a grand ceremony in the city of David. At this point in his life, David was a promising king, military leader, and iconoclast of Baal (an ancient Semitic fertility god).[2] David and his army had just recovered the Ark of the Covenant—a receptacle that contained the tablets of the Ten Commandments—from enemy territory. The Bible describes a festive atmosphere complete with musicians, singers, and feasting. Clearly, the dance of David was the festival's tour de force: "And David danced with all his might before the Lord [saltabat totis viribus ante Dominum]: and David was girded with a linen ephod [ritual robe]. And David and all the house of Israel brought the Ark of the Covenant of the Lord with joyful shouting and with sound of trumpet" (2 Samuel/ Regum 6:14–15).[3]

Despite these ritualistic overtones, David's wife, Michol, was not pleased with his performance: "And when the ark of the Lord was come into the city of David, Michol the daughter of Saul, looking out through a window, saw King David leaping and dancing [subsilientem atque saltantem] before the Lord: and she despised him in her heart" (2 Samuel/Regum 6:16). What warranted Michol's contemptuous reaction to her husband's dance? The Vulgate provides some clues. The text employs the Latin verb *saltare*, which connotes "dance," as well as "jump," "leap," "spring," and "hop." Occasionally the word suggests a salacious, sensational movement quality (Miller 2000, 236n19; see Gruber 1990). Rather than a dignified processional fit for a king, David's dance may have resembled more of a prance or jig. Four verses later, the Vulgate states that David was *nudatus* (naked), even though the text had already mentioned his ephod, a garment that ancient Jewish priests wore during rituals. It is likely that David's explosive *saltatio* momentarily lifted his robes and, in turn, exposed his nether regions (Smith 1995; Juriansz 2013, 1–14).[4] Evidently, this unintentional striptease infuriated his wife.

Given the problematic nature of David's dancing, early Christians strove to distance him from the pagan dancing body. For the church fathers writing during the Roman Empire, David could have been dangerously reminiscent of Greco-Roman spectacle. For instance, full nudity of men and women was ubiquitous in Roman theater (Webb 2008, 100–102). The obscene gesticulations of pantomime artists inspired virulent critiques from Christian authors and bishops, including Tertullian (died ca. 240), John Chrysostom (d. 407), and Augustine (d. 430). When confronting the questionable content of 2 Samuel/ Regum 6, I posit that the ancient Christian response was to depaganize David, to sanitize his *saltus*.[5] For example, in the third century, Cyprian insisted that David and the Israelites did not dance like the performers of Greek spectacles ([Pseudo] Cyprian of Carthage 1871). Archbishop of Constantinople John Chrysostom assured his congregants that, unlike diabolical women and prostitutes, David performed as if he were in a church, not a theater (Chrysostom 1862). Contrary to pantomimes' contortionist choreography, Procopius (d. 565) proclaimed that David's dancing body exuded valor and virtue (Procopius of Gaza 1865; 2007, 45–51). Bishop and theologian Ambrose of Milan (d. 397) forged a direct correspondence between David and penitence, that is, the nature of sin, repentance, and redemption. In his treatise *Concerning Penitence*, Ambrose resituated the dance of David into Christian worship: "The dancing [*saltationem*] which David practiced before the ark of God is commended. For everything that is seemly is done for religion, such that we need not be ashamed of a service that tends to the worship and honoring of Christ" (1955, 615–16, translation mine).

Following Ambrose's analysis, medieval clergy repurposed the dance of David to consecrate Christian proselytization and institutionalization. In texts, images, and ritual practice, David reemerged as a sort of "born-again Christian," a martyr of the Roman amphitheater, or even Christ himself. The French liturgist Amalarius (d. ca. 850) identified David's dance as the first Christian rite (Amalarius of Metz 1864). Eudes Rigaud (d. 1275), the bishop of Rouen, reported that the nuns at Villarceaux (northwest of Paris) justified their dancing by appealing to David's example (Schmitt 1999, 91). In their devotional books, German nuns recorded how King David appeared at sisters' deathbeds to sing and dance their souls out of their bodies (Ancelet-Hustache 1930, 435; G. Lewis 1995, 167). Moreover, Dante features King David in his vision of Purgatory (*Purgatorio*, canto 10). Exemplifying humility, his dance disciplines the souls of the proud (Dickason 2017). Through the figure of David, might we reconstrue the Bible as a dance manual for medieval Christians?

The book of Psalms was perhaps David's most significant gift to Christian devotion. Medieval Christians believed that David authored the Psalms, a book of the Old Testament composed in verse. Hybridizing poetry and song, David's Psalms praised God and asked for his forgiveness. In medieval monasteries, novice monks and nuns had to recite the Psalms in Latin to prove their spiritual commitment. The Psalms' lyrical quality facilitated chanting, musical accompaniment, and ceremonial gesture. As the first psalmist, David's image appeared in medieval psalters (manuscripts containing the Psalms), often playing his harp or praying. A less conventional illustration from an Italian psalter depicts David as an old man clutching his psaltery while youthful descendants dance around him. The artist pictured the performers within a large initial *E*, which corresponds to the beginning of Psalm 81 / 80 Vulgate: "Rejoice in God our helper" (Exultate Deo, adjutori nostro). Together the text and image replicate David's dance cross-generationally. For devotees using this object as a devotional manual, the imagery would imply a performative transmission of the biblical dancing body. As the next section reveals, pictorializing dance enabled medieval Christians to reinhabit sacred time. And, rather disturbingly, such imagery helped redefine the categories of good and evil.

FIGURE 1. Psalter with King David and his descendants (detail) with a historiated initial *E* (Exultate) for Psalm 81 / 80 Vulgate. Master of Isabella di Chiaromonte, Matteo Felice, illuminators Naples, ca. 1465–70. (The Hague, Koninklijke Bibliotheek [the Netherlands], 131, fol. 86v, used with permission)

Christianizing Dance / Picturing Otherness

The most salient accomplishment of medieval approaches to David was the explicit typology between David and Christ. By typology, I refer to a mode of biblical interpretation in which events or figures from the Old Testament prefigured those in the New Testament (Auerbach 1984). The intimate relationship between David and Christ helped sanctify dance in the medieval West. Incorporating primary source evidence, this section of the chapter articulates the exegetical logic supporting a Christian David. Moreover, typological imagery stereotyped medieval Jews. As such, medieval Christian dance became equally complicit in the degradation and demonization of religious otherness.

In his *Moralia in Iob*, a moralizing commentary on the biblical book of Job, Pope Gregory the Great (d. 604) reformulated the identity of King David. For Gregory, David's dancing rendered him abject (*abjecta*). Upon reflection, Gregory concluded that David's debasement proved more awesome than any military conquest: "I am more surprised at David dancing than fighting. For by fighting he subdued his enemies; but by dancing before the Lord he overcame himself" (Ego David plus saltantem stupeo quam pugnantem. Pugnando quippe hostes subdidit, saltando autem coram Domino semetipsum vicit) (Gregory the Great 1979, translation mine). David's self-effacement was essentially self-sacrifice. The archaic, uncivilized quality of his dance both suspended and enhanced his kingship. Moreover, David's embodied piety prefigured the inversional crux of Christianity: the high become low, and the low become high (Matthew 5).

The Gregorian gloss on David's dance unleashed diverse avenues of intertextual associations that influenced centuries of medieval theology. Gregory's *Moralia* interpolated additional Latin terminology absent from the Vulgate. According to Gregory, David's humility unfolded in the choreography of the wheel (per saltum rotat). The wheel was a multivalent signifier in Christian thought. Evoking the revolutions of celestial bodies, *rotare* (to rotate, revolve, or whirl) aligned David with the cosmic dance. David's *rota* recalibrated martyrdom, given that imperial Roman authorities used to persecute Christians with spiked wheels. Elsewhere Gregory interpreted the wheel as the Old Law / Judaism turning into the New Law / Christianity (Gregory the Great 1990). Gregory interpreted David as a technology of the Christian dancing body, actively transforming a frenzied spectacle into voluntary suffering and thus advancing the progression of sacred time.

In their approaches to sacrifice, religious studies scholars offer complex understandings of the valorization of victimization. Thinkers as diverse as Søren Kierkegaard (2006), Émile Durkheim (1995), and Maurice Blanchot (2009) have theorized the conditions under which divine and human worlds intermingled—sociologically and experientially—in the context of sacrifice. In the 1890s, Henri Herbert and Marcel Mauss pushed sacrificial discourse beyond the simplistic *pars pro toto*, or the draining of one's lifeblood for the sake of the collective social body. Rather, for these thinkers, sacrifice erects a bridge between humanity and divinity that is made possible by the sacrificial victim's intermediary role. In his famous "gift theory," Mauss (2011) took these insights further, drawing attention to ceremonious exchanges that surpassed the logic of quotidian economic transactions. In short, sacrifice, a simultaneous destruction and consecration, allows religious practitioners to (re)articulate the rift between sacred and profane (Robbins 1998, 29–90).

Georges Bataille's work crystallized the dynamics of sacrificial rituals. In Bataille's estimation, religion at its most authentic reestablishes the intimacy between humankind and the sacred. By exhausting the economy of exchange through generosity and consumption, sacrifice transcends the mundane realm (Robbins 1998, 290). Bataille's position on excess and transgression is perhaps more concrete when applied to the prehistoric cave paintings at Lascaux: "A work of art, a sacrifice contains something of an irrepressible festive exuberance that overflows the world of work, and clashes with, if not the letter, the spirit of the prohibitions indispensable to safeguarding this world" (1955, 39). As Bataille explained, the so-called birth of art emerged out of the violent, all-consuming excesses of festival and sacrifice. By negating utilitarianism, accumulation, and ethics, art—like ritual—originated from transgression (Bataille 1988, 55–61; Guerlac 1996, 10–12; Taussig 1998, 356–59).

Bataille's framework resonates with the Christianization of the dance of King David. In consonance with Bataille's theory of sacrifice, due to its exuberance David's dancing transgressed the boundaries of ordinary existence. His taboo action threatened his kingship. Yet through his self-abandonment to "holy play" (*sacer ludus*), David ushered in a radical immanence. Given Christianity's internalization of sacrifice through Christ, the dance's disruption of the normative order rendered David an archetype of piety.

An unfortunate outcome of Christianizing dance was its effect on medieval Jews. Again, the dance of David anecdote provided theologians with a precedent. In the Vulgate, David's wife, Michol, was an easy target for anti-Judaizing polemic. Reacting to her husband's flagrant display, Michol remarked, "How glorious was the king of Israel today, uncovering himself before the handmaids of his servants and was naked, as if one of the buffoons should be naked [quasi si nudetur unus de scurris]" (2 Samuel/Regum 6:20). In response, David defended dance: "I will both play and make myself baser than I have done: and I will be little in my own eyes: and with the handmaids of whom you speak, I shall appear more glorious" (2 Samuel/Regum 6:22). As retribution for her spite, Michol remained infertile, effectively ending her father's dynasty. Within the context of royal succession, 2 Samuel 6 foreshadowed the genesis of Davidic lineage (made possible through his younger wife, Bathsheba). According to the Gospels, it was this very bloodline that culminated in the birth of Jesus Christ.

Medieval commentaries on Michol denounced her Jewishness. For Christians of the era, Jews were synonymous with those who mocked and killed Christ. Consider a passage from the *Glossa ordinaria*, or *Ordinary Gloss*, a twelfth-century compilation of biblical interpretation. Citing Ecclesiastes 3:4 ("a time to mourn and a time to dance"), the *Gloss*'s commentators morph Hebrew scripture into a template for Christian salvation: "We mourn now and we will dance [*saltemus*] in the future, that dance [*saltationem*] which David testified around the ark. The daughter of Saul [Michol] scorns [the dance], but it was pleasing to God" (Froehlich, Gibson, and Rusch 1992, 3:214, translation mine; see also Ambrose of Milan 1955, 181).⁶ The implications of these words transcend the confines of the Bible per se. The text conflates all Jews, ancient and contemporary, arguing that they lack spiritual understanding, flout repentance, and reject grace. The eschatological effects of such behavior are devastating and permanent. In medieval Christian visions of the afterlife, good Christians dance among the blessed for eternity. By contrast, unrepentant sinners and those who spurned Christ suffer eternal damnation.

The anti-Judaic tendencies of medieval biblical interpretation are particularly piquant in the *Bible moralisée* (Moralized Bible). First appearing in thirteenth-century France, these luxury manuscripts combined commentary (often in the Old French vernacular) with rich illustrations, all devoted to biblical themes. Here, I will draw from one of the earliest manuscripts of this genre, which most scholars believe was commissioned by or for Louis VIII, king of France (d. 1226) (Lipton 1999, 1–8; Lowden 2000, 50–51). The folio addressing the dance of King David is most relevant to this study. In the top register, David dances while Michol observes. A figure descends from the heavens to bless David. The caption corresponding to this imagery reads, "Here the ark comes into Jerusalem and David undresses before all the others and takes off his robe as far as his chemise and comes before the ark and dances and is joyous [bale et trippe et dance et kerole et mene ioie] in honor of the ark, and Michol is at a window and sees David and despises him in her heart" (Anon. ca. 1215–29, fol. 44; Guest 1995, 121). In the lower register, David has transformed into Christ, whereas Michol, now ugly and disfigured, is accompanied by Jewish men. A similar figure descends from the heavens and gestures toward Christ. The corresponding caption reads, "The ark, which came into Jerusalem, signifies the Holy Church, which came into the world. David, who danced before

FIGURE 2. Dance of King David, from the *Bible moralisée* (detail), French, early thirteenth century. (Österreichische Nationalbibliothek [Vienna], cod. 2554, fol. 44, used with permission)

the ark [bala devant l'arche], signifies Jesus Christ, who celebrated the Holy Church and celebrated the poor and the simple and showed great humility. Michol, who mocked David and despised him, signifies Synagoga, who mocked Jesus Christ and despised him" (Anon. ca. 1215–29, fol. 44; Guest 1995, 121).

The *Bible moralisée*'s polarization of Judaism and Christianity is self-evident. The text states explicitly the correspondence between David / the ark and Christ / the church. Conversely, the rapport between Michol and Synagoga (the feminine personification of Judaism) identifies Jews as the tormentors of Christ and, by extension, equates the dance of David to the Passion of Christ.

The *Bible moralisée* appeared during an escalation of anti-Jewish activity in Western Europe. Pogroms, blood libel, and the burning of rabbinic books comprised some of the atrocities inflicted on medieval Jews (M. Cohen 2008, 30–51, 139–94; Nirenberg 2013, 135–245). More specifically, the illustrations abound in demeaning caricatures that may reflect actual governmental policy concerning Jews. Under Capetian control—the dynasty to which the manuscript's most likely patron, Louis VIII, belonged—France taxed and administered justice to Jewish territories. Capetians reportedly raided synagogues and expelled Jews from certain areas. Louis VIII himself fought heretics in the Albigensian Crusade in southern France (Lipton 1999).

As historian Sara Lipton has shown, the *Bible moralisée* exploited the primacy of its imagery to develop an aesthetic of unprecedented anti-Jewishness. In her assessment of numerous manuscripts, the artists and commentators who cocreated these works branded Jews as symbols of avarice, usury, pollution, idolatry, heresy, and diabolism (Lipton 1999). Accordingly, the manuscript's Michol (lower register) reappears with Orientalized and distorted features, whereas the Jewish men next to her wear the stereotypical "horned hat" (*pileum cornutum*), all of which exacerbate the aura of discrimination. Within the larger context of premodern anti-Semitism, the *Bible moralisée*'s manipulation of biblical dance helped fabricate an iconography of evil Jews. Pictorializing sacred history wielded powerful effects on the present. As the next section shows, biblical dance imagery could inflict violence, both rhetorical and actual, against religious otherness.

From the Bible to the Battlefield:
Dancer Becomes Crusader

Recent biographies of King David contend that violence was integral to his identity. The Bible may paint him as pious and humble, but the historical David manifested ruthlessness and bloodlust (McKenzie 2000; Baden 2013). The remainder of this chapter shows a reverse strategy, namely, how medieval rulers and warriors appropriated the sacred king and his pious performance to support their own political agendas. Indeed, the sources demonstrate how representations of biblical dance could be wielded to justify and incite violence against non-Christian foreigners.

Content from a French picture Bible (ca. 1244–54) offers direct evidence for the militarization of biblical dance. This codex contains several images of King David, including his dance before the Ark of the Covenant. Here David plays his harp while prancing ebulliently. Musicians play trumpets, viols, timbrels, pipes, bells, and the bones (Weiss 1998b, 290). Others prepare rams for ritual sacrifice, draining their blood into ornamented chalices. Michol peers and gestures from her window in disapproval.[7]

While the iconography itself is not unusual, the politics and patronage concerning this image generate complex layers of meaning. This manuscript, commonly called the Morgan Crusader Bible, belongs to the Pierpont Morgan Library in New York. Likely a collaboration between four Paris-based artists during the Crusades, the manuscript's large-scale illustrations depict Old Testament kings, patriarchs, and military generals. Successive owners added marginal inscriptions in Latin, Persian, and Judeo-Persian, which testify to the manuscript's unusual provenance before the banker John Pierpont Morgan Jr. acquired it in 1916.[8]

FIGURE 3. Dance of King David (detail), Morgan Crusader Bible, Paris, ca. 1244–54. (Pierpont Morgan Library and Museum [New York], MS M 638, fol. 39v, used with permission)

By the term "Crusades," I refer to a succession of military ventures (1095–1291/1396) by which medieval Christians tried to reclaim the Holy Land from Muslims, or the "Saracen infidels" (Claster 2009, xv). Crusaders conjoined warriors and pilgrims. Thus, crusading constituted a religious act. If a crusader died fighting abroad, he would be martyred in heaven. By sanctifying soldiers, the Crusades were considered holy wars authorized by God, not entirely unlike Islamic *jihad* (Constable 2008, 18, 144–46, 155–56; Riley-Smith 2011, 9–28; Claster 2009, xviii). With varying success, the crusaders established a Latin kingdom in the Middle East until the Ottoman Turks forced them to retreat to Europe in 1396.

Scholars surmise that King Louis IX of France (d. 1270) commissioned the picture Bible as propaganda for the Crusades. Louis launched both the Seventh Crusade (1248–54) and the Eighth Crusade (1270) to recapture Jerusalem from the Persians and Egyptians (Claster 2009, 247–52, 260–63). Apparently, Louis was the *rex christianissimus* (most Christian king) due to his remarkable piety, charity, and asceticism. In 1297 the papacy canonized him as a saint (Jordan 1979, 183–93). Louis's spirituality manifests itself in the Crusader Bible. Art historians observe that its biblical episodes are depicted in a French Gothic style, making them appear more contemporary than archaic. With his architectural commission of the Sainte-Chapelle in Paris, Louis sacralized the Capetian dynasty, and specifically his kingship, by re-creating the Ark of the Covenant and the Temple of King Solomon, David's son. In addition to faith and military prowess, David possessed fears and regrets that made him immediately relatable to Louis and his failed Crusade. Accordingly, the Morgan manuscript depicts the crusaders as the new Chosen People and makes a spiritual connection between Paris and Jerusalem (Weiss 1998a, 179–86; 1998b, 229–45; Strayer 1971).

The Morgan artifact is well studied and was the center of a 2014–15 exhibition (*The Morgan Crusader Bible: A Gothic Masterpiece*). Yet analysis of its dance iconography remains paltry. Consider another image that imbricates festive movement and military conquest, here illustrating David's triumph over Goliath from 1 Samuel/Regum 17–18.[9] Courtiers, warriors, musicians, and dancing cheerleaders celebrate David's victory as he enters the city with the head of Goliath on a shepherd's crook. Given the medieval parallel between David and Christ, as well as David and Louis IX, the Crusader Bible's dance imagery differentiates the Christian warrior / David from the Muslim "other" / Goliath. The potency of medieval images comes from theorizations of *imago*. The English "image" does not possess the semiotic richness of the Latin *imago*. For medieval mystics, monastics, and philosophers, *imago* was not merely representational or mimetic; it was a transportative tool of meditation and contemplation.

Both prescriptive and proleptic, *imago* could exemplify sanctity and envision salvation. In the Crusader Bible, dance imagery communicated the ideology of holy war by bridging sacred time to human time. Fueling warriors' morale and mobilizing aggression toward Islam, dance in the Bible addressed contemporary concerns (see also Deshman 1980; A. Cohen 2016).[10]

Intertextually and intervisually, the Morgan Crusader Bible recalls representations of Islamic Others in popular literature. When discussing the Outremer (crusader colonies beyond the sea), medieval travelers described "monstrous" races and grotesque giants inhabiting Africa and the Middle East (Wollesen 2013, 343–44). Read alongside the Crusader Bible, these fanciful accounts facilitated an equation between Goliath and Muslims. Moreover, literary representations of Muslim dancers exuded idolatrous sensuality. In "Malanquin," a story from a thirteenth-century collection of pious tales, a Muslim duke tried to tempt a saintly hermit into sin. After many unsuccessful attempts, the duke confronted him with a beautiful, shapely woman: "She danced before him [tresces devant lui], often peeking through her veil, as proof of her beauty" (Lecoy 1993, 25–26).[11] The hermit resisted and converted the duke to Christianity. The text's French author exoticized the Muslim dancing body, investing it with sexuality, seduction, and perdition, thereby authorizing Western invasion (Galderisi 2005, 81–82, translation mine; Tudor 2005, 47–48, 114–15, 412, 431–37, 577–79).[12]

FIGURE 4. David presents the head of Goliath and Israelite women rejoice (detail), Morgan Crusader Bible, Paris, ca. 1244–54. (Pierpont Morgan Library and Museum [New York], MS M 638, fol. 29, used with permission)

I am not arguing for a direct, or causal, relationship between the Crusades and dance. Rather, I call attention to dance's capacity to signify multiple and even contradictory incentives and to be repurposed for multiple agendas. In fact, Louis IX was concerned about the moral laxity dancing could engender. To sanctify his surroundings, Louis reiterated dance prohibition from earlier centuries, incurring mockery from the satirical poet Rutebeuf (Rutebeuf 1969; Levy 2000, 111–12). However, Louis's personal psalter contains several images of biblical dancers, which suggests that Louis recognized the devotional function of dancing (Anon. [Pseudo] David. ca. 1270, fols. 53, 66, 87). Moreover, medieval chroniclers reported that dances occurred during Louis's wedding celebration (Le Goff 2009, 91). When residing in the Middle East during the Crusades, Louis and his associates welcomed foreign entertainment. Louis's biographer, Jean de Joinville (d. 1317), described three Armenian acrobats who performed before the crusaders and Eastern royalty. They had "les voiz des cynes" (the voice of swans) and delighted the court with acrobatic marvels:

> These men also performed amazing leaps [merveillous saus]. When a mat was put under their feet they would execute a somersault [tournoient tout en estant] from a standing position and finish with their feet back again on the mat. Two of them could make a somersault backward [tournoient les testes arieres]. The eldest did this too, but whenever he was asked to make one head foremost, he would cross himself, for he was afraid of breaking his neck as he turned [il se seignoit; car il avoit paour que il ne se brisast le col au tourner]. (Joinville 1874, 286–88; 1963, 297)

Other crusading monarchs reportedly appreciated foreign, non-Christian dancing bodies. The Holy Roman emperor Frederick II (d. 1250) partook in the Fifth and Sixth Crusades and observed dances in the so-called Saracen style. Frederick spoke Arabic and Greek, employed Muslim soldiers, had a Muslim colony, enjoyed Middle Eastern entertainment, occasionally wore Arab fashions, and allegedly showed religious tolerance toward Muslims (Kantorowicz 1957, 312; Claster 2009, 225, 230–31). Matthew of Paris (d. 1259), an English chronicler who documented Frederick's crusading, described Muslim dancers at Frederick's court: "Two Saracen girls of fine form [due enim puelle Sarracene corporibus elegantes] stood upon four spheres placed upon the floor, one on two balls and the other on the other two, and they danced across the spheres to and fro; and in a festive spirit they gesticulated with their arms, singing in various contorted ways, and twisting their bodies according to the tune, beating cymbals or castanets together with their hands, and prodigiously twirling themselves around in fun. And indeed they afforded a marvelous spectacle [mirabile spectaculum]" (Paris 1888, 18–24; S. Lewis 1987, 280–81). Like Joinville, Matthew praised rather than denounced the performers' skills. Despite the anti-Islamic tendencies of medieval Christianity, Frederick's court provided a space for the valorization of cultural difference. And indeed, recent scholarship reveals the influence of Islamic / Middle Eastern dance culture on the West via musical notation and the visual arts (Temple 2001, 34, 66–75; Zeitler 1997, 36; Folda 2005, 421, 471).

In the crusader chronicles cited above, live performance created a confluence rather than conflict between East and West. These documents challenge a simplistic binary that would divide rhetoric and reality. Westerner nobility clearly appreciated and admired foreign dancing bodies. However, the Saracen performers in Frederick's court were likely "imported," rendering them closer to war booty than autonomous individuals (Wollesen 2013, 345–57). Did dancing Others temper conquest and colonization? Or did dance, reduced to a recreational diversion, mask the brutality of intolerance and warfare? The scope of this chapter cannot begin to address such fraught questions. Nevertheless, a study of medieval dance underscores the tension between politics and pleasure, appropriation and assimilation. In doing so, it asks us to reconsider the many afterlives of dance, in which they become repurposed and reimagined in textual and imagistic reference.

In conclusion, expanding the dance archive to include ancient and medieval materials can challenge dance history periodization, namely, the presumed Renaissance origins of ballet (Homans 2010, 3–11). An excavation into premodern materials suggests that medieval history—with its political, religious, and cross-cultural entanglements—constitutes a prehistory of Western dance. Perhaps, then, to look to the future of our field we can begin to more robustly unearth its past. The fruitful intersections of dance studies and religious studies that have proven so vital for the study of modern dance can be extended to the ancient and medieval world productively, as even in the archive we can chart the repurposing of dance from sacrilege to sanctity and beyond.

Notes

1. The medieval sources often contrast David, the sacred dancer, with Salome, the sinful dancer (Mark 6; Matthew 14; Dickason 2017, 61–74).

2. For a militaristic approach to David's dance, see McNeill (1995, 68–70).

3. All English translations of the Vulgate come from http://vulgate.org/ (accessed April 9, 2019).

4. In medieval art, David is never nude, though he occasionally appears topless with a simple undergarment. Some imagery paralleled the (near) nudity of David with the idealized humility of medieval kings.

5. However, some noncanonical texts may relate David to Dionysius (Dilley 2013).

6. Interestingly, in a sixteenth-century Jesuit apology on dance, the author coined the neologism *micholaiser* (to micholize). This term applied to those who blamed all dance as scandalous, lustful, or vicious, as well as those who relived Michol's erroneous judgment (Anon. 1572; Arcangeli 2000, 214).

7. Interestingly, the Persian inscription (added centuries later) misread Michol's expression as "joyous" (Anon. ca. 1244–54, fol. 39v).

8. Historians believe that the manuscript belonged first to Louis IX and then to his younger brother Charles of Anjou. The first documented owner was cardinal and bishop of Cracow Bernard Maciejowski (d. 1608), who eventually gave it to Shah 'Abbas the Great, king of Persia. The shah displayed religious tolerance toward Christians and was an ally of the Vatican against the Turks. Thus, the codex is also known as the Maciejowski Bible or the Shah 'Abbas Bible (Weiss 1998a, 1998b).

9. For additional dance imagery, see folios 9, 13v, and 17. It is possible that a chronicler recounting Clotaire I's victory over the Saxons in 555 appropriated this same Bible story. See *Vita Faronis.*

10. It is noteworthy that during the First Crusade, crusaders massacred German Jews on their way to the Holy Land, which resulted in medieval Jewish commemorative poetry that integrated biblical dances (Einbinder 2002, 77, 105). For medieval Jewish dance practice, see Salmen (1995); Sparti (2011).

11. *Tresces/tresque* denoted diverse dancing (group dance, a ball, of a sprightly nature, etc.). See Godefroy (1881–1902, 8:47).

12. However, Western crusaders' sack of Constantinople in 1204 and desecration of Hagia Sophia was so brutal that Byzantine chroniclers referred to them collectively as a "dancing harlot" (Choniates 2014, 235–36).

Works Cited

Amalarius of Metz. 1864. *De Ecclesiasticus Officiis*. In *Patrologia Latina*, vol. 105, 985–1242, edited by J.-P. Migne. Paris: Migne.

Ambrose of Milan. 1955. *De poenitentia*. In *Corpus Scriptorum Ecclesiasticorum Latinorum*, vol. 73, edited by O. Faller.

Ancelet-Hustache, J. 1930. "Les *Vitae Sororum* d'Unterlinden: Édition critique du ms. 508 de la Bibliothèque de Colmar." *Archives d'Histoire Doctrinale et Littéraire du Moyen Âge* 5:317–509.

Anon. ca. 1215–29. *Bible moralisée*. Österreichische Nationalbibliothek cod. 2554, Vienna.

Anon. ca. 1244–54. Morgan Crusader Bible. Pierpont Morgan Library MS M 638, New York.

Anon. (Pseudo) David. ca. 1270. The St. Louis Psalter. Bibliothèque Nationale de France ms. lat. 10525, Paris.

Anon. (Pseudo) David. 1465–70. Medieval psalter. Koninklijke Bibliotheek 131, The Hague.

Anon. 1572. *Apologie de la ieunesse, sur le fait & honneste recreation des danses: Contre les calomnies de ceux qui les blasment*. Bibliothèque Mazarine 80 40909–11. Anvers: Grégoire Baldhazar.

Arcangeli, Alessandro. 2000. *Davide o Salomè? Il dibattito europeo sulla danza nella prima età moderna*. Rome: Viella.

Auerbach, Erich. 1984. "Figura." In *Scenes of the Drama of European Literature*, translated by Ralph Manheim, 11–76. Minneapolis: University of Minnesota Press.

Baden, Joel. 2013. *The Historical David: The Real Life of an Invented Hero*. New York: Harper Collins.

Bataille, Georges. 1955. *Prehistoric Painting: Lascaux or the Birth of Art*. Translated by Austryn Wainhouse. Lausanne: Skira.

———. 1988. *The Accursed Share, Volume I*. Translated by Robert Hurley. New York: Zone Books.

Blanchot, Maurice. 2009. *The Unavowable Community*. Barrytown, NY: Station Hill.

Choniates, Niketas. 2014. *Historia Byzantina*. In *The Crusades: A Reader*, edited by S. J. Allen and Emilie Amt, 228–33. Toronto: University of Toronto Press.

Chrysostom, John. 1862. *Expositio in Psalmis*. In *Patrologia Graeca*, vol. 55, 35–526.

Claster, Jill. 2009. *Sacred Violence: The European Crusades to the Middle East, 1095–1396*. Toronto: University of Toronto Press.

Cohen, Adam. 2016. "King Edgar Leaping and Dancing before the Lord." In *Imagining the Jew: Jewishness in Anglo-Saxon Literature and Culture*, edited by Samantha Zacher, 219–36. Ithaca, NY: Cornell University Press.

Cohen, Mark. 2008. *Under Crescent and Cross: The Jews in the Middle Ages*. Princeton, NJ: Princeton University Press.

Constable, Giles. 2008. *Crusaders and Crusading in the Twelfth Century*. Surrey: Ashgate.

(Pseudo) Cyprian of Carthage. 1871. *Liber de Spectaculis*. In *Corpus Scriptorum Ecclesiasticorum Latinorum*, vol. 3, 1–13.

DeFrantz, Thomas. 2004. *Dancing Revelations: Alvin Ailey's Embodiment of African American Culture*. New York: Oxford University Press.

Deshman, Robert. 1980. "The Exalted Servant: The Ruler Theology of the Prayerbook of Charles the Bald." *Viator* 11:385–442.

Desmond, Jane. 1991. "Dancing Out the Difference: Cultural Imperialism and Ruth St. Denis's *Radha* of 1906." *Signs* 17 (1): 28–49.

Dickason, Kathryn. 2017. "Discipline and Redemption: The Dance of Penitence in Dante's *Purgatorio*." *Dante e l'Arte* 4:67–100.

Dilley, Paul. 2013. "*Christus Saltans* as Dionysos and David: The Dance of the Savior in Its Late-Antique Cultural Context." *Apocrypha* 24:237–53.

Durkheim, Émile. 1995. *The Elementary Forms of Religious Life*. Translated by Karen Fields. New York: Simon and Schuster.

Einbinder, Susan. 2002. *Beautiful Death: Jewish Poetry and Martyrdom in Medieval France*. Princeton, NJ: Princeton University Press.

Folda, Jaroslav. 2005. *Crusader Art in the Holy Land: From the Third Crusade to the Fall of Acre, 1187–1291*. Cambridge: Cambridge University Press.

Franko, Mark. 1995. *Dancing Modernism / Performing Politics*. Bloomington: Indiana University Press.

Froehlich, Karlfried, Margaret Gibson, and Adolph Rusch, eds. 1992. *Biblia Latina cum Glossa Ordinaria: Facsimile Reprint of the Editio Princeps Adolph Rusch of Strassburg 1480/81*. 4 vols. Turnhout: Brepols.

Galderisi, Claudio. 2005. *Diegesis: Études sur la poétique des motifs narratifs au Moyen Âge, de la Vie des pères aux lettres modernes*. Turnhout: Brepols.

Godefroy, Frédéric. 1881–1902. *Dictionnaire de l'ancienne langue française, et de tous ses dialectes du IXe au XVe siècle*. 10 vols. Paris: F. Vieweg.

Gregory the Great. 1979. *Moralia in Iob*. In *Corpus Christianorum Series Latina*, vols. 143 and 143B. Edited by M. Adriaen. Turnhout: Brepols.

———. 1990. *Homilies on the Book of the Prophet Ezekiel*. Translated by Theodosia Tomkinson. Etna: Center for Traditionalist Orthodox Studies.

Gruber, Mayer. 1990. "Ten Dance-Derived Expressions in the Hebrew Bible." In *Dance as Religious Studies*, edited by Doug Adams and Diane Apostolos-Cappadona, 48–67. New York: Crossroad.

Guerlac, Suzanne. 1996. "Bataille in Theory: Afterimages (Lascaux)." *Diacritics* 26 (2): 6–17.

Guest, Gerald. 1995. *Bible Moralisée: Codex Vindobonensis 2554, Vienna, Österreichische Nationalbibliothek*. London: Harvey Miller.

Homans, Jennifer. 2010. *Apollo's Angels: A History of Ballet*. New York: Random House.

Joinville, Jean de. 1874. *Jean, sire de Joinville: Histoire de Saint Louis; Credo; et lettre à Louis X*. Edited by Natalis de Wailly. Paris: Librairie de Firmin Didot Frères, Fils et Cie.

———. 1963. *Chronicles of the Crusades*. Translated by Margaret Shaw. London: Penguin.

Jordan, William Chester. 1979. *Louis IX and the Challenge of the Crusade*. Princeton, NJ: Princeton University Press.

Juriansz, Allen. 2013. *King David's Naked Dance: The Dreams, Doctrines, and Dilemmas of the Hebrews*. Bloomington: iUniverse.

Kantorowicz, Ernst. 1957. *Frederick the Second, 1194–1250*. Translated by E. O. Lorimer. New York: Frederick Ungar Publishing.

Kierkegaard, Søren. 2006. *Fear and Trembling*. Edited by C. Evans and Sylvia Walsh. Cambridge: Cambridge University Press.

LaMothe, Kimerer. 2006. *Nietzsche's Dancers: Isadora Duncan, Martha Graham, and the Reevaluation of Christian Values*. New York: Palgrave Macmillan.

Lecoy, Félix, ed. 1993. *La vie des pères*. Vol. 2. Paris: Société des Anciens Textes Français.

Le Goff, Jacques. 2009. *St. Louis*. Translated by Gareth Gollrad. Notre-Dame: University of Notre-Dame Press.

Levy, Brian. 2000. *The Comic Text: Patterns and Images in the Old French Fabliaux*. Amsterdam: Rodopi.

Lewis, Gertrud. 1995. "Music and Dancing in the Fourteenth-Century Sister-Books." In *Vox Mystica: Essays on Medieval Mysticism in Honor of Professor Valerie M. Lagorio*, edited by Anne Bartlett, Thomas Bestul, Janet Goebel, and William Pollard, 159–69. Rochester, NY: D. S. Brewer.

Lewis, Suzanne. 1987. *The Art of Matthew Paris in the Chronica Majora*. Berkeley: University of California Press.

Lipton, Sara. 1999. *Images of Intolerance: The Representation of Jews and Judaism in the Bible Moralisée*. Berkeley: University of California Press.

Lowden, John. 2000. *The Making of the Bibles Moralisées*. Vol. 1. University Park: Pennsylvania State University Press.

Manning, Susan. (1993) 2006. *Ecstasy and the Demon: The Dances of Mary Wigman*. Berkeley: University of California Press.

Manor, Giora, ed. 1992. "The Bible in Dance." Special issue, *Choreography and Dance* 2 (3).

Mauss, Marcel. 2011. *The Gift: The Form and Reason for Exchange in Archaic Societies*. London: Routledge.

McKenzie, Steven. 2000. *David: A Biography*. Oxford: Oxford University Press.

McNeill, William. 1995. *Keeping Together in Time: Dance and Drill in Human History*. Cambridge, MA: Harvard University Press.

Miller, James. 2000. "Christian Aerobics: The Afterlife of Ecclesia's Moralized Motions." In *Acting on the Past: Historical Performances across the Disciplines*, edited by Mark Franko and Annette Richards, 201–37. Middletown, CT: Wesleyan University Press.

Nirenberg, David. 2013. *Anti-Judaism: The Western Tradition*. New York: W. W. Norton.

Paris, Matthew. 1888. *Chronica Majora*. In *Monumenta Germaniae Historica, Scriptores*, vol. 28, 107–389.

Procopius of Gaza. 1865. *Commentarii in Libro II Regum*. In *Patrologia Graeca*, vol. 87, edited by J.-P. Migne, 511–1201.

————. 2007. *Secret History*. Translated by Richard Atwater. New York: Cosimo Classics.

Riley-Smith, Jonathan. 2011. *Crusades: Christianity and Islam*. New York: Columbia University Press.

Robbins, Jill. 1998. "Sacrifice." In *Critical Terms for Religious Studies*, edited by Mark Taylor, 285–97. Chicago: University of Chicago Press.

Ross, Janice. 2014. *Like a Bomb Going Off: Leonid Yakobson and Ballet as Resistance in Soviet Russia*. New Haven, CT: Yale University Press.

Rossen, Rebecca. 2014. *Dancing Jewish: Jewish Identity in American Modern and Postmodern Dance*. Oxford: Oxford University Press.

Rutebeuf. 1969. *Oeuvres complètes de Rutebeuf*. Edited by Edmond Faral and Julia Bastin. Paris: A. et J. Picard et Cie.

Salmen, Walter. 1995. "Jüdische Hochzeit- und Tanzhäuser im Mittelalter." *Aschkenas: Zeitschrift für Geschichte und Kultur der Juden* 5 (1): 107–20.

Schmitt, Jean-Claude. 1990. *La raison des gestes dans l'Occident médiéval*. Paris: Gallimard.

Scolieri, Paul. 2012. "Rhythms of Resurrection: The Comebacks of Ruth St. Denis." *Women and Performance: A Journal of Feminist Theory* 22 (1): 89–107.

Smith, Susan. 1995. "The Bride Stripped Bare: A Rare Type of the Disrobing of Christ." *Gesta* 34 (2): 126–46.

Sparti, Barbara. 2011. "Jewish Dancing-Masters and 'Jewish Dance' in Renaissance Italy: Guglielmo Ebreo and Beyond." In *Seeing Israeli and Jewish Dance*, edited by Judith Brin Ingbar, 235–50. Detroit: Wayne State University Press.

Strayer, Joseph. 1971. "France: The Holy Land, the Chosen People, and the Most Christian King." In *Medieval Statecraft and Perspectives on History: Essays by Joseph Strayer*, 300–314. Princeton, NJ: Princeton University Press.

Taussig, Michael. 1998. "Transgression." In *Critical Terms for Religious Studies*, edited by Mark Taylor, 349–64. Chicago: University of Chicago Press.

Temple, Michele. 2001. *The Middle Eastern Influence on Late Medieval Italian Dances: Origins of the 29987 Istampittas*. Lewiston: Edwin Mellen Press.

Tudor, Adrian. 2005. *Tales of Vice and Virtue: The First Old French "Vie des Pères."* Amsterdam: Rodopi.

Vita Faronis. Turnhout: Brepols, 2010.

Webb, Ruth. 2008. *Demons and Dancers: Performance in Late Antiquity*. Cambridge, MA: Harvard University Press.

Weber, Robert, and Roger Gryson, eds. 2007. *Biblia sacra iuxta vulgatum versionem*. Stuttgart: Deutsche Bibelgesellschaft.

Weiss, Daniel. 1998a. *Art and Crusade in the Age of Saint Louis*. Cambridge: Cambridge University Press.

———, ed. 1998b. *Kreuzritterbible = The Morgan Crusader Bible = La Bible des croisades*. Lucerne: Facsimile Verlag Luzern.

Wollesen, Jens. 2013. "East Meets West and the Problem with Those Pictures." In *East Meets West in the Middle Ages and Early Modern Times: Transcultural Experiences in the Premodern World*, edited by Albrecht Classen, 341–48. Berlin: De Gruyter.

Zeitler, Barbara. 1997. "'Sinful Sons, Falsifiers of the Christian Faith': The Depiction of Muslims in a Crusader Manuscript." *Mediterranean Historical Review* 12 (2): 25–50.

Zimmermann, Julia. 2007. *Teufelsreigen—Engelstänze: Kontinuität und Wandel in mittelalterlichen Tanzdarstellungen*. Frankfurt am Main: P. Lang.

Dancing Dahomey at the World's Fair

Revising the Archive of African Dance

JOANNA DEE DAS

The Dahomeyans dance, of course.

—"Odd Shows at the Fair"

On May 29, 1893, the Dahomey Village opened along the Midway Plaisance at the World's Columbian Exposition in Chicago. For the next five months, performers from the Kingdom of Dahomey (now the country of Benin) put on multiple shows a day in their compound. There were approximately twenty-six million admissions to the fair at a time when the US population was only sixty-five million.[1] Even when factoring in repeat attendees and international visitors, an astonishingly large percentage of Americans walked down the Midway Plaisance. Some paid the extra twenty-five cents to enter the Dahomey Village to witness a staged performance of music and dance; others merely gaped at the Dahomeans, who, in a refusal to remain barricaded inside their compound, danced and sang atop the wall that served as the threshold between the street and the interior.[2] Nor did their dancing remain sealed within the temporal and spatial confines of the Columbian Exposition. A different group of Dahomean dancers resurfaced at the California Midwinter International Exposition (the Midwinter Fair) in 1894 in San Francisco and toured with the Barnum & Bailey circus. Even when their physical bodies departed from the North American continent, their performances remained.[3] The Dahomey Village had an afterlife in minstrelsy, vaudeville, and musical theater, most notably in the George Walker and Bert Williams production *In Dahomey* (1902) and as inspiration for the "In Dahomey" song-and-dance number in the musical *Show Boat* (1927).

Though dance is an ephemeral art form, we can recover the significance of the Dahomey Village performances by following embodied traces from the world's fairs to *Show Boat* and beyond, or what Priya Srinivasan calls a "bodily archive" (2012, 71). Black dance scholarship in particular remains invested in tangible traces of Africanist aesthetics as a challenge to cultural erasure (R. Thompson 1966; Asante 1985; Gottschild 1996; DeFrantz 2014b). Srinivasan argues that modern dance in the United States started not with Ruth St. Denis staring at a cigarette advertisement but rather with the unmarked labor of South Asian women at Coney Island (2012, 73). I make a related move by suggesting that Africanist aesthetics shaped black American performance not only during the centuries of the slave trade but also during the late nineteenth century via the laboring modern bodies of world's fair performers.

I also turn to what I call a colonialist archive to understand the significance of dance at the Dahomey Village.[4] Recent attention to embodied archives has often implied that the traditional material archives of the (colonialist) state have little to offer scholars of performance (Taylor 2003; Schneider 2011). While the colonialist archive cannot reveal how the Dahomeans danced, it uncovers important social and political meanings of that dancing. I read newspaper articles, pamphlets, commemorative books, speeches, and photographs against the grain to show that while late nineteenth-century authors wrote about Dahomean dance to justify white supremacy, dance as a force of resistance is revealed in what Ranajit Guha calls the "distorting mirror" of these authors' discourse ([1983] 1999, 333). The "of course" of the *New-York Tribune* epigraph that opens this chapter implies that the Dahomean Villagers fulfilled the white American expectation that primitive people dance. Yet how, where, and when the Dahomeans danced defied expectations about primitivism and proved to be a means of expressive freedom.

The tension between black performance as object of an oppressive white gaze and black performance as a means of liberation has continued well into the twenty-first century, in which debates about hip hop aesthetics often follow the same contours (DeFrantz 2014a). The Dahomey Village also reflects a diasporic conundrum articulated by Paulla Ebron: not only colonial powers but also people of African descent have conflated the lived realities of people in Africa with the performance of Africa, eager to "sustain their own oppositional version to the ill effects of 'Western' culture" (2002, 3). Performance "is thought to provide a sense of hope and the possibility for the powerless to speak back, indeed, to act out, in response to the West" (5). Ebron criticizes two of the characteristics dance scholars have used to define Africanist aesthetics— namely, polyrhythm and "community feeling"—for "constrain[ing] the range of possibilities" of what Africa can be (33–34). Pinning hopes of resistance on performance threatens to reconfirm Euro-American regimes of representation that continuously fail to imagine African people as full, complex subjects.

With Ebron's cautionary note in mind, I embark on a journey of colonialist archival readings and tracings of the bodily archive in order to imagine dance in the Dahomey Village as capaciously as possible. I recognize the agency of the Dahomeans in making choices that reverberated for decades after in black American performance while acknowledging the limits of interpretation when African dance is imbricated in what Jasmine Johnson (forthcoming) calls the "psychic black project" of liberation.

Reading Dance in the Colonialist Archive

In May 1893 the Chicago World's Fair, officially known as the Columbian Exposition in honor of the four hundredth anniversary of Christopher Columbus's arrival in the Americas, opened its gates to the curious masses. Occurring at the zenith of US imperialism, scientific racism, and industrial growth, the fair promoted Anglo-Saxon superiority, trumpeted the success of capitalism, and showcased the vast technological advances that were purportedly leading the United States to greatness. The San Francisco Midwinter Fair, which occurred a year later, was smaller in scale but operated under similar principles.

A central attraction of both fairs was the Midway Plaisance, which in Chicago was a one-mile-long, six-hundred-foot-wide strip that consisted of a series of ethnic villages populated by "natives" from various locales around the world who cooked, sold handicrafts, and performed in shows. It was "the one quarter most talked about and investigated in the whole Exposition," and its success subsidized the cost of the rest of the fair (Leslie 1893, 99). Organizers insisted on the educational value of the Plaisance as an "illustrated encyclopedia of civilization," but in truth it borrowed much of its organizing principles from minstrelsy, circuses, and curiosity museums (Rydell 1984, 5, 40, 45). The various villages were theatricalized spaces fully invested in the capitalist desire to sell difference.

Visitors expressed a range of responses to the Midway Plaisance. Some sardonically commented upon the blatant commercialism. One reporter declared, "P. T. Barnum should have lived to see this day," and observed a woman in the Laplander village speaking "English with an accent blended of Stockholm and Chicago" (M.S. 1893, 9). Others insisted on its ethnological truth, asserting that the villages "are not make-believes; they are the genuine article," or that the people "are not a part of a show—they are the people themselves" (Hawthorne 1893, 150; Millet 1893, 122–23). Such views were not necessarily contradictory, for as Louis Chude-Sokei points out, "The desires for ethnographic authenticity and the secret desire to be potentially hoodwinked and deceived" are "interlinked" (2006, 164).

Nowhere were these twinned desires more evident than at the Dahomey Village, one of the Plaisance's central attractions. Christopher Robert Reed asserts that the performers were Fon people, subjects of Behanzin, King of Abomey (2000, 144). They may have been from other ethnic groups, however, for by the 1890s Dahomey was a polyglot kingdom that included Yorubans from Nigeria and Afro-Brazilians who had returned from slavery (Bay 2008, 3–5). Thus, this chapter refers to the performers with the broader term "Dahomeans." Xavier Pené, an amateur French geographer and a labor contractor who had spent time in West Africa, brought the group to Chicago, with what mix of coercion and persuasion is unclear. At that time, France and Dahomey were at war, so it is entirely possible that the performers were captives or living under extreme conditions of duress. Pené negotiated a contract with the Chicago fair managers in 1892 that included stipulated performances of "military maneuvers," "modes of combat," and religious ceremonies daily at the village site (Rydell 1999, 137–38).

Though the Plaisance featured Algerian, Egyptian, and Sudanese groups, Dahomey represented black Africa, standing in both for the whole of the continent and for a specific place with which Europeans and Americans were relatively familiar. As early as 1793, one Englishman remarked that the path from the port of Whydah to the inland city of Abomey was "perhaps the most beaten track, by Europeans, of any in Africa" (Dalzel 1793, 19). Despite such familiarity, wild stories persisted about Dahomeans' ruthlessness, savagery, and thirst for blood, myths that were used to justify France's attempts to conquer and colonize the kingdom (Herskovits [1938] 1967, 3). According to Robert Rydell, the Dahomey Village represented the "pornography of power" that "was so vital to the efforts of imperialists trying to build public support for their expansionist schemes" (1999, 140). The supposed savagery and debasement of the villagers became data points in social Darwinist arguments legitimizing racism against African Americans and part of "an enduring and successful propaganda effort aimed at reinforcing a racial hierarchy of white supremacy" (Reed 2000, 144).

Fairgoers mentioned dance as evidence to support their view of Africans as less than human. Hubert Bancroft, who published one of the most influential works on the fair, wrote a description of the Dahomey Village. In his words, the performances began with the "drum-major" tapping his drum in a "gentle, rhythmic" pattern; eventually all the musicians joined in. Once the full band was hard at work, the dancers were "aroused from sleep or stupor"—at least, they performed the idea of being unable to resist the insistent rhythm. The dancers began to "beat time to the music" and then, on the leader's cue, commenced a "war-dance." They marched back and forth, "brandishing war-clubs and grinning as only Dahomeans can grin." After a few minutes, "the posturing begins; but in this there is nothing of the graceful or sensuous; simply a contortion and quivering of limb and body" (Bancroft 1893, 878).

One way to read Bancroft's description against the grain is to pair it with footage of Dahomean dance filmed by the white American anthropologist Melville Herskovits in 1931. Inevitably circumscribed by Herskovits's world-view and shot decades after the fair on a different continent, the films are not without their own limitations as source material. Herskovits recorded several dances, though none of them are war dances. Instead, the people on the cel-luloid dance to mourn the dead, venerate ancestors, honor kings, and worship gods. Certain characteristics prevail. Throughout there is the consistent pulsing of the torso front to back, or what one might consider rapid contractions and releases of the spine. Sometimes, as in the procession for a returned ancestor, these pulses are gentle, subtle. In the dances for the thunder god, the articula-tion of the back is sharper, more forceful, and faster.[5] Perhaps Bancroft observed this rapid contraction and release of the spine, which in a need to justify white supremacy he characterized as ungraceful "quivering" and "contortion."

Bancroft also noted the use of props, writing that the Dahomeans engaged in the "swinging of weapons as though nothing would delight them more than to kill and destroy" (1893, 878). Herskovits filmed the Ghungan, a chief's dance honoring the king in which the performer holds a machete or hatchet. The dancer's movements are precise, controlled, and defined. As he keeps a steady beat with the stepping of his feet, he rolls his shoulders and articulates his torso in the frontal plane at a faster tempo, embodying polyrhythm. His left hand holds the hooked blade, and he strikes it at exactly the same place each time he slices diagonally through the air in front of his body. Perhaps the Dahomey Village dancers, too, had a directional energy and force in their bodies as they swung their props. Perhaps the performers delighted in inject-ing some fear into their audiences; perhaps they enjoyed performing power. What we can take away from Bancroft's description of the Dahomean "grin" is a sense of the acting abilities of these performers. After weeks of putting on the same repetitive marching dance, they still wore the smiling mask to draw in the curious visitors.

The source pairing can also be done with a report from a *New-York Tribune* journalist. He wrote that to perform Dahomean dance, "it is only necessary to stand on one foot for several seconds, leap in the air suddenly, come down on the other foot, stand on that for a while, hop across the floor, and yell" (*New-York Tribune* 1893, 17). Like Bancroft's description, his characterization must be read as a distortion to justify colonial subjugation of Africa. Can we actually envision how the Dahomeans traveled through space? In Herskovits's film of a ceremony to honor the Loko tree, the main motion is not the contraction and release of the spine as in other dances but the turn. Dancers rotate in place, knees slightly bent, torsos slightly pitched forward, skirts twirling out. Sometimes the turns involve pushing off of one leg, then placing it back down once the rotation is complete. Other dancers jump from one leg to the other as they turn, occasionally leaning on the diagonal in a barrel leap fashion. Were these the *New-York Tribune* reporter's "hops"?

A more learned observer of the Dahomey performances who avoided sensationalism but still employed the language of "savage" and "primitive" was musicologist Henry E. Krehbiel. He complimented the skill and complexity of the Dahomean music: "The players have the most remarkable rhythmical sense and skill that have ever come under my observation. Berlioz, in his supremest effort, with his army of drummers, has nothing to compare in artistic interest with the harmonious drumming of these savages" (Krehbiel 1893, 14). He wrote that the performers of a war dance "moved with measured steps, keeping admirable time, up and down the dancing floor, sometimes in direct, but oftener in oblique movement" (14). One of Krehbiel's companions observed another performance, during which the dancers "began to keep step with absolute precision" even as the tempo and rhythm changed "from double to compound triple time" and the singers sang an "antiphonal allegro phrase" (14). These descriptions offer a skeletal sense of the geometric and rhythmic patterns that the Dahomeans created for their performances. They raise the intriguing possibility that certain Africanist aesthetics in twentieth-century black American performance, such as polyrhythm and ephebism (Gottschild 1996, 13–17), were at least in part the result of exchanges between African Americans attending the fair and the Dahomey villagers. Such a possibility affirms Nadine George-Graves's way of theorizing diaspora as a web of connections that can form contemporaneously rather than only chronologically (2014, 37).

Descriptions of the Dahomey Village at the California Midwinter Fair, however, undo any sense of certainty about aesthetic qualities of Dahomean movement in the 1890s. Like the Columbian Exposition, the San Francisco fair included a Midway Plaisance with reproductions of ethnic villages. Most of the villages came directly from Chicago and arrived in late January 1894. Some sources mistakenly state that the Dahomey Village was a part of this transplantation (Lipsky 2002, 71). Instead, the Dahomey Village opened five months later, in late May, with a new group of performers under the same manager, Xavier Pené (*San Francisco Chronicle* 1894a, 1894b). In describing the performances of this troupe, one journalist likened the dancing to a striptease: "The principal danseuse purposely removes the top pin from the folds of [her] dress so as to let the garment fall lower. She keeps smiling the while. When she finishes her dance she retires to the group of females in the rear and another of the dusky beauties advances to go through the same performance." The reporter also noticed a "faint suggestion of the hula-hula" (*San Francisco Chronicle* 1894c). Chicago observers had never mentioned disrobing or circular movement. Instead, they had stressed jumping, leaping, marching, and "quivering." Were the San Francisco performers from a different ethnic group within the Kingdom of Dahomey, with different movement aesthetics? Had Pené or San Francisco fair organizers demanded more seductive performances this time around, inspired by the success of the dancing women of Cairo Street in Chicago (Carlton 1994)?

Photographs provide another failed insight into the embodied performances of Dahomeans at the fairs. As Robin Bernstein contends, "things" such as photographs "script" human behavior to construct race (2009, 68). A script offers directions for action but leaves open the possibility for resistance and human agency. The photographs of the Dahomey Villagers were certainly staged by either Pené, fair organizers, or photographers, scripting viewers' responses to emphasize black primitivism and thus justify European or American imperialist endeavors. Even more so than the written texts, the photographs reveal the gendered dynamics of the scripted performance of racial Otherness. "Amazons," or female soldiers in King Behanzin's army, captured the American imagination more than any other aspect of Dahomean culture. Myths multiplied about these women warriors, known in Dahomey as *ahosi*, "king's wives," or *mino*, "our mothers" (Law 1993, 245). Their existence contradicted Victorian gender ideals of female passivity and domesticity, and visitors to the fair clamored to see Amazons in battle mode, naked to the waist and waving weapons.

Photographs from both fairs reveal how these women, like the representations of most people of African descent in European and Euro-American visual art, were "hypervisible and disappeared, spectacularly present and not seen" (K. Thompson 2011, 28). In a large group photograph from the Chicago fair (Figure 5), the men wear long robes or fabric that drapes across their torsos, whereas the women wear knee-length pants and no tops—the opposite of high-necked, long-skirted Victorian garb. Both men and women raise their arms, some wielding hatchets or long spears. The mixed-sex grouping also defied Victorian social codes of separate spheres for men and women, though world's fairs were primary sites where Americans began to challenge gender separation (Sotiropoulos 2006, 5). The photograph scripts viewers to see Dahomeans as warrior-like and Dahomean women as particularly unfeminine. It is tempting to read boredom, resentment, and defiance on the faces of the performers in a desire to destabilize such a script. Nineteenth-century photographic technology, however, required people to sit still for several minutes, with the result that virtually all photographed subjects of the era exude a stiff and serious demeanor. The Dahomeans' facial expressions may simply be a result of exhaustion from posing for so long.

The performance of masculinist aggression scripted by the first photograph was apparently not borne out in the live performances of song and dance. In a commemorative book of the Chicago fair, one writer remarked of the Dahomean women that "no proof of their fierce nature was displayed in Midway life," though he assured readers that their "frightfully scarred" bodies proved that they had been warriors in their homeland. The writer called them "hideous looking" and, paradoxically, "objects of attraction and even admiration" (*Chicago Times Portfolio* 1893). The ambivalence of his commentary is borne out by the photograph accompanying it. Someone seemingly superimposed clothing on the Dahomean women after the photograph was taken. While still not in what would be considered proper Victorian style, the scarves and shirts cover their breasts. They no longer carry weapons or make gestures

FIGURE 5. The Dahomey Village, Chicago, 1893. (Photo by C. D. Arnold, Chicago Public Library, Special Collections, C. D. Arnold Photographic Collection, 1891–1893, vol. 10, plate 70)

of attack. The caption guides viewers to believe that the Dahomean women embody a ferocity unknown to white women, but the nonconfrontational poses and suggestion of "civilization" with the semiclothed bodies and unscarred skin script a more ambivalent read.

Retreating even further from the masculinist warrior image, photographs from the San Francisco fair emphasize Dahomean women's sexual desirability. Figure 6 appeared in *The Official History of the California Midwinter International Exposition* with the caption "Dahomey Girls in Picturesque Poses" (1894, 150). The women carry weapons, but they are not aimed at the viewer. In fact, the woman in front has laid her weapon on the ground. The obvious arrangement of the composition renders the women as objects rather than subjects, moveable parts to create a pleasing picture. The author calls them "girls" rather than "women," suggesting a playful rather than homicidal nature. The women's breasts are only partially revealed, either seen in profile or covered in part by other limbs such as a shoulder or hand. The carefully choreographed tableau forefronts sexual desirability in a manner that photographs with the women fully facing front attempt to deny.

One incident at the Chicago fair reveals how dance laid bare the desirability of Dahomean women, though like all materials from the colonialist archive the stories still deny the women their full subjectivity (K. Thompson 2011). On August 16, 1893, the concessionaires' club of the fair had sponsored an International Ball. The American entrepreneur George Francis Train led the initial grand march with his chosen partner, Zahtoobe, a Dahomean woman who created a dress for the occasion made out of small American flags. After performances from various nations, the dance floor opened up for waltzes, quadrilles, polkas, and other European social dances. American men in "dress suits" quickly partnered up with "black Amazons" to dance the night away (*Boston Daily Globe* 1893; *Chicago Daily Tribune* 1893b). No articles mentioned white women dancing with Dahomean men—such a transgression would have been too much in 1890s America. Even the inverse, however, was a startling breach of racial norms that caused a scandal. The story appeared on the front pages of both the *Boston Daily Globe* and *Chicago Daily Tribune*. It acknowledged, first, black women's desirability and, second, the ease with which they could dance European genres. The barriers between purportedly primitive and civilized cultures broke down on the dance floor.

Even in materials not officially reporting on Midway Plaisance performances, Dahomeans dance constantly across the colonialist archive. Framed as evidence of unruly or uncivilized behavior, the stories reveal how the Dahomey villagers embodied freedom. At the June 16, 1893, parade along Chicago's Midway Plaisance, William Cameron records that the Dahomean men "persisted in

FIGURE 6. "Dahomeyan Girls with War Hatchets and Knives, Dahomeyan Village, C.M.I.E.," 1894. Souvenir of the California Midwinter International Exposition (graphic), presented to F. A. Haber, chief of the Viticulture Department, San Francisco. (Photograph taken by I. W. Taber, BANC PIC 1976.029:86A-ffAI-8, courtesy of the Bancroft Library, University of California, Berkeley)

progressing with a one-two-three side shuffle that threatened to delay the procession several hours, until their 'boss' told them to march straight ahead. Then
they struck out on a loping dance" (1893, 682). Moving sideways and accelerat-
ing forward, the performers jammed the imperial machinery of the "straight"
march. Multiple sources report that the Dahomeans danced on top of the
ten-foot-high wall overlooking the Plaisance instead of fulfilling their contractual obligation to remain inside their compound (Hawthorne 1893, 148; *Chicago Daily Tribune* 1893a). Instead of merely being objects of the gaze, they
reversed it to gaze down at the visitors promenading along the thoroughfare.
Finally, the Dahomeans used embodied refusal to protest conditions at the
Chicago fair. Underpaid and tired of the cold weather, they went on strike.
The dancing bodies sat still. At first they negotiated a compromise with Pené,
but, unsatisfied with the result, they eventually forced him to take them home
a full month before the fair ended (*Chicago Daily Tribune* 1893a, 1893c).

Dance also factored into how African Americans responded to the Dahomey
Village. The fairs occurred during a historical moment considered the "nadir"
of black life in the United States (Logan 1954), in which violence against African
Americans rose precipitously and rights that had accrued under Reconstruction from 1865 to 1877 vanished as southern "Redeemer" governments regained
power. Several white visitors to the Chicago fair wrote about the Dahomeans
as proof of the debasement of the black race and cracked jokes about African
American pretensions toward difference, seeing the two groups as interchangeable (Benedict 1994, 53).

The first impulse of many African American visitors, then, was to reject such
an easy equation. Missionaries from the AME and Baptist Churches, emigra-
tionists, and many others converged in characterizing the Dahomeans as backward, savage, and in need of tutelage from their civilized brethren in the United
States (Reed 2000, 168). Frederick Douglass, in a famed speech given on Colored American Day at the Chicago fair, used the Dahomeans as a point of contrast to showcase African American progress: "Look at the progress the Negro
has made in thirty years! We have come up out of Dahomey unto this. Measure the Negro. But not by the standard of the splendid civilization of the
Caucasian. Bend down and measure him—measure him from the depths
out of which he has risen" ([1893] 2000, 194). We cannot know to what extent
Douglass genuinely believed such rhetoric or whether he was strategically
adopting Progressive Era language to further the political goals of African
Americans. Either way, what Douglass did not condemn, interestingly, were
the "dance and ceremonies," which he claimed "were all on the same principle,
if not quite so well developed, as those of people living nearer to civilization"

(quoted in Rydell 1999, 142). This concession to the performers' dance abilities provided an opening, a way for the representation of African life at the fair to have a positive rather than a negative effect on the fight for racial equality.

The response of the many black entertainers who visited the Chicago fair is unknown. It seems impossible that they did not engage with Dahomeans on some level, however, given that according to multiple sources ragtime music had its creative birth at the fair as a synthesis of black American and Midway Plaisance rhythms (Sotiropoulos 2006, 39). Will Marion Cook, who composed the music for the musical *In Dahomey*, worked at the fair for its duration (Carter 2008, 27). Jesse Shipp, who wrote the script, performed in *The Creole Show* in Chicago during the fair (Sotiropoulos 2006, 37). Presumably they were two of the twenty-six million visitors who passed by the Dahomey Village compound. If they did not venture inside, did they at least see the men and women dancing atop the wall or hear their music from a distance?

In San Francisco the relationship between African Americans and the African performers had clearer lines of alliance. According to one history of the Midwinter Fair, black San Franciscans "treated the Dahomeans as envoys from a foreign country, and invited them to local lodges for formal receptions" (Chandler and Nathan 1993, 19). The curious circumstances of the Dahomey Village setup may have contributed. According to George Walker, the San Francisco organizers hired him and Bert Williams to impersonate Dahomeans in the village during the months before the group's arrival (1906, 248). Though Walker implies that visitors failed to notice the difference, the press had made it clear that the "real" Dahomeans did not arrive until May, five months after the opening. Thus the fairgoers were in on the charade and did not seem to mind, perhaps already having decided on the fluid interchangeability of blackness. Once the Dahomeans arrived, the two vaudevillians stuck around, developing camaraderie with their continental counterparts and observing their performances.

Embodied Traces of Dahomey

In 1902 Williams and Walker premiered *In Dahomey*, the inspiration for which Walker explicitly attributes to their experiences at the Midwinter Fair eight years prior. Walker wrote that the duo decided "we would delineate and feature native African characters as far as we could, and still remain American, and make our acting interesting and entertaining to American audiences" (1906, 248). Daphne Brooks calls this approach a "kind of Afro-diasporic alienation effect," in which the performers explored "ways to articulate the dissonant multivocality of black identity in performance space" (2006, 224). They neither completely rejected nor fully accepted the conflation of African or African

American, instead attempting to show the connections and disjunctures simultaneously. Louis Chude-Sokei sees *In Dahomey*'s incorporation of "the gestures, sounds, and clothing of Dahomeyans" as a means "to wage war with the racist stereotypes that were celebrated and disseminated by the colonial expositions" and to challenge African American ambivalence about connections to Africa (2006, 166–67). Therefore, Chude-Sokei argues, *In Dahomey* anticipated the Harlem Renaissance's "strategies of performance in the struggle for racial liberation" and "paved the way for Garveyite pan-Africanism" (171, 188). While no sources mention choreographer Aida Overton Walker's relationship to the Dahomey Village, it is clear that in the wake of the world's fairs of 1893 and 1894 the embodied performance of Africa became a key feature of black vaudeville.

Williams and Walker's influence on future generations of black musical theater is well established. The reemergence of the Dahomey Village in another setting—the interracial musical *Show Boat*—reveals a second, less well known path by which Dahomey endured in black performance. In 1927 Jerome Kern and Oscar Hammerstein, upon hearing of Williams and Walker's origin story for *In Dahomey*, incorporated the tale of impersonation into *Show Boat*. At the beginning of act 2, the characters Ravenal and Magnolia visit the 1893 Chicago World's Fair. When the couple exits, the white chorus stays onstage, moving upstage to form a crowd of onlookers as the "Dahomeys" come out of the "Village." The Dahomeans begin to sing nonsense lyrics:

Dyunga doe
Dyunga doe
Dyunga hungy ung gunga
Hunga ung gunga go.

The script gives no notes about the dancing that accompanies such syllables, but the movements combined with the chanting scare the white chorus offstage ("Play Script: 'Show Boat'" ca. 1927).

Once the white chorus flees, the black chorus breaks out of their performance of Africanness, revealing that they are in fact Americans. They sing,

We're glad to see them go;
We're glad to see those white folks go;
We've had enough
Of all this stuff—
We wish we'd never come here
To join a Dahomey show! ("Play Script: 'Show Boat'" ca. 1927)

They proceed to sing nostalgically about their hometown, New York City, and the fun parties they attend there. In contrast, they characterize Dahomey as populated by boring "mild folks," upending the savage imagery of Africanness ("Play Script: 'Show Boat'" ca. 1927). They then begin dancing to jazz music, more typical of the 1920s than the 1893 setting (Decker 2013, 117–18).

One review called the "In Dahomey" scene a "raucous interruption of static on a radio waltz" (Bellamy ca. 1927). That "raucous interruption of static" is the moment in *Show Boat* where the black characters get to break with their roles in the rest of the musical: as nostalgic background for a false image of the South in 1890s, as victims of the tragedy of racism, or as wise and worldly black sages. The African Americans playing Dahomeans sing longingly of New York, resisting the plantation nostalgia of the rest of the production. They scare the white chorus offstage, break with the false performance of African savagery, and find expressive freedom in dancing among themselves. Neither the choreographer, Sammy Lee, nor the chorus members attempted anything like African dance; instead, they used the performance of it to expose white ignorance and critique racial assumptions.

By the time the 1946 revival appeared on Broadway with dancer Pearl Primus as a featured member of the chorus, new political and artistic developments had necessitated a shift in the performance of Africanness. Pan-African thought, which until the 1930s had still largely followed imperialist assumptions about African American superiority, increasingly turned to anticolonial solidarity after Emperor Haile Selassie of Ethiopia successfully repelled Italy's 1935 invasion (Von Eschen 1997, 8). In 1934 Asadata Dafora of Sierra Leone performed *Kykunkor*, or what was called a "folk opera," on Broadway. For many American audiences, it was the first time a performer from Africa had presented "authentic" dances, and it set a new standard for the performance of Africa in the realm of so-called high art (Perpener 2001, 108–10; Manning 2004, 44–54). Increasing anticolonial activism and the legitimacy now afforded African dance opened up new possibilities when invoking the Dahomey Village.

The white modern dancer Helen Tamiris officially choreographed the 1946 version of *Show Boat*, but it was widely acknowledged that either she encouraged Primus to create her own movement or the two collaborated closely. For "In Dahomey," Primus and the dance chorus, which included former Katherine Dunham dancers Talley Beatty, Claude Marchant, and La Verne French, did not sing fake lyrics or suggest that they were African Americans burlesquing African dance. Instead, Primus was called in sincerity a "Dahomeyan Queen" and performed a series of powerful jumps and leaps meant to signify as authentic African dance. Walter Terry of the *Herald Tribune* wrote that "In Dahomey" had "the intensity of an incantation as the pounding feet and vibrating bodies generate rhythmical magic" (quoted in Decker 2013, 176). Primus had not been to Africa at that point. She most likely drew upon her interactions with Nigerian students from Columbia University, books at the New York Public Library, and Trinidadian dance that she learned from her family and dancer Beryl McBurnie, the three primary sources she drew upon to teach African dance at the New Dance Group (Schwartz and Schwartz 2011, 30–31). Regardless of how nearly or distantly Primus's movement aesthetics mirrored those of the 1893 Dahomey villagers, she invoked the political memory of their expressive freedom.

Primus's "Dahomeyan Queen" became the template for the 1948 touring production, which featured La Verne French as the "Dahomeyan King." Reviews across the country lauded French's "splendid acrobatic dancing" and called him "superbly lithe and rhythmic in movement and strikingly dramatic in pantomime, particularly in the native sketch in 'In Dahomey'" (Rodgers 1947–49, 45–57). Eventually, Geoffrey Holder and Alvin Ailey also played the "Dahomeyan King," leading musicologist Todd Decker to proclaim that "In Dahomey" germinated "historic innovation of new, danced, black masculinities that would emerge with great power in the late 1950s" (2013, 178). The "In Dahomey" number disappeared from *Show Boat* revivals precisely at the time when nations in Africa gained their independence and began sending their own dance companies on tour internationally. Self-representation became a new factor in the performance of Africa across the diaspora. Nevertheless, the impact on the future of black concert dance had been made.

The African men and women at the 1893 Columbian Exposition and 1894 Midwinter Fair left an indelible imprint on black American performance. Their dances, regardless of the authenticity of reproduction of actual traditions from the Kingdom of Dahomey, were certainly authentic creations of that group of performers themselves. In what one could think of as the most exploitative of conditions, the Dahomey Village performers exerted choreographic agency, compelled audiences to recognize their humanity, and staged acts of resistance. Through bodily mobility and immobility, they insisted on the value of their lives and labor. They precipitated a wave of imitation and inspiration that rebounded throughout the twentieth century and beyond, raising questions about the linkages of diaspora, the political utility of dance, and the timelines of Africanist aesthetic influence in the Americas.

Notes

1. Figures range between twenty-five and twenty-seven million. See Larsen (2004) and Chicago Historical Society (1999).

2. I will use the most commonly accepted spelling, "Dahomean," but "Dahomeyan" is an accepted variant. In citing historical material, I will use whichever spelling the author has chosen.

3. In using this language, I draw upon Rebecca Schneider (2011).

4. The United States did not colonize Africa in the 1890s, but its interactions with Dahomeans were *colonialist* in their power dynamics.

5. Descriptions based upon my viewing of the 1931 Melville Herskovits film. See Herskovits (1931).

Works Cited

Asante, Kariamu Welsh. 1985. "Commonalities in African Dance: An Aesthetic Foundation." In *African Culture: The Rhythms of Unity*, edited by Molefi K. Asante and Kariamu Welsh Asante, 71–82. Trenton, NJ: Africa World Press.

Bancroft, Hubert Howe. 1893. *The Book of the Fair: An Historical and Descriptive Presentation of the World's Science, Art, and Industry, as Viewed through the Columbian Exposition at Chicago in 1893*. Chicago: Bancroft Company.

Bay, Edna G. 2008. *Asen, Ancestors, and Vodun: Tracing Change in African Art*. Urbana: University of Illinois Press.

Bellamy, Francis R. ca. 1927. "Lights Down." Box 14, folder 23, Flo Ziegfeld–Billy Burke Papers, New York Public Library for the Performing Arts, Jerome Robbins Dance Division.

Benedict, Burton. 1994. "Rituals of Representation: Ethnic Stereotypes and Colonized Peoples at World's Fairs." In *Fair Representations: World's Fairs and the Modern World*, edited by Robert W. Rydell and Nancy E. Gwinn, 28–61. Amsterdam: VU University Press.

Bernstein, Robin. 2009. "Dances with Things: Material Culture and the Performance of Race." *Social Text 101* 27 (4): 67–94.

Boston Daily Globe. 1893. "Ball of Wickedness: Midway Plaisance People Have a Dance." August 17, 1.

Brooks, Daphne A. 2006. *Bodies in Dissent: Spectacular Performances of Race and Freedom, 1850–1910*. Durham, NC: Duke University Press.

Cameron, William. 1893. *The World's Fair: Being a Pictorial History of the Columbian Exposition*. Chicago: J. R. Jones.

Carlton, Donna. 1994. *Looking for Little Egypt*. Bloomington, IN: IDD Books.

Carter, Marva Griffin. 2008. *Swing Along: The Musical Life of Will Marion Cook*. New York: Oxford University Press.

Chandler, Arthur, and Marvin Nathan. 1993. *The Fantastic Fair: The Story of the California Midwinter International Exposition*. San Francisco: Pogo Press.

Chicago Daily Tribune. 1893a. "Dahomey to Remain till Oct. 30: Manager Pene Effects a Compromise with the Fair and Striking Natives." September 24, 3.

———. 1893b. "The International Ball at the Fair." August 17, 1.

———. 1893c. "The Midway: Success of the Street." November 1, 16.

Chicago Historical Society. 1999. "The World's Columbian Exposition." https://www.chicagohs.org/history/expo.html.

Chicago Times Portfolio of the Midway Types. 1893. Pt. 12. Chicago: American Engineering Company.

Chude-Sokei, Louis. 2006. *The Last "Darky": Bert Williams, Black-on-Black Minstrelsy, and the African Diaspora*. Durham, NC: Duke University Press.

Dalzel, Archibald. 1793. *The History of Dahomey, an Inland Kingdom of Africa*. London: T. Spilsbury and Son.

Decker, Todd. 2013. *Show Boat: Performing Race in an American Musical*. New York: Oxford University Press.

DeFrantz, Thomas. 2014a. "Hip Hop Habitus v2.0." In *Black Performance Theory*, edited by Thomas DeFrantz and Anita Gonzalez, 223–42. Durham, NC: Duke University Press.

———. 2014b. Introduction to *Black Performance Theory*, edited by Thomas DeFrantz and Anita Gonzalez, 1–18. Durham, NC: Duke University Press.

Douglass, Frederick. (1893) 2000. "Speech at Colored American Day." Reprinted in *"All the World Is Here!": The Black Presence at White City*, by Christopher Robert Reed, 193–94. Bloomington: Indiana University Press.

Ebron, Paulla. 2002. *Performing Africa*. Princeton, NJ: Princeton University Press.

George-Graves, Nadine. 2014. "Diasporic Spidering: Constructing Contemporary Black Identities." In *Black Performance Theory*, edited by Thomas DeFrantz and Anita Gonzalez, 33–44. Durham, NC: Duke University Press.

Gottschild, Brenda Dixon. 1996. *Digging the Africanist Presence in American Performance: Dance and Other Contexts*. Westport, CT: Greenwood Press.

Guha, Ranajit. (1983) 1999. *Elementary Aspects of Peasant Insurgency in India*. Durham, NC: Duke University Press.

Hawthorne, Julian. 1893. *Humors of the Fair*. Chicago: E. A. Weeks.

Herskovits, Melville. 1931. "Herskovits' Film Study of West Africa, 1931." Human Studies Film Archives, Smithsonian Institution, Washington, DC.

———. (1938) 1967. *Dahomey: An Ancient West African Kingdom*. Evanston, IL: Northwestern University Press.

Johnson, Jasmine E. Forthcoming. *Rhythm Nation: West African Dance and the Politics of Diaspora*. New York: Oxford University Press.

Krehbiel, Henry E. 1893. "Folk-Music in Chicago: Songs and Dances of the Dahomans." *New-York Tribune*, August 20, 14.

Larsen, Erik. 2004. *The Devil in the White City: Murder, Magic, and Madness at the Fair That Changed America*. New York: Vintage.

Law, Robin. 1993. "The 'Amazons' of Dahomey." *Paideuma* 39:245–60.

Leslie, Amy. 1893. *Amy Leslie at the Fair*. Chicago: W. B. Conkey Company.

Lipsky, William. 2002. *Images of America: San Francisco's Midwinter Exposition*. Chicago: Arcadia Publishing.

Logan, Rayford. 1954. *The Negro in American Life and Thought: The Nadir, 1877–1901*. New York: Dial Press.

Manning, Susan. 2004. *Modern Dance, Negro Dance: Race in Motion*. Minneapolis: University of Minnesota Press.

Millet, Frank D., et al. 1893. *Some Artists at the Fair*. New York: Charles Scribner's Sons.

M.S. 1893. "Wonderful Place for Fun; What the Money Catchers Offer in Midway Plaisance." *New York Times*, June 19, 9.

New-York Tribune. 1893. "Odd Shows at the Fair: Theatrical Performances on the Midway Plaisance." June 25, 17.

The Official History of the California Midwinter International Exposition: A Descriptive Record of the Origin, Development and Success of the Great Industrial Expositional Enterprise, Held in San Francisco from January to July, 1894. 1894. San Francisco: H. S. Crocker Co.

Perpener, John O. 2001. *African-American Concert Dance: the Harlem Renaissance and Beyond.* Urbana: University of Illinois Press.

"Play Script: 'Show Boat.'" ca. 1927. T-MSS 1987-010, box 5, folder 5, Flo Ziegfeld–Billy Burke Papers, New York Public Library for the Performing Arts, Jerome Robbins Dance Division.

Reed, Christopher Robert. 2000. *"All the World Is Here!": The Black Presence at White City.* Bloomington: Indiana University Press.

Rodgers, Richard. 1947–49. Scrapbook, bk. 17, Billy Rose Theatre Collection, New York Public Library for the Performing Arts.

Rydell, Robert W. 1984. *All the World's a Fair: Visions of Empire at American International Expositions, 1876–1916.* Chicago: University of Chicago Press.

———. 1999. "'Darkest Africa': African Shows at America's World's Fairs, 1893–1940." In *Africans on Stage: Studies in Ethnological Show Business,* edited by Bernth Lindfors, 135–55. Bloomington: Indiana University Press.

San Francisco Chronicle. 1894a. "Beauty Is Their Fad: Queer Folks from Darkest Africa." May 27, 16.

———. 1894b. "Oration by Talmage: He Will Speak at the Fair To-Day." May 30, 5.

———. 1894c. "Pictures in Powder: Fireworks at the Fair To-Night." June 2, 8.

Schneider, Rebecca. 2011. *Performing Remains: Art and War in Times of Theatrical Reenactment.* New York: Routledge.

Schwartz, Peggy, and Murray Schwartz. 2011. *The Dance Claimed Me: A Biography of Pearl Primus.* New Haven, CT: Yale University Press.

Sotiropoulos, Karen. 2006. *Staging Race: Black Performers in Turn of the Century America.* Cambridge, MA: Harvard University Press.

Srinivasan, Priya. 2012. *Sweating Saris: Indian Dance as Transnational Labor.* Philadelphia: Temple University Press.

Taylor, Diana. 2003. *The Archive and the Repertoire: Performing Cultural Memory in the Americas.* Durham, NC: Duke University Press.

Thompson, Krista. 2011. "A Sidelong Glance: The Practice of African Diaspora Art History in the United States." *Art Journal* 70 (3): 6–31.

Thompson, Robert Farris. 1966. "An Aesthetic of the Cool: West African Dance." *African Forum* 2 (2): 85–102.

Von Eschen, Penny M. 1997. *Race against Empire: Black Americans and Anticolonialism, 1937–1957.* Ithaca, NY: Cornell University Press.

Walker, George. 1906. "The Negro on the American Stage." *Colored American Magazine,* October, 243–48.

Critical Memory

Arthur Mitchell, Dance Theatre of Harlem,
and the Rise of the Invisible Dancers

GILLIAN LIPTON

Shot diagonally from behind, the black-and-white photograph of a dancer poised at a ballet barre draws attention to her elongated leg, extended backward in a basic warm-up exercise—a tendu derrière. Dressed in leotard, tights, and pointe shoes, with her hair styled in an Afro, she turns over her right shoulder toward a distant point beyond the image's frame. Though her upper body carriage reveals her to be a ballerina still in training, the dynamism and far-reaching line of her gesturing leg command attention first to her figure, then beyond to the unhinged basketball net dangling from a metal rim overhead, and finally to a wall-size mural of a fist holding an illuminated cross.

Taken by Martha Swope circa 1970, the photo resides in box 45 of the Arthur Mitchell Collection and captures Ronda Sampson, a company member of the Dance Theatre of Harlem (DTH), warming up in the gym at Church of the Master on 122nd Street in Harlem. Founded two years earlier in 1968 by Arthur Mitchell with the help of his former teacher Karel Shook in response to the assassination of Martin Luther King Jr., DTH started with thirty students and a company of two professional dancers in the basement gym of the Harlem School of the Arts on St. Nicholas Avenue and 141st Street. Months later, the operation moved up the block, using Mitchell's own funds to convert a garage into a studio with a more forgiving floor and intimate theater (Shook 1978). In the heat of that first summer, the open doors attracted crowds of onlookers, many of whom asked to join. Within a year, DTH had more than one hundred students and sixteen dancers. It rapidly became a community fixture.

By the time Mitchell and Shook moved to the gym at Church of the Master in October 1969, DTH had a school enrollment of six hundred and a company of twenty dancers.[1] To match a $150,000 seed grant they received from the Ford Foundation, Mitchell and the dancers embarked on a circuit of

FIGURE 7. Ronda Sampson at Church of the Master, ca. 1970. (Box 45, Arthur Mitchell Collection; photo by Martha Swope © The New York Public Library for the Performing Arts, Jerome Robbins Dance Division)

lecture-demonstrations and master classes at performing arts centers, high schools, and colleges across the country, including one at Spelman College attended by Ronda Sampson and her younger sister Roslyn. In Atlanta, both had studied with Robert Barnett, formerly of the New York City Ballet (NYCB). Mitchell invited them to join him in New York, and within months, Ronda Sampson was dancing in the Harlem gym (Bryant 2017).

Having worked alongside Mitchell on the development of his archive and aware of his lifelong commitment to excellence, even perfection, I pause over this enlarged photograph and its backstage vulnerabilities—torn net, practice towel, crumpled paper on the floor—in tension with its goal of display. And what was displayed? For whom?

Mitchell told me he hired Martha Swope, the white photographer who often worked with the NYCB, to photograph company rehearsals at the Church of the Master.[2] Journalists, funders, artistic collaborators, and school groups were invited on Wednesday afternoons to watch company rehearsals from a viewing galley, a tiered platform along one wall of the gym (Shook 1978). In the mirrorless space, DTH dancers became accustomed to being on view for others.

The photograph of Sampson exposes a new assemblage of practice, politics, and place called into relation by Mitchell and Shook's project. Here the dancer's technique and satin pink toe shoes, her fashionable Afro, and the hoop and cross index, respectively, a dance tradition originating in the royal courts of Italy and France, a new black radicalism, and the long-standing link between the black church and black activism in Harlem. Sampson stands as the articulator of this new assemblage who self-consciously performs for the camera and the gaze of the white photographer. Yet what stays with me in a manner Roland Barthes described as the *punctum*, the prick or sting felt when observing a photograph (1981, 26), is that Sampson's gaze is directed to an area beyond the frame, where I imagine other DTH company members are readying their muscles for action. Her focus—determined but also weary—critically turns the assemblage in relation to this blind field. Though pictured as a lone dancer at the barre, Sampson's critical turn reminds us that in this scene she is not the exception.

Mitchell's goal and achievement with DTH were to develop African American expression and bring visibility to the black dancing body in American ballet. This ambition was illustrated by an early promotional flyer featuring the company of twenty-three dancers configured in a V shape, with Mitchell at the center. Women in black leotards and tights on pointe and men in black tights and white T-shirts press their chests forward and stare directly into the camera above. Their collective stance is firm. It would become an iconic image of the

The Dance Theatre of Harlem, Inc.

presents

"The rise of the invisible dancers"

with
Arthur Mitchell, Artistic Director
and
Karel Shook, Associate Artistic Director

produced by
SUNYAB Norton Hall
Minority Cultural Affairs
UUAB Dance Committee

FIGURE 8. Dance Theatre of Harlem company, promotional flyer, ca. 1970. *Left (back to front)*: Derek Williams, Cassandra Phifer, Edward Moore, Roslyn Sampson, Clover Mathis, Llanchie Stevenson, Ronald Perry. *Center front*: Patricia Ricketts. *Right (back to front)*: Lazar Dano, Pamela Jones, Rodney Swan, Gayle McKinney, Walter Raines, Lydia Abarca, William Scott. *Center section (left to right)*: Arthur Mitchell, Susan Lovelle, Sheila Rohan, Ronda Sampson, Virginia Johnson, Olinda Davis, Samuel Smalls, Gerald Banks, unknown dancer. (Courtesy of Dance Theatre of Harlem)

DTH company, but uniquely this version of the photograph is underscored by the caption: "The Dance Theatre of Harlem, Inc.: The rise of the invisible dancers." The phrase suggests the bringing into view of the formerly unrecognized presence of the African American dancer in American ballet.

To the degree that the black dancer in American ballet had been overlooked or denied opportunities, that is, made invisible in the sense Ralph Ellison (1995) articulated, visibility was an important political and artistic goal. Yet as Peggy Phelan (1993, 1–33) and Fred Moten (2003, 1–24) have put forth, simply being seen does not guarantee an acknowledgment of one's legitimacy, as demonstrated by the hypervisibility of the (fictional and real) black body on minstrel stages. Might the upright carriage of ballet and its associations with European royalty defuse the minstrel stereotype? Several short-lived African American ballet companies appeared in the 1930s and 1940s, and some black dance artists considered the high art of ballet a means to gain acceptance in a racist society, reflecting the racial uplift ideology articulated by Alain Locke that influenced Harlem Renaissance artists in the second half of the 1920s and early 1930s(1992, xxv–xxvii, 3–18, 47–53).

Mitchell came of age in the mid-1940s, in the wake of the Harlem Renaissance, when ballet was experiencing a surge in popularity with American choreographers and audiences across dance genres (Reynolds and McCormick 2003). When attending auditions in his last year at the High School for the Performing Arts, he encountered overt racism and decided to intensify his study of ballet, "At this time, racism was very high, I said, what could I do that would make me so good that people would use me? . . . [C]lassical ballet, that would make me unique and people would use me" (Mitchell 2004a). In addition to his preference for the discipline and line of ballet, Mitchell's decision reflects the uplift ideals that black distinctiveness and universality could be expressed in the mastery of European elite cultural forms (Gaines 1996). Mitchell was also tasked with helping his single mother support their family, and his turn to ballet ensured his employment, given ballet's rising popularity. Upon graduation from high school, he accepted a scholarship to the School of American Ballet (SAB) and three years later joined the NYCB. Under the leadership of Lincoln Kirstein and George Balanchine, Mitchell experienced firsthand the impact of Africanist aesthetics on Balanchine's modern ballet—influences that were largely unacknowledged by audiences and critics at the time. As Thomas DeFrantz has noted, "While there is nothing inherently racist in ballet technique, its institutions of teachers, artistic directors, managers, patrons and critics live in a racist society and succumb to its vicissitudes" (2004, 146). Just as the ballet idiom is not inherently racist, neither is it innately recuperative. Practices are rooted in and controlled by discourses of their time.

The system of rules that controls the discourse—that is, who can speak and what is said about a memory, tradition, and history—is defined by Michel Foucault as the archive: "The archive is first the law of what can be said, the system that governs the appearance of statements as unique events" (1972, 129). In the Foucaultian sense, the archive of ballet and its traditions have served the function of the state or, at the very least, a majoritarian masculinity—from the sixteenth-century dance manuals of Thoinot Arbeau, which theorized the basic classical dance positions as a military march (Lepecki 2007); to the court dance of Louis XIV, which mobilized dancing bodies to spell out the dictates of the king (Franko 2015); to the eighteenth-century reformulation of classicism, which choreographed an obedient, politically nonthreatening modern subjectivity to serve an unstable monarchy (Foster 1998). Furthermore, Richard Iton argues that the dialectics of modernity necessitated the subordination of a racialized "other," "The bundle of cultural, philosophical, political and technological iterations and reiterations of Renaissance and Enlightenment 'requires an alterity.' . . . [I]t implies and requires an antonymic and problematic 'other' that resulted in a primal tendency to read issues that make race salient as pointing toward either the pre-modern or anti-modern" (2008, 13). Iton challenges whether those who have been marginalized can change their circumstances without altering the logic and language of their exclusion. In the context of American ballet, the language of exclusion is fundamental not to the classical movement idiom but to the discourse controlling access to its study and performance. With their formation of DTH and its promotion through publicity materials and the press, Mitchell and Shook aimed to significantly shift the terms of the discourse.

Following the assassination of Martin Luther King Jr. in April 1968, Mitchell radically repurposed his career to start DTH. While the aim was to eventually integrate the organization, he claimed the necessity for an autonomous school and company of African American administrators, teachers, and dancers at its inception (Mitchell 1968, 1). His was an act of critical memory, a rhetorical mode of black modernity that Houston Baker (1995) explains as the call for decisive change in response to the past. For Baker, black critical memory challenges the universalism of modernity in its refusal to relinquish racial roots and its illumination of an American history based in a "troubling racial idea" (2001, 10). Mitchell's critical memory was born of his feeling for the urbanity of the Harlem Renaissance, a knowledge of the social fabric of black urban impoverishment, and frustration over a stalled civil rights agenda made evident by the assassination of King. As the lone African American dancer in a predominantly white NYCB, he was keenly aware of his exceptionalism and motivated to break down barriers for other black dancers.

Mitchell understood the interconnections of race and power in America that determined how visibility was granted. By selecting the photographers who attended rehearsals, constructing narratives about the company, holding lecture-demonstrations to build an African American public, and developing teachers and choreographers to work with the company during this initial period, Mitchell, together with Shook, aimed to strategically recalibrate "the rules of what could be said" in the archives of American ballet. The photograph of Sampson in the gym evidences their efforts to render visible these altered rules of practice, redistributing the sensibility of classical ballet to new players, publics, and places.

In what follows I demonstrate the singularity of Mitchell's career by briefly tracing a history of African Americans in ballet. I then show how his role in Balanchine's company and the new politics of black radicalism enabled and delimited opportunities for DTH. I discuss how Mitchell's critical memory developed African American expression and brought visibility to the black dancing body in DTH's official premiere performance at the Guggenheim Museum in January 1971. Finally, in a close reading of lecture-demonstrations and the Guggenheim performance, I discuss how ballet, with roots in European modernity, becomes a discursive arena in which American racial and social tensions of the 1960s and 1970s were debated.

An Exceptional Dancer

In his own career as a dancer, Mitchell's remarkable visibility was both an empowerment and limitation. As a performer with the New York City Ballet since 1955, he had achieved international acclaim for his artistry and unparalleled status as the first African American principal dancer in a major US ballet company. Born and raised in Harlem, Mitchell became the first in his family to formally study dance when he started at the High School for the Performing Arts in New York in 1948. At the suggestion of Mary Hinkson, a modern dance teacher at Performing Arts and a black soloist with the Martha Graham company, Mitchell began ballet classes with Karel Shook at the Katherine Dunham School. After a year of study with Shook, he graduated from high school in 1952 and was accepted to study at the SAB (Shook 1971). He joined the NYCB three years later in 1955, premiering in Balanchine's *Western Symphony*.

Mitchell's career took off with his performance of the pas de deux in Stravinsky's *Agon* (1957), which George Balanchine choreographed for him and his white dance partner, Diana Adams. Some critics later saw the entangled partnering between a black man and a white woman as a metaphor for the simmering racial and sexual tensions of the time, but Balanchine often referred to the modern *Agon* as "the IBM ballet, more tight and precise than usual, as if controlled by an electronic brain," attributing the motivating logic of the dance to the neutral machine rather than to contemporary social tensions (Reynolds and McCormick 2003, 310). Mark Franko explains dance modernism as "the reduction of art to the essence of its formal means," which facilitates the "depersonalized ('universal') embodiment of subjectivity" (1995, x–xi). Balanchine's rhetoric of detachment from the mundane and from history emphasized the modernism of medium specificity in *Agon*.

Despite Balanchine's rhetoric of universalism, dance scholars have shown that his choreographic innovations compressed classical dance steps in response to everyday life: the postwar anxiety of his time; speed on the city street; and a host of cultural influences, including Africanist dance and music aesthetics (Gottschild 1996; Banes 1994). In an analysis of the company's 1962 Soviet Union tour, Clare Croft argues that Balanchine's casting of an interracial couple in *Agon* and Mitchell's performance style made visible the Africanist influences on modernist music and choreography (2015, 75–83). In so doing, Balanchine's plotless ballets showed the repressed and racialized underpinnings of modernism's abstraction.

At the time of Dance Theatre's founding in 1968, Mitchell had been the sole black dancer in the NYCB for more than thirteen years. In a lecture at Harvard, "Ethnicity and Classicism: A Beautiful Connection," Mitchell reflected on his frustrations about enduring racial hierarchies in classical dance: "I was ready to break the myth that blacks could not do ballet. I would point out that I was black, and a ballet dancer, only to be told by everyone that I was an exception. I got very, very tired of hearing that statement. So I'd say, 'No, I had the opportunity.' Rather than keep arguing the question, I decided to prove my point. I would develop black ballet dancers" (1984, 147). Mitchell responds to the racist, irrational views held by some leading dance critics of the time who wrote of a black dancer's unsuitability for ballet because of "tight joints, a natural turn-in rather than the desired ballet turn-out, hyperextension of the knee, [and] weak feet" (McDonagh 1968, 44). Dance Theatre, however, was more than a reactionary project aimed at opposing racist critics. Echoing Mitchell, Shook explained in a 1971 interview, "Black people can do ballet. . . . So we didn't want to prove that it could happen—we just wanted it to happen." Their insistence on action rather than rhetoric reflected the strategies of a new radicalism of the time. Together, Mitchell and Shook would create opportunities for African American dancers to study and perform ballet that had not existed before.

A History of African Americans in Ballet

The African American presence in classical ballet grew alongside a rising American interest in the form, beginning with the Ballets Russes tours of the

1930s (DeFrantz 2006). Audiences for the Ballets Russes included many future notables: Alvin Ailey, Betty Nichols, Cleo Quitman, and Arthur Mitchell, among others (Dunning 1996; Classic Black Symposium 1996). Yet racial divisions meant that black ballet dancers had to seek separatist all-black companies. These attempts, however, were largely short-lived and are generally absent from ballet histories.

In 1930 Katherine Dunham partnered with ballet dancer Mark Turbyfill to open a school in Chicago and train dancers for their company, Ballet Negre (Das 2017, 21–24). Known for her choreography that integrated European and African diasporic aesthetics, the young Dunham believed ballet was the ideal form to express black cultural content in the realization of her vision for an innovative black dance distinct from black social forms. Her artistic philosophy reflected the ideology of racial uplift articulated by Alain Locke and New Negro artists. Due to a lack of funding, Dunham's school closed within a year. Her later effort to establish a black ballet company in New York during the mid-1940s was also short-lived, but Dunham would continue to integrate ballet into her dances throughout her career (Das 2017, 112).

In 1937 Eugene von Grona, son of a white American mother and a German father, started the American Negro Ballet. His company of thirty Harlemites performed his choreography to Duke Ellington, Igor Stravinsky, and Johann Sebastian Bach at Harlem's Lafayette Theater and later appeared at the Apollo Theater (DeFrantz 1996, 2006). Von Grona used the term "ballet" to indicate that the dances on the program contained narratives, but no dancers in these productions went on pointe. Limited critical success and the onset of World War II made funding difficult, and the company folded (Classic Black Symposium 1996).

After World War II German émigré Joe Rickhart started the First Negro Classic Ballet on the West Coast in 1949. The group performed classical works on pointe such as *Variations Classiques* to music by Bach and a reworking of *Cinderella*. Embraced by integrated audiences and critics, the company merged in 1956 with the East Coast company New York Negro Ballet, started by Edward Flemyng, an African American dancer with private patronage. The combined group toured England under the name Ballet Americana. Dolores Brown, a dancer with the company, explained that the publicists changed the name to New York Negro Ballet to create a sense of exotic novelty (Classic Black Symposium 1996). Although both companies were established to "express the racialist purpose of proving the ability of the black body to inhabit classical ballet technique," DeFrantz argues that their choreography curiously succumbed to the negative stereotypes of the minstrel stage (1996, 11).

During the immediate postwar years, when the New York Negro Ballet toured Europe, Balanchine and Kirstein engaged several black dancers, namely, Betty Nichols and Talley Beatty, for their short-lived venture, Ballet Society.[3] In 1948 they founded the NYCB and hired black dancer Arthur Bell. More often, however, black dancers performed as guest artists with the NYCB, including Louis Johnson, who danced in Jerome Robbins's *Ballade* (1952), and Mary Hinkson, who partnered Mitchell in Balanchine's *The Figure in the Carpet* (1960) (Reynolds 1977). No African American ballet dancer, however, gained professional recognition in the United States or internationally on a scale that rivaled Arthur Mitchell.

Black Critical Memory and the
Founding of DTH

Despite his remarkable visibility, Mitchell's statement "I became very very tired" reveals his frustration with the entrenched racial hierarchies of the dance world and his readiness to respond to the new momentum of black radicalism's demands for the new and structurally significant visibility of marginalized black constituencies. In the spring of 1968 Mitchell was both a featured dancer with the NYCB and the new artistic director of the Brazilian ballet company Companhia de Brasileira de Ballet.[4] Within two weeks of King's assassination, Mitchell left his post in Brazil and began contacting potential company members (see Mitchell's 1968 proposal to the Ford Foundation). Reacting to this moment of social fracture, Mitchell decisively turned his life and career to the needs of the black community, "When I heard the news about the assassination of Martin Luther King, I was very upset and I guess I became very introspective. I began to question what I was doing running off to Brazil, when *my own people* had major problems here at home. . . . I started looking around me, and I saw so much rage and hostility. I saw all that pent up energy; it would most certainly erupt into violence unless it could be channeled into something positive" (Mitchell 1984, 146–47, emphasis added). With an awareness of the urban unrest of the time and memories of the 1943 Harlem riots of his youth, Mitchell's turn "to my people" was an act of critical memory that would connect his leadership as the artistic director and cofounder of a separatist ballet school and company to a black collectivity. Baker explains that critical memory is composed of acts of decisive change that seek liberation realized through connections between black leadership and a black public: "[The] operation [of critical memory] implies a continuous arrival at turning points. Decisive change, usually attended through considerable risk" (1995, 7). Baker sees critical memory at work in the changed tactics of Martin Luther King Jr.'s leadership—from the slow, noble reform he had advocated in the South toward demands for the comprehensive restructuring of political and economic power. He understands King's radical criticality in 1967–68 as a response to the new "black visibility" evident in the urban uprisings and the emergent Black Power movement in the mid-1960s (1995, 35). King's changed rhetoric made the needs of the black and the poor visible as a matter of American structural concern.

Mitchell and Shook's project used artistic means to participate in the fight for racial justice in America at that time. In their respective lectures, proposals, and essays, they explain that the assassination of King propelled them both to leave their posts with major ballet companies in order to start an autonomous black arts institution. While Mitchell had been in Brazil, Shook had been the ballet master first at the Netherlands National Ballet and then the Dutch National Ballet for almost ten years. Mitchell claimed that ballet—and that arts more broadly—would offer "something positive" for "my people" in the face of impending violence (1984, 147). As Baker explains, "The essence of critical memory's work is the cumulative, collective maintenance of a record that draws into relationship significant instants of time past and the always uprooted homelessness of now" (1995, 7). Mitchell's proposals, program notes, and lectures narrated the DTH project as a response to the period of fracture following King's death and distilled this moment in the collective memory of Americans, especially African Americans.

The midsixties saw newly radical and visible forms of black activism that exposed the isolation, spatial confinement, and abandonment of black Americans and created a new conceit for black modernist artists to figuratively address the harsh realities of their lives (Baker, 1995). Mitchell and Shook could have established an integrated school elsewhere in New York City, but chose Harlem. Mitchell claimed, "The arts belong to the people . . . we are training black dancers for a black ballet. Where else would it be if not in Harlem?" (quoted in Vaglio 1971).

Yet by 1968 the integrationist spirit of the civil rights era had given way to the militarism and separatism of the Black Power movement in northern cities. The Black Arts Movement espoused a politics of protest and the development of a black aesthetic with its own symbolism, mythology, and iconography (DeFrantz 1999; Manning 2008). Young dance artists strove to find forms that would conform to an emergent black aesthetic, while artists of earlier generations unwilling to relinquish their technique were viewed by black nationalists as maintaining the racist status quo (DeFrantz 1999, 85–86).

Although a ballet school and company in Harlem may not have aligned with the aesthetic philosophy of the Black Arts Movement, as a separatist organization DTH conveyed a black pride and power in the elegance and strength of classically trained African American dancers. As an institution, it stood for the restructuring of the racial hierarchy in American ballet and benefited from new resources made available to cultural programs in black communities in response to the pressure from black radicals. As James Smethurst argues, the urban unrest of the mid-1960s created an environment in which "radical cultural and political projects, institutions and actions seemed practical not only to radicals, but to many people hitherto outside black radical circles" (2016, 93). Large amounts of money and other resources were made available for public arts and education initiatives, especially within black communities.

A few years earlier, when Mitchell was still a principal dancer with the NYCB, the company received Ford Foundation funding to teach ballet at the Jones-Haywood Dance School, a ballet center for students of color in Washington, DC. The goal was to select thirty students for scholarships at the SAB. Mitchell explains that teaching these classes and witnessing the determination that the study of ballet gave the children inspired him to start his own school (1968, 5). While the NYCB project aimed to integrate African American students into an overwhelmingly white ballet school, by 1968 Mitchell was developing plans for an autonomous black school in Harlem.

Newly funded programs were often interpreted as complicit with hegemonic efforts to discipline the black freedom struggle unless they concretely served the black community (Smethurst 2016). In practical terms alone, DTH created jobs in Harlem—for dancers in the company, teachers at the school, designers and musicians, and administrators to keep the school and company running. As the photograph of Sampson makes apparent, DTH also received support from the black church. Yet by Mitchell's own admission, the idea of a classical ballet school in Harlem in the late 1960s and early 1970s was not immediately welcomed by the local community or perceived as relevant to black self-determination or the material difficulties of urban life in Harlem (Mitchell 2004b).

Mitchell and Shook would have to develop a constituency of students, dancers, and audience members. DTH's school curriculum and lecture-demonstration program redistributed the sensibility of classical ballet to a black collectivity. Like Katherine Dunham's New York school, where Shook and Mitchell had taught, the curriculum of the DTH school included African, modern, and tap dance classes alongside ballet, but unlike Dunham's school, DTH characterized itself as a ballet school with a social mission. Jacques Rancière illuminates how aesthetic regimes, specifically, sensory experience, can radically recalibrate social relations and generate new ways of being in common: "This distribution and redistribution of places and identities, this apportioning and reapportioning of spaces and times, of the visible and the invisible, and of noises and speech constitute what I call the distribution of the sensible. Politics consists in reconfiguring the distribution of the sensible which defines the common community, to introduce into it new subjects and objects, to render visible what had not been" ([2009] 2012, 25). Mitchell and Shook began to define a black consciousness in relation to classical dance by developing lecture-demonstrations and performances that publicly explored new connections between ballet and black vernacular culture before integrated audiences. This redistribution was a means to develop black self-determination and build toward their long-term goal of an integrated school, company, and classical dance public.

The company's first official lecture-demonstration and performance at the Guggenheim Museum on January 8–10, 1971, exemplified its method of redistributing the sensible. The company had already appeared publicly on an extensive lecture-demonstration circuit of public schools in the New York area, as well as on tour in the summer of 1970 to Bermuda, the Bahamas, Curaçao, and Jacob's Pillow in Massachusetts. With the Guggenheim performance, Mitchell and Shook introduced their company to an established arts institution in New York City.

At the Guggenheim, Dance Theatre of Harlem performed two lecture-demonstrations to a thousand predominantly African American secondary students. Baker writes that critical memory not only exposes difficult aspects of a racist history but also mobilizes new potential through institution building and education (2001, 19). With the goal of developing an African American dance public and student body, the company presented a series of ballet exercises and repertoire excerpts with verbal narration by Mitchell, who explained the function of the exercises and the meaning of the choreography. The middle section of the program focused on connections between ballet and vernacular dance and sport. Mitchell aimed to make explicit the links between a black collectivity, African American culture, and the classical movement tradition. Structured as a call-and-response session with the audience, this section related the classical dance of DTH to the everyday embodied practices of the student audience.

In a 1973 lecture-demonstration for broadcast, Mitchell asked the crowd of grade schoolers to name a popular dance. When they called out "the Penguin," he invited an African American girl, Susan, to the stage. Dressed in a green jumper, knee socks, and loafers, Susan demonstrated the Penguin in sync with Mitchell's sounding of a syncopated beat: pitched onto the balls of her feet, she snapped her legs in and out at her hips and circled her arms up and down at her sides while maintaining an air of cool in her upper body. In antiphonic gestures, Mitchell repeated his version of her dance and drew comparisons to both James Brown's popular Slop and balletic footwork, including port de bras (*Rhythmetron* 1973).

The invocation of Brown, the father of soul, who by 1968 had become known for his hit "Say It Loud—I'm Black and I'm Proud," is critical because it relates the girl's kinesthetic universe both to the black pride of James Brown and to the whiteness of European-derived forms of ballet. In the space-time of the lecture-demonstration, Susan's dance, as analyzed by Mitchell, carried political promise because it drew European and African diasporic forms into a common space. Rancière explains that aesthetic education "changes aesthetic idleness into the action of a living community that the redistribution of the sensible invites a 'consensual community,' which is not to say a community in which everyone is in agreement, but one that is realized as 'a community of feeling'" ([2009] 2012, 37). In this presentation, Mitchell cast Susan as the articulator of that connection between sensibilities when he anointed her, upon her return to her seat, by stating, "See, you are a little ballerina!" During this public venue broadcast for television, he challenged the limits of the discourse of ballet to encompass that connection as new potential for American ballet.

Dance Theatre of Harlem's formal performance at the Guggenheim Museum featured an all-Mitchell program, including the neoclassical *Tones* (1970), set to music by Tania Leon; the classically based *Fête Noir* (1971), set to Dmitri Shostakovich's Piano Concerto no. 2; and *Rhythmetron* (1971), set to Marlos Nobre's score for thirty-three percussion instruments. Taken together, the three dances showcase the expressive range of the black ballet dancer, demonstrating the company's virtuosity in neoclassical and classical ballet while highlighting a new style that combined Africanist aesthetics and classical movement idioms to express African diasporic content. Of the three works, critics noted that *Rhythmetron*'s combination of "classical and ethnic styles" introduced a "new subtlety" and "individual style" (Kisselgoff 1971). Described by Mitchell as an exemplar of DTH style, *Rhythmetron* became a signature work in the company repertoire and lecture-demonstrations.

Staging the African Diaspora in American Ballet: Choreographing the Break

Mitchell had choreographed *Rhythmetron* for his ballet company in Brazil and the work draws on Afro-Brazilian influences in its score and choreography, performed by nine women on pointe who are often joined by eight men. Like Nobre's music, known to integrate African diasporic musical forms and serial music, Mitchell's choreography combines Africanist aesthetics with a classical movement idiom (Gusmão 2009). Calling *Rhythmetron* an "abstract version of an African ritual," Mitchell was inspired by seeing Afro-Brazilian candomblé to choreograph a formalized version of a trance ceremony (*Rhythmetron* 1973). The dance unfolds across three movements: "The Preparation," a designation of the ritual space and gathering of the community; "The Chosen," a pas de six for three men and three women; and "The Ritual," a "trance" dance for the full company (Dance Theatre of Harlem 1971). *Rhythmetron* introduced an African diasporic theme and Africanist aesthetics into a program billed as classical ballet. The performance at the Guggenheim gathered a newly desegregating audience for American ballet, including public school children and critics from the black presses. *Rhythmetron* challenged black and white spectators alike to consider the staging of African diaspora in the context of American ballet. A novelty in 1971, the proposal was met with ambivalence and mixed critical reception.

Rhythmetron opens in silence with a gesture of metamorphosis: a large red cape, draped from the shoulders of a woman standing at center stage, peels open to reveal her majestic figure in leotard and tights, pointe shoes, and a jeweled cap framing her face. She sends her arms upward into a commanding V while rooting her legs firmly downward, a powerful conduit between distinct domains of spirit and earth, past and present, Africanist and classical, Africa and America. The priestess runs into the spotlight downstage and suspends on pointe with her arms held in a circle overhead. In a sudden release of verticality, she bends her knees, contracts and releases her spine, and sharply turns away. She repeats these gestures twice more in lit areas of the stage, as if sanctifying the space. Returning upstage, she bows and on the beat of a drum snaps her head up and sharply draws her arms in to her sides, ushering in six women, who dart across the stage from both sides to a propulsive drum rhythm, cutting the visual field on sharp diagonals. With the clash of cymbals, the dancers punctuate this stream of movement by striking an arabesque or passé on pointe in solos, duets, and trios. They are eventually joined by eight men, staging the bold arrival of a community in preparation for a ritual (*Rhythmetron* 1973).

In this opening, visual and aural gestures of rupture make apparent a structuring device common to African American performance known as "the break." Thomas DeFrantz defines the term: "The break is an unexpected, uncontrollable space. It is where an insistent beat is interrupted by a flash of contradictory rhythmic ideas. For me, the break is the most significant gesture of African American performance, as it contains both the tie to a ubiquitous rhythmic flow and the potential for anarchy and disruption. . . . [I]t is relational, interstitial, and contingent" (2010, 31). The priestess introduces the break in her sudden change in spatial orientation and movement idiom. The break is also emphasized when women emphatically strike a balance at center, interrupting the stream of running movement, and again with the clash of cymbals, which disrupts the rhythmic continuum of the drum. The title, *Rhythmetron*, a combination of the terms "rhythm" and "meter," turns our attention to the timed patterning of gestures of rupture.

As a structuring device, the break is made evident throughout the dance in the juxtaposition of flow and rupture. In *Rhythmetron* the sensation of flow is created by the pulse of the drum and the lyricism of the predominantly classical movement vocabulary in the work. More than the apposition of Africanist and European diasporic forms, the gestures of break announce the decisive change in the animating force of the ballet. Throughout *Rhythmetron*, the reiterated gestures of rupture define spatial and temporal thresholds in the choreographic field, moments of suspension that make sensibly apparent the convergence of Africanist sensibility and the classical movement idiom. In *Rhythmetron* the break choreographically enacts critical memory by structurally and affectively announcing the pivotal turn in the aesthetics of ballet toward an Africanist sensibility.

In the opening of *Rhythmetron*, the priestess, danced by Patricia Ricketts in the Guggenheim premiere, introduces an Africanist percussive attack in her quick and emphatic release from suspended verticality of a classical pose and the Africanist undulation of her torso. These gestures respectively reorient the established *sensible* coordinates of classical ballet: verticality, continuous flow, and weightlessness are juxtaposed with dynamism, sharpness, and the complete expression of the pose. While classical sensibilities are also present, *Rhythmetron* newly foregrounded Africanist aesthetics within a work of ballet.

In his formulation of the political potentiality of aesthetics, Rancière explains that "[sensory experience] is given in a specific experience that suspends the ordinary connections not only between appearance and reality, but also between form and matter, activity and passivity, understanding and sensibility" ([2009] 2012, 30). In *Rhythmetron* the repeated intervals of breaking mark the redistribution of a relationship between African diasporic sensibility and the European diasporic forms in ballet to allow the force animating the movement to be recognized as black.

Still, critics white and black who reviewed the official premiere performance avoided describing *Rhythmetron* as black dance. Reviewing the evening for the *Los Angeles Times*, Marcia Siegel (1971) expressed agitation: "That evening left me with some strong and confused emotions. Anger, first, at the persistent prejudice that keeps black dancers out of classical ballet. . . . And the puzzling feeling that DTH was somehow out of its time, that a black separatist dance organization should be doing black dance—whatever that is—and not carrying on the legacy of the seventeenth-century French monarchs." Though she

lamented the institutionalized racism that had historically barred African
American dancers from white ballet schools and companies, Siegel delimited
ballet to expressions of whiteness when she claimed that a company of African American dancers should be doing black dance. She shifted the terms
of debate regarding the presence of African American dancers in ballet from
the question of physical capability to ethnic suitability. Perhaps Siegel's views
reflected a broader anxiety and confusion about changing racial boundaries in
American culture. Writing for the *New York Amsterdam News,* Carol Vaglio
(1971) referred to DTH dancers as black but not the choreography, describing
"natural abandon" and "ethnic style" in *Rhythmetron*. Vaglio's reticence may have
been a response to pressures both from the Black Arts Movement to define a
separatist black aesthetic and from a traditional white ballet establishment
resistant to change. Responding to the Guggenheim premiere, critics black
and white showed ambivalence about defining *Rhythmetron* as black dance.

Significantly, in the months following the museum event the discourse regarding an African American presence in ballet seemed to be changing. Carole
Johnson (1971) included ballet in her definition of "Black Dance" for the *Feet,*
linking black dance artists' freedom of aesthetic expression to the black liberation struggle of the time. The *Saturday Review* also ran Walter Terry's article

FIGURE 9. The priestess, Melva Murray White, with the Dance Theatre of
Harlem company in *Rhythmetron*. (Photo by Martha Swope © The New York
Public Library for the Performing Arts, Jerome Robbins Dance Division)

"Black Ballet Can Be Beautiful," in which he refers to black ballet as the artistic range showcased by DTH: "modern movement styles, jazz, as well as the most aristocratic of ballet pas" (1971, 49). Accompanying Terry's article are three photographs of DTH principal dancers—Pamela Jones, Rosalyn Sampson, and Ronda Sampson—representing the diverse virtuosity of the ballerina of black ballet. Roughly eighteen months after the rehearsal in the Church of the Master and no longer a dancer in training, Ronda Sampson appears in pointe shoes extending her leg backward, twisting her shoulders, and shooting her arms straight backward like radials bursting from her torso. In this striking assemblage of modern, jazz, and classical styles, she critically turns to the camera—an image of the freedom and power of the ballerina in black ballet.

Notes

1. Dance Theatre of Harlem was officially incorporated on February 11, 1969.

2. Unless otherwise specified, all paraphrases of Arthur Mitchell's statements are from conversations with the author between April 2014 and July 2017 in my role as archivist for the Arthur Mitchell Project (AMP). The Arthur Mitchell Collection is housed at Columbia University's Rare Book and Manuscript Library.

3. Betty Nichols appeared in Todd Bolender's *Zodiac* (1946) and later partnered Tally Beatty in Lew Christensen's minstrel show–themed ballet, *Blackface* (1947).

4. Mitchell was first sent to Brazil by the US State Department in 1967 to organize a federally funded national ballet company. Since the company was short-lived, he moved on to organize Companhia de Brasileira de Ballet, privately funded by the Brazilian entrepreneur Paulo Ferraz at the encouragement of his dancer wife, Regina Ferraz.

Works Cited

Baker, Houston. 1995. "Critical Memory and the Black Public Sphere." In *The Black Public Sphere*, edited by the Black Public Sphere Collective, 3–38. Chicago: University of Chicago Press.

———. 2001. *Critical Memory: Public Spheres, African American Writing, and Black Fathers and Sons in America*. Athens: University of Georgia Press.

Banes, Sally. 1994. *Writing Dancing in the Age of Postmodernism*. Middletown, CT: Wesleyan University Press.

Barthes, Roland. 1981. *Camera Lucida: Reflections on Photography*. New York: Noonday.

Bryant, Homer. 2017. Interview with the author. April 28.

Classic Black Symposium. 1996. New York Public Library for the Performing Arts, February 12 and 26. New York Public Library for the Performing Arts, Jerome Robbins Dance Division.

Croft, Clare. 2015. *Dancers as Diplomats: American Choreography in Cultural Exchange*. New York: Oxford University Press.

Dance Theatre of Harlem. 1971. Guggenheim Museum Program, January 8–10. New York Public Library for the Performing Arts, Jerome Robbins Dance Division.

Das, Joanna Dee. 2017. *Katherine Dunham: Dance and the African Diaspora*. New York: Oxford University Press.
DeFrantz, Thomas. 1996. "Simmering Passivity: The Black Male Body in Concert Dance." In *Moving Words: Re-writing Dance*, edited by Gay Morris, 107–20. New York: Routledge.
———. 1999. "To Make Black Bodies Strange: Social Critique in Concert Dance of the Black Arts Movement." In *A Sourcebook of African-American Performance: Plays, People, Movements*, edited by Annemarie Bean, 83–93. New York: Routledge.
———. 2004. *Dancing Revelations: Alvin Ailey's Embodiment of African American Culture*. New York: Oxford University Press.
———. 2006. "Ballet." In *Encyclopedia of African American Culture and History*, 2nd ed., edited by Colin A. Palmer, 1:179–84. Detroit: Macmillan Reference USA.
———. 2010. "Performing the Breaks: Notes on African American Aesthetic Structures." *Theater* 40 (1): 31–37.
Dunning, Jennifer. 1996. *Alvin Ailey: A Life in Dance*. New York: Da Capo Press.
Ellison, Ralph. 1995. *Invisible Man*. New York: Vintage.
Foster, Susan Leigh. 1998. *Choreography and Narrative: Ballet's Staging of Story and Desire*. Bloomington: Indiana University Press.
Foucault, Michel. 1972. *The Archeology of Knowledge*. New York: Vintage.
Franko, Mark. 1995. *Dancing Modernism / Performing Politics*. Bloomington: Indiana University Press.
———. 2015. *Dance as Text: Ideologies of the Baroque Body*. New York: Oxford University Press.
Gaines, Kevin. 1996. *Uplifting the Race: Black Leadership, Politics and Culture in the Twentieth Century*. Chapel Hill: University of North Carolina Press.
Gottschild, Brenda Dixon. 1996. *Digging the Africanist Presence in American Performance: Dance and Other Contexts*. Westport, CT: Praeger.
Gusmão, Pablo da Silva. 2009. "A Synthesis of Modern and Brazilian Elements: An Investigation of *Variantes e Toccata* Opus 15a by Marlos Nobre." PhD dissertation, University of North Carolina, Greensboro.
Iton, Richard. 2008. *In Search of the Black Fantastic: Politics and Popular Culture in the Post Civil Rights Era*. London: Oxford University Press.
Johnson, Carole. 1971. "Black Dance." *Feet* 2 (4): 2.
Kisselgoff, Anna. 1971. "Harlem Dancers Excel at Guggenheim." *New York Times*, January 10, 71.
Lepecki, André. 2007. "Choreography as Apparatus of Capture." *Drama Review* 51 (2): 119–23.
Locke, Alain. 1992. "Forward," "The New Negro," "Negro Youth Speaks." In *The New Negro: Voices of the Harlem Renaissance*, edited by Alain Locke, xxv–xxvii, 3–18, 47–53. New York: Simon and Schuster.
Manning, Susan. 2008. *Danses Noires/Blanche Amérique*. Paris: Centre National de la Danse.
McDonagh, Don. 1968. "Negroes in Ballet." *New Republic* 159:41–44.

Mitchell, Arthur. 1968. Proposal to Ford Foundation. Arthur Mitchell Collection, Rare Book and Manuscript Library, Columbia University, New York.

———. 1984. "Ethnicity and Classicism: A Beautiful Connection." *Journal of Education* 166:144–49.

———. 2004a. Interview with Martin Duberman. Arthur Mitchell Collection, Rare Book and Manuscript Library, Columbia University, New York.

———. 2004b. Visionary Leaders Project Interview, July 18. Arthur Mitchell Collection, Rare Book and Manuscript Library, Columbia University, New York.

Moten, Fred. 2003. *In the Break: The Aesthetics of the Black Radical Tradition*. Minneapolis: University of Minnesota Press.

Phelan, Peggy. 1993. *Unmarked: The Politics of Performance*. London: Routledge.

Rancière, Jacques. (2009) 2012. *Aesthetics and Its Discontents*. Cambridge: Polity.

Reynolds, Nancy. 1977. *Repertory in Review: 40 Years of the New York City Ballet*. New York: Dial Press.

Reynolds, Nancy, and Malcolm McCormick. 2003. *No Fixed Points: Dance in the Twentieth Century*. New Haven, CT: Yale University Press.

Rhythmetron: The Dance Theatre of Harlem with Arthur Mitchell. 1973. Capital Cities Communications, Inc. (US); McGraw-Hill Book Company. Film.

Shook, Karel. 1971. Interview with John Gruen. New York Public Library for the Performing Arts, Jerome Robbins Dance Division.

———. 1978. "The First Ten Years." Manuscript, Dance Theatre of Harlem Archives.

Siegel, Marcia. 1971. "Arthur Mitchell Brings Ballet Home to Harlem." *Los Angeles Times*, February 14, R10.

Smethurst, James. 2016. "The Black Arts Movement." In *Black Power 50*, edited by Sylviane A. Diouf and Komozi Woodard, 89–101. New York: New Press.

Terry, Walter. 1971. "Black Ballet Can Be Beautiful." *Saturday Review*, February 27, 48–49.

Vaglio, Carol. 1971. "22 Gifted Young People from Harlem Exciting." *New York Amsterdam News*, January 23, 20.

Breathing Matters

Breath as Dance Knowledge

LAURA KARREMAN

> For the breath is the mysterious great master who reigns unknown and
> unnamed behind all and everything—who silently commands the function
> of muscles and joints—who knows how to fire with passions and to relax,
> how to whip up and restrain—who puts the breaks in the rhythmic structure
> and dictates the phrasing of the flowing passages—who above all this regulates
> the temper of expression in its interplay with the colourfulness of rhythm
> and melody.

—MARY WIGMAN, *The Language of Dance*

Over the past three decades, the emergence of dance studies as an autonomous field of research has coincided with critical turns that have firmly directed the attention to practice, embodiment, and (kinesthetic) experience. Often referred to as "the body as archive" (Baxmann 2007; Lepecki 2010), the embodied mnemonic role of the dancer's body has received significant attention in dance studies. At the same time, many features of embodied knowledge of the dancer continue to receive scant attention. One example of such embodied expertise is the dancer's use of breath in performance. Mary Wigman's expressive description above of the breath as "the mysterious great master who reigns unknown and unnamed" points to the significance of breath in dance, but it also highlights the breath's perceived obscurity. Indeed, the ways in which dancers make use of breath may be characterized as what Michael Polanyi (1958) has termed "tacit knowledge." This is a type of embodied knowledge that is "tacit," which means "silent" or "unspoken."

The goal of this chapter is to contribute to a demystification of breath in dance performance. How can we move from the established view of the breath as "unknown and unnamed" to a knowing and naming of how breath matters in dance? In addition, I will demonstrate how this move toward an articulation of breath as a vital feature of dance knowledge is connected to contemporary developments of digital technologies.

How technological design affects corporealities is a topic that is gaining relevance in the current cultural moment, which can in part be defined by the widespread use of digital capturing tools such as smartphones, laptops, and other devices that enable lifelogging and quantified selves. This development has sparked a multitude of practices, so much so that it has become impossible to imagine everyday life without these tools. While they are primarily concerned with capturing and measuring physical and physiological features, these tools also inevitably restructure ways of seeing and understanding dance.

The critical evaluation of the abstraction and reduction of the dancing body, which are part of its digital transfer into data, requires further inquiry. In fact, I believe that questions emerging in this research area will represent some of the most pressing tasks for the field of dance studies in years to come. In this chapter, I zoom in on this topic from a specific angle. I argue that in response to digital capturing technologies and the specific challenge they generate to make motion data speak, breath is emerging as a particular topic of interest because of its potential to relate physical movement to intentions, emotions, and other layers in the semantic realm of performance.

This is a new line of inquiry that represents an exciting avenue for future research. Research into the role of breath in dance performance not only leads to deeper insight into the embodied knowledge in dancers. The study of breath may also be instrumental to strengthening bridges between research areas such as dance studies and corporeal computation, in which research is based on the transposition of moving bodies into data. In order to set the stage for such a future inquiry, I draw on a wide range of sources that are concerned with *the relationship between performance and respiration.* I take my inspiration from Luce Irigaray's philosophy of breath; draw on breath studies in dance and somatic practices; and examine relevant case studies in the interrelated realms of dance, performance, film, and human-computer interaction (HCI) design.[1]

The Forgetting of Air

Breath is a key topic in the work of Belgian philosopher and cultural theorist Luce Irigaray, the influential author of writings on ethics and sexual difference. The beginning of Irigaray's philosophical exploration of breath is marked by *L'oubli de l'air chez Martin Heidegger* (1983), translated as *The Forgetting of Air in Martin Heidegger* (1999), part of a series that was devoted to the elements water, earth, and air. "It was only with Heidegger's and Irigaray's theories that we started to be fully and radically aware of the meaning of our being oblivious to the notions of being and breath in our history," Slovenian philosopher

Lenart Škof noted in reflecting on the book's importance (2015, 3). By pointing out the importance of breath, Irigaray aims to draw awareness back to the
body. By redirecting attention to embodied experience, Irigaray joins in the
often-expressed critique of the logocentric bias of Western thinking. However,
rather than merely articulating this critique, Irigaray conceptualizes breath as
essential for an embodied ethics of difference. Awareness of breath, in Irigaray's
(2013) view, offers the possibility "to attend to our own bodies and the bodies
of others, to animals, nature, other cultures, oppressed minorities, and the
other of sexual difference." Breath is vital for human existence and is in constant flux. At birth, a baby is given breath, is given inspiration, but at the same
time, one can never hold on to breath, one cannot appropriate it and keep
it to oneself. Breath is necessarily shared with others. Irigaray recognizes this
"giving-sharing one's breath" as an ethical gesture that offers a fundamental
possibility for compassion and understanding. In her essay "A Breath That
Touches in Words" (1996), Irigaray considers the relation between breathing
and speech. She identifies speech as a phenomenon that, in Western society,
is favored over listening and silence. Speech represses breath and draws the
attention away from the embodied reality of beings. Irigaray argues that this
actually puts lives at risk:

> Speech, instead of bearing breath, takes its place, replaces it, which invariably
> stifles and preoccupies the place for silence. People who pay no heed to respira-
> tion, who breathe poorly, who are short of air, often cannot stop speaking, and
> are thus unable to listen. . . . It is, therefore, important to reflect upon the fact
> that a language, spirituality or religion that is founded on speech, yet pays no
> need to the silence and breath making it possible, might well lead to a lack of
> respect for life; for one's own life, for the other's life, for others' lives. (1996, 122)

To incite a reflection on the potential of silence and breath, Irigaray (2004,
2013) has proclaimed "le temps du souffle" (the age of the breath), which can
be understood as "a spiritual shift in human awareness to the needs of the
other figured through breathing." The age of the breath means a commitment
to the body and the senses and involves "a process of accepting and sharing
vital energies of the cosmos" (Škof 2015, 148).

   When Irigaray's thought is considered from the perspective of dance studies, the dancer would seem the incontestable heroine of the age of the breath.
Irigaray's philosophy certainly destabilizes the established prejudice about the
dancer, namely, that being a *nonspeaking* performer represents a challenge
rather than an advantage. Following Irigaray, a radically different perspective
on dance performance becomes apparent. In this view of dance, it is precisely

the absence of speech that inspires mutual respect, an appreciation of the body and the senses, and a "giving-sharing" of vital energies. Breath, then, is fore-grounded as a powerful aspect of the exchange between dancer and audience. In appreciating the core of Irigaray's writings, the fundamental possibility that is offered by this exchange is nothing less than a cultivation of humanity or, perhaps more comprehensively put, a cultivation of *being*.

Why Does Breath Matter in Dance?

Despite its crucial role in dance performance, breath has rarely been consid-ered a principal topic within dance studies. This is remarkable, because breath has various functions in dance and often figures as the foundational element of specific techniques and practices. Following Irigaray's notion of "the for-getting of air," the underacknowledgment of breath can be understood as a result of the problematic position of bodily practices in Western academia, which has long been permeated by logocentrism. This deep-rooted focus on the expression of speech and written language has concealed the strength of the body as a meaning-producing force. This focus has also been apparent in traditional dance studies, as has been observed by Susan Foster (1995, 2011). The dominance of propositional ways of knowing in scholarly research has not been conducive to the study of the corporeal-experiential realm of the dancer, including the ways in which breath functions in performance. The following overview should by no means be understood as exhaustive; instead, it serves to provide principal reference points for further research in this area. At issue is the question, Why does breath matter in dance?

In many long-established bodily practices, breath takes a central position. In hatha yoga, breathing exercises (*pranayama*) are of equal importance to the practice of postures (*asana*). The rising and falling sensation of the breath is the primary focus of Buddhist meditation. In Eastern martial arts and related practices, such as Aikido, Kendo, Wushu, and Chi Kung, breath is used to create a correct state of mind and body, to focus strength. The continuous flow of breath is used as an instrument that supports the anticipation of the opponent by facilitating a *moving together with* an opponent. In Japanese per-formance traditions, such as Noh performance but also in the more recent Butoh, specific breathing techniques are used. Indeed, Sreenath Nair notes in his study *Restoration of Breath* that the "fundamental approach to breath in relation to the psycho-physical energy level of the body is the basic method found in many systems of actor training available in some of the traditional performance forms like Kathakali, Kudiyattam and Noh" (2007, 63). Laurence Louppe points to the influence that the "pneumatic thought of the East" has had on Western dance practice: "In all phases of its history contemporary dance has, in a reflexive or remedial way, called upon the great Eastern or Mediterranean techniques in which breathing represents, physically and metaphorically, the source of any search for the self" (2010, 57).

This notion of the "pneumatic body" was also present in the work of Antonin Artaud, whose systematic reflection on the actor's use of breath is one of the most prominent examples of the acknowledgment of breath as a vital element of physical knowledge within Western performing arts traditions. "Thus with the whetted edge of the breath the actor carves out his character," writes Artaud in *The Theatre and Its Double*, conjuring up a metaphorical image of the breath as a weapon of combat ([1938] 1958, 137). An important clue that explains the meaning of Artaud's breath-oriented body emerges from the analogy he draws between the lungs and the brain. Both of these organs, says Artaud, either act unconsciously or can be directed by the will. "We can keep ourselves from breathing or from thinking, can speed up our respiration, give it any rhythm we choose, make it conscious or unconscious at will, introduce a balance between two kinds of breathing: the automatic, which is under the direct control of the sympathetic nervous system, and the other, which is subject to those reflexes of the brain which have once again become conscious" (21). The analogy of the working of the brain and lungs is a compelling way of empowering performers because it makes them aware that they are in charge and have the capacity to unleash their bodily potential through their breath. The lasting influence of Artaud's work remains visible in recent work on the subject of the role of breath in expression, such as Brandon LaBelle's *Lexicon of the Mouth*, which describes how gasping, grunting, and sighing give shape to expression and are created by breath: "Controlled breathing allows for directing intensities, and grunting appears as a sonic register of this, where the energy of breath is held in the lungs until the optimal moment of release and attack" (2014, 78).

As many dancers will answer when asked, in dance, *the breath is everything*. For example, the breath was a central point of attention in interviews I conducted with dancers of the Belgian dance company Rosas on their practices of performance and transmission (Karreman 2015). These interviews illustrated various ways in which dancers use breath: as a means to sustain rhythm and strength, as a way to support synchronicity and communication between dancers, as an instrument to shape movement qualities, as a method to avoid mechanical repetition of dance phrases, and as a way to give "color" to their movement.

Indeed, the work of many prominent choreographers is entangled with a specific understanding of the use of the breath. In Martha Graham's work, the key principle of contraction and release in dance phrases relates to the inhaling and exhaling of breath (Freedman 1998, 56). Breath is also a central element in the teaching of modern dance icons such as Mary Wigman and Doris Humphrey. (The epigraph at the beginning of this chapter gives a taste of Wigman's eloquent writing on the subject.) Sally Banes notes that for Humphrey, "the breath pulled the body out of two possible kinetic and symbolic 'deaths'—the stable positions of standing upright and lying down—into fall and recovery, creating an asymmetric arc" (1987, 4). In Limón technique, breath is emphasized as a motivating force. Suzanne Youngerman explains how this emphasis distinguishes Limón from ballet as a dance technique: "A leg extension to the side, for instance, might be done in ballet with the goal of reaching as high a point as possible, whereas for the Limón dancer the intent would be for the leg to travel only as far as the forceful impulse of the breath would send it" (1984, 117). Laban's design for a comprehensive movement analysis system recognized breath as a connective force that supports the connection between the physiological and expressive qualities of the body.

In the exchange between choreographers and dancers, the breath is often used in a sense that is simultaneously physical and metaphorical. For instance, dancers are invited to "breathe life" into their movement phrases, a metaphor that emphasizes the entwinement of the meaning-making and life-giving qualities associated with breathing. At other times, breath plays a role in more complex metaphorical images that may help dancers to imagine and explore movement beyond their familiar range of motion. This breath-imbued imagery is abundantly present in many somatic practices and movement techniques that are used to support dance practice, such as the Alexander Technique, the Skinner Releasing Technique, and the Feldenkrais Method.[2] In these and other somatic practices and techniques, breath has also often been identified as an essential connecting force between inside and outside. The dynamic connection between inward and outward experience that is associated with breathing also characterizes the work of breathing therapist Ilse Middendorf, who wrote, "Breath is a connecting force. It creates a bodily equilibrium and balance and helps us to make inner and outer impressions interchangeable. It connects the human being with the outside world and the outside world with the inner world" (1995, 77).

My Breathing Is My Dancing

My Breathing Is My Dancing (2015), by the dance company Rosas, is a work that explicitly positions breath at the core of dance performance. The piece was created by choreographer Anne Teresa De Keersmaeker during a nine-week residency that ran parallel to the exhibition *Work/Travail/Arbeid* at the gallery space WIELS in Brussels in the spring of 2015. Aptly described by Rosas's

(2015) website as "an elegant study on motion from breath to space," the piece is performed by a flutist and a dancer. Breath is rendered audible by a flutist, Chryssi Dimitriou, who performs parts of *L'opera per flauto* (1947) by Salvatore Sciarrino and Bach's *Partita in A Minor for Flute*. The dancer—De Keersmaeker herself—dances "in the steps of the flutist's breath" (Rosas 2015).

As in the large-scale performance exhibition *Work/Travail/Arbeid*, which ran parallel to the creation process of this piece, in *My Breathing Is My Dancing* the audience could move around freely in the gallery space. There were no seats for the audience, nor was there any indication of the position the audience was supposed to take. Indeed, when I went to see the performance, members of the audience often stood or sat in close proximity to the flutist and dancer. There was no guarantee that spectators would not eventually end up in De Keersmaeker's trajectory, and in fact this happened quite frequently.

A result of this proximity and shared space was that the conventional spectator-performer divide of "watching and being watched" was blurred. This divide seemed to be partially lifted and transformed into a shared complicity. As Marie Pons (2015) remarks in her review of the performance, "To create space for the human, for a smile and for physical proximity, is the true strength of this proposal. A complicity is established among the spectators, not without a sense of drama." This complicity among the spectators is induced by

FIGURE 10. Rosas, *My Breathing Is My Dancing*, 2015. Dancer: Anne Teresa De Keersmaeker. Flutist: Chryssi Dimitriou (Photo by Anne van Aerschot, reprinted with permission of Anne Teresa De Keersmaeker / Rosas)

De Keersmaeker, who subtly yet deliberately changes course, at times physically confronting and provoking audience members. Will they move out of her way or not? And if not, what will their encounter look like? Pons observes one such encounter: "[De Keersmaeker] does not shy away from gently pushing aside a female spectator who persists in systematically placing herself in [De Keersmaeker's] trajectory, spreading out her arms in protest." In this way the dancer-choreographer continues to test the invisible limits of the space of the dance. How much space does this dance occupy? And how much distance does a spectator need to watch the dance? The performance revealed—perhaps not surprisingly but still spectacularly—that this space had to be continuously renegotiated. Spectators responded in different ways. Some remained standing right next to De Keersmaeker as she danced in one spot. Her flowing pants revealed one bare leg, a leg that is both slender and compactly muscled. Other spectators gave her ample room, quickly moving away as soon as she started heading in their direction. This prompted a heightened physical awareness of the spectators, who became quite conscious of their own attitude. Spectators of *My Breathing*, then, could never "merely watch"; they could not escape from performing, from dancing along *themselves*.

In *My Breathing Is My Dancing*, De Keersmaeker employs her idea of a "stepping phrase," which is a "phrase that literally transposes, step by step / note by note, the rhythmic aspect of the music with which it appears. It is a way to 'walk' or 'step' the music, rendering it visible or inscribed on the floor by movement" (De Keersmaeker et al. 2013, 186). The piece also employs the coupled principle of "Mickey-Mousing," described as "the principle of literal transposition of music into dance. . . . [I]t indicates whichever way of maintaining a correspondence between what the spectators can hear in music and see in movement" (186). In *My Breathing*, the tones of the flute have a clear relationship to the breath of the flutist. The swirling sounds of the flute performance of Sciarrino—which vary greatly in color, frequency, and amplitude—work as a focalizer for the audience to read the phrasing of De Keersmaeker's dance.

When the flute stops, the musician comes to a standstill. De Keersmaeker continues her dance in silence, tentatively at first, as if trying to pick up on the breath that still reverberates in the space but no longer carries the music. Then her dancing becomes more energetic. The Rosas vocabulary is unmistakable. It consists of running, walking, and jumping. There are the extended arms and legs swinging in the air. As always, however, De Keersmaeker's dancing stays far from becoming completely airborne. While there are definitely qualities of elegance, focus, precision, and refinement, the dance does not include the detached ethereality associated with ballet. The dance makes a connection with the ground that is at the same time dynamic and firm. The phrasing and movement qualities of the dance continue to be communicated through breathing, but in the absence of the flute, the dominant source of the breath has now shifted to the dancer's body. Standing close enough to see, hear, and even feel the dancer's breath, members of the audience are invited to notice how their kinesthetic awareness of the dance changes in accordance with this shift.

As a result of its minimal yet powerful setup, *My Breathing Is My Dancing* triggers an intimate awareness of the breath as a reverberating, vital energy that binds and attunes performers to audience members. The performance is imbued with a deep sense of sharing that sparks a *respirational empathy*.[3] By continuing to teach herself to dance, De Keersmaeker teaches others. De Keersmaeker transforms the pure joy she emanates when dancing into a generous gesture toward spectators. It is a gesture that seems to say, "Look, this is how movement is turned into dance. Do you think it looks simple from up close? I assure you, *it is not*." *My Breathing Is My Dancing* thus underlines the importance De Keersmaeker attributes to the breath as a vital element in her ongoing reflection on choreography, on dancing, and on the relationship between music and performance.

Mediating Breath

Digital technologies such as motion capture currently play a pivotal role in supporting a wide range of animation processes, as well as the design of HCI applications in thriving industries such as robotics, films, and games.[4] A central pursuit in this rapidly developing area of research is the simulation or re-creation of lifelike movement. Although motion data may still be understood as indexical traces of captured performance, processes of corporeal computation necessarily mean a radical abstraction of the complex embodied phenomenon of a moving performer. When motion data are used to make other bodies—both virtual and real—move, the challenge is to render motion data in an effective and convincing way. Movement that is re-created in this way is ideally expressive and *believable*. This complicated pursuit has triggered a novel interest in the nature of expressive movement. Computer scientists, engineers, animators, digital artists, and others involved in these creative industries express much interest in the body of knowledge that is harbored by dance and performance traditions. Computer scientist Michael Neff has explained the main reasoning behind this interest as follows: "The performance literature defines what issues the computer animation research community must pay attention to if it wants to create effective tools for producing engaging, rich, nuanced expressive characters. Simply put, the performance literature defines the problem we as computer science researchers are trying to solve and provides part of the solution" (2005, 51). The urgent demand for such meaning-making frames is also evidenced by the widespread appropriation of Laban Movement Analysis and Labanotation as conceptual frameworks to support the analysis, recognition, and re-creation of gestures, emotion, and movement qualities.

In order to grasp the implications of motion capture and wearable physiological sensors as capturing tools for dance, it is important to differentiate between the ways in which various media conceptualize dance. How can an embodied dance feature, such as breath, be mediated by these technologies? Video, the most established capturing tool in the dance field, can make breath visible and audible and thus, to a certain degree, provide useful insights into the kinesthetic basis of a live performance. When researching how the subtle body movements of a performer in standstill may be used in an interactive dance/music performance, musicologists found that "micro-movements can be felt by the performer, can to some extent be seen by an observer, and can easily be picked up by a motion capture system" (Jensenius and Vadstensvik Bjerkestrand 2012, 7). Indeed, motion capture and wearable sensors are able to track breathing movements and transfer these movements into three-dimensional data trajectories. This yields a range of options to adapt and render these data into visualizations or to map these data onto other bodies or entities.

When considering the relationship between breath data and meaningful constructs of dance, such as movement qualities and other expressive features, breath data can be a source through which different types of dance knowledge can be brought to the surface. Such an approach would be in line with existing research, in which qualitative inferences are made based on motion data of the performer's gestures. Indeed, in experimental setups of interaction between performer and performance systems, the computation of breathing sounds has been used to facilitate the interaction of performers with generative performance systems. For example, HCI researcher Gregory James Corness explored how by incorporating breath as part of a system's feedback, the interaction design could leverage the performer's sense of intuition, allowing for an expanded sense of connection and understanding toward the system and leading to synchronization, collaboration, and trust during the performer's interaction with the system (2013, 5).

Another example of the computation of breathing sounds in an interactive performance system can be found in research performed at the Institute for Research and Coordination in Acoustics/Music (IRCAM) in Paris. Breath was used as part of a "gesture follower," an interactive system that was designed to provide real-time feedback to dancers when they were performing a dance phrase (Bevilacqua 2007). A central motivation for a focus on breath in HCI, thus, is that breath is a physiological feature that is not only measurable but also considered to be closely related to the affective and semantic layers of performance.

Making Motion More Alive

Gaining awareness of the importance of breath is also of great importance to digital artists who are working on the animation of films and games. Adding or amplifying breathing movements may have a decisive impact on rendering the performance of a character compelling and lifelike. This has also become apparent in the research project "How to Make Human Motion More Alive" (2013), in which Dutch software developer, dancer, and movement analyst Sandra Hooghwinkel analyzes the movement expression of human characters in film animation. Hooghwinkel observes that characters with a realistic outward appearance but a flawed movement signature run the risk of evoking an uncanny response in the viewer. With regard to the role of breath in "making motion more alive," Hooghwinkel writes, "We 'say' a great deal with our breath and we perceive much about another person's mood and/or intentions by how they are breathing. Breath defines many things, for example life, emotion, phrasing and intent. . . . However, in most of the animated characters, breath is almost never shown. . . . Especially in motion capture movies I was amazed that so little breath is conveyed in the characters" (2013, 54–55). This observation is substantiated by Hooghwinkel's movement analysis of the character Jake Sully in James Cameron's celebrated movie *Avatar* (2009). As part of this analysis, Hooghwinkel uses the notion of breath support, "which underlies and informs every part of human movement" in accordance with Laban Movement Analysis (Bradley 2009, 71). Jake comes across as a distant character. Even though his upper body is uncovered, he can hardly be seen to be breathing. However, eventually, a close-up shows him taking one deep breath. Hooghwinkel observes, "This is almost a relief for me, since I then feel I can allow myself to release my own breath, which I tend to hold when watching Jake. This one breath suddenly makes Jake alive, too!" (2013, 40). Whether or not animated characters in films and games are allowed to take a breath, then, is a matter of design. The choices that directors and designers make will likely have a significant impact on the degree of empathy, sympathy, and identification the viewer experiences in response to the character.

Breath and Body States

The emergence of digital capturing technologies has also triggered an increased interest in breath as a meaning-making dimension in dance practice. Recent experimental approaches of this topic have taken place in an area that combines input from arts and sciences. Breath sensors have become more available,

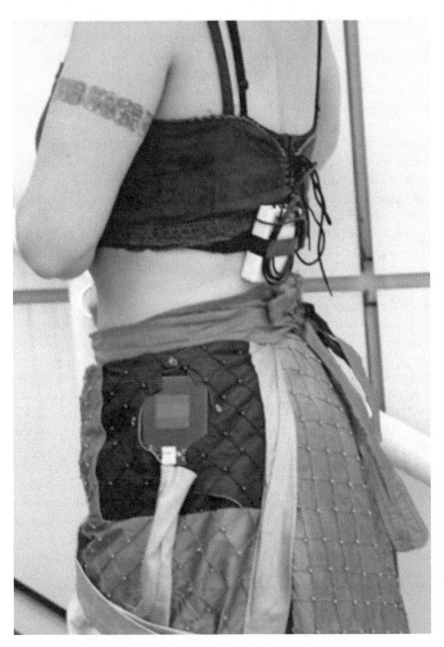

FIGURE 11. Breath-sensing technology integrated in costumes for the performance *exhale*. The breath-sensor waistband measures breath, while the radio-frequency identification tag enables breath exchange. (Reprinted with permission of Thecla Schiphorst, Simon Fraser University)

more affordable, and less intrusive to wear. These sensors have been used in performances that explore the use of "wearable technologies" to transpose the breath into visual and audiovisual output.[5]

An example of such a project is the wearable technology art piece *exhale* (2003–5), which was part of the movement research project "breath between bodies," conducted at Simon Fraser University (Schiphorst et al. 2007). A central question of this project was, How can movement research based in performance and somatics be applied to design strategies for digital interfaces? In *exhale*, participants wear garments with an integrated breath-sensor waistband.

When several participants breathe simultaneously, the color and rhythm of the lights that are attached to their garments change accordingly.[6] Explicitly considering breath as a feature of performance, the researchers tried to relate specific tools of performance analysis, such as Laban Effort/Shape Analysis, to embodied computing and HCI. In this way, the project specifically searched for meaningful ways to transpose breath to a digital network set up through wearable technologies. Thecla Schiphorst points out how the work of neurophysiologist Antonio Damasio (2003) on the relationship between feelings and body states helps to grasp what is happening in *exhale*: "[Damasio's] research suggests that these 'feeling' body-states are an interconnected set of feeling, thought, emotion and physiological functioning: each of these being present and affecting the other. He asserts that the induction of a body-state can be brought about through attention to *any* one of the interconnected patterns: so that attention to physiological patterning (for example breath) can induce a body state, or conversely, attention to other associated patterns, such as the occurrence of certain thought patterns can also induce the body state" (2006, 178). The interconnectedness that is suggested by Damasio gives an important clue as to why breath is such an interesting phenomenon to focus on in technologically based exchanges. Because breath corresponds with physical movement, it can be captured and transposed into data by wearable sensors or motion capture technology. Furthermore, Damasio's notion of interconnectedness points to the possibility that such data may hold a bigger potential than merely capturing breathing aspects as part of a physiological state. Because breath is an element that is part of the interconnected set of feeling, thought, and emotion, breath data may well be understood as indexical traces of these elements, which together constitute a body state.

Breathing Machines

The interconnectedness that lies at the basis of body states also helps us understand why breath is such a rewarding lead in the continuing endeavor to design intuitive ways to relate to a continually expanding technological realm. This is shown by many examples of technological design that tap into the sensitivity to the perception of breathing movements, even when such movements are clearly mapped onto inanimate objects. An everyday example of such design is the way in which breath is suggested by the "sleep mode" of a Mac laptop. The gently increasing and then dimming of the LED light on the laptop imitates the rising and falling sensation of the breath. The even rhythmical pattern of the light not only invokes a relaxed and calm body state but also subtly invites users to embrace the computer as a *living being* and accept it as an intelligent partner that may function as an extension of themselves.

In another striking example, breathing movements are mapped onto a machine to suggest intelligence and trigger fear. The opening scene of Ridley Scott's *Blade Runner* (1982) features the Voight-Kampff machine, a polygraph-like machine and "replicant" detector. Replicants, genetically engineered creatures composed entirely of organic substances, are designed to look and act like humans. In *Blade Runner*, replicants are perceived as a dangerous threat and are hunted down by special human agents called "blade runners." Standing on the table that separates interrogator and suspect, the Voight-Kampff machine has bellows that move in a breathing rhythm. The machine is able to sniff air samples to detect if a subject is nervous in support of its task to determine if a suspect is truly human. A publication of the sketchbook with the original production artwork for the film notes that "Ridley Scott specifically wanted the unit to appear to breathe, hence the bellows. . . . This added to the 'life-like' features of the machine, while underscoring its threatening nature" (Scroggy 1982, 51). Through its breathing bellows, the machine conveys the message to both humans and replicants that it is not to be provoked. The Voight-Kampff machine can be interpreted as a cultural artifact that quite accurately premediated the current interest of creative industries in the business of re-creating movement based on bodily expression.

Conclusion

The renowned breathing therapist Ilse Middendorf states that "breathing is an original unceasing movement and therefore actual life" (1995, 77). It seems to be particularly this conceptualization of breath—breath as movement—that provides the main basis for emerging practices of breath capture and the re-creation of breath. In these practices, breath is mapped onto virtual, animate, and inanimate bodies. These practices take advantage of humans' highly developed sensitivity to perceiving bodily expression through the principle of interconnectedness of feelings and body states. The emergence of digital capturing tools can be understood as a stimulating force that fosters interest in embodied experience in performance and thus opposes the commonly held view that digital technologies ignore the corporeal and the material in favor of the virtual. Making sense of the streams of data that are generated by these devices is a difficult task. But it is exactly this challenge that encourages new investigations of performance techniques and that presents opportunities to articulate the corporeality of dancers in different ways.

The pursuit of this research area to "make motion data speak" adds a new urgency to the understanding of the role of breathing in dance because, for instance, animations of motion data are found to be more compelling when breathing movements are added or amplified. One reason for the focus on breath as a dance feature in HCI research is that breath, even though it is rather complex, is a physiological feature closely related to the affective quality of a performance. It seems that a sensory highlight of breath—be it auditory, visual, or tactile—makes motion data visualizations of dance performance easier to interpret. This observation can be confirmed when looking at an analysis of motion capture–based films in which explicit visualization of the breath increases the lifelike appearance of their characters.

This chapter thus signals a fundamental shift in attention in dance studies that may be boldly phrased by the following question: How can dance be imagined *from the outside in* instead of *from the inside out*? The hypothetical image of the dancer as the uncontested heroine of the age of the breath—conjured up at the beginning of this chapter in response to Luce Irigaray's philosophy of breath—then acquires a new meaning and potential. In tandem with the search for intuitive technological design that is more and more attuned to corporeality, current artistic and scientific research invites a new appreciation and articulation of breathing as the key to intentions and intensities at the core of the dancer's expression.

Notes

1. This chapter is based on my PhD dissertation, "The Motion Capture Imaginary: Digital Renderings of Dance Knowledge" (Ghent University, Belgium, 2017). The research for this dissertation was funded by a four-year grant from Research Foundation Flanders (FWO).

2. For an outline of the historical development of somatic movement practices, specifically as they relate to dance, dancers, and dance education, see Eddy (2009).

3. I am indebted to Janice Ross for suggesting this term after reading an earlier draft of this chapter. Also see Foster (2011).

4. Optical motion capture is a technology that makes use of cameras that emit and detect infrared light and track the three-dimensional trajectories of reflecting markers connected to a body in submillimeter detail.

5. For the use of breath sensors and other measurements of physiological parameters in interactive performance systems, see Bevilacqua, Schnell, and Fdili Alaoui (2011).

6. Another example is the work of Myriam Gourfink, who has used breath sensors and gyroscope sensors in the performance *This is my house* (2005), a collaboration with Frédéric Bevilacqua (Gourfink 2013).

Works Cited

Artaud, Antonin. (1938) 1958. *The Theater and Its Double.* Translated by Mary Caroline Richards. New York: Grove Press.

Banes, Sally. 1987. *Terpsichore in Sneakers: Post-modern Dance.* Middletown, CT: Wesleyan University Press.

Baxmann, Inge. 2007. "The Body as Archive: On the Difficult Relationship between Movement and History." In *Knowledge in Motion: Perspectives of Artistic and Scientific Research in Dance*, edited by Sabine Gehm, Pirkko Hussemann, and Katharina von Wilcke, 207–16. Bielefeld: Transcript.

Bevilacqua, Frédéric. 2007. "Momentary Notes on Capturing Gestures." In *Capturing Intention: Documentation, Analysis and Notation Research Based on the Work of Emio Greco*, edited by Scott deLahunta, 26–31. Amsterdam: Amsterdam School of the Arts.

Bevilacqua, Frédéric, Norbert Schnell, and Sarah Fdili Alaoui. 2011. "Gesture Capture: Paradigms in Interactive Music/Dance Systems." In *Emerging Bodies: The Performance of Worldmaking in Dance and Choreography*, edited by Gabriele Klein and Sandra Noeth, 183–93. Bielefeld: Transcript.

Bradley, Karen K. 2009. *Rudolf Laban.* London: Routledge.

Corness, Gregory James. 2013. "Breath as an Embodied Connection for Performer-System Collaborative Improvisation." PhD dissertation, Simon Fraser University.

Damasio, Antonio R. 2003. *Looking for Spinoza: Joy, Sorrow, and the Feeling Brain.* Orlando: Harcourt.

De Keersmaeker, Anne Teresa, Bojana Cvejić, and Michel François. 2013. *En Atendant & Cesena: A Choreographer's Score.* Brussels: Mercatorfonds and Rosas.

Eddy, Martha. 2009. "A Brief History of Somatic Practices and Dance: Historical Development of the Field of Somatic Education and Its Relationship to Dance." *Journal of Dance & Somatic Practices* 1 (1): 5–27.

Foster, Susan Leigh. 1995. "Choreographing History." In *Choreographing History*, edited by Susan Leigh Foster, 3–21. Bloomington: Indiana University Press.

———. 2011. *Choreographing Empathy: Kinesthesia in Performance.* London: Routledge.

Freedman, Russell. 1998. *Martha Graham: A Dancer's Life.* New York: Clarion Books.

Gourfink, Myriam. 2013. "Dance, Borrow, Create? From the Breath to Ideas, from Ideas to Gestures." *International Journal of Performance Arts & Digital Media* 9 (1): 14–30.

Hooghwinkel, Sandra. 2013. "How to Make Human Motion More Alive: Viewing Human Animation through the Lens of Laban Movement Analysis." LIMS / Agape Modular Certification Programme.

Irigaray, Luce. 1983. *L'oubli de l'air chez Martin Heidegger.* Paris: Les Éditions de Minuit.

———. 1996. "A Breath That Touches in Words." In *I Love to You: Sketch of a Possible Felicity in History*, 121–28. New York: Routledge.

———. 1999. *The Forgetting of Air in Martin Heidegger*. Translated by Mary Beth Mader. Austin: University of Texas Press.

———. 2004. "The Age of the Breath." In *Luce Irigaray: Key Writings*, edited by Luce Irigaray, 165–70. New York: Continuum.

———. 2013. "About Breathing with Luce Irigaray." Accessed August 1, 2017. http://www.bloomsbury.com/us/breathing-with-luce-irigaray-9781441115485/.

Jensenius, Alexander Refsum, and Kari Anne Vadstensvik Bjerkestrand. 2012. "Exploring Micromovements with Motion Capture and Sonification." In *Arts and Technology: Second International Conference ArtsIT 2011*, edited by Anthony L. Brooks, 100–107. Berlin: Springer.

Karreman, Laura. 2015. "Repeating 'Rosas Danst Rosas': On the Transmission of Dance Knowledge." *Performance Research* 20 (5): 98–107.

LaBelle, Brandon. 2014. *Lexicon of the Mouth: Poetics and Politics of Voice and the Oral Imaginary*. New York: Bloomsbury Publishing.

Lepecki, André. 2010. "The Body as Archive: Will to Re-enact and the Afterlives of Dances." *Dance Research Journal* 42 (2): 28–48.

Louppe, Laurence. 2010. *Poetics of Contemporary Dance*. Translated by Sally Gardner. Alton, Hampshire: Dance Books Ltd.

Middendorf, Ilse. 1995. "The Perceptible Breath: A Breathing Science (Preface)." In *Bone, Breath & Gesture*, edited by Don Hanlon Johnson, 74–79. Berkeley: North Atlantic Books.

Nair, Sreenath. 2007. *Restoration of Breath: Consciousness and Performance*. Amsterdam: Rodopi.

Neff, Michael P. 2005. "Aesthetic Exploration and Refinement: A Computational Framework for Expressive Character Animation." PhD dissertation, University of Toronto.

Polanyi, Michael. 1958. *Personal Knowledge*. Chicago: University of Chicago Press.

Pons, Marie. 2015. "Souffles en choeur." In *Les trois coups: Le journal du spectacle vivant*, translated by Laura Karreman. May 17. Accessed August 1, 2017. http://lestroiscoups.fr/my-breathing-is-my-dancing-de-et-avec-anne-teresa-de-keersmaeker-chryssi-dimitriou-dans-le-cadre-du-kunstenfestivaldesarts-brux/.

Rosas. 2015. *My Breathing Is My Dancing*. Accessed August 1, 2017. http://www.rosas.be/en/productions/371-my-breathing-is-my-dancing.

Schiphorst, Thecla. 2006. "Breath, Skin and Clothing: Using Wearable Technologies as an Interface into Ourselves." *International Journal of Performance Arts and Digital Media* 2 (2): 171–86.

Schiphorst, Thecla (artistic director, concept, systems design), Susan Kozel (performance and dramaturgical design), et al. 2007. *exhale*. Accessed August 1, 2017. http://www.sfu.ca/~tschipho/exhale/index.html.

Scroggy, David, ed. 1982. *Blade Runner Sketchbook*. PDF version, 2008, by Fans for Fans ed., Blue Dolphin Enterprises.

Škof, Lenart. 2015. *Breath of Proximity: Intersubjectivity, Ethics and Peace.* Dordrecht: Springer.

Wigman, Mary. 1966. *The Language of Dance.* Translated by Walter Sorell. Middletown, CT: Wesleyan University Press.

Youngerman, Suzanne. 1984. "Movement Notation Systems as Conceptual Frameworks: The Laban System." In *Illuminating Dance: Philosophical Explorations*, edited by Maxine Sheets-Johnstone, 101–23. Lewisberg: Bucknell University Press.

Desires

Gender and sexuality emerge as crucial categories for analysis in this section of essays. Bodies in motion—at the lecture podium and in the newspaper column, on the theatrical stage, in song lyrics and on music videos, in the street during Carnival—articulate images and ideas of masculinity and womanhood, same-sex bonding and intimacy, heterosexist logics, and queer and feminist subversions of the status quo. What constitutes desire in these diverse scenarios? Do the desires of participants and onlookers coincide or move in opposing directions? And how does the racialization of bodies in US culture—the larger scene for all the case studies explored in this section—inform enactments of gender and sexuality?

In "Lesbian Echoes in Activism and Writing: Jill Johnston's Interventions" Clare Croft highlights a 1971 town hall in New York City that pitted Norman Mailer against leaders of the emergent feminist movement. Jill Johnston, a columnist for the *Village Voice*, upstaged her colleagues by ending her remarks with a comic and erotic make-out session with two other women. Undoing the bifurcation of Johnston's career into an early phase dedicated to dance criticism and a later phase dedicated to activism, Croft demonstrates how the writer deployed embodiment throughout her career to disrupt the status quo. Johnston's appearance at the town hall becomes a test case for a lesbian counterpublic, for a lesbian dance. "Lesbian arises as not just an identity," Croft argues, "but a strategy—a mode of disruption that makes visible misogyny, heteronormativity, and the limits of feminist respectability politics."

Whereas Croft shows what attention to movement in public can add to dance studies, Daniel Callahan deepens the analysis of theatrical dance through attention to choreomusicality, the relation between dance/choreography and music/score. In "Accent, Choreomusicality, and Identity in *Rodeo* and *'Rōdē,ō*" Callahan compares Agnes de Mille's 1942 choreography, set to a commissioned score from Aaron Copland, with Justin Peck's 2015 work, set to a concert arrangement of the ballet score. Zeroing in on "Corral Nocturne," Callahan argues that Peck's choreography for the New York City Ballet (NYCB) more vividly realizes the scenario de Mille sent to Copland—dancing "intoxicated with space"—than does her own choreography. The male quintet in Peck's "Corral Nocturne" realizes this spaciousness through "tenderly partnering each other in flowing lyrical movement," a movement quality that Callahan interprets as "lovingly homosocial or even queer," an interpretation supported by his interviews with performers in the work. Even in 2015, and especially in the aftermath of the Pulse Nightclub shootings, which shadowed the research and writing of his essay, Callahan finds Peck's choreography a welcome departure from the status quo at NYCB.

Both Croft and Callahan acknowledge their desire to see queer dance. Croft also acknowledges how Jill Johnston's whiteness enabled her staging of a lesbian dance at the 1971 town hall, an event that presented only white panelists for a largely white audience. In that time and place, an African American, Asian American, Latina, or Native American woman would have encountered an entirely different set of risks in making out with other women in public. Callahan addresses the question of racialization more obliquely than does Croft. Although he notes that two of the men in Peck's original casting for "Corral Nocturne" were nonwhite, he chooses not to emphasize how the mixed-race casting of the quintet intersected with its homosociality or queerness. As Gillian Lipton's essay demonstrates, Arthur Mitchell had challenged the whiteness of American ballet with his founding of the Dance Theatre of Harlem in 1969. Fifty years later, Callahan recognizes that "the larger question . . . is not new: to what extent can ballet . . . speak to and reflect the increasingly diverse set of identities, cultures, and histories of its performers and audiences today?"

It is telling that both Croft and Callahan illustrate their topics, whereas the final two authors in this section do not. From very different perspectives, Jasmine Johnson and Adanna Kai Jones approach the social dancing of black women, aware that the visibility, indeed the hypervisibility, of the black female body is at issue. As Johnson writes, "Overdetermined from without, black women are understood as caricatures." How, then, does it become possible for black women to dance their desires?

In "Flesh Dance: Black Women from Behind" Johnson examines the lyrics and accompanying music videos of hip hop songs that "direct black women to move in sexually mimetic ways," a subgenre she calls "flesh dance." Her examples—50 Cent's "Down on Me" (2010), Waka Flocka's "No Hands" (2010), Travis Porter's "Bring It Back" (2011), among others—feature a male rapper instructing female dancers "to move their behinds percussively" for the erotic pleasure of the male singer and viewer. Applying Hortense Spillers's astute analysis of the "hieroglyphics of the flesh," Johnson understands flesh dance as paradigmatic of black social dance and, indeed, of black women in public: "Flesh dance polices sex, intimacy, and expectations of kinship, yet this objectification does not entirely foreclose the potential for pleasure, self-identification, and self-possession." Johnson calls for black feminist approaches to dance studies to rely less on visuality and to cultivate alternate modalities, attending to what Callahan would term "choreomusicality" and what Hannah Kosstrin has called "kinesthetic seeing."

Whereas Johnson imagines how black women might take pleasure in their performance of flesh dance, Jones writes about her own pleasure in performing winin', "a rolling hip/butt dance informally learned at a very young age and commonly performed at Trinidadian-style Carnivals." Scripting an autoethnographic account of her participation in the 2011 West Indian American Day Carnival in Brooklyn, Jones reveals the pleasures of sneaking past a police barricade with her friends, jumping on the truck carrying her favorite soca singer of the season, and flirting with a handsome man during the all-night festivities. In these ways, "winin' in public works as a pleasure-filled strategy for masqueraders to push back against, renegotiate, and undermine the contending racial meanings they wear upon their bodies." In contrast to Jones's participatory account of the Carnival, news accounts circulated via the media focused on crime along the parade route (grossly exaggerated). At least one site on the internet posted a video of a white policeman daggering black female dancers (a Jamaican dance hall move in which the man thrusts his pelvis into the woman's backside). Isolated from the surroundings of the Carnival, where such corporeal exchanges potentially subvert the authority of the police, the video clip visualizes the colonialist gaze and stance of the police. It is such (mis)readings of winin' that compel Jones's desire: "Because her disembodied hypervisibility became a necessary part of her racial and gendered existence, it is both necessary and radical for the black dancing woman to take up public space."

In their explorations of black social dancing, Johnson and Jones recognize that the desires of onlookers and participants may not coincide. While many male rappers and viewers of flesh dance likely focus on the female dancers' sexualized moves, the dancers themselves may well attend to their own rhythmic and corporeal mastery and pleasure. Similarly, while the white policeman caught on video at the 2011 Carnival likely interpreted the black dancers' moves as erotic, Jones and her friends experience their own moves as a means for playing with and hence defusing the sexualized meanings projected onto their bodies. In contrast, the desires of Croft and Callahan as onlookers—and historians—seem more congruent with the desires of their subjects to stage lesbian and queer subversions of the status quo. To be sure, Croft and Callahan recognize the heterosexism that reimposes the values of the dominant culture in Norman Mailer's heckling of Johnston and the male-female duet that follows Peck's "Corral Nocturne" (not to mention the scenario for de Mille's *Rodeo*). But they seem able to bracket the heterosexism in their case studies in a way that Johnson and Jones cannot bracket the sexism that onlookers bring to black women dancing in public, and this asymmetry underscores how racialization shapes images and ideas of gender and sexuality in US culture.

Lesbian Echoes in Activism and Writing

Jill Johnston's Interventions

CLARE CROFT

In 1971 dance critic turned lesbian feminist provocateur Jill Johnston reoriented a public debate about feminism. With her luscious language and provocative spectacle, Johnston forced an evening initially pitched as a debate of women versus men into an exploration of the *many* ways to be a woman in public. Johnston paired the linguistic and the embodied to thrust her own identity position as a lesbian into an otherwise heteronormative, masculinist display. The occasion of Johnston's lesbian spectacle was a gathering of writers and activists assembled in the immediate wake of the publication of author Norman Mailer's antifeminist screed, *The Prisoner of Sex*. The group included Mailer, Johnston, British feminist poet/critic/provocateur Germaine Greer, National Organization of Women (NOW) New York chapter president Jacqueline Ceballos, and literary critic Diana Trilling.[1]

Deft deployment of language was likely to animate the event. These were mostly people known for their excellent writing; thus Johnston—a well-known, shrewd, yet experimental writer for New York alternative weekly *The Village Voice*—fit well within the group. She had first come to the *Voice* as a dance critic and became the foundational voice of New York's postmodern dance scene. By 1970 she was using her column to poetically chronicle her coming out process, making herself America's most famous out lesbian—not a position many were vying for in the early 1970s and one that often put her at odds with both the male establishment and mainstream feminists. Johnston's explicitly lesbian challenge to patriarchy and white straight feminist respectability took on new fervor at the 1971 event, a town hall organized by the Theatre of Ideas.

That the event would be antagonistic was no surprise, and not just because of Johnston's reputation. Panel organizers first proposed the event as "Feminists v.

Mailer," forecasting the discussion as one predicated on "Man versus Women" or, more accurately, "Man versus *Woman*," imagining only a singular possibility for the latter category. The event gave Mailer outsized status, as evidenced by the choice to initially name him in the title and also by making him moderator, a role he inhabited not as a mere referee but as a platform to interrupt whenever he liked. In contrast, the initial title grouped together the women as though they were a monolithic unit. Mailer carried that sentiment into the room, calling them "lady critics" in his introduction. The eventual format also carefully curtailed the women's individual voices. Each had ten minutes to speak, but all faced frequent interruptions from Mailer as he narrated and disagreed with each at will.

The evening was staged as a battle of words, but Johnston's physical actions highlighted the real stakes of the exchange: any debate about feminism is not a mere intellectual exercise but a battle over how a woman can be a person, with a mind and a body, in public. Greer (1971) later described that night not as a town hall but as "town bloody hall," a quip later borrowed to title the 1979 documentary that captured the evening's event. Greer's "bloody" indexes the event's physical and affective intensity.

Even as advertising for the event positioned Greer as the panel's controversial voice, Johnston's speech and physicality stole the room from Mailer. Once at the microphone for her allotted ten minutes, Johnston spun her signature associative style: lilting and poetic ("The lover should resemble the beloved and be the same, and the greater is the likeness brighter will the ruptured flame"), provocative ("I am a woman and therefore a lesbian"), and pointedly funny ("He said, 'I want your body,' and she said, 'You can have it when I'm through with it'").[2] The room grew raucous, charged by Johnston's heat and wit. Still Mailer interrupted, loudly grasping for the audience's attention. Johnston finally overwhelmed him with bodies and desire. She invited two women onstage and began a make-out session with both, complete with loud kisses and falls to the floor. All Mailer could do was yell, "C'mon Jill; be a lady." He, however, was in no position to determine what it meant to be a "lady."

In Pennebaker's 1979 documentary, Johnston's emergence as the night's most charismatic and brilliant figure is clear. She is the figure who sears herself most intensely into the historical record, and she does it against layers of odds. The evening's debate was never meant to be hospitable to women at all, and certainly not to a broad range of women. It was predicated on patriarchy (giving Mailer nearly unchallenged power), compulsory heterosexuality (pairing of men and women in the title, Mailer's many homophobic comments), and racism (only white people were invited to speak). Johnston's *physical* insistence on the fact of

FIGURES 12 AND 13. Jill Johnston looks aghast at Norman Mailer (*center*) as he tells her to stop speaking and then walks from behind podium, arms open, inviting two women onstage to make out with her. (From the film *Town Bloody Hall* by Chris Hegedus and D. A. Pennebaker, courtesy Pennebaker Hegedus Films, PHFilms.com.)

her lesbianism disrupted if not the event's racism, then certainly its misogyny and homophobia.

This essay considers the nature of Johnston's lesbian disruption through her work as an activist as seen in the 1971 panel and, in a perhaps surprising turn, in her work as a dance critic. While Johnston herself, as well as most historians, has drawn a firm line between her dance writing in the 1950s and 1960s and her lesbian feminist work, I think across this bifurcation of her life, taking a cue from Johnston's own emphasis on embodiment as a social tool to examine the possibility of lesbian as a political strategy that resonates in both postmodern dance and second wave feminism. Literary theorist Annamarie Jagose has shown how, in literature, the lesbian is often framed as a figure that is "elsewhere," a figure "less an absence than a presence that can't be seen" (1994, 1–5; 2002, 3). The lesbian, in Jagose's analysis, is a figure imagined "elsewhere" because of the entanglement of heteronormativity and misogyny, but her specter, her "presence that can't be seen," produces a sense of possibility (even utopia), even as it is also evidence of her abjection. Moving Jagose's observations into the realm of dance—a category I take up broadly as both an art form and an insistence on paying attention to bodies—requires thinking the paradox of absent present bodies, a kind of queer possibility of embodiment.

To think the lesbian dancing body as a form of public disruption, I first situate Johnston's work in the historical and social context of feminist and queer politics of the 1960s and 1970s. Next, I discuss the role of lesbians in public space by examining how dancing, moving bodies challenge ideas of publicity and how specifically lesbian bodies create not just publicity but counterpublicity. I then use these ideas as a way to more carefully examine the 1971 panel. Finally, I return to Johnston's earlier dance criticism to see how the absent presence of Johnston's lesbianism returns a politics of gender and sexuality into the now often depoliticized realm of postmodern dance. In all these considerations, lesbian arises not just as an identity but as a strategy—a mode of disruption that makes visible misogyny, heteronormativity, and the limits of feminist respectability politics. Importantly, this is not just a lesbian strategy of "raising awareness"; instead, it is a strategy that offers, indeed enacts, other possibilities for ways a woman can appear in public.

Johnston in Context

The year 1971 was crucial in Johnston's life. In 1971 EP Dutton published Johnston's self-edited volume, *Marmalade Me*, a collection of her writing from her *Village Voice* column that was titled as a "dance journal." Also in 1971 Johnston had the standoff with Mailer described earlier. As Johnston turned to lesbian activism, reviewers of *Marmalade Me* commented on and usually derided the shift in Johnston's focus from dance to lesbianism. She began to be described as once a thoughtful, wide-ranging critic now limited by a marginal identity marker. One review of *Marmalade Me* celebrated the volume for being a reminder of Johnston's prose as something other than the more personal, lesbian-centered prose she was writing by 1971. The reviewer described Johnston now as "*just*" being a "professional lesbian" (emphasis in text) (David quoted in Gever 2003, 56). The pronouncement—as superficial critiques of identity politics often do—vilified a woman's assertion of herself as having an identity meaningful enough to her to label with a term of her choosing. From this suspicious vantage point, identity categories can only be limits, not the naming of possibilities. Performance scholar Kareem Khubchandani has termed this reductive notion of identity, especially around experimental queer performances, as the "clott[ing of] identity" (2017, 200). To give oneself a label is to announce something about oneself to an audience, not necessarily to imagine that name as one's only identity or even as a coherent identity. Theorist Ann Cvetkovich has argued that this recognition of importance, as well as partiality, is particularly salient when thinking about the term "lesbian," a label that has proved forceful but also stubbornly linked to whiteness and thus often requiring additional terms to encompass racial identities, among other vectors of identity (2003, 11).

Johnston's writing, however, helped expand "lesbian" as a label that conjured not just an identity but also a practice. She did this through her very public coming out in the *Voice*, first in 1970 and then again in 1971 (sometimes people don't hear you the first time) (Johnston 1970, 1973). She also manifested lesbian as a disruptive practice by drawing on the tone and strategies for making radical stands in public that had been central to the postmodern dance scene Johnston chronicled.

As a dance critic, Johnston did not just describe performance for readers; instead, she sought to ignite a sensuous, often personal experience of what it felt like to attend a performance. Her visceral, playful language conjured the space and the scene, often positioning the audience not as passive spectators but as fully present, active, participants within the larger frame of the experience. This positioning draws on the characteristics of many of the performances Johnston wrote about, most notably, the Judson Church scene now usually described as the origin of US postmodern dance's bucking of balletic and high modernist traditions in favor of an embrace of the egalitarian and pedestrian. Johnston's positioning of the audience (and subsequently her readers) as within the performance also extended from Johnston's role in the art world: she was a critic, but a very much embedded, physically present one.

Like the artists most often associated with Judson—Yvonne Rainier, Trisha Brown, Steve Paxton, Lucinda Childs, and Deborah Hay, among others—Johnston was invested in displacing the dance world's institutional and aesthetic hierarchies. Johnston challenged hierarchies by upending them through physicality. As a critic she observed physical possibilities in her writing and in her spectatorship, and she tracked how physical encounters in public produced unexpected interactions and critiques. For instance, in May 1968 Johnston reviewed the "Destruction in Art" symposium at Judson, an evening she termed "the most unusual manifestation of a performer-audience situation I have witnessed in a decade of attending theatre in which the performer-audience relationship has been pushed in every conceivable direction" (1968b, 132). In a tumbling, sometimes hilarious review, Johnston tracks how audience members sought to intervene in a series of performances, climaxing with an audience member named Saul Gottlieb getting a bloodied face after putting his body in the way of performance artist Charlotte Moorman's destruction of a violin in Nam June Paik's *One for Violin* (1961). After charting how the intervention unfolded—including her own yelling from the audience to try to get Moorman to accept Gottlieb's offered trade of his coat for the violin's safety—Johnston assessed, "It wasn't so much a question who was right or wrong (I thought, if pressed, both were right and both wrong), but what might have been done to avert the inevitable" (1968b, 134). Evenings like this provided Johnston ample experience in witnessing what happens when people confront one another in public, using their bodies, and how participating fully in these events forces everyone present to reckon with the ethics of encounter.

Art had no special purchase on the notion of the physical as a form of social critique in the 1960s. As historian Alice Echols has noted, feminist movements, especially the radical feminism of the late sixties—which would, to some degree, give rise to lesbian feminism—emphasized physical, body-centered spectacles as central to public protest. In 1968 feminist activists gained national attention protesting the Miss America pageant in Atlantic City, parodying the event by marching outside the venue and eventually crowning a live sheep "Miss America" (Echols 1989, 92–93). Creating this kind of physical spectacle as social action was not just limited to those theatrically inclined (as several Miss America protest planners were). Some radical feminist groups, like New York Radical Feminists, required interested women to stage at least one public action to gain membership (190). Other groups made physical practice part of their regular training. For instance, the women of Cell 16 trained in karate (158). Radical feminists trained their bodies and used their bodies in public to make statements about inequality and to draw attention to women's issues—issues often focused on the body (e.g., birth control and abortion).

Doing It in Public

While both the postmodern dance scene and the radical feminist scene studied and manipulated physical possibility toward social critique, neither openly invited questions of homosexuality, particularly lesbianism, into their lexicons. While certainly many within the Judson scene engaged in homosexual relationships, many of the artists of the period now name the inattention to sexuality in Judson as rising from a combination of ignorance about sexuality and/ or homophobia (Hay 2017; Rainer 2017). Radical feminism was often openly homophobic and excluded lesbians. In Echols's examination of four major radical feminist groups, one of the few constants across all was hostility toward lesbians (1989, 139–202). The rejection of lesbians often pivoted on an accusation that lesbians were not really women but were rather women who wanted to be men.

Johnston's public displays arise from this painful rejection of women by women even as they also challenge the dominance—even the necessity—of men. Hers was a lesbian physical spectacle, not just a feminist one. The braiding of public protest, lesbianism, and the physical is a complicated collage that brings together an understanding of public and counterpublic, sameness and difference that bears further elaboration.

Public sphere theory, originating with political theorist Jürgen Habermas (1991), considers how people form spaces of debate and connection beyond structures provided by the state, and these theories have been a critical buttress for many performance scholars interested in the political possibilities of people gathering in the live space of the theater. For performance scholars more focused on embodiment than on text or language, however, the model of public debate proffered within Habermas's writings has proved fraught, since he ignores physicality as a path toward public sphere formation. This inattention to embodiment in public sphere theory has racial, gender, and class implications, since the modes of rational engagement Habermas highlights—writing, voting, and rational debate—generally unfold in settings that privilege and protect white men (Black Public Sphere Collective 1995; Berlant and Warner 1998).

Habermas's disregard for the physical as a mode of debate in the public sphere would not surprise dance scholars accustomed to physical action being disregarded as a form of discursive engagement (1991, 38–40).[3] In contrast, dance studies recognizes the role bodies play in public debate and that physical expression is an important mode for minoritarian communities, specifically women and communities of color. Dance studies seeks to highlight the physical as doing work in public space and to honor that the work done might happen in marginalized, even subversive ways.

Dance is not essentially "special" or "different" from other art forms or other modes of communication. But in situations where written and oral speech are prized over physical communication as the primary forms through which a group executes what Habermas calls the "properly political tasks of a citizenry acting in common" (1991, 52), dance is more likely aligned with resistance. Dance in public, with its marginalized status and often populated by minoritarian groups, is more likely to promote not the formation of a Habermasian public but what feminist theorist Nancy Fraser has termed a "counterpublic." "Subaltern counterpublics" are, in Fraser's language, "parallel discursive arenas where members of subordinated social groups invent and circulate counterdiscourses to formulate oppositional interpretations of their identities, interests, and needs" (1992, 123). The tendency toward thinking of writing and speech as the only, or at least the preferred, modes of engaging in public intellectual debate gives the physical a unique vantage point for challenging social norms.

In text-centric situations, like the 1971 panel with Johnston and Mailer, the physical seems disposed to invite the formation of a counterpublic, and Johnston's physical work conjures a specific counterpublic: a lesbian one. Johnston's announcement of herself as a lesbian through text—but even more so through kissing and falling—makes visible the possibility of "lesbian" countering a monolithic, homogeneous category called "Woman." Johnston's lesbian counterpublicity is one that insists on difference and multiplicity. Lesbian, like gay, is often described as being based in "same-sex" attraction and/or partnership. Queer phenomenologist Sara Ahmed, however, has argued for lesbian not only as an orientation that is about a draw to another woman but also, more importantly, as an attraction predicated on difference *among* women. For Ahmed, lesbian desire undoes the "fantasy that women are 'the same'" (2006, 96). The very side-by-sideness of women in lesbian community makes apparent the multitude of ways to be a woman. Critic and poet Maggie Nelson, writing about relationships among lesbians and transmen, reimagines what it is that might be the "same" in lesbian connection, arguing that what these groups share is not something essential to their gender but rather a social condition aware of patriarchy and misogyny: "Whatever sameness I've noted in my relationships with women is not the sameness of Woman. . . . Rather, it is the shared crushing understanding of what it means to live in a patriarchy" (2015, 25). For Nelson, the possibility of lesbianism comes from a shared experience of social norms and their constant imposition of limitations. Dance theorist Petra Kuppers (1998) has argued that to dance as a lesbian—a position Kuppers acknowledges has often been difficult to identify in concert dance—requires a choreography that makes female desire explicit *and* refuses to be merely an "other" to heterosexuality. To be a lesbian body in public, then, is to challenge a monolithic notion of Woman, to challenge patriarchy and misogyny, and to develop terms of representing the lesbian that make the lesbian body visible not only in opposition to heterochoreographies.

Johnston's performance on the 1971 panel is the most lesbian of lesbian dances. In her speaking and moving, she insists on her difference from the other panelists and the lesbian stereotypes Mailer posed in his writing and speech—all homophobic ideas forged from/of the male gaze. This lesbian choreography, then, is never one fully inscribed in language; instead, it is a spectacular event that counters how the community of the room assembles. Through a performance of desire, Johnston undermines the definitions of feminism, gender, and sexuality that organized the panel.

Johnston spoke third among the four women at the panel. Unlike the two preceding speakers, Johnston immediately began her comments in a comedic register. From the first moments of her talk—a beautifully crafted, fluid example of her associative style of argumentation—she regularly cracked herself up and eventually drew guffaws from the panel and the audience. This seems a prime example of what queer theorist Sara Warner has referred to as Johnston's "joker citizenship," a comedic activist gesture Warner argues allowed Johnston a critical outsider perch from which to critique mainstream feminisms (2013, 121). What is intriguing about Johnston's panel comments is how this joker sensibility registers as not just comedy but physical comedy. Her moments of cracking herself up are particularly notable, as when she laughs so hard that she rears back from the microphone, unable to keep talking, and when she makes out with the women, a moment that is erotic, funny, and slightly awkward.

Johnston's joker status is essential to her creation of lesbian counterpublicity, but it is important to note that it is a strategy made possible not just by her lesbianism but also by her whiteness. Public physical performances of white women and women of color in 1960s and 1970s feminist movements had remarkable differences. White women could take on the mantle of public frivolity, in essence overfilling the boundaries of public respectability in order to make feminist critique. As was the case with crowning the sheep beauty queen at the 1968 Miss America protest, silliness was an effective tool for white feminist protest. When black feminists appeared in public, they often did so with intense seriousness. It was less safe for them to use comedy; they could not even smile, except for when that smile was one of ironic disapproval of white ignorance. Take, for instance, the close-ups on Angela Davis's face as she speaks in a 1972 interview from her jail cell (Olson 2011). She looks directly into the camera and offers no hint of a smile except for when she is exasperated with the interviewer's thoughtless line of questioning. The very fact that she speaks from a jail cell also notes the heightened stakes for women of color's physical self-regulation: one self-polices to avoid being policed by the state.

While Johnston's jokester, staged only months before the Davis interview, is made partially possible by whiteness, her jokester is also a specific tool used against the male gaze. Without the layer of humor and awkwardness, a public display of lesbian erotics could be read as presented for a male audience's gaze. Johnston uses humor to make clear how much Mailer is not her audience, especially at the end of her performance. While Johnston is at the podium, Mailer sits at the table, first trying to get her to finish her talk and later trying to get her to stop making out with her kissing interlocutors. His shouts from the table, where he sits with the female speakers, have no impact. In response, he announces that he will introduce the next speaker, Trilling, from the "rostrum." As Mailer comes to the lectern, Johnston leans her make-out partner against it, so he comes to a microphone he can only partially stand behind. His voice is amplified, but Johnston has quite literally taken space from him. Mailer is put on the defensive, displaced from center stage, contorted around the women, and no longer blasting them out of his way with volume and talktalktalk. The public display of lesbianism is tinged with the comedic in a move that makes space for a lesbian visibility while importantly keeping the moment from seeming like lesbian erotics framed for heterosexual male viewership. Johnston's choreography does not invite Mailer to be titillated by the women. Instead, they literally force him to edge away from center stage, away from the microphone, where he is publicly, visibly uncomfortable, not pleasured in any way.

Through physical choices, Johnston and her kissing partners mark Mailer's sexism as ridiculous *and* overpower it. It is key that it is many women who overpower Mailer, not just Johnston as lone lesbian superhero. Equally important is the egalitarian relationship among the women. As they kiss, fall, and tumble, there is no sense of leader and follower—or at least not a sense of those roles as stable or hierarchical. To be valued in the kissing trio is to be responsive, not to be in control.

Yet Johnston does not cede control entirely. Putting Mailer on the sidelines, Johnston fully becomes the evening's central character, a shift to the center that makes her exit possible. Eventually, seemingly on her own time, Johnston takes one of the women's hands and strolls offstage. She never returns. Through the remaining portion of the evening, Mailer often shouts, "I would ask Jill Johnston this, if she were here!" These comments evoke Johnston in her very present absence. Johnston's ability to linger in the space seems evocative of Jagose's articulation of a lesbian style of exercising power, an ability to be "less an absence than a presence that can't be seen" (2002, 3). Johnston is a lesbian echo, a powerful lingering of women's bodies, women touching, a woman being funny, a woman seen on her own terms.

Lesbian Echoes in Writing

The lesbian echo is a spatial invocation in the 1971 panel but a temporal one in Johnston's criticism. Johnston was "out" to some degree in the 1960s—publicly involved with women in her personal life, including at the many parties that were almost as significant to the 1960s avant-garde scene as was the art itself. To read for a lesbian echo in her 1960s dance writing is to read for the specificity of politics in the writing, as opposed to the more universalized notion of democracy more frequently associated with Judson as it has been canonized. I follow these lesbian echoes to examine radical political challenges to hierarchy Johnston makes in her writing.

Johnston began covering what would become known as New York's postmodern dance scene in the late 1950s, primarily for the *Village Voice*. The scene's egalitarianism compelled her, particularly that of a young Merce Cunningham. In a 1968 review of a performance of the José Limón Dance Company, Johnston explains her preference for Cunningham's directness with his audience, looking them "straight in the eye," an approach she vastly preferred to the heavenward gaze of modernists like Limón, whom she chastised for always having his chin "tilted . . . to the sky" (1968e, 126). Displays of superiority disgusted Johnston. She devoted her writing and her activism to challenging hierarchies in whatever form they occurred, even if that disturbance of hierarchy created discomfort (maybe even *especially* if that disturbance created discomfort).

Johnston deployed discomfort and playfulness as tools to unsettle hierarchies prior to her lesbian activism. For instance, in 1968 she organized a panel at NYU—a performance of sorts—explicitly focused on undermining expertise, a notion often used to justify hierarchies. The performance score Johnston (1968f) devised invited audience members to tackle panel speakers whenever they felt the speaker should stop talking. The afternoon event ended with all the original panelists in the audience, a small child left alone in a panelist's seat onstage, and a pig loose in NYU's Loeb Student Center.

As seen in this 1968 scene and in the 1971 panel, Johnston choreographed her challenges to hierarchy, directing bodies and ideas in space. Reordering the physical is something she did in writing, too—a difficult act she managed in concert with the dances about which she wrote. Writing, especially writing in newspapers, unfolds in a particularly linear form. Sequence may be naturalized in journalistic prose and thus its hierarchies may be easily overlooked, but information is prioritized. One idea or word precedes another, and what goes

first is what is marked as most important. Among the most powerful characteristics of Johnston's writing is her ability to overwhelm this sense of unfolding
knowledge—through rhythm, through language choice—as a way to create an
egalitarian sensibility that defies journalistic prose's naturalization of sequence.
Jagose has argued that the position of the lesbian critic is often one critical of
sequence, especially of a social sequence that often places heterosexuality first
and homosexuality second or that sees the lesbian as always derivative of either
straight women or gay men (2002, xi). In her dance criticism, Johnston played
with populating a scene with a number of queer characters all presented on
one plane. In other criticism less focused on gender and sexuality she denatu-
ralized sequence with an egalitarian aim that could still be recognized as feminist and queer.

In Johnston's writing there is no one thing to which to become attached:
the thing is the whole arising from many items commingling and spilling forward. The many specific elements, connected but not coherent, thwart attempts
to organize them into hierarchies. In the writing, specifically in the extraordi-
narily long lists that often appear in Johnston's performance description, there
is a sense of overflow that can be read as feminist and queer. Her frequent use
of these long lists in her prose creates associative, accumulative logic; refuses to
elevate specific referents among others; and redistributes power among many.
The multiple, specific elements, connected but not coherent, thwart any attempt
to organize the scene she describes into hierarchies. Perhaps the best example
of this kind of writing—a prose style that creates, intentionally or not, a horizontal field of queer possibility—comes at the end of a 1968 review of Steve
Paxton's *Satisfyin' Lover*:

> And here they all were in this concert in the last dance, thirty-two any old
> wonderful people in "Satisfyin' Lover" walking one after the other across the
> gymnasium in their any old clothes. The fat, the skinny, the medium, the
> slouched and slumped, the straight and tall, the bowlegged and knock-kneed,
> the awkward, the elegant, the coarse, the delicate, the pregnant, the virginal, the
> you name it, by implication every postural possibility in the postural spectrum,
> that's you and me in all our ordinary everyday who cares postural splendor. Like
> the famous ordinary people who are certain they will see and be seen whether
> they fall down or keep walking in a forest with or without other famous ordinary
> people there is a way of looking at things which renders them performance. Let
> us now praise famous ordinary people. (Johnston 1968c, 137)

In this passage, Johnston directs readers' attention in several directions: toward
how difference unfolds among bodies; how weight and gravity produce the

idea of a person; and how all these elements—differences, weight, gravity, and rhythm—create a mass that is simultaneously individually differentiated and collective. Juxtaposition sparks every phrase: "the coarse, the delicate, the pregnant, the virginal." So many juxtapositions in close proximity produce the counterintuitive effect of making contradictions true: there *can be* such a thing as "famous ordinary" people. Passages like this amass details upon details that themselves become performances of excess. The writing becomes a choreography of sorts: it has rhythm, a sense of affective connection, and, in a particularly postmodern turn, a claim to the ordinary and the excessive.

Another 1968 review turns these strategies more explicitly toward gender and sexuality. In an essay about a wide-ranging, mixed repertoire performance in Central Park—an evening ranging from the dance/mime of Lotte Goslar to the black dance of Rod Rodgers—Johnston most explicitly imagines a queering of notions of gender and sexuality through dance criticism. As is often the case in Johnston's reviews, the Central Park review ends with a cluster of sentences that share many formal and spectatorial qualities of the list from the *Satisfyin' Lover* review: a juxtaposition of opposites, a repetition that creates rhythmic force, mounting collisions that eventually body forth a larger idea that is *almost* contradictory, and an invitation to the reader to join the "we" that begins as a reference to the performance's audience but then extends outward temporally and spatially.

The Central Park review ends with this passage: "A queen is a queen is a boy is a girl is a ballerina is a boy is a dyke is a fag is a butch is a boy is a girl is just a kinky son of a gun like the rest of us. Hello all you sexes. We're too good to be true" (Johnston 1968a, 184). This review and certainly this selection are perhaps less a performance description, except, again, for Johnston, the performance very much includes the audience. The review's ending, if imagined as a description of the audience (and there is context for this, as, earlier in the review, she described overhearing audience conversations and how audience members looked as they socialized during the show), feels like a description that swirls each viewer/reader around and around, placing a range of types side by side and repeatedly repositioning everyone through the string of multiple "is-es." This string equalizes all these queer types and asks each to see one another. The writing has the characteristics often imagined as particular to performance, able to hold contradiction by holding multiple times and spaces together. The work describes a heterogeneous world and writes that world into existence. The sentence takes a roll call of queer characters and then greets them (us?) as an assemblage, a force, and individuals at once specific and distinct. But they (we?) are more than just those specific identities, we (we!) are in one another's sights. This sentence is a protoqueer articulation of what queer theorist Eve Kosofsky Sedgwick would write decades later as she described queerness as a politics necessarily emerging from practice and from heterogeneity, a set of "political adventures" carried out by "a motley crew engaging in queer practices" (2013, 7).

This is not just queer writing. It is also lesbian. Much like Johnston's physical display at the 1971 panel, lesbian as writing strategy insists upon the category of Woman as one category among many categories of gender *and* that the category of Woman holds many possibilities within it. Johnston's writing is lesbian, too. At a formal level, she clearly positions herself within a longer trajectory of lesbian experimental writing. Johnston's long lists obviously invite associations with Gertrude Stein's writing. Johnston (1962) frequently mentioned Stein in her dance writing, turning to Stein as not just a writer but a theorist of repetition and familiarity—a way of thinking that puts Johnston's writing and the Judson work she described into a lineage of queer experimentation. Both Johnston and Stein deploy language to draw readers into a present relationship with words, as opposed to seeing words as documenting a moment already passed. Johnston's lists accomplish this via rhythm and force, much as Stein's did, and there is also a sense of looping that both writers share. At the syntactical level, both women eschew common punctuation rules, including a reimagining of commas, which Stein described as "servile" in a 1934 lecture she gave at Harvard (published the next year in *Lectures in America*; Stein quoted in Nordquist 2016). Understanding writing as speech-in-the-moment is perhaps even a trait of lesbian experimental writing, as Stein and Johnston linguistic heir and poet Eileen Myles (2017) has pondered.

To read Johnston's dance writing as lesbian is not just about placing it within traditions and lineages. To read Johnston's dance writing is to imagine the body and the person who writes it, and how her embedded quality—describing her own yelling from the audience at the Charlotte Moorman performance and more—keeps her body in the frame. Her lesbianness bodies forth. The rhythm, too, causes the reader to sense the insistent woman who writes it. In the language on the page and in filmed documentations of Johnston reading (including at the 1971 panel), the writing sings lesbian labor as its multiple, colliding elements upend patriarchy and heteronormativity. Johnston writes like someone who knows she could be interrupted at any moment, like someone trying to push into the world an identity for which there is not yet a place. She writes like someone coming out. She writes like someone who knows a man will try to interrupt her at any minute. She writes like a lesbian.

What does it mean for this woman to be writing about herself in a newspaper? This is an urgent question in *Marmalade Me*. Even as Johnston describes her own genealogy of writers and thinkers, a list she builds from the New York

School of poets, the Beats, and the Black Mountain School, all her references are male (Johnston 1968g, 21–22). Johnston herself, writing in the collection's expanded and revised version, published in 1998, described the writing in *Marmalade Me* as, at most, a protofeminist text. She made this description, as have many others, in comparison to her later *Village Voice* writing, which followed the column's name change from "dance journal" to "jill johnston."[4] But in *Marmalade Me* Johnston celebrates messiness, collision, and the dissolving of boundaries, and those concepts have everything to do with the demands she makes later as a lesbian feminist activist.

The periodization—of protofeminist versus feminist, nascent lesbianism versus full-on making-out-in-public lesbianism—needs to be messed with. In the final sentence of *Marmalade Me*'s final essay, Johnston ponders how meaning gets made:

> What does it mean, I'm wailing the phrase into the hallway down the steps under an armful into another journey, what does it mean, I know it means something if a glass container and a plastic container go flying out of a cellophane bag into their glassy and plasticky fragments in pools of goo on the landings below my wailing complaining questioning what in the name of any great god good is the present design in the total scheme. There is a design and I am not a free agent and I will to mine own self be true by not knowing and not pretending that I know whatever it is at the moment which is not to be known. (1968d, 113)

Johnston's turn to the personal is not a turn to the personal as though there is one person at the center, a consolidated subject; instead, it is a notion of what one knows as always shifting, a self that is important but without a defining referent. A queer self, we might say, in the sense that David Halperin says that queer might be anything that positions itself as against the norm (1995, 62). Johnston's queer lesbian self is wailing and falling down the stairs and doing description and analysis and slyly offering a politics of meaning making all at once—intercut, interspliced, and always moving in a never-ending project of disruption.

Lesbian Splashes

Prior to the 1971 panel, Johnston's best-known performance of lesbian antics came as she stripped down and swam laps in Gloria Vanderbilt's pool during a NOW fund-raiser. She splashed her way into feminist history as second wave icon Betty Friedan began speaking to the gathered guests (Warner 2013, 105–7). Like a dive into a pool in which one was not invited to swim, Johnston

used her lesbian body again and again to physically mark and displace heteronormative and misogynist structures. "You're not supposed to do this in public? Why? Let's see what happens when I do."

We should be grateful that Johnston's dives splashed onto dance. She is here
in our history to remind us again and again that there are many ways to be a
woman. To be a lesbian is to be a woman, with a body, with a mind—loud,
brash, funny, and full of desire spilling forth.

Notes

1. Jacqueline Ceballos's surname suggests Latinx origins, but Ceballos is her mar-
ried named, taken from her Colombian husband. All the women on the panel are white
by heritage and were also visibly white.

2. All descriptions are drawn from *Town Bloody Hall: A Dialogue on Women's Liberation* (1979).

3. Habermas doesn't overlook the arts completely. He gives brief attention to how
European music education, with its creation of techniques and modes of notation,
made possible a sonorous public. Despite the development of training institutions that
might have functioned similarly in dance in the time period on which he focuses,
however, he does not consider physical training and exchange to have the same capacity he ascribes primarily not only to verbal but also to musical exchange.

4. Deborah Jowitt, like most dance historians, primarily focused on Johnston's writing as egalitarian and experimental and does not address the lesbian writing, whereas
queer performance theorist José Esteban Muñoz celebrates the experimental dance
criticism and charges Johnston with being less adventurous as she turns toward the
identitarian focus.

Works Cited

Ahmed, Sara. 2006. *Queer Phenomenology: Orientations, Objects, Others*. Durham,
    NC: Duke University Press.
Berlant, Lauren, and Michael Warner. 1998. "Sex in Public." *Critical Inquiry* 24 (2):
    547–66.
Black Public Sphere Collective. 1995. Preface to *The Black Public Sphere*, edited by the
    Black Public Sphere Collective, 1–15. New York: Oxford University Press.
Cvetkovich, Ann. 2003. *An Archive of Feelings: Trauma, Sexuality, and Lesbian Public
    Cultures*. Durham, NC: Duke University Press.
Echols, Alice. 1989. *Daring to Be Bad: Radical Feminism in America 1967–1975*. Minne-
    apolis: University of Minnesota Press.
Fraser, Nancy. 1992. "Rethinking the Public Sphere: A Contribution to the Critique of
    Actually Existing Democracy." In *Habermas and the Public Sphere*, edited by Craig
    Calhoun, 123–46. Cambridge, MA: MIT Press.
Gever, Martha. 2003. *Entertaining Lesbians: Celebrity, Sexuality, and Self-Invention*. New
    York: Routledge.
Greer, Germaine. 1971. "My Mailer Problem." *Esquire*, September, 82–85.

Habermas, Jürgen. 1991. *The Structural Transformation of the Public Sphere: An Inquiry into a Category of Bourgeois Society.* Translated by Thomas Burger. Cambridge, MA: MIT Press.

Halperin, David. 1995. *Saint=Foucault: Towards a Gay Hagiography.* New York: Oxford University Press.

Hay, Deborah. 2017. Interview with the author.

Hegedus, Chris, and D. A. Pennebaker, dirs.. 1979. *Town Bloody Hall: A Dialogue on Women's Liberation.* New York: Pennebaker Hegedus Films.

Jagose, Annamarie. 1994. *Lesbian Utopics.* New York: Routledge.

———. 2002. *Inconsequence.* Ithaca, NY: Cornell University Press.

Johnston, Jill. 1962. "Fresh Winds." *Village Voice*, March 15, 13–14.

———. 1968a. "Hello Young Lovers." In *Marmalade Me*, 180–84. New York: E. P. Dutton. Originally published in *Village Voice.*

———. 1968b. "Over His Dead Body." In *Marmalade Me*, 132–35. New York: E. P. Dutton. Originally published in *Village Voice.*

———. 1968c. "Paxton's People." In *Marmalade Me*, 135–37. New York: E. P. Dutton. Originally published in *Village Voice.*

———. 1968d. "Three American Pennies." In *Marmalade Me*, 113–15. New York: E. P. Dutton. Originally published in *Village Voice.*

———. 1968e. "Time Tunnel." In *Marmalade Me*, 125–27. New York: E. P. Dutton. Originally published in *Village Voice.*

———. 1968f. "The Unhappy Spectator." In *Marmalade Me*, 188–95. New York: E. P. Dutton. Originally published in *Village Voice.*

———. 1968g. "Untitled." In *Marmalade Me*, 18–23. New York: E. P. Dutton. Originally published in *Village Voice.*

———. 1970. "Of This Pure but Irregular Passion." *Village Voice*, July 2, 29–30, 38–39.

———. 1973. "Lois Lane Is a Lesbian." In *Lesbian Nation: The Feminist Solution*, 135–47. New York: Simon and Schuster.

Jowitt, Deborah. 1998. Introduction to *Marmalade Me,* new and expanded ed., 3–15. Lebanon, NH: University Press of New England.

Khubchandani, Kareem. 2017. "Aunty Fever: A Queer Impression." In *Queer Dance: Meanings and Makings*, edited by Clare Croft, 199–204. New York: Oxford University Press.

Kuppers, Petra. 1998. "Vanishing in Your Face: Embodiment and Representation in Lesbian Dance Performance." *Journal of Lesbian Studies* 2 (2–3): 51–54.

Myles, Eileen, with Erica Schwiegershausen. 2017. "Eileen Myles on the Book That Made Writing Like Talking." *Cut*, August 29. https://www.thecut.com/2017/08/eileen-myles-on-lectures-in-america-by-gertrude-stein.html.

Muñoz, José Esteban. 2009. *Cruising Utopia: The Then and There of Queer Futurity.* New York: New York University Press.

Nelson, Maggie. 2015. *The Argonauts.* Minneapolis, MN: Gray Wolf Press.

Nordquist, Richard. 2016. "Punctuation in Prose, in Gertrude Stein." Thought.Co., March 2. https://www.thoughtco.com/punctuation-in-prose-by-gertrude-stein-1690751.

Olson, Göran, dir. 2011. *Black Power Mix Tape.* https://www.youtube.com/watch?v=6
    bryhoIFMhg.
Rainer, Yvonne. 2017. Interview with the author.
Sedgwick, Eve Kosofsky. 2013. "Queer and Now." In *The Routledge Studies Queer Reader,*
    edited by Donald Hall and Annamarie Jagose with Andrea Baell and Susan Porter,
    1–25. New York: Routledge.
Warner, Sara. 2013. *Acts of Gaiety: LGBT Performance and the Politics of Pleasure.* Ann
    Arbor: University of Michigan Press.

Accent, Choreomusicality, and Identity in *Rodeo* and *'Rōdē,ō*

DANIEL CALLAHAN

Agnes de Mille recounts that in 1942 she invited composer Aaron Copland to her studio in New York's Greenwich Village. She wanted him to compose a score about a cowgirl in the West. Copland, however, had no interest in "another cowboy ballet"—just four years prior he had composed the score for Eugene Loring's *Billy the Kid* with Ballet Caravan. After de Mille detailed her scenario, the composer sat silently. She ventured, "Well, it isn't *Hamlet*. But it can have what Martha Graham calls 'an aura of race memory.'" Copland burst out laughing and replied "Couldn't we do a ballet about Ellis Island instead?" At this, de Mille told him to go to hell. Within twenty-four hours, however, he started composing (de Mille 2015, 271). Copland worked not only with the general scenario de Mille gave him but also from detailed notes about the action of the ballet, including her suggestions for preexisting cowboy tunes he should include (Copland and Perlis 1984, 355–57). *Rodeo*, Copland's result-ing five-movement work, follows de Mille's suggestions to the letter and con-sists almost entirely of arrangements of folk music. "Corral Nocturne," *Rodeo*'s second section, is the only one not based on folk music.

Over seventy years later, Justin Peck turned to Copland's slightly slimmer four-movement concert version of the work, *Rodeo: Four Dance Episodes*. Peck wanted to choreograph a piece for the New York City Ballet that would *not* be mistaken for another cowboy ballet. His focus would be the music itself in an avowedly plotless work without any cowboy connotations. The section of *Rodeo*'s score that should most easily be denuded of chaps and lassos is the "Corral Nocturne," free as it is of folk music, whip-snapping cowboy tunes, and fiddle reels like the one in the famous "Hoe-Down." In this essay, I examine the spatial and temporal affordances that the music of *Rodeo*, especially its less celebrated "Corral Nocturne" section, offered, first to de Mille for her 1942 choreography about a misfit cowgirl trying to find herself and acceptance, and second to Peck for his 2015 choreography, 'Rōdē,ō, where the "Corral Nocturne" section is for five men whose movement Peck likens to "weather patterns." Close analyses of how these two choreographies engage Copland's score highlight the different meaning each suggests. De Mille's Cowgirl, although she occasionally signals her resilient individuality, repeatedly collapses and seems small compared to the vastness of Copland's music and the wide-open space implied by Oliver Smith's drop, depicting empty corrals and a huge Texas sky. In Peck's choreography—despite its stress on accents in the danced steps of its outer sections and in the stylization of its title, and despite its avowed plotlessness—the male quintet more fully realizes the "Corral Nocturne" as an exploratory space of desire and identity. Ironically, Peck's dance hews closer to the scenario for the "Corral Nocturne" that de Mille originally sent Copland, and on which Copland based his music, than it does to what de Mille choreographed in 1942.

Comparison of *Rodeo* and *'Rōdē,ō* is an object lesson in the relationship between music/score and dance/choreography, or what I term *choreomusicality*. De Mille's choreography, though clearly responsive to the score, often treats it as a background against which her dances stand out. Notably, some of her most iconic choreography (the running set, the Champion Roper's tap solo) occurs between sections without musical accompaniment, or in an especially long pause in the middle of the music. Peck's choreography, on the other hand, often approaches a step-for-note level of synchronization with the music, so much so that—as in the dances of George Balanchine or Mark Morris—an audience might feel as if it sees the music. Contemporary dance scholarship too often disregards this audiovisual reality: dance is effectively treated as if it occurs in silence. Given the centrality of choreomusicality to the experiences of performing and witnessing dance, an audiovisual turn in dance studies yields new insights both historical and critical-theoretical. Beyond formal concerns (the focus of most previous research on music-dance relationships), choreomusicality, I suggest, inflects our understanding of larger cultural issues, such as the relationship between a dancer's performance of a choreography and his or her identity. Drawing on my interview with Taylor Stanley (2016), which ranges over topics from the specifics of Peck's choreomusicality in *'Rōdē,ō* to gay pride and shame both on- and offstage, this essay concludes by noting that dancing "on the needle" of the beat, to use Stanley's words, can just as equally highlight as hide a dancer's identity.

De Mille's *Rodeo, or the Courting at Burnt Ranch*

Aaron Copland—Brooklyn-born, cosmopolitan, city-loving, rarely west of the Hudson, communist-sympathizing, HUAC-interrogated, Jewish, and homosexual—composed music in the late 1930s and 1940s that has remained the symphonic signifier of Americana ever since, as the soundtracks of mass culture reveal. *Rodeo*'s famous "Hoe-Down" was used in television commercials across the 1990s to sell "Beef, it's what's for dinner." Using Copland exclusively for his movie's score, Spike Lee memorably opens his 1998 *He Got Game* on amber waves of grain and solitary young people shooting hoops on farms and city lots to the muted trumpet and simple clarinet melody of *John Henry*. To conclude the dedication of the National September 11 Museum on May 15, 2014, the New York Philharmonic played *Fanfare for the Common Man*. Copland's music has also been widely imitated; Coplandesque music resounds in everything from PBS documentaries to a homophobe-baiting Rick Perry 2012 presidential campaign commercial. Three of Copland's most famous Americana scores were originally yoked to choreographies depicting scenes from frontier life: Eugene Loring's *Billy the Kid* for Ballet Caravan in 1938; Agnes de Mille's *Rodeo* for the Ballet Russe de Monte Carlo in 1942; and Martha Graham's *Appalachian Spring* for her company in 1944.[1] Today, dancing cowboys might seem camp; it is therefore unsurprising that Justin Peck would want to dewesternize his ʹRōdē̄,ō. When de Mille approached Copland, however, this Americana sound and "American ballet" were still fresh. Audiences in the late 1930s and early 1940s relished the settler-colonial national mythography that undergirded the development and consolidation of multiple "American" arts—consider *Stagecoach*, John Ford's 1939 Hollywood western. Long before Loring's *Billy the Kid* and John Wayne's "Ringo Kid," de Mille danced as a "Forty-Niner" in her eponymous 1927 solo, an audience favorite. In "Rodeo," the final section of her 1938 *American Suite,* presented in London, de Mille transformed her quirky forty-niner into a rodeo rider. "Rodeo" was the audience's favorite section, and the scenario and choreographic notes for it reveal the great extent to which de Mille's later 1942 *Rodeo* is based on the all-female 1938 "Rodeo" (Barker 1996, 136–39).

Much of Copland's 1942 *Rodeo* consists of recompositions of cowboy and work songs. The score's novelty and excitement are found in how the "Brooklyn Stravinsky" arranged these songs, adding levels of syncopation that spoke to Copland's love of jazz and modernist music. Consider "Buckaroo Holiday," which opens *Rodeo*. Copland's melodic material here includes two folk songs that he selected from John and Alan Lomax's *Our Singing Country*, both found in section III, "Men at Work." One, "If He'd Be a Buckaroo," is found in section III.3, "Cowboy Songs"; the other, "Sis Joe," is found in section III.4, "Railroaders and Hobos." Shortly, we'll consider how the dances of de Mille and Peck each respond to the "Sis Joe" material (figure 14). First, let's highlight the most basic way that de Mille's outsider Cowgirl is choreomusically marked as "off beat": she sometimes dances to the rhythm of her own drummer. This is especially clear just before her exit offstage in "Buckaroo Holiday." After the orchestra plays a loud unison passage with the "Sis Joe" motive and during which all of the cowboys come to a halt, there is long silent pause (figure 14d).

While the cowboys are all frozen, the Cowgirl loudly shuffles in place on her imaginary horse. When she finally jumps to a halt, she looks around sheepishly and realizes that she had been noisily bucking around on her own. She tries to play it cool, but the Head Wrangler signals for her to scram. She exits ungracefully, as if not entirely able to control her horse. Together with the audience's laughter, this all happens with the orchestra silent, on average, for over half a minute. In the first section of *Rodeo* the Cowgirl does not fit in with the soundscape but clashes against it. Her antics even silence the orchestra.

"Corral Nocturne," the second section of *Rodeo*, is the only one that does not use preexisting folk music. De Mille originally wanted this section to reveal the consolation her lonely Cowgirl finds in the West's expansiveness. In the scenario Copland used as the basis of his composition, de Mille writes:

> The cowgirl sits on a post of the corral forgotten. The men and their sweethearts stroll in the evening. The twilight deepens. The sky goes green. They walk in the dusk. (This is a dance entirely of mood, lyric, quiet, almost mystic, a dance of courting, but abstracted, impersonal. It is more a dance between people and darkness than between people and people.) The few stragglers move like moths in the darkness. They are barely visible, outlined only against the deepening sky. The girl still sits. She is lonely. But she is in love with the land around and the great glowing night sky, and the smells and the sounds. She leaves the fence and moves across the moonlit space. Someone hurries by with an oil lantern. She runs through the empty corrals intoxicated with space, her feet thudding in the stillness. She stops spell-bound. A coyote calls. (de Mille, *Early Papers*)

Copland's slow nocturne captures the sense of stillness at dusk and the Cowgirl's loneliness in several ways (figure 15).[2] The nocturne is composed almost entirely of tonic, subdominant, and dominant chords (the three most common chords in tonal Western music), just as in the simplest folk song. The unusual $\frac{5}{4}$ meter, which opens and closes the movement, suggests an extended sense of time (unlike common time, $\frac{4}{4}$, there's an extra beat that extends the measure), as well as the Cowgirl's own unusual nature.

Examples of $\frac{5}{4}$ meter in classical music are fairly rare. Perhaps the most notable example is the queer version of a waltz in the second movement of Tchaikovsky's Symphony no. 6 (*Pathétique*), which had long been received (if never intended) as a veiled suicide note signifying homosexual suffering. Just

Figure 14a. "Sis Joe" concluding three lines, as sung by Henry Truvillion and transcribed in *Our Singing Country*. Figures 14b, 14c, and 14d. Aaron Copland, *Rodeo* (piano reduction), I. Buckaroo Holiday, excerpts from rehearsal numbers 38, 39, and 41.

Figure 15a. Aaron Copland, *Rodeo* (piano reduction), II. Corral Nocturne, opening (measures 1–16). Figure 15b. Copland, *Rodeo* (piano reduction), II. Corral Nocturne, conclusion (measures 47–53).

under a minute into "Corral Nocturne" at the second measure of rehearsal 1, Copland's harmony poignantly strives to go elsewhere (specifically, he introduces a flattened seventh, lending a blue sound) as the music widens its range and reaches upward hopefully. After peaking, the melody descends, but without cadential closure. Two measures of somber chromatic harmonies follow before a return to the main theme. Like much of Copland's music (consider the opening of *Billy the Kid*), the nocturne capitalizes on simple harmonies orchestrated with wide registral spaces between them. This culminates in an expanse of six octaves between the highest and lowest notes in the *pianississimo* fifth-to-last measure of the movement (figure 15b). For many listeners, even without the stage picture, these stratospheric notes conjure a wide, open sky on a quiet night.

De Mille had requested just this sort of spatially suggestive music. However, the choreography she finally devised for the "Corral Nocturne" differs from her original vision, found in her scenario referenced above. The dance is spare and simple, so much so that in the Agnes de Mille Papers, in which there are dozens of pages of choreographic notes for the other sections of *Rodeo*, there are, comparatively, hardly any notes for the "Corral Nocturne." The cast slowly strolls across upstage, while center stage features a brief duet between the Rancher's Daughter and the Head Wrangler, with whom the Cowgirl is infatuated. The Rancher's Daughter's movement consists of a gentle relevé passé into a turn upstage, followed by a graceful fall to her knee with a lunge away from the Head Wrangler. The movement suggests coyness, not trying too hard. With each turn by the Rancher's Daughter back to the Wrangler, we understand that this is how a woman gets a man's attention—demurely. Their courtship is sealed by a lift. The Cowgirl watches the reserved Daughter and quietly confident Wrangler finish their moment together and walk off. Before the couple exit, three women who have been frozen upstage in profile thrice extend their arms out and forward from their chest, as if to suggest women's expected willingness to give all that men ask of them.

The Cowgirl now attempts to perform femininity as she just witnessed it. As the couple and upstage women exit, the $\frac{5}{4}$ meter briefly returns, and the Cowgirl attempts a relevé arabesque forward. She cannot maintain it and collapses to the floor. She tries again. She collapses. Her inability to perform the arabesque marks her inability to "correctly" perform her gender. Throughout the section she performs textbook shame by the "lowering of [her] head and eyes" (Tomkins 1995, 135). Her contained hesitant movements are not supported by the music, which seems especially vast. This is the case in the film version of Christine Sarry performing the role in 1973, and it is even clearer in the theater. Watching Misty Copeland as the Cowgirl in the "Corral Nocturne" with American Ballet Theatre in May 2015, I wrote in my notebook: "She is alone, the music is big." I reiterated in all caps: "THE MUSIC IS BIG, she is small." Copland's music captures de Mille's scenario, but the movement onstage is a far cry from the choreographer's original vision of the Cowgirl "run[ning] through the empty corrals intoxicated with space."

Only a few lines later, however, I scribbled "time step." Throughout the "Corral Nocturne" so far, de Mille's choreomusicality has been very loose: the choreography seems to float above the orchestral score, paying it little attention. Now the choreography actively sets itself *against* the musical soundscape. In an effort to maintain her self-composure in the face of pressure to conform, the Cowgirl turns to her own rhythm. She taps. Her time step offers her only a brief respite, but it foreshadows a possible theme clear only at *Rodeo*'s conclusion: before dancing to the beat of the community, one must find and celebrate one's own rhythm. The "Corral Nocturne" ends with the Championship Roper traveling across upstage, his movement punctuated by taps. The Cowgirl, however, falls completely to the floor. This section conveys that the Cowgirl, outside of gender and sexual normativity, can only collapse alone in shame, "the affect that most defines the space wherein a sense of self will develop . . . the place where the *question* of identity arises more originarily and most relationally" (Sedgwick 2003, 37). She is not positively identified with the great space around her, as de Mille originally intended; instead, we understand her negatively, through an interrupted identification that reveals "the double movement shame makes: toward painful individuation, toward uncontrollable relationality" (37).

De Mille's original scenario specified that a running set would follow the "Corral Nocturne":

> In the dark there is the sound of clapping and running feet. The lights rise to disclose a running set in progress. (4 boys and 4 girls.) There is no sound but the beat of feet, clapping hands and the cries of the caller—"Single File, Indian Style, Swing your honey Once in a while" "Running down the river Indian style, Ladies in the lead and gents hog-wild"—As the dance is paced up in speed and intensity, the dancers themselves cry out in excitement—"Daddy catch a rat!" "All chaw Hay!" (This dance is abstracted, timeless, placeless. The figurations are formal, there is no attempt at characterization or story-telling.) The light dims on the spinning circle. (de Mille, Early Papers)

Although de Mille describes this as "abstracted, timeless, placeless . . . formal" her decision to present her audience's ears with nothing but the sound of the dancers further advances a reading where being apart from the score represents a kind of personal freedom. The point is driven home most forcefully when later in *Rodeo*, in a protracted silence in the middle of rousing music, the Champion Roper wins the Cowgirl's respect and heart with a tap solo.

The paradox of autonomy presented at the heart of *Rodeo*—in order to be a happy member of the community, the Cowgirl has to put on a dress and learn to dance in time with others—is presented rather lightly. In the original scenario, the "Corral Nocturne" was to be a space where we could see the Cowgirl's "intoxication with space," her sense of self on her own. Instead, we see only her pain. Edwin Denby, in a review of a Ballet Russe de Monte Carlo performance, writes that the Cowgirl should project "the sense of a girl who only gradually discovers what it means to be a girl. It is this gradual, painful, and at the end happy discovery that is the dramatic heart of the piece" (1986a, 215). Happy though the Cowgirl seems, has she betrayed her true self? Marcia Siegel felt that *Rodeo* should be unequivocally "denounced and picketed" by feminists (1985, 127–28). In the context of the late 1940s and 1950s retrenchment of women's wartime progress and recognition in the workplace, the Cowgirl might have still seemed to stride forward in gender-challenging ways. We can hope that audiences today recognize the ugly sexual politics of the chipper musical comedy even if they are swept away by the propulsive music and dance rhythms of the "Hoe-Down" that concludes *Rodeo*.

Peck's *'Rōdē,ō: Four Dance Episodes*

The focus on phonetic symbols suggested by the stylization of Peck's title, *'Rōdē,ō*, is matched by the careful correspondence between dance and music accents throughout the work. Following the 2015 premiere, critics were mystified by the diacritics, apparently forgetting their introduction to phonics as children. Peck uses macrons to represent long vowels in his pronunciation. The pronunciation of the second syllable is especially important here: Is it a long *a*, as in "day," or a long *e*, as in the first syllable of "delight"? For Peck, it is the latter. He apparently wanted the word "rodeo" pronounced and accented as it most commonly is in vernacular American English and not as in Spanish or other Romance languages. At one point in 2015, the New York City Ballet updated its webpage for *'Rōdē,ō* to note that "the punctuation marks in the title indicate the common pronunciation of 'rodeo,' distinguished from the de Mille ballet." Beyond differentiating between the de Mille and Peck titles, this phonetic gesture might also be understood as checking the pretentiousness of a balletomane who feigns incomprehension when someone pronounces *Serenade* so that it rhymes with "neighed" instead of "nod," as in French. By this interpretation, Peck the Populist comes to the rescue. The literally marked insistence of pronouncing *'Rōdē,ō*, however, could just as easily be seen as ethnocentric, denying the word's origins on *la frontera*. A year after the premiere, Peck and the NYCB dropped the diacritics from the title. Musical accents, dance accents, and linguistic accents all point to identities, cultures, and histories. The larger question this points to is not new: To what extent can ballet—an art form that delights in and depends on gestures, forms, hierarchies, and other traditions established long ago—speak to and reflect the increasingly diverse set of identities, cultures, and histories of its performers and audiences today?

In the repertoire of the New York City Ballet, Justin Peck's *'Rōdē,ō* stands out for its preponderance of men.[3] The ballet opens with fifteen of them, and the sole female dancer is not highlighted until the third of the dance's four sections. Throughout the work Peck's attention to choreomusical detail is striking, even in the Balanchine-dominated NYCB repertoire. Despite Peck's stated focus on the musical and plotless aspects of the dance, however, the contrasting choreography and affect of the second section capture the sense of an outsider exploring space, as de Mille originally intended and as Copland's music is meant to suggest. Taken in context with the other three sections and with the rest of the NYCB's repertoire, it also suggests the possibility of moving beyond long-standing limits of how the company's men should be presented onstage. The second section quintet, set to the "Corral Nocturne" music, might not be explicitly sexual, but the sight of five NYCB danseurs tenderly partnering each other in flowing lyrical movement was new and exciting for the company and its audiences, even in 2015.

Peck's '*Rōdē,ō* opens with an image of speed and athleticism. Lined up across the depth of stage right, the men are crouched with their eyes on the stage left wing, as if they are all in starting position on runner's blocks on a track. The closest guys-running-around-together analogues in the NYCB's repertoire, to my mind, are by Jerome Robbins: the male sextet in the third movement of *Glass Pieces* (1983) and the prologue section of *West Side Story Suite* (1995). Peck has noted that he always wanted to combine his love of athletics with his love of dancing, and the first movement of '*Rōdē,ō* achieves this with high energy and a varied movement vocabulary. This opening section also creates an especially strong contrast with the second section, the "Corral Nocturne." In a statement first published in NYCB's promotional 2014–15 *Guide to the Repertory*, Peck notes: "In creating the choreography, I divided the score into four distinct choreographic interpretations: The first movement takes on a kinetic, engine-like quality; the second movement elicits recurring weather patterns; the third movement calls to mind the synchronicity illustrated by two birds in flight; and finally, the concluding fourth movement communicates a sense of total vitality, bright fervor, and healthy competition" (New York City Ballet 2014). Achieving the "kinetic, engine-like quality" of the first movement up to the "healthy competition" of the last, the choreography of '*Rōdē,ō* depends on rhythmic precision and attacked accents even more than on speed, height of jumps, or sections of unrelenting movement.

This sharper, more step-for note choreomusicality becomes even more apparent when one compares the choreomusicality of Peck's and de Mille's choreographies. Consider their respective choreographies in the first section for the climactic presentations of the "Sis Joe" tune, recomposed from the rail liners' song. The backbreaking, repetitive, rhythmic work of rail lining is captured in the original tune of "Sis Joe" by an accented downbeat on which the men would heave forward into the rail. The short-short-DOWNBEAT rhythmic motive is especially insistent in the final three repeated lines of the song. Copland recomposes the regularity of the plodding work tune into a play of punchy syncopations, which de Mille and Peck respond to with very different degrees of attention.

De Mille's choreography for the climactic presentation of the "Sis Joe" motive in "Buckaroo Holiday" suggests that even though she wanted to capture the sense of accent, she might have been limited by how well her dancers could internalize Copland's score and synchronize their movement to it. On three separate occasions, starting roughly three-quarters into the first movement, the entire orchestra plays the "Sis Joe" motive in unison (figures 14b, 14c, 14d). On the first occasion (figure 14b), the motive is immediately preceded by a thunderous strike of the bass drum and whip (two hinged pieces of wood that create a sharp loud crack when clapped together) on the downbeat. In synch with the drum hit, the circle of lassoing, galloping cowboys comes to an abrupt halt: they thrust their elbows into their waists as if reining in their horses and simultaneously raise and hold their right leg parallel to the floor. They remain frozen while the orchestra blares the powerful "Sis Joe" motive in unison. They continue to stand motionless during the downbeat whack of the bass drum in the next measure. When in the following measure starting rehearsal 38 the bass drum is now heard in unison with the "Sis Joe" motive two beats later than one might expect and now *fortississimo* (i.e., very, very loud), only the two cowboys in the center of the circle are responsible for marking the massive accent as their turns come to a halt. While not entirely unresponsive to the score, de Mille's choreography doesn't harness or highlight Copland's accents. Ultimately, the music seems more energetic than her cowboys.

Peck's choreography at rehearsal 38 makes de Mille's seem comparatively unmusical. By coordinating his choreography with the bass drum's accents, the choreomusicality feels tighter and more energetic. Peck has the nine men onstage take off in two big leaps, each right on the bass drum and whip downbeats of the two measures before rehearsal 38. They then move to finish the phrase with the arms in fourth position on the final *fortississimo* hit of the drum and whip in the first measure of rehearsal 38. This synchronization here makes the corps's impressively precise unison seem even more explosive. When a similar rhythmic pattern with the "Sis Joe" motive occurs at rehearsal 39 but with the third iteration of the short-short-LONG occurring a beat later than expected (figure 14c), Peck's choreography captures the energy of the syncopation. After the men have been literally imitating the snare's drumroll with their forearms drumming against the stage while lying flat on their stomach, the dancers in three groups of three from upstage to downstage pop up into the runner's-block position from the beginning of the dance. Each group pops in sync with the score: accented downbeat, accented downbeat, accented syncopation. The effect is sharp. De Mille's cowboys, however, are unresponsive to the snap of the score here: they stand still during the syncopated accent in the third measure of rehearsal 39, letting it pass by like a huge tumbleweed.

In his choreography for the "Corral Nocturne" section, Peck continues to respond to Copland's score at a detailed level. The dancing here also seems loaded with meaning: its actions, gestures, and affect are as referential as what we see in de Mille. Peck has analogized the quintet's movements to "weather patterns," and perhaps the very opening of the quintet suggests this, as the fluid formation alternately coalesces and diffuses as it travels downstage right.

The quintet's movement here falls neatly within the beginning and ending of each of these opening $\frac{5}{4}$ measures, adding to the sense of purpose and order. This five-man "weather pattern" progresses measure by measure. Whereas de Mille here presents the Cowgirl in the "Corral Nocturne" as awkward and aberrant, Peck presents five men who seem so "natural" that he uses a weather metaphor to describe them. Further unlike de Mille's "Corral Nocturne," the dancers here seem not to pass over the music but to embody it. Taylor Stanley (2016) highlighted the close synchronization of the second movement's choreomusicality in my interview with him: "There's just as much clarity and precision needed for the slower section, but there's more room for elongation

FIGURE 16. Taylor Stanley and the New York City Ballet in Justin Peck's *'Rōdē,ō: Four Dance Episodes*, second episode ("Corral Nocturne"), end of the second measure. (Photo by Paul Kolnik)

in our movement." That added "room for elongation" is not only because of the slower tempo but also because Copland uses the fifth beat of his opening $\frac{5}{4}$ measures only to sustain notes, not to introduce new ones (figure 15). The music sounds like $\frac{4}{4}$ measures, each of which doesn't want to let go and move forward. Time and space seem expanded. Peck underlines this unusual $\frac{5}{4}$ meter in multiple ways. Stanley enters the stage before the orchestra even begins the second movement. He describes the entrance this way: "[I assume] a contemplative position, and I stroke my chin a little bit. It's like thinking, daydreaming." He then taps his foot five times. It's as if he dreams up the "Corral Nocturne," starting with its unusual meter. Five men then start dancing to music in $\frac{5}{4}$, savoring and stretching out in the space of that fifth beat.

Initiating the "Corral Nocturne," Stanley is singled out as special; Peck has referred to him as the "nucleus" of the movement in promotional material (Peck 2015, 2:01). "Protagonist" might be more appropriate: the dance revolves around him and also is about him. About thirty seconds into the nocturne, after the members of the quintet all rise into relevé with their left leg high, Stanley falls to the floor, where he is cradled by another dancer (originally Craig Hall, now retired; in recent performances, Preston Chamblee). After I viewed this poignant moment live for the first time in 2015, my focus quickly shifted from the details of stage patterning, at which Peck excels, to the sense of the quintet as a community. While images of men lovingly partnering men are common in many dance companies, seeing two men of color in the NYCB express care for each other onstage felt momentous.

After Hall/Chamblee cradles Stanley, the two dancers look skyward, as if seeking energy to get on their feet again. Regarding this moment, Peck instructed Stanley in rehearsals to "look up into the sun and let the warmth of the sun shine over you, take in the warmth of the sun" (Stanley 2016). The dance continues to conjure the space of the sky. At the third measure of rehearsal 1, as the violins reach for their highest notes in the movement so far, each of the four men quickly slinks down to lie with his back on the floor. As they all do so, Stanley also slinks backward so that he too is on his back and held aloft by the four men below him. The movement is liquid and happens in an instant. Supported by the men, Stanley rests a moment with his hands behind his head, staring skyward as if lying in a field and stargazing. The choreography here reflects the violins reaching into the stratosphere. After moving like a weather pattern, the five men now wonder at the expanse around them. Reflecting Copland's score so closely, Peck's choreography inadvertently captures de Mille's original scenario, on which the music is based: the dancers are "intoxicated with space." That five men explore this space while also supporting each other's weight offers at last the perspective and possibility that the NYCB male dancers can perform onstage relationships that are lovingly homosocial or queer, just as they and their audiences do offstage.

When the violins come back down from their heights, the men shift Stanley forward back onto his feet. The quintet now stands in a row, holding hands and facing the audience. Stanley runs downstage, stretching the chain of linked hands, as if in a game of crack the whip, and reaches out into the house with a yearning expression. But instead of cracking the whip, the whip cracks him. At two measures before rehearsal 2 in the score, the men unlock hands just as the music chromatically shifts to a suddenly darker place. Stanley reacts with a contraction of pain and a look of shock and loss that in May 2015 was visible even from the third ring of the house. "Justin has me put my hands to my stomach . . . like something painful occurred," he told me (Stanley 2016). This seems anything but "plotless." Desiring to explore and extend the space around him, Stanley is ultimately held back, his possibilities limited (figure 17).

Like de Mille's choreography for the "Corral Nocturne," Peck's also ends with a sense of loss, deferred potential, and even shame. Stanley's character is ultimately just as sad as the Cowgirl; this is made clear in the silent transition between the "Corral Nocturne" and the following, third episode, "Saturday

FIGURE 17. Taylor Stanley and the New York City Ballet in Justin Peck's '*Rōdē,ō: Four Dance Episodes*, second episode ("Corral Nocturne"), sixth measure after rehearsal 1. (Photo by Paul Kolnik)

Night Waltz," a male-female pas de deux premiered by Sara Mearns and Amar Ramasar. At the end of the second episode Stanley is alone onstage, his face projecting forlornness. Of the end of the "Corral Nocturne," Stanley told me that he is

> looking into the corner of the house [the rear audience left corner of the fourth ring of the theater], and I envision looking up at the moon, like it's nighttime, and like I've kind of left everything behind me. It's like the five men kind of gathered to this place to express and emote, and then we kind of all wake up from maybe a daydream or a nap. We all kind of disperse and go back into reality a little bit and perhaps just looking up at the sky and [then] seeing another person [Sara Mearns] enter this space that we just gathered to, is just kind of like, "Oh, there's somebody. . . . Oh, we're back in the world, we aren't dreaming anymore, we aren't hurting anymore, we aren't really unified anymore, we're just kind of—we're back in reality." (2016)

The dance's sole female enters and touches Stanley's shoulder as if to console him. He leaves the stage. One senses a narrative here more strongly than at any other point in Peck's *'Rōdē,ō*. Whereas de Mille's Cowgirl's desires must be repressed in the face of a heteronormative community, here the male soloist's sensitive expressivity and space-creating potential are cut short by the beginning of the male-female pas de deux that Peck choreographed for the third movement. The "Corral Nocturne" second movement, in which men partner men and share each other's weight, was just a dream. By the final movement the dance has returned to the athletic virtuosity, complex group forms, and explosive synchronization with the music that we saw in the first episode. At the work's conclusion, the three male soloists from the first movement are onstage pointing upward. Following the blackout and rapturous applause—like de Mille's choreography, Peck's is a crowd-pleaser—the three male soloists of the first movement and the male-female partner of the third take front-of-curtain bows. Stanley, who provides the emotional core of *'Rōdē,ō*, is not highlighted.

On the Needle and on the Horizon

In 1942 de Mille's *Rodeo* seemed to be just as focused in its sense of attack and accent as Balanchine's *Concerto Barocco* to many, including Edwin Denby. In his article "Rockettes and Rhythm," the critic bemoans that the Music Hall's Rockettes and its ballet dancers perform so that "the dramatic punch of the number lies in the unique (and apparently effortless) synchronization of all the dancers and of the entire dance with the music" (1986b, 201). Denby claims this is fine for tap but not ballet:

You don't follow a ballet beat by beat. Ballet dancing probably once had a good deal of this percussive quality—so eighteenth-century dance music suggests. In 1890s ballet you can see a percussive dance number in the Cygnet quartet in *Swan Lake*. Contemporary American ballet tends to use this device more sharply— you see it in parts of *Rodeo* and particularly in *Concerto Barocco*. Here the sound of the dancers' toe steps is part of the effect. But these passages are details. More generally the rhythmic interest in ballet dancing isn't fixed on the beat or on the dancers' relation to it; the interest is in their relation to the musical phrase, to the melody, to the musical period. At such times their rhythm is a "free" one, more like that of a singer in its variety of emphasis than like that of a tap dancer. . . . In ballet you often look at a free meter and listen to a strict one. Complete synchronization of ballet and music is a special effect that works by contrast to other rhythmic possibilities and it satisfies only when used for such a contrast. (1986b, 201–2)

Denby's understanding of accent demonstrates that one's sense of choreo-musicality is historically and culturally contingent. Denby associates a tightly synchronized movement with commercial entertainment, *not* with nineteenth-century ballet. Being "fixed on the beat," however, quickly became associated with much twentieth-century ballet, from Bronislava Nijinska and Balanchine up to William Forsythe and Christopher Wheeldon.

Taylor Stanley noted that dancing with the NYCB more closely aligns with Denby's understanding of tap. When I asked him to describe his understanding of an "NYCB choreomusicality," Stanley sat up very straight. He placed his hands together, back of the hands facing me, with the two middle fingers aligned and pointing down on a specific spot on the table in front of him, as if his two fingertips were pointe shoes in a fifth position relevé: "I'm imagining this needle. You're standing on top of the needle, and that's the only place you can be; it's all about precision and clarity, and you can't fall off of that needle. There's no time or space for any other extra things" (Stanley 2016). Stanley noted that this precision is similar for him whether the choreography is Balanchine's or Peck's.

I wanted Stanley to compare the choreomusicality of de Mille's and Peck's choreographies, so we watched the televised recording of the 1973 performance of de Mille's "Corral Nocturne" section together. "How much of the story do you know?" I asked him beforehand. He paused and replied, "Isn't there a tapper in it?" Stanley had never seen *Rodeo*, although he had a vague sense that he "probably should have," given that it gets talked about and even occasionally performed by the American Ballet Theatre across the Lincoln Center

Plaza, as it was in May 2015. After the conclusion of the "Corral Nocturne," Stanley exclaimed, unbidden, "It's really sad!" When I asked him why, he replied, "I don't know. It makes me sad. I don't know why. I think she's trying so hard to fit in and everyone—no one is accepting, embracing her. The way she— [He stopped speaking and did the Cowgirl's signature movement in the "Corral Nocturne" from his chair, suggesting a relevé and reaching out and then collapsing.] That's what I got from it. Is that the story line?" (Stanley 2016).

Our discussion about the Cowgirl's performance of gender led into a discussion about the performance of gender by male ballet dancers today. Speaking just weeks after Stanley was promoted to principal in the company, I asked him if he ever felt that success and recognition required him "to self-police, to be more—" He finished my question:

> Like, "manly"? Yeah, all the time. I think a lot of us feel that way because, I don't know, the sexuality game is so difficult in the ballet world, where it's a place where it *should* be accepted and embraced and used as a tool to showcase the different sides of a person, male or female. You get cast in these roles, and you're expected to be a "man," whatever a "man" is supposed to be. What being a "man" is supposed to be is just based on tradition, on videos and old tapes. We all look at Baryshnikov and Nureyev and Peter Martins. It kind of makes you shameful. There's a lot of shame that goes along with being gay, of course, and then having to be a ballet dancer. It can be a really dangerous place to be in if you're not totally comfortable with yourself yet, and having to play these roles doesn't really help when you're trying to figure out who you are and—It can just be very unnurturing sometimes. (Stanley 2016)

When I asked Stanley how Peck's work and *Rodeo* compares to the rest of the NYCB repertoire, he noted that it is "the most athletic-feeling piece that [Peck has] done. There's a lot of running, and there's a lot of testosterone, since there's fifteen men. . . . I feel like a soccer player because of our costumes." He also noted that while the precision of movement required in a unison passage is the same in ballets by Peck and Balanchine, in Peck "there is freedom to be more diverse in the *expression* of the movement. [In Balanchine] more of a uniform image is expected" (Stanley 2016).

The horizon of what a dance by the New York City Ballet can look like and its possibility for representing queer selfhood seems to have expanded, if only slightly, with Peck's quintet.[4] Stanley noted that even though he and his fellow dancers are becoming ever more aware of the need for racial diversity in the company and in ballet more generally, during the rehearsal for and performance of the quintet "we don't really think about it. We kind of just dance." It was only upon reflection after the premiere that he and the other dancers realized that their partnering in the quintet was special: "Four out of the five guys, I think, are gay, myself included. . . . [T]here is something so tender about [the quintet], and it's such an important image to relay to people. I think we all—gay or straight, white, black, Asian—I think we all just felt this . . . equal care for each other in the movement, falling into each other's arms. And not spiritually but just energetically caring for one another. . . . [T]hat image of men caring for other men, regardless of sexuality or race or anything" (Stanley 2016). That this image occurs in a dance that its choreographer likens to weather patterns and sees as abstract and primarily concerned with formal interactions with the music that inspired it seems slightly less ironic when we consider that the music was composed to suggest a lone figure exploring both the possibilities of the vast space around her and the horizons of her own sense of self. "There's no time or space for any other extra things," Stanley said of being "on the needle" in the NYCB's choreomusicality. In the present moment of performance, an audience member and/or the dancer onstage might not be able to tell the dance from the music, the dancer from the dance, or even the dancer from the music. At other times, their separateness might seem obvious. Either way, the intermedial reality deserves attention. Future dance studies could only benefit from considering choreomusicality's important role in a dance's performance and production of meaning and identity.

Notes

1. For an overview of Copland's music for dance, see Lynn Garafola (2005). For an overview of Copland's music's relationship to the American West, see Levy (2012).

2. Among the options for those wishing to view the dance, the most widely available is the filmed performance of the first two sections of *Rodeo* found in *A Close-Up in Time*, the WNET television special later released on video.

3. It includes almost double the eight-man ensemble in Balanchine's *Kammermusik No. 2* (1978).

4. As this essay underwent final revisions during the fall 2017 New York City Ballet season, Taylor Stanley danced a pas de deux with Preston Chamblee in the premiere of Lauren Lovette's *Not Our Fate*. That same week, Peck cast Stanley in the female role of the previously male-female central pas de deux of his *The Times Are Racing*, in which Stanley was partnered by Daniel Applebaum, who also dances in the "Corral Nocturne" quintet. Applebaum also discussed *Rodeo* at length with me, as did Russell Janzen, in June 2016, just a week after the Pulse nightclub shooting, when talking about men dancing with men felt more important and urgent than usual and was also especially emotional. I am grateful for how generously they shared their time and how openly their thoughts, which could not fit here due to space limitations but which I hope to incorporate in an expanded version of this essay.

Works Cited

American Ballet Theatre, Agnes de Mille, et al. 1973. *A Close-Up in Time*. VHS. New York: WNET.

Barker, Barbara. 1996. "Agnes de Mille, Liberated Expatriate, and the *American Suite*, 1938." *Dance Chronicle* 19 (2): 113–50.

Copland, Aaron, and Vivian Perlis. 1984. *Copland: 1900 through 1942*. New York: St. Martin's Press.

de Mille, Agnes. 2015. *Dance to the Piper*. New York: NYRB Classics.

———. Early Papers, (S)*MGZMC-Res.27. New York Public Library for the Performing Arts, Jerome Robbins Dance Division.

Denby, Edwin. 1986a. "A Monte Carlo Matinee." In *Dance Writings*, edited by Robert Cornfield and William Mackay, 214–15. London: Dance Books.

———. 1986b. "Rockettes and Rhythm." In *Dance Writings*, edited by Robert Cornfield and William Mackay, 200–202. London: Dance Books.

Garafola, Lynn. 2005. "Making an American Dance: *Billy the Kid*, *Rodeo*, and *Appalachian Spring*." In *Aaron Copland and His World*, edited by Carol Oja and Judith Tick, 121–47. Princeton, NJ: Princeton University Press.

Levy, Beth. 2012. *Frontier Figures: American Music and the Mythology of the American West*. Berkeley: University of California Press.

New York City Ballet. 2014. *2014–2015 Guide to the Repertory*. New York: New York City Ballet.

Peck, Justin. 2015. "Justin Peck and Taylor Stanley on Rodeo: Four Dance Episodes." Repertory video created for and archived on nycballet.org.

Sedgwick, Eve Kosofsky. 2003. *Touching Feeling: Affect, Pedagogy, Performativity*. Durham, NC: Duke University Press.

Siegel, Marcia. 1985. *The Shapes of Change: Images of American Dance*. Berkeley: University of California Press.

Stanley, Taylor. 2016. Interview with the author. New York City, June 20.

Tomkins, Silvan. 1995. *Shame and Its Sisters: A Silvan Tomkins Reader*, edited by Eve Kosofsky Sedgwick and Adam Frank. Durham, NC: Duke University Press.

Flesh Dance

Black Women from Behind

JASMINE ELIZABETH JOHNSON

Let's face it. I am a marked woman, but not everybody knows my name.

—HORTENSE SPILLERS, "Mama's Baby, Papa's Maybe:
An American Grammar Book"

In her canonical essay "Mama's Baby, Papa's Maybe: An American Grammar Book" ([1987] 2000), literary and feminist theorist Hortense Spillers argues that the history of antiblack violence rendered black women's bodies "marked." The institution of chattel slavery depended on a black woman's kinlessness through the impermissibility of her exercising unbound and self-possessed familial care. Simultaneously, the institution capitalized on her anatomy, or womb, to produce future slave property. A physical and discursive violence sundered black bodies into maimed flesh. Slavery depended on objectifying the black enslaved; as such, black women became subject to slavery's uses *for* (rendered as "markings" on) them. These "hieroglyphics of the flesh," Spillers writes, "come to be hidden to the cultural seeing by skin color" (66). Overdetermined from without, black women are understood as caricature. For Spillers, racialized tropes ("Peaches," "Brown Sugar," "Sapphire," and "Earth Mother," to evoke a few that the author herself lists) stand in for black women's identity. These "hieroglyphics," although understood by black women themselves as markings, go (mis)recognized by others as authentic. Thus, the black female body is "marked up"—signified on—while black *womanhood* evades a broader public optic. What we "see" or come to know in looking at a black woman is rarely a black woman's "truer word" (80).

"The problem before us," Spillers writes, "is deceptively simple: [terms such as "Peaches," "Brown Sugar" and so on] isolate overdetermined nominative properties. . . . [T]hey are markers so loaded with mythical prepossession that there is no easy way for the agents buried beneath them to come clean" (57). If, as Spillers argues, black women struggle as agents to disembalm from the heft of overdetermination, how do dance scholars confront such "nominative properties"? What, I ask, can black feminist theories of embodiment teach dance scholars about black bodies in motion and the limits of looking? As a field that is in many ways dependent on sight, what do we do with America's grammar of misrecognition and the unreliability of seeing black women at all, much less black women's bodies in motion?

In this essay I draw from black feminist and social dance scholarship to consider the politics of black women's movement through what I call *flesh dance*. I conceptualize flesh dance as a choreographic/sonic coupling through which hip hop lyrics direct black women to move in sexually mimetic ways. Flesh dance, I argue, italicizes a tension that black social dance has always embodied: it polices black intimacy and gender while extending a vehicle through which individual and communal pleasure might be instantiated. This double bind— that of potentially eroding and titillating—calls scholars of race, gender, and dance to examine embodied consent, creative labor, and black self-making. By holding this tension (of finding pleasure at the site of racial and gendered injury), we are better equipped to tackle the nuanced relationship between sex, dance, and self-articulation. Might we be able to move beyond understanding explicitly libidinal dance as derogatory (and, as such, bankrupt of feminist possibility) and toward an analytic in which pleasure is conjoined to pain—where power might be appropriated, usurped, and reigned through the execution and mastery of the flesh? This essay invites critical pause rather than prescription.

Flesh dance is a genre of instructional dance; instructional dance belongs to the broader category of social dance. Social dances convene, entertain, and concretize a community. Black social dance describes movements intended for and which in their doing produce black social worlds. It crops up, in other words, from the material conditions that structure black living. I follow Thomas DeFrantz, who (by way of Martiniquan postcolonial theorist Frantz Fanon) "make[s] a gesture towards blackness as an existential and corporeal reality" (2001, 11). Like black bodies, black social dance is political, consequential, and historical. Black social dance might also be described as vernacular dance: choreographies exacted for and during social, communal occasions. As Julie Malnig writes, "The labels 'social,' 'vernacular,' and 'popular' are used interchangeably and often inconsistently in the social dance literature" (2009, 4). Dance scholars have examined histories of black social dance in the United States; most draw connections between social dance forms in the New World and West African cultures (Gottschild 1998; Emery 1988; Hazzard-Donald 1990; Malone 1996; Murray 1989; Stearns and Stearns [1968] 1979). They call our attention to the efficacy of movement to concretize community and carve out social spaces within political contexts that bridle black life.

Black social dance embodies the retentions and contingencies that shape(d) black culture. Scholars such as Robert Farris Thompson (1984), Kariamu Welsh-Asante (1997), Lawrence Levine (1978), and Katrina Dyonne Thompson (2014) draw our attention to the centrality of dance to African and black diasporic self-making and survival. Outlining broad themes among dances in West African cultures, through the Middle Passage, during slavery, in minstrelsy, and in band culture, Jacqui Malone, for example, argues that choreography indexes the politics of the historical moments during which certain dances emerge. How black bodies moved through the diaspora is indexical of linkages and breaks inevitable in black transatlantic history (Malone 1996, 24). Like black social dance at large, instructional dances speak to the sociopolitical climates from which they emerge.

A subset of social dance, instructional dances rehearse bodies through lyrical direction; they can be understood as choreographies rendered through verse that direct the stylization of the body. Black social dances were introduced to white audiences through instructional, or pedagogic, songs. In their article "From 'Messin' Around' to 'Funky Western Civilization': The Rise and Fall of Dance Instruction Songs," Sally Banes and John F. Szwed examine the 1920s and 1960s American instructional dance waves, charting their emergence, popularity, and eventual decline. They define instructional dance songs as a kind of dance notation that privileges the aural over the written and is popular rather than elite (2002, 170). Instructional dances grew in popularity through black American social instruction. Evidencing what Brenda Dixon Gottschild (1998) has described as "Africanisms," Banes and Szwed note that the dance instructional song that emerged before World War I "is *about* the mass distribution of dance and bodily knowledge and thus has served crucial aesthetic, social, and political functions. It has played an important part in the democratization of social dancing; it has spread African American dance forms and styles throughout Euro-American culture and other subaltern cultures; and it has helped create a mass market for the work of black artists. In short, the dance instruction song has contributed to the formation of a syncretic dance culture— and bodily culture—in multicultural America" (2002, 170). Through the instructional dance song, African American dances circulated beyond the black social contexts from which they emerged. At different periods, dances like the twist, the mashed potato, the hustle, the smurf, ballin', the jerk, and the bump, to name a few, became national dance crazes with black American origins that spread through performance mediums like minstrel shows, black vaudeville, and musicals. Reflecting this historical trend, Banes and Szwed center nonblack audiences' tutoring in African American movement vocabularies, thus focusing on white reception of largely black music and choreographic repertoire. For example, Banes and Szwed write that instructional songs of the early 1920s and 1960s waves "seem[ed] to indicate that the white mass audience/partici-pants needed tutoring in all the moves, postures, and rhythms of black dance" (182). After the 1960s, artists assumed that audiences already had some dance skill and prior experience. Consequently, instructions became conveyed with less choreographic detail, and elements like exhortation and style made their way more centrally into the songs. Despite this shift, the dance instruction song functioned as a resource for white tutelage of black movement.

Generalized instructional songs and dances permeate contemporary hip hop too. Mr. C's "Cha Slide" (2006), the 69 Boyz' "Tootsee Roll" (1994), Ciara's "1-2 Step" (2009), Cali Swag District's "Teach Me How to Dougie" (2011), and Silento's "Watch Me (Whip / Nae Nae)" (2015) represent instructional songs. Indeed, this genre of directive music is so popular that songs have now emerged that catalog a body of contemporary social dances and challenge the listener to execute a range of popular dance styles with both precision and flair. DJ Challenge's "Hit That Bit for the Gram" (2015) and DLow's "Bet You Can't Do It Like Me" (2015), for example, skip detailed tutelage, asking listeners to per-form a body of popular movements. Flesh dance differs from the earlier black instructional songs described by Banes and Szwed. It emerges out of hip hop culture, centers black singers/rappers addressing and instructing black danc-ing bodies, and features dances that simulate sex acts. It is also distinguished by its songs' titles, which do not immediately signal specific dance moves but broadcast sexual commands. Songs like Travis Porter's "Bring It Back" (2011), Juvenile's "Slow Motion for Me" (2007), Jeremih's "Put It Down on Me" (2010), and Waka Flocka's "No Hands" (2010) instruct predominantly black female-identified bodies to move their behinds percussively in order to instantiate male pleasure. Thus black women's moving bodies (and their attendant sig-nifications of hypersexuality) are hailed through direct lyrical commands atop an embodied rhythmic percussion that constitutes the beat.

These songs and attendant choreographies conflate dance and sex, empha-size execution and style (rather than a detailed string of choreographic direc-tives), and shift from first to second person (from "I" or "we" to "you"). For the most part, a speaker gendered as male addresses a female-identified dancer. Flesh dance centers "ass-clapping"—that is, moving one's backside repetitiously so that it generates the rhythmic sound of applause. Flesh dance incorporates sexualized commands into the lyrics, thereby shaping notions of black sexual-ity in both black social contexts and the public sphere. It asks us to consider the power of the sonic and embodied to impact meanings of race and sexuality and reveals the complicated relationship between being "marked" as Spillers writes and being a "truer word."

My use of *flesh* deliberately engages the complexities around black women's agency and subjectivity that Spillers theorizes. In "Mama's Baby" she writes that under the institution of slavery, reproduction, motherhood, pleasure, and desire were thrown into "unrelieved crisis" ([1987] 2000, 59). Black flesh became a commodity of capitalist exchange. Captive African bodies became the source of an irresistible sensuality while being simultaneously reduced to a thing. The enslaved were thus made available for being signified on: a receptacle for others' desires, fears, and capitalist ambitions. As Brittney Cooper writes (reflecting on Spillers), "Enslavement was predicated on a dialectical doing and undoing of gender that frequently rendered the Black body a space of indeterminate gender terrain" (2017, 20). It is against this historical context that Spillers makes a distinction between the body and the flesh—a difference distinguished "between captive and liberated subject-positions. In that sense, before the 'body' there is the 'flesh,' that zero degree of social conceptualization that does not escape concealment under the brush of discourse, or the reflexes of iconography" ([1987] 2000, 61). A black woman's flesh was unprotected because the institution of slavery exploited her form to generate wealth; a black woman only carried gendered potential when her body increased her owner's stock. A black woman navigated a political position of utter sexual endangerment while being refused the right to care for her kin. "In this play of paradox," Spillers writes, "only the female stands *in the flesh* both mother and mother-dispossessed" (80). She continues, "In order for me to speak a truer word concerning myself, I must strip down the layers of attenuated meanings, made an excess in time, over time, assigned by a particular historical order, and there await whatever marvels of my own inventiveness. The personal pronouns are offered in the service of a collective function" (80). Flesh, then, indexes the relationship between discourses around black womanhood and black womanhood itself. It recognizes that black women are most often interpreted through "attenuated meanings." "Peaches," "Brown Sugar," or "Sapphire"—while mapped onto her skin—tell us more about her *uses* for others rather than her "truer word." Flesh dance, I argue, activates these attenuated meanings. I use the term both to examine the role of dance in reinscribing "property relations" and to suggest that these relations tell us more about the "collective function" of the black woman than they tell us about the ends of black women's interiority (71). I suggest that black women's flesh being "marked" should not be confused with black women being legible.

The lyrical and percussive repetition within the songs and lucid instructional details might make flesh dance appear legible, if not obvious, in terms of its choreographic and political operations. The movement, however, blurs the boundaries between sex and dance and between public and private acts. Within the aggressively heterosexist worlds from which flesh dance emerges, a black woman's dance aligning with a "marking" is not synonymous with her availability. Executing flesh dance does not mean consent; nor does it imply total impossibility for joy inside of sonic contempt. Ultimately, I call for a black feminist reading of these instructional dance songs to trouble the problem of black women's hypervisibility. How might being so regularly beheld actually obscure being seen?

Flesh dances index the political valences of black women's bodies in motion. Rather than landing on analyses that only understand sexually mimetic music and dance forms as regressive and, by extension, antifeminist, I describe the injurious work of flesh dance alongside its potential capacity to mobilize flesh in service of the body. Later, I consider African American studies professor Alexander Weheliye's question: "Can we conceive of a black body politic in ways that do not depend on discreteness and modesty as measures of worthwhile art and performance?" (2005, 184).

If we understand social dances as kinds of movements that, in their enactment, shape individuals' sense of group membership, then contemporary hip hop music belongs to this tradition. Dance instruction songs teach not only "the quantitative aspects of the dance (the steps, postures, and gestures) but also the qualitative aspects" (Banes and Szwed 2002, 189). As important as the choreography are the social, sexual, and classed norms that inform and contextualize the dances. Considering flesh dances as social dances reveals how, in a contemporary context, black social life is made through movement both embodied and lyrical.

Flesh dance emphasizes technique more than "new" choreographic material. This can be gleaned from the song titles alone: "No Hands," "Bring It Back," "Slow Motion for Me" all direct the stylization of the (black) female body; all are double entendres for both choreographic and sexual acts. Although the kinds of songs under discussion here may not immediately register as instructional dances in that their titles do not name a narrow dance "craze" (like Chubby Checker's "The Wah-Watusi," Sam Cooke's "Shake," or E.U.'s "Da Butt"), they belong to the same genre of dance and musical style in their calling on bodies to move in specialized ways. It is perhaps because they do not announce themselves and yet carry the same social-world shaping power that flesh dance songs are differently efficacious from their instructional dance relatives.

With very few detailed directives, flesh dance's lyrical content rests on inculcating pliant sexual flexibility. The dances themselves all figure women dropping low, splitting or clapping their backsides, bouncing up and down, and performing other sexual acrobatics. In "Bring It Back," Travis Porter instructs women to

> Run and hit that pussy like a crash dummy
> Bend it over, touch ya toes;
> Shake that ass for me
> Bounce that ass on the flo', bring it back up
> Hit a split on the dick, shawty act up
> Now bring it back. (2011)

In this song the dance shifts into sex, dissolving the line between public dance and personal intimacy. Lyrically, the voice shifts between describing the rapper's own movements and instructing the dancing woman. While the first section of the lyrics describe action to be carried out by the male rapper ("Run and hit that pussy like a crash dummy"), the lyrics pivot to describe the activity of the female dancer ("Bend it over, touch ya toes; / Shake that ass for me") (Porter 2011). Porter moves from instructing himself (or another man) to the woman's movement, to affirming her success. In so doing he underscores the evaluative and rehearsed nature of the social space. That women are routinely congratulated for "performing well" in these songs underscores the paternalism at play. The congratulation also countersignals the reality that dancers are indeed working, practicing, and thus performatively constituting their own presentation of self. Here, "going hard," meaning performing well, is proven by the woman's ability to control her butt cheeks: "Shawty goin' hard, concrete / She can shake her ass, one cheek / two cheeks, both cheeks, both cheeks" (Porter 2011).

Flesh dance songs (which I use to describe both music and movement, since they are inextricably tied) are sung predominantly by male rappers and call for women to move in sexually stylized ways. The songs thus performatively construct black masculinity despite the fact that men do little dancing during them. The rappers work as interlocutors, toggling between conducting women's bodies and anticipating subsequent social protocols. They serve as both directors and authenticators of women's movement. "Slow Motion for Me" by Juvenile (2003) demonstrates this lyrical command and attendant choreographic execution. The title itself works as a declarative rather than a question: Juvenile elects his partner to move *for*, not with, him. This rehearses a strip club dynamic in which women move with the goal of satisfying the spectator's and perhaps her own pleasure while pursuing financial procurement.

Like Porter, 50 Cent insists on and evaluates women's dance techniques as a guest artist on Jeremih's single "Down on Me." Here, club dancing and f*cking (choreographic reality and sexual fantasy) slip into one another. He raps,

Systems thumping, party jumping, shorty, she's a perfect 10
She rock her hips, then roll her hips, then drop it down like it's nothing
She shaped just like an hour glass, she see how fast an hour passed
Time flies when I'm on that ass but I won't put our shit on blast

Work it like a pro, sit and watch it go
Do her thing all on the floor, she bounce it fast and shake it slow
So sexual incredible, she beautiful, she edible
I got her, I won't let her go, I ain't seen nothing better yo

Look at how she twurk it, the way she work it
Make me wanna hit it, hit it, heaven when I'm in it, in it
If I do not fit, I'm gonna make it
Girl, you can take it, don't stop, get it, get it (Jeremih 2010)

50 Cent's lyrics index the violence of heterosexism that emerges via flesh dance; the song also raises urgent questions around consent and gendered power relations within hip hop. Here, public dance is dangerously conflated with consent, and a "successful" flesh dance leads to anticipated sexual violence as 50 Cent shares that the dancer's comfort ("If I do not fit, I'm gonna make it") is of no consequence to this foreseen assault. The repetition of "I see you baby," uttered later in the song, calls attention to the illegibility of the dancing black female body. While "I see you" in black vernacular culture is often evoked to communicate that "whatever you are doing, you happen to be doing well" (a recognition of a mastery of one's own body), here "I see you" predatorily calls a woman into sight, making her dangerously available to sexual violence. Flesh dance indexes the heterosexism within black social dance spaces.

Men direct flesh dance. While they do not execute the kind of sexually mimetic choreography that women are called to do ("And no darlin' I don't dance," explains Wale), they perform other physical tasks that highlight their wealth, attractiveness, and power over women. In "Bring It Back," Porter raps:

Back that ass up like a dump truck
If you havin fun in the club, throw ya pumps up
All my ballas in the building throw ya 1s up
If you ain't throwin no money then get ya funds up (2012)

Monetary excess functions as a sign and source of masculinity. Not having cash to throw works to mobilize one's ambition to earn more. This theme runs throughout "No Hands," too. Waka Flocka explains:

> Girl the way you movin' got me in a trance
> DJ turn me up, ladies this yo jam
> Imma sip moscato and you gon' loose them pants
> And Imma throw this money while you do it with no hands
> Girl drop it to the floor I love the way yo booty go
> All I wanna do is sit back and watch you move and I'll proceed to throw this
>   cash (2010)

The sexually animated fabric of flesh dance, alongside its flagrant reification of differentiated gender power, mechanizes this genre of music and dance. Putting it directly, T. Denean Sharpley-Whiting writes that "the impact of these sexually suggestive videos is undeniably regressive in terms of gender politics and young girls' and women's self-identity" (2008, 27). But other black feminists have drawn our attention to black women's nuanced mobilization of discursively harmful hip hop songs—a mobilization that appropriates and sometimes subverts the music's originally sexist operations. In writing about the Punany Poets, for example, Raquel Monroe contends that "the black feminist analysis of the dancing bodies as passive commodities and mere props of misogyny elides the dancers' physical labor, usurps their agency, and suppresses further conversations and explorations of what else this body might do and does, and the pleasures of those watching and performing" (2017, 250).

While the lyrics position women as useful insofar as they instantiate male pleasure, the dancing and its spectatorship open the possibility of the dancer's commitment to tending to the self. Here I am reminded of Karrine Steffans, a hip hop video model whose *New York Times* best-selling memoir *The Vixen Diaries* cataloged the dynamics and labor of being a woman working in the flesh dance industry. An interview with *NPR* indexes the reporter's discomfort with Steffans's unapologetic position on her life and choice to disclose sexual encounters, alongside Steffans's insistence on self-possession.

INTERVIEWER: But your financial independence, at the root of it, is men. It's either being with men, or writing about your being with men. Do you find that contradictory at all?

STEFFANS: No, because I don't write about being with men. I write about my life. I do have a personal private life. . . . I'm all the things that people hate to hear about.

INTERVIEWER: So what do you think you represent?
STEFFANS: I represent me. (Steffans 2007)

Flesh dances shape public discourse about black women (hieroglyphics, perhaps?) while concurrently shaping how black women understand their gendered, sexed ("truer"?) selves. Inside the repetition of dance is also the making of racialized and gendered meaning. As Sharpley-Whiting writes, "Just as important as the complex motivations behind young women's suggestive performances in hip hop videos—rumps moving with the alacrity of a jackhammer, hips gyrating like a belly dancer on amphetamines, limbs akimbo, mouths agape in a perpetual state of orgasmic 'oh'—is the repetition of particular ideals of femininity" (2008, 27).

Flesh dance music videos are rich sites for understanding the central role that black communal gatherings play in the execution of the dancing, for they accentuate the genre's steady evocation of financial gain and dominance over women. Changing meanings of black sociality are central tropes in contemporary instructional songs. Like jook joints and rent parties, the club, lounge, or block party may be considered as a potential counterpublic in which black intimacies are exchanged. Although mired with the same political economies that complicate if not determine black people's lives generally, these scenes also represent the singers' staged social utopia. In addition to the club, lounges, hotel rooms, streets, and stoops are places where groups of black folk gather and dance. Rappers position these public spaces as sites of rehearsal for how to get ready for sexual encounters. In this light, the group dynamics that are applied to populated social situations are then transferred to intimate, private ones, and vice versa. For example, the distance is murky between the dance that is being "taught" on the dance floor and the sex that it promises after. In a few short bars, a dance floor transforms into a bedroom and back. The sonic power of flesh dance (and the promiscuous way music circulates) allows for a kind of traveling that supports the permeation of the dance/sex pedagogy.

In Travis Porter's video for "Bring It Back" (2011) he maneuvers his iPad to literally rearrange the women on his screen. Watching a video of himself on the street as black women walk by, Porter puppeteers the video's sequencing, rewinding women back into his field of vision. His community of peers laugh while Porter casts additional women into the moving image, only to pour a bucket of water onto one unsuspecting female pedestrian. The majority of the video takes place at a house party where women in body-hugging dresses sway near Porter and his friends. The men do not dance; they move from the street, to the house party, to the bedroom. Throughout, they stand with outstretched arms and clap their hands, the clap representing both the musical beat and a woman's drilling backside, which the men demand, again and again, for her to "bring back."

In Juvenile's "Slow Motion for Me" (2006) the rapper stands perched in front of a megabus. Videos of working-class black America weave between scenes of a block party where children ride bikes, adults traipse atop broken bottles, grill-masters flip hamburgers, Juvenile kisses babies, and women churn their hips. The production is reminiscent of a pedestrian home video; this underscores the distance between the financial success implied by the tour bus (in front of which Juvenile raps) and the black working-class modesty of the house party. The distance between the song's central referent (sex) and the backdrop of the video (a family picnic) evidences the informality of the song's content and dance. Black women dance everywhere and nowhere: there is no receipt of their embodied labor from the guests at the party or from Juvenile. Even while women stir their hips, the black elders do not acknowledge the women's presence. And yet the angle from which the scenes of black women dancing are shot is from below (suggesting, perhaps, an erotic dancer/specta-tor field of visual relationship), as opposed to the remainder of the video, which rests at eye level.

The social arena where the dance takes place—whether the club, the family picnic, or the street—becomes a field of sexual rehearsal. On the dance floor, power relations are manifested, affirmed, corrected, or denied through dance. Waka Flocka's "No Hands" (2010) (which has over forty-one million views on YouTube) is a classic "club video": big city rooftops, glistening floors, black women evidencing a mastery of polyrhythms. Cutting scenes between the club and a hotel room, "No Hands" positions sex acts as both central to the club's sociality and promised at the end of a night. The dancers move with mouth open; their dance is slowed to half-time, elongating their smooth descent to the floor and slow levitation to standing. Waka Flocka, Wale, and Roscoe Dash fling cash, while a crowd of dancers entertain them.

Framing these performances of black sexuality as flesh dance works to keep feminist critiques of heterosexism activated while holding the possibility that a black woman's "truer word" might live as and beyond the stereotyped eroticization of her body. There is a potential for black women's enjoyment within antiblack and sexist contexts. Indeed, to understand that black women, since the event of slavery, have been "marked" is to acknowledge that there has never been a context in which black women have been, as a gendered and racial group, outside of racism, sexism, and homophobia. Spillers writes that "whether or not 'pleasure' is possible at all under conditions that I would aver as non-freedom for both or either or the parties has not been settled" ([1987]

2000, 77). Flesh dance positions women as the property of men; yet this fact does not foreclose the possibility that these public and popular performances of femininity, authored by misogyny, could also be a source of subversive power.

Dance scholars have addressed the importance of resisting a "success/failure" dichotomy in evaluating movement. As Susan Manning outlines in her literature review on feminist readings of early modern dance, choreographers practiced a "double move of subverting the voyeuristic gaze while projecting essentialized notions of identity" (1997, 154). This simultaneity—of intervening and perpetuating—is a concurrence at work in flesh dance as well. Black feminists have for nearly four decades now produced nuanced work on gender and sexuality in the hip hop era (Rose 1994; Collins 2000; Durham 2014; hooks 1990, 2000; Pough 2004). These authors extend robust analyses of the workings of gender and sexuality within hip hop culture. In its indivisible coupling of the lyrical and embodied (within social contexts mired with racism, sexism, and homophobia), flesh dance extends a productive entry point through which to analyze race and gender performativity.

Building on Albert Murray (1989), Jacqui Malone argues that black social dances "[help] drive the blues away and [provide] rich opportunities to symbolically challenge societal hierarchies by offering powers and freedoms that are impossible in ordinary life" (1996, 1). Does flesh dance drive the blues away, or does it fondle them? The ritual of a party holds the potential to empower in ways that may not be available in everyday black life. Executing flesh dance in social spaces is at once proof of one's facility with one's own body and evidence of a pop cultural knowledge. This notion of the potentially restorative power of contemporary social dance differs from Paul Gilroy's argument in *Against Race: Imagining Political Culture beyond the Color Line* (2000) that "love songs" are increasingly obsolete: the body has become an end to itself as opposed to a site for spiritual transcendence, he argues. Gilroy writes about the shift in black cultural production from a space that was explicitly derived out of a state of black unfreedom to a sexually obsessed public sphere. In Gilroy's estimation, there has been a transformation from aurality to visuality: the image usurps the musical listening. Yet I want to both extend and push back on Gilroy's argument by proposing that dance and movement are central factors to this changing nature of black cultural production and that a consideration of flesh dance can help us understand how this shift can be both damaging and freeing.

Sexual excess dominates the black public sphere, Gilroy posits, and an addiction to specularity has usurped aurality (2000, 191). Today, "stylized tales of sexual excess" dominate black public life and have threatened, if not completely deadened, other modes of black expressivity (178). Gilroy's reading of contemporary black life underestimates the power of the "bump and grind" (to use his language). By investing in nostalgic notions of "real" music and black love, Gilroy forecloses the possibility of black female joy in the face of discursive impairment.

In *Phonographies: Grooves in Afrosonic Modernity* (2005) Weheliye examines sound technologies that have produced black modernity and black cultural production more broadly. Within his analysis is a counterreading of Gilroy that I extend through flesh dance. Weheliye troubles the connection Gilroy draws between the increasing pornification of black music and black folks' presumed devaluing of spiritual transcendence. Weheliye writes that "the body Gilroy refers to gains its freedom in and not through sex, making sex an end unto itself rather than a means through which to acquire freedom" (2005, 184). Weheliye's inquiry—"How can we conceive of black body politics in ways that do not depend on discreteness and modesty as measures of worthwhile art?"— helps us think through flesh dance (185). Flesh dance centers the body and therefore centers sex, creating contexts for both sexual policing and potential pleasure.

Flesh dance polices sex, intimacy, and expectations of kinship, yet this objectification does not entirely foreclose the potential for pleasure, self-identification, and self-possession. Black women are not inherently excellent at flesh dance; their dexterity is the result of physically repetitive work, control, and selective withholding. Indeed, as Sharpley-Whiting writes, hip hop "shower[s] [black women] with contempt," but closing the shutters on fleshy scenes does not fully constitute a black feminist strategy for dismantling patriarchy (2008, 8). How might we effectively call out detriment (the physical and discursive objectification of black women's bodies) without denying black women's capacity to draw their own cartographies of self, which may or may not align with stereotype?

With regard to the aforementioned flesh dance videos, we do not have access to the dancers' sentiments about how they interpret their own dancing. (Indeed, such an ethnography would no doubt deepen and complicate what I have heuristically laid out here.) Without access to the interiority of these flesh dance ensembles, we do have entrance to black female authors' writing on their individual relationships to hip hop music/choreography—movement that I would argue falls into the flesh dance category. Among these authors are the Crunk Feminist Collective, a rhetorical community for hip hop generation feminists of color. In their anthology, the authors write that "Crunk feminism gives us the nerve to make our way off of the dance floor, where we were shaking our asses just a moment ago, when a song comes on that dares to suggest that ass-shaking constitutes desire and consent. Ass-shaking is whatever we say it is, and our hip hop feminism means you will either respect that or you will learn today" (Cooper, Morris, and Bollard 2017, 170). Across the span of the volume, the contributing authors raise questions around the complicated association between pleasure, constraint, and black women's agency to decide their own flexible relationship to hip hop. In the above excerpt, the authors privilege the meanings they make for themselves in light of lyrical content, gratification of dance, and safety of social space. Black women exercise agency through self-possessed social dance practice.

Within the broader sociocultural world of flesh dance is the possibility that racial scripts that demean blackness might also titillate and employ. Black feminists have long theorized black women's practices of sexual contentment within political contexts that work to starve them of this erotic pleasure.[1] To draw from Jennifer Nash's language in reference to the silver age of pornography, we should consider the potential agency of erotic labor and the possibility that black women may "find pleasure at the site of racial injury" (2014, 86).

What would it mean to practice black feminist dance studies? I suggest that this would first require, in some ways, loosening our fidelity to sight. If black women are, from the moment of their "invention," a sum of uses, then surely black women in choreographic motion would invite a different set of questions around enactment, principally: What is the simultaneous play between seeing and invisibility in black women's dance? A black feminist dance reading would also reserve the head of the analytical table for the black woman in motion. With this understanding, a black woman's flesh dance, so regularly understood as "excessive" (as black women's bodies in motion, fully clothed or not, are read), would be understood as the mobilization of a "mark." Whether or not her drilling backside is her "truer word" will always be beyond us. That she mobilizes the flesh, though, is clear: it is an embodied practice of controlling a marked body. Flesh dance, in other words, forces us to understand black women's standpoint (Collins 2000) from the back.

Flesh dance takes behindness as a productive lens through which the embodied labor of black women can be complicatedly examined. After all, black feminism has long taught us that how we are trained to see a black woman is rarely her actual image. Hypervisibility is more of a blindness than a clarity. Flesh dance asks us to consider the possibility that black female sentience might very well be unavailable in plain sight. "Let's," as Spillers insists, "face it."

Note

1. See Brittney Cooper and Treva Lindsey's special issue "On the Future of Black Feminism" in the *Black Scholar* (2015).

Works Cited

Banes, Sally, and John F. Szwed. 2002. "From 'Messin' Around' to 'Funky Western Civilization': The Rise and Fall of Dance Instruction Songs." In *Dancing Many Drums: Excavations in African American Dance*, edited by Thomas DeFrantz, 169–204. Madison: University of Wisconsin Press.

Collins, Patricia Hill. 2000. *Black Feminist Thought: Knowledge, Consciousness, and the Politics of Empowerment.* New York: Routledge.

Cooper, Brittney C. 2017. *Beyond Respectability: The Intellectual Thought of Race Women.* Urbana: University of Illinois Press.

Cooper, Brittney C., Treva Lindsey, Joan Morgan, Tanisha Ford, and Kaila Story, eds. 2015. "On the Future of Black Feminism." "Black Feminisms." Special issue, *Black Scholar* 45 (1): 1–69.

Cooper, Brittney C., Susana M. Morris, and Robin M. Bollard. 2017. "Introduction: Hip Hop Generation Feminism: Feminism All the Way Turned Up." In *The Crunk Feminist Collection*, edited by Brittney C. Cooper, Susana M. Morris, and Robin M. Bollard, 169–71. New York: Feminist Press at the City University of New York.

DeFrantz, Thomas F. 2001. "Foreword: Black Bodies Dancing Black Culture—Black Atlantic Transformations." In *Embodying Liberation: The Black Body in American Dance*, edited by Dorothea Fischer-Hornung and Alison D. Goeller, 11–16. New Brunswick, NJ: Transaction Publishers.

Durham, Aisha S. 2014. *Home with Hip Hop Feminism: Performances in Communication and Culture.* New York: Peter Lang Publishing Inc.

Emery, Lynne Fauley. 1988. *Black Dance from 1619 to Today.* Princeton, NJ: Princeton University Press.

Gilroy, Paul. 2000. *Against Race: Imagining Political Culture beyond the Color Line.* Cambridge, MA: Harvard University Press.

Gottschild, Brenda Dixon. 1998. *Digging the Africanist Presence in American Performance: Dance and Other Contexts.* Westport, CT: Praeger.

Hazzard-Donald, Katrina. 1990. *Jookin: The Rose of Social Dance Formations in African American Culture.* Philadelphia: Temple University Press.

hooks, bell. 1990. *Yearning: Race, Gender, and Cultural Politics.* Boston, MA: South End Press.

———. 2000. "Black Women: Shaping Feminist Theory." In *The Black Feminist Reader,* edited by Joy James and T. Denean Sharpley-Whiting, 131–45. New York: Blackwell.

Jeremih. 2010. "Down on Me." *All About You.* Island Def Jam Musical Group. MP3.

Juvenile. 2003. "Slow Motion for Me." *Juve the Great.* Cash Money Records. MP3.

Levine, Lawrence. 1978. *Black Culture, Black Consciousness.* Oxford: Oxford University Press.

Malnig, Julie, ed. 2009. *Ballroom, Boogie, Shimmy Sham, Shake: A Social and Popular Dance Reader.* Urbana: University of Illinois Press.

Malone, Jacqui. 1996. *Steppin' on the Blues: The Visible Rhythms of African American Dance.* Chicago: University of Illinois Press.

Manning, Susan. 1997. "The Female Dancer and the Male Gaze." In *Meaning in Motion: New Cultural Studies of Dance*, edited by Jane Desmond, 153–66. Durham, NC: Duke University Press.

Monroe, Raquel. 2017. "'Oh No! Not This Lesbian Again': The Punany Poets Queer the Pimp-Ho Aesthetic." In *Queer Dance: Meaning and Makings*, edited by Clare Croft, 243–62. New York: Oxford University Press.

Murray, Albert. 1989. *Stomping the Blues*. Cambridge, MA: Da Capo Press.

Nash, Jennifer. 2014. *The Black Body in Ecstasy: Reading Race, Reading Pornography*. Durham, NC: Duke University Press.

Porter, Travis. 2011. "Bring It Back." *From Day 1*. Jive Records. MP3.

Pough, Gwendolyn. 2004. *Check It, While I Wreck It: Black Womanhood, Hip-Hop Culture, and the Public Sphere*. Boston: Northeastern University Press.

Rose, Tricia. 1994. *Black Noise: Rap Music and Black Culture in Contemporary America*. Middletown, CT: Wesleyan University Press.

Sharpley-Whiting, T. Denean. 2008. *Pimps Up, Ho's Down: Hip Hop's Hold on Young Black Women*. New York: NYU Press.

Spillers, Hortense. (1987) 2000. "Mama's Baby, Papa's Maybe: An American Grammar Book." In *The Black Feminist Reader*, edited by Joy James and T. Denean Sharpley-Whiting. Malden, MA: Wiley-Blackwell.

Stearns, Marshall, and Jean Stearns. (1968) 1979. *Jazz Dance: The Story of American Vernacular Dance*. Cambridge, MA: Da Capo Press.

Steffans, Karrine. 2007. "Former 'Video Vixen' Talks Sexuality and Power." *NPR*. http://www.npr.org/books/titles/138281789/the-vixen-diaries. Accessed July 16, 2017.

———. 2007. *The Vixen Diaries*. New York: Hachette Book Group.

Thompson, Katrina Dyonne. 2014. *Ring Shout, Wheel About: The Racial Politics of Music and Dance in North American Slavery*. Urbana: University of Illinois Press.

Thompson, Robert Farris. 1984. *Flash of the Spirit: African & Afro-American Art & Philosophy*. New York: Vintage Books.

Waka Flocka. 2010. "No Hands." *Flockaveli*. Warner Bros. Record. MP3.

Weheliye, Alexander G. 2005. *Phonographies: Grooves in Afrosonic Modernity*. Durham, NC: Duke University Press.

Welsh-Asante, Kariamu. 1997. *African Dance: An Artistic, Historical and Philosophical Inquiry*. Philadelphia: Africa World Press.

Winin' through the Violence

Performing Carib[being]ness at the Brooklyn Carnival

ADANNA KAI JONES

Also known as the wine, winin' is a rolling hip/butt dance informally learned at a very young age and commonly performed at Trinidadian-style Carnivals. Although winin' continues to be practiced by Caribbean people of various ethnicities, races, genders, and classes, it remains linked to black/African histories and female bodies, especially due to the historical link between big bottoms and the African female body (Gottschild 2003). Moreover, the erotic potency of the wine and its associations with black and deviant sexuality frame winin' Afro-Caribbean women, in particular, as immoral, violent, sexually manipulative, and ultimately tragic. In practice, the colonizing gaze often displaces the black dancing female with an imago—or, rather, a disembodied, floating signifier (Fleetwood 2011)—of blackness, hypersexuality, and self-sabotage, termed here the "winin' fatale" (Jones 2016). This further leaves Afro-Caribbean women vulnerable to misogynistic discourses, such as the belief that skilled female winers are predisposed to prostitution, out-of-wedlock motherhood, or sexual violence. As a result, the ways in which winers of all ages are interpreted and thus policed (by both the state and other individuals) reveal a long history of colonizing the black dancing female body through violence and shame. For when we take up public space in a *foreign* place—namely, a place that recognizes or presents our winin' bodies as in but not of that nation—our very livelihoods are at stake.

As a Trinidad-born, US-raised, always ready to *bus' ah wine* (read: wine at a moment's notice), black female, I remain determined to reveal the unapologetic ways winers use their writhing hips and jiggling bottoms to produce a sense of sociality and Carib[being]ness, a term I use to describe the experience of feeling, being, and belonging to the Caribbean. Using an autoethnographic approach, I begin this *tale* by focusing on the gyrating *tails* of the Afro-Caribbean women who wined through the crime-laden neighborhood of Crown Heights during the 2011 Brooklyn Carnival. Officially titled the West Indian American Day Carnival, the Brooklyn Carnival is heavily influenced by the pre-Lenten Carnival of Trinidad and is used to promote aspects of various Caribbean cultures. The Brooklyn version of Carnival was established in 1967, and the main event, known as "the parade of bands," continually features thousands of masqueraders (myself included) winin', dancing, and parading along Eastern Parkway in bright, colorful costumes. Through dance analysis, I focus on the politics of winin' specific to the context of Trinidadian-style Carnivals in order to reveal the intimately microscopic ways winers use every roll and gyration to navigate and renegotiate the contested ways blackness and public pleasure are both experienced and performed at the level of the body. Because the act of winin' is a labor of and for pleasure, winin' in public works as a pleasure-filled strategy for masqueraders to push back against, renegotiate, and undermine the contending racial meanings they wear upon their bodies. In effect, winers must constantly learn and relearn themselves as black subjects while toggling between multiple constructions of (trans)nationality and citizenship.

In order to tackle these intermeshing constructions vis-à-vis modes of resistance, I thread an autoethnographic vignette throughout the essay based on my experience of the 2011 Brooklyn Carnival. Referred to as "My Version *ah Tings*" (read: of Things), this vignette works as the glue that holds everything together, especially since the aforementioned intermeshed constructions entrap the winin' body within disparate political discourses. I use the subsequent two sections to conscientiously decipher the nuanced ways the winin' body further operates as a site through which power is both enacted and subverted. Because the way in which winers experience pleasure gets policed according to the gendered and racial histories and genealogies of the foreign site of the United States, winin' at this particular street festival mediates not only the antiblack violence that haunts Crown Heights but also the tense ties that the New York City Police Department (NYPD) maintains with that overwhelmingly black community. In "Their Version ah Tings," I spotlight the "No More West Indian Day Parade Detail" Facebook scandal that followed the 2011 Brooklyn festivities to discuss the ways in which Carib[being]ness remains vulnerable to the colonizing gaze of the state, or in this case the NYPD, which ultimately reimagined the winin' body as savage, violent, and always already black. Finally, in the section "Another Version ah Tings," I analyze a scandalous video clip of an NYC police officer gyrating on and with Caribbean masqueraders at that very same Carnival. Written along the vein of Joan Morgan's endeavors to reveal the politics of pleasure "as a liberatory, black feminist project," which she argues elevates "the need for sexual autonomy and erotic agency without shame to the level of black feminist imperative" (2015, 39), I assert the pleasure of winin' as an important and relevant feminist undertaking. In theorizing the winin' tales/tails that play out *on di road* (read: at Carnival), my essay thus attempts to disrupt the inextricable link Morgan shows between "trauma and violence to black women's lived and historical experiences" (38). As such, the ways in which winers tirelessly labor of and for pleasure remain necessary tools for resisting fatalism and creating intimacy, both among winers themselves and between winers and the state.

My Version ah Tings

My version ah tings exists somewhere along the chafing borders of antiblack violence and the sweaty politics of winin' for pleasure. As the essay develops, my version ah tings will be interrupted and remembered by way of other ethnographic and archival data, including evidence from social media and casual conversations with my informants. Doing so allows me to engage with the multiple consciousnesses that winers partake in and take on while coming to terms with the violence, fear, blackness, and pleasure that get circumscribed within the Brooklyn Carnival.

> *As I remember it, the 2011 Labor Day Carnival was the best I had yet to experience in Brooklyn. That year I was determined to get into a band so I could mash up di streets wit' meh wais'line thunda!*

Before continuing my ethnographic vignette, I want to contextualize this autoethnographic tale/tail with the acknowledgment that the labor it took to "mash up di streets wit' meh wais'line thunda" (read: mash up the streets with my waistline thunder) was not only exhausting but also purposeful and pointed. The phrase "mash up" implies that some kind of disruption is imminent. Here, the wine itself and thus the winer embody both flattery and slander. In effect, when one attempts to mash up something or someone with one's winery (read: the work of winin'), one's intentions can encompass (1) using exceptional winin' skills to physically challenge, emotionally bewilder, or sexually overwhelm those who are witnessing or experiencing one's winery, (2) changing the space, energy, or flow of events in some way, shape, or form with one's spectacular winery, such as bringing the party to a stop and/or leaving a mess behind, and (3) partying excessively by winin' on everything and everyone with fervor and rhythmic precision. The act of mashin' up is ultimately a commitment to pleasure at the risk of enduring physical pain or exhaustion, even in the face of hardship, misery, or violence.

Such behavior, however, is not uncommon. This bodily logic is not only the expected behavior for the Trinidadian-style Carnival but also one of the inherited legacies of the nineteenth-century *jamette* (feminine form). Because I am focusing on winers who participate in Carnivals that are heavily influenced by Trinidad's own Carnival, the corporeal legacies of the jamettes must be recognized as an important historical lineage that informs today's Carnival winery. *Jametres* (unisex) were a subculture of mostly Afro-Creole ex-slaves, especially associated with the post-emancipation Trinidadian Carnival after 1838 (Noel 2010). The jamettes defiantly politicized the female hip/butt area through their controversial masquerade performances and forever changed how the festival was practiced. Their bodily legacies circumscribe winin' in such a way that the act of winin' during Carnival also works as a citation of the jamette's defiant use of her waistline.

This brings me to the second half of my proclamation: wais'line thunda. Like the clapping sound of rolling thunder, this type of winin' is meant to send shock waves through the dance floor or, at the very least, through the person with whom you are dancing. Moreover, it implies that these "reverberations" will be done with a skillfully rolling bottom (i.e., a butt that could rel mash up di place). Herein lies the hidden gendered and racial element. The use of the word thunda indicates an expectation of a heavy-weightedness with each roll of the butt. Therefore, this kind of wine promotes the image of a big, round, jiggling bottom, which is then stereotypically imagined as both black and feminine. However, seeing that I do not quite fit this prototype—descriptors such as *mahgah* (read: narrow and skinny) have been used to describe my non-jiggling rear end by friends, family, and even strangers—I had to use my superb winin' skills (namely, my rhythmically dynamic use of my waistline) to mash up di place. This compensation, however, further points to the insidious ways in which the black dancing female (read: the nineteenth-century jamette) has set the standard for mashin' up di place.

After we had scouted the scene and navigated through the densely overcrowded sidewalks of Eastern Parkway for about an hour, a moment of serendipity arrived. One of the officers standing in front of the metal barriers that separated the masqueraders (in the street) from the onlookers (on the sidewalk) looked over his right shoulder, just long enough for us to slip through one of its broken bars and jump into the passing band. "Hide behind their feathers," I screamed out to my three girlfriends as we pushed through the band, making sure to also avoid the band's security crew. After some time had passed and our fears of getting caught had subsided, we began our search for someone to bus' ah sweet wine on. My friend was the first to locate someone. As Machel Montano's "Slow Wine" blasted through speakers strapped onto the music truck, she called him to her by deliberately gesturing toward him with her rolling bottom. With impeccable musicality, she made sure to hit every gyrating contour of that man with her sultry hips as Montano sang, "Slooooo-ohh-oh-ohhh." Even I blushed a bit at her winery, but as with everything in Carnival, the song came to an end, her winin' came to an end, and we continued our search for more sexy men to wine up on. It was rel pace (read: keep going at all costs).

Then, in the midst of all the feathers, screaming, jumping, waving, and winery, I heard the words "Ah Wot-leeeeeeh-sss" bleed through the speakers; I remember quickly looking up at the DJ to let him know that this was my absolute favorite soca song for the season. As I did so, I saw Kees Dieffenthaller himself (known simply as Kes) step out on top of the truck to sing the very tune that won him the 2011 International Groovy Soca Monarch title.[1] In that moment, I remember thinking, "Now this is freedom!"

The term *wotles* is an Anglophone-Caribbean Creole term that derives from the word "worthless." In the Trinidadian Creole dictionary *Côté ci Côté la*, *wotles* is defined as a term used to describe a person, not an inanimate object, who is seen as being "no good" (Mendes 2012, 209). As I was growing up in a middle-class Trinidadian household, the term *wotles* was synonymous with behaviors that were deemed undesirable or morally loose and often punishable via shaming or even legal action. These associations further link the term *wotles* to the figure of the jamette. The term *jametre* itself is a product of the colonial encounter, for it was not a self-appointed name but rather a slanderous name of disgust created by the white elite class and overwhelmingly assigned to poor Afro-Creoles who were said to be transitioning from chattel slavery into (disenfranchised) citizenship (Noel 2010, 61–63). Nonetheless, when it comes to winin', being called wotles can be easily embraced as a compliment in addition to an insult. In turn, it is within this discursive space that the performance of wotlesness, shame, fatality, pleasure, pride, and erotic power/agency profusely bleed into one another.

I had successfully stormed (read: entered uninvited) a band, and even better, one of my absolute favorite soca singers was here, in the flesh, straight from Trinidad and on Brooklyn soil, singing my favorite tune for the season. All I could do was scream aloud, throw my hands above my head, and bus' the sweetest wine in di middle ah di road. The nearby masqueraders must have felt my excitement, because the next thing I knew, I was being sandwiched by two men and two other women, who not only wined all around me but challenged me to wine down low to the ground on more than one occasion. I did not mind it, so I stayed with the groove for a bit; but when Kes started to sing out "Just show me whey yuh from," I had to break free from the sandwich. With my Trini flag in my right hand and my left hand on one of the speakers, I latched onto the moving truck and began to jog and wine. The music was just too sweet to let go, so I made sure to grab my girls as well. They loved Kes too! And jus' so, di Ca'nival jumbie in we jump out. We had no choice but to surrender to the moment and the good vibes. We then began to furiously jump up and down behind di truck, making sure to scream out loud "WE LOVE YOU, KES" on more than one occasion!

Like the concept of thunda and wotles, the word *jumbie*, meaning a "ghost, spirit, or demon" or an "overwhelming energy," is also a coded citation of the jamette figure. In that moment, my winery was deeply rooted within the *fete* mentality (note: in Trinidad, *to fete* means "to party"), which began with my conviction to "mash up di streets wit' meh wais'line thunda" and was intensified when "di Ca'nival jumbie in we jump out," ultimately "forcing" us to enhance our winery, fete harder, have more fun, and enjoy the moment intensely. The sweaty labor of both wotlesness and jumbieness allowed my friends and me to feel the pleasure of performing our own understandings of Carib[being]ness. During this visceral moment, our winin' performances revealed us as slippery and playful dancing bodies that desired pleasure not only for ourselves but also for the entire Caribbean community at large.

I was running on fumes at that point, meaning I had been up for over twenty-four hours with little to no sleep. My best friend, who was born to a Haitian mother and a Dominicano father, and I had spent much of the previous night covered in mud and paint, which was thrown and rubbed onto our bodies by revelers on their way to the pre-Carnival J'Ouvert festivities. We even encountered an impromptu jam session somewhere off Nostrand Avenue, where baby powder and black oil were being thrown onto any and every passerby. This of course was a prelude to the official J'Ouvert festivities, held near Prospect Park, a few miles up from where we had been roaming. High off this energy (and the rum), I soon fell in love with a young, strapping, African American man who ended up escorting us throughout the rest of the night. He bought me a roti with curry channa (freshly made by one of the Trini vendors) and a ginger and lemon juice (freshly squeezed and blended by a Jamaican Rastafarian vendor). I was in my glee.

Then on the morning of Carnival itself, around sunrise, I returned to my car, somewhere on Pacific Street, and just as I put the key to the car door, my friend called my attention to the massive numbers of people running toward us. We both started to freak out, for the sight of dozens of people running toward us was quite alarming. But just as we were about to join in on the frenzy, we noticed that members of the crowd started slowing down. My friend then heard one of them mumbling something about how black people can't gather in one place without someone getting shot. So with that we jumped in my car. We were not trying to stick around and face the possibly dangerous situation that had just occurred. For in that moment of fear, the magic from the night's ecstasy and euphoria flowed through my veins so forcibly that it became necessary for me to return to safety for the sole purpose of mashin' up di streets wit' meh wais'line thunda. So I quickly drove back to New Jersey to drop my best friend off, took a quick shower, picked up my three Haitian American girl-friends, and returned to Brooklyn for the parading of the bands. I mean, Carnival was calling me, and I felt like a Super-Trini, invincible from anything that threatened to put a damper on my fun. I wanted this Carnival to be only about togetherness, letting go of worries, and mischievously challenging any rules of authority. My opportunity to mash up di place had arrived, and I was ready. Or, as I heard a comedian say at a post-Carnival comedy show in Trinidad, "When life gives you soca, WINE!"

In my version ah tings, the allusion to gunshots is not intended to overlook the violence that continually haunts the Labor Day festivities. Rather, I am pointing to the ways in which winers actively pursue and labor for pleasure—which, as an act of resistance, rejects the violence that threatens to exterminate their very existence. On that particular Labor Day, falling in love and getting hit by a stray bullet were very real possibilities. From ecstasy to peril to feelings of solidarity and moments of social pariahdom, winers that day had to negotiate multiple states of being in order to ascertain an embodied sense of freedom and euphoria, all while remaining conscious of the very real threat of violence. In effect, my version ah tings points to the entangled ways the politics of Carib[being]ness, blackness, sexuality, violence, romantic love, freedom, fear, and pleasure constantly flowed in, out, through, and around my winin' body along the Eastern Parkway.

Their Version ah Tings

It is clear that on the very public streets of Brooklyn, the winin' masquerader's rolling production of sweat remains vulnerable to the colonizing gaze of anti-black racism. Due to the fact that this Carnival is held in a predominantly black area, the space of the Brooklyn Carnival is as much a black space as it is a Carib[being] space. That year it became a public scandal when members of the NYPD referred to the Brooklyn Carnival as the "'West Indian Day Massacre' [. . .] a 'scheduled riot'" (Roberts 2012), and as "Savage Day" (johnd7463 2011). Here, the colonizing gaze replaced Carib[being]ness with the winin' fatale imago. A pair of Brooklyn lawyers uncovered "over 70 pages worth of racist, violent comments directed at parade-goers" on Facebook (Mathias 2011), including "let them kill each other," "drop a bomb and wipe them all out," and "maybe next year they should hold it on Rikers Island" (johnd7463 2011). The

New York Times reported that the Facebook group was created later in September 2011, after I had already mashed up di Eastern Parkway wit' meh wais'line thunda (Glaberson 2011). Although the "No More West Indian Day Parade Detail" Facebook group has since been taken down, "a comparison by *The Times* of the names of some of the more than 150 people who posted comments on the page with city employee listings showed that more than 60 percent matched the names of police officers, and [the Police Department's deputy commissioner for public information] did not deny that they were officers" (Glaberson 2011).

As offensive and deplorable as those police officers' commentaries were to West Indians in particular and to the predominantly African American community of Crown Heights, the feelings of frustration that drove these police officers to create the Facebook page seemed to be driven by the consistent violence that continually occurs during the Labor Day festivities. Nonetheless, pouring their frustrations into the Carnival and its participants falsely promotes the idea that the festival itself is the cause of the violence. Too many of those police officers viewed Caribbean Carnival-goers as uncivilized (black) savages who deserved to die, especially because their Carib[being] behavior was seen as a threat to the rest of the city (johnd7463 2011). According to these police officers, the uncivilized, "disgraceful," "disgusting behavior" of winin' Caribbean revelers should be reason enough not only to stop serving and protecting this community and its people but also to end the Carnival in its entirety (johnd7463 2011).

Contrary to my version ah tings, the New York City police and the media both donned colonizing lenses as they misrecognized the work of Carib[being] ness as a sign of antiblack fatality. According to many local new stations, a recap of the Carnival consisted of the total number of stabbings, shootings, and killings that had occurred by the completion of Monday's festivities. In fact, countless news outlets reported that the year's festivities were "marred by violence" (*Huffington Post* 2011a). Journalists' use of such phrases as "the parade-related shootings," "gun battle," "terror-filled," and "bloodshed" worked to retranslate or rather recode my version ah tings (Burke et al. 2011). In a 2012 interview, the then president of the West Indian American Day Carnival Association (WIADCA), Thomas Bailey, commented on this recoding: "You have statements like the carnival was very colorful, with beautiful weather and a large crowd, but it was marred by three murders, then you look at the murders and there was one in the Bronx, one in Queens, one in Yonkers" (Richardson 2012). Bailey's assessment is a general sentiment not specifically about the 2011 Brooklyn Carnival but rather about how the media discusses the Carnival in relation to all the violence that takes place throughout New York City every Labor Day. For instance, of the sixty-seven shootings and thirteen homicides originally reported in relation to the 2011 Brooklyn Carnival, the actual violence that took place in the vicinity of the parade route resulted in three deaths, three gun-related wounds, and one stabbing, none of which I witnessed or felt while on di road (Burke et al. 2011).

Fundamentally, the winin' Caribbean body remains inextricably marked as the border against which violence is both produced and deflected. Because these bordered tensions must be negotiated with each wine, winers' public displays of erotic agency and cultural pride on di road further implicate their pursuit of pleasure as yet another border that is in need of being policed. In her discussion of Trinidad's relationship to Carnival as a representation of the nation itself, Patricia De Freitas defines nations as "bounded entities which require the constructing and policing of borders. . . . 'Soft' borders," she continues, "are easily penetrable while 'hard' borders maintain the integrity of the Self-Other distinction" (1999, 13). From this perspective, winin' on di road positions men and women as the feminized "soft borders" between the US national "Self" and the Caribbean "Self" that threaten the limits of Western civility.[2] On the other hand, the NYPD, which was both embodying and policing the metal barriers along the Carnival route, represented the "hard" US border that my friends and I serendipitously slipped through in my version ah tings.

Although the NYPD demands that the spectators' space (the sidewalk) and the masqueraders' space (the street) be separated by a metal barrier, the Carib[being] masquerader knows that during a Trinidadian-style Carnival the wine has no boundaries. Both masqueraders and spectators have permission to "misbehave" and "get on bad," which includes blurring the lines between chaos and order, spectacle (participating) and spectator (watching), or appropriate (winin') and inappropriate (nonwinin') behavior. On di road, one has unspoken permission to wine up, down, around, in between, and through anything and everything, whether it be still, moving, nonhuman, inanimate, or even off-limits. As a result, Caribbean winers strategically mediate the very palpable tension between their own desires to wine and "misbehave" in public and the tendency of the policing gaze (a colonizing gaze) to control such performances of Carib[being]ness by recoding their winery as markers of violent blackness, savagery, and fatality. A winer's pursuit of pleasure, therefore, becomes dependent on whom or what one wines up with or on. The said difference between winin' *on* versus winin' *with* a partner is permission. If someone does not give their permission for you to wine "with" them, you are said to be winin' "on" them, as they are not willing participants. This is also known as *tiefin'* (read: stealing) a wine. Most of the time, however, such interactions are playful and easily forgiven. Using this distinction, the next section analyzes the "dagger" (a thrusting hip movement) that went viral.[3]

Another Version ah Tings

When the Carnival jumbie jumps out and possesses an onlooker, the possession can very easily come in the form of a winin' bottom, which is exactly what happened to many on-duty police officers standing along the Carnival route. One, however, was caught on video indulging in the intoxication of the day's winery and soca music. One week later, the video was posted on WorldStarHipHop .com, a popular entertainment media outlet that especially targets young black urban audiences, under the title "NY Cops Wilding Out on Labor Day 2011: Daggering on the Parkway! (Grinding and All)." The internet quickly went into a frenzy, and the video went viral. From Facebook to the *New York Post*, everyone seemed to have an opinion about the officer's candid dancing, caught on tape. As a result of the scandalous attention, the NYPD launched an investigation of the events to see if the officers broke any codes of conduct (Gardiner 2011; Doll 2011). However, unlike the video itself, the actual investigation was downplayed and almost dismissed by then police commissioner Ray Kelly. And although none of the officers lost their jobs (*Huffington Post* 2011b), the NYPD banned all patrolling officers from winin' with masqueraders in the future (Tyson 2017).

The original video clip shows four white male police officers standing along the Carnival route in full uniform being approached throughout the day by several female Afro-Caribbean masqueraders hoping to tief a wine or two from the officers. Looking at these women's faces in the film, I could tell they had intentions to "cause trouble" or, rather, to mash up those police officers with some wais'line thunda. For example, two of the women, both of whom were wearing green bikini-style costumes, looked at the officer with their heads tilting downward while their eyes stared directly at the officer, as if to playfully say, "I'm doing something naughty." One of them even winked at him as she flicked a button on his shirt. In casual conversation with an NYPD officer, I was told that although it was okay to wine and enjoy the festivities then, their rule of thumb was to limit their dancing with masqueraders (Tyson 2017).

However, as the video revealed, one officer in particular went above and beyond the call of duty that day. In the video, every time a winin' woman approached him, he would thrust his crotch into her gyrating behind. At times, he daggered so hard that he would then have to hold on to the winin' masquerader's hips or lower back to maintain his own balance and momentum. At one point, he even stepped over one woman's legs to widen his stance and meet her challenge to drop down low to the ground. Even though he was unable to actually roll his waistline in rhythm and time with each masquerader, his thrusting ability to engage with each winer blurred the line between spectator and spectacle. Within these almost fleeting, yet spectacular, moments—specifically when the officer's and a masquerader's sweaty labor of and for pleasure came together on di road—an important space of intimacy was forged.

As each winin' Afro-Caribbean female masquerader and her dance partner—a white male police officer—pressed their bodies against each other, the intimacy created in those moments allowed everyone involved, including the witnesses, to *un*learn the living memories of mistrust generated by long histories of perpetual crime and police brutality in that particular neighborhood. In other words, the work it took for these ladies to mash up di streets wit' their wais'line thunda was not only evident but also successful. For it was within those particular moments of public intimacy that their winery became acts of *un*raveling colonization. With each roll and thrust of the women's waistlines, this particular cop was no longer seen as an enforcer of white supremacist laws and values legally perpetuated within the United States, nor did he continue to represent the personification of antiblack racist oppression. Instead, under the public gaze of those witnessing these moments of winery, the power dynamics between the two dancing bodies began to shift. For the officer, his pursuit of pleasure literally became dependent upon and tied to the pleasure of his winin' partner. In fact, when some of the winin' masqueraders pushed back on him, he quickly learned that he needed to push back on them with an equal amount of force for both of them to maintain balance. In those brief moments, their winin' bodies worked in tandem to mash up the antiblack racist practices propagated within that neighborhood, forging a counterhegemonic intimacy that was experienced at the level of the body and deciphered throughout cyberspace.

During these wined choreographies, Caribbean masqueraders were literally able to use their bodies and push back against the racist ideologies of black savagery as propagated by the Facebook group. Many commentaries on the posted video ("NY Cops Wilding Out") echoed a similar sentiment:

BREE-BREE (September 3, 2012): gah headddd nypd . . . finally see them acting like humans . . . i love itttt!

JOSHUA (January 17, 2012): see cops aren't so bad.

DWAYNE LEE (November 8, 2011): It's a lose lose situation it seems. . . . Police don't bend, people say no community spirit. . . . They have fun & go with it, then they not doing their jobs!!! WTF Everybody there looked safe & community looked pleased. job well done!!! (john7463 2011)

In that finite moment of winin' revelry, that cop was seen as human, as down to earth, or, as a few of the masqueraders said aloud as they laughed and high-fived him, "Yuh gud, yuh gud, yuh gud." In this case, this expression loosely translates to "you're cool with us."

Notwithstanding, there was another side of intimacy brought into the light during these winin' sessions. Among Trinidadians the phrase "yuh gud" can also mean "you've had enough," which can then be applied as a question or an assumption. After reviewing the clip, I realized that the masquerader quoted above was not implying that the police officer should stop daggering because his white patriarchal colonizing desire for dancing black female bodies should have been more than satisfied at that point. On the contrary, this Afro-Caribbean woman, implying that the cop was "cool with her," even went as far as to pat the officer on his shoulder. However, as she repeated the phrase, I became painfully aware of my discomfort in watching his thrusting crotch on a webpage that did not contextualize the space, energy, or purpose of Carnival. In my version ah tings, I did not see the officers from the video get wined on. I did, however, see other officers being approached and indulging in the day's winery every now and again. However, outside the context of Carnival itself (i.e., cyberspace), there were a few of the officer's vigorous daggers that actually made me worry about the safety of each of his winin' partners. Although this type of daggering never lasted more than a handful of thrusts, when his dancing became too hard to watch, I became painfully aware of his whiteness, his maleness, and his colonizing gaze.

As winers perform and embody Carib[being]ness on di Eastern Parkway, the link between violence and the black female body continually haunts their attempts to take up public space. Even in these moments of intimacy, winin' Caribbean women are always already left to confront the potential for institutionalized, gendered, and racial violence that continually presses against their black dancing bodies. This particular interplay of racialized desire and power is also a residual effect of the colonial encounter. The white man's desire for the black woman's flesh remains tainted by a long history of desire and violence (Young 1995). Consequently, the uneven power dynamic between the white male and the black female perpetuates an abusive relationship between the two. In fact, a few of the commentaries for the posted video, "NY Cops Wilding Out," addressed the racialized and sexualized tension between the black dancing women and the white male officer:

SHAKINGMYHEADD (January 24, 2012): They wanna piece of that chocolate loving lmao.

GUEST (September 24, 2011): everybody know the jacks love black p*ssy, slave masters had no problem raping their women slaves then hangin the men . . . like styles said i know u scared of me mister but you dont really seem to be

scared of my sister . . . in a couple weeks those f***in craker nypd prolly will
be shootin down a black man . . . s*** is crazy son (john7463 2011).

Regarding the semantics of daggering, when a woman is being daggered by
a man, the thrusting can become so forceful that she may lose her balance,
or, at the very least, her own winin' rhythm gets viciously disrupted. In these
moments, the police officer and the winin' masquerader were no longer dancing with each other; instead, he was winin' on her. As a result, some of the
women's rhythmic wiggles and jiggles became dominated by the officer's
thrusting body. My point here is that as practiced, each wined moment does
not represent a universal or utopian sentiment of harmony, trust, or cultural
understanding, especially when considering the precarious position of the
black dancing woman in public. To use the words of Caribbean literary scholar
Faith Smith, "*Intimacy* implies a colonizing gaze as much as anything else"
(2011, 201). In addition to forging counterhegemonic intimacies, the intimacy
forged while winin' can also solidify "a naturalization of what [would] otherwise [be] understood as a violation" (202). Taking this into account, these
thrusting moments reveal the microscopic cultural chafing that occurs when
dancing bodies from different historical and cultural traditions crash into one
another in public.

Afterthoughts on "My Version ah Tings"

In a poll entitled "Should the city cancel the annual West Indian Day Parade?"
posted a day after the 2011 Labor Day Carnival, 60 percent of the respon-
dents voted "No. The vast majority of parade participants have a fantastic
time and do not cause any trouble. They shouldn't lose out because of a few
bad apples" (*Crain's New York Business* 2011). In spite of the violence and the
stilting attempts to colonize the winin' body, winers' relentless desire to maintain a space where Caribbean people can gather and experience themselves as
Carib[being]s further substantiates the importance of embodying pleasure in
the face of fatalism. Caribbean winers' visceral and affective understanding of
blackness and Carib[being]ness gravely differs from the US racial constructions
imposed on their bodies. Thus, Caribbeans' participation in the Trinidadian-
style Carnival allows them to blur the imagined boundaries that define blackness, who or what is foreign and native, and where pleasure can or cannot
be reclaimed. Because masqueraders' winery not only teases foreigners' and
locals' senses alike with promises of unabashed naughtiness and unpoliced
pleasure in the Caribbean, each wine also projects back toward the foreign US
homeland these same exotic promises, which were also seen as threats (by the

NYPD) to US civility. And as these projections play out on the streets abroad, Caribbean winers further fall victim to and play into the national and cultural regulations, translations, and contradictions that reside along the chafing borders of colonization and decolonization.

Throughout this essay, my intention has been to highlight the mundane, intimate, and spectacular ways Caribbeans use their winery to push against, renegotiate, or undermine the overlapping tensions that circumscribe their gyrating bodies within the Trinidadian-style Carnival held in Brooklyn. In taking up public space, especially under the colonizing gaze of the NYPD, winin' women both literally and figuratively push their bodies against the barriers that seek to uphold the gnarled history of trauma and violence branded onto the black dancing female body. For it was on the auction block that the black woman lost the right to claim her own body, where she was sexualized and constructed as public property. Because her disembodied hypervisibility became a necessary part of her racial and gendered existence, it is both necessary and radical for the black dancing woman to take up public space. Ultimately, these very public streets must be the space where she reclaims her right to life, liberty, and the pursuit of happiness—or, in this case, the pursuit of pleasure—if she intends to be seen in all of her complexity.

Notes

1. This is an annual international music competition held in Port of Spain, Trinidad. For more information, see "International Soca Monarch: Home," *Caribbean Prestige Foundation* (2013), www.socamonarch.net/home/ (accessed March 14, 2015).

2. Note that I am using this concept of the "Self" hermeneutically, as the Caribbean is *not* a nation or even a homogeneous community with a homogeneous identity or "Self." My intention here is to convey the ways in which Caribbean people's identities get homogenized within the US imagination *as if* the Caribbean is one place. Literary Caribbeanist Silvio Torres-Saillant explains that within the United States there is a rule of homogeneity, "the presumption that we have one root, not many, [such] that . . . to claim more than one origin is to be less" (2009, 14). For instance, in representing my own Trinidadianness during Carnival, I simultaneously represent a homogenized comprehension of "The Caribbean" to the US colonizing gaze.

3. Daggering is a dance style derived from Jamaica's dance hall culture in which the man thrusts his crotch vigorously into his dance partner's butt (who is always expected to be a woman). The thrusting is usually so daring—sometimes men jump from high heights to meet their dance partner's hip and/or butt cheeks—and so brutal that women must often brace themselves in anticipation of the forceful impact of each thrust. The word itself literally means "to stab," but it is often used to mean "fucking." In the Trinidadian-style Carnival context, daggering is often reinterpreted as a thrusting type of wine known as jukkin'. Because my research focuses on winin' that is

contextualized by soca music and Trinidadian-style Carnivals, this essay does not unravel the complex gendered, racial, and sexual elements of this particular dance style from a Jamaican dance hall point of view.

Works Cited

Burke, Kerry, et al. 2011. "Two Cops Shot in Brooklyn Gun Battle, Caps Terror-Filled NYC Labor Day Weekend of Shootings." *New York Daily News,* September 6. http://nydn.us/1Dza97v.

Crain's New York Business. 2011. "Should the City Cancel the Annual West Indian Day Parade?" September 6. http://mycrains.crainsnewyork.com/blogs/polls/2011/09/should-the-city-cancel-the-annual-west-indian-day-parade/.

De Freitas, Patricia A. 1999. "Disrupting 'the Nation': Gender Transformations in the Trinidad Carnival." *New West Indian Guide / Nieuwe West-Indische Gids* 73 (1–2): 5–34.

Doll, Jen. 2011. "NYPD Investigated for Excessive Use of Dance at the West Indian Day Parade." *Village Voice,* September 13. www.villagevoice.com/news/nypd-investigated-for-excessive-use-of-dance-at-the-west-indian-day-parade-6710283.

Fleetwood, Nicole R. 2011. *Troubling Vision: Performance, Visuality, and Blackness.* Chicago: University of Chicago Press.

Gardiner, Sean. 2011. "Dancing Cops Draw NYPD Investigation." *Wall Street Journal,* September 13. http://blogs.wsj.com/metropolis/2011/09/13/dancing-cops-draw-nypd-investigation/?mod=WSJBlog.

Glaberson, William. 2011. "N.Y.C. Police Maligned Paradegoers on Facebook." *New York Times,* December 5. www.nytimes.com/2011/12/06/nyregion/on-facebook-nypd-officers-malign-west-indian-paradegoers.html.

Gottschild, Brenda Dixon. 2003. *The Black Dancing Body: A Geography from Coon to Cool.* New York: Palgrave Macmillan.

Huffington Post. 2011a. "2011 West Indian Day Parade Marred by Violence." December 6. http://www.huffingtonpost.com/2011/09/06/west-indian-day-parade-2011_n_950135.html.

———. 2011b. "Mayor Bloomberg, Commissioner Kelly OK with Dirty Dancing Cops at West Indian Day Parade." September 14. http://www.huffingtonpost.com/2011/09/14/mayor-bloomberg-commissio_n_961918.html.

johnd7463. 2011. "No More West Indian Day Detail." *Scribd, Inc.* September 7. https://www.scribd.com/doc/74938745/No-More-West-Indian-Day-Detail-9-7-11-612-Pm.

Jones, Adanna Kai. 2016. "Can Rihanna Have Her Cake and Eat It Too? A Schizophrenic Search for Resistance within the Screened Spectacles of a Winin' Fatale." In *The Oxford Handbook of Screendance Studies,* edited by Douglas Rosenberg, 1–23. New York: Oxford University Press.

Mathias, Christopher. 2011. "NYPD Group, 'No More West Indian Day Parade Detail,' Calls Paradegoers 'Animals,' 'Savages.'" *Huffington Post,* December 6. http://www.huffingtonpost.com/2011/12/06/nypd-group-no-more-west-i_n_1131830.html.

Mendes, John, ed. 2012. *Côté ci Côté la: Trinidad and Tobago Dictionary (The Signature Edition).* Port of Spain: Zenith Services, Ltd.

Morgan, Joan. 2015. "Why We Get Off: Moving towards a Black Feminist Politics of Pleasure." *Black Scholar* 45 (4): 36–46.

Noel, Samantha A. 2010. "De Jamette in We: Redefining Performance in Contemporary Trinidad Carnival." *Small Axe* 14, no. 1 (31): 60–78.

"NY Cops Wilding Out on Labor Day 2011: Daggering on the Parkway! (Grinding and All)." 2011. *WorldStarHipHop.com.* September 12. www.worldstarhiphop.com/videos/video.php?v=wshh119k832Gb7nAfp16.

Richardson, Clem. 2012. "Murder, They Wrote, Was Caused by the West Indian Day Carnival; Not So, Say Parade Organizers." *New York Daily News*, August 27. http://www.nydailynews.com/new-york/brooklyn/murder-wrote-caused-west-indian-day-carnival-not-parade-organizers-article-1.1144860.

Roberts, Arlene M. 2012. "The West Indian Day Parade: An Island Woman's Perspective." *Huffington Post*, February 7. http://www.huffingtonpost.com/arlene-m-roberts/the-west-indian-day-parad_b_1133643.html.

Smith, Faith. 2011. "'Only His Hat Is Left': Resituating Not-Yet Narratives." *Small Axe* 35, no. 2 (35): 197–208.

Torres-Saillant, Silvio. 2009. "One and Divisible: Meditations on Global Blackness." *Small Axe* 13, no. 2: 4–25.

Tyson, Fitzalbert Roy, Jr. (NYPD patrol officer). 2017. In conversation with the author via text messaging. July 30.

Young, Robert J. C. 1995. *Colonial Desire: Hybridity in Theory, Culture, and Race.* New York: Routledge.

Sites

The essays in this section examine how spaces and places—cities, neighborhoods, museums, theaters—always carry meanings of their own and how bodies in motion configure and reconfigure these meanings. How do the hyperlocal connotations of second lining in New Orleans's black neighborhoods alter when artists adapt the form for theatrical stages? What happens when dance enters the museum? How does what is commonly called "site-specific performance" reveal the choreography of urban geography and why does it matter?

In "Second Line Choreographies in and beyond New Orleans" Rachel Carrico looks at how three choreographers incorporated second lining into stage works after Katrina. Camille A. Brown created *New Second Line* (2006) just a year after Katrina, prompted by the experiences of two of her dancers whose families were impacted by the hurricane and its aftermath. Much like a jazz funeral, *New Second Line* moves from mourning to celebration, underscoring the dance's "capacity for spiritual healing and community building." In 2009 Jawole Zollar, artistic director of Urban Bush Women, revised *Shelter*, a work originally created in response to homelessness in New York City, in order to also allude to Katrina. The most significant change came with the addition of second lining at the end—an addition that electrified the opening-night audience in New Orleans and one which closes the work with what Carrico defines as "defiant hope." In 2013 Latanya d. Tigner contributed her precise re-creation of second lining, titled *St. Ann and North Rampart Street*, to a suite of works, *Down the Congo Line: The Rhythms of Life*, premiered by Dimensions Dance Theater in San Francisco. Other sections are set in Cuba, Brazil, and Congo, and within this context the company's second lining suggests the multiple sites of the African diaspora. Rather than recycle the binary of appropriation and authenticity often applied to theatrical adaptations of social and popular dance, Carrico argues that each choreographer highlights one of the several functions of second lining. Thus their works engage with the city of New Orleans as port and portal—a port through which many African peoples entered the United States and a portal through which their descendants and contemporary publics can experience the power and resilience of black expressive culture.

While Carrico follows the transfer of second lining from the street to the concert stage, Amanda Jane Graham follows the transfer of modern dance from the private studio and commercial theater to the public museum. In "The Dance in the Museum: Grant Hyde Code and the Brooklyn Museum Dance Center" Graham recovers a three-year experiment in the late 1930s when Grant Hyde Code founded a center for dance training and production at the Brooklyn Museum. Funded partly by the Works Progress Administration, the Dance Center offered free classes for youth and adults and free lecture-demonstrations and performances. Code also cocurated an exhibit, *The Dance in Art*, that featured works by immigrant, first-generation, and Indigenous artists. In all these ways, the Dance Center participated in leftist culture, promoting access to the arts, fair compensation for artists' labor, and an expansive view of American culture. Graham considers the Dance Center's "bilateral emphasis on aesthetic innovation and social concerns . . . an aspirational but realistic model for museums today." She also views the Dance Center as a starting point for future initiatives integrating dance into museum spaces, from *An Evening on American Dance* at the Museum of Modern Art (MoMA) in 1948 to the landmark exhibit *Judson Dance Theater: The Work Is Never Done* at MoMA seventy years later.

In "Dancing the Image: Virgilio Sieni's Choreographic Tableaux" Giulia Vittori focuses on one of many instances of contemporary dance in European museums. Her case study, *Vangelo secondo Matteo* (Gospel of Matthew), was staged at the Gallerie dell'Arsenale, a former shipbuilding complex now used as exhibition space for the Venice Biennale. As part of the Dance Biennale in 2014, artistic director and choreographer Virgilio Sieni created the work for more than 150 dancers, many nonprofessionals. Divided into three cycles of nine dances, these twenty-seven choreographic tableaux make reference to tropes from Matthew and to iconography from Renaissance painting illustrating these tropes. Zeroing in on two of the tableaux performed by professional dancers, "Pietà" and "Pietà-Deposition," Vittori describes Sieni's method of "figural dance," an approach to choreography that indexes iconic gestures in Renaissance painting but that mutates the meanings of the gestures through embodiment. In defining figural dance, Vittori turns to Giorgio Agamben's writing about gesture. In fact, Sieni had collaborated with Agamben a few years before creating *Vangelo secondo Matteo*, one of several recent collaborations between a contemporary choreographer and a philosopher in Europe. Similar to how Laura

Karreman turns to Luce Irigaray to illuminate Anne Teresa De Keersmaeker's *My Breathing Is My Dancing*, Vittori demonstrates the interdependence of philosophy and performance as topic and method for dance studies.

While Vittori recalls Karreman, Alana Gerecke recalls Adanna Kai Jones's autoethnographic method in her essay, "Sidewalk Choreographies: The Politics of Moving Along in Battery Opera's *Lives Were Around Me*." Having herself performed with Battery Opera in other works, Gerecke describes her role as spectator for *Lives Were Around Me* (2009), a site-specific work in which guides from Battery Opera led three or four spectators from a local pub to a street corner a few blocks away in the neighborhood called Downtown Eastside (DTES) in Vancouver. In 2009 DTES was a severely underresourced neighborhood just starting to gentrify, and the performances subverted the conventions of a "walking tour": the guides gave neither clear directions nor coherent narratives; hence the spectators became aware of their "physical lexicon . . . scored around ambivalence, confusion, and unease." This in turn made them aware of the "sidewalk ballet" theorized by Vancouver geographer Nicholas Blomley, his expression for how the design of urban sidewalks facilitates middle-class commuting, an imperative to "move along" that criminalizes alternate use of the sidewalk such as a space for socializing or sleeping. In the end, Gerecke concludes that *Lives Were Around Me* "magnifies the various choreographies that structure Vancouver's DTES even as it also reenacts the exploitation it seeks to critique."

Like Carrico and Vittori, Gerecke is intimately familiar with the place and the choreography shaping her case study. Carrico, herself a second liner, interviewed the choreographers for all three works she describes in her essay. Vittori also interviewed Sieni and attended the final three weeks of rehearsal and performances of *Vangelo secondo Matteo*. Is such direct access necessary in order to probe the intersection of space, place, and dance? Not necessarily, for Graham shows that careful archival research also can recover the meanings of this intersection. In the past and in the present, bodies in motion are continually negotiating meanings in tandem with space and place.

Second Line Choreographies in and beyond New Orleans

RACHEL CARRICO

For more than one hundred years, brass bands have gathered crowds of people to dance through the streets of New Orleans's African American and Afro-Creole neighborhoods in processions known as second lines. Today, second lines accompany many occasions, including weddings and music festivals, but are rooted in mourning death, celebrating life, and claiming a community's home. Thus, after the Katrina disaster in 2005, many black New Orleanians second lined to grieve, rejoice, and declare ownership of their contested city.

This essay follows second line dancing as it moved beyond New Orleans's streets during the post-Katrina years, when three African American female choreographers adapted second lining for the concert stage: Camille A. Brown and Jawole Willa Jo Zollar, both in New York City, and Oakland-based Latanya d. Tigner. When Hurricane Katrina made landfall, these women—although at different stages in their careers—were already making deeply researched, ensemble-created dances that probed histories of racism and resistance in the African diaspora. In different ways, their responses to Katrina (re)shape cultural memory of the event. Each work presents a respect for second lining's unique form, but the artists are more concerned with its functions. They invite audiences worldwide to experience the parades' capacity to generate spiritual healing, issue social critiques, and strengthen communal ties. Their works address how Katrina's impacts spread far beyond the flood lines to force a reckoning with US histories of racism.

In and beyond the Flood Lines

In order to understand the choreographers' street-to-stage processes, it is important to historicize second lines within the post-Katrina context. For more than a century, black benevolent societies, known today as a social aid and pleasure clubs, have employed brass bands to accompany their anniversary parades and members' funerals (Malone 1996, 167–86). The musicians and club members form the first line. The event's name comes from the second line of paraders who follow the band. Second line also denotes the improvised dance form showcased, which encompasses forward-moving footwork and "buck-jumping," or high-energy drops and leaps.

Second lining was one of many living traditions threatened by the devastation of New Orleans in 2005. Even though the region's black culture was lauded as a reason to rebuild, resources were repeatedly denied the African Americans who maintain the culture (Carrico 2013). The city's poorest residents, many of them African American, received few means to evacuate before Hurricane Katrina's landfall. Days after the levees were breached, rescue teams dispersed stranded victims to far-flung locations, tearing families and social networks apart. During the recovery, policies and economic decisions systematically blocked the road home for the disenfranchised (Adams 2013). As some social aid and pleasure club members began to rebuild their homes and lives, they organized parades to bring pained communities together and give displaced neighbors a reason to come home, if only for a weekend. When excluded from rebuilding plans, second liners performatively insisted upon their right to return and, more fundamentally, their humanity (Johnson 2010).

Katrina's impact rippled far beyond the Gulf Coast, and just as losses split along race lines in New Orleans, so did affective impacts nationwide. Initial media coverage characterized victims as criminals and framed the situation as an urban insurgency rather than a catastrophe (Tierney, Bevc, and Kuligowski 2006). This media coverage made a deeper emotional impact on African Americans than white Americans (Harris-Lacewell 2008, 164–65). Katrina and its representations revealed the enduring legacies of US slavery and contemporary ideologies about race, citizenship, and social value.

In this political climate, three US dance artists intervened into national conversations about Katrina. Camille A. Brown and Dancers created *New Second Line* (2006); Jawole Willa Jo Zollar's Urban Bush Women restaged a twenty-year-old classic, *Shelter* (2008); and Latanya d. Tigner choreographed *St. Ann and North Rampart Street* (2013) for Dimensions Dance Theater. Dancers utilized the concert stage to tell the story of black New Orleans to multiracial audiences in New York City, the San Francisco Bay Area, and cities in between. Additionally, Urban Bush Women performed *Shelter* in New Orleans before touring it across the United States and Europe. All three companies continue to perform these works in prestigious theaters, on college campuses, at arts festivals, and onscreen.[1] They articulate the histories of black New Orleanians that have been either obscured by media images of dysfunction and danger or romanticized in narratives of the city's cultural significance. Furthermore, each artist incorporates second lining into her choreography, not only sharing a story about New Orleans but also inviting audiences to participate in it. When the trumpet sounds, everyone is invited to heal from the disaster's trauma and understand a dimension of Katrina not portrayed in media accounts.

Notably, none of these choreographers is from nor based in New Orleans. Jawole Zollar was aware that her artistic response to Katrina could have been received as appropriative. Soon after the floodwaters receded, a number of East Coast foundations subsidized high-profile theater and visual art events in New Orleans that included local artists but featured well-known outsiders (Decter 2009, 28). Some New Orleans artists rightly wondered why such resources were not funneled directly to them (Michna 2013, 63). This gave Zollar pause. She "felt like it was a risky decision" to add a piece about Katrina to her company's repertoire, but at the same time, she trusted that she and her dancers "were in an authentic place" (Zollar 2014).

What should we make of Brown, Zollar, and Tigner—East and West Coast choreographers—responding to Katrina through staged second lining? Second lining is, after all, profoundly rooted in place. As the procession moves through carefully chosen streets and pauses at locations significant to club members, it documents neighborhood histories. Simultaneously, second lining's symbolism often connects the local with the global. One group signals second lining's West African origins by wearing suits custom-made from kente cloth, while other clubs design outfits in step with the latest hip hop fashions. Some clubs hold funeral processions for prominent black figures, such as Michael Jackson and Nelson Mandela, associating neighborhood culture and fights for freedom with celebrities and global leaders. Second lines thus enact both a collective local memory and a global present to resist traditional narratives of New Orleans as geographically isolated or stuck in a romanticized past (Richardson 2007, 261n22).

Brown, Zollar, and Tigner have produced similar local/global enactments by situating New Orleanians' struggles and creative pathways to recovery within an expansive geography of cultural memory (Cahill-Booth 2013, 90). They engage with New Orleans as both port and portal: the port through which many enslaved Africans entered North America, and the portal through which their dispersed descendants make contact with them and their homelands. As detailed below, each work's development relied on the artists' sustained investments of time, resources, and personal relationships in southeast Louisiana. Yet the performances illustrate that physical travel is not necessary to enter New Orleans's portal; the place is regularly re-membered through imaginative and spiritual journeys (Cahill-Booth 2013). All three choreographies expand and extend the city's borders into psychosocial terrains of the past, present, and future. These terrains, within and beyond the flood lines, mark the co-ordinates of what Zollar calls an "authentic place."

These works' authenticity does not hinge upon faithful reproductions of an original; instead, that authenticity indexes the artists' commitment to sensitive witnessing. The artist as witness accepts the dangers and responsibilities of acting (or dancing) on what she has seen and in her performance makes witnesses of others (Taylor 2003, 211). These choreographers do not simply re-create second lining's *form* for viewing pleasure; instead, they invite onlookers to join in second lining's *functions* as a spiritual ritual, a venue for social critique, and a mechanism for building solidarity. The artists' authenticity includes not only personal commitments to individual New Orleanians but also ongoing artistic commitments to dance as witness to the pain and perseverance of the African Atlantic diaspora. By including New Orleans in their bodies of work, they ask their audiences, regardless of race or origin, to remember Katrina not only as a singular tragedy in one location but also as an accumulation of violent histories within the circum-Atlantic sphere. Furthermore, they locate second lining at the heart of the African Atlantic diaspora's creative resistance to violence. Like second lines on the street, these onstage second lines dissolve the line between performer and audience, inviting all present to share in the parade's multiple capacities for healing, protesting, and communing.

Camille A. Brown's *New Second Line*

In 2006, while parts of New Orleans were beginning to recover, New York–based choreographer Camille A. Brown choreographed *New Second Line* to create a venue for healing in the way that New Orleanians have done for generations: by dancing to brass band music. Brown was connected to the disaster through two of her closest friends and fellow dancers, Francine Ott and Clarice Young, whose families are located in southeast Louisiana and were personally impacted by the storm (Brown 2013). When Brown was commissioned to create a piece for the Reflections Dance Company in Washington, DC, she sifted through records in her uncle's basement and found a 2001 LP recording of the brass band classic "New Second Line," which became her soundtrack and title.[2] Brown defines second lining as "praise dance, honoring a past, celebrating culture, history, tradition," and "a celebration of the spirit" (2013). *New Second Line* could be described in precisely those terms. Brown's choreography taps into the heart of *why* New Orleanians second line: to access spiritual transcendence in community as a recourse for survival and resistance.

Accompanied by a musical dirge, five dancers enter carrying umbrellas and holding handkerchiefs.[3] They hunch over, step slowly, and wipe their eyes. Their procession ceases just left of center stage, when two dancers kneel and touch the ground, as if scooping up a handful of dirt. Behind them, the projected photo of a young boy playing a full-sized trombone fills the entire cyclorama, the first in a series of nine photographs by Moses Ball that accompany the eight-minute piece. One woman steps away from the group. Softly, she squats, brushes her thighs, and pats the air with flat palms, shifting from right to left. A tuba begins to pulse through the sound system. Trumpeter Kermit Ruffins chants: "Work it out! Work it out! . . . Second line, second line!" As the horn section swings in, the dancer repeats the sequence, stretching farther and accenting sharper. The other four dancers join in, losing the props as they move into unison. Legs wide and knees bent, they execute syncopated step-touches and compact tuck-jumps as arms swing and wrists flap, all while gazing intently at the audience.

New Second Line reflects the temporal structure of a jazz funeral, in which celebration follows mourning. Much like the vernacular tradition, Brown does not abandon the mourning once the celebration begins but presents dirge stepping and buckjumping as interconnected paths to spiritual experiences. The group executes percussive movements while one woman pauses in the middle of the action. She reaches behind her, palm braced as if to stop an encroaching force. Two dancers lie on their backs and slowly push themselves

FIGURE 18. Camille A. Brown and Dancers, featuring Keon Thoulouis (*center*) and Francine E. Ott (*right*), in *New Second Line*. (Photo by Christopher Duggan, courtesy Camille A. Brown and Dancers)

in a circle with their feet, providing quiet contrast to the others who leap and stretch. A male dancer kneels down once more to touch the ground, seemingly oblivious to the kinetic frenzy around him. These stilled moments, glimpsed amid energetic movement, keep the dirge alive in the second line.

Brown only had a week to put the piece together with the twelve-member Reflections ensemble in 2006, but she dug into it with her newly formed company, Camille A. Brown and Dancers (CABD), a year later (Brown 2013). As CABD members and Louisiana natives, Francine Ott and Clarice Young were integral to the process. They held many discussions with their fellow company members to relate second lining to the dancers' experiences. As Ott explained, "One of the dancers is from Trinidad," so they made connections between the two cultures (2013). For dancer Juel D. Lane, the connection was more personal than cultural, and the piece became a way to pay homage to "loved ones that have transitioned" (2014). Discussions allowed the dancers to infuse the movement with personal meaning. At the same time, the process also required them to master second lining's specific movement vocabulary. It's a fine balance. As Brown still tells her dancers, "It's less about your facility in terms of what we think is technical, but this is a technique as well" (2017). When coaching the movement, Brown, Ott, and Young oscillated between specificity of form and open expression. "Anybody can do the dance," Brown instructed, "but you have to bring your spirit to it, and that's what makes the dance come alive" (2017). Movement coaching often involved refining weight placement. Ott found it easier to teach second lining to those who had experience with African dance in addition to ballet or modern. "Not that, 'Oh, the second line is African dance,'" she explains, "but for people who haven't had any connection with grounded movement or anything, [second lining is] very different." She reflects, "We have a tendency as trained dancers to want to be up. We want to be lifted" as a way to show "we have technique" (2013). But in order to move through spirit, CABD dancers must also find their connection with the earth.

Ott's links between weight, technique, and spirit apply equally to second lining in the studio and street. The second liner must lift her weight away from the earth while grounding that lift with a downward drive, finding a posture that, much like the "get-down" or "ready for anything" stance of many African diaspora dance forms, is both utilitarian and symbolic (Thompson 1979, 44–47; Daniel 2005, 160). Practically, this stance allows dancers to scissor the legs quickly enough to keep up with a fast-moving band and readies the dancer for endless improvisations. Symbolically, it yokes opposites into an interdependent relationship wherein boundaries dissolve: celebration and mourning, life and death, body and spirit, and self and community.

Ott sees the second liner's bodily lift as a signal that she is "letting the spirit move." Simultaneously, "the groundedness of it is staying connected to the people around you" (Ott 2013). CABD members bring individual motivations and histories to *New Second Line*, but they perform it as a community. Ott remembers that during the creation process she, Young, and Brown stressed that genuine interaction "in spirit and in body" was paramount: "We've known each other for a really long time, you know. It was easier to do that, because it was like doing it with your family" (2013). Much like the social aid and pleasure clubs that provide a family-like social network for New Orleanians, CABD reinvigorates dancers' familial relationships each time they second line together.

Given the immediacy with which Brown created *New Second Line*, she could be considered as one of Katrina's first responders. Lara Cahill-Booth uses this term to identify those artists, like Jamaican choreographer Rex Nettleford, whose post-Katrina aid came "in the form of shaping, or reshaping, the cultural memory of the event" (2013, 93). Brown's work offered such aid during the storm's aftermath. Since then, her relationship to New Orleans has changed. In June 2009, while Brown was teaching at the New Orleans Dance Festival, Ott's mother took Brown to the Lower Ninth Ward to show her the devastation still evident four years after the levees broke. She also attended a jazz funeral for Michael Jackson, witnessing a second line parade in situ and in person for the first time. Her perceptions of second lining as praise dance, formed by televised and filmic depictions and later Ott's and Young's descriptions, were confirmed.

New Second Line was one of the first pieces in CABD's repertoire, and as new dancers join the company, Brown asks them to expand the choreography's context beyond Katrina to include more recent assaults on black life, namely, the police killings of African Americans. She reflects, "We think about death and black bodies being shot down and killed, and the mourning that comes with that, the pain, and then the resilience that comes with that, and the celebration of perseverance" (2017). Brown and her dancers understand that second lining's myriad functions—to mourn, gather strength, commune, celebrate, and move through spirit—are not limited to one event or city.

Like all of the works considered here, *New Second Line* places material specific to New Orleans within a broader context. By moving between the groundedness of second lining's funeral mourning and the liftedness of its spiritual celebration, CABD honors the second line's capacity as a vehicle for spiritual transcendence. As first responders, the dancers helped to shape the cultural narrative of Katrina. More than ten years after its premiere, *New Second Line* continues to narrate Katrina by placing it within continuing histories of struggle, legacies of resistance, and the endurance of spirit.

Urban Bush Women's *Shelter*

When Urban Bush Women (UBW) performed their restaged version of *Shelter* in New Orleans on February 5, 2009, they filled the 960-seat Dixon Hall on the campus of Tulane University. The packed house welcomed UBW founder Jawole Willa Jo Zollar onstage for her curtain speech with hearty applause. "Thank you," she said. "This really is home." Zollar explained that New Orleans has a special place in UBW's heart as the first place where they developed their community engagement model: "This is our birth place."

When Zollar first traveled to New Orleans in 1987, she attended several second line parades and jazz funerals. "For me, it was just phenomenal to see the culture and the uniqueness of it," Zollar recalls. "And the dancing was an alive tradition. . . . I was just amazed" (2014). Shortly after this trip, Zollar's four-year-old company premiered *Shelter*, which responded to the homeless epidemic among African Americans and identified UBW as a group that made dance about social justice issues (Curtis and Berryhill 2012). In 1991 Zollar returned to New Orleans with her company to undertake UBW's first residency (Chatterjea 2004, 43; George-Graves 2010, 184–85). After Katrina, Zollar decided to restage *Shelter* as a comment on the displacement caused by the disaster. She also reinvested in UBW's activism in New Orleans by moving the company's annual Summer Leadership Institute from Brooklyn to New Orleans a few months after the premiere of *Shelter* at Dixon Hall.[4]

Upon recounting this story for her New Orleans audience, Zollar offered *Shelter* as a gift: "Ultimately, this piece is about strength, it is about resilience." Gesturing to the seats, she concluded, "This piece is about you and for you. Thank you."

As Zollar exited, the lights faded to black. A tambourine rattled, and a voice rang out through the auditorium's speakers.[5] Zollar chose a track that Wynton Marsalis, one of New Orleans's best-known jazz musicians, recorded during the aftermath of Katrina. Marsalis's tune, "Ring Shout (Peace of Mind)," sailed into a steady beat, tambourine thumping and a chorus of voices singing in call-and-response.[6] The lights gently rose as six dancers walked onstage and lowered into a heap. Once the final woman, Catherine Dénécy, laid her head down, recorded music gave way to the live drumming of Bashir Shakur. Dénécy jerked upright as if she had become aware of some danger. From that moment on, the women were on a constant search for stability, rest, and, above all, high ground.

This opening sequence was one of the few alterations Zollar made to *Shelter* when she remounted it as "the New Orleans version" (Zollar 2014). Originally, the piece started with live percussion and the dancers already huddled onstage.

Significantly, the ending also changed to include second line dancing, as discussed below. Beyond the beginning and end, the choreography changed very little. Marked by relentless relocations, powerful outbursts, and moments of tender care, the movements already reflected the displacement caused by Katrina. Zollar replaced some of the original text by Hattie Gossett and Laurie Carlos with a poem, "nawlins nightmare," written by New Orleanian DeWanda Wise during the 2006 Summer Leadership Institute.[7] By combining existing choreography and percussion with new text and recorded music, Zollar created a haunting comment on, as stated in the program note, "the contemporary and the historical relationship of disempowered people affected by displacement."

One particularly impactful moment occurred when Christine King read the following lines from Wise's poem: "New Orleans don't raise no chumps, so don't victimize me, because I ain't fled nothing; my country fled me." Shakur hit one forceful drumbeat as all dancers dropped into a second-position plié, right arms reaching toward the audience with index fingers extended. In silence, they slowly scanned the audience from house right to left with pointing fingers and unflinching stares.

FIGURE 19. Urban Bush Women featuring (*left to right*) Smantha Spies, Marjani Forté, Paloma McGregor, Bennalldra Williams, Catherine Dénécy, Maria Bauman, and Keisha Turner in their New Orleans version of *Shelter*. (Photo by Ayano Hisa, courtesy of Urban Bush Women)

In the original version, the dancers' finger-pointing scan follows the lines from Gossett's poem, "Living on the streets, it's so easy. It could happen to you, too." For Ananya Chatterjea, this text and the gesture destabilize a "comfortable and distanced viewing" of a homeless woman by insisting that we see ourselves in her (2004, 315–16). *Shelter* suggests the precarity that many share, regardless of race, while living under global capitalism. Gossett's poem, for example, mourns the fact that "ill-advised policies and simple greed" threaten all life. At the same time, because the text connects homelessness to the Middle Passage, it insists that African Americans are particularly endangered by threats to literal and figurative homes (Chatterjea 2004, 315–16; George-Graves 2010, 125).

In the New Orleans performance, the dancers' pointing fingers seemed to say many things at once, starting with, "Your country fled you." The gesture also conjured up accusations made against local politicians, developers, business executives, and law enforcement officials who abandoned their fellow residents with "ill-advised policies and simple greed." When performed outside of the Gulf Coast, perhaps UBW's pointing fingers could mean, "You are the country that fled New Orleans." The dancers might also issue a warning, as in the original version: "It could happen to you too." Understanding the restaged *Shelter* through the lens of the original illuminates the piece's connections between Katrina and global mechanizations of neoliberal capitalism. Thus, as UBW toured *Shelter* in the post-Katrina years, they offered a multiplicity of reactions to the disaster: embodied rage, a recognition of shared precarity, pleas for accountability, and a call to action. As they perform it today, their confrontational stance rejects popular post-Katrina discourses that referred to New Orleanians as victims of their own circumstances, blameworthy for their own misfortune, and refugees undeserving of protection.

In *Shelter*'s final moments at Dixon Hall, the dancers entered with rippling lunges, holding white handkerchiefs. When Shakur played a recognizable second line beat, the ensemble grooved to the rhythm while slowly backing offstage, that is, all except Bennalldra Williams, who broke into second line footwork. She bounced on one leg while tapping the other toe out and in, bending forward and waving her handkerchief in the air. She stepped backward with a confident swag, digging a heel in front while pumping her shoulders. As the lights faded, she punctuated her solo with a nod of her head that contrapuntally complemented her footwork.

When Stephanie McKee recalls watching that performance, she wipes tears from her eyes. McKee is a dancer, community organizer, and New Orleans resident who has worked with UBW in many capacities and played a key role in relocating the Summer Leadership Institute. The memory of watching *Shelter* was moving, in no small part, because of whom she was watching it with. "We organized our asses off . . . to make sure that people from the community were present," she said. "And what I remember the most is that you could hear a pin drop" (2014). But when Williams began her second line solo, the audience erupted. McKee "heard somebody say, 'You did that! That's right!' . . . And so it was this beautiful affirmation from community that . . . 'You represented us well.' You know? 'That's our story.'" Williams, who is from Alabama and has learned to second line from family and friends in New Orleans (including McKee), understood the import of her solo. She remembers thinking, "'Let me make sure I can do it the way they taught me'" and not simply for formal precision. "It was more than just second lining. It was like, 'I am the voice right now of millions of people'" (2013). Williams accepted the responsibility of the artist as witness. As UBW toured *Shelter* internationally, she and her fellow dancers reshaped the cultural narrative of Katrina from one of victimization to one of strength and resilience.

UBW's restaged *Shelter* can be characterized by what Chatterjea calls a "politics of defiant hope" (2004, 42). It connects Katrina to structural and historical violence but refuses to victimize those most affected by the levee failures and floods. By tying the forced movement of New Orleanians to 1980s homelessness, Zollar places Katrina-induced displacement within US histories of structural racism. The final image of second lining, handkerchief in hand, asserts the defiant hope that mobilizes black people in New Orleans to take to the streets as a way of claiming home.

Dimensions Dance Theater's
St. Ann and North Rampart Street

All eyes gaze at a darkened stage when a tuba announces itself from the back of the house.[8] Heads turn as lights come up on the aisles and a second line parade moves toward the stage. The San Francisco–based band MJ's Brass Boppers accompanies approximately twenty paraders who high-step their way through the house. The dancers belong to the Oakland-based Dimensions Dance Theater (DDT), but in this moment, they are also members of the Fonktional Equation Social Aid and Pleasure Club. The company created this club for the performance, and, accordingly, they don parade-day accoutrements: color-coordinated blazers, wide-brimmed hats, and sashes (known in New Orleans as streamers). The leader carries a large umbrella emblazoned with DDT, and others carry feathered fans bearing the initials FE. Choreographer turned drum major Latanya d. Tigner brings up the rear, blowing

FIGURE 20. Postcard advertisement for Dimensions Dance Theater's fortieth-anniversary performance featuring *(left to right)* Chelsea Morris, Noah James, Denice Simpson-Braga, and Erik Lee in Latanya d. Tigner's *St. Ann and North Rampart Street*. (Photo by Edward Miller, courtesy of Dimensions Dance Theater)

her whistle in rhythm. The audience responds to the trumpet's call to join, clapping in rhythm and dancing in front of their seats.

Tigner wants her audience to feel swept into a second line parade the way she first encountered one. When Tigner was visiting New Orleans in November 2008, a local friend encouraged her to attend a second line. While growing up in the Bay Area, Tigner had heard about second lines from two of her New Orleans–born dance instructors, including DDT's artistic director, Deborah Vaughan, but she was still unsure of what to expect. She followed her friend's directions to the appointed street corner, only to find a large crowd of people standing around, eating sandwiches, and drinking beers sold by ambulatory vendors. Before too long, Tigner heard a tuba's bass line thump and was subsumed by the river of music and dancing. She soon learned that she was following Original New Orleans Lady Buckjumpers Social Aid and Pleasure Club's annual anniversary parade and emerged hours later and miles away with no idea how to find her car. Tigner recalls that afternoon with wonder: "But just getting swept up in that energy, and seeing people dancing on the crypts and on the cars and the utility workers dancing. . . . [It] was just amazing to me" (2014). Thereafter, she dedicated herself to studying the second line tradition, journeying to New Orleans regularly.

In 2010 Tigner and Vaughan took a research trip to the Democratic Republic of the Congo. Upon their return, Vaughan was inspired to create an evening-length work that traced retentions of Congolese movement in the diaspora. She commissioned pieces by four choreographers, Tigner included, to represent different locations.[9] Vaughan wove it all into a two-hour work complete with live music and spoken word. *Down the Congo Line: The Rhythms of Life* premiered at the Yerba Buena Center for the Arts in San Francisco in October 2013 to celebrate DDT's fortieth anniversary.

The entire suite opens with *The Last Dance*, a funeral procession also choreographed by Tigner. A vocalist sings the hymn "Just a Closer Walk with Thee," accompanied by MJ's Brass Boppers. Dancers rock in the dirge step typical of jazz funeral processions, punctuating their procession with deep, sudden contractions and hands thrust skyward. They carry a six-foot-by-three-foot rectangle of cloth framed with lightweight pipes. It appears to be a coffin when carried and a gravesite when placed on the ground, connecting the funeral processions of New Orleans and the Congo. It is a spiritual, spatial, and historical invocation that positions the continent of Africa and the city of New Orleans as two locations on a diasporic map that spans oceans and centuries. This is not only a celebration of cultural retentions but also a sobering ritual to mourn the retentions' violent conditions of possibility, namely, the transatlantic slave trade, which brought so many Congolese through New Orleans's port. Next, poet Marvin White stands alone onstage. "Dance brings forth history," he reads. "We have not lost anything, because we remember all the moves." With that, DDT takes its audience on a journey through Cuba, Brazil, and Congo before returning to New Orleans via the second line with Tigner's *St. Ann and North Rampart Street*.

The concert references the African diaspora at large and engages a specific segment of it: the post-Katrina diaspora in the Bay Area (*New York Times* 2005; Bliss 2016). Following any performance of *St. Ann and North Rampart Street* with New Orleanians in attendance, Tigner receives text messages and emails that say, "'Thank you. You hit the nail on the head. Thank you. . . . I never knew somebody could put that on the stage like that'" (2016). Dancer Valerie Sanders notices that some audience members leap to their feet as soon as they hear the tuba and imagines that they get "a piece of home . . . that *feels* like home" (2016). Furthermore, the company recognizes that black people from Louisiana had been coming to California long before Katrina, initially fleeing the Jim Crow South (Moore 2000, 45–51, 127–28). In fact, several company members are the descendants of people who undertook this migration. *St. Ann and North Rampart Street* speaks to this diaspora too. Tigner's mission was to embody a dance tradition that many Bay Area residents have heard about but never experienced: "I wanted it to be exact" (2014). With exactitude, Tigner transports people through New Orleans's portal. Each performance re-members New Orleans within an expansive geography of cultural memory.

Tigner and Vaughan included New Orleans in their journey down the Congo line due to the importance of Congo Square. Second liners commonly claim that parading on Sunday afternoons started in the antebellum era, when bondspeople gathered there to play music and dance. Congo Square is widely understood as an incubator for creolized, African-derived cultures that profoundly impacted US culture at large, and its name points to the routes that Kongo-Angolan dance forms have traveled via forced migrations of the transatlantic slave trade (Evans 2011, 47–48; Floyd 2002, 51; Thompson 1983, 131–32). With her funeral and second line processions, Tigner stakes an embodied argument about diasporic routes through and roots in Congo Square.

Once on the stage, Fonktional Equation converts it into a street grid. One group forms a horizontal line, creating a narrow corridor with the lip of the stage. Another group dances through this corridor as if flanked by ropes, with struts spins, heel-to-toe footwork, and high-knee hops. Sometimes Tigner assigns DDT's youth company to carry ropes. Even without them, viewers can imagine a street scene taking shape. When the dancers reach the corridor's end, the imaginary rope line simply pivots—now forming a column stretching from the lip of the stage to the cyclorama—and the dancers continue on, as if rounding the corner from one street to the next. In fact, Tigner asked her dancers to visualize their spatial patterns as a parade route through New Orleans's streets: "I told them, 'Now you're on Claiborne [Avenue], when we turn this corner you're going to be on Orleans [Avenue]'" (2014).

Tigner's emphasis on exactitude expands beyond the dancers' spatial patterns to include their mastery of second lining's movement vocabulary. In rehearsal, Tigner shares insights gained on each trip to New Orleans and supplements her research with videos posted to social media sites by second liners. Meeting her high standards has been both a challenging and a transformative process for the company. Denice Simpson Braga confessed that "the only way I could execute the technique that she wanted was to pull on my black roots, and say, 'OK, well, back at the army base we used to do this,' and then I could connect the two. Otherwise it was just super foreign to me" (2016). Her reflections hold true for many of the dancers in the original cast, who drew upon their various backgrounds in hip hop and other black social dances. Once the company began dancing with a live band, however, things changed. They first took a field trip to see the New Orleans brass band Hot 8 on tour in San Francisco. Then they became regulars at MJ's Brass Boppers' monthly set in Oakland.

Eventually, Tigner brought that band into rehearsals, and, as dancer Erik Lee put it, "it cemented everything" (2016).

Another important aspect of Tigner's process includes taking DDT dancers and drummers on annually organized trips to New Orleans. Since 2014 Tigner has led a group to experience a second line parade, take a second line dance class, and experience the food and humidity. The itineraries also ask the artists to engage with Louisiana's histories of racism and resistance. Tigner schedules day trips to nearby plantations, plans boat tours of the swamps once inhabited by Maroons, and hires a local historian for tailored tours of the city's sites of the slave trade, Reconstruction-era massacres, and black-led social movements. For Valerie Sanders, the trip helped her to understand "the historical why, the contemporary why, and why it continues" (2016). Erik Lee discovered a personal "why": "Knowing that I have family from Louisiana is one thing, but actually being on the ground, dancing in New Orleans, I felt like . . . I was embodying my ancestors, like I had taken on this energy that I had never [felt before] and this spirit that I had never felt before" (2016). Physical travel to New Orleans allowed Lee to enter its portal in new ways, and he brings this experience to every performance, transporting audiences through imaginative and spiritual journeys.

Importantly, even as *St. Ann and North Rampart Street* brings forth histories of New Orleans, it does not present second lining as something stuck in the past. Tigner's meticulous efforts to replicate a parade as it is done today honors second lining as a living, changing, contemporary tradition. DDT / Fonktional Equation's second line evokes overlapping diasporas born of historical and contemporary conditions and allows Bay Area audiences to experience something that feels like home.

Conclusion

The creative processes utilized by Brown, Zollar, and Tigner engage with New Orleans as port and portal. Their works constitute acts of sensitive witnessing that absorb the bodies of the dancers and their audiences into "vibrations of history," memory, and real and imagined places (Lee 2017, 76). Their methods— which include place-based research, building a network of New Orleanians who will hold them accountable, and choreographic approaches that communicate New Orleans's unique place within the African Atlantic diaspora—trouble binary value judgments of street-to-stage adaptations as either appropriation or appreciation. That they created these works post-Katrina meant that they intervened into public discourse about the disaster to (re)shape cultural memory of the event and its aftermath.

Importantly, each choreographer utilizes second lining's movement vocabulary to not only tell a story about New Orleans but also, in call-and-response fashion, to invite her audiences to participate in it. Reflecting on *Shelter*, Stephanie McKee explains, "By using second line as the form," UBW dancers embody "the way [New Orleanians] turn around and that we're alright" (2014). This assessment can be extended to Brown and Tigner as well. Brown highlights the second line's capacity for spiritual healing and community building; Zollar utilizes second lining to punctuate political commentary with defiant hope; and Tigner's second line brings forth histories of multiple diasporas. With deft footwork, these artists and their dancers invite multiple publics to experience second lining's myriad functions, offering audiences a chance to heal, opening a portal to "home," insisting upon a reshaped narrative of Katrina, and issuing a call to action.

Notes

1. The 2014 documentary film *Restaging Shelter* follows Urban Bush Women as they set the New Orleans version of *Shelter* on student dancers at Virginia Commonwealth University. A 2018 performance of Camille A. Brown and Dancers' *New Second Line* was recorded by the viral video phenomenon TED (Technology, Entertainment, and Design). Both are easily accessible online.

2. Los Hombres Calientes, "New Second Line—Mardi Gras 2001," *Vol. 3: New Congo Square*, Basin Street Records, 2001.

3. My description of *New Second Line* is based on two viewings: a video recording of Camille A. Brown and Dancers' performance at the Bates Dance Festival (Schaeffer Theater, Bates College, Lewiston, Maine, July 15, 2011; New York Public Library for the Performing Arts, Jerome Robbins Dance Division) and the company's live performance at Bryn Mawr College (McPherson Auditorium, Bryn Mawr, Pennsylvania, December 8, 2014).

4. The institute remained in New Orleans for seven summers before returning to Brooklyn in 2016.

5. My description of *Shelter* is based on my viewing of the 2009 performance at Dixon Hall and video footage of that same performance shared with me by UBW.

6. Wynton Marsalis, "Ring Shout (Peace of Mind)," *Congo Square*, Jazz at Lincoln Center, 2007.

7. Two poems were written in collaboration with Zollar during the development of *Shelter* in the late 1980s: "Between a Rock and a Hard Place at the Intersection of Reduced Resources and Reverberating Rage" by Hattie Gossett and "Belongo" by Laurie Carlos. These and DeWanda Wise's 2006 poem, "nawlins nightmare," are featured in performances of *Shelter* and were previously unpublished.

8. My descriptions are based on a live performance at Contra Costa College (John and Jean Knox Performing Arts Center, San Pablo, California, May 21, 2016) and video recordings of two performances, both shared with me by Tigner: *The Last Dance:*

St. Ann and N. Rampart Street at the San Francisco Ethnic Dance Festival (Lam Research Theater, Yerba Buena Center for the Arts, San Francisco, California, June 29, 2013); and *Down the Congo Line: The Rhythms of Life* (Yerba Buena Center for the Arts, San Francisco, California, October 5, 2013).

9. Besides Tigner, the other choreographers were Herve Kayos Makaya (Brazzaville, Congo), Isaura Oliveira (Brazil), and José "Cheo" Rojas (Cuba).

Works Cited

Adams, Vincanne. 2013. *Markets of Sorrow, Labors of Faith: New Orleans in the Wake of Katrina*. Durham, NC: Duke University Press.

Bliss, Laura. 2016. "10 Years Later, There's So Much We Don't Know about Where Katrina Survivors Ended Up." *Atlantic: City Lab*, August 25. http://www.citylab .com/politics/ 2015/08/10-years-later-theres-still-a-lot-we-dont-know-about-where -katrina-survivors-ended-up/401216/.

Brown, Camille A. 2013. Interview with the author. December 10.

———. 2017. Interview with the author. July 28.

———. 2018. "New Second Line." Performance, TED2018, Vancouver, BC. Accessed April 8, 2019. https://www.ted.com/talks/camille_a_brown_new_second_line.

Cahill-Booth, Lara. 2013. "Re-membering the Tribe: Networks of Recovery in Rex Nettleford's *Katrina*." *TDR: The Drama Review* 57 (1): 88–101.

Carrico, Rachel. 2013. "On Thieves, Spiritless Bodies, and Creole Soul: Dancing through the Streets of New Orleans." *TDR: The Drama Review* 57 (1): 70–87.

Chatterjea, Ananya. 2004. *Butting Out: Reading Resistive Choreographies through Works by Jawole Willa Jo Zollar and Chandralaekha*. Middletown, CT: Wesleyan University Press.

Curtis, Martha, and Bruce Berryhill, dir. and prod. 2012. *Restaging Shelter*. Richmond, VA: Curtis/Berryhill Productions. Vimeo. Video, 26:49. http://vimeo.com/60658021.

Daniel, Yvonne. 2005. *Dancing Wisdom: Embodied Knowledge in Haitian Vodou, Cuban Yoruba, and Bahian Candomblé*. Urbana: University of Illinois Press.

Decter, Joshua. 2009. "Art and the Cultural Contradictions of Urban Regeneration, Social Justice and Sustainability: Transforma Projecs and Prospect.1 in Post-Katrina New Orleans." *Afterall: A Journal of Art, Context, and Enquiry* 22 (Autumn/Winter): 16–34.

Evans, Freddi Williams. 2011. *Congo Square: African Roots in New Orleans*. Lafayette: University of Louisiana at Lafayette Press.

Floyd, Samuel A., Jr. 2002. "Ring Shout! Literary Studies, Historical Studies, and Black Music Inquiry." *Black Music Research Journal* 22: 49–70.

George-Graves, Nadine. 2010. *Urban Bush Women: Twenty Years of African American Dance Theater, Community Engagement, and Working It Out*. Madison: University of Wisconsin Press.

Harris-Lacewell, Melissa. 2008. "'Do You Know What It Means . . . ?' Mapping Emotion in the Aftermath of Katrina." In *Seeking Higher Ground: The Hurricane Katrina Crisis, Race, and Public Policy Reader*, edited by Manning Marable and Kristen Clarke, 153–72. New York: Palgrave Macmillan.

Johnson, Zada. 2010. "Walking the Post-disaster City: Race, Space and the Politics of Tradition in the African-American Parading Practices of Post-Katrina New Orleans." PhD dissertation, University of Chicago.

Lane, Juel D. 2014. Email correspondence with the author. April 15.

Lee, Anna Paulina. 2017. "Memoryscapes of Race: Black Radical Parading Cultures of New Orleans." *TDR: The Drama Review* 61(2): 71–86.

Lee, Erik. 2016. Interview with the author. May 4.

Malone, Jacqui. 1996. *Steppin' on the Blues: The Visible Rhythms of African American Dance*. Urbana: University of Illinois Press.

McKee, Stephanie. 2014. Interview with the author. February 5.

Michna, Catherine. 2013. "Performance and Cross-racial Storytelling in Post-Katrina New Orleans: Interviews with John O'Neal, Carol Bebelle, and Nicholas Slie." *TDR: The Drama Review* 57 (1): 48–69.

Moore, Shirley Ann Wilson. 2000. *To Place Our Deeds: The African American Community in Richmond, California, 1910–1963*. Los Angeles: University of California Press.

New York Times. 2005. "Katrina's Diaspora." October 2. http://www.nytimes.com/inter active/2015/08/25/us/ mapping-katrina-and-aftermath.html?_r=0.

Ott, Francine. 2013. Interview with the author. December 6.

Richardson, Riché. 2007. *Black Masculinity and the U.S. South: From Uncle Tom to Gangsta*. Athens: University of Georgia Press.

Sanders, Valerie. 2016. Interview with the author. May 4.

Simpson Braga, Denice. 2016. Interview with the author. May 4.

Taylor, Diana. 2003. *The Archive and the Repertoire: Performing Cultural Memory in the Americas*. Durham, NC: Duke University Press.

Tierney, Kathleen, Christine Bevc, and Erica Kuligowski. 2006. "Metaphors Matter: Disaster Myths, Media Frames, and Their Consequences in Hurricane Katrina." *Annals of the American Academy of Political and Social Science* 604 (March): 57–81.

Tigner, Latanya d. 2014. Interview with the author. May 15.

———. 2016. Interview with the author. May 4.

Thompson, Robert Farris. 1979. *African Art in Motion: Icon and Act*. Los Angeles: University of California Press.

———. 1983. *Flash of the Spirit: African & Afro-American Art & Philosophy*. New York: Random House, Inc.

Williams, Bennalldra. 2013. Interview with the author. December 9.

Zollar, Jawole Willa Jo. 2014. Interview with the author. January 19.

The Dance in the Museum

Grant Hyde Code and the
Brooklyn Museum Dance Center

AMANDA JANE GRAHAM

> The fairly new idea that the dance belongs in the museum, together with
> and in relation to other arts traditionally collected and exhibited in museums,
> evokes two very pertinent questions: What is the museum, and what is the
> dance?
>
> —GRANT HYDE CODE, "The Dance in the Museum," January 1939

In June 1936 Grant Hyde Code, editor of Brooklyn Museum publications, began a regular correspondence with Hallie Flanagan, national director of the Federal Theatre Project. Code's initial letter expressed the broad public appeal of a series of dance recital demonstrations that he had been organizing at the Brooklyn Museum since 1935: "There are thousands of children and adults who are interested in the contemporary development of dance as an art form, a group or community activity, a means of helpful recreation and artistic expression, thousands who cannot afford to attend the private schools and dance centers" (GHCP 1936). Code then made an impassioned appeal for federal financial support both to expand his dance programming into a sanctioned museum Dance Center and to develop the nascent and underfunded Dance Unit of the Federal Theatre Project (FTP), a Works Progress Administration (WPA) program initiated by the Dancers Association in January 1936. Like the better-known WPA programs for theater, arts, music, and writers, the Federal Dance Project sought to mitigate Depression-era unemployment and was conceived of as an alternative to relief payments. Moreover, as dance historian Ellen Graff explains, not only were the WPA arts programs created "to provide relief to unemployed artists, but they democratized American culture, creating 'art for the millions'" (1997, 76). Indeed, Code, a leftist sympathizer, pragmatist, and dance aficionado, imagined the Brooklyn Museum and museums in general as ideal sites for introducing dance to a broad spectrum of Americans. Free museum dance lessons and demonstrations in the heart of Brooklyn, he felt, would make conventionally theater-sited concert dance forms, including modern dance and ballet, more accessible and popular. By (re)siting dance in the museum, Code also strove to further a new, progressive mission for the conventionally object-oriented museum institution: to financially support dancers while legitimizing their work as both art and entertainment. In doing so, he opened up new and generative spaces for social and aesthetic experimentation at the intersection of dance and visual art.

Drawing primarily on archival correspondence, newspaper articles, dance concert programs, and early exhibition catalogs, this essay begins to recuperate dance's history with the American art museum through one case study: Code's partially WPA-subsidized Dance Center at the Brooklyn Museum, which unofficially opened in 1935 and officially closed its doors just three and a half years later. The Brooklyn Museum's "recognition of the dance as one of the important art forms," as *Brooklyn Daily Eagle* reporter Henry Lamb wrote, "mean[t] that *something* ha[d] happened" (1936, 78). The critic explained, "Not so many years ago dance was little more than a subject for ridicule in America, even among sophisticated and 'art-conscious' people," and the Brooklyn Museum, like most museums, preferred its "art dead and well documented" before consenting to let it through the front door (78). However, in the mid-1930s museums and visitors alike were changing their minds about dance and its place in art museums. Nowhere was this more evident than at the Brooklyn Museum, where dance was recognized as a valid form of labor and promoted as an art form "existing with great vitality in the present as well as in the past" (78).

This Undying Quest

Grant Hyde Code is quite possibly the first museum curator of dance in the United States. Code began his tenure at the Brooklyn Museum as the editor of museum publications. However, after his first year managing the museum's Dance Center, he officially requested that his colleagues at the FTP identify him as "the acting Director [of the] Dance Center of the Brooklyn Museum" (GHCP 1937). By the beginning of 1938 he was signing his professional correspondence "Manager Brooklyn Museum Dance Center." By the end of that year he had settled on the title "Curator, Brooklyn Museum Dance Center" (GHCP 1938). Although Code kept this designation for only a few months before the Dance Center closed, the fact that he specifically identified himself as a curator of dance is significant.

As art historian Beatrice von Bismarck (2010) notes, the term "curator" historically originated in the visual arts. While the moniker began to gain traction in the late eighteenth century with the emergence of art museums and galleries, it was not until after 1945 that a curator became an official position. Performance scholar Bertie Ferdman explains that the idea of performance curation and the job title "performance curator" materialized when performance and visual art began to share the space of the art museum: "Initially, the job and function of the curator as caretaker of collections expanded as art became more discursive and attuned to context, in particular in the sixties with the rise of immaterial production such as installations, happenings, and performance art" (2014, 8). Indeed, the title "performance curator," no less "dance curator," is relatively new. Even today it is uncommon. Thus, Code's professional identification suggests not only that he was ahead of his time but that he purposefully deployed the title "curator" to expand the bounds of its associations. In the process, he demonstrated that dance, like visual art, necessitated a gatekeeper and an institutional interpreter.

Code's apparent co-optation of the then nascent title "curator" from the visual arts is all the more incisive given his professional history with language. For the entirety of his career, Code wrote criticism and composed plays, stories, and poems. A little-known but well-respected poet, Code published his final poetry collection in 1971, only three years before his death. The book, *This Undying Quest*, is comprised of sonnets, odes, blank verse, and other forms that represent "the totality of [the author's] experience" (Code 1971, front book jacket). Code's lifelong professional passions were varied and often overlapping. His occupation with poetry and, in his later years, his acting career on Broadway, on television, and in film never eclipsed his utmost quest: to promote the art of the dance. In fact, *This Undying Quest* includes many references to dance, notably, a poem titled "Terpsichore" in which Code addresses the Greek goddess of dance. The poet asks his muse, "Ah, Terpsichore, how shall we know that a man is loyal to you" (6). If Terpsichore could have responded, she might well have proclaimed, "Compare his actions to those of Grant Hyde Code."

A lifelong dance enthusiast, Code made a concerted effort to advance many styles of dance. Although he had a clear personal preference for modern dance, especially for the work of his friend the modern choreographer Helen Tamiris, Code's public statements and programmatic efforts illustrate that he was supportive of diverse dance forms; indeed, he considered dance "*highly necessary in contemporary life*" (Code 1939a, 5; emphasis in the original). Code articulated his investment in dance as a medium rather than in any particular style of dance in his correspondence with jazz dancer Roger Pryor Dodge. Dodge, who worked closely with Code at the Brooklyn Museum as a member of the Young Choreographers Laboratory, wrote to the curator to express his intense

FIGURE 21. Grant Hyde Code in *Mexican Dance*. ("The Dance in the Museum," *Journal of Health and Physical Education* 10, no. 1 [1939]: 8)

distaste for the modern dance of the 1930s, which he associated with "intellectual or emotional revolt." He also conveyed his dislike of "group dance" (as opposed to solo works) and for "content" (as opposed to formal execution) (GHCP 1937). Rather than defend modernism or entertain the binaries that Dodge proposed, Code's return letter underlines his open but hardly apolitical position on dance aesthetics:

> Personally I am very shy about assuming an ethical attitude toward aesthetic problems. I do not like to say such and such a thing should be or should not be, also I try to be careful about giving too much importance to my own taste in aesthetic matters. If anyone is interested in knowing what I like or how I feel, I am very glad to tell them, but I try to do so with the understanding that I have no idea that my statement is anything more than a description of my personal taste and feeling. (GHCP 1937)

Code recapitulates this egalitarian stance on dance in his published writing, including "The Dance in the Museum," in which he bemoans the scant dance literature of the 1930s. He describes the existing dance scholarship and history of the period as primarily "polemical," judgmental, and ultimately detrimental to the popularity of dance as an art form for the people: "The thesis is usually that this type of dancing is utterly and completely different from that type of dancing, that such and such a characteristic is the mark of this type and something else the mark of that type, that this is bad and that is good" (Code 1939a, 5). Here, Code is positing that it is important for scholars, critics, and dancers to look for the porosity between "types" of dance; such a connective approach to dance analysis would, in his mind, encourage audiences to be more open to dance in general, especially dance forms with which they have less familiarity or affinity, thus creating a more democratic and willing viewership.

As a dance curator, Code arranged programs that brought together dancers performing in a variety of dance styles and organized exhibitions that combined or aligned dance performance and dance ephemera with visual art. His decisive presentation of dance was pedagogical in that it revealed significant aesthetic and conceptual affinities between dance forms and artistic mediums. In other words, through his curation he was teaching the museum audience to make comparisons between and among different dance forms and between dance and visual art. However, Code's pedagogy not only was an aesthetic venture but also was steeped in the politics of his time.

In sometimes subtle and other times overt ways, Code's curatorial approach and his general public advocacy for manifold dance forms were compelled by the dance labor movement taking place in New York City beginning in the early 1930s. With his rhetoric and institutional connection he strove to support the Dancers Union, spearheaded by his compatriot, Tamiris. Tamiris's New York City–based Dancers Union (also referred to as the Dancers Emergency Association or the Dancers Association) called for "much needed unity among dancers in all fields" (Graff 1997, 79). Unification was necessary for successful mobilization and for "raising . . . standards all along the line": better conditions, more venues, and salaried positions for dancers in all sectors and career stages (79). Given the historical and cultural context of Code's statements and the progressive networks within which he operated, his mission at the Brooklyn Museum takes on new meaning. That is, Code's investment in advancing varied dance forms and in negating aesthetic and media hierarchies was reflective of the Dancers Union's promotion of worker equity. If read through this lens, Code's appeals to Flanagan and others might be considered an extension of contemporaneous dance labor negotiations.

The Dance in Art

In 1935, when Code began taking steps toward the creation of a program for dance at the Brooklyn Museum, the United States was in the midst of the

Great Depression. President Roosevelt's New Deal–sponsored WPA relief program made the government the largest single employer in the nation. By 1935 the WPA had created the FTP. One year later, and following a significant organizing effort led by Tamiris, FTP director Flanagan approved the creation of the Federal Dance Project, with a starting operating budget of $155,000 (Graff 1997, 82). Approximately six months after the Federal Dance Project's budget was set, Code sent his first appeal for Dance Center funding to Flanagan and Works Progress administrator Harry Hopkins. After some consideration and a site visit to the museum to meet with Code and museum director Philip N. Youtz, Flanagan enthusiastically agreed to support the dance initiative in Brooklyn, which she called "a splendid idea" and "exactly the kind of tie-up we wish to make" (GHCP 1936).

Flanagan was on board with Code's initiative in part because it was already successful. The regular public dance recitals Code hosted in the museum's sculpture court—a space that could comfortably seat twelve hundred people—generally attracted between one thousand and three thousand spectators (GHCP). Often there was standing room only. The free Saturday performances, which demonstrated "contemporary dance techniques" and featured dancers such as Tamiris, Holm, and students from the Wigman School and the School of American Ballet, were initially arranged without any budget (Code 1936, 178). Code and the dancers worked long hours and without pay in order to establish the potential of such programs and make a case for future funding.

Also involved in advancing dance at the Brooklyn Museum was contemporary art curator Herbert B. Tschudy, who oversaw the new Gallery for Living Artists. This gallery, created expressly for contemporary artwork by living artists, was, much like the dance program, a means of enlivening the museum. Together, Tschudy and Code established a connection between the institution and the contemporary social and cultural worlds beyond its walls. United in their mission, the art and dance curators organized a series of exhibitions in the gallery that expressly linked the museum's performance programs to the visual arts. The first of these exhibitions, *The Dance in Art*, opened in January 1936. It featured 135 paintings, drawings, and sculptures by artists who sought to represent and interpret human movement, especially dance. The artists participating in the show were as diverse in medium and style as they were in background and identity. They included sculptor Dorthea Denslow, best known for her Clay Club, which would later become the SculptureCenter; Russian-born modernist painter Rifka Angel; costume designer Betty Joiner; Mexican-born Miguel Covarrubias, a well-known caricaturist and muralist; Japanese American artist Isamu Noguchi, whose stage sets for Martha Graham's productions were as iconic as the dances themselves; and painter Oqwa Pi, from San Ildefonso Pueblo in New Mexico, whose watercolor *The Eagle Dance* was an audience favorite (Code 1937). Code also exhibited two of his own paintings: a watercolor entitled *Elaine* and an oil piece entitled *The Swan*.

The mélange of artists and works highlighted the cross-cultural ubiquity of dance, a genre that interested visual artists not only for its aesthetic appeal but also for its ability to convey social and cultural systems, mores, and values. Unlike previous exhibitions of dance in painting by primarily European artists (notably, Edgar Degas) and exhibitions of dance-related ephemera (like the 1933 show *Twenty-Five Years of Russian Ballet* at Julien Levy Gallery), the Brooklyn Museum exhibition had a strong focus on American dances rendered by American artists (Udall 2012). Although Code never explicitly acknowledged it, the artists and works included in the exhibition not only linked dance and visual art but also portrayed American dance through the eyes of many first-generation non-European immigrant and first-generation artists, like Covarrubias and Noguchi, and Indigenous artists, including Pi. Together, the pieces in the show made manifest the curators' inclusive notion of American identity. In many ways, their project was reflective of a larger inclusive nationalist movement in the art world of the 1930s, one that arose at least in part because of artists' and art institutions' reliance on WPA funding, which was made available to artists and institutions that purported to further democratic ideals. As art and cultural historian A. Joan Saab explains, "Cries for a national art form and desires to link democracy to the arts seemed to escalate during the 1930s, as debates over what constituted 'America,' and who defined the arts took new form and reached a much larger audience than ever before. Many of the participants in the debates were already aware of the constructed nature of the idea of 'America,' and they self-consciously attempted to include those previously outside of its purview within their new constructions and in so doing democratize cultural capital" (2004, 8). To be sure, Code and Tschudy "attempted to include those previously outside" of "the idea of 'America'" in their exhibition. By displaying contemporary art by many immigrants and Indigenous artists alongside work by white artists, the curators sought to challenge the homogeneity of the idea of "America," American visual art, and American dance. Through the exhibition, the artists and the dance styles that the curators chose to represent were assimilated into the "great melting pot of America" (Fanya Geltman quoted in Graff 1997, 19). At the same time, the show and its related publications celebrated the artists' distinctive ethnic identities, highlighting the cultural specificities of the dances in their works. The progressive curators astutely proposed an inclusive version of "American" art and

dance and in so doing subtly challenged the pervasive anti-immigration policies of the era such as Mexican Repatriation (1929–39) and the ethnic quotas
established by the Immigration Acts of 1921 and 1924.

Code's preface for *The Dance in Art* exhibition catalog also positioned dance
as a uniquely American art form. However, according to the curator, dance's
singular American identity developed in spite of or as a result of its marginalization by some audiences and institutions: "There have been times and
places in which dancing was regarded with disapproval by the typical opinion
of society in general, when the name dancer was a term of reproach, no matter
what ardent devotees of some particular form of the dance might exist in society. This is certainly not true at present in America. Such opinion exists here,
but it is in a minority, and typical American opinion regards such attacks on
the dance as narrow-minded, bigoted, ridiculous" (Records of the Department, September 1935–June 1936). The defensive tone that Code takes in his
introductory remarks is intriguing, for it betrays his position on dance and
politics. Considered within its historical context, Code's essay in the program
and perhaps even *The Dance in Art* exhibition as a whole might be read as a
platform for the curator's critique and subtle derision of the federal government's limited support of dance. This was certainly worthy of criticism. However, even nominal federal support for dance demonstrates that a number of
individuals working under the auspices of the WPA, including Flanagan, *were*
responsive to dancers' concerns and demands. The fact that there was federal
funding for dance at all was in itself a fairly new and enlightened concept.
However, there were a number of kinks to work through.

One such issue was the federal freeze on dancer registration for the Federal
Dance Project. As Graff notes of the March 1936 hiring hiatus, "Only eighty-five
dancers had been hired at this time, although the quota had been set at one-
hundred more" (1997, 82). In response, a group of dancers picketed in front of
the FTP offices in New York City. During the second day of these protests, ten
dancers were arrested and charged with "walking a coicle and shouting some-
thin' about unemployed dancers wantin' jobs" (Geltman 1936, 58). The dancers'
trial, which Code would later write about in *Dance Observer*, was, according
to the curator and critic, "the first recorded public performance of the dance
project" (Code 1939b, 6). Code's tongue-in-cheek comment had gravity. With
it, he established the clear connection between the dance onstage and "the
dance offstage, orchestrated by the techniques of organized labor—pickets,
sit-ins, delaying tactics" (Graff 1997, 83).

It seems hardly inconsequential that the hiring freeze and dancer protest
took place at the tail end of *The Dance in Art*. While the exhibition was reviewed through a primarily aesthetic lens, the tone of Code's catalog text hints

that it was (also) a tactical project, one that brought together dancers and artists, as well as dance and art audiences, in a moment of unity. Moreover, establishing dance's legitimacy as an art form during a precarious cultural transition and potential uprising was in itself a political tactic. Code and Tschudy's curatorial casting of dance in a positive and serious light would have influenced the public's perception of the medium and its practitioners and, by extension, forwarded the favorable popular perception of dancers and the dance labor mission.

The enthusiastic reviews of *The Dance in Art* make few allusions to the political stakes of the show and no reference to its possible connections to the radical performances of New York dancers onstage or off. However, critics were remarkably open-minded about the relationship between dance and visual art and Code's contention that the art of the dance had a place in the art museum. Art critic Elisabeth Luther Cary of the *New York Times* remarked of the movement studies in the exhibition, which were "of different degrees of expertness," "[The sketches were] refreshing to eyes a trifle surfeited with art prepared for those to whom finish is the sauce without which—no pudding" (1936, X9). Cary's focus on the "fragmentary" motion studies by artists such as Ruth Taylor and Alfred H. Stein reveals as much about the exhibition and its public appeal as the critic herself. An outspoken advocate for the creation of industrial art schools and the introduction of factory machines to the artist's studio, Cary had a preexisting interest in the mechanics of movement, in visualizing process, and in exposing the artist's labor (Hagelstein Marquardt 1988). Her modern view of art and industry and the studio and the museum is especially overt when she professes, "When a breath of the studio blows across an exhibition it does bring refreshment" (Cary 1936, X9). Like Code, who programmed dance performance demonstrations and works in progress, Cary was of the opinion that process was part of the product, and as such it should be made publicly visible. But was a process-based approach to art and dance or, for that matter, art and dance curation too experimental for the Brooklyn Museum of the 1930s?

The Dance Experiment

In December 1936 John Martin reviewed the activities at the Dance Center in an article titled "The Dance: Experiment." As the title of his *New York Times* article made clear, Martin considered the Dance Center an "experiment" "conducted" by the museum and "watched with the closest interest, not alone by those who are particularly concerned with the welfare of the dance, but also by the many other museums which are seeking to serve their communities in a living manner." In other words, Martin presented the initiative as a test case for dance in the museum. The scientific nature of Martin's language and the overall discourse that surrounded the Dance Center at the Brooklyn Museum illustrated a connection between dance, the museum, and the scientific method: a set of trial-and-error techniques used to prove or disprove a hypothesis.

This is no wonder, considering there was a strong cross-disciplinary interest in the scientific method in the 1930s. As Daniel P. Thurs explains, it was a decade during which the scientific method became popular as "a mindset rather than a technique." "Sometimes associated with virtues such as honesty and healthy skepticism," the method was often viewed as important to "the continued functioning of democracy" (Thurs 2011, 323). Outside the world of the natural and biological sciences, the method was adopted and adapted by thinkers in a variety of fields, including education and philosophy. One of the most well known proponents of the scientific method in these fields was John Dewey, whose writings on an "inductive method of knowledge acquisition" influenced professionals in museum education and pedagogues and performers in dance (Ross 2000, 126). Considering Code had a foot in both worlds, it is not surprising that he portrayed the Dance Center as an experiment. Code expanded that experiment through the development of the Young Choreographers Laboratory—originally referred to as the Young Choreographers Forum. His deliberate framing of the group as a laboratory is again indicative of Dewey. The name evoked Dewey's turn-of-the-century Laboratory School in Chicago, which championed experiential learning (Phillips 2014).

The Dance Center and its offshoot, the Young Choreographers Laboratory, sponsored a number of diverse initiatives that Code detailed in his publications, including "The Dance in the Art Museum," and in professional correspondence with a number of art museum directors and curators around the country who were, as Martin (1936) anticipated, watching the Dance Center with "the closest interest." Throughout the 1930s and afterward, Code was the primary consultant on programming dance in the art museum in the United States. Among those who conferred with Code were Anne W. Olmstead, director of the Syracuse Museum of Fine Art; Siegfried R. Weng, director of the Dayton Art Institute; and Gertrude Lippincott, founder of the Modern Dance Center of Minneapolis, who would go on to organize a dance event at the Walker Art Center in 1940.

Code's correspondence with museum directors, curators, and performers was generous and frequent, and his advice was humble and pragmatic. In a letter to Olmstead, Code admits, "We [at the Brooklyn Museum] got into this work more or less by accident." But, he adds, "the development has been quite extraordinary and has convinced us that the dance is an art which should be regularly included in the program of a museum, not only on account of its very close relation with figure composition in painting and sculpture but also for its own sake as one of the liveliest of contemporary arts and certainly here one of the most popular" (GHCP 1938). Code's enthusiasm for dance in the museum and the many successes of the Dance Center—visual art exhibitions, recitals, free dance lessons for children and adults, lectures by dance scholars, and publications—inspired Olmstead to organize a special interest group for dance at her institution. Supervised by Margot Krolik Harper, dance teacher at Syracuse University, the group began brainstorming collaborations between local dancers and the museum in 1936. Dayton Art Institute director Weng contacted Code with questions regarding a proposed museum performance by the Experimental Group for Young Dancers, a new dance company organized by local sisters Josephine and Hermene Schwartz. After conferring with Code, Weng agreed to the 1938 performance, now remembered as the first public performance of the dance collective, which would later become known as the Dayton Ballet (GHCP 1938).

Code's influence on dance in art museums during the 1930s not only inspired one-off programming in Syracuse, Dayton, and elsewhere but also most likely motivated and informed Lincoln Kirstein's donation of dance paraphernalia to the Museum of Modern Art Archives in the 1940s. Kirstein, who was critical to the founding of the Museum of Modern Art Dance Archives in 1939 and subsequently MoMA's Department of Dance and Theatre Design (1944–48), first expressed his enthusiasm for programming dance in museums during his three-week term in 1936 as the director of the Federal Dance Project. Flanagan enticed Kirstein to stay with the FTP by proposing that he help Code undertake a program at the Brooklyn Museum focusing on "the changing trends in the American dance." According to Flanagan, the unrealized production, set to be called *America Dances*, would broadly focus on "the entire history of dance forms in America including Indian and Negro, early Colonialist, etc. right down through the dancers such as Ruth St. Denis, Ted Shawn, up to the present" (GHCP 1938). Although this event never solidified and Kirstein never committed to Flanagan or the FTP, his stated enthusiasm for the *America Dances* endeavor anticipates Kirstein's future engagement with art museums, in particular, MoMA, which notably hosted a similar program in 1948, *An Evening on American Dance* (Elligott 2009).

Code's Dance Center had a definitive and lasting impact on the whole of the museum world; however, no one felt the effect of his initiatives more immediately than the dancers who were involved in the Young Choreographers Laboratory. The core members of the laboratory were dancers Nadia Chilkovsky,

Saida Gerrard, Mattie Haim, William Matons, Lillian Mehlmann, Mura Dehn, Roger Pryor Dodge, and Ailes Gilmour. The first recital of the select group took place in 1937 and was free to the public. Comprised primarily of solos and in a variety of dance styles, the performances drew on diverse sources and inspirations. Russian-born Dehn was especially interested in creating dances inspired by the art and artifacts in the Brooklyn Museum. In *Dance of Plenty* Dehn wore a costume created by Doris Kaminsky based on an African Likishi dance costume, and in *16th Century Venus* the dancer donned a gold necklace borrowed from the museum's permanent collection. The latter dance was based on a painting by the German Renaissance painter Lucas Cranach the Elder (GHCP 1937). While most of the dancers did not engage with the museum collection as expressly and extensively as Dehn, all considered the implications of the museum as a new site of reception and production.

Given his devotion to enlivening the space of the museum and celebrating process, Code arranged for the Young Choreographers to use the museum's sixth floor as a rehearsal space. He set up screens as dressing room partitions, a mirror, and tables and chairs. The Museum Studio, as the choreographers called it, became a space for dance and for dance discourse (GHCP 1937). Although the curator was welcoming to the dancers, the museum's linoleum-over-concrete floors were not. The floors left many dancers with metatarsal bruises. Doubting whether the museum was an ideal site for dance, a number of dancers chose to rehearse their pieces off-site.

Audience reactions to the Young Choreographers' recitals were overwhelmingly positive. Dozens of Brooklyn residents wrote to the museum to express their high regard for the dancers' presentations. Ruthann Raskin gushed, "This is the second time that I have attended your Saturday morning Dance Recitals. I think that they are beautiful. I don't think I have ever seen such graceful people. . . . I wish that the Young Choreographers Society would give us more recitals in the future" (GHCP 1937). Similarly, local minister Frederick Reustle reached out to Code following a 1937 performance:

> For two hours I felt that we were really civilized with a new art taking form under our eyes in such appropriate surroundings. This performance constitutes an achievement which restores ones faith in a Federal Theatre. Without knowing much about it I got the feeling that you were conducting an experiment. If so, you deserve great credit for thus presenting such opportunities for experimental work that we need in art and religion by giving these young people an opportunity to appear in public and present their work with fine simplicity and sincerity with which they performed Saturday morning. You have made possible that which commercial theatre does not appreciate. (GHCP 1937)

Unlike Raskin, who primarily conveys her appreciation for the look and "grace" of the performers, Reustle, echoing Martin, underlines the experimental nature of Code's endeavor. By framing the performances as social and artistic experiments, Reustle acknowledges the risks of staging dance performances in the museum. He also recognizes the institutional and cultural potential of the initiative, which not only challenged the role of the museum and the definition and bounds of art but also sought to create a sustainable economic and creative home for dancers. Finally, Reustle indicates the fundamentally liberatory nature of Code's project from "commercial theatre" and suggests the emancipatory possibilities of the museum.

No matter the praise for the Young Choreographers, the administrators from the Federal Dance Project were unhappy with what they perceived as an unprofessional presentation and one which ultimately did not reflect the goals or the standards of the FTP. National director Flanagan, for one, expressed the concern that the Young Choreographers were "suffering from a disease afflicting the dance itself—a lack of relation to life, a lack of discipline, a reliance on subjective emotion in place of objective craftsmanship. Certainly the dance today, like all art, needs a reorientation in everyday life" (GHCP 1937). Flanagan's criticism was warranted. Most of the Young Choreographers had experience as company dancers but were relatively new to performing their own choreography. On top of that, they were performing solos or duets for thousands of audience members, many of whom had never attended a dance concert before. Hence, establishing what Flanagan calls "a reorientation in everyday life" was especially critical. Her comment might also have pointed to a lack of connection between the dances and the social and political concerns of the day. Many of the dances (like Dehn's) were historically oriented and citational. Others (with "a reliance on subjective emotion") expressed the interior feelings of the dancer rather than more universal thoughts or concerns. Although Flanagan had a long history of supporting experimental theater and was historically an advocate for dancers, she generally championed artists who made an overt attempt to connect with their audiences, especially through social and cultural critique. Quite possibly, many of the Young Choreographers were simply too artistically formal in their approach for Flanagan and the FTP.

The Failure of the
Museum of the Future

The Young Choreographers Laboratory was denied funding in 1938 and closed after less than a year in operation. Not long afterward, the Brooklyn Institute trustees voted to close the entire Dance Center. Robert E. Blum, president of the Brooklyn Institute of Arts and Sciences, claimed that the museum could not afford the cost of Dance Center operations or fulfill its spatial needs (GHCP 1938).

Brooklyn Museum visitors and those in dance and museum programming were enraged by the decision and unsatisfied by Blum's justification for the closing. Walter Crittenden, chairman of the Governing Committee of Museums, Brooklyn Institute of Arts and Sciences, and Laurence P. Roberts, who succeeded Youtz as Brooklyn Museum director following his 1938 resignation, received numerous letters expressing concern over the news. Arthur Prichard Moor, Brooklyn resident and author of *The Library-Museum of Music and Dance,* wrote, "The Brooklyn Museum Dance Center, I have just been told, is about to be closed. As this has seemed to me such a worthwhile effort, I should like to enquire, if it is in order, why the Committee has deemed it necessary to terminate this project at present, and whether there is some prospect of its being continued at a later date." Toward the conclusion of his letter Moor noted, "The Dance Center seemed to me a particularly inspiring enterprise, not merely for what it accomplished, but especially for what it looked toward. It had pioneered for the whole country in an important new field" (Moor quoted in GHCP 1938). Moor's letter reflected the sentiments of many New Yorkers who saw the Dance Center as indicative of what Youtz called "the museum of the future."[1] These museum patrons, some of whom canceled their Brooklyn Museum memberships in protest after the closing, saw it not only as a shift in programming but as a betrayal of the members of the Brooklyn community who had come to see dance and the museum as part of their everyday lives.

Conclusion

Even though Blum, Crittenden, and Roberts cited a shortage of space and funds as the primary reason for closing the Dance Center, Code realized their decision was politically complicated. For one, Code's ally, Youtz, had recently resigned from his post. Frustrated by "the aloof policy inherited from old private collections" and resistance to his educational, curatorial, and architectural innovations, Youtz (1932) sought a more progressive workplace. Youtz's replacement, Robertson, had a more conservative view of art than his successor. He aligned dance with the "folk" rather than with "high" art and believed it belonged in the museum only in the form of family programming.

Internal issues at the museum were exacerbated by the depletion of external support. In October 1937 the Federal Dance Project was incorporated back into the Federal Theatre Project due to congressional cutbacks. In June 1939, only months following Youtz's departure, the House Un-American Activities Committee determined that the Federal Theatre and Dance Projects would be terminated in part because of the leftist political tone of some of their productions and the alleged Communist activities of many of their artists. Thus, the federal funding that the museum would have received for the continuation of the Dance Center was no longer available.

Although Code was certainly devastated by the closing of the Dance Center, which, in its short life, had attracted approximately sixty-five thousand museum visitors and programmed performances by more than sixty-five professional dancers, he understood its failure as indicative of a shift in American cultural life and social policy (Code 1936, 178). He therefore did what many desperate and angry Americans did in 1939: he wrote to his president. Code's letter to President Roosevelt, dated June 4, 1939, is at once a plea for federal support of the arts, a call to arms regarding national labor practices, and an expression of his antiwar sentiments. He shares his good impression of the WPA, "one of the noblest and most constructive achievements of your administration," and makes suggestions regarding its reimplementation (GHCP 1939). While Code penned his letter in the wake of the institutional reorganization at the Brooklyn Museum and his own resignation, it has an overall hopeful tone. The letter is clearly written by an idealist who is resilient and flexible in the midst of defeat.

The consequences of siting dance in the museum were numerous, varied, and crucial to resuscitating underfunded and underappreciated Depression-era dance. The financial support and exposure the Brooklyn Museum provided transformed American concert choreographers, dancers, and companies long after this period of acute economic and labor crisis, ultimately resulting in federal and civic ingenuity. For one, dancers who did not have the necessary fiscal support or connections to perform in theaters or host dance classes in studios realized there were alternative performance and rehearsal spaces. They were liberated from the conventional constraints of the theater. Consequently, dancers had more freedom in how they marketed themselves and, artistically, in the kind of work they could pursue. Freedom, in turn, inspired a greater sense of agency and stimulated creativity across the field. Just as important, Code's venture established that museum dance performances had mass appeal. Although museum audiences knew little to nothing about modern dance and ballet, they nonetheless consistently and enthusiastically attended performances, even making connections between dance and visual artwork in the museum's collection. Thus, the so-called failure of the Brooklyn Museum Dance Center was ultimately rich and productive in that it perpetuated experimentation and acknowledged parallel and hybrid practices in dance and art. All the while, the Dance Center addressed issues of dancer labor and public access to the arts. Given its bilateral emphasis on aesthetic innovation and social concerns, the Dance Center remains an aspirational but realistic model for museums today.

Note

1. Youtz's phrase was a reference to George Brown Goode, "The Museums of the Future: A Lecture Delivered at the Brooklyn Institute, February 28, 1889."

Works Cited

Cary, Elisabeth Luther. 1936. "Dance in Art at the Brooklyn Museum." *New York Times,* February 2.

Code, Grant Hyde. 1936. "Brooklyn Museum Presents the Dance in Art." *Bulletin of the Brooklyn Institute of Arts and Sciences* 16 (11): 178, 184.

———. 1937. "The Dance at the Brooklyn Museum." *Dance Observer* 4 (10): 125–26.

———. 1939a. "The Dance in the Museum." *Journal of Health and Physical Education* 10 (1): 3–8, 56.

———. 1939b. "The Dance Theatre of the WPA: A Record of National Accomplishment." *Dance Observer,* October 6, 8.

———. 1971. *This Undying Quest.* Sauk City, WI: Stanton & Lee.

Elligott, Michelle. 2009. *Another Modern Art: Dance and Theater.* Museum of Modern Art Interactive Exhibitions. Accessed March 10, 2016. http://www.moma.org/interactives/exhibitions/2009/anothermodernart/.

Ferdman, Bertie. 2014. "From Content to Context: The Emergence of the Performance Curator." *Theater* 44 (2): 5–19.

Geltman, Fanya. 1936. "Letters." *Dance Observer,* May, 57–58.

GHCP (Grant Hyde Code Papers). 1936–1938. (S)*MGZMD 8. New York Public Library for the Performing Arts, Jerome Robbins Dance Division.

Graff, Ellen. 1997. *Stepping Left: Dance and Politics in New York City, 1928–1942.* Durham, NC: Duke University Press.

Hagelstein Marquardt, Virginia. 1988. "Louis Lozowick: From 'Machine Ornaments' to Applied Design, 1923–1930." *Journal of Decorative and Propaganda Arts* 8 (Spring): 40–57.

Lamb, Henry. 1936. "I See America Dancing! The Brooklyn Museum Establishes a Dance Center in Recognition of the Oldest of the Arts." *Brooklyn Daily Eagle,* December 20.

Marshall, John. 1935. "Interview with Philip N. Youtz." In *100 Years: The Rockefeller Foundation.* Accessed March 4, 2018, https://rockfound.rockarch.org/digital-library-listing/-/asset_publisher/yYxpQfeI4W8N/content/interview-with-philip-n-youtz.

Martin, John. 1936. "The Dance: Experiment." *New York Times,* December 20.

Phillips, D. C., ed. 2014. *Encyclopedia of Educational Theory and Philosophy.* Vol. 2. Thousand Oaks, CA: Sage.

Records of the Department of Painting and Sculpture: Exhibitions. September 1935–June 1936. *Dance in Art* exhibition, January 24, 1936–March 15, 1936. Brooklyn Museum Archives.

Ross, Janice. 2000. *Moving Lessons: Margaret H'Doubler and the Beginning of Dance in American Education.* Madison: University of Wisconsin Press.

Saab, A. Joan. 2004. *For the Millions: American Art and Culture between the Wars.* Philadelphia: University of Pennsylvania Press.

Thurs, Daniel P. 2011. "Scientific Methods." In *Wrestling with Nature: From Omens to Science*, edited by Peter Harrison, Ronald L. Numbers, and Michael H. Shank, 307–36. Chicago: University of Chicago Press.

Udall, Sharon R. 2012. *Dance in American Art: A Long Embrace*. Madison: University of Wisconsin Press.

von Bismarck, Beatrice. 2010. "Relations in Motion: The Curatorial Condition in Visual Art and Its Possibilities for the Neighboring Disciplines." "Curating Performing Arts." Special issue, *Frakcija* 1 (55): 50–57.

Youtz, Philip. 1932. "The Sixty-Ninth Street Branch Museum of the Pennsylvania Museum of Art." *Museum News* 10 (December 15): 6–7.

Dancing the Image

Virgilio Sieni's Choreographic Tableaux

GIULIA VITTORI

Venice, Gallerie dell'Arsenale, Dance Biennale, July 2014. Two performers occupy a small taped-off area of a large room in which other performances are simultaneously happening. They are a woman and a man in their midsixties. They are not professional dancers—perhaps this is their first time on a stage. They perform a contemporary dance with movements that are neither pedestrian nor technical. A peculiar, savant grace marks their relationship. At one moment they perform at a slow pace: the woman stands still, watching straight ahead; the man is seated in a chair, looking down. As the dance develops through many situations, the woman stands now behind the man, who is also standing, and gently holds his head, swinging it to either side, again and again—he abandons himself to her, he trusts her. In their composed dance, they retain a harmonious precision in the rhythm, a special grace in their relationality, and a strong affect in their gaze. They must understand each other deeply—they might be husband and wife.

These performers are dancing "Pietà." It is a danced interpretation of the biblical episode in which the Virgin Mary mourns Christ, her dead son. The title refers to the many painted pietà of art history, such as Bellini's *Pietà* (1460) and Rogier van der Weyden's *Pietà* (ca. 1441). A symbol of a mother's pain, the image was made famous by Michelangelo's statue *Pietà vaticana* (1497–99). In the dance there is no pose that attempts to re-create any specific artwork. Still, artworks are there, an invisible presence stimulating spectators' memories to imagine yet another pietà. This dance suggests that *pietà*—an Italian word that could be translated as "compassion"—is an emotion that can go beyond the specific biblical episode of maternal grief. Pietà might reach the many folds in any number of relationships that manifest between partners.

"Pietà" is a dance within a much larger choreography, *Vangelo secondo Matteo*, a contemporary dance work that Italian choreographer Virgilio Sieni staged for the Venice Dance Biennale in 2014. With a background in visual arts, Sieni (who was born in Italy in 1957 and is now an established contemporary dance choreographer based in Florence) largely draws on paintings to make his choreography through the use of both art historical citations and site-specific works embedded in museums. Having developed his study of the relationships between painting and dance over several years, Sieni choreographed *Vangelo secondo Matteo* as the conclusion of his mandate as the artistic director of the Venice Dance Biennale. *Vangelo secondo Matteo* takes inspiration from the episodic Gospel of Matthew, the main source for painters who have depicted Christian episodes. Interestingly, in this work—which is a summa of the many site-specific choreographies Sieni has presented in front of paintings in cenacles, galleries, and museums during the last decade—artworks were not present in the performance space. This time, Sieni studied his iconographic sources mostly on his own in preparation for the rehearsal process. Paintings were a ghostly presence within this large choreographic work. As his work stimulated spectators to recognize some of the artworks that inspired his dances, Sieni invited them to contemplate religion and art history through the somatic, affective, and kinetic point of view of choreography, invested with his aesthetic.[1]

Vangelo secondo Matteo involved 163 dancers, of which only a few were professional dancers from Sieni's company. The work was composed of twenty-seven dances split into three distinct cycles counting nine dances each. Sieni calls the twenty-seven dances "choreographic tableaux," making explicit the connection between dance and visual art history in the subtitle of the work: *27 Quadri Coreografici* (translated into English as *27 Choreographic Tableaux*). Some of the choreographic tableaux from the three cycles presented episodes from the Gospel—such as "Flight into Egypt," "Crucifixion," and "The Last Supper"—whereas others performed themes characterizing the Gospel—such as "Healing," "Pietà," and "Beatitudes." *Vangelo secondo Matteo* was performed in three subsequent long weekends, each dedicated to one cycle. During each cycle, live music and different layouts delimited the performance space: the dancers performed inside squares of different sizes marked on the floor with tape. Spectators were invited to freely wander around them, following a handout with a map of the space that indicated the title of the religious episode interpreted in each choreographic tableau. Each spectator was free to engage with the choreographic tableaux without attention to chronicle development, much as one might visit the Stations of the Cross in a church according to personal orientation, mirroring the itinerant and anachronistic medieval mode of navigating the Gospels. Personal, structural, and qualitative connections were available to the spectators. Periodically, synchronic sound cues and silent gestures (hand clapping, stick beating, hand rising) coordinated collective actions among the different groups of dancers. Titles of the episodes, well-known iconographic symbols, *crescendo* and *diminuendo* in the dance, and the spatial perception derived from different-size groups of dancers guided the spectators to navigate the lack of explicitly structured narration. Each spectator could design a unique path for experiencing each cycle, thus reading from the Gospel anew.

In *Vangelo secondo Matteo*, Sieni's choreography refers to visual art history beyond the literality of single artworks and their historical period. Imaginative association guides Sieni's choreography of *Vangelo secondo Matteo*. We have seen the theme of pietà transitioning from a mother-and-son bond to what might be a husband-and-wife relationship, such that the interpretation of a theme goes well beyond the roles assigned in the biblical episode and its traditional iconographic portrayals. In other cases, the interpretation sticks to the episode but not to a single iconographic source of interpretation. The same choreographic tableau, for example, can be based on one or more religious paintings from the Italian and Flemish Renaissances, as we will see.

With a multilayered response to paintings, Sieni's choreographic tableaux bring together the concepts of image representation and image engagement. If, on the one hand, the choreography cites art historical painting, on the other hand, it does not aim at translating the painting into dance solely at the level of image. Rather, through a twofold perspective, Sieni's dancer both *refers to* and *engages* the painting. As a dancer dances the painting, Sieni guides her dancing body to reinterpret its subject. She starts from one or more paintings, develops her dance through them, and arrives at a performance of the same episode that retains only some of the elements from the original images. By focusing on its structure (e.g., the spatial relation between bodies or between bodies and landscape) and by selecting small details from the painting (such as the pose of a hand, the intensity of a gaze, the torsion of a limb), Sieni guides a live process of reelaboration of the episode that arrives quite far from the painted image. Thus, in Sieni's work, the choreography does not focus on representing the painting. Rather, the work engages with the structural, affective, and somatic relationship between dance and painting.

Sieni's work is decidedly intermedial. He not only draws attention to the continuous passage between two distinct artistic means but also suggests how this action of passing between media reveals new insights about possible interpretations of a subject. Dance, in particular, makes such a "passing" *flow* between living body and painted image. At times present in the dancer's posture and detailed gestures, at times modified by the dancer's movement, the painting is finally transported and overcome as the dance takes a spectator's attention elsewhere, allowing her mind to wander through analogies. It is as if the painting breathes through the dancer's body and flows away before repetitions of initial gestures and movements, like intake of breath, bring it back again.

Encouraging his dancers to adopt an embodied and personal perception of the painting, Sieni uses dance to help spectators access the painting beyond its perceptual reification. In "Choreographing You: Choreographies in the Visual Arts," Stefanie Rosenthal reads the relation between contemporary art and choreography through the idea of artwork as object: "An engagement with choreography seems to offer us the opportunity to free art—and hence the world—from the predominance of the object" (2010, 20). Going beyond such premises, Sieni supports the idea of a type of choreography that, by fusing artwork and dance in the performer's gestures, revitalizes the object through performance. That is, instead of rejecting the idea of art as object per se, as Rosenthal does, Sieni invites his dancers and their audiences to engage the object (here, the painting), reinterpreting it through embodiment. If we were to juxtapose the dance to the paintings, we would see that the dance motivates an embodied perception of the painting, which is not comprehended within the visual quality of perception we often apply to flat and still images as museumgoers who treat them as reified artworks. The choreographic engagement of the image aims to find kinetic, affective, and somatic ways of understanding paintings, and the Gospel they reinterpret, beyond visual perception and semantic interpretation of the written text.

Sieni's *Figural Dance*

Existing analytical lenses are insufficient to examine the complex way in which Sieni's work intertwines dance and painting, for his aesthetic mingles philosophy with religion and anthropology, dance with the visual arts, and performance theory with community work. Neither choreographic or image analyses, sociological approaches, nor critical theory or performance studies readings of choreography and painting, taken alone, can provide satisfactory tools to investigate how Sieni structures the embodiment of the image in what I call *figural dance*: a dance that enacts figures from visual artworks.[2] To analyze his sophisticated aesthetic, I use a formal approach that has been developed through philosophy and relies on philosophical ideas based on performance practices: *gesture, inactivity/inoperativity, gap/interval*, and *passing*.

A tool for accessing the structural relation between image and embodiment, gesture is a fundamental concept useful for understanding Sieni's figural dance, as it allows for investigating the transition from the painted pose to the lively domain of performance. It is important to clarify how, with gesture, I look not at a social signifier or a pedestrian expression but at an aesthetic phenomenon. I draw from Giorgio Agamben's (2011a) concept of aesthetic gesture as processual experience freed from teleological purposes. Following Agamben, I use gesture here to mean a movement done for no purpose other than feeling the body dance and think through such an experience. My choice of analyzing the gesture as the dancer's aesthetic experience serves Sieni's formal approach to the Gospel. Instead of starting his work from sociocultural readings of the Gospel text, Sieni chose to study how the dancer's body would respond to the very *shapes* in the painting—what the dancer's live gesture and expressivity would add to the painted still image and how the image would affect the dancer's experience. Such a work in turn offers reflections on the function of the Gospel as a reservoir of cultural relations that undergo an ongoing process of redefinition. This shifting perspective derives from Sieni's work rather than being the source for it.

In his choreography of the Gospel, Sieni draws symbolic gestures from religious painting (such as the mother and son's embrace in *Pietà*), filtering them through gestures coming from the performers' own gestural lexicons and their embodied responses to the episodes they took up in performance. Where dance is a potential reservoir of both repeated and innovative gestures, the gestures in paintings offer a repertoire of fixed behaviors that mark and transmit cultural values. The dancer's gesture, occurring live, invites a critical gaze toward the cultural codes portrayed in the painting. The dancer's gesture can recall distinct variations on the symbolic gestures that have accumulated over time within a cultural and geographic zone. The dancer's interpretation of the painting thus works as a sieve, filtering the accumulation of repeated symbolic gestures by replaying and reinterpreting them across the live body. Such moves support a critical awareness of their sedimentation, as a dancer uses her own gestures to either transmit, modify, or even overcome specific signs in the image by training her body to replicate, interpret, and even counteract them.

To Sieni, the gesture is the form holding the choreography. Conceived as an abstract shape rather than a semantic text, Sieni's concept of gesture is based on a plastic idea of form, emphasizing the passages in between instead of the design. Sieni observes, "The gesture is not a productive action made to arrive at a final point. The attention of the gesture is directed toward all that stays in the middle and is called process, but in fact is not a process, as it is a set of infinitesimal moments" (2013). Here, I refer to Sieni's work as processual but ask the reader to bear in mind that for Sieni, process refers to an ever-shifting set of minute temporal intervals through which the dancer passes. Thus, focusing on the "processual" nature of gesture, Sieni shows the temporality of passage as *the* crucial moment that the performer's gesture discloses—moment after moment after moment in process but not as progression. The dancer's final goal is to eliminate, through gestural flow, the borders between intention and action, gesture and pause, gesture A and gesture B, and painted figure and dancer. Such gestural fluidity between passages helps the dancer float between the shapes of the painted figures she embodies.

The "processual" and open-ended conception of gesture described above shifts the focus from the painting as final product—in Agamben's words, "oeuvre" (translatable as opera in Italian) (Agamben 2008, n.p.)—to the painting translated into a plastic dance of minimal passages. Philosophy is embedded in Sieni's work. In 2008 Agamben and Sieni collaborated over fieldwork sessions, exchanging notes about the potential *inoperativity* of dance. To describe Sieni's dance, Agamben used the concept of *inoperosità*, provisionally translated from Italian into English as "inactivity" in their written exchange from 2008. This same concept, later applied in a different context in *Nudities*, was later translated as "inoperativity" (Agamben 2011b, 104–12). The inactive quality in the dancer's performance seems to embrace the "particular modality of acting and living" (105) typical of inoperativity. Sieni's dancers seek a deformation, or better, a de-formation of gesture that allows them to challenge the conceptions of dance as final product made of finished form, thus deactivating the operatic in the dance, making it inoperative—or inactive. Agamben wrote to Sieni: "Recently the idea to which all the lines of my research seem to converge is something whose provisional name is 'inactivity'—not in the sense of inertia, but in one of an active operation that consists of making the action inactive, to the '*des-oeuvre*' to open it up from the inside for another possible use. . . . In short, it was this that I was thinking whilst watching you dance yesterday, and, in a certainly inadequate way, I was suggesting to you to accentuate all the parts in which you seemed to undo, dis-locate, disjoint (and then revertebrate) your gestures in a sort of constitutive 'diphonia' or '*dismorphing*'" (Agamben 2008, n.p.). In Sieni's dance, Agamben observes a project of *des-oeuvrization* (deactivating the oeuvre) against the final product the word "oeuvre" implies. To make his dance inoperative, Sieni *de-forms* the dancer's gesture. The neologism *dismorphing* Agamben uses—once more meaning to deform (hence de-form)—inserts a positive nuance into the idea of de-formation; it implies not destruction or unaccomplishment of form as such but an act of resistance against the function of form as oeuvre.

On his part, Sieni is interested in the process of formation of the gesture, imagining a type of restless gesture that never inscribes a pose: "I have tried to give the body a singularity, where everything comes into being, decays and collapses all at the same time, in unison; where each movement crystallizes from a multitude of forces, collapses and flexions. With Giorgio [Agamben], with his eye, and in his notes and reflections, space tended to be seen as a wave of forces and images. With him the work is infiltrated by action seen at the moment of its disappearance; not a point of suspension but a time that brings things together" (Sieni 2008, n.p). This philosophical vision of the dancer's gesture broadly affects Sieni's work, including his work with paintings. Breaking the representation of an action into fragmented and scattered gestures, the dancer attempts to dance the painting beyond its operatic meaning. In his figural dance, Sieni focuses on the very moment of performing the gesture as the crucial point necessary to reverse one gesture into the other, "dismorphing" them alongside their reference to the painted gestures. In eliminating borders, definition also diminishes. The dance purposely ends up missing the replication of the initial shape alongside the purpose of communicating the meaning illustrated in the painting. In attempting to have the painted shapes disappear in her movement, the dancer offers an inoperative version of the painting, avoiding representing it in its final, product-oriented form.

"Dismorphing" and inactivity/inoperativity are, ultimately, acts that dance uses to complicate shared form. In figural dance, this form is the painted figure that the dance both refers to and engages, both cites and alters. If we were to think of this in a Foucaultian register, we might say that the dancers undo the discourse delimited by the painting even while engaging discursively with the form. Through the enactment of form as undoing, dance engages the painting and its representational scene to rethink our inheritances of figural form, iconic history, and gestural symbolisms. Moreover, as dance explores these aspects of iconography, it manifests in the dancer's body a contemporary response to an ongoing history of Gospel (re)interpretation.

"Pietà-Deposition": Plastic Falls and Rigid Immobility

In the second cycle of *Vangelo secondo Matteo*, one dancer couple from Sieni's company executes a choreographic tableau titled "Pietà-Deposition." The duet is built on the contrast between the organic shapes of the Italian Renaissance and the sharp lines of the Flemish Renaissance. The aesthetics of the two Renaissance traditions merge to influence the structure of the choreography and, with it, the dancers' postures, gestures, and states of mind, as well as their spectators' reflection on the plurality of perspectives deriving from mingling in the same dance two distinct styles of painting portraying the same theme.

Executed by dancers Giulia Mureddu and Jari Boldrini, "Pietà-Deposition" offers another example of figural dance. The choreographic tableau is comprised of two parts and a coda. It shows a complexity in terms of themes, iconographic sources, rhythm, dance technique, gestural expressivity, and use of the gaze. Sieni explores the idea of Deposition together with that of pietà, as if the two consequential episodes reinforced each other's message. As previously mentioned, in art history the term *pietà* (compassion) captures the instant when the Virgin Mary holds the body of the dead Christ, deposed from the cross. Instead of staging the whole episode narrated in the Gospel or literally reproducing the iconographic sources in the dance, in Mureddu and Boldrini's "Pietà-Deposition" Sieni creates the performance by working on the simple act of holding a body against the gravity provoked by the weight of the body as it is being lowered. Sieni connects the embrace (which he derives from the idea of pietà) with the body's fall to the ground (which he derives from the biblical episode of Christ's Deposition). The act of holding extends the tragic moment of the Deposition into an emphatic embrace that attempts to give life again.

In part 1 the action of holding repeats in a loop; once the body touches the ground, the dance starts over. The catalog of the performance recites: "The two bodies refuse a definitive departure from earthly life. They cyclically depose and rise again in a suspension that seems animated by the desire to engage in a relationship with the body of the other" (Di Paolo and Sieni 2014, 106, my translation). The dancers' physical effort to hold and resist, alongside gravity, identification with the experience of death enhances the affective surround of pietà as emotions pass among the dancers and the spectators. In terms of dance actions, such emotions emerge through the action of embracing, which develops through enduring a fight against the abandonment to the ground.

Let us look for a moment at the image of dancers Mureddu and Boldrini performing "Pietà-Deposition" (figure 22). The photograph, taken from the rehearsals, shows a woman (Mureddu) performing in place of Christ and a man (Boldrini) in place of Mary. The shifting of gender roles (alongside age and ethnicity) with respect to the written and iconographic source is a constant element of Sieni's work. Dancing Sieni's Gospel is an occasion for all participants to explore the existential charge of its extreme situations, such as grief, mourning, and death, beyond the categories inscribed in the written text. Here, the Christian episode of the Deposition becomes an occasion for meditating on life well beyond the metaphysical perspective of Christian religion and well past the historical occasion of Christ's particular death.

In the image, the proximity of the dancers' heads, the placement of their hands and arms, and the angle of the legs of the deposed dancer recall the realistic anatomy, the dramatic poses, and the plastic space of Rosso Fiorentino's *Deposition from the Cross* (1521) (figure 23).[3] Fiorentino's painting, reproduced here, shows a composition typical of the Italian Renaissance, in particular of the Florentine and Roman schools. The cross marks a rigid structure, which the characters' movements (some taking down Christ's body and others crying because of his death) and positions in space make dynamic. By occupying

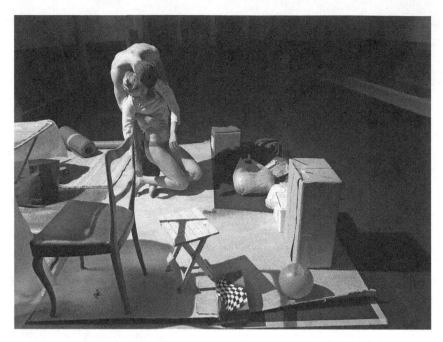

FIGURE 22. Giulia Mureddu and Jari Boldrini in rehearsal for "Pietà-Deposition." (Photo by Virgilio Sieni)

FIGURE 23. Rosso Fiorentino, *Deposizione dalla croce*, 1521, oil on wood. (Comune di Volterra, Pinacoteca e Museo Civico)

several planes and directions in perspective, the characters contribute to creating a sense of depth in turn enhanced by the contrast of the brown cross with the blue sky and the green land. The figures' faces are individually marked and expressive of their feelings as they witness the event of Christ's death.

Using contact improvisation in rehearsal, the dancers worked through passages to incorporate the image source into the structure of their dance, showing a choreographic approach to the image that combines structural poses with details. From Sieni's notes on the creative process pursued during rehearsals, three main steps emerge. First, the dancers concentrated on the encounter between the hand of the dancer who will hold the body and the arm of the dancer who will be supported. They examined how this first touch makes the body of the person held fold. Second, they studied the physical pressure exercised by this encounter on their dancing bodies. Then, using this pressure to guide the gaze, they built a spiral that takes the gaze from the horizon to the centralized hidden position of their folded heads. Expanding the main action of such an embrace with rhythmical changes in the fall and ascent and through repetitions, they appropriated other poses from the figures in the painting as steps through which the choreography proceeds (such as elongating and folding the holding arms).

When the dancers slow down their rhythm, part 2 takes place with another interpretation of "Pietà-Deposition." In figure 24 we can see Mureddu and Boldrini perform this other part of the dance, which, as the two dancers continue the action of holding, draws on the stiff poses, stylized anatomy, and flat surface of Flemish schools. The dancers' roles shift; we can now see the woman holding the male body to be deposed. The held dancer keeps his legs slightly bent and his torso straight, twisted toward the other dancer and avoiding the viewer's gaze, whereas the holding dancer carries a certain detachment in her posture and emotion. The dancers' limbs are stiff and elongated. With its hieratic rigidity from one pose to the next, this second part of the choreography contrasts with the intricate combination of the voluminous shapes of the two bodies marking the first part. Their gestures take inspiration from Rogier van der Weyden's style, in particular his *Pietà* (ca. 1441) (figure 25), which shows a different version of the Deposition episode that contrasts with the emotional situation portrayed in Fiorentino's plastic painting. In van der Weyden's painting, the characters' facial expressions, postures, and details show elegant composure, slightly disturbed by the characters' flexed torsos, as if conveying their pain. The held dancer keeps his heels joined, like Christ; the hands' action softens the fingers' elongation. The metaphysical horizon of a future resuscitation present in Fiorentino's image, given by the homogeneous blue sky, which contrasts with the crudeness of the cross, is absent in this other image. Instead,

FIGURE 24. Giulia Mureddu and Jari Boldrini in rehearsal for "Pietà-Deposition." (Photo by Virgilio Sieni)

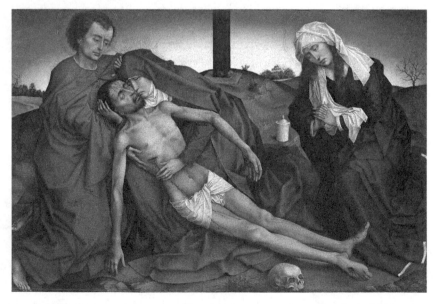

FIGURE 25. Rogier van der Weyden, *Pietà*, ca. 1441, oil on oak panel. (© Royal Museums of Fine Arts of Belgium, Brussels; photo by J. Geleyns— Art Photography)

the viewer's attention is retained in the tragic moment of death, emphasized by the dim light and gathering darkness. In Sieni's choreography, this part of the dance consists of an almost still tableau insistent on the action of holding. For about five minutes the dancers seldom rotate in their taped square, switching the spectators' perspective of the same situation from left to right and back.

Passages between Gap and Gaze

In composing their choreography from painted images, the dancers must deal with the distance between the painting and the dancer, which is both temporal and physical. First, they encounter a temporal (and consequently sociocultural) type of gap. The interaction between painting and dancer echoes multiple temporalities, including the date of the painting, the period of the episode illustrated in the painting, and the date of the performance; in turn, the distance between the time of the painter and that in which the dancers live emerges. Second, they face a physical type of gap depending on the intermedial perspective of the work: the dancers' three-dimensional living bodies must find ways of transferring the two-dimensional artwork out of flatness into movement. Because of Sieni's formal approach to dance, the work on the physical gap affects the way in which the temporal gap is addressed by the dancers and perceived by the spectators.

Exercising a close observation of the image is part of the somatic practice the dancers employ to deal with physical gaps. Although in *Vangelo secondo Matteo* no painting is present in the performance space, Mureddu and Boldrini had already worked on pietà and Deposition in other performances, often performing in front of the artworks engaged to inform the choreography. Sieni observed: "It is beautiful, this relationship with the two-dimensionality, this space that it creates; it is beautiful because to me it is a meditative space. . . . I must say that this is an opportunity, from time to time standing in front of the work and watching it—doing nothing, watching it. This is, to me, a very fertile territory: to allow that it enters you . . . and then to forget it . . . to forget it" (2013). From an attentive observation of the painting, Sieni derives a set of gestures to compare with and modify through the dancers' habitual gestures and their dance technique. This moment of concentration while observing takes, for the choreographer, the form of a "duet between dancer and painting" (Sieni 2013). The painted shapes pervade the dancer's body, guiding her movement as she imagines that the painting space reaches her space. The dancer's own gaze is important here, as she uses her gaze across and into the painting as information for movement.

Using her gaze in capturing the painting and informing her movement, the dancer employs her subsequent gesture to support her duet with the painted work. Sieni's choreographic process sets the dancer's gaze and the gesture on the same level of importance, as if they were corresponding parts of the same creative process. Working on embodiment against the separation between vision and bodily expression, Sieni emphasizes a plastic motility of the gaze and its synesthetic qualities. In fact, Sieni teaches his dancers to use a "tactile gaze" (2010, 4, my translation), that is, a process of observation that emphasizes their *physical* response to the painting. The tactile gaze imagines the figures three-dimensionally, which is the first step necessary to pass through the physical gap between the flat surface of the painting and the dancer's body and kinetically develop the painted poses. Sieni's choreography invites the spectator to engage with such a somatic quality of perception, for a correspondence also exists between the spectator's gaze and the dancer's gesture. As Rodolfo Sacchettini explains, "In these works it is as if the artistic image became a mirror at which eyes look, discovering themselves as body, a sort of doorway into gestures, positions, articulations" (2010, 10, my translation). The observer's eyes (whether dancer or spectator) linger on the curves and chiaroscuro of the painting, learning to embrace the painted volumes. Aiming to engage the body as the means of response to the image makes visual perception plastic. The act involves a fully sensing body instead of one confined by visual perception, as traditional studies on the perception of artworks suggest (Gombrich [1960] 2000, 291–329; Baxandall [1972] 1988, 29–108).

In figural dance, the figure is composed of a dynamic interaction between performed gestures and painted forms that depends on the use of the gaze but does not limit perception to the eye. During the process of dancing, the artwork is the source to which the gaze returns for each sequence of gestures. The reiterated gesture from the figure in the painting to the dancer initiates, to borrow Rebecca Schneider and Lucia Ruprecht's terminology, a relational dynamic of "call and response" between painting and performance that promotes space for a critical attitude (2017, 110, 113, 119). Such a critical attitude relies on the expansion of one's perception—the dancer's and the spectator's—from visual and still to somatic and kinetic. In this relational process, the gap between dancer and painting becomes a connecting "interval" (111). While *gap* might imply lack and distance, when envisioned as an interval, the gap becomes a tool to stimulate the relationality of the dancer's gesture. "Interval" implies passage and reciprocity between painting and performer. By imposing the perception of distance, the gap invites the dancer to establish an interval that engages such distance, finding her connection as a matter of relation, existing between the image and her gestic performance. The interval that the dance makes evident becomes a dimension where the gesture is not immobilized but (re)*passes* previous gestures, traversing spaces, ages, and cultures.

Passing through the Gap

The study of figural dance encourages us to ask how the dancer deals with the gap between her movements and the painted figure that triggers them. The concept of "passing" that Schneider uses in her book *Performing Remains: Art and War in Times of Theatrical Reenactment* clarifies the role of the gap in the embodiment of figures: "If a pass has been thrown from one medium to another, from dance to statuary or from statuary to dance, the emphasis should be placed on *passing*, and the spaces between our overly sedimented medial distinctions" (2011, 135, emphasis added). The idea of passage inscribed in the action of passing supports the intermedial approach of figural dance. In the context of Sieni's work with paintings, "passing" helps bring our attention to the smallest movement fragments that are necessary to build gestic transitions and smooth the gap. As a choreographer, Sieni guides the dancer to see within and move from the figure. Where "tactile gaze" offers an idea of the dancer's embodied visualization of the painted figure, "passing" points to *how* dancers transform the poses of the flat figures into movement and live instants.

The choreographic tableau "Pietà-Deposition" introduces in parts 1 and 2 distinct bodily plasticities and movement qualities depending on two distinct painting styles (Italian and Flemish) and ends with a coda that goes beyond those pictorial traditions. The coda takes the form of a variation on the theme of Deposition that furthers the dancers' work on the gap/interval and enables their passing of the gesture from painting to dance as a dynamic intermedial form. This variation is fast and frenzied, contrasting with the slow tempo of part 1 (Italian Renaissance) and the almost still performance of part 2 (Flemish Renaissance). In it, as in part 1, a male Madonna (Boldrini) holds a female Christ (Mureddu). The male Madonna attempts to keep alive the rigid deposed body of the female Christ by involving it in a frantic puppeteer-marionette dance. The dance dramatically performs the effort of impeding the body from reaching the ground. As if to postpone the acknowledgment of death, the dancers elaborate a sequence of movements that, interrupting the status of stillness, put the deposed dead body in motion. This part of the choreographic tableau is made of fragments of oppositional gestures that occur as if pulled by invisible strings—pushes and pulls, highs and lows, torsions and plunges. In the coda, the dance serves to ultimately disrupt the seeming permanence of any of the various iconographic sources that make up its referential painting. Relying on speed and abrupt rhythm change, the dance avoids any rest, and the dancers make their acts of passing across gaps the very core of the dance. Quick passages seem to retain the dancers' gestures and carry the dancers' emotions away, as if denying them any final abandonment.

The result is that the dance purposefully lacks, in its final movements, the paintings' completed sense of Agamben's "oeuvre." Sieni's gesture is a work of de-formation that undoes the oeuvre in the painting. His aesthetic counteracts the perception of a painting as a final product. The scene of the painting is reduced to one action, repeated. No other gesture contextualizes or develops its narrative. Agamben wrote to Sieni:

> Since the moment I started to love your work, or should I say "your joy," it has seemed to me that you dance "diphonicly." As the voice of the singer, who is often a shaman, emits two sounds contemporaneously, it is as if you carry out two movements at the same time. Or better, one gesture plus something that, inside and through it, undoes it, moves it, accelerates it and slows it down, twists and disarticulates it, loses and rediscovers it. It is as if in all your gestures and all your "creations" there is a *de-creative* force at work, which interrupts and keeps it hanging there, only to resume immediately, all whilst the action is being accomplished. (Agamben 2008, n.p.)

Agamben characterizes Sieni's gesture as an oxymoronic action of forming and de-forming. By emphasizing the gesture as a process of de-formation, Agamben and Sieni envision gestures that counteract the circumscription of the artwork. Sieni offers figural dance to challenge an image's integrity. Passing between painting and dance becomes a strategy to reveal, compose, vary, and potentially even negate the habitual self-enclosure of images and open them instead to choreographic passages for semantic and embodied reinterpretation.

In his work with painting and figures, Sieni's terrain of inquiry is not the discursive text describing the iconographic episode but the very shape of the image included in the episode as that image leans off the painting into its relations. As the dancers do and undo the painting through their gestures, continually citing the iconographic source and exiting the citation, their de-formed gestures "dismorph," to use again Agamben's word, the image, making it inoperative. Undone, its message is modified as dancers switch roles in embodying the figures in the painting and reinterpret the characters' ages. Further, the undone painting's message is enriched through subtraction. "Pietà-Deposition" undoes falling in two ways: by never allowing the body of the dancer who is held to descend to the ground completely and by having the dancer who holds it pull it up each time that it falls, reinitiating its possibility to stand, move, and live. As the choreographic tableau finishes with a loop of movement in place of an ending, the dancer passes from one gesture to the next without waiting for each gesture's completion. Through de-forming gestures, the dance attempts to capture the formation of movement when it is not at its full ending but stopped at an intermediate climax. Such an intermediate position transforms its integral meaning. In "Pietà-Deposition" the inactive dance makes the paintings inoperative because it fights back against the episode's ending—the falling of the body the dancers illustrate. The dancers emphasize the potential of the act instead of its function and insist on the process as the possibility of *both* doing *and* not doing: "Human beings are the animals capable of their own impotentiality" (Agamben 2011b, 44). Reinventing the paintings through danced forms that pass beyond those painted, the choreographic tableau reiterates the act of passing. By passing through the gap, making it an interval, Sieni's choreography undoes the oeuvre in the finished paintings. While dance undoes death, it also undoes the paintings' iconographic narration and eschatological mission.

Dancing a Tale

In Sieni's figural dance, the danced gesture is not limited to its sociocultural significance. Discovered through a somatic awareness and supported by a philosophical lexicon that expresses such awareness, the dancer's gesture can be seen as an exquisitely aesthetic phenomenon that serves an anthropological and cultural interpretation of its use. On the one hand, the philosophical stakes of figural dance make thinkers of the choreographer and the dancer, putting them in the position of the philosopher's interlocutors. As figural dance emphasizes the gap between the performers and the figures in the image, it also reveals the potential of the gap/interval as a moment for thinking. Built on the gap with de-forming gestures, Sieni's *Vangelo secondo Matteo* invites dancers and spectators to push their imaginations beyond their usual understandings of the Gospel. The "dismorphing" quality of the dancers' gestures challenges received doctrinal interpretations, creating fractures that open up space for a fresh understanding of well-known contents recurring in the Gospel.

On the other hand, the intermedial approach inherent in figural dance invites us to further elaborate on the relation between contemporary Italian culture, its Renaissance artistic heritage, and its Catholic tradition. Choosing to enact the Gospel is not an anachronistic or unusual move in Italian society. Because of the Catholic history of the country, Italian culture, albeit relying on a democratic constitution that separates religion and government, is in fact influenced by the cumbersome presence of the Roman Catholic Church in communities and media. With *Vangelo secondo Matteo*, Sieni reflects on the position of religion in Italian society as a terrain of free interpretation beyond the canons and prescriptions of the doctrine. Sieni's choreography emphasizes a vision of religion as a domain of agency, consciousness, and participation and offers the Gospel as an occasion for sharing episodic stories as common human experiences. The intermediation of iconography is essential to move away from the doctrine. Sieni does not use the visual artwork to make his performers' gestures more readable and accurate, nor is it the dancers' goal to support the narration in the image. Sieni uses the paintings *and* dance to open up imagination. Most Italian spectators are familiar with the Gospel's content and its iconography, which they can admire in many churches and museums. Moreover, art history is part of their education. Thus, as Sieni presents new depictions of the sacred book, his figural dance conjures the spectators' memories and stimulates new associations in their thinking.

Creating dance from religious iconography makes the dancer's gesture a means to filter and engage cultural history. Sieni's *Vangelo secondo Matteo* offers an investigation of the gestural provenance of our contemporaneity. It provides a reading of the Gospel that is not only contemporary but also, according to Sieni (2013), anthropological. In a perspective influenced by Aby Warburg's practice of iconology as a repertoire of anthropological symbols that return under variations through time, Sieni engages through dance the returning symbols of a specific culture. "One cannot know the symptom—the pathos of Antiquity, the unconscious gesture of the nymph—without comprehending it. Comprehending it? 'To comprehend' means to take with," observes Georges Didi-Huberman, commenting on Warburg's iconological study of the nymph (2004, 19). The phrase "to take with" implies gesture, movement; it encourages an embodied, choreographed vision of knowledge. In such a possibility for a type of danced knowledge, *Vangelo secondo Matteo* itself becomes part of a Warburgian atlas that collects painted images. Warburg encouraged the detection of embodied connections between variant images of variant time periods, and in this vein we can also see Sieni encouraging an understanding of the dancer's gesture as an anthropological reservoir that can embody accumulated symbols frozen in paintings across time. As the dancer's action collects and transforms the paintings, prolonging them, as it were, as an archaeological understanding of the present, it offers a contemporary version of its ancient gestures.

Sieni's choreography ghosts dance with the repetitious forms of art history. Figural dance locates in the dancer's gesture the potential to dive into the poses inscribed in still images. In painting, the gesture supports the pose. In dance, the gesture marks the process of the movement, unfolding other meanings in the image that are revealed as the dancer embodies the material. In Sieni's work, the gestures, figures, and symbols in the paintings return as contemporary signs that change meanings according to the community of dancers and spectators who embrace them. Cut off from their sources and displaced from their context, their original background fades out, facing our contemporaneity.

Vangelo secondo Matteo identifies in the painted gesture an important cultural heritage and in the dancing body its heir. Where the painting presents gestural codes, the *performed* gesture hovers just beyond that codification.

Notes

1. I attended the performance and observed the final three-week rehearsal phase at the Venice Biennale in July 2014.

2. I borrow the concept of the *figural* from Gilles Deleuze (2004) and Giuliana Altamura (2013).

3. In every choreographic tableau, Sieni draws from a rich variety of images such that no dance is isolable to one work. Here, I am analyzing the sources documented in his unpublished notes or those that emerged in my conversations with him (Sieni 2013).

Works Cited

Agamben, Giorgio. 2008. "From Giorgio Agamben." In Virgilio Sieni, Stefano Scodanibbio, and Giorgio Agamben, *Interrogazioni alle vertebre / Questioning the Vertebrae*. Florence: Maschietto Editore.

———. 2011a. "Giorgio Agamben: Gesture, or the Structure of Art. 2011." European Graduate School Video Lectures. Accessed August 1, 2017. https://www.youtube.com/watch?v=v4bKAEz3TF0.

———. 2011b. *Nudities*. Translated by David Kishik and Stefan Pedatella. Stanford, CA: Stanford University Press.

Altamura, Giuliana. 2013. "Il figurale a teatro: Bacon e l'evento sulla scena del novecento." *Mimesis Journal* 2 (1): 4–36.

Baxandall, Michael. (1972) 1988. *Painting and Experience in Fifteenth Century Italy: A Primer in the Social History of Pictorial Style*. Oxford: Oxford University Press.

Deleuze, Gilles. 2004. *Francis Bacon: The Logic of Sensation*. Minneapolis: University of Minnesota Press.

Didi-Huberman, Georges. 2004. "Forward, Knowledge: Movement (the Man Who Spoke to Butterflies)." In *Aby Warburg and the Image in Motion*, by Philippe-Alain Michaud, 7–20. Translated by Sophie Hawkes. New York: Zone Books.

Di Paolo, Stefania, and Virgilio Sieni. 2014. *Vangelo Secondo Matteo*. Venice: La Biennale di Venezia.

Gombrich, E. H. (1960) 2000. *Art and Illusion: A Study in the Psychology of Pictorial Representation*. Millennium ed. Princeton, NJ: Princeton University Press.

Rosenthal, Stefanie. 2010. "Choreographing You: Choreographies in the Visual Arts." In *Move: Choreographing You*, edited by Stephanie Rosenthal et al., 7–21. London: Hayward Publishing.

Sacchettini, Rodolfo. 2010. "Notte Beccafumi." In Virgilio Sieni, Rodolfo Sacchettini, and Anna Maria Guiducci, *Notte Beccafumi*, 8–14. Florence: Marsilio.

Schneider, Rebecca. 2011. *Performing Remains: Art and War in Times of Theatrical Reenactment*. London: Routledge.

Schneider, Rebecca, and Lucia Ruprecht. 2017. "In Our Hands: An Ethics of Gestural Response-Ability." *Performance Philosophy Journal* 3 (1): 108–25.

Sieni, Virgilio. 2008. "Questioning the Vertebrae: Studies in Learning to Walk Again." In Virgilio Sieni, Stefano Scodanibbio, and Giorgio Agamben, *Interrogazioni alle vertebre / Questioning the Vertebrae*. Florence: Marsilio.

Sieni, Virgilio. 2010. "Scarlatti alla porta del gesto." In Virgilio Sieni, Rodolfo Sacchettini, and Anna Maria Guiducci, *Notte Beccafumi*, 4–7. Florence: Marsilio.

———. 2013. Interview with the author. August 8.

Sidewalk Choreographies

The Politics of Moving Along in
Battery Opera's Lives Were Around Me

ALANA GERECKE

To an outside eye, this does not look like a dance. A small group, four people, stretch into a trailing line before closing again into a tight, traveling knot as they pass through the streets and sidewalks of Vancouver's Downtown Eastside (DTES), one of Canada's most contested city quarters. It takes the man at the front of the group a fraction of a moment to notice that the guide, who had been situated a body width behind him on the right, has stopped walking. The man's momentum carries him slightly past the group, stretching the spatial boundaries of relation before he redirects, shifting his weight back and turning toward the bodies that have clustered around the guide. These bodies lean in, stiff with taut attention, presumably laboring to make out the guide's words. Eventually, the guide finishes talking but lingers in the moment, occupying the authoritative space he has carved out in the midst of these bodies, these city blocks, but hesitantly, deferring the charge to lead. When the guide begins to move again, he does so searchingly, as though he, too, is following a directive. A physical sense of confusion (even dull panic) moves through the group in a subtle choreography of over-steps, catch-steps, stutter-steps, delayed and jolted starts as the group attempts to follow an uncertain, disappearing, and reluctant guide. The physical lexicon is scored around ambivalence, confusion, and unease.

I have just described an excerpt from Battery Opera's intimate choreographic "walking tour," *Lives Were Around Me* (2009).[1] The show left from the then relatively quiet (now trendy and perpetually bustling) Alibi Room pub (location 1 in figure 26) every hour on the hour, five times per night on Tuesday nights throughout January and February 2009 and again in November and December of the same year. Led first by creator and director David McIntosh and then in turn by two other performers, Paul Ternes and Adrienne Wong,

Lives Were Around Me navigated east and then southward from the pub toward Hastings Street before winding around the 200 block of East Cordova. Audience members entered the Empress Hotel Bar on Hastings (location 2 in figure 26), just east of Main Street, and settled there for a sleeve of beer before winding through the streets again and into the Vancouver Police Museum (location 3 in figure 26), with its eerie homage to some of Vancouver's grisliest unsolved homicides. Taking the museum's back exit, the performance then drifted through the alley and street before it deposited audience members a few blocks shy of the Alibi Room again, directing them to make their way back, unguided, to retrieve the belongings they left with greeters at the pub. Performed for a maximum of three audience members per show (with an occasional exception made for a fourth), the performance had an intimate and demanding aesthetic.

    Lives is markedly different from the standard walking tours that have been so controversial in this neighborhood. Consider, for example, the *Sins of the City* DTES walking tour, which is run by the Police Museum. *Sins of the City* has been critiqued for imposing widely held assumptions of the DTES as a hotbed of violence, illness, and addiction (Aoki and Yoshimizu 2015). Local frustration with "poverty pimping" in the neighborhood (Puri 2016) is also evidenced by

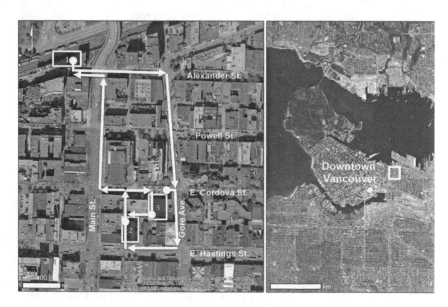

FIGURE 26. Route of the Battery Opera's performance of *Lives Were Around Me*. (Map created by the author with Ersi's ArcGIS® software and online World Imagery basemap)

the public outcry in response to Jenn Potter's recent *Socially Responsible Van* tour. Potter's walking tour has incited reciprocal and ironic "Yuppie gazing" tours (Zeidler 2016), performed in response to this aestheticization of poverty by DTES residents who would be the objects of observation. Unlike these tours, *Lives* is largely invisible as a tour. McIntosh explains, "I did some experiments with what size of audience doesn't disrupt the street, and it seemed like three was good" (2015a). In the outdoor portions of the show, locals and passersby did not recognize *Lives* as either walking tour or performance, a quality of incognito that generated its own set of ethical quandaries.

McIntosh's choreographic tour departed from traditional walking tours in various ways, but it remained ensnared in issues of exploitation. Instead of adhering to walking tour conventions of tracking and lingering at significant locations animated by a guide's historical narrative, audience members of *Lives* were invited to follow a seemingly unsure guide who was rapidly delivering intentionally obscure text.[2] Throughout, engagement with the particular features of the physical space felt abrupt, understated, and almost off-hand: a curt nod or a wave of the hand. Indeed, the guide's seeming lack of interest in the details of site prompted criticism of the show as abstruse and self-involved (Dickinson 2009). Without disputing these criticisms, I seek to resituate the performance's remove from its site as one force in a productive tension that is germane to the more significant criticism the performance enacted. The show's relationship to its site was designed to foreground the place politics that always structure site-based performance—and are so often sidelined (Deutsche 1996; Gerecke 2016; Harvie 2013; Kwon 2002; Levin 2014; Levin and Solga 2009). *Lives* occupied an uncomfortable set of frictions, bristling against the poverty tourism rampant in the area while also inhabiting the preferred structure of this same trend. By generating a choreographic score structured by these contradictions, *Lives* asked its audiences to reflect on how they moved with the economic and social disparities that attend gentrification, particularly an aesthetic consumption of poverty.

In this essay, I draw considerations of urban geography and of site-specific and immersive theater together with my own kinetic experience of *Lives* to develop a notion of *audiencing bodies*. This gerund allows me to explore the doubly choreographic quality that grounds the critical force of this dance: how the movement pathways that comprised the dance in turn choreographed the performance's temporary publics, its audiences. Of course, the kinetic arrangements and kinesthetic experiences in any performance can and will vary widely between audience groups and individual members along gendered, classed, raced, and other lines, as Susan Leigh Foster has insisted (2011, 158–59). Combining the internal mapping of *Lives* I hold in my white, middle-class, cis-female, and dance-trained body with my observations of the ways the piece interacted with its site, I trace the choreographic invitations imbedded in the structure of *Lives*.[3] I ask, how were the audiencing bodies choreographed—socially, spatially, and affectively—through this tour? How did this mode of choreographic knowledge reorient understandings of movement through the city? What was the relationship of this instance of formal choreography to urban choreographies of the everyday and to the socially and spatially mandated ways bodies navigate through city spaces?

To address these questions, I supplement theoretical support for my notion of the city as a choreographic force with historical and urban planning perspectives on Vancouver's DTES. Even as I am invested in context specificity, I also seek to sketch a model for analyses of other performances in other locations. Using *Lives* as a case study, I examine how these choreographic imperatives result in asymmetrically distributed movement vocabularies within particular urban spaces. *Lives,* I argue, magnified the various choreographies that structured Vancouver's DTES at that time even as it also reenacted the exploitation it sought to critique.

Audiencing Bodies and Ambivalent Choreographies

Expanding on the work of Alexandra Boutros and Will Straw (2010), SanSan Kwan (2013), and Gretchen Schiller and Sarah Rubidge (2014), I approach the city as a choreographic force, one that invites us to move in particular ways alongside and within architectural, social, and affective frameworks. I understand the moves that constitute a dance as only one collaborator in a site-specific *cochoreography* that folds together the social, spatial, and environmental elements of a given site with the responsive bodies that people the scene.[4] For the purposes of this small study, I focus on the choreographic impulses built into and orchestrated by urban North American sidewalk spaces.

Crucially, these social, aesthetic, and architectural choreographies are not ideologically neutral. Spaces choreograph bodies differently along the crosscutting and convoluted lines of class, gender, race, ability, age, and sexual orientation. Precisely how bodies are moved in and through city spaces has direct bearing on the possibilities and limitations of both spatial and social engagements and orientations. Put otherwise, the built environment directs everyday trajectories, shapes movement vocabularies, disciplines bodies, and choreographs the social. I will return to unpack the specific choreographies that play out daily on these city sidewalk blocks in Vancouver's DTES. For now, let me bring this notion of urban choreographies to bear on the audiencing bodies in *Lives*.

My understanding of audiencing bodies builds on Kwan's "kinesthetic eth-nography" (2013, 127). For Kwan, a practice of "autoethnographic choreogra-phy" is "a way of studying space" or "knowing geography" (7). Kwan draws from Lena Hammergren's (1996) "re-turn[ed]" notion of the flaneuse.[5] Moving away from earlier conceptions of the (ubiquitously male) flaneur, Hammergren's flaneuse privileges the kinesthetic over the ocular, "observing and responding in the flesh" (55). Following Kwan, I filter the possibilities of Hammergren's flaneuse through my movement training; I combine my "personal kinesthesia" (7) with attention to how audience members were choreographed by *Lives*.

I think of the movement of *Lives'* audiences through the DTES as an exag-gerated form of embodied spectatorship that yielded a subtle participatory choreography, one that built on a long tradition of walking tours in site-specific performance.[6] In her online review of the first run of *Lives* for the local *Plank Magazine*, Rachel Scott recounts her frustration at her inability to grasp the logic within the show's route or narrative. "But then," Scott notes, "I real-ized that the _feel_ of what was happening was the real story—not the linear events that I might piece together out of the script" (2009, underscores in original).[7] Like Scott, I locate the primary aesthetic object of *Lives* in the intro-spective kinetic experience of each audience member, a set of somatic sensa-tions and micromovements coproduced by audience, site, and performer.[8] The show guided its audiencing bodies inward, elevating a self-conscious attention to a "personal kinesthesia" (Kwan 2013, 7)—or "_feel_" in Scott's terms—with an emphasis on the kinetic and affective ambivalences that surfaced during the tour.

Let me offer an example drawing from my personal kinesthetic experience of *Lives*. By the time we left the comfort of the Alibi Room—assured by our host that we would find our guide outside—dark had settled over the DTES. Without addressing us, McIntosh led us away from the pub and away from the small, rapidly gentrifying strip of businesses at the edge of Gastown. (If not for my familiarity with McIntosh, I am not sure that I would have known that he was, in fact, the guide we had been sent out to encounter.)[9] McIntosh was both a gracious host and an unreliable one. He guided us in stops and starts. It almost seemed as if he had forgotten the route he had intended to follow; he appeared to be continually (if only mildly or, perhaps, guardedly) surprised by where he found himself. He paused at each intersection and looked around with a lightly masked searching quality. After a barely perceptible lag, he prof-fered a softly spoken directive, "This way."

We wound east and then south for a few blocks in a mostly awkward, jit-tery silence. Eventually, McIntosh asked us if we had been "here" before, and, repeatedly (though not comfortingly), he muttered, "You can't always understand what you hear." One block from Hastings Street, McIntosh pulled out his cell phone and appeared to take a call. Putting his phone away, he addressed us, "Actually, I have to go find the other group; I left them rather abruptly." As he left, he uttered a cryptic promise: "If you wait here, I'm sure your guide will be along shortly. I can't describe what they look like because they're always changing. But I'm sure they'll make themselves known to you if you wait here." And then we were left again, standing in the dark, waiting for our guide. "What [McIntosh's abrupt departure] did," according to reviewer Kevin Griffin (2009), "is turn every passerby into a potential performer." More than a few people wandered by, seemed to approach us, but then passed without a look—or at least without a look of recognition. We waited for a few beats too long before a young woman (our next guide, we soon learned) seemed to materialize out of nowhere, suddenly standing behind us.

From this point, *Lives* moved its small audience through other spaces in this three-block radius, and as it did so, it also moved us through various forms

FIGURE 27. Although the only existing documentation of *Lives* is dim video footage that yields still images that are too grainy to print, this image captures the feel of the walking aesthetic McIntosh cultivated in *Lives*. Pictured here is a performance of another of Battery Opera's DTES-based walking projects, *Vancouver, Crawling, Weeping, Betting,* 2014. (Image by and courtesy of Yvonne Chew)

and degrees of unease, a quality that culminated in our visit to the dimly lit Police Museum, with its brined human body parts, murder scene evidence, and morbid framing of a performer's nude body lying on an autopsy table not a meter in front of us. Yet this opening sequence—with its stops and starts, exaggerated uncertainties, and dark surroundings—established the sense of nervous, internally preoccupied, and intensely physical awareness that defined the show and determined its affective and aesthetic heft. It was not only the mobility and the possibility of proximity that worked productively in *Lives*; the ambivalence built into its structure directed its audiencing bodies to attend to their own physical responses to their changing environments.

With its careful choreography of the multipart outdoor walking route and its "worked" physicality throughout (McIntosh 2015b), *Lives* generated a sense of perpetually shifting and catching weight in the bodies of its audience members. Audiencing bodies are themselves transformed into the terrain in/on which a dance of uncertain partial physical commitment takes place. In McIntosh's words, "The site of the performance is the body of the audience" (2015a). It is the audience who does the dancing. Throughout the show, audiencing bodies were constantly on their toes, on the move, and out of sorts. A feeling of missing something, of being consciously led astray, or led alongside rather than toward, characterized the performance and the way the piece worked on its audience. The show traded in spatial and social disorientation, of half-committed and half-demanded actions. *Lives* failed—pointedly and intentionally—to offer its audience the comfort or security of a clear and tangible structure, of intelligible theatrical content, or even of a sure-footed route. It is this subtle dance that contains the critical commentary embedded in *Lives*, despite (or, indeed, because of) its problematic relationship to its site: a microdance of ambivalence articulated McIntosh's politics of disorientation. With this cultivation of awareness of the small shifts and catches that constitute both everyday movements and stillnesses, *Lives* invited its audiencing bodies to "_feel_" (recall Scott's review) the unevenness of the social and urban choreographies that structure movement through Vancouver's DTES, a set of dynamics to which I will now turn.

On Moving Along

As I have argued, *Lives* reworked and upset the formal properties of a traditional sightseeing walking tour. Instead, *Lives* offered a kinetic corollary, an ambivalent choreography led by seemingly unsure guides who privileged restless movement over the specificities of site. But the specific context of the DTES was far from irrelevant to *Lives*; indeed, a tension between gawking and overlooking is precisely what the performance explored.

In order to situate the narrative of the DTES that *Lives* simultaneously called up and called out, it is worth highlighting a few elements of the area's complex social history. Oral histories and material evidence (middens of clam shells) indicate that Coast Salish Peoples used and stewarded the area as a seasonal village site for thousands of years prior to colonial settlement (Birmingham et al. 2008, 19). In the late nineteenth and early twentieth centuries, the section of the Hastings Street corridor along and around which *Lives* traversed—land that was never ceded by the Musqueam, Squamish, or Tsleil-Waututh First Nations—became central to the local colonial logging industry, hence the area's nickname of the time, Skid Road (a reference to log skidding).[10] Skid Road was home to the men who labored there and, as such, reflected the gendered and classed imbalance of this section of the workforce (Blomley 2004, 33). Over time, immigrant communities collected in Skid Road neighborhoods: subsections of the area became home to Vancouver's Chinatown and Japantown and, as such, were targets of ensuing racist, "anti-Asiatic" violence (Sommers and Blomley 2002, 30). In the 1950s a postwar exodus of industry to cheaper parts of town rendered Skid Road an area associated less with employment and more with gendered and racialized poverty (31–33). Indeed, even beyond Chinatown and Japantown, narratives of racialized belonging and displacement continue to define the area. The current-day DTES is home to a significantly higher density of Indigenous Peoples than the rest of city (City of Vancouver 2013, 10) and remains a hotspot for resistances by, services for, as well as abuses to Indigenous Peoples.[11] In a neighborhood where residents are instructed by security guards to "go back to the reserve" (Robertson 2007, 528), it is not possible to discuss class-based sociospatial regulation without also acknowledging the systems of racism that underpin so many instances of its expression.[12]

Financially, the area experienced a "slow decline" (Sommers and Blomley 2002, 31) in the postwar period, despite coordinated local efforts to "halt the skid" in the 1960s and 1970s (33) and attempts to render the city attractive on a global stage in the run-up to Expo '86 (Punter 2003, 192). An intersection of poverty, illness, and drug-use resulted in a pathologization of the neighborhood that still dominates discourses about the DTES, overlooking the vibrant communities that reside there (Sommers and Blomley 2002). Meanwhile, surrounding areas of downtown Vancouver continued to gentrify, supporting the city's rising international profile. Mere yards to the south, north, and west, buildings are, "economically and socially, worlds apart," visibly part of the "enfolding sphere of civic entitlement and reimagination" (Shier 2002, 10). Gentrifying forces along the Hastings Street corridor accelerated in support of the Vancouver 2010 Winter Olympics. Characteristics of what Neil Smith

(1996) has called a "revanchist city" became manifest in a renewed wave of evictions of tenants from single room occupancy accommodations, building renovation projects like the SFU Woodward's development (Dickinson 2014), "antihomeless" public space policies that criminalize the movement pathways of those who live and sleep on the streets, and the hiring of private security forces that monitor movement behaviors of neighborhood residents (Freiler 2009, 23). Actions by local residents resisting the ever-advancing effects of gentrification in the area evidence the strength of community forces at work in the DTES, from the "Woodsquat" occupation of the Woodward's development in 2002, to anti-Olympic demonstrations, to ongoing protests outside various high-end caterics in the area. Indeed, the DTES has a strong reputation for its local microclimate of social activism and community resilience. Yet as economic disparity runs deep in Vancouver, the DTES continues to serve as "the site for intensifying regulation of the outcast poor" (Sommers and Blomley 2002, 42).[13] These are precisely the dynamics to which *Lives* attended by implicating its audiences in the classed tensions inscribed in physical placement.

The class politics of McIntosh's approach become clear when we consider the particular choreographies inscribed in sidewalk spaces along and around the Hastings Street corridor. To develop this idea, I turn to Vancouver-based geographer Nicholas Blomley's research on sidewalk spaces in North America. It is telling that Blomley, quoting Jane Jacobs ([1961] 2011), uses the term "'sidewalk ballet'" to describe the processes by which "people occupy and use the sidewalk in intricate, yet patterned forms of community-based surveillance and encounter" (2011, 19). Working with notions of "shy distances" that are informally maintained between pedestrians who share sidewalk space and a two-foot "no-touch zone" that structures ideal sidewalk usage and design, Blomley's kinetic theory of passage draws from civil engineering guidelines to foreground the sidewalk's ability to "choreograph urban encounters between subjects," including the proximity between bodies and between bodies and buildings (28).

In an effort to articulate the friction between humanist expressions of distress at the shrinking public sphere and on-the-ground decisions that shape the design and regulation of cities, Blomley assembles from interviews, urban histories, and planning documents a notion of an ostensibly apolitical organizational system that he terms "pedestrianism," a "functional logic of pedestrian circulation" (2011, 62). Pedestrianism is "a view of the sidewalk as a system of movement" (15). This, Blomley argues, is the principle according to which city engineers design sidewalks and city bylaws regulate them. It is a networked system of flow (and blockage) that serves a "traveling public" and is upheld by an adherence to the "right to pass" (63, 59). Anything or anyone that impedes

Basic pedestrian dimensions

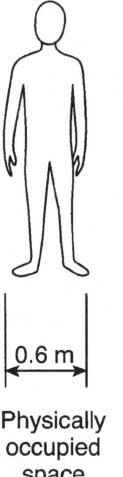

0.6 m

Physically
occupied
space

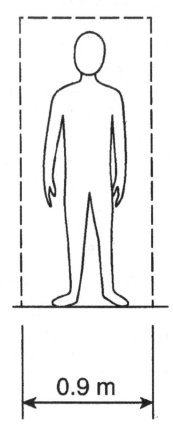

0.9 m

Occupied space
plus
"no touch zone"

FIGURE 28. "Basic Pedestrian Dimensions," American Society of Civil Engineers, 1981. (Image used with permission from the ASCE)

the steady flow of movement along the sidewalk corridor is not only undesirable but also rendered illegal in many cases by various city bylaws, including the contentious sit-lie ordinances so common in North American cities. Crucially, in the logic of pedestrianism, "bodies and objects are viewed as broadly interchangeable" (89); "duly licensed," Blomley insists, "the panhandler is on the same plane as the street vendor or sidewalk café owner, or electrical pole or bus stop" (88). Indeed, the function (if not the intention) of pedestrianism is to depoliticize contestations over access to public spaces and, crucially, to "deactivate rights claims" by presenting issues in "highly spatialized terms" wherein "users are not persons, but *peds*" (89, 97, 106, emphasis added). Pointing to the fraught social consequences of this depoliticization, Blomley insists that pedestrianism's use of an "alchemical language of space" and of "use" is itself "a remarkable political move that needs to be taken seriously" both in and on its own terms (110). In the logic of pedestrianism and thus in the design of city sidewalks, "what is important about the body is whether (rather than why) it is in motion or static" (9), and, as Blomley insists, this "lack of curiosity as to how we walk, and to what ends, is a curious one" (107).

As various strains of dance scholarship have convincingly argued, the imperative to move and to keep moving is itself deeply political; consider Randy Martin (1998) and André Lepecki's respective studies of, in Lepecki's terms, "the political ontology of modernity's investment in its odd hyperkinetic being" (2006, 5). Choreographic knowledges understand that running, walking, wheeling, walking slowly, crawling, strutting, stumbling, drifting, driving, moving with or against the flow, and any number of other variations on mobility effect and affect the space differently. And the imperative to move along, choreography structured into the flow logic of North American sidewalks, acts differently on the bodies that pass through, depending on their needs and desired uses of these spaces. Consider, for example, one policy enacted in a host of North American cities, particularly in the run-up to megaevents like the Olympic Games. Dubbed "the 'move on' power," this policy tends to target "young people, street workers, the homeless and Aboriginal people," people who, for a variety of systemic reasons, may use the sidewalk for purposes other than commuting, prompting them to "move along" (Freiler 2009, 9). In *Lives* the imperative to keep moving was kinetically grounded in a self-conscious sense of how, when, and where we move.

What *Lives* achieved in its exterior tour portions was to call the physical attention of its audiencing bodies to the ways in which the sidewalk orchestrates an urban choreography—that is, how the structure of the sidewalk choreographs bodily movement through the city. As I followed McIntosh (and then Wong and then Ternes and then McIntosh again) through the streets, I remember thinking: *I don't know where I'm going, and I'm not convinced that my guide knows where we're going, but I know I should continue to go, to keep moving.* In the first leg of the tour, we collected at the stoplight at the southwest corner of Alexander and Main Streets and shifted restlessly as we waited for the cue (green means go) to move forward again. We followed McIntosh across the street with a temporarily clear trajectory before our pace slowed again as we approached the sidewalk on the other side. McIntosh had not yet indicated a direction; he had not telegraphed his trajectory with a clear physical commitment, a hand or head gesture, or a verbal cue. We pooled for a moment on the east side of the street, not quite coming to a stop, before McIntosh decided—on the spot, it seemed—to progress straight ahead.

Structured as a walking tour but without a clear or confident trajectory and without a narrative of the route to justify the pathways selected, *Lives'* emphasis on the physicality of *keeping up* cultivated a sense of mandated motion for the sake of motion. McIntosh's approach to the choreographed walking tour complied with and magnified Blomley's pedestrianism. Yet, particularly in the opening portion, our guide's hesitancy cut through this choreographic impulse of forward motion; his unreliability—articulated by his vague sense of disorientation, his stops and starts, his seeming spatial confusion—undermined even as it foregrounded the architectural and legislative choreography of constant flow that characterizes movement through the city. Precisely by obeying the prevailing "logic of uninterrupted flow," the choreography of *Lives* asked its audiencing bodies to "register their passage"—to borrow Fiona Wilkie's formulation (2015, 17)—and to do so kinesthetically, in all its various complexities. The wondering, hesitant breed of inertia that McIntosh's tour performed produced an ongoing pressure to move (purposefully) through city spaces.

But to characterize all the restless movement in *Lives* as hesitant would miss some important information about how the performance choreographed its audiences. Although the exterior portions of *Lives* were dominated by a kind of stilted meander, there was a stretch in which the walking was brusque and clearly directed. Once we turned west onto Hastings Street, through the ad hoc markets set up along the sidewalk, the pace quickened and focus sharpened. McIntosh (2015b) reflected on this choice, noting that this was an effort to complete the desired trajectory (into the Empress Hotel Bar) uninterrupted. Like the determined stride of the commuting worker, among a variety of other slants of direct trajectory, we scurried quickly along the Hastings corridor in the hopes of passing if not unnoticed, then at least ignored by the downmarket dealers and dealings along the sidewalk. Indeed, blockage of flow is a factor motivating recent and renewed city efforts to relocate this informal street market in what critics argue is yet another instance of revanchist city efforts with decidedly choreographic a/effects (Alliance Against Displacement BC et al. 2015; Woo 2015). Our increased pace along Hastings Street was motivated by an interest in keeping up with our ever-revolving guide; but, or perhaps more accurately *and*, it was also bound together with issues of class. By exaggerating a kinesthetic of moving along, *Lives* invited audiencing bodies to register kinetically the physical and social sensations yielded by a bourgeois sidewalk choreography, the "choreopolicing" of "imposed circulation," as Lepecki conceptualizes it (2013, 20). By enacting an aesthetic of *moving along* against a backdrop of those who live and work on the streets—those who do not or cannot move in accordance with these swift trajectories—*Lives* exposed the (classed) choreographies inscribed in these purportedly nontheatrical spaces.

Backgrounded Bodies

Audiencing bodies, as I have insisted, were cast into the choreography of *Lives*, but they were not alone. By virtue of placement, the performance also cast as its background the lives and environs of the DTES—the *lives that are around us*. Recall my description of McIntosh's abandonment of my group on Gore Street; during those long moments between his departure and the arrival of our new "guide," every passerby was conditionally conscripted into the show as a possible (and thus temporary and unwitting) performer. This is, of course, fraught. In her application of Una Chaudhuri's (1995) foundational critique of environmental theater's imperialist "resourcism" to site-specific theater practices, Laura Levin points to the underexamined "politics of (back)ground" in site-based performance, insisting that "traditionally, women and other historically marginalized persons (non-white, lower class, queer, etc.) have been relegated to the background or have been made to stand in for the formal properties of space itself" (2014, 17). While *Lives'* transformation of its audiencing bodies into site or terrain—its resourcing of its audience—was a voluntary, optional luxury, the show's parallel transformation of the DTES into theatrical background operated without the sanction (indeed, sometimes without the knowledge) of those who populated the neighborhood.

Not at all immune to the social dynamics of his work, McIntosh (2015b) understands the troubling ethics of casting a theatrical frame on public sites in general and on the DTES in particular, especially in the context of what he identifies, baldly, as the "bourgeois" theatrical tradition to which his work belongs.[14] As McIntosh puts it, "I was really self-conscious about exploiting. And [*Lives*] *was* exploitative" (2015a). Exploitation is precisely what the show investigated and critiqued, even as it was also what it achieved. The show lingered over the differences between the optional, leisure-based performance of its audiencing bodies and the exploitative, backgrounded theatrical labor of those who belong to a sector of Vancouver's population whose relationship to labor is, in turn, exclusionary, precarious, compulsory, dangerous, and poorly compensated.

Moments of the performance were particularly attuned to classed discord. Whereas audiences had been invisible as such outdoors, fading into the foot traffic along sidewalk corridors, *Lives* groupings were conspicuous inside the Empress bar. Mostly middle class, we were the wrong clientele for the establishment. During my *Lives* tour and overwhelmingly throughout both runs of the show, locals tended to respond by ignoring audience presence in the bar (McIntosh 2015b). I remember some long looks as we followed our guide to the back of the bar where our prepoured beer awaited us; otherwise, I felt peripheral to the scene—except in one crucial moment. Peter Dickinson and I attended *Lives* together, and, as he details in his blog review (2009), a local seated nearby engaged with us enthusiastically, telling us about his life and repeatedly offering physical embraces. Throughout the encounter, our guide insisted (though feebly) that she had to "keep to her schedule" and deliver her text, a response that rendered the juxtaposition between the show and its site particularly stark. The show's design strained against this site-specific contribution, seeming to perform its own failure by explicitly and pointedly sidelining its environs.

The theatrical frame ushered through the doors with the arrival of *Lives* effected an aestheticization of the bar and its patrons that was inflected with a different version of the same ambivalence that structured the rest of the show. Just as we had been guided past significant locations without due pause or description, our audiencing bodies were now escorted into a dynamic and peopled space only to be turned inward, physically choreographed away from the greatest theatrical contributions of the peopled environment. Our guide's only somewhat successful persistence through a relentless, rapid, and barely audible delivery of text demanded that I lean in and watch her lips. Her performance proffered a set of unspoken physical directives that overrode the contextual invitation to experience the bar and the bodies in it as performance objects. Anxious and tight, my audiencing body contracted under the imposed self-reflexivity of my position as privileged flaneuse. I felt the classed tension embedded in *Lives'* hyperbolic demand to attend to the performance over the *lives around* that the show promised to explore. The show set up its audiencing bodies to "_feel_" (Scott 2009) the processes of simultaneously conscripting into and excluding from the performance a group of people routinely ignored by site-based and immersive performance's reworking of the city into an ad hoc performance space—"those for whom the city is not simply about play, but is also about work, about safety issues, and about struggle" (Levin and Solga 2009, 52).

Lives magnified its own structural privileges, including the bourgeois luxuries of attending the show, casting a theatrical frame on the DTES, passing through the DTES's particular "sidewalk ballet," participating in a kind of metacritically privileged flaneurie, and (very likely) leaving the area at the end of the night's entertainment. *Lives* prompted a set of thorny questions that apply beyond a kinesthetic and theatrical exploration of the DTES. Under what conditions do you watch the lives around you? Whose lives do you ignore? What does it "_feel_" like to look, or to look away? Asking audience members to critically consider their roles as distanced and displaced cultural and aesthetic tourists in the DTES, *Lives* pressed them to recognize their complicity with the maintenance of the poverty on display. The restless urban choreography of audience physicality throughout functioned to expose mandated and classed movement built into the DTES while calling attention to the troubling dynamics of art consumption sited in the midst of and as continuous with poverty. *Lives* did not attempt to quiet or occlude its contentious insistence on laying temporary claim to public space: instead, the performance geared its entire theatrical machinery toward exposing its own structuring inequities. With its cultivation of a classed kinesthetic, *Lives* tracked and critiqued, even as it also re-created, how the city—a built, legislated, lived, and perpetually unsettled structure—orchestrates a set of quiet and *uneven* choreographies of the everyday.

Notes

I thank Peter Dickinson, Susan Bennett, Carolyn Lesjak, Rebecca Schneider, Susan Manning, Janice Ross, Laura Levin, Marlis Schweitzer, Carolyne Clare, and the jury of the Canadian Association for Theatre Research's 2016 Robert G. Lawrence Prize, as well as participants in the Mellon Dance Studies Summer Seminar on Publication 2016, for feedback on earlier iterations of this article. This research was supported by a Trudeau Foundation Doctoral Scholarship, a SSHRC Doctoral Scholarship, and a Banting Postdoctoral Fellowship.

1. A Vancouver-based contemporary dance company that produces interdisciplinary work, Battery Opera Performance has been in operation since 1995 under the joint direction of choreographer, musician, and sommelier David McIntosh and dancer-choreographer Lee Su-Feh. Their works have been presented widely within Canada and beyond. My descriptions of this piece are drawn from my live viewing (February 10, 2009) and from video footage of a rehearsal (February 23, 2009).

2. The driving script of *Lives* is drawn from "lives were around me," a chapter in the obscure (though award-winning) Scottish author James Kelman's *Translated Accounts* (2002).

3. A professional dancer based in Vancouver, I am trained in contemporary dance techniques in the Western theatrical tradition.

4. Consider the foundational understandings of movement in and through the city as formulated by Michel de Certeau (1984), Edward Soja (1980), and Edward Casey ([1993] 2009), among others. Urban geography's "mobility turn" (Cresswell 2006), "non-representational theory" (Thrift 2007), explorations of "emotional geography" (Davidson, Bondi, and Smith 2005), and "deep mapping" or "deep geography" (Bodenhamer, Corrigan, and Harris 2015) flesh out considerations of moving bodies in public spaces.

5. For foundational theory and criticism of the flaneuse, see Janet Wolff (1985) and Susan Buck-Morss (1986).

6. While McIntosh's performance as an uncertain guide has many precedents in the tradition of site-specific walking tours—for example, consider the guides in Forced Entertainment's *Nights in This City* (1995)—the kinesthetic emphasis of the ambivalence *Lives* cultivates set it apart.

7. With her use of underscores in "_feel_" Scott implies a folding together of physical sensation, emotional experience, and meaning making in a way that resonates with Josephine Machon's formulation of the fusing together of "making-sense/*sense*-making" in her study of "(syn)aesthetic" performance (2009, 14, emphasis in the original).

8. In my attention to the internal somatic dimensions of audience participation, I build on critiques of audience participation, activation, and passivity raised in recent scholarship on immersive theater by Adam Alston (2016) and Gareth White (2013), among others.

9. My approach to and analysis of this work is complicated and informed by my history as a performer with Battery Opera in numerous other projects over the past decade.

10. As Vancouver's city council acknowledged in 2014, the land remains unceded: "The modern city of Vancouver was founded on the traditional territories of the Musqueam, Squamish, and Tsleil-Waututh First Nations [and] these territories were never ceded through treaty, war, or surrender" (as cited in McCue 2014).

11. For more on the DTES as a site of resistance and erasure of Indigenous women, see Dara Culhane (2003). For an analysis of how daily embodied acts in the DTES challenge the dominant (post)colonial organization of Vancouver as a "settler city" sited on unceded Indigenous territories, see Blomley (2004).

12. For a fuller account of sociospatial experiences in the DTES at the intersection of race, gender, and class, see Leslie Robertson (2007).

13. The median income of DTES residents is currently the lowest in the city, $13,691 per annum compared to the citywide median of $47,299 per annum (City of Vancouver 2015, 19).

14. See Nicolas Ridout (2008) for more on the specifically bourgeois discomforts of consuming theatrical experiences.

Works Cited

Alliance Against Displacement BC, Association for People on Methadone, Carnegie Community Action Project, Chinatown Action Group Drug Users Resource Centre (DURC), DURC Political Action Group, No One Is Illegal Vancouver, Vancouver

Area Network of Drug Users, and Western Aboriginal Harm Reduction Society. 2015. "Open Letter: Displacing Hastings Street Vendors Is Social Cleansing." *Georgia Straight*, December 2. Accessed 5 June 2017. http://www.straight.com/news/588 226/open-letter-displacing-hastings-street-vendors-social-cleansing.

Alston, Adam. 2016. *Beyond Immersive Theatre: Aesthetics, Politics and Productive Participation*. London: Palgrave Macmillan.

American Society of Civil Engineers. 1981. *A Guide to Urban Arterial Systems*. Prepared by the Committee on Urban Arterial Systems of the Urban Transportation Division. New York: ASCE.

Aoki, Julia, and Ayaka Yoshimizu. 2015. "Walking Histories, Un/making Places: Walking Tours as Ethnography of Place." *Space and Culture* 18 (3): 273–84.

Birmingham & Wood Architects and Planners. 2008. *Historical and Cultural Review: Powell Street (Japantown)*. Vancouver: City of Vancouver. Accessed April 6, 2019. https://vancouver.ca/files/cov/powell-street-japantown-historical-cultural-review.pdf.

Blomley, Nicholas. 2004. *Unsettling the City: Urban Land and the Politics of Property*. New York: Routledge.

———. 2011. *Rights of Passage: Sidewalks and the Regulation of Public Flow*. London: Routledge.

Bodenhamer, David J., John Corrigan, and Trevor M. Harris, eds. 2015. *Deep Maps and Spatial Narratives*. Bloomington: Indiana University Press.

Boutros, Alexandra, and Will Straw. 2010. Introduction to *Circulation and the City: Essays on Urban Culture*, by Alexandra Boutros and Will Straw, 3–20. Montreal: McGill-Queen's University Press.

Buck-Morss, Susan. 1986. "The Flaneur, the Sandwichman and the Whore: The Politics of Loitering." *New German Critique* 39 (October): 99–140.

Casey, Edward. (1993) 2009. *Getting Back into Place: Toward a Renewed Understanding of the Place-World*. 2nd ed. Bloomington: Indiana University Press.

Certeau, Michel de. 1984. *The Practice of Everyday Life*. Berkeley: University of California Press.

Chaudhuri, Una. 1995. *Staging Place: The Geography of Modern Drama*. Ann Arbor: University of Michigan Press.

City of Vancouver. 2013. *Downtown Eastside Local Area Profile 2013*. Vancouver: City of Vancouver Community Services and City of Vancouver Planning and Development Services. Accessed June 4, 2017. http://vancouver.ca/files/cov/profile-dtes-local-area -2013.pdf.

———. 2015. *Downtown Eastside Plan*. Vancouver: City of Vancouver. Accessed March 28, 2017. http://vancouver.ca/files/cov/downtown-eastside-plan.pdf.

Cresswell, Tim. 2006. *On the Move*. New York: Routledge.

Culhane, Dara. 2003. "Their Spirits Live within Us: Aboriginal Women in Downtown Eastside Vancouver Emerging into Visibility." *American Indian Quarterly* 27 (3–4): 593–606.

Davidson, Joyce, Liz Bondi, and Mick Smith, eds. 2005. *Emotional Geographies*. Aldershot: Ashgate.

Deutsche, Rosalyn. 1996. *Evictions: Art and Spatial Politics.* Cambridge, MA: MIT Press.

Dickinson, Peter. 2009. "$1 Billion." *Performance, Place, and Politics* (blog), February 12. http://performanceplacepolitics.blogspot.ca/search?q=lives+were+around+me.

———. 2014. "PuShing Performance Brands in Vancouver." *Theatre Research in Canada* 35 (2): 130–50.

Foster, Susan Leigh. 2011. *Choreographing Empathy: Kinesthesia in Performance.* London: Routledge.

Freiler, Alex C. 2009. "Public Space in Vancouver's Downtown." Master's thesis, Simon Fraser University.

Gerecke, Alana. 2016. "Moving Publics: Site-Based Dance and Urban Spatial Politics." PhD dissertation, Simon Fraser University.

Griffin, Kevin. 2009. "4-Person Audience Sees City Spaces through New Eyes; Performers Conduct a Disorienting, Rewarding Downtown Walkabout." *Vancouver Sun,* January 8.

Hammergren, Lena. 1996. "The Re-turn of the Flâneuse." In *Corporealities: Dancing Knowledge, Culture and Power,* edited by Susan Leigh Foster, 54–71. New York: Routledge.

Harvie, Jen. 2013. *Fair Play: Art, Performance and Neoliberalism.* Basingstoke: Palgrave Macmillan.

Jacobs, Jane. (1961) 2011. *The Death and Life of Great American Cities.* New York: Modern Library.

Kelman, James. 2002. "lives were around me." In *Translated Accounts: A Novel,* by James Kelman, 50–60. London: Vintage.

Kwan, SanSan. 2013. *Kinesthetic City: Dance and Movement in Chinese Urban Spaces.* Oxford: Oxford University Press.

Kwon, Miwon. 2002. *One Place after Another: Site-Specific Art and Locational Identity.* Cambridge, MA: MIT Press.

Lepecki, André. 2006. *Exhausting Dance: Performance and the Politics of Movement.* New York: Routledge.

———. 2013. "Choreopolice and Choreopolitics: Or, the Task of the Dancer." *Drama Review* 57 (4): 13–27.

Levin, Laura. 2014. *Performing Ground: Space, Camouflage, and the Art of Blending In.* New York: Palgrave Macmillan.

Levin, Laura, and Kim Solga. 2009. "Building Utopia: Performance and the Fantasy of Urban Renewal in Contemporary Toronto." *Drama Review* 53 (3): 37–53.

Machon, Josephine. 2009. *(Syn)aesthetics: Redefining Visceral Performance.* Basingstoke: Palgrave Macmillan.

Martin, Randy. 1998. *Critical Moves: Dance Studies in Theory and Politics.* Durham, NC: Duke University Press.

McCue, Duncan. 2014. "Vancouver's Oppenheimer Park Protest Raises Question of Aboriginal Title to Urban Centres." *CBC News,* July 22. http://www.cbc.ca/m/touch/aboriginal/story/1.2714731.

McIntosh, David. 2015a. Interview by the author. Vancouver, January 22.

———. 2015b. Interview by the author. Vancouver, June 23.

Punter, John. 2003. *The Vancouver Achievement: Urban Planning and Design*. Vancouver: University of British Columbia Press.

Puri, Belle. 2016. "Walking Tours Exploit Vancouver's Downtown Eastside, Advocates Say." *CBC News*, August 9. Accessed April 12, 2017. http://www.cbc.ca/news/canada/british-columbia/walking-tours-exploit-vancouver-s-downtown-eastside-advocates-say-1.3713724.

Ridout, Nicholas. 2008. "Performance in the Service Economy: Outsourcing and Delegation." In *Double Agent*, edited by Claire Bishop and Mark Sladen, 126–31. London: Institute of Contemporary Arts.

Robertson, Leslie. 2007. "Taming Space: Drug Use, HIV, and Homemaking in Downtown Eastside Vancouver." *Gender, Place and Culture* 14 (5): 527–49.

Schiller, Gretchen, and Sarah Rubidge, eds. 2014. *Choreographic Dwellings: Practicing Place*. Basingstoke: Palgrave Macmillan.

Scott, Rachel. 2009. "*Lives Were Around Me*: A Deliciously Eerie Walk About." *Plank Magazine*, April 13. Accessed October 22, 2015. http://www.plankmagazine.com/review/theatre/lives-were-around-me-deliciously-eerie-walk-about.

Shier, Reid. 2002. Introduction to *Every Building on 100 West Hastings*, by Stan Douglas, 10–17. Vancouver: Contemporary Art Gallery and Arsenal Pulp Press.

Smith, Neil. 1996. *The New Urban Frontier: Gentrification and the Revanchist City*. London: Routledge.

Soja, Edward W. 1980. "The Socio-spatial Dialectic." *Annals of the Association of American Geographers* 70 (2): 207–25.

Sommers, Jeff, and Nick Blomley. 2002. "The Worst Block in Vancouver." In *Every Building on 100 West Hastings*, by Stan Douglas, 18–61. Vancouver: Contemporary Art Gallery and Arsenal Pulp Press.

Thrift, Nigel. 2007. *Non-representational Theory: Space, Politics, Affect*. New York: Routledge.

White, Gareth. 2013. *Audience Participation in Theatre: Aesthetics of the Invitation*. Basingstoke: Palgrave Macmillan.

Wilkie, Fiona. 2015. *Performance, Transport and Mobility: Making Passage*. Basingstoke: Palgrave Macmillan.

Wolff, Janet. 1985. "The Invisible *Flâneuse*: Women and the Literature of Modernity." *Theory, Culture & Society* 2 (3): 37–46.

Woo, Andrea. 2015. "In East Vancouver, A Street Market's Growing Pains." *Globe and Mail*, May 20. Accessed June 5, 2017. https://www.theglobeandmail.com/news/british-columbia/in-east-vancouver-a-street-markets-growing-pains/article24505241/.

Zeidler, Maryse. 2016. "VANDU's 'Yuppie Gazing Tour' Takes Aim at Downtown Eastside Walking Events." *CBC News*, August 16. Accessed April 12, 2017. http://www.cbc.ca/news/canada/british-columbia/yuppie-gazing-tour-downtown-eastside-1.3724109.

Politics

The essays in this section demonstrate how political movements and state policies impact dancing bodies and how dancing bodies in turn shape politics. The first two case studies—drawn from visual art and theatrical dance in Canada—look at the interaction between artists and movements for social and political change. How does an Indigenous artist's work intentionally contribute to the movement for First Nations sovereignty? How does the founding of Les Ballets Jazz de Montréal in 1972 parallel the Québec separatist movement of the time—a parallel not necessarily intended by the choreographer involved? The final two case studies, drawn from theatrical dance in Cuba and Argentina, look at how artists find ways to comment on state policies even when the public sphere is limited or censored. At issue is how dancing bodies enact and elude the politics of their era.

In "Convening Muses and Turning Tables: Reimagining a Danced Politics of Time in Jordan Bennett and Marc Lescarbot," VK Preston juxtaposes an acoustic sculpture by contemporary Mi'kmaq artist Jordan Bennett with an early seventeenth-century travelogue by Marc Lescarbot recounting his visit to New France, including his encounter with the Mi'kmaq. Reading both sculpture and travelogue as "imagined dances," Preston shows how Bennett's *Turning Tables* (2010), a DJ setup made of wood, figuratively turns the tables on the assumptions of settler colonialism, thus joining the Indigenous sovereignty and resistance movement, Idle No More. The tree rings visible in the acoustic sculpture, which records Bennett's attempt to learn the Mi'kmaq language, recall First Nations' epistemologies of the animate life of trees, in contrast to the assumptions of the Anthropocene, when Europeans separated themselves from nature. Not incidentally, Lescarbot's travelogue was published in 1609, exactly the moment when some historians date the emergence of the Anthropocene. *Turning Tables* toured as part of an exhibit titled *Beat Nation: Art, Hip*

Hop, and Aboriginal Culture, and Preston describes how the exhibit "embraces a cultural language of resistance and resilience . . . [by] foregrounding entanglements of black and First Nations histories and solidarities."

Whereas Preston sees First Nations' engagement with black histories as part of a progressive alliance, Melissa Templeton queries the way that activists in the Québec separatist movement made reference to Black Power. In "Les Ballets Jazz and White Mythologies of Blackness in Québec," Templeton examines images of blackness in early works by Les Ballets Jazz de Montréal against the backdrop of the separatist movement of the 1970s. The movement redeployed the rhetoric of Frantz Fanon, Aimé Césaire, and Black Power writers in the United States to claim that French-speaking citizens of Québec were "nègres blancs" (white Negroes) within English-speaking Canada, that is, citizens who demanded liberation from their oppression through independence. Echoing the equation of blackness and liberation in the separatist rhetoric, Les Ballets Jazz deployed a jazz-inflected ballet vocabulary for its predominantly white company and audience. *Jérémie* (1973), the company's first major work, followed a libretto by Marcel Dubé, a French Canadian playwright engaged in the separatist movement. With choreography by Eva von Gencsy, the Hungarian-born cofounder of Les Ballets Jazz, *Jérémie* depicts its eponymous protagonist seduced by the Pimp into a "downward spiral . . . of drugs and sex" before finding salvation through Love, impersonated by a white female dancer. The Pimp was performed by Eddy Toussaint, the Haitian-born cofounder of the company, and when Templeton asked him why he was cast in this role rather than as the protagonist, he acknowledged that "his complexion likely had something to do with it." Toussaint nonetheless praises von Gencsy for supporting his career, and Templeton in turn acknowledges multiple interpretations of *Jérémie*. In her reading, the work "demonstrates the limits of white mythologies of blackness and freedom," mythologies that underlay local audiences' hailing of Les Ballets Jazz in the 1970s for its distinctive Québécois identity.

Multiple interpretations of theatrical dance also ground Elizabeth Schwall's argument in "Cuban Modern Dance after Censorship: A Colorful Gray, 1971–74." Like Templeton, Schwall reconsiders works in their immediate political context, drawing from contemporary reviews and surviving film, photographs, and archival documents. Echoing authors in the opening section, "Archives," she believes that "imagining the many possibilities of political intent honors gaps in the archive." Schwall starts with the first major event of censorship in Cuban concert dance since Fidel Castro assumed power in 1959: the cancellation of Ramiro Guerra's *El Decálogo del Apocalipsis* (The Ten Commandments of the Apocalypse) two weeks before its premiere in 1971. Twelve years earlier Guerra had founded the modern dance ensemble, the Conjunto Nacional de

Danza Moderna Cuba, and after the cancellation he did not choreograph again for many years. His effective departure left Danza Moderna in a period of uncertainty at the same time that artists in other fields were facing similar restrictions, what scholars of the arts in Cuba have called the *quinquenio gris* (five gray years). But within a few years Danza Moderna had reestablished its artistic authority, an accomplishment that Schwall attributes both to an influential dancer's negotiations with state leaders and to young choreographers staging innovative works that took Guerra's legacy in new directions. Eduardo Rivero's *Súlkary* (1971), Gerardo Lastra's *Negra Fuló* (1971), and Víctor Cuéllar's *Con los puños cerrados* (1972), *Diálogo con el presente* (1972), and *Panorama de la música y danza cubana* (1973) all could be interpreted as, on the one hand, upholding Castro's mandate for art to serve the revolution while, on the other hand, challenging state policy in subtly different ways. That all three choreographers were of African descent and, in varying ways, explored Africanist aesthetics alongside revolutionary politics expanded the repertoire of Danza Moderna. Meanwhile, Lorna Burdsall, an American-born member of the company and wife of a highly placed government official, argued behind the scenes for more resources for the company. The ascent of Danza Moderna after 1974, Schwall notes, "ultimately points to the complexities of Cuban cultural policies and the impossibility of a single chronology across the arts."

Whereas the artists of Danza Moderna work within a system of national patronage for the arts, the Argentinian choreographers profiled by Victoria Fortuna find patronage both in Europe and in their country of birth. In "Tango and Memory on the Contemporary Dance Stage," Fortuna examines how artists deploy tango in contemporary dance works to evoke and work through the trauma of the Argentinian dictatorship from 1976 to 1983 and its aftermath, when successive governments pardoned the military officials involved in the disappearance of an estimated thirty thousand citizens. Although incorporating tango into theatrical dance has a long tradition on the Argentinian stage, Fortuna focuses on two artists whose works and careers have been the subject of European film documentaries: Silvia Vladimivsky and Silvia Hodgers. Vladimivsky lived and worked in Buenos Aires during the dictatorship, and the 2007 Italian film *Alma doble* (Double soul) highlights her memories of those years alongside the creative process for her 2006 stage work, *El nombre, otros tangos* (The name, other tangos), performed in both Turin and Buenos Aires. In contrast to Vladimivsky, Hodgers did not remain in Argentina during the military dictatorship. She was arrested in 1971 for militant activism and spent two years in prison before going into exile in 1976 and settling in Geneva. A 2001 Swiss documentary, *Juntos: Un retour en Argentine* (Together: A return to Argentina), follows Hodgers on a return visit to Buenos Aires, her memories intercut with rehearsals and performances of her widely performed 1990s work, *María Mar*, an all-female work that evokes the choreographer's own experiences of torture. In a detailed performance analysis, which incorporates interviews with both choreographers, Fortuna shows how tango functions in their works "as a privileged corporeal repertoire for moving into, dwelling in, and sifting through the pieces of the past."

Fortuna's focus on transnational exchange points toward yet other ways of interrelating the essays in "Politics" with other essays in *Futures of Dance Studies*. Together with Alana Gerecke's essay on site-specific performance in Vancouver and José L. Reynoso's essay on the Centro Nacional de Investigación, Documentación e Información de la Danza José Limón, the center for dance research in Mexico City, the essays in this section demonstrate the potential for a hemispheric perspective within dance studies. Following dancers and dance practices across North and South America, we can trace how Eva von Gencsy brought her jazz studies in New York City to Montreal and how Silvia Hodgers was inspired by the Cuban Revolution to work toward revolution in Argentina. From other sources, we learn about Trinidadian dancer Noble Douglas's study in Canada and about the extensive exchange between dancers in Cuba and Mexico. Yet a transnational approach is not limited to one hemisphere, as Fortuna's essay also makes clear. Indeed, many of the essays in *Futures of Dance Studies* take a global perspective, decentering dance studies' earlier emphasis on the United States and Western Europe.

Convening Muses and Turning Tables

Reimagining a Danced Politics of Time in Jordan Bennett and Marc Lescarbot

VK PRESTON

Newfoundland artist Jordan Bennett's *Turning Tables* (2010) opened at the ImagineNATIVE film and media arts festival in Toronto. The acoustic sculpture played at The Rooms, a cultural center in St. John's, Newfoundland, before its vernissage on unceded Salish lands in Vancouver in the celebrated exhibition *Beat Nation* (Ritter and Willard 2012). The sculpture then toured to Toronto, Montreal, and Halifax with *Beat Nation* before joining the French exhibition *Hip Hop*, curated by the legendary IAM rapper Akhenaton, at the Arab World Institute in Paris. Handmade from cut wood and electronics, Bennett's DJ setup enacts a potent substitution. Its records are made from the cross sections of trees, and its grooves are tree rings spinning on platters of solid oak. The sculpture convenes a palpable dance in the gallery, activating the listener and the space in rippling relation. As the turntables hiccup and crackle over breaks in the wood, they beat out a reminder of cyclical time.

Bennett (Mi'kmaq), a DJ, powwow dancer, performance artist, and traditional tattoo artist, studies Mi'kmaq and Beothuk First Nations visual culture and histories. Asserting, as a point of entry into Indigenous epistemology, that matter remembers and things speak, Bennett describes the voices of this sculpture as sylvan witnesses, suggesting that cut wood may "hear" and recall past generations (Bradbury 2012). *Turning Tables* evokes both the pleasures of the turntable and a history of ethnographic recording as the artist's voice rises and falls, replaying Bennett's voice as he learns the Mi'kmaq language, a First Nations language endangered in centuries of colonial cultural policies. Here, the DJ's stylus seems to hiccup over breaks in the record, converting wood grain into a beat as it interlinks black and Indigenous political resurgence. The

FIGURE 29. Photograph of *Turning Tables*, by artist Jordan Bennett. (Image credit to Mark J. Bennett)

work bespeaks shared histories, peoples, and expressions, intimacy and solidarity, the space of the learner and of the artist, the kinetic memory of the beat, and dances past, present, and future.

In what follows, I syncopate critical approaches to two imagined dances: Bennett's sculpture and Marc Lescarbot's four-hundred-year-old calls to reform Indigenous dance and music (Lescarbot 1609a, 1609b). This remix of forms and histories addresses an ideological and historiographical silence in the routine asymmetry assigning value to writing over dance. The persistence (or ephemerality) of performance here is a site that Bennett shows to be intimately entangled. By placing historical writing and contemporary art side by side, I counterpose cultural histories across a longue durée of settlement and colonization. This approach observes complex rhetorical and cultural calls on dances' relationships to time, voice, and silence. Writing on dance in the Americas pre-1850 reveals a great deal about histories of negotiation and treaty, sovereignty, assembly, resiliency, and diplomacy in North America. As a trope of proto-colonial writing, dance description in these sources takes shape as foreigners' cultural theory of knowledge. Lescarbot's *History of New France* imagines empire in the songs and dances of a future "New France." The writer's *Muses of New France* imagines new solemnities invested in "trans-marine" dance and song he traces back to Antiquity and intermixes with French-language accounts of early seventeenth-century northeastern North America (1609b, 765–66; Preston 2015).

European publications of this period routinely contained passages on dancing, establishing settlement in North America and interweaving dance with descriptions of land and resources within a logic of claiming land. With a few exceptions (Scolieri 2013; Cabranes Grant 2016), dance scholars have not understood such passages as performative theories of dance and cultural memory.[1] Lescarbot's writing on dance is preoccupied with harmonizing and subduing empires, appraising resources from fish to fur and from mining to forestry as a means of financing a French empire in North America.[2] In his introduction to the *Muses*, celebratory dances and song mark the imagined future of the early seventeenth century Port Royal settlement in Mi'kma'ki, Mi'kmaw homelands, in the region today often called Nova Scotia.

In Lescarbot's poetic imaginary, the dance form of the branle extended to environmental movements of water and tides. His writing extends a choreographic imaginary of the maneuver European sailors used to cross the Atlantic: the Volta, or leap, a term also evoking a popular dance step of the time (Foster 2011, 90). This technological and navigational innovation metaphorically leaped over the ocean, interweaving dancing and the imperial project in a shared site of "kinesthetic imagination" (Roach 1996, 27). Preoccupation with dance as a cultural, kinetic, and perceptual form also retraced the meetings and observations of Indigenous and settler groups who did not always share languages, despite massive baroque-era undertakings in translation. Entangling a description of a medicine ceremony with European dance theaters, for instance, Samuel de Champlain compared the protocols of an Algonquin healing dance, likely along the Ottawa River in 1615, to the "entries of a ballet" (1619, 98[v]).[3] This early seventeenth-century description deployed the dramaturgical structure of baroque-era ballets, transposing ceremony into the mimetic registers of performances beloved by France's elites. These festive genres, with which Champlain was clearly familiar, also draw on shared cultural reference points with potential patrons for the project of settlements in North America. Such insistence elaborates dramaturgical theory to choreograph a future empire while claiming French presence in North American lands.

Invoking imagined dances is a recurring motif in the earliest published writings on the Americas. Alongside baroque theories of cultural transmission and political authority, Lescarbot describes dances as celebrations of the harmony of empire. Dances' appearances in these writings amount to theories of performativity, leapfrogging across times and continents. To borrow Lescarbot's metaphor, the "Muses of New France" present a willing reform and the subjection of the arts and knowledges of North America to a French empire, joining this imagined empire as dancers would a dance and singers a harmony. Such politicized imaginaries of art and empire illuminate dances' baroque and allegorical scope, while discourses of empire reveal a cultural history of inscribing political theories of order onto mobile imaginaries of the body and of time—a cultural project that I am also terming "performance extractivism," extending spectatorship's reach into colonial rhetorics claiming land and resources.

To cross-temporally juxtapose works by *Beat Nation*'s artists and curators with a complicated protocolonial figure like Lescarbot illuminates a cultural and political theory of dance and memory embedded in the writing of history. Opposition to such political discourse, however latent, illuminates artists' embrace of danced knowledges in contemporary political art and curation. Joining the resurgence of Indigenous knowledges and concepts of creation, this reconsideration of both archive and danced rhetorics also dismantles a long history of pernicious conflations of dance and the Americas in colonial discourse. Bennett's work shows the power of contemporary artists reclaiming and dismantling cultural forms while exposing violent cultural stereotypes embedded in histories of dance writing, recording, and composition. By contrast, the accumulated writings of this colonial archive of dances in travel writings, routinely constituting unreliable texts, nonetheless have political and legal significance, as well as cultural force, appearing as authenticating detail in works published to instantiate Europeans' legal presence on North America's east coast. This cultural and linguistic detail is performative, participating in logics of claiming land and resources. Such descriptions of dances and songs reveal notions of time and cultural devaluation in a region that would ultimately witness explicitly genocidal proclamations and institutionalized cultural destruction. Reading against the grain of such history, as suggested by the cycles of Bennett's sculpture, contemporary calls upon imagined dances are also calls for emancipatory political and cultural engagements. Theorizing performance extractivism in relationship to a history of seizing land and resources, I investigate material relationships between records made of colonially extracted substances and cultural labor to the performative, asking specifically how dance and music transcribed on paper or recorded onto vinyl might constitute material records relying upon extractive substances, colonial industries, and plunder.

Turning the Tables on Settler Colonialism

Emerging from a 2008 digital web curation project on Indigenous hip hop, the *Beat Nation* exhibition focuses its geographic and political scope on Indigenous cosmologies and political resurgence (Willard and Reece 2008; Ritter and Willard 2012). The touring exhibition designated its cultural engagement with the geography and cosmology of Turtle Island (North America), thereby disavowing the partitioning of the continent into settler states (Canada, Québec, the United States, or Mexico) while citing a creation story shared by many Indigenous nations, making the world an island on a great turtle's back. This assertion deprioritizes a colonial partitioning of North America in favor of multilateral nation-to-nation relationships.

Beat Nation curated works whose collective spirit traversed hip hop's embrace of sound, dance, poetry, visual art, graffiti, and political speech. This pluridisciplinary approach, refuting colonial partitionings of knowledge, also reimagines the cultural work of the dancer and the dance. Bear Witness, of the Ottawa electronic DJ group A Tribe Called Red, projects VJ sets in galleries, exposing the ideological and choreographic imaginaries shaped in made-up "Indian" dance, gesture, and movement. Witness's montages deftly expose racialized imaginaries in settler-colonial media such as danced choruses for twentieth-century film and television, animation, and early ethnographic film. Bear Witness's VJ sets dismantle these gestures as choreographic forms of "playing Indian" even as Witness's videos, when viewed from the dance floor, assert spectatorship activated in motion as fans join the press of the dance floor, experiencing these mediatized dances through the amplified, kinesthetic experiences of the concert and the club (Deloria 1998). This "Electric Pow Wow" (Campeau and Bear Witness 2016) undoes the spectatorial position of an immobile viewer whose understanding of the dance, as theorized in Lescarbot, exceeds that of the dancer.

Dance rather than theater lies between the works of *Beat Nation*.[4] Heather Igloliorte, who curated many of *Beat Nation*'s artists in earlier exhibitions, writes of "indigeniz[ing] the Western institutional framework of the art exhibition by incorporating song, movement, and performance" (2010, 25). Foregrounding entanglements of black and First Nations histories and solidarities, *Beat Nation* embraces a cultural language of resistance and resilience (Madden 2009). As such, these artistic works avow resilience and illuminate histories of violence, where attempts to convert the Indigenous inhabitants of North America and seize their land and resources were themselves intertwined with the Caribbean plantocracies and slave trade (Pestana 2009).[5] The emergence of Atlantic-world dances as contested "performative commons" disputed over centuries (Dillon 2014) here presents a powerful counterplay between the political art of Bennett and Bear Witness and the cultural reform imagined through dance and music in Lescarbot.

Bennett's hand-crafted DJ set, *Turning Tables*, mimics the pop and hush of recorded silence on vinyl. Asking what trees and woody matter might also tell us of a violently silenced past, the sculpture indicates a kinesthetic and ontological invitation that, like Eduardo Kohn's *How Forests Think*, asks how "living thoughts" and beings decenter the human (2013, 100). Trees' memories and perceptions offer models of communication quite otherwise than the human exceptionalism embedded in "living" plant or "dead" wood. Considering the impact of colonization on forests and trees, as well as on archives and mnemonic systems, the felling of forests has affected global ecologies, as well as material records, libraries, and wooden theaters (Nardizzi 2013). Importantly too, the woods Bennett crafts into *Turning Tables* also possess medicinal properties, participating in Mi'kmaw conceptions of being and knowledge.

Mi'kmaw language articulates what speaks and what lives according to hierarchies of grammatical animacy or inanimacy (McKegney 2007; Julian 2016; Little 2016). As an engagement with animacy hierarchies, as well as linguistic and mnemonic records, Bennett's sculpture raises important interconnections between voice, language, and semantics: wood, paper, and books participate in both the suppression and the preservation of language, just as crude oil and the metamorphoses of the laboratory materially constitute the vinyl LP. Providing a model of resilience and (re)learning in the skillful playing of multiple tracks, Bennett's complex homage to the DJ set nonetheless also puts a motif of deforestation on display—as a violence done not simply to land but to land-based knowledges and pedagogies. As Jussi Parikka writes in *The Anthrobscene*, "[Even] if media theory might have *partly* forgotten the existence of the earth as a condition of media, the arts did not" (2014, 4). The author continues: "In addition to the history of media derivable from the earth sciences, artistic practices from sculpture to painting [have] had a close relationship to earth's materials. Art has turned chemicals, clays, pigments, into expressions of . . . the existence of the earth: an understanding of the earth's tendencies to create sound, light, and more" (4). Similarly, in examining the history of the book, as well as of performance, we do well to consider the entanglement of deforestation and its ecologies with the stage, the printing press, and the ship (Nardizzi 2013), producing early modern media and material conditions that also globalize conceptions of performance through ecocide.

Playing back samples of Bennett learning Mi'kmaq, *Turning Tables* activates a history of the artist learning the language of his occluded First Nations ancestry. Simulating historical recordings, he cites and subverts the acoustic tropes of "salvage ethnography" (Gruber 1970; Mills 2017). Without reproducing these tropes, he records himself learning the language in spite of histories of violent repression, removal, and "linguicide" (Julian 2016). This sampling distills a conceptual "challenge to historiographical assumptions—about time, place, and space; genres of performance" (Carter, Recollet, and Robinson 2017, 205), an interrogation that cultural theorist and dance writer Karyn Recollet also powerfully describes as "a refusal of being stilled" (213). Investigating the remix in the curatorially polysemic *Beat Nation*, Recollet hones in on Indigenous cosmologies that remain irreducible to Western conceptions of linear time and cadence. Moreover, in a 2015 Skype interview, Bennett told me how wax cylinders and recordings that might provide a complex, mediated access to Beothuk and Mi'kmaw practices and histories, including family history, were shipped away to collections abroad, notably, the Musée du Quai Branly in Paris, and thus participate in yet further dispossessions. This insight de-centers records' relationships to accumulation and collections, amplifying the relevance of *Beat Nation*'s remixes as strategies for taking up practices of ethnography when sources are complicatedly entangled in survival, as well as in institutionalized and industrialized logics of assimilation and genocide. They also underscore the political and artistic insurgency of Indigenous artists reclaiming and redefining such records from the archives—most prominently of late in Jeremy Dutcher's internationally acclaimed 2018 debut, post-classical album *Wolastoqiyik Lintuwakonawa*, recorded in untranslated passages drawn from 1904–17 wax cylinder recordings of Wolastoqiyik peoples' traditional songs in the artist's ancestral language. This work refuses but also reimagines anthropological collections founded on seized and recorded fragments of community knowledges extracted and dispossessed from First Nations during extended and ongoing histories of colonization.

In performance extractivism, relationships between print and recording underscore their relation to practices and materials plundered in the course of settler colonialism and imperialism. This relation becomes audible in the sonic worlding of Bennett's sculpture, suggesting an intimate, nonlinear remixing of times and sources brought into relation otherwise than by linear principles. By switching out PVC and plastics (both petrochemicals) for wood, Bennett also brings attention to mining and deforestation. In what I read as a political moment of protest, Bennett's title, *Turning Tables*, evokes the legal position of "turning the tables" articulated by the Idle No More movement, the "round dance revolution" launched in 2012 to assert Indigenous sovereignty and resistance to extractivism, access to safe housing and water, and insistence upon cultural resilience. Idle No More emphasizes a mutuality of treaty that "is also our best chance to save entire territories from endless extraction and environmental destruction" (Idle No More 2014). This strategy, pursued in round dances, flash mobs, and social media, demands that settler cultures not forget but rather respect and honor treaties that have bound settlers and Indigenous persons for more than four centuries. In Canada these reach to the era of "New France" of Lescarbot's publications, negotiated in the early seventeenth century by Mi'kmaw leader Henri Membertou with the Holy See. Known as the Concordat of 1610, the earliest known treaty in this region between European and Indigenous parties included Membertou's baptism and was marked with a wampum belt that is still held at the Vatican despite a growing movement for its repatriation. In a diplomatic mode, Indigenous scholars argue, the treaty enhanced nation-to-nation clarifications of Mi'kmaw sovereignty and harmonized First Nations and European spirituality according to Indigenous practices (McKegney 2007, 112). Not incidentally, some scientists also identify the year of this first treaty as the inauguration of the Anthropocene, the moment at which humans came to have unprecedented impacts on the planet (Lewis and Maslin 2015).

By returning to reasserting mutual responsibility, the principle of "turning the tables" underscores self-determination and Indigenous jurisdiction, disavowing the perversity of the notion that "land claims" mean relinquishing previous negotiation. This approach asserts historical and cultural memory, even as Indigenous sound recordings in archives today may play significant legal roles as "records of land use that can be vital in modern assertions of sovereignty over traditional territory" (Mills 2017, 116). Given that written documents have proven unreliable (and at times forged), these uses honor a spectrum of memory practices that can contend with prioritizing writing over other cultural knowledges (Battiste 2006; Glover and Cohen 2014; Recollet 2015a, 2015b; Recollet quoted in Carter, Recollet, and Robinson 2017; Hudson, Ibrahim, and Recollet 2019).

Within historians' troubling history of recording and collecting Indigenous practices (Mills 2017), their tendency to privilege alphabetic writing over other forms of transmission, including dance, inevitably raises questions about acts of cultural suppression such as dance bans (Shea Murphy 2007), which I believe are rooted in colonial discourses imagining dances in the Americas. Current thinking also involves deepening awareness of a plurality of media supports and formats for culturally distinct North American cultures and nations (Glover and Cohen 2014). For instance, Heidi Bohaker, citing Arjun Appadurai's "mediascape," argues that "historians of 'early modern' America have much to gain by jettisoning Western conceptions of what constitutes history and historical sources in favor of categories grounded in Indigenous epistemological frameworks" (2014, 126); such a model "requires a different way of thinking about historical sources" (127).[6] Citing the petroglyph as distinct from epistemologies of choreo-graphy's entanglement with the written, Recollet (2015b) offers movement across materials, as well as mediatized and performative spaces, inter(in)animating dance, glyph, music, carving, graffiti, story, bodies, and stones.[7] In her recent contributions on Indigenous dance and hip hop, she decenters alphabetic writing as the privileged metaphor for cultural sharing, offering an Indigenous media spectrum in which apprehending time and narrative across dance and stone becomes a creative and political act, uprooting dances' devaluation in settler epistemologies (Recollet in Shea Murphy 2016; Carter, Recollet, and Robinson 2017). This "glyphing" of a dance, Recollet writes, evokes the petroglyph, or rock carving, as a model traversing practice, as well as material culture, story, and land-based knowledges.

Bennett's autorecordings draw attention to material support while attending to wood's cross-temporal witness. In an interview, the artist imagines *Turning Tables* playing back the voices of grandfathers and grandmothers once heard by the trees, replaying heard worlds and knowledges that invite listeners to consider which substances and practices enact and carry mnemonic transmission (Bradbury 2012). Listening in this remediated mode to tree rings, a mode of times nested in other times, *Turning Tables* evokes colonial deforestation, transforming the ecologies and lifeways of a continent.

Bennett's transposition—of petrochemical consumer and professional media crafted into handcrafted walnut, spruce, and oak parts—makes a conceptual move that engages the remix as agential and ethical labor, and perhaps also as a healing medicine, creating and reiterating relationships to materials, selection, and sources. Enriching relationships to cultural memory, along with the felt and audible time of the breach, Bennett's artwork denaturalizes the conventional materials of mnemonic commodities and reminds viewers and listeners of the substances with which mnemonic machines are made, decentering petrochemicals with the medicinal and healing agencies of nonhuman entities. Against the legacy of settler colonization and programmatic cultural violence, Bennett's approaches to media and performance take up popular forms, from postering to the remix, in an ecology with beadwork, microfiches and petroglyphs, books and birch bark scrolls, recordings, songs, dances, and alphabetic writing.[8] Each of these memory systems inter(in)animates relationships of matter and memory. Where Bennett's records speak, the tree rings spin both materially and metaphorically, holding times within other times. Cycles of historiography, as the sculpture's stylus writes with and against the grain of wood, (re)play both matter and voice.

Critics exposing this translocalizing of substance, voice, and signal provide insight into the performativity that Bennett's wooden turntables propose as models of the DJ's archive: matching and syncopating sources, recomposing forms and temporalities.[9] Where, Fred Moten writes, "montage renders inoperative any simple opposition of totality to singularity," the remix affords agential selection and relationships that "[make] you linger in the cut between them, a generative space that fills and erases itself" (2003, 89). In convoking such a proposal, *Turning Tables* emphasizes both continuity and rupture, heeding a call to dance in the seeming stillness of the gallery and its silencing inheritances of settler modalities of knowledge. The work instead convenes the participatory, ecstatic thinking-feeling of the dance floor. Its possibility of experience shared between those who dance together, between nations, cosmologies, and materiality illuminates the possibility of interrelationship while also resisting extractivism.

Polyvinyl chloride (PVC) composes the late twentieth-century vinyl record, extracted from crude oil in the laboratory. The concentric nesting of tree rings, suggesting cyclical notions of time, here offers a model of expanding growth in a plurality of directions. This principle, rendered audible in *Turning Tables*, decenters settler histories' presumptive models of linear and developmental structure, recomposing practice with the DJ's stylus. Like the sample, this structure models kinesthetic interplay and pluralism, "obliterat[ing] conventional distinctions between performing (or practicing) and recording" (Schloss 2014, 46). This "obliteration" is not an act of destruction. It pluralizes and asserts interrelationships: the archive that the DJ *does*. Making an ethics of such breaks and samplings makes community not only through listening and movement but through sensory immersion in a kinesthetic possible, interrelating the spiral temporality of the vinyl LP and the circular time of the trees' growth.

Reading against the Colonial Grain

Dance, as a practice of convening and of medicine and healing, is a recurring preoccupation in early print histories of North America. Writings by Samuel de Champlain and Lescarbot recount dances within codified dance-theatrical models in a genre of dance writing and publishing that, as Paul Scolieri (2013) notes, engages writing on dance as an active theorization of memory and historiography. Yet at the same time, colonial accounts routinely silence and ultimately devalue the knowledges of the Indigenous inhabitants of the Americas, even as they offer a massive, albeit complicated, archive of Indigenous performance alongside maps and itemizations of land and resources. Lescarbot's chapter on dance and song theorizes a binary of benevolent and corrupt dancing, leapfrogging from David of the Hebrew Bible to transcriptions of Indigenous dances and songs. Interpreting the misheard cry "Hallelujah" as a ceremonial inversion of Christian ceremony, Lescarbot links it to the devil (1609a, 691–92). Such misunderstandings in the colonial, sensorial archive explain why historians have routinely ignored such dance descriptions, yet this silence also erases how such theories of dance, ceremony, the body, and gesture circulated, even scripted, and eventually congealed stereotypes of subjection and colonization, with dances as minor knowledges and ephemeral conceptions of community.

Lescarbot's writings on dance, song, and oratory insinuate a call to reform Indigenous arts and culture within both a "history" and a "theater" of "New France" (Lescarbot 1609b; Seed 1995; Bloechl 2008, 149; Welch 2011; Preston 2015). Emerging from baroque-era theories of cultural reform, the writings of Lescarbot and his peers have persisted in strategies regulating collective and bodily movement. These protocolonial writings on dancing, I would argue, constitute cosmologies and systems of belief elaborating mnemonic theories of the Americas and of bodies, with material, legal, corporeal, economic, and philosophical consequences that participate in devaluations of cultural transmission.

Not unlike Jacques in William Shakespeare's *As You Like It*, evoking a forest of trees as expanded books in which to write the name of the beloved (act 3, scene 2),[10] Lescarbot's motif of the book of nature in a *History of New France* imagines engraving the French minister of finance's name, Nicolas Brullart de Sillery, on the trees, rocks, and features of the landscape. Designating the coast of North America "New France" and deploying the motif of an imagined theater as the space, organization, and purview of European political hierarchy, Lescarbot offers theatricalizing proof of the early French settlers' presence on the land. His conceptual organization of a theater imagines a political relationship of Europe to North America's peoples and to its landscapes, ceremonies, and resources. Writing to Pierre Jeannin, the king's councilor and general comptroller of finances, Lescarbot makes his appeal, advising him to "send French colonies to civilize the people . . . and make them Christians"; he adds, "God gives you the most eminent seat in the great theatre of France so you will see and consider these things and bring them your assistance" (1609a, 13–14, my translation).[11] This allusion to the construction of a theater of conversion as a relationship to political leadership decenters performance and the human. As Vin Nardizzi (2013) observes, public theaters and mass deforestations coemerged in the early seventeenth century at the cusp of what is called the Anthropocene, which comes into view as a transformation not only of the earth and its atmosphere but also of performance and its mnemonic traces. Such changes maintain and materialize the formats and spaces of publications and architectures, producing theaters that perform in, with, and on felled wood at industrial scales—not simply in England, as in Nardizzi's thesis, but also in the Americas. With prayers likened in Lescarbot to a stylus, engraving possession through prayer onto the land, the entanglement of these cultural histories of spectatorship, religion, performance, and extractivism scripts a theatrical modeling of relationships of power and subjection imagined through danced motifs as well as of records.

Lescarbot's introduction to what has long been framed as the first works of European theater in the region, the "Theatre of Neptune" (1609b), and the epistles to his *History* (1609a) and *Muses* (1609b) invoke claims on plant and animal life, the mining of sacred copper, laurels, lands, and waters. Claiming land in North America for France, his writing assigns economic, political, and theological meaning to theatricalized models of sovereignty, fame, and ceremony. Lescarbot's formulation of prayer and spectatorship imagines a course toward future empire, promising North America viewed from Europe as a "theater of the world."

Read against the grain, such texts constitute a cultural history in which Lescarbot's calls to reform Indigenous music and dance toward a "more responsive" rhythm resonate with his urgent cry to found an empire (1609b, 3). "Few early writers have expressed the cultural assimilationist aims of French colonization so succinctly," writes Olivia Bloechl. "In Lescarbot's vision of colonial relations, the Mi'kmaqs required settlement, development of agriculture, pacification, and Christianization, but also the reform of their comportment and expression through song and dance" (2008, 149). Lescarbot emphasizes dances' origins in the sacred, suggesting his opposition to antidance stances of the late sixteenth and early seventeenth centuries (1609a, 848).[12] As Lescarbot disputes the "learned" baroque-era definition of dance as a "mute Rhetoric" (Arbeau 1589, 5v), he also asserts that "[all] dances [in the Americas] are sung [like those of Greek antiquity] and do not make mute gestures [*gestes muets*]" (1609a, 768). Lescarbot then traces this teaching on the dancer's silence to the oracle of Delphi in the Greek writings of Lucian, insinuating a performance genealogy into his accounts of New France that prioritizes the spectator's understanding over the dancer's practice. This eruption of dance theory is most clear when Lescarbot asserts that the "*spectator* [of a dance] *must understand the performance itself, and so it must be mute and is measured by the extent it does not speak*" (1609a, first edition 768; third edition 1617, 849; revised with emphasis in the third edition above). The consequence of such a theory in a political history of diplomacy and treaty in North America, where dances have ceremonial and cosmological consequence, cannot be underestimated.

Turning Tables: Redux

Bennett's remix reconfigures acoustic and kinesthetic imaginaries in a model that is never linear. The DJ's performative practice turns upon itself here, honoring complex histories of recording ancestors' voices and songs while also proposing that the trees and the land also, definitively, remember (Katz 2012). The hushes and warbles of the artist's acoustic installation mimic ethnographic recordings, making Bennett's amplified tree rings evoke, yet reconfigure, wax cylinders and phonographs in collections and museums. The DJ's stylus, the needle, here counters the engraving of prayer as an act of possession inscribed on the land. This virtuality of the felt dance in the museum or gallery also draws out the potential of ontological and epistemological recomposition. Where the stylus skates over and replays cracks in the wood, suggesting histories of systemic cultural violence with the sound of rupture, it both visually and sonically refuses pride of narrative, dismantling an opposition of liveness and deadness, performativity and record. Grammatologically, Bennett seems to draw voice from wood, activating animacies along with Mi'kmaq syntax (Bradbury 2012). Calling things and the cosmos into motion, this insight retraces a performative making and maintaining of worlds by way of arboreal memory. The sculpture's mode of remembering audible pasts and its materialization of an ethic of honoring sources and of convening spectators to dance invite us to listen to these hushings and cracklings of syntax and song. Thus Bennett proposes an ethics of remembering, to "bend time in another way" (McLeod 2016, 6), while recognizing the voice in the recording as a relation, a relative (Schneider 2011, 59; Mills 2017). This engagement also reminds us that the future "is not just a technical or neutral space, but is shot through with affect and with sensation," where futures offer scripts of both exclusion and belonging (Appadurai 2013, 286–87).

Bennett's very deployments of mnemonic machines and categories displace a petrochemical format, the LP, with a hand-crafted wooden one. With this act of substitution, the artist honors intercultures between elders and global youth cultures. Evoking an imagined dance floor, convening dancers past, present, and future to the floor, the record speaks and repeats, calling treaty-making peoples into linguistic and cultural revitalization through the "turning of tables" and treaty. In contradistinction with violent and strategic acts of cultural suppression, this approach calls upon a closer scrutiny of the record, treating its mnemonic and material structures as relationships to land and rupture written into hidden histories of dance and theater.

Notes

The passages from early modern sources are drawn from special collections research at the Bibliothèque nationale de France (BnF), Bibliotheque et archives nationale de Québec (BAnQ), and the John Carter Brown Library. The translations are mine, and their pagination by default references first editions of these works (unless otherwise indicated). Readers may note, however, that both page numbers passages vary in different versions of these texts. The BnF has recently created new digital versions of Thoinot Arbeau and Samuel de Champlain for the French digital resource Gallica. Québec's BAnQ has digitized new first editions of Marc Lescarbot's publications. These sources appear in the bibliography. Gallica offers a low-resolution scan of the 1617 edition of *History of New France* and links to the BAnQ for first editions of Lescarbot.

1. On sound, networks, technologies, and what he terms *performance*, see Grant (2016, 88–89, 94–95).

2. Further close readings and translations from Marc Lescarbot on dance and theater appear in Preston (2015).

3. See https://gallica.bnf.fr/ark:/12148/bpt6k8705145s/f224.image.

4. *Beat Nation*'s Toronto tour included an all-styles dance battle at the Power Plant Gallery. See http://www.thepowerplant.org/ProgramsEvents/Programs/Live/Beat -Nation-Break-Dance-Battle.aspx.

5. In *Beat Nation,* dance traverses Maria Hupfield's jingle dance works; Nicholas Galanin's screen dances *Tsu Heidei Shugaxtutaan, parts 1 and 2*; Kent Monkman's *Dance to Miss Chief*; and Bear Witness's *Assimilate This*. For A Tribe Called Red's superb videos, see the band's website.

6. On Indigenous and colonial media beyond the page, see Battiste (2006) and Cohen and Glover (2014), especially Bohaker (2014). On Mexico and the Caribbean, see Scolieri (2013) and Grant (2016). On contemporary Indigenous art and curation's critical reconfigurations of encounter narratives and records, see Racette (2011).

7. In *Performing Remains*, Rebecca Schneider describes her conception of inter(in) animation as "a constant (re)turn of, to, from, and between states in animation," writing that "'survival' . . . may be a critical mode of remaining, as well as a mode of remaining critical: passing on, staying alive, in order to pass on the past *as past*, not, indeed, as (only) present. Never (only) present" (2011, 7).

8. For more on a spectrum of Indigenous archives and media, see Battiste (2006) and Glover and Cohen (2014).

9. Joseph Schloss writes of "consciousness about the significance of the turntable" in his account of the ethics of sampling as an account of both the art form's and the artist's histories (2014, 41, 52).

10. *The Yale Shakespeare: The Complete Works*, edited by Wilbur L. Cross and Tucker Brooke (New York: Barnes and Noble, 1993).

11. Lescarbot rewrote the dedicatory epistles and front matter for *History of New France* in each edition, reflecting a volatile political situation in France following the king's assassination in 1610 and queen's 1617 ouster. The pages' numbering varies in these differing versions. This phrasing closes the third edition's letter to Pierre Jeannin, the France's finance comptroller and advisor to the king. See https://gallica.bnf.fr/ark:/ 12148/bpt6k1095053/f12.image.

12. The emphasis on reforming and containing dance in the Americas, penned into early writings on Atlantic-world empire and colonization, suggests that the seeds of North America's dance bans began to take root in writings published very early in the history of transmarine travel and publication. European assertions on dancing can be found in other European travel accounts, for example, in Spanish-language travel narratives. For more, see Scolieri (2013, 7–14, 49–55).

Works Cited

Appadurai, Arjun. 2013. *The Future as Cultural Fact: Essays on the Global Condition.* London: Verso.

Arbeau, Thoinot. 1589. *Orchésographie et traicté en forme de dialogue*. . . . Lengres: Johan des Preyz. For a digital edition, see https://gallica.bnf.fr/ark:/12148/btv1b86107 61x/f9.image.

Battiste, Marie. 2006. "Print Culture and Decolonizing the University: Indigenizing the Page: Part 1." In *The Future of the Page*, edited by Peter Stoicheff and Andrew Taylor, 111–23. Toronto: University of Toronto Press.

Bennett, Jordan. 2015. Interview with the author.

Bloechl, Olivia Ashley. 2008. *Native American Song at the Frontiers of Early Modern Music*. Cambridge: Cambridge University Press.

Bohaker, Heidi. 2014. "Indigenous Histories and Archival Media." In *Colonial Mediascapes: Sensory Worlds of the Early Americas*, edited by Jeffrey Glover and Matt Cohen, 99–137. Lincoln: University of Nebraska Press.

Bradbury, Tara. 2012. "Jordan Bennett's Art Based on His Mi'kmaq Heritage." *Western Star*, May 4. http://www.thewesternstar.com/living/2012/5/4/jordan-bennetts-art -based-on-his-mikma-2971269.html.

Cabranes Grant, Leo. 2016. *From Scenarios to Networks: Performing the Intercultural in Colonial Mexico*. Chicago: Northwestern University Press.

Campeau, Ian, and Bear Witness. 2016. "The Creation of 'Electric Pow Wow Drum: A Tribe Called Red.'" Interview, *CBC Music*. https://www.youtube.com/watch?v=L8 YQFjpgTBk.

Carter, Jill, Karyn Recollet, and Dylan Robinson. 2017. "Interventions into the Maw of Old World Hunger: Frog Monsters, Kinstellatory Maps, and Radical Relationships in a Project of Reworlding." In *Canadian Performance Histories and Historiographies*, edited by Heather Davis-Fisch, 205–31. Toronto: Playwrights Canada Press.

Champlain, Samuel de. 1619. *Voyages et descourvertes faites en la Nouvelle France, depuis l'année 1615 iusques à la fin de l'année 1618*. . . . Paris: Chez Claude Collet, au Palais, enlaGalleriedesPrisonniers.https://gallica.bnf.fr/ark:/12148/bpt6k870514s?rk=42918;4.

Deloria, Philip Joseph. 1998. *Playing Indian*. New Haven, CT: Yale University Press.

Dillon, Elizabeth Maddock. 2014. *New World Drama: The Performative Commons in the Atlantic World*. Durham, NC: Duke University Press.

Foster, Susan. 2011. *Choreographing Empathy: Kinesthesia in Performance*. New York: Routledge.

Glover, Jeffrey, and Matt Cohen, eds. 2014. *Colonial Mediascapes: Sensory Worlds of the Early Americas*. Lincoln: University of Nebraska Press.

Gruber, Jacob. 1970. "Ethnographic Salvage and the Shaping of Anthropology." *American Anthropologist*, n.s., 72 (6): 1289–99.

Hudson, Aubrey, Awad Ibrahim, and Karyn Recollet, eds. 2019. *In This Together: Blackness, Indigeneity, and Hip Hop*. New York: Do It Ourselves Press.

Idle No More. 2014. "Turn the Tables." Legal analysis. http://www.idlenomore.ca/turn_ the_tables.

Igloliorte, Heather, ed. 2010. *Decolonize Me / Decolonisez-moi*. Ottawa: Legacy of Hope Foundation.

Julian, Ashley. 2016. "Thinking Seven Generations Ahead: Mi'kmaq Language Resurgence in the Face of Settler Colonialism." Master's thesis, University of New Brunswick.

Katz, Mark. 2012. *Groove Music: The Art and Culture of the Hip-Hop DJ.* New York: Oxford University Press.

Kohn, Eduardo. 2013. *How Forests Think: Toward an Anthropology Beyond the Human.* Oakland: University of California Press.

Lescarbot, Marc. 1609a. *Histoire de la nouvelle France: Contenant les navigations, découvertes, & habitations faites pare.* Paris: Iean Milot.

———. 1609b. *Les Muses de la Nouvelle France.* Paris: Iean Milot. http://numerique. banq.qc.ca/patrimoine/details/52327/2036224.

Lewis, Simon L., and Mark A. Maslin. 2015. "Defining the Anthropocene." *Nature* 519: 171–80.

Little, Carol Rose. 2016. "Inanimate Nouns as Subjects in Mi'gmaq: Consequences for Agreement Morphology." In *Proceedings of the Workshop on the Structure and Constituency of Languages of the Americas* 21, University of British Columbia Working Papers in Linguistics, edited by Megan Keough. http://conf.ling.cornell.edu/carol roselittle/WSCLA21Little.pdf.

Madden, Paula. 2009. *African Nova Scotian-Mi'kmaw Relations.* Halifax: Fernwood.

McKegney, Sam. 2007. *Magic Weapons: Aboriginal Writers Remaking Community after Residential School.* Winnipeg: University of Manitoba Press.

McLeod, Neal, ed. 2016. *mitêwâcimowina: Indigenous Science Fiction and Speculative Storytelling.* Penticton: Theytus.

Mills, Allison. 2017. "Learning to Listen: Archival Sound Recordings and Indigenous Cultural and Intellectual Property." *Archivaria* 83: 109–24.

Moten, Fred. 2003. *In the Break: The Aesthetics of the Black Radical Tradition.* Minneapolis: University of Minnesota Press.

Nardizzi, Vin. 2013. *Wooden Os: Shakespeare's Theatres and England's Trees.* Toronto: University of Toronto Press.

Parikka, Jussi. 2014. *The Anthrobscene.* Minneapolis: University of Minnesota Press.

Pestana, Carla Gardina. 2009. *Protestant Empire: Religion and the Making of the British Atlantic World.* Philadelphia: University of Pennsylvania Press.

Preston, VK. 2015. "Un/becoming Nomad." In *History, Memory, Performance*, edited by Yana Meerzon David Dean and Kathryn Price, 68–82. Basingstoke: Palgrave Macmillan.

Racette, Sherry Farrell, ed. 2011. *Close Encounters: The Next 500 Years.* Curated by Candice Hopkins [et al.]. Exhibition catalog for the Winnipeg Art Gallery, *Urban Shaman: Contemporary Aboriginal Art.* Winnipeg: Plug In Editions.

Recollet, Karyn. 2015a. "For Sisters." In *Me Artsy*, edited by Drew Hayden Taylor, 91–104. Madeira Park: Douglas & McIntyre.

———. 2015b. "Glyphing Decolonial Love through Urban Flash Mobbing and *Walking with Our Sisters*." *Curriculum Inquiry* 45 (1): 129–45.

Ritter, Kathleen, and Tania Willard. 2012. *Beat Nation: Art, Hip Hop and Aboriginal Culture.* Vancouver: Vancouver Art Gallery.

Roach, Joseph. 1996. *Cities of the Dead: Circum-Atlantic Performance.* New York: Columbia University Press.

Schloss, Joseph. 2014. *Making Beats: The Art of Sample-Based Hip-Hop.* Middletown, CT: Wesleyan University Press.

Schneider, Rebecca. 2011. *Performing Remains: Art and War in Times of Theatrical Re-enactment*. Abingdon: Routledge.

Scolieri, Paul. 2013. *Dancing the New World: Aztecs, Spaniards, and the Choreography of Conquest*. Austin: University of Texas Press.

Seed, Patricia. 1995. *Ceremonies of Possession in Europe's Conquest of the New World, 1492–1640*. Cambridge: Cambridge University Press.

Shea Murphy, Jacqueline. 2007. *The People Have Never Stopped Dancing: Native American Modern Dance Histories*. Minneapolis: University of Minnesota Press.

———, ed. 2016. "Indigenous Dance Today." Special issue, *Dance Research Journal* 48 (1).

Welch, Ellen R. 2011. "Performing a New France, Making Colonial History in Marc Lescarbot's Théâtre de Neptune (1606)." *Modern Language Quarterly* 72 (4): 439–60.

Willard, Tania, and Skeena Reece. 2008. "Beat Nation: Hip Hop as Indigenous Culture." Curatorial statements. http://www.beatnation.org/curatorial-statements.html.

Les Ballets Jazz and White Mythologies of Blackness in Québec

MELISSA TEMPLETON

Les Ballets Jazz de Montréal is a dance company steeped in ambiguity. After the group's founding in 1972, Canadian critics and funding agencies struggled to categorize the jazz-ballet style, seemingly unable to resolve the two competing genres at work onstage. Still, audiences were enthusiastic about the company, and despite equivocation in the press, Les Ballets Jazz was supported avidly by its public (Templeton 2012). The ambiguity of the company, however, runs deeper than a seeming contradiction between "ballet" and "jazz" in the dance world of the 1970s. In one of only a handful of academic texts written about Les Ballets Jazz de Montréal, Iro Tembeck describes the company as a "québécois invention" but also one that "does not particularly reflect a québécois sentiment" (1994, 112–14). For Tembeck, the company's movement quality, especially its use of jazz, reflected American trends in dance more so than the French Canadian heritage typically associated with Québec culture. Still, looking at reviews of the company's early performances, it is striking just how often the press claims the company as an important part of Québec (Côté 1973; Quensel 1973; Maynard 1974). The question remains, how did the public come to identify a company performing ballet and jazz dance as "québécois"?

Les Ballets Jazz began at a pivotal moment in Canadian politics. The 1960s and 1970s witnessed a dramatic shift in Québec's political landscape. Québec nationalism was on the rise, and an emerging sovereigntist movement, one that sought to establish Québec as its own nation separate from Canada, was shaping cultural and political discourses. In many ways, identifying Les Ballets Jazz as a part of Québécois culture helped strengthen provincial claims that Québec was distinct from the rest of Canada. The unusual hybrid movement vocabulary of the company highlighted this difference.

But the ambiguity of Les Ballets Jazz speaks to a racial ambiguity that shaped Québec's social history as well. Numerous scholars have pointed out that during centuries of British rule, French-speaking Canadians were racialized as "less white" than English-speaking Canadians (Dorsinville 1974; Makropoulos 2004; Austin 2013; Scott 2015). This ambiguity took on new significance in the 1960s, when political rhetoric seeking to empower French Canada began borrowing heavily from writers speaking to black oppression like Frantz Fanon, Aimé Césaire, and Black Power leaders in the United States. Claiming to be "les nègres blancs d'Amérique," many Québec writers harnessed global black political discourses to help reclaim nationalist sovereignty for Québec and, ironically, the privileges of whiteness lost during British colonization. Counter to what Tembeck suggests, I argue that Les Ballets Jazz was more than just a "québécois invention" and reflects a "québécois sentiment" in its appropriation of jazz dance and interest in blackness, echoing a similar trend in Québec politics at this time.

In this essay, I analyze Les Ballets Jazz and the paradoxical relationship between blackness and whiteness in Québec cultural nationalism by offering a reading of the company's first major ballet, *Jérémie* (1973), with choreography by Eva von Gencsy, a script by Marcel Dubé, and music by Lee Gagnon. In studying the appropriations of blackness that appear in both the repertoire of Les Ballets Jazz de Montréal and Québec's own political rhetoric of the 1970s, I argue that a fictitious notion of "blackness," one imagined and mythologized by whites in Canada, emerges as a metonym for social freedom in Québec. Whether we consider how Les Ballets Jazz founder Eva von Gencsy idealizes jazz dance as a liberating force or the allusions to blackness in separatist-leaning literature by Québec writers, these white voices equate the performance of blackness, whether in writing or through movement, with a desire to be "free."

However, such imagined or idealized connections between freedom and blackness manifest in ways that ignore the actual experiences of racism of black Canadians; these appropriations of blackness seem to be at the expense of Québec's own black community and create an erasure of the struggles black men and women face in the province. I further argue that the way *Jérémie* consumes blackness while marginalizing black bodies reveals much about how whiteness is constructed through the simultaneous consumption and marginalization of nonwhite cultures. Further studies of Les Ballets Jazz might also consider how First Nations are represented in the company's repertoire and the relationship between these representations and Québec's own discourses on colonialism.[1]

This essay takes part in what Anthea Kraut calls an "attempt to racialize whiteness" in dance studies (2016, 30). While the last two decades have witnessed the emergence of foundational literature connecting dance and racial construction (Gottschild 1996; Albright 1997; DeFrantz 2004), relatively few of the numerous books and articles written about white dancers and choreographers bring these subjects into conversation with critical race theory (McMains 2001; Manning 2004; Kraut 2011). As a result, the concessions and advantages that accompany whiteness often go unacknowledged, contributing to what Richard Dyer calls "the invisibility of whiteness as a racial position" (1997, 3). Race is often treated as a central issue in the study of nonwhite artists, yet it is peripheral in the study of white artists, despite the fact that race and especially racial privilege deeply inform their work. The case of Les Ballets Jazz highlights the power and privileges accorded to whiteness, as well as the gradations of whiteness that see some as more white than others in Québec.

There are, however, potential hazards in this kind of project. As Kraut notes, there is some danger in reclaiming whiteness as a racial identity in dance studies, as it recenters conversations about race on white subjects, enacting its own kind of white privilege (2016, 33). This chapter attempts to balance out efforts to make whiteness visible with the need to mitigate this privilege. My discussion of black politics in Montreal (particularly those taking shape alongside the development of the concept of "nègres blancs" in the late 1960s), as well as the experiences of Eddy Toussaint and André Lucas, who danced with Les Ballets Jazz in its early years, attempts to decenter and critique whiteness within this framework. With the goals of racializing whiteness and tempering its privilege, this project contributes to literature that tactically studies whiteness in order to displace it from its position of authority and power.

Although dance studies increasingly uses critical race studies as a methodological lens, the intersection of these fields has been made largely on US terrain and about US subjects. However, race surreptitiously works differently in different sociopolitical, economic, and historical conditions, continually adapting itself to perpetuate its effects. Casting a blind eye to race's power outside of the United States narrows our understanding of race and racism as global phenomena that shape local understandings in multifaceted and nuanced ways. This essay calls attention to the importance of studying race in conjunction with Canadian dance studies, which I argue is significant not just for scholars working inside Canada but for scholars outside Canada as well, especially US scholars. Although Canadian artists and scholars push back vehemently against it, there is an assumption that persists, especially in the United States, that Canadian culture is a counterfeit or imitation of American culture. While there are certainly similarities between the cultural products of Canada and the United States, as is often the case between nations that share a border, there are also foundational differences in the political structures, cultural policies, and nationalist rhetorics that shape Canadian and American societies— differences that are often assimilated in international settings. Studying racial construction in Québec adds to the project of distinguishing similarities and differences between Canadian and American cultures, as well as garnering a better understanding of global manifestations of race as they exist beyond US national boundaries and take up new meanings in new contexts.

While there is limited footage of Les Ballets Jazz's *Jérémie*, I have used the archival material available (rehearsal videos of sections of the choreography, a published script of the work, photos, and critical responses in the press) to construct my reading. I also rely on interviews with dancers and choreographers involved in the process to build my analysis. These resources, in conjunction with extensive research about the social context surrounding the work's production, demonstrate a parallel between Les Ballets Jazz's appropriations of blackness with those of sovereigntist rhetoric of the 1960s and 1970s, in particular in their mythologizing of blackness as a symbol of freedom. At the same time, this research also demonstrates the limits of that identification, as these appropriations of blackness ultimately work to secure the privileges of whiteness.

"Blackness" and "Liberation" in Québec Politics

In Canada, language has historically served as an important racial marker and has been one of the many ways French Canadians have been discriminated against. The oppression felt by French Canada has had tangible cultural, economic, and political ramifications (McRoberts 1997). Though there is not the space in this essay to outline these details, I will mention that until the 1960s, Québec's French-speaking population was mostly rural, and those few residents in the city often lived on the edge of poverty. At the federal level, there was still relatively little political representation for French speakers, and business was conducted largely in English, often to the exclusion of French speakers. Overall, English Canadians made up a relatively small portion of Québec's population but carried far more political and economic clout.

In the 1960s, a period in Québec marked by the gradual development of a French-speaking middle class, French Québécois intellectuals began voicing their concern over English domination in the province. At this time, influential political journals began printing works by black revolutionary writers, in particular Aimé Césaire and Frantz Fanon, whose writings about decolonization resonated with prominent French Québécois thinkers. Scholar of black Canadian history David Austin writes, "Césaire spoke a language that French Canadians, after being battered and bruised by the Anglophone minority in Québec, could relate to. As they peered into the mirror of Césaire's world, many of them saw their own reflection" (2013, 57). Austin suggests that the idea of French Québecers as "nègres blancs" started to take shape at this time. For example, it was in the 1960s that Québec poet and essayist Paul Chamberland

began to write in a style he called "négritude blanche" and that the writings
of Frantz Fanon, especially *The Wretched of the Earth*, were used by revolutionary groups like the Front de Libération du Québec, itself based loosely on
the Front de Libération Nationale in Algeria, to justify acts of violence against
the state (Bothwell 2006, 447; Austin 2013, 58–60). As literary scholar Max
Dorsinville explains, "In the early sixties . . . the Black man, as a symbol, image
and myth emerges in the French Canadian consciousness" (1974, 9–10).

However, these myths of blackness permeated the sovereigntist imagination
so powerfully that they erased the black men and women living in Québec
from these narratives of oppression. This is perhaps most powerfully observed
in Pierre Vallières's infamous book *Nègres blancs d'Amérique* (1968). While describing various parallels he sees between African American and French Canadian history, Vallières claims that Québec does not have a "Black problem"
(quoted in Austin 2013, 67). His comment, which suggests that Québec does
not have a black population to oppress, fails to recognize the struggles of
Québec's black communities, whose histories date back to at least the nineteenth century and at times as far back as the seventeenth.

In fact, the late 1960s was an important moment for black politics in Montreal. In October 1968, just months after *Nègres blancs d'Amérique* was published,
the Congress of Black Writers took place at McGill University in Montreal and
brought together prominent black intellectuals from around the world to discuss the social challenges facing black communities in the aftermath of slavery
and colonialism (Austin 2013, 20–21). In January 1969, spurred in part by the
political momentum of the October Congress, Montreal witnessed a group of
protestors, led by black activists, occupying the computer lab of one of the
main buildings on the Sir George Williams campus in downtown Montreal to
voice their disapproval of the school's racist, discriminatory policies. The Sir
George Williams Affair (as it was later named) came to a head when miscom-
munication between school officials, protestors, and police officers led to a fire
in the lab and ninety-seven arrests and resulted in surveillance of Canada's
Black Power movement by the Royal Canadian Mounted Police (Austin 2013,
159). These very public events inserted Montreal's black community and its concerns over racial discrimination more prominently into the Canadian public
imaginary, adding another dimension to the discourses on English oppression
in Québec and complicating the idea of French Québecers as "nègres blancs."
Yet despite the visibility the Sir George Williams Affair brought to Québec's
black population, an imagined connection between black oppression and French
Canadian oppression continued to permeate much of the political discourse
of the time and still finds its way into these discourses today, often at the expense of Québec's black communities.[2]

In the 1960s and 1970s Québec intellectuals may have appropriated "blackness" to articulate their sense of oppression, but ultimately, this was done in an effort to restore the powers and privileges associated with whiteness lost during British colonization. By the 1990s Québec separatist rhetoric had become obsessed with asserting Québec's whiteness; this is especially apparent in the comments made by sovereigntists during the 1995 referendum and more recently in the reasonable accommodation debates.[3] This obsession with whiteness suggests that sovereigntists' sense of affiliation with blackness was a temporary strategy that allowed them to express a sense of oppression, but it could not be sustained, given French Canada's precarious position within the framework of Canadian whiteness. The romanticized connection between blackness and liberation that flourished in the 1970s helped articulate the plight of French Canada, yet it would have limited currency when it came to reestablishing the province's whiteness.

Jazz Dance and Myths of Blackness in Les Ballets Jazz

In the late 1960s Eva von Gencsy, a Hungarian-born ballet dancer who had already had a formidable career performing across Canada, began to study jazz dance.[4] She traveled regularly from her home in Montreal to New York to take classes with famous jazz dance pedagogues like Luigi (Eugene Faccuito) and Matt Mattox. Although Luigi's and Mattox's dance practices might already be seen as a blend of African American and Euro-American forms (and their styles exemplify America's troubled history of white artists appropriating African American cultural practices), von Gencsy (2011) began teaching her own hybrid style of "ballet jazz," believing that the additional emphasis on ballet would be more appealing to Canada's white dance community. Her classes were highly popular with young Montreal dancers, and in 1972 the success of her teaching led her to found the professional dance company Les Ballets Jazz de Montréal with two of her former students, Geneviève Salbaing and Eddy Toussaint.[5]

In a film made to celebrate the fortieth anniversary of Les Ballets Jazz, von Gencsy discusses what drew her to jazz dance. On a split screen, her 2012 interview plays alongside video footage of her teaching class in the 1970s. She speaks emphatically about the importance of jazz dance and its connections to histories of oppression:

The origin of jazz, it was taken from the streets; they call it the folk dance of America. What kind of a folk dance when it started with the *slaves* who were *oppressed*. They couldn't even play the drums, therefore they started to do tap. . . . They had to have a way to express themselves—to escape the misery, to find freedom. And somehow I was caught up in a beautiful, magical experience.

Something got a hold of me—a creative force—and I found in jazz everything
I was dreaming about. Freedom of expression, this dynamic rhythm, feeling
human feelings, and it was so wonderful. I found myself, and I fell in love with
it. (BJM Danse 2012, emphasis added)

While watching the video, it is hard to reconcile the highly stylized balletic
movements Gencsy teaches her students with her comments about jazz's origins.
Her oversimplified historical account contains many omissions. In particular,
von Gencsy excludes much of the complicated interaction between black and
white artists in the history of jazz and tap, from the influence of blackface
minstrelsy on the development of tap dance to white appropriations of Africanist dance practices on Broadway and the erasure of black cultural labor in
promoting a canon of individual white geniuses creating "American" culture.
Her omissions, whether intentional or not, allow her to skirt some of the more
complicated questions that call attention to her participation in these pathologies. The fact that she sees jazz dance as "magical" subtly confirms the fantasy that shapes her understanding of this history.

For the sake of this argument, however, what is most crucial here is that von
Gencsy associated her jazz practice with African American culture and African
American culture with freedom. Though von Gencsy is not French Canadian,
her words resonate with discourses on sovereignty linking blackness with a
desire for freedom that was also common in Québec's nationalist rhetoric at
that time. Although von Gencsy (2011) has explained that she is not interested
in politics, her vision and appropriations of jazz dance are similar to those seen
in the sovereigntist movement of the time. I suggest that von Gencsy's interest
in jazz dance speaks to Québec sentiments about political freedom and helped
pave the way for the company's association with Québec identity.[6]

Though von Gencsy herself did not have any direct ties to Québec sovereignty, one of her collaborators, Marcel Dubé, was very active in the movement.
Dubé, a well-respected playwright and nationalist in Québec known for his
sympathetic stance on separatism, was invited to write the story for *Jérémie*.
Though not as explicitly political as his second Ballets Jazz script, *Fleur de
lit* (1976),[7] *Jérémie* contains numerous subtle allegories that speak to Québec
nationalism and constructions of race all the same. Here I would like to mention that even the way Dubé describes his involvement in the process is coded
in potentially racialized terms, especially in the language that he uses to describe the labor involved in this project. In the introduction that prefaces his
script for *Jérémie* he writes, "So I was there with my usual shackles [*carcan*],
leaning over an unmanageable chore. Images and symbols came to help me.
These shadows that fluttered in the night, I had to give them their freedom,

FIGURE 30. Newspaper advertisement for Les Ballets Jazz, May 1975. (Photo BJM—Les Ballets Jazz de Montréal)

permit them to attend to the elasticity of the moving poem. I endeavored to get there" (1973, 10, my translation).[8] Though not explicit references to black political movements, Dubé's description of his shackles and the image of him freeing the moving dark figures potentially allude to slavery. The sense of confinement he speaks of, juxtaposed next to the shadows he wants to liberate, evokes imagery associated with blackness and freedom. Even in this description of his creative process, Dubé hints at an interest in using blackness as a symbol for catharsis or liberation.

While von Gencsy and Dubé demonstrate artistic interests in and fantasies of blackness, the marketing of the company capitalized on such racialized imagery as well. In a newspaper ad from 1975 three dancers appear in a black-and-white photograph, heavily shadowed such that their skin tone is somewhat obscure. Featured most prominently in the image is a tall slender figure, hips tilted to one side, with an Afro hairstyle that associates this image with "blackness." Next to the company's name is written, "L'expression de la joie de vivre au rythme Québécois" (The expression of the joy of living to the rhythm of Québec).[9] Since the company used mainly jazz music, the implication is that Québec's own rhythm is a jazzy one. Images associated with blackness circulated prominently around the company in the early 1970s, and whether intentionally or not, the company temporarily capitalized on the connections it drew between French Québécois culture and "blackness."

However, what of the central dancer in this photograph? What might he offer the conversation about "blackness" in Les Ballets Jazz? While this chapter focuses largely on white myths of blackness, this kind of analysis potentially privileges whiteness by foregrounding its interpretations despite attempts to critique it. In the next section, I include my conversations with André Lucas (the central dancer in the advertisement) and Eddy Toussaint (one of the company's founders and a choreographic contributor to *Jérémie*). While their stories are mediated by my own words (and, in the case of Toussaint, my own translation), I aim to highlight their perspectives, including the tension between my own more critical take on the company and their support for Eva von Gencsy's work.

Les Ballets Jazz and Experiences of Antiblack Racism

In 2011 I had the opportunity to speak with André Lucas, a featured dancer with Les Ballets Jazz in its early years. He invited me to take his class and chat with him about his work. A tall, slender man, clearly built for a mainstream dance career, Lucas has an exuberant, generous presence in one-on-one conversation but a fiery persona in the studio. He teaches a relentless class, best described as a combination of ballet, modern, and jazz techniques, while he stands at the front of the room banging intimidatingly on a drum and spewing witty criticism at his students—to their delight. I waited patiently after class for the other students to leave so Lucas and I could slip away from the group and find a quiet spot upstairs to speak.

Lucas grew up in Little Burgundy, a black Canadian enclave in Montreal's Saint-Henri district. He began his dance training as a child, studying tap and ballet with former Montreal nightclub performer Olga Spencer Foderingham and later as a teenager at Les Grands Ballets Canadiens before joining Les Ballets Jazz. With my concerns about the company's portrayals of blackness in mind, I asked Lucas if he ever felt discriminated against in the dance community. He said he did not, with the possible exception of his experiences in ballet. He recalled an awkward first meeting with Mme Chiriaeff, founder of Les Grands Ballets Canadiens, upon receiving an invitation to attend her ballet school: "When she saw me [chuckles], and in those days I had this incredible Afro and had on a buckskin jacket and purple corduroy pants and boots . . . she was sort of taken aback because my name was André Lucas. . . . She thought I was French. And she was very nice, she offered me a scholarship, but . . . I did not want to dance with Les Grands Ballets Canadiens, that wasn't my thing" (2011). I asked him to elaborate on why he didn't want to dance with Les Grands Ballets Canadiens. He said he wanted the training but also explained, "I could see that because I was black, that was sort of the reason why, you know . . . but it didn't matter to me really." Although his remarks were equivocal, and he seemed not to want to linger on it too long, Lucas briefly touched on the subject of racial biases in the ballet field. He assured me, however, that he did not feel discriminated against with Les Ballets Jazz. He mentioned that he really considered himself a modern dancer and initially looked down at jazz dance, though he spoke highly of Eva von Gencsy for sparking his interest in it while he was there. His concern about racism in ballet resonates with accounts from other dancers as well.

Eddy Toussaint, cofounder of Les Ballets Jazz, expressed a similar frustration with the world of ballet but an appreciation for the opportunities and support he found in Eva von Gencsy. Toussaint trained extensively in ballet in Haiti before moving to Montreal in his teens, and his first encounter with jazz dance was when he began taking class with von Gencsy. He was only in the company for a year, leaving to found his own group, Ballet Montréal: Eddy Toussaint, which was itself quite successful in the 1970s. While his company was funded by the Ministère des Affaires Culturelles du Québec, the Canada Council never funded him. I spoke with him over lunch in September 2011, and the mention of the Canada Council sparked an impassioned response. Toussaint explained to me that ballet was his preferred movement vocabulary.

However, when he spoke with a member of the Canada Council for the Arts (he has asked that I do not mention this person's name), he was told (as he retells it), "with all due respect, because of your origins I personally recommend that you stick to jazz" (Toussaint 2011). In spite of Toussaint's ballet background, this member of the council saw Toussaint as a jazz dancer not because of his training (which was in ballet) but because she associated his Haitian background with jazz.

In the cases of both Toussaint and Lucas, it appears that racial prejudice in the Canadian dance community was something that was present but often unspoken. Just as Lucas struggled to say explicitly what it was about the ballet world that seemed less welcoming and how the representative from Canada Council implied without plainly saying that she saw Toussaint as a jazz dancer because of his heritage, racism seemed to be a kind of "public secret" in Canada—an idea that is known but difficult to articulate (Francis 2011, 4–5). But adding to this complication is the fact that both Toussaint and Lucas spoke highly, even protectively, of von Gencsy, who they felt had been an important figure in their training and supportive of their early careers. While my reading of Les Ballets Jazz critiques the representations of blackness in the company's image, my conversations with Toussaint and Lucas suggest that the company may have also been an important stepping stone for the careers of black Canadian dance artists in Montreal.[10] Again, Les Ballets Jazz occupies an ambiguous space when it comes to race and representation in Canada. On the one hand, it provided opportunities for black ballet dancers when the ballet world had been less welcoming, but on the other hand, it often depicted blackness onstage in deeply problematic ways.

Jérémie (1973) and the Whitening of French Québec

Jérémie premiered on May 7, 1973, and featured choreography by Eva von Gencsy, music by Lee Gagnon, and a script by Marcel Dubé.[11] As the program explains, the story's protagonist, Jérémie, is a veteran of war (though what war is not specified) caught up in a life of "sex, drugs, money, and compromise" but discovers a refuge in a world of fantasy and dreams ("Les Ballets Jazz" program, 1973). The story line lends itself to the idea that jazz dance can be used as a vehicle of pleasure and escapism, as a way to free oneself from the suffering of daily life, which, again, resonates with white mythologies of blackness and liberation. But alongside this romanticizing of blackness, the ballet's appropriations, narrative tropes, and casting choices work to reinforce codes of white normativity.

Based on the limited footage available of this piece,[12] much of the movement in Jérémie resembles what dance scholars might call "modern jazz"—a popular studio and stage practice that merges African American dance traditions with Euro-American styles and was popular in Broadway musicals beginning in the mid-1930s (Stearns and Stearns 1968; Mahoney 2005). Polycentrism, a trait often associated with Africanist dance aesthetics, characterizes much of the company's movement, especially the mobile pelvis and ribs. But while traces of Africanist influences might be identified in the choreography, the dancers' leg extensions and partnering rely heavily on ballet conventions. Though I would hesitate to call jazz "black" and ballet "white," an oversimplification that masks the years of cross-pollination that have influenced both forms, it's important to note that qualities associated with both Africanist and European-ist aesthetics are present in the work (Gottschild 1996, 11–19).

At first glance, the Africanist qualities of the choreography potentially undermine the company's whiteness. Yet the act of appropriating Africanist culture is itself a signature of whiteness, and the predominantly white company's ability to perform and ostensibly master Africanist dance aesthetics appeals to white notions of European superiority. Dance scholar Brenda Dixon Gottschild writes, "There seems to be a general assumption on the part of Europeanist cultures that African visual arts, music, and dance are raw materials that are improved upon and elevated when they are appropriated and finessed by European artists" (1996, 41). In other words, paradoxically, the attempt to show white dancers' proficiency and skill in performing Africanist art is itself a quality associated with Europeanist culture, and the ability to transcribe the cultural codes of both forms affirms the privileged status of whiteness.

Another strategy that centers whiteness involves casting choices. The title role of *Jérémie* went to white ballet dancer James Boyd, which may be somewhat surprising, considering the fact that Eddy Toussaint, who was one of the company's cofounders, a choreographic contributor on the project, and an extraordinary ballet dancer, was not cast as Jérémie but rather in the role of the Pimp.[13] I asked Toussaint (2011) why he was given this role. He explained that he had the right assertive personality for it, although after an awkward pause, he conceded that his complexion likely had something to do with it. A similar trend occurs in the casting of the female lead. Jérémie is saved from a life of debauchery by the character LOVE, also known as "the girl continent," and Dubé's stage directions state that this role should be played by a woman who "is Asiatic (or Black African, it all depends)" (1973, 66). In spite of these directions—problematic in their own right—the role of LOVE went to a young white ballet dancer, Nathalie Breuer. Marie-José Robinson, the company's only black female dancer, ended up in the more minor role of a prostitute. In discussing this choice with Eva von Gencsy, she explained to me that Robinson was too tall. Von Gencsy (2011) felt Breuer was her strongest dancer and partnered

well with Boyd. But it is also crucial to note the different types of intimacy
these two women came to represent in the ballet: as LOVE Breuer embodied
pure and chaste courtship, while Robinson, in the role of a prostitute, represented promiscuity and commodified sexual labor, surreptitiously echoing
white interpretations of black female sexuality inherited from slavery. Despite
the potential to cast black dancers in lead roles, *Jérémie* instead centered its
story on white dancing bodies.

The relationships between these characters and the narrative arc of the story
also privilege whiteness, often while presenting blackness in derogatory ways.
The Pimp, likely a reference to Hollywood stock characters and blaxploitation
films of the 1970s, becomes the individual responsible for Jérémie's increasingly downward spiral: the Pimp seduces Jérémie into a life of drugs and sex
that he is almost unable to escape. In one scene, the Pimp offers Jérémie wine
while the Pimp's two prostitutes (one being Robinson) begin to perform a
sensual dance; while Jérémie is distracted, the Pimp empties Jérémie's pockets
and robs him. The miscegenation, intoxication, homoeroticism, and illicitness
of this scene are complex. On the one hand, the depiction of this scenario
through dance might be read as an invitation to contemplate and perhaps even
celebrate the social defiance of these characters. On the other hand, the story
arc speaks to Christian myths of redemption, suggesting that these transgressions must be overcome; despite being tempted by the Pimp, Jérémie eventually escapes this existence of sin and is saved by LOVE (both the character and
the sentiment). Richard Dyer explains that one of the major tropes associated
with whiteness, which is again deeply linked to Christianity, is its ability to
transcend the material world (1997, 15–18). In this scenario, Jérémie's spirit is
able to overcome his body and its material conditions (his injuries, his addic-
tions, and his financial hardships). And indeed, by the end, Jérémie is cured,
while the rest of the cast, including the Pimp and the prostitutes, become,
according to the script, "motionless shadows" (Dubé 1973, 69). Overall, the
arc of the narrative shows how Jérémie is able to overcome his physical limitations, echoing narratives of whiteness in which white men are understood as a
strong spirit, while racialized others are relegated to the realm of the body.

The Pimp and the prostitutes embody a different kind of "blackness" here.
Rather than a symbol of liberation, these black bodies come to represent criminality and deviant sexuality, eventually receding into the background; they act
as character foils that illuminate Jérémie's whiteness all the more through their
own blackness. Robinson and Toussaint take on symbols of eroticism and
delinquency, of living outside the norms and codes of society, while Jérémie,
the universal (read: white) man, dabbles in misadventure before being saved by
a virtuous and chaste (read: white) woman, LOVE. In many ways Les Ballets

Jazz reinforces familiar gendered and racialized patterns that see white women as pure and virginal, black men and women as lascivious and dangerous, and white men in a constant struggle against temptation.

What makes *Jérémie* a fascinating case study is that it demonstrates the limits of white mythologies of blackness and freedom. Appropriating images of blackness might speak to an ambiguous desire for liberation, but performing blackness potentially compromises the authority of whiteness. *Jérémie* speaks to white audiences all the same as it mitigates this racialization by emphasizing the whiteness of its lead characters. The predominantly white company's ability to master embodied codes of "blackness" and "whiteness," the casting, and the parallel between this ballet and familiar Christian myths about fall and redemption reinscribe the ballet's white protagonists with privileges associated with whiteness. At the same time, the company's black dancers take on minor roles that reinforce negative sterotypes surrounding "blackness" rather than the freedom that "blackness" supposedly represents when appropriated by white bodies.

Les Ballets Jazz and Racial Ambivalence

In this essay I have used Les Ballets Jazz—the company's artistic interests, public image, and first major work, *Jérémie*—as a lens for thinking through racial dynamics in Québec. In particular, the company's performances of "blackness" through jazz dance in the early 1970s became a way to articulate an ambiguous desire for liberation that resonated with sovereigntist aspirations and Québec nationalism. Paradoxically, these cross-cultural borrowings, which might seem to compromise the company's whiteness, also strategically preserve the privileges associated with whiteness through the ballet's tactical appropriations, casting choices, and stereotypes, which simultaneously consume and marginalize blackness.

However, Les Ballets Jazz is a polysemous dance company open to many interpretations and multiple simultaneous meanings. Its ambiguity stems not just from the seeming incongruousness of its influences, ballet and jazz, but also from the cultural significance it holds more generally in Québec. Canadian critics struggled to reconcile the simultaneous presentation of Africanist and Europeanist aesthetics onstage, yet the company was extremely popular with Canadian audiences. Les Ballets Jazz also appeared to be a representation of Québec national identity despite the fact that its connection to French Canadian heritage is not immediately obvious. The company's racial identification reaffirmed white normativity in its appropriation and marginalization of blackness, yet despite the potential harm such images create for Canada's black community, the company was also, according to some of its company members, an important space for the development of black dance artists. Speaking to all these resonances, the company's ambiguity occupies an important place in the study of Québec cultural identity of the 1970s and the complexities that distinguish racialization in Canada.

Notes

1. Representations of First Nations find their way into the 1976 work *Fleur de lit*. Marcel Dubé's script depicts French settlers and "Indians" living a peaceful coexistence until the seductive English colonizer destroys them. Contemporary examples exist as well, as in choreographer Rodrigo Pederneiras's *Rouge* (2014), which, according to the website of Les Ballets Jazz de Montréal is "a discreet tribute to Native peoples and their musical and cultural legacies" (BJM—Les Ballets Jazz de Montréal 2014) but which has been panned in the press (Kourlas 2016).

2. During a 2012 demonstration in Montreal, a group of white students donned blackface to allude to the oppressiveness of proposed tuition hikes. Many in the press defended the students' use of blackface as politically symbolic, while others pointed out how offensive such representations were to Montreal's black communities (Morgan 2012).

3. This may be seen in Jacques Parizeau's comments blaming "money and ethnic votes" for the separatists' loss of the 1995 referendum; in Lucien Bouchard's comments, made around the same time, disparaging French Québecers for being the white race with one of the lowest birthrates; in the reasonable accommodation debates from 2006–7 that saw major media outlets in Québec debating the limits of social tolerance for ethnic and religious minorities; and in the proposed 2013 Charter of Values, which would have taken particular aim at public displays of Muslim symbols and attire in Québec.

4. Von Gencsy was born in Csongrád but left her family when she was just nine to pursue a professional dance career in Budapest. Near the end of World War II she moved to Salzburg to dance professionally with the Salzburger Landestheater. When the war ended, von Gencsy's family warned her not to return to communist Hungary; she moved to Winnipeg in 1948.

5. Ironically, none of the company's founders were originally from Québec; Toussaint migrated to Montreal from Haiti as a teenager, and Geneviève Salbaing came from France via Morocco and the United States. However, Les Ballets Jazz featured Québécois dancers and composers and two important collaborations with Marcel Dubé, helping ground the company in an emerging French Québécois identity.

6. Though von Gencsy did not speak much about her time in Hungary and Austria during and immediately after World War II, her desire for "freedom" may resonate with the tumultuous politics of Europe at that time and her own experience in those conditions.

7. *Fleur de lit: 300 Years of Québec History* was made for Montreal's 1976 Olympics. The reference to *lit* (bed) rather than *lis* (lily, a symbol of France) was meant to highlight how Québec had been exploited by the English (von Gencsy 2011).

8. As in the original translation, the word *carcan* could refer to "shackles" or "iron collar" (less commonly used in English); both terms refer to images associated with slavery. *Carcan* can also mean "straitjacket." However, as Dubé is describing his writing process, it seems more apt to use "shackles" than "straitjacket" to emphasize that he is still able to write but does experience restraint.

9. Although this is the literal translation of the French text, the English version of this 1975 advertisement reads, "An expression of our lifestyle."

10. Constantine Darling is another black Canadian artist who worked with Les Ballets Jazz. He choreographed the warrior scenes in *Jérémie* and went on to have a successful career as a dance artist in British Columbia. Sadly, Darling passed away shortly before the research for this project began.

11. Eddy Toussaint and Constantine Darling also contributed to the choreography of *Jérémie*, but von Gencsy is typically listed as the main choreographer (though occasionally Toussaint, as cofounder of the company, is mentioned in the press). In my interview with her, von Gencsy acknowledged the work that Toussaint and Darling contributed to *Jérémie*; in fact, it was through von Gencsy that I first learned of Darling's input. Darling and Toussaint went on to choreograph other works for the company for which they received credit, so it is curious that these dancers did not receive more formal acknowledgment for the first production of *Jérémie*.

12. The only available video of *Jérémie* is rehearsal footage on three-quarter-inch film, consisting of clips of danced phrases out of context without the score. As such, my analysis can only speak about the movement of the work in a general sense.

13. Lucas (2011) also occasionally played the Pimp after Toussaint left the company.

Works Cited

Albright, Ann Cooper. 1997. *Choreographing Difference.* Hanover: University of New England Press.

Austin, David. 2013. *Fear of a Black Nation: Race, Sex, and Security in Sixties Montreal.* Toronto: Between the Lines.

BJM—Les Ballets Jazz de Montréal. 2012. "XL: Les 40 ans des Ballets Jazz de Montréal." Accessed May 15, 2016. https://vimeo.com/45817836.

———. 2014. "Rouge." Accessed August 30, 2017. http://www.bjmdanse.ca/en/repertoire/rouge/.

Bothwell, Robert. 2006. *The Penguin History of Canada.* Toronto: Penguin Canada.

Côté, Fernand. 1973. "Avec Monsieur B on fête le 90e anniversaire de *La Presse.*" *Ici Radio-Canada.* 8:44. BJM Danse Archive.

DeFrantz, Thomas. 2004. *Dancing Revelations: Alvin Ailey's Embodiment of African American Culture.* New York: Oxford University Press.

Dorsinville, Max. 1974. *Caliban without Prospero: Essay on Quebec and Black Literature.* Erin, ON: Press Porcepic.

Dubé, Marcel. 1973. *Jérémie: Argument de ballet.* Ottawa: Éditions Leméac.

Dyer, Richard. 1997. *White.* London: Routledge.

Francis, Margot. 2011. *Creative Subversions: Whiteness, Indigeneity, and the National Imaginary.* Vancouver: University of British Columbia Press.

Gottschild, Brenda Dixon. 1996. *Digging the Africanist Presence in American Performance Art: Dance and Other Contexts*. Westport, CT: Greenwood Press.

Kourlas, Gia. 2016. "Review: Les Ballets Jazz de Montreal, with No Jazz and Lots of Head Scratching." *New York Times*, May 25. https://www.nytimes.com/2016/05/26/arts/dance/review-les-ballets-jazz-de-montreal-with-no-jazz-and-lots-of-head-scratching.html?mcubz.

Kraut, Anthea. 2011. "White Womanhood, Property Rights, and the Campaign for Choreographic Copyright: Loïe Fuller's *Serpentine Dance*." *Dance Research Journal* 43 (1): 3–26.

———. 2016. *Choreographing Copyright: Race, Gender, and Intellectual Property Rights in American Dance*. New York: Oxford University Press.

"Les Ballets Jazz" program. 1973. Bibliothèque de la Danse Vincent Warren (archive).

Lucas, André. 2011. Interview with the author. Montreal, Canada, November 6.

Mahoney, Billie. 2005. "Jazz Dance." In *The International Encyclopedia of Dance*, edited by Selma Jeanne Cohen. New York: Oxford University Press.

Makropoulos, Josée. 2004. "Speak White! Language and Race in the Construction of Frenchness in Canada." In *Racism Eh? A Critical Inter-disciplinary Anthology of Race and Racism in Canada*, edited by Camille Nelson and Charmaine Nelson, 241–58. Concord, ON: Captus Press.

Manning, Susan. 2004. *Modern Dance, Negro Dance: Race in Motion*. Minneapolis: University of Minnesota Press.

Maynard, Olga. 1974. "Les Ballets Jazz: Dance le style québécois." *Dance Magazine*, January, 72–75.

McMains, Juliet. 2001. "Brownface: Representations of Latin-ness in Dancesport." *Dance Research Journal* 33 (2): 54–71.

McRoberts, Kenneth. 1997. *Misconceiving Canada: The Struggle for National Unity*. Toronto: Oxford University Press.

Morgan, Anthony. 2012. "La grève et les minorités." *HuffPost Blog*, March 27. Accessed May 14, 2016, http://quebec.huffingtonpost.ca/anthony-morgan/greve-etudiante-minorites_b_1383521.html?ref=fb&src=sp&comm_ref=false.

Quensel, Peter. 1973. "Les Ballets Jazz: Spectacles ombres et lumières." *Le Droit*, December 20.

Scott, Corrie. 2015. "How French Canadians Became White Folks, or Doing Things with Race in Quebec." *Ethnic and Racial Studies* 39 (7): 1280–97.

Stearns, Marshall, and Jean Stearns. 1968. *Jazz Dance: The Story of American Vernacular Dance*. New York: Schirmer Books.

Tembeck, Iro. 1994. *Dancing in Montreal: Seeds of a Choreographic History*. Madison, WI: Society of Dance History Scholars.

Templeton, Melissa. 2012. "Polyrhythmic Dance Currents: Race, Multiculturalism, and the Montreal Dance Community." PhD dissertation, University of California, Riverside.

Toussaint, Eddy. 2011. Interview with the author. Montreal, Canada, September 13.

Vallières, Pierre. 1968. *Nègres blancs d'Amérique*. Montreal: Éditions Parti Pris.

Von Gencsy, Eva. 2011. Interview with the author. Montreal, Canada, September 22.

Cuban Modern Dance after Censorship

A Colorful Gray, 1971–74

ELIZABETH SCHWALL

For over a year, Cuban choreographer Ramiro Guerra worked with the Conjunto Nacional de Danza Moderna (National Ensemble of Modern Dance, CNDM) to stage his magnum opus, *El Decálogo del Apocalipsis* (The Ten Commandments of the Apocalypse). It was to last two hours without intermission and take place in different locations outside the Teatro Nacional de Cuba (National Theater of Cuba, TNC) in Havana, requiring the audience to move during the performance. Architectural spaces inspired the choreography, and the content alluded to the Ten Commandments. The work combined psychedelic elements with Cuban pageantry. Using burlesque and satire, it reflected on the international social upheavals of the 1960s with vignettes featuring polemical images like the crucifixion of a black man, prostitution in exchange for luxuries, a heterosexual orgy, homosexual abduction, and quasi-tribal phallic worship in ironic counterpoint to biblical poems. The residents of the neighborhood near the TNC, known as La Timba, provided an attentive audience during months of rehearsal. Although the work was widely advertised, two weeks before its scheduled premiere on April 15, 1971, the government canceled the performance in the first clear instance of censorship in concert dance since the 1959 Cuban Revolution (Mousouris 2002, 67, 69–70).

The cancellation happened immediately prior to the First National Congress of Education and Culture in late April 1971. During the congress, a commission on mass media discussed "pornography in Cuban art" and mentioned Guerra's *Decálogo* (Burdsall 1973a). Indeed, according to the US-born, Cuban modern dancer Lorna Burdsall, "During the course of rehearsals, word spread that there were pornographic elements and phallic symbols flying. . . . All of this was just too much for some of the pseudo-puritanical 'cultured' bureaucrats"

303

(2001, 173). This dispute compelled Guerra to leave the company that he had founded in 1959. For many years thereafter, he choreographed nothing.

Though the 1971 censorship has become an often-cited indication of repressive realities in Cuba (Mousouris 2002; John 2012, 110–18), here I am more interested in what happened next, especially how dance makers continued after losing a formative creator and encountering expressive limits. New choreographers filled the void that Guerra left behind. Their work made public statements about the vitality and sociopolitical importance of Cuban modern dance. Behind the scenes, modern dancers complained to cultural bureaucrats about deteriorating conditions in the company, caused in large part, they argued, by official mistreatment and underappreciation. By 1974 these choreographic and discursive tactics had worked, and the company enjoyed unprecedented opportunities and support.

The crisis and recuperation of modern dance from 1971 to 1974 occurred during a period that became known as the *quinquenio gris* (gray five years) from 1971 to 1976. The early years of unbounded revolutionary experimentation in Cuban arts ended in 1961 when the government censored the short film *P.M.* At that time, Fidel Castro told intellectuals and artists, "all within the revolution, nothing without," meaning that the state had a right to police expression in order to protect the revolution (L. Guerra 2012, 338). As the 1960s continued, artists faced new challenges, including a virulent homophobia that ended careers and led to public humiliation and even imprisonment. Then, the year 1971 was one of hardship and crisis (Fornet 2013). In March 1971 the award-winning poet and essayist Heberto Padilla was arrested and forced to apologize for his allegedly counterrevolutionary work. A few weeks later, the government declared homosexuals unfit to teach or present work abroad because their morals were "not in accord with the prestige of [the] revolution" (Young 1982, 106–7). During the next five years, Luis Pavón Tamayo directed the National Council of Culture (Consejo Nacional de Cultura, CNC). His tenure became known as the *pavonato* (the period of Pavón) and the *quinquenio gris* because of the marginalization of experimental artists and official preference for didactic art. A reorganization of the cultural bureaucracy in 1976— with the Ministry of Culture directed by Armando Hart replacing Pavón's CNC—resulted in a more open environment.

Although this narrative accounts for some aspects of the arts in Cuba, scholars have questioned its accuracy. Several have suggested that repression far exceeded the misnomer *quinquenio gris* and in fact 1968 to 1983 was a *trinquenio amargo* (bitter fifteen years; Coyula 2007) that was "not gray but black for many intellectual lives and works" (Navarro 2002, 198). Others have pointed out that the standard 1971 to 1976 chronology applies mostly to writers (Miller

2008). Work on Cuban music, for instance, has dated the *quinquenio gris* to 1968 through 1973 and recognized repression and self-censorship at other moments as well (Moore 2006, 104–5). Analysts of visual arts and film, on the other hand, have described the Cuban government's relatively liberal approach to these forms. In the essay "Socialism and Man in Cuba," revolutionary leader Ernesto "Che" Guevara famously criticized socialist realism, the preferred artistic approach of the Soviet Union, calling it dated and limiting ([1965] 2003, 223). Cuban officials embraced abstract and experimental visual arts more than their counterparts in the Soviet Union and Eastern Bloc (Craven 2002, 75). Filmmakers also seemed to push the boundaries of expression at least partially thanks to the good relationship between the film institute director Alfredo Guevara and Fidel Castro (Chanan 2004, 7). However, artistic leeway had its limits. For instance, the innovative documentary filmmaker Nicolás Guillén Landrián was sentenced to two years of hard labor at a prison camp, electroshock therapy, and house arrest for supposed ideological diversion in the late 1960s (L. Guerra 2012, 343).

This essay contributes to reassessments of post-1959 cultural policy by focusing on dance, an arena of cultural production previously overlooked in scholarship on the early 1970s. With this novel perspective, I argue that during the gray period, modern dancers created decidedly "colorful" work, that is, repertoire with great range and dynamism. Particularly impressive was the diversity of politics expressed by Cuban dances, which reflected on race, sexuality, class, and nationalism in distinct ways. These choreographies pushed the boundaries of revolutionary politics beyond state paradigms to include individual opinions and aspirations. Along with innovation onstage, modern dancers made claims against the state in the wake of censorship and under the threat of further sanction. As dancers made aesthetic and administrative choices in conversation with expressive strictures, they moved Cuban modern dance in new directions. Adding to understandings of artistic repression and reaction in the early 1970s, I examine the vivid moves of Cuban modern dancers in a grim political moment.

This history moreover addresses a series of dance makers who have not received much attention in existing work on Cuban modern dance. Scholars have concentrated on Ramiro Guerra (John 2012; Mousouris 2002; Pajares Santiesteban 1993), who has merited these attentions not only because of his integral role in developing Cuban modern dance but also due to his prolific writing on Cuban dance history and theory (R. Guerra 1989, 1998, 2000, 2003, 2010, 2013). Although scholars have provided insights on the priorities and aesthetics of modern dance during later decades by publishing edited interviews (Pajares Santiesteban 2005) and contextualized participant-observer experiences

(Burdsall 2001; Guillermoprieto 2005; John 2012), a narrative of key historical developments in Cuban modern dance during the early 1970s remains untold. This essay provides line and definition to the blurry past by focusing on works by three Cuban choreographers—Eduardo Rivero, Gerardo Lastra, and Víctor Cuéllar—who filled the creative void left by the 1971 censorship and Guerra's sudden departure. I also analyze previously unexamined archival materials that shed light on crucial behind-the-scenes maneuvers by Lorna Burdsall, who helped to secure the company's fate during this period. Looking on and off the stage, I demonstrate how performative and administrative labors worked in tandem as modern dancers dealt with censorship and asserted agency. Though decentering Guerra's 1960s oeuvre, I nevertheless honor his legacy by examining the achievements of his students and longtime colleagues.

This history of Cuban modern dancers in the 1970s also contributes to the futures of dance studies, especially historical approaches to dances in a limited public sphere. The Cuban modern dancers under examination operated in a tense moment when the state's Manichaean ideology divided the world into revolutionary friends and counterrevolutionary foes. Yet their choreography troubled the stark moral universe by not necessarily resisting or conforming to state mandates. Instead, a single work held many potential political readings. Borrowing from scholar Sara Johnson, who makes compelling use of "speculation" in her analysis of nineteenth-century Haitian women, I examine textual and visual material and then speculate about possible choreographic meanings (2012, 122–56). This approach responds to gaps in available records and testimonies, given that statements about dance politics appeared in the state-controlled press and all three choreographers have since passed away. Rather than generating any definitive conclusions, which would be an impossible undertaking, I instead imagine the scope of political possibility within a single dance action. In dialogue with recent scholarship on artists in the Soviet Union, East Germany, and China (Ezrahi 2012; Giersdorf 2013; Ross 2015; Wilcox, in this volume), I demonstrate how state strictures did not foreclose originality, as artists found ways to express personal beliefs about politics and society. By not categorizing artists as either critical or complicit, I seek to represent the many shades of political thought that a single dance maker articulated through movement.

Modern Dance and Revolution

In the months after Castro and his 26th of July Movement overthrew Fulgencio Batista, the new government passed measures to eliminate racial segregation, improve access to housing, health care, and education, and build cultural institutions. As part of the cultural campaign, the TNC was nationalized in June 1959, placed under the jurisdiction of the Ministry of Education, and organized into five departments: Music, Dramatic Arts, Modern Dance, Folklore, and Publications and Cultural Exchange, renamed Theatrical Extension in 1960 (Sánchez León 2001, 47–49). Guerra, who had trained in Havana and New York, became the director of the Department of Modern Dance.[1]

Around this time, Guerra published an article about dance, race, and nation in Cuba. He critiqued previous dance approaches and laid out a plan for better practices in the field. Guerra asserted that the country lacked adequate institutions for conserving and developing folklore. Folklore, for mid-twentieth-century Cubans, denoted cultural practices of the nonelite majority and became associated with blackness, since class was racialized in Cuba.[2] According to Guerra, folklore previously had been distorted in commercial venues, tourist attractions, and misguided official troupes (1959, 10). In order to redress past wrongs, Guerra contended that a true national dance needed "the direct intervention of individuals of the black and mestizo race" (1959, 11). Their contributions had been inhibited, Guerra continued, because of persisting prejudices and the fact that "black and mestizo artists, owners of the powerful expression of their race, escape the grasp of serious art for economic reasons . . . [as] they end up involved in the vulgarity of commercial art" (1959, 11). Capitalizing on the political moment, Guerra called for expanding folkloric and modern dance as part of "current profound changes of our nation and its strengthening of national principles" (1959, 11). To Guerra, folklore and modern dance were instrumental to nationalistic revolution.

Guerra soon put these thoughts into practice. On September 11, 1959, an advertisement in the newspaper called for people of all backgrounds and physical types to audition for scholarships to take dance theory and technique classes at the TNC with the possibility of becoming a permanent member of the new company (Teatro Nacional de Cuba 1959). In the audition, Guerra accepted dancers of "different races" and training, from individuals with ballet or cabaret background to those without formal instruction or stage experience (de la Torriente 1960, 75; Pérez León 1985, 21–22). Along with a diverse group of Cubans, Burdsall also joined the new modern dance company.

Burdsall had worked as a professional dancer in New York before meeting and marrying Manuel Piñeiro, a Cuban student at Columbia University. Burdsall moved to Cuba to be with her husband in 1955 (2001, 48, 54). Soon after, Piñeiro joined the 26th of July Movement in the Sierra Maestra, earning the moniker Barba Roja, or Red Beard. Following the 1959 regime change, Piñeiro became the vice minister of the interior. Early in 1959 Burdsall lived in Santiago de Cuba with her husband, but in June they relocated to Havana. By October she was working with Guerra and his modern dancers (Burdsall 2001, 125, 129; Conjunto Nacional de Danza Moderna 1965).

Because of her husband, Burdsall enjoyed a privileged position in revolutionary society. In a letter written in March 1959 Lorna described a trip to the beach with her son, her husband, one of her two maids, and "two rebels," all piled into a jeep, leaving their air-conditioned Cadillac at home. Burdsall wrote that once the group arrived at the beach, they "were surrounded by admirers taking pictures, etc. The children especially love M[anuel] & the rest of the 'bearded ones' [*barbudos*, a moniker assigned to the unshaven guerrilla fighters of the 26th of July Movement]. After being so afraid of the former regime, they love the rebels like Santa Claus" (Burdsall 1959). Her memoir reveals that in the 1960s and 1970s she had a comfortable situation complete with nice homes, maids, cars, and diplomatic trips all over the world (Burdsall 2001, 116–74). With undeniable privileges, Burdsall nevertheless worked hard over the years, as a dancer, teacher, choreographer, and, eventually, an artistic director of the CNDM.

Burdsall and her fellow dancers took classes from and performed choreography by Guerra, who created works that explored race, folklore, and nationalism in Cuba. For instance, in 1960 Guerra choreographed *Suite Yoruba*, inspired by the *orishas* (deities) of the African diasporic religion Santería and performed to sacred vocal and drum music. The piece explored religious syncretism, as conveyed with great theatricality in the opening scene, when a dancer standing in an oval cutout of the Virgin Mary stepped through it to dance with her attendants as the orisha Yemayá. Guerra saw Santería syncretism encapsulating Cuba's national identity, which he defined in an interview as one of racial integration (Arrufat 1960). In 1964 Guerra created *Orfeo Antillano* (Antillean Orpheus), based on the story of Orpheus transposed to a modern Cuban setting with the orishas in place of the Greek pantheon. Along similar lines, in 1968 Guerra created *Medea y los negreros* (Medea and the enslavers), which set the Greek myth of Medea and Jason in the Caribbean during the Haitian Revolution at the end of the eighteenth century. Jason was a European adventurer traveling from Haiti to Cuba with his lover, Medea, an enslaved princess of an African tribe. When Jason abandoned Medea for another woman, she used Haitian Vodou against Jason, only to be murdered by elements of the violent slaveholding society (R. Guerra 2003, 261–62). Linking African diasporic religions to Greek mythology, Guerra showed how divinities shaped human lives across cultures and epochs.

Guerra struggled as a result of exploring racial difference and African diasporic faith in his work. In February 1962 Castro declared that the revolution had eradicated discrimination based on race or sex (de la Fuente 2001, 279). Castro's statement made discussions about race taboo and, by extension, Guerra's choreographed explorations of African heritage in Cuba potentially

problematic. Moreover, Guerra's work highlighted the contemporary importance of Santería, while the state increasingly cast African-descended religions
as obstacles to socialism and linked to criminality. By the late 1960s the government had implemented measures to prohibit Santería initiation ceremonies.
Although the state revoked the rule in 1971, adherents still needed special permission for ceremonies, and minors could not attend (de la Fuente 2001, 291–
92, 295). In interviews conducted decades later, Guerra recalled the numerous
battles he fought with cultural bureaucrats in the late 1960s: "When my work
about folklore brought me close to the traditional religious cults . . . I was
summoned by officials who threw in my face the fact that I was encouraging . . . religious practices outside the prevailing ideology of that time" (quoted
in Pajares Santiesteban 1993, 202). Guerra was engaged in an uphill battle to
secure a place for folklore-inspired modern dance in Cuban society.

Compounding the struggles Guerra faced due to his choreographic interests,
the state believed him to be homosexual (Schwall 2016, 182). Starting in the
mid-1960s, reigning political discourse labeled homosexuals, Jehovah's Witnesses, Seventh Day Adventists, Catholic priests, Protestant preachers, and
young peasants who resisted collectivization as "antisocials." Between 1965
and 1968 the government "reeducated" such individuals in forced labor camps
(L. Guerra 2012, 227–331). Guerra's perceived homosexuality put him at odds
with prevailing sexual norms and likely contributed to the state's eventual
censorship of his work in 1971.

Colorful Choreography

After Guerra left the CNDM, his students Eduardo Rivero, Gerardo Lastra,
and Víctor Cuéllar filled the void that he left behind. Rivero trained in ballet,
Cuban folklore, and popular dances like *danzón* and rumba at a Havana studio from 1953 to 1959 and then was a founding member of the CNDM (Pajares
Santiesteban 2005, 48–49; Pérez León 1985, 21). Although information about
Lastra's early dance background is scarce, he began performing with the CNDM
in the early 1960s, as evidenced by a September 1960 performance program
("Danza Moderna" 1960). Cuéllar started his career in musical theater and television and joined the CNDM in 1967 ("Víctor Cuéllar" 1989). These dancers,
all men of African descent, had different dance backgrounds and choreographic
styles but similarly worked with Guerra and contributed to the development of
Cuban modern dance. Looking at their choreographic output for the CNDM
in the early 1970s demonstrates how modern dance went in many aesthetic
and political directions during the *quinquenio gris*.

On May 13, 1971, about a month after the censorship of *Decálogo*, the CNDM
premiered Eduardo Rivero's *Súlkary*, a work inspired by African sculpture and

fertility rites. It featured three male-female pairs, all dancers of African descent. According to Rivero, *Súlkary* portrayed the "plastic beauty of the people who make Africa a strong and majestic continent full of great mysteries and rhythms" (n.d.). An article described the work as "strong and lyrical at the same time" as male and female dancers interacted in a "harmonious, ancestral confrontation" ("Danza Moderna" 1974). According to Burdsall, the choreography reflected Rivero's impressive talent, which she described in a letter to her family as "more organic than Ramiro" and resulting in works that "would be a hit anywhere in the world" (1973b).

As depicted in a film version of *Súlkary* (1974), the "ancestral confrontation" accentuated gender difference and heterosexual attraction. Soaring Yoruban chants set a mystical, solemn tone. Three women wearing nude leotards move through space slowly and heavily. The air surrounding their bodies appears viscous as they advance forward and flow in and out of various poses. The women dance in unison and then suddenly break away into different sequences to suggest a universal femininity that has both individual and collective aspects. When the women end their opening section, three men enter wearing nude loincloths and holding staffs. They parade out to more energetic vocals, moving their chest and shoulders to pulsating rhythms as the women watch, seated. Each man has a solo, captured in turn by the camera. In contrast to the heavy, grounded women, the men jump, turn, and enact showy handlings of their staffs. After the men complete their solos, the music pauses, the women stand, and the aural ambience becomes quieter, though still charged. The men and women, now in three couples, dance together, creating sculptural designs with their bodies, including those suggestive of copulation. The final sequences feature the women on their male partner's shoulders and then back down on the ground, pressed to their respective male counterparts. Each couple has become one, and in this fused state, they leave the stage.[3]

What does Rivero's sculptural, sensual work reflect about dancing politics in 1971? On the surface, *Súlkary* seems to dodge conventional political messaging, choosing instead to meditate on the beauty and vitality of African aesthetics. It is possible that after the scandal of Guerra's *Decálogo*, Rivero sought to avoid controversial material by portraying heteronormative relationships onstage. Yet another hypothesis would be that Rivero refused to articulate a particular message, choosing instead to give audiences space to contemplate and interpret *Súlkary* on their own. This intention would have contrasted sharply with ubiquitous state propaganda, which daily called for revolutionary sacrifices. Moreover, in a context where revolutionary antiracism and racism paradoxically coexisted (Benson 2016), Rivero's effort to deepen audience appreciation for Africanist culture in Cuba importantly promoted ideals of

FIGURE 31. *Súlkary*, 1971. (Photograph courtesy of Danza Contemporánea de Cuba)

racial equality. Finally, Rivero's homage to Africa in Cuba continued his mentor's work and thus refused to allow state censure to define the company's future. Years later, Rivero revealed how Guerra remained firmly on his mind as he began choreographing: "A very important, for me, definitive, factor in my dedication to choreography, without abandoning dance completely, was the absence of Maestro Ramiro. When it happened we were all a little disoriented and even helpless [*desamparados*]. We needed to continue his line of work to keep the pace of creation we were used to, so I decided . . . to fill the void that we suffered, and I gave classes and did choreography" (Rivero quoted in Pérez León 1985, 24). Indeed, *Súlkary* and other works by Rivero built on Guerra's long-standing commitment to examining Afro-Cuban culture through modern dance.

Along with Rivero, Lastra began choreographing regularly for the CNDM in the early 1970s. The same May 13, 1971, program with Rivero's *Súlkary* featured Lastra's *Negra Fuló* (Black Fuló), set in colonial Brazil and inspired by Brazilian poet Jorge de Lima's poem about a beautiful slave woman who overpowers the slaveholder through her sensuality. There were five characters: a slaveholder and his wife, two enslaved men, and an enslaved woman, Fuló.

The enslaved men upset the slaveholder's wife, and the slaveholder tries to castigate Fuló but becomes enamored with her beauty. In a final sequence, the different characters dance around a chair, which "is a symbol of power," until Fuló ends up enthroned in the seat (Lastra n.d.). In his choreography, Lastra showed protagonists prevailing despite their historical positions of enslavement.

Negra Fuló celebrated successful rebellions by enslaved peoples, an idea that resonated with contemporary state efforts to cultivate international solidarity against imperial exploitation.[4] With this content, Lastra may have hoped to regain broader official support and bolster the political capital of modern dance in the wake of the 1971 censorship. However, the plot's revolutionary legibility also potentially allowed Lastra to posit racial politics that diverged from the official line. Lastra told a history of racial violence that was resolved only when Fuló, an embodiment of black endurance and beauty, overthrew exploitative powers. Thus, the piece intentionally or unintentionally presented a more radical vision of revolutionary justice than the Cuban government had proposed or enacted. Rather than shoring up official ideals of a classless, raceless society, Lastra explored racial difference to address and even undermine enduring structural inequalities.

FIGURE 32. *Negra Fuló*, 1971. (Photograph courtesy of Danza Contemporánea de Cuba)

Lastra and his colleague Víctor Cuéllar created along similar lines, choreographing overtly political pieces that heralded contemporary revolutionary icons and struggles. For instance, Lastra's *Con los puños cerrados* (With clenched fists) premiered on June 3, 1972. Inspired by African American activist Angela Davis, it depicted African American politics from slavery to the civil rights movement to a "more progressive position of armed struggle, as a way to achieve rights and total liberation" ("Danza 'Puños Cerrados'" n.d.). The timely piece coincided with extensive coverage of Davis's activism and trial in the United States, as well as her trips to Cuba.[5] Premiering on the same night was Cuéllar's *Diálogo con el presente* (Dialogue with the present), which paid homage to "all guerrilla fighters who, through the figure of Commander Ernesto Che Guevara, will achieve the ultimate expression of the new man," according to program notes (Conjunto Nacional de Danza Moderna 1973). Guevara had died in 1967 but still remained (and remains) a powerful symbol of leftist politics throughout the world. These two works aligned with prevailing political discourses. Like *Negra Fuló*, the pieces could be seen as exhibiting modern dancers' continued revolutionary devotion. Such political performances made state sanctions seem unwarranted and, more importantly, not necessary in the future. However, it is just as likely that Lastra and Cuéllar explored Davis and Guevara to connect with internationalist progressive struggles for justice, choosing to bypass the Cuban government and its singular definition of revolution.

Another important work from this colorful gray period, Cuéllar's *Panorama de la música y danza cubana* (Panorama of Cuban music and dance), premiered on March 10, 1973. Program notes described the piece as exploring "the fusion of Spanish and African cultures" through the historical development of transcultural music and dance (Conjunto Nacional de Danza Moderna 1974). Cuéllar aimed to valorize Cuban popular culture, as he explained in an interview: "It has always bothered me a lot—the criteria that have devalued popular music by applying the label 'popular' with a pejorative sense. . . . Yet it is one of the most difficult to interpret in the world" ("Danza Moderna" 1974). Cuéllar viewed popular music and dance as having "true and profound social-historical value" (quoted in González Freire 1974).

Indeed, *Panorama* has great interest in history. It starts with a scene portraying Spanish boats traveling to the Americas. A clash occurs between Spanish colonizers (portrayed by women) and enslaved peoples of Africa (all men). From this violent confrontation comes the development of Cuban colonial culture, which included dances like the *contradanza* and later the *danzón*. Traditional and modern dance interpretations of popular rhythms happen simultaneously, differentiated by costuming, with some men and women in period dress dancing traditional versions and others in leotards enacting modern dance

FIGURE 33. *Panorama de la música y danza cubana*, 1973. (Photograph courtesy of Danza Contemporánea de Cuba)

stylizations of popular dances. Moving into the republican period, the choreographic journey includes the *son*, cha-cha-cha, rumba, and mambo, among others.

In interviews, Cuéllar carefully aligned his work with revolutionary tenets. For instance, he gestured to pedagogic priorities, claiming to teach Cuban audiences about the centrality of popular culture through time. As he put it, "My intention is historical, and thus I have produced a didactic spectacle" (quoted in González Freire 1974). With "didactic" intentions, Cuéllar answered the state's call to artists during the early 1970s to educate the masses with their work (Fornet 2013, 165–86). Cuéllar also described the piece as expressing his political ideology: "Before *Panorama* I was lost. . . . This new way, I feel, ties the choreographic work in a close manner to ideological formation. It has been fifteen years of a revolution that arrived when I was a youth; it is why I think that all my work has to do with political content developed within the concepts of the revolution" (quoted in "Danza Moderna" 1974). Cuéllar suggests that he "found" his artistic voice by expressing himself "within" the revolution. This word choice evokes Castro's 1961 mandate that only art "within the revolution" had a right to exist. However, despite these militant statements, *Panorama* did not have a politicized plot or symbols. Perhaps Cuéllar strategically asserted revolutionary meanings to the press about his less obviously political choreography. Or he may have believed that his work clearly promoted current campaigns to educate the masses and valorize their cultures. Regardless, the piece remains a canonical representation of Cuban modern dance that is admired for its popularity and celebration of national culture (Pajares Santiesteban 2005, 76, 81–82).

The works by Rivero, Lastra, and Cuéllar differed considerably; however, they all explored Africanist aesthetics and revolutionary politics. As these choreographers interpreted Cuba's African roots, they evidenced Guerra's continuing influence on the company. Yet they also took Guerra's long-standing interests in new directions. Rivero explored the beauty and power of African culture through nonnarrative productions, while Lastra choreographed tales about colonial Brazil and African American struggle. Cuéllar also forged his own path as he created a militant homage to Guevara and pedagogic depiction of Cuban popular music and dance history. This variety evidences that the early 1970s was a fruitful era of Cuban modern dance creation. Further proof came several decades later. While on tour in 2011, Cuban modern dancers performed *Súlkary,* forty years after its premiere, at the Joyce Theatre in New York. The fact that *Súlkary* was included in the program indicated its durability. It had weathered not only restrictive cultural policies but also the test of time (John 2012, 96–99).

Backstage Maneuvers

Though the CNDM presented an impressive array of choreography, turmoil existed behind the scenes after Guerra's departure. The company changed directors five times in a year and a half, and four of the five simply imposed new rules, never asking for input from longtime company affiliates (Burdsall 1973a). In late 1972 Burdsall decided to write a report on Cuban modern dance history that registered formal complaints about years of bureaucratic mistreatment. It would go "to everybody important" in hopes of starting a necessary conversation about better policies moving forward (Burdsall 1972). She sent her essay to CNC president Pavón, among others, as revealed in a handwritten note accompanying her report that requested an in-person meeting with him to discuss pressing issues further (Burdsall 1973a).

Now housed in the Ministry of Culture archives, the report protested years of bureaucratic failure and demanded immediate resolutions. The essay detailed the history of the CNDM and Cuban modern dance training. After several pages of exposition, Burdsall flagged internal and external problems in a section titled "Críticas y autocríticas" (Criticism and self-criticism). According to Burdsall, when the CNC took charge of dance enterprises in 1962, modern dancers "had the first impressions of a lack of support" from cultural officials. This manifested in numerous ways over the years, such as constant difficulties in getting theater space. Burdsall also complained about the labeling of Guerra's *Decálogo* as pornography during the 1971 congress: "The act of criticizing the work before the participants of the Commission VI . . . without deeply analyzing the labors and works that had been realized since the beginning or having someone of modern dance present to defend the national line of the said group was in our opinion a great mistake and an injustice. The result was the implementation of an extremist policy, eliminating from the repertoire all the works of the choreographer of the work in question" (1973a). Along with this complaint, Burdsall claimed that the CNC had failed to fix a studio in need of repairs and never invited the CNDM to perform for official foreign visitors. Burdsall then suggested steps to improve the situation, which included ensuring regular theater space, allowing the company to perform abroad more frequently, and repairing its studios as soon as possible. She concluded with a humble but pointed reiteration of the CNDM's value to Cuban and international culture: "In spite of all these limitations and incomprehension, we can affirm that modern dance in these twelve years has made a modest contribution to the culture of our country and to Latin America."

Conditions improved for the CNDM soon after Burdsall's report. It is possible that Burdsall's status as the wife of a high-level government official allowed her to protest so boldly and effect change. Regardless, in March 1973, a couple of months after she submitted the report, the CNDM performed for a Peruvian delegation, and Fidel Castro was at the performance for the first time in the company's history (Burdsall 2001, 170). He congratulated the dancers after the performance, which left everybody in the company "floating on air," Burdsall wrote (1973c). In letters to her family, she detailed upcoming "ambitious plans" (1973d) and happily asserted, "Modern dance has finally been 'discovered,' and we are at last coming into the fore. . . . In October we celebrate our fifteen[th] anniversary and will perform 15 of our best works. There is also talk of tours to Europe, etc." (1974). The company indeed toured widely for the remainder of the decade (Schwall 2016, 260–321).

Dancing in and beyond Cuban History

The company's achievements and eventual recuperation from 1971 to 1974 challenge sweeping characterizations of the early 1970s as a period of unrelenting repression that resulted in lackluster creativity. Although the CNDM indeed experienced harsh treatment on the part of the state, modern dancers also persisted and found unprecedented support in the span of a few years. For instance, CNC president Pavón wrote a congratulatory letter to the CNDM on its fifteenth anniversary, hailing the company's recent name change to Danza Nacional de Cuba (National Dance of Cuba, DNC) as "a sign of maturity" (1974). The plight and then ascent of modern dance in the early 1970s ultimately point to the complexities of Cuban cultural policies and the impossibility of a single chronology across the arts.

These modern dance histories and speculation about dancing politics also have relevance beyond Cuban cultural history. Modern dancers in the early 1970s experienced the bitter sting of censorship but continued to promote revolutionary ideals choreographically. Perhaps the politics they staged came from genuine conviction, survival instinct, or some combination of the two. However, imagining the many possibilities of political intent honors gaps in the archive and makes clear the necessity of speculative leaps. And this analysis provides only a beginning. Along with choreographers embedding gestures and sequences with multiple meanings, dancers and audience members undoubtedly layered on their own beliefs and perspectives. As the Cuban example shows, the limitless horizons of choreography allow dance makers to create moving moments of color even in the grayest of times.

Notes

All translations are by the author unless indicated otherwise.

1. For more on Guerra's training, see Pajares Santiesteban (1993).

2. For more on the racialization of Cuban folklore, see de la Fuente (2001, 285–96).

3. This reading is based on the version filmed in Cuba (*Súlkary* 1974). This same version is available to view online at https://www.youtube.com/watch?v=leijJDdiUiU.

4. For instance, Cuban fighters supported guerrilla militants throughout Latin America in the 1960s and African anticolonial struggles in the 1970s. For more on this, see Harmer (2013).

5. In June 1972, when Lastra's piece premiered, articles in the main magazine, *Bohemia*, covered Davis's visits and political struggles.

Works Cited

Arrufat, Antón. 1960. "Al hablar con Ramiro." *Lunes de Revolución*, April 4, 15.

Benson, Devyn Spence. 2016. *Antiracism in Cuba: The Unfinished Revolution*. Chapel Hill: University of North Carolina Press.

Burdsall, Lorna. 1959. Letter, March 27, folder 1, box 1, Burdsall Family Papers (BFP), Cuban Heritage Collection, University of Miami Libraries, Miami, FL (CHC).

———. 1972. Letter, November 19, folder 3, box 1, BFP, CHC.

———. 1973a. "12 años de danza moderna en Cuba." Folder Conjunto de Danza Nacional 1962/1975, box 229, Fondo Consejo Nacional de Cultura (CNC), Biblioteca

Juan Marinello, Archivo General del Ministerio de Cultura, Havana, Cuba (BJM, AGMC).

————. 1973b. Letter, February 11, folder 3, box 1, BFP, CHC.

————. 1973c. Letter, March 13, folder 3, box 1, BFP, CHC.

————. 1973d. Letter, October, folder 3, box 1, BFP, CHC.

————. 1974. Letter, April 7, folder 3, box 1, BFP, CHC.

————. 2001. *More Than Just a Footnote: Dancing from Connecticut to Revolutionary Cuba.* Québec: AGMV Marquis.

Chanan, Michael. 2004. *Cuban Cinema.* Minneapolis: University of Minnesota Press.

Conjunto Nacional de Danza Moderna. 1965. Memorandum to Arsenio Pandiello, May 18, folder CDN Asistencia Técnica 60, box 224, CNC, BJM, AGMC.

————. 1973. "Uruguay Hoy" performance program, folder 1973 Ballet—Danza, Centro de Documentación y Archivo Teatral, Teatro Nacional de Cuba, Havana, Cuba (CDAT, TNC).

————. 1974. Performance program, December 1973–January and February 1974, folder 1974 Ballet—Danza, CDAT, TNC.

Coyula, Mario. 2007. "El trinquenio amargo y la ciudad distópica: Autopsia de una utopía." Conference paper, Instituto Superior de Arte, Havana, Cuba. www.crite rios.es/pdf/coyulatrinquenio.pdf.

Craven, David. 2002. *Art and Revolution in Latin America, 1910–1990.* New Haven, CT: Yale University Press.

"Danza Moderna." 1960. Performance program, Danza Moderna del Teatro Nacional, September, folder Programoteca 1959–61, Archivos de Danza Contemporánea de Cuba, Teatro Nacional de Cuba, Havana, Cuba (DCC, TNC).

"Danza Moderna hoy y mañana en el teatro Mella." 1974. *Juventud Rebelde*, July 2, 4.

"Danza 'Puños Cerrados' (Simbólica)." n.d. Folder Con los Puños Cerrados 1972, Fondo Repertorio, DCC, TNC.

de la Fuente, Alejandro. 2001. *A Nation for All: Racial Inequality and Politics in Twentieth-Century Cuba.* Chapel Hill: University of North Carolina Press.

de la Torriente, Lolo. 1960. "La danza, disciplina de la Mente y Alegría del espíritu." *Bohemia*, October 10, 34–35, 75.

Ezrahi, Christina. 2012. *Swans of the Kremlin: Ballet and Power in Soviet Russia.* Pittsburgh, PA: University of Pittsburgh Press.

Fornet, Jorge. 2013. *El 71: Anatomía de una crisis.* Havana: Letras Cubanas.

Giersdorf, Jens Richard. 2013. *The Body of the People: East German Dance since 1945.* Madison: University of Wisconsin Press.

González Freire, Nati. 1974. "El *Panorama* de Víctor Cuéllar." *Bohemia*, July 19, 28.

Guerra, Lillian. 2012. *Visions of Power in Cuba: Revolution, Redemption, and Resistance, 1959–1971.* Chapel Hill: University of North Carolina Press.

Guerra, Ramiro. 1959. "Hacia un movimiento de danza nacional." *Lunes de Revolución*, July 13, 10–11.

————. 1989. *Teatralización del folklore y otros ensayos.* Havana: Letras Cubanas.

————. 1998. *Calibán danzante: Procesos socioculturales de la danza en América Latina y en la zona del Caribe.* Caracas: Monte Ávila Editores Latinoamericana.

———. 2000. *Eros baila: Danza y sexualidad.* Havana: Letras Cubanas.

———. 2003. *De la narratividad al abstraccionismo en la danza.* Havana: Centro de Investigación y Desarrollo de la Cultura Cubana Juan Marinello.

———. 2010. *Siempre la danza, su paso breve: Escritos acerca del arte danzario.* Havana: Ediciones Alarcos.

———. 2013. *Develando la danza.* Havana: Ediciones ICAIC.

Guillermoprieto, Alma. 2005. *Dancing with Cuba: A Memoir of the Revolution.* Translated by Esther Allen. New York: Vintage Books.

Guevara, Ernesto "Che." (1965) 2003. "Socialism and Man in Cuba." In *Che Guevara Reader: Writings on Politics and Revolution,* 2nd ed., edited by David Deutschmann, 212–30. North Melbourne: Ocean Press.

Harmer, Tanya. 2013. "Two, Three, Many Revolutions? Cuba and the Prospects for Revolutionary Change in Latin America, 1967–1975." *Journal of Latin American Studies* 45: 61–89.

John, Suki. 2012. *Contemporary Dance in Cuba: Técnica Cubana as Revolutionary Movement.* Jefferson, NC: McFarland.

Johnson, Sara E. 2012. *The Fear of French Negroes: Transcolonial Collaboration in the Revolutionary Americas.* Berkeley: University of California Press.

Lastra, Gerardo. n.d. "Desarrollo de la Danza *Negra Fuló.*" Folder Negra Fuló 1971, Fondo Repertorio, DCC, TNC.

Miller, Nicola. 2008. "A Revolutionary Modernity: The Cultural Policy of the Cuban Revolution." *Journal of Latin American Studies* 40 (4): 675–96.

Moore, Robin. 2006. *Music and Revolution: Cultural Change in Socialist Cuba.* Berkeley: University of California Press.

Mousouris, Melinda. 2002. "The Dance World of Ramiro Guerra: Solemnity, Voluptuousness, Humor and Chance." In *Caribbean Dance from Abakua to Zouk: How Movement Shapes Identity,* edited by Susanna Sloat, 56–72. Gainesville: University Press of Florida.

Navarro, Desiderio. 2002. "In Medias Res Publicas: On Intellectuals and Social Criticism in the Cuban Public Sphere." Translated by Alessandro Fornazzari and Desiderio Navarro. *boundary 2* 29 (3): 187–203.

Pajares Santiesteban, Fidel. 1993. *Ramiro Guerra y la danza en Cuba.* Quito: Casa de Cultura Ecuatoriana.

———. 2005. *La danza contemporánea cubana y su estética.* Havana: Ediciones Unión.

Pavón Tamayo, Luis. 1974. Letter, December 17, folder Conjunto de Danza Nacional 1962/1975, box 229, CNC, BJM, AGMC.

Pérez León, Roberto. 1985. *Por los orígenes de la danza moderna en Cuba.* Havana: Departamento de Actividades Culturales Universidad de la Habana.

Rivero, Eduardo. n.d. "*Sulkari.*" Folder Súlkary 1971, Fondo Repertorio, DCC, TNC.

Ross, Janice. 2015. *Like a Bomb Going Off: Leonid Yakobson and Ballet as Resistance in Soviet Russia.* New Haven, CT: Yale University Press.

Sánchez León, Miguel. 2001. *Esa huella olvidada: El Teatro Nacional de Cuba (1959–1961).* Havana: Editorial Letras Cubanas.

Schwall, Elizabeth. 2016. "Dancing with the Revolution: Cuban Dance, State, and Nation, 1930–1990." PhD dissertation, Columbia University.

Súlkary. 1974. Directed by Melchor Casals. Havana: ICAIC.

Teatro Nacional de Cuba. 1959. "Convocatoria." *Hoy*, September 11.

"Víctor Cuéllar: Imaginación y conjuro en la danza moderna." Performance program, 1989, Sala de Arte, Biblioteca Nacional José Martí, Havana, Cuba.

Young, Allen. 1982. *Gays under the Cuban Revolution.* San Francisco: Grey Fox Press.

Tango and Memory on the Contemporary Dance Stage

VICTORIA FORTUNA

From 1976 to 1983 Argentina suffered a brutal military dictatorship. During this period, known as the last military dictatorship, the government launched a campaign against the civilian population on the Cold War pretext of fighting "subversion," generally construed as communist or anti-Argentine sentiment. The government forcibly disappeared, tortured, and murdered an estimated thirty thousand citizens. This chapter examines the prominence of tango themes in contemporary dance works that engage the physical and psychic trauma of Argentina's last military dictatorship. Contemporary dance choreographers' engagement with the tango, a social dance that first emerged in Buenos Aires at the turn of the twentieth century, began in the years immediately following the country's return to democracy in 1983 and stretched into the early 2000s. The move to blend tango movements, music, and themes with modern and contemporary dance vocabularies and creation processes was not a new or uniquely postdictatorship phenomenon in Argentine concert dance.[1] However, in the wake of the dictatorship, choreographers repeatedly invoked tango as an embodied rubric for approaching the individual and collective trauma of political violence.

In the decades following the return to democracy, Argentina faced the tremendous task of publicly reckoning with state violence and rebuilding democratic processes suspended under military rule. Following his democratic election in 1983, President Raul Alfonsín appointed the National Commission on the Disappearance of Persons, and a 1985 civilian trial found military leaders guilty of war crimes. Two of the original junta leaders, Jorge Videla and Emilio Massera, were sentenced to life imprisonment, while the third member of the initial junta, Orlando Ramón Agosti, and later leaders received shorter sentences. While the government initially investigated the military's crimes, its actions and rhetoric soon implored the population to move on and forget the violent past. The year following the convictions, the Full Stop Law set a cutoff date for the investigation and prosecution of human rights violations by high-ranking military officials. In 1987 the Due Obedience Law declared that sub-ordinate military officers were simply following orders and could therefore not be prosecuted. Shortly after assuming the presidency, Carlos Menem (1989–99) pardoned first military officers awaiting trial and later Videla and Massera, releasing them from their life sentences. In the absence of juridical account-ability and national recognition, tango-inflected choreographic works joined a broad range of activist and cultural movements that played a critical role in reconstructing the past, providing spaces for mourning, and advocating for change on national and international scales.[2]

This chapter charts two principal ways in which postdictatorship contem-porary dance works mobilized tango to engage with trauma. On the one hand, tango's historical ties to immigration and marginalization allowed choreogra-phers to situate their lived experience of dictatorship violence and exile within a broader historical continuum of social exclusion in Argentina. Tango culture and movement function as palimpsests of embodied responses to collective trauma across the twentieth century and combine with contemporary dance vocabulary and creation processes to offer a way of dwelling in the recent past. In this sense, tango's presence emphasizes the collective experience of dictator-ship trauma and dance's role in the construction and transmission of cultural memory. On the other hand, the improvisational, leader-follower movement structure that characterizes tango's social practice allowed choreographers to explore deeply personal experiences of trauma, particularly the violent, sexual-ized power dynamics that marked practices of imprisonment and torture, as well as the experiences of losing loved ones to forced disappearance. While the leader (traditionally danced by a man) generally prompts the steps of the follower (traditionally danced by a woman) through subtle physical cues, the follower has agency over the interpretation of the movement prompt and can thus influence how a dance develops. As a meditation on personal trauma, this exploration of tango theorizes dance as a site for recuperating agency. This chapter argues that both these collective and individual approaches—and the crossings between them—situate dance as a modality for making sense of vio-lent histories.

Documentary films on and concert works by choreographers Silvia Vladim-ivsky and Silvia Hodgers exemplify how tango-inflected contemporary works engage trauma. I begin by analyzing the Italian-produced documentary *Alma doble* (Double soul, 2007), which centers on Vladimivsky's recollections of her life during the last military dictatorship and documents the creative pro-cess behind *El nombre, otros tangos* (The name, other tangos, 2006), a concert work developed in Argentina and Italy that calls on tango's historical roots to speak to collective experience of national trauma, as well as the form's ability to articulate Vladimivsky's personal loss of a loved one to forced disappearance. Vladimivsky's choreography moves between staging partnered, *milonga*-style tango—how tango would be danced socially—and virtuosic, shape-driven, contemporary dance–based movement. Both movement genres combine to depict the experience of loss and to represent the violence of the last military dictatorship.

While Vladimivsky lived and worked in Buenos Aires during the dictatorship, Hodgers's membership in the People's Revolutionary Army (Ejército Revolucionario del Pueblo, ERP), the armed branch of the Marxist-Leninist Workers' Revolutionary Party (Partido Revolucionario de los Trabajadores, PRT), forced her to seek exile in Geneva, where she continues to live today. The Swiss-produced documentary *Juntos: Un Retour en Argentine* (Together: A return to Argentina, 2001) documents Hodgers's return to Buenos Aires and is intercut with selections from her concert work *María Mar*. First presented in Geneva in the late 1990s, *María Mar* features an ensemble female cast and enlists tango to confront Hodgers's experience as a political prisoner in the early 1970s, the loss of her partner to forced disappearance, and her exile. Unlike Vladimivsky's work, Hodgers's piece does not explicitly stage partnered tango. Rather, the piece reimagines tango movement vocabulary through contemporary dance–based choreography to locate the steps for negotiating trauma.

While Vladimivsky's and Hodgers's projects are not the only choreographic works to link tango to histories of political violence, the choreographers' transnational careers and shared status as subjects of European-produced documentaries offer particular insight into how dictatorship-themed works negotiate tango as a fraught national and international icon.[3] Across the twentieth century, tango became synonymous with Argentine and, more broadly, "hot" and "passionate" Latin dance. Marta Savigliano's influential *Tango and the Political Economy of Passion* (1995) traces how a social dance that first grew out of the experiences of marginalized bodies became central to the global exotification and hyper-sexualization of Latin American bodies, as well as a symbol of national identity.[4] Notably, many credit the emergence of Broadway-style theatrical productions such as *Tango Argentino* (1983), which heavily marketed macho tango men and seductive tango women on stages across the United States and Europe, with reinvigorating national and international interest in the tango in the postdictatorship period (Savigliano 1995, 3; J. Taylor 1998, 43). In my analysis of their works, I examine how both Vladimivsky and Hodgers negotiated the pressure of the international stage to sell an exoticized and hypersexualized tango.

Relatedly, this chapter resists a reading of Vladimivsky's and Hodgers's works that reduces their turn to tango as the search for something more "authentically" Argentine than contemporary dance in the wake of a national trauma. In fact, tango's hyperpresence in the international imaginary and in English-language dance scholarship has eclipsed Argentina's extended concert dance history.[5] This essay honors the past work of dance studies and gestures toward the field's future at this juncture. It joins a dance studies conversation that has broken down the "Dance" versus "world dance" dichotomy, untangling the hierarchies that figure "Dance" (modern, contemporary, ballet) as racially unmarked, universal, and from the United States and Europe and "world dance" ("ethnic" or "cultural forms" like tango) as culturally particular, racialized, and from the Global South.[6] Influential studies have demonstrated how white concert dance choreographers historically obscured the contributions of artists of color, as well as the influences of social and vernacular forms, and recent monographs have traced a transnational history of concert dance that extends beyond the United States and Europe.[7] Additionally, a rich body of work reflects on choreographers who blend "traditional" and vernacular forms with contemporary dance vocabularies and creative processes.[8] By examining how Hodgers's and Vladimivsky's works blend marked (tango) and unmarked (contemporary dance) genres, this chapter reveals both as equally potent sites of cultural expression and contestation.[9]

Dancing Tango's Remains

Vladimivsky's prolific career began during the last military dictatorship. In 1981 she cofounded the Fantastic Theater of Buenos Aires (Teatro Fantástico de Buenos Aires) with her husband, actor Salo Pasik. In our conversations, Vladimivsky (2009) characterized much of her work with the Fantastic Theater as a project "que liga el teatro danza con el tango como expresión cultural argentina" (that links dance theater with tango as [a form of] Argentine cultural expression). Vladimivsky noted that this project frequently came into conflict with expectations of and demands for an exoticized or what she calls an "export" version of the tango, especially during periods she spent living and working in Italy. To illustrate her point, Vladimivsky highlighted an instance in which she turned down a likely lucrative offer to codirect an Italian tango school and performance venue. She did so because she felt that the venture sold sexualized and racialized intrigue to its European clientele and limited tango's creative potential— a potential Vladimivsky thought that she could best explore in dance works that incorporated contemporary dance vocabularies and creation methods.

Vladimivsky explained during an interview in 2009 that she agreed to appear in *Alma doble* precisely because the film promised to offer international audiences an alternative perspective on the tango that attended to both the form's historical roots among socially excluded populations and its contemporary link to the exile and loss that dictatorship violence produced. *Alma doble* also features prominent tango composer Gustavo Beytelmann's narrative of exile (he left for Paris in 1976) and follows the development of his score for an improvised concert with Vladimivsky's dancers. Vladimivsky became involved in the documentary through Patrizia Pollarolo, a Turin-based tango performer and instructor who proposed collaboration between Vladimivsky and Beytelmann on the theme of memory of political violence. La Sarraz, a Turin-based independent company specializing in documentaries and art films focused on social issues, produced the film. The project was filmed in Buenos Aires and Turin while Vladimivsky developed a new version of *El nombre, otros tangos*, which she first had begun showing in Buenos Aires in the early 2000s. The piece explores the trauma of political disappearance through the danced narrative of a heterosexual couple.

Alma doble begins with a site-specific rehearsal of *El nombre, otros tangos* in an antique shop in the Colegiales neighborhood of Buenos Aires. In the opening scenes, clips of Pollarolo interviewing Vladimivsky among the antiques alternate with shots of dancer Karina Filomena improvising on the sidewalk outside the shop. Filomena moves in relationship to multiple tables and chairs, at times invoking a café space where tango might be danced socially. She manipulates a collection of worn, mismatched shoes as Beytelmann's score plays. Her movement does not explicitly employ a tango vocabulary; rather, it draws on shapes associated with contemporary dance, including dramatic leg extensions, floor work, lunges, and back arches (Bosso and Gentile 2007).

In the interview clips, Vladimivsky explains the location of the rehearsal and the ideas that ground Filomena's movement:

This is a very special neighborhood where the antiques in Buenos Aires end up, when they are apparently no longer useful. However, this shop is magical because it holds the story of people's lives. I'm working poetically to get at what we harbor inside ourselves. In Argentina, a country devastated by the dictatorship where so many young people died, it is very important to recuperate every last thing. Ultimately, tango is not something that you just dance for entertainment. Tango is also a way of being, in a word, metaphysics. It's mystical, where the past is important. . . . She [the dancer] is looking for an answer in her innermost being. These are classic themes in the tango, but brought to a level of theatrical drama. She opens the coat and these men's and ladies' shoes fall out and she gets her memory back. Her hidden memories come out. (Bosso and Gentile 2007)[10]

FIGURE 34. Still from *Alma doble*, directed by Ivana Bosso and Francesca Gentile and produced by La Sarraz Pictures srl-Italy, 2007.

The antique shop scene ends with Vladimivsky recounting the painful story of her boyfriend's disappearance during the early years of the last military dictatorship. His name, she notes, is missing from government records. The absence of his name among the recorded disappeared is reflected in the title of the stage work.

By surrounding Vladimivsky and Filomena with objects from the past charged with the mystique of their own unknown stories, the antique shop setting gives allegorical form to Vladimivsky's mission to "recuperate every last thing." In Vladimivsky's usage, recuperate implies both "official" reckoning with dictatorship violence in the form of public commemoration and juridical trials of military officials and performance's capacity to transmit the embodied experience of trauma, itself fundamentally marked by absence and fragmentary knowing. Vladimivsky makes clear that she will never be able to recuperate her boyfriend's body or know how he died. Rather, her choreography comes from "el lugar de intentar cerrar yo una situación poéticamente que no cierra ni históricamente ni legalmente" (the place of me trying to poetically close a situation that isn't closed historically or legally) (Vladimivsky 2009). Vladimivsky, then, does not purport to recuperate literal facts or complete narratives through dance; instead, she invokes dancing as a site that allows pieces of the past to "flash up," to borrow Walter Benjamin's phrase (2003, 391). This flashing up defies juridical impunity and government discourses that insisted that Argentines simply move on. The collection of mismatched shoes, however, symbolizes the inevitable incompleteness of the past's returns.

Vladimivsky's notion that the dancer's movement in the antique shop improvisation recuperates "hidden" memories invokes Cathy Caruth's theorization of trauma's repeats. In *Unclaimed Experience: Trauma, Narrative, and History*, Caruth draws on Sigmund Freud to suggest that "trauma is not locatable in the simple violent or original event in any individual's past, but rather in the way that its very unassimilated nature—the way it was precisely not known in the first instance—returns to haunt the survivor later on" (1996, 4). Caruth is interested in how literary language might invoke the aspects of trauma that escape available modes of comprehension and representation, that is, "a language that defies, even as it claims, our understanding" (5). Performance scholar Diana Taylor has demonstrated how both staged and protest performance's efforts to recuperate dictatorship memory both encompass and expand what she considers the "individual" focus of foundational trauma studies concepts like Caruth's (2003, 165). Taylor extends Caruth's argument to performance, noting that performance's own basis in repetition assists survivors in coping with trauma not only as it represents the incommensurability of individual experience but also as it publicly interpolates witnesses and grounds political mobilization around collective experience (2003, 165).

In Vladimivsky's theorization, contemporary dance, combined with "classic" tango themes, creates a potent choreographic language for publicly hosting the collective and individual aspects of trauma's returns. The antique shop scene develops this choreographic language vis-à-vis tango as a "way of being . . . where the past is important." As a social practice, tango first developed in Argentina amid the intense modernization projects that marked the late nineteenth and early twentieth centuries. Beginning in the post-Independence period, nation-building projects aimed to modernize Buenos Aires and populate Argentina's vast countryside with northern Europeans. Immigration to Argentina boomed; however, the newly arrived population was largely southern Italian, poor, male, and concentrated in the capital city. Poor migrants—from abroad and from rural Argentina—lived in *conventillos* (tenement houses) and gathered in bars now remembered as birthplaces of the tango. The oligarchical ruling class racialized the immigrant bodies most closely associated with early tango practice in opposition to the desired "whiter" northern Europeans and constructed immigrants as "sexual inverts"—the plethora of young men in Buenos Aires had fostered an active sex trade linked with the tango (Salessi 1997, 151). In these early years, tango became swept up in a national panic over mass immigration, race, class, and gender as its movement and lyrics captured experiences of marginalization, failed romance, broken families, and nostalgia for distant

homelands. Savigliano reads these tensions in the evolution of tango movement, particularly in the tightening of the embrace and shifts in footwork over
time, demonstrating how tango's steps are quite literally imbued with past struggles (1995, 31). For María Olivera-Williams, early tango music is likewise an
aural ruin whose diverse African and European musical influences and melancholic lyrics allow us to hear the exclusions executed in the making of modern
Argentina (2009, 97).[11] She understands tango "as a nostalgic invention that is
always fragmentary and inconclusive" (96).

While Savigliano and Olivera-Williams see tango as an embodied and aural
palimpsest of the struggles of the early twentieth century, anthropologist Julie
Taylor considers how the socially danced tango's historical residue accrued
new meaning during the last military dictatorship:[12]

> The tango is one of the ways Argentines have given me to think about vio-
> lence. I wrote that the tango expresses suffering under terror imposed initially
> by economic violence that formed the context of the invention of the dance and
> its songs among impoverished immigrants who did not share a language but
> who managed to share a dance. This economic violence has been linked again
> and again in the minds of its victims with the political violence that has caused
> repeated exiles from Argentina. I wrote that the tango taps this link when it tells
> of human ties destroyed. (1998, 61)

The *Alma doble* sidewalk scene extends the palimpsestic tradition that Savigliano, Olivera-Williams, and Julie Taylor identify in the socially danced tango
to a contemporary dance–based improvisation by taking tango sounds and
themes as occasions for dancing through trauma's—and modernization's—
repeats. Turn-of-the-century economic violence is not comparable, in scale or
kind, to the political violence of the last military dictatorship. However, the
periods share a focus on modernization; the military envisioned the dictatorship as a project that combined economic liberalization with Western,
Christian values. The antique shop improvisation inscribes the trauma of dictatorship violence onto the tango as an aural and embodied ruin, visually lit-
eralizing this idea by surrounding Filomena and Vladimivsky with antiques.
Ultimately, the *Alma doble* antique shop improvisation invokes tango as an
established repertoire for expressing the traumatic effects of national projects
on the body. Like Julie Taylor's description of socially danced tango, Vladimivsky's choreography calls on the form to "tell of human ties destroyed." At
the same time, the contemporary dance vocabulary and inclusion of props
(i.e., the shoes) allow Vladimivsky to choreograph absence and trauma beyond
specific tango steps.

Vladimivsky completed *El nombre, otros tangos* in 2006. She presented two versions of the work that year, one in Turin (presented under the title *¿Cómo te llamás? . . . Azul* [What is your name? . . . Blue]) and a second in Buenos Aires.[13] Vladimivsky's continual return to and revision of the piece, since developing the first version in the early 2000s, embody engagement with trauma as a process based in repetition.[14] Both 2006 versions are duets between a female and male dancer and incorporate tango music and partnered tango dance interludes alongside the contemporary dance vocabulary exemplified in Filomena's antique shop improvisation. The Italian version features a video design that literalizes the conflation between tango, turn-of-the-century economic violence, and political violence that Julie Taylor describes and the antique shop improvisation implies. Projection juxtaposes images of archival tango photographs, the Argentine flag, impoverished immigrants standing outside a *conventillo*, and shots of the Mothers of the Plaza de Mayo, the activist group well known for protesting the disappearance of their children, in front of the government palace in Buenos Aires. While the worn shoes employed in the *Alma doble* improvisation appear in the Buenos Aires version of the work, in the Italian production they are replaced with suitcases, scattered clothing, and mannequin busts. In both versions, these various artifacts signal "a story inevitably in pieces" (J. Taylor 1998, 72).

The Italian production makes legacies of torture explicitly present. In the opening moments of the piece, the male dancer appears alone onstage—naked, bound, gagged, and lying supine across the top of a metal structure that resembles a freestanding ballet barre. His pose evokes stress positions frequently incorporated into torture practices. This intense image brings to light the horror of clandestine torture practices, whose absence from public view allowed the military government to feign innocence. This act of making the invisible visible, frames the choreography's subsequent journey into the history of the couple, making clear that their separation is the result of devastating physical violence. It also acts as an enduring reminder of the past in the context of continued activist efforts to advance juridical accountability for human rights violations committed during the last military dictatorship.

In both *El nombre, otros tangos* and the *Alma doble* documentary, tango helps to establish the embodied conditions of possibility for exploring the trauma of dictatorship violence on the concert dance stage. In Vladimivsky's own construction, her work proposes a hybridized movement language for approaching the specificity of the Argentine experience—and claiming Argentineness—on its own terms. In the following, I turn to Silvia Hodgers's engagement with tango in the *Juntos* documentary and her concert work *María Mar*. While Vladimivsky's work emphasizes how tango's historical relationship to exclusion lends itself to dancing memories of dictatorship violence, in *Juntos* and *María Mar* the structure of the dance form creates a space to reflect on agency and interpersonal connection in the wake of torture, the disappearance of loved ones, and exile.

An Argentine Return

Like *Alma doble* and *El nombre, otros tangos, Juntos* and *María Mar* employ tango as a framework for moving through the pieces of the dictatorial past. *Juntos*, like *Alma doble*, explores the loss of loved ones. Viewers heart-wrenchingly witness Hodgers learning that her disappeared partner most likely died in one of the military's death flights, during which officials threw detainees (often drugged but still alive) from planes into the Río de la Plata, which borders Buenos Aires. However, unlike Vladimivsky, Hodgers participated in organized political activity and personally experienced the physical violence of political repression. *Juntos* and *María Mar* both center on Hodgers's narrative as a torture survivor and trace the intersections between her artistic and political careers (Hodgers 2014).

As a dancer, Hodgers began training in Buenos Aires at a young age. Her interest in political mobilization first developed during her time dancing in Europe in the mid-1960s. While living in Paris, Hodgers began working with Peruvian theater maker Emilio Galli, who had close connections with the Peruvian Left. Hodgers's performance work with Galli catalyzed her interest in joining the leftist movements that had spread throughout Latin America in the wake of the Cuban Revolution (Hodgers 2014). Following her return to Buenos Aires in late 1970, Hodgers joined the PRT-ERP. This militant organization fought against the military government that had assumed control in 1966. In September 1971, soon after she began training to serve as a nurse with the PRT-ERP, federal police arrested Hodgers. Officials tortured her and other political prisoners during this period, a practice that anticipated the intensification of state violence in the late 1970s. Between 1971 and 1973, she remained incarcerated at the Villa Devoto and Rawson penitentiaries, located in Buenos Aires and near the southern city of Trelew, respectively. At Rawson, Hodgers took part in an attempted prison escape that resulted in the military's execution of sixteen political prisoners on August 22, 1972.[15] Following her release, Hodgers continued to work with the PRT-ERP until 1976, when she fled Argentina following the disappearance of her partner, Héctor Fernández Baños, a University of Buenos Aires law professor and fellow PRT-ERP member.

Hodgers taught briefly in Buenos Aires under an assumed name following her release from prison; however, she did not resume full-time work in the dance field until she settled in Geneva. Hodgers restarted her dance career as a professor at the University of Geneva and director of Atelier de l'Antichambre (Antechamber Workshop), the dance company with which she developed *María Mar*. The work, which explores Hodgers's memories of her periods of incarceration, was performed broadly in Switzerland in theaters and schools, as well as under the auspices of international human rights organizations (Lifschitz 2010). *María Mar*'s successful run inspired filmmaker Raphaëlle Aellig Régnier to propose a documentary project featuring rehearsals and a performance of *María Mar* alongside footage of Hodgers's return to Buenos Aires in 2000. Aellig Régnier's small, independent company coproduced *Juntos*; the documentary circulated through film festivals in Switzerland and France following its 2001 release (*Juntos* 2016).

While *Alma doble* and *El nombre, otros tangos* explicitly foreground tango, its presence in *Juntos* and *María Mar* is subtler. In *Juntos*, clips of Hodgers dancing and spending evenings at Buenos Aires *milongas*, or events where tango is danced socially, frame her journey into the past. In between these clips, Hodgers speaks with ex-PRT-ERP members about their unrealized political project and visits notable memory sites in the city, including the Navy Petty-Officers School of Mechanics (Escuela de Suboficiales de Mecánica de la Armada, ESMA), a former clandestine detention center. Given that the documentary primarily addressed a European audience, the *milongas* indeed lend the film an air of "authenticity" as they introduce the viewer to Buenos Aires through Hodgers's eyes. That is, *Juntos* does not feature the flashy, tourist-oriented tango presented at expensive dinner shows; instead, it brings viewers to a traditional space with "real" tango dancers. At the same time, the persistent presence of the *milongas* in the documentary (scenes in the *milongas* accompany charged emotional scenes in which Hodgers directly confronts her past) visually marks one of her early statements: "You can never erase the past. I carry it with me every day. Part of me is made of that past" (Aellig Régnier and Wiedmer 2001). Hodgers makes only one direct comment about the *milongas*. In a final scene, she recounts to a friend that a chance dance partner, a businessman, revealed that militants kidnapped him twice. In that instant, the improvisatory space of the *milonga* brought together two experiences of the 1970s otherwise unlikely to find a space for dialogue and physical (even intimate) proximity. As a framing device in the documentary and in the *milonga* encounter, the tango embrace creates "a space to reflect on power and terror" (J. Taylor 1998, 71).

Juntos dedicates ample time to footage of Hodgers rehearsing *María Mar* in Geneva and narrating clips of a performance of the work. In the following descriptions of *María Mar*, I draw on excerpts of the piece featured in *Juntos* and Hodgers's descriptions of additional scenes.[16] The piece features an all-female cast, with five dancers clad in light-blue pants and tops reminiscent of prisoners' garb. Hodgers understands two of these dancers as embodiments of the same character, María; her doubling suggests the fracturing of self and returns that characterize trauma. A sixth dancer wearing a suit represents a prison guard. Notably, *María Mar* and the *Alma doble* antique shop improvisation share several scenographic elements. Both employ tables and chairs, and both turn to collections of worn shoes that symbolize absence. While the table and chair in the antique shop improvisation evoke a *milonga*, in *María Mar* the furniture represents a prison cell. The imprisoned dancers engage the table and chairs with the full length of their bodies and from every angle, wrapping, arching, sliding, and occasionally striking their torsos and limbs against the objects (Aellig Régnier and Wiedmer 2001). In Hodgers's description, one of the Marías pushes the shoes off the surface of the table and scatters them around the stage in a gesture similar to Filomena's release of the shoes onto the sidewalk in *Alma doble* (Hodgers 2014).

As in the documentary, tango plays an unassuming yet constitutive role. It blends seamlessly into Hodgers's contemporary vocabulary, which in *María Mar* emphasizes sharply controlled floor work. The specter of tango emerges twice: once as part of a series of scenes featuring the guard and one María, and once in a moment danced by the prisoners. In *Juntos* a series of clips conclude with a close embrace reminiscent of tango upper body positioning that comments on power relationships between guards and prisoners. In the first clip, the guard stands on top of a small platform wearing a pair of flamenco shoes. The dancer who performed this role happened to be a flamenco dancer, and Hodgers prompted her to perform flamenco's characteristic foot strikes as if she were giving orders to the prisoners (Hodgers 2014). In the next clip, one María repeatedly slams her knee against the table in a gesture of self-discipline as the guard looks on. In the final clip in the series, the guard moves into a lead dancer's arm positioning in a close embrace, one arm positioned around an absent partner's back and the other extended to meet an invisible hand. Eyes closed, the guard slowly shifts back and forth in a moment of private reverie before lowering herself to her knees in front of one María. She gropes María's thighs and buttocks before pulling her into an embrace. María's body goes limp in the guard's arms as the guard sways her body. María's blank stare and limp posture while she is fondled and manipulated signal the loss of agency over her body as it becomes the object of sexualized violence (Aellig Régnier and Wiedmer 2001).

In our interview, Hodgers explained that this scene stemmed from her memories of a female prison guard's repeated attempts at sexual assault. In this scene, the leader-follower structure of tango and its association with sexual encounters offer steps for denouncing the frequent incorporation of assault

FIGURE 35. The guard and María in Silvia Hodgers's *María Mar.* (From *Juntos*, directed by Raphaëlle Aellig Régnier and Norbert Wiedmer and produced by RaR Film and Biograph Film, Switzerland, 2001)

and rape into torture practices. The guard's structured posture, juxtaposed with María's motionless body, exaggerates the leader's determination of how a dance can unfold, in turn mirroring the guard's position of power over the prisoners. By occupying the leader position (traditionally danced by a man), the guard's movements comment on the military's repeated masculinization of government power and feminization of "subversives." As Diana Taylor has demonstrated, torture practices, which often involved the insertion of instruments into the anus or vagina, operationalized the military's "reorganization of the social and political 'body' into active (male) and passive (feminine/effeminate) positions" (1997, 156).

While the tango embrace employed in this scene alludes to uneven gendered and sexualized power dynamics, an additional episode cites tango elements to rechoreograph possibilities for self-determination and healing. In Hodgers's recollection, the imprisoned dancers apply makeup and each dancer puts on one high-heeled shoe as Mariano Mores's instrumental tango "Taquito militar" (Military heel) plays. The title of Mores's song references early men's tango shoes, which derived from military boots. The heel provided a forward pitch that facilitated turning and the close embrace, and it accented the foot strikes male tango dancers performed before asking a partner to dance (Del Priore and Amuchástegu 2001, "Taquito militar").

Lying facedown on the floor, the prisoners perform movements typically associated with a follower's steps in a tango pairing, particularly *ochos* (figure-eight steps; Hodgers 2014). Though the leader's movements generally prompt the follower in socially danced tango, followers have agency over the interpretation of the lead's signal and options to add flourishes. These possibilities arise precisely from an intercorporeal awareness and responsiveness between leader and follower, completely foreclosed in the guard scene. In her work on tango, theorist Erin Manning locates politics in this leader-follower negotiation: "Tango as a political gesture is the exhibition of the between: between my interpretation and your creation, between my lead and your response. Tango allows the mediality of experience to shine through, exposing the ethical dimension of that relation" (2007, 17). Manning's comment might be extended to encompass tango's staging of mediality not only between two bodies but also, as *María Mar* and *El nombre, otros tangos* so powerfully demonstrate, between experiences of the past and the present.[17]

The steps performed while lying flat on the floor, or the "stomach tango," as Hodgers (2014) referred to it, might be read as a play on tango's possibilities for improvisation and individual expression within a determinant structure. In this case, the "ethical dimensions" of the "medial" experience that Manning describes stage the possibility of reconnecting with one's own body and agency, a link that torture and imprisonment severed. By performing tango movements lying facedown, a position associated with a number of violent disciplinary acts (from arrest to rape), *María Mar* asks if tango might provide the literal steps for recovering the body's history and identity from a physical position often used to strip those elements away. It adapts tango movements and puts them to work in a context literally designed to discipline the body into stillness and silence. The "Taquito militar" musical reference makes present tango's historically heteronormative power dynamics (and the military's) at the same time that *María Mar*'s choreography creates the space for the tactical negotiation that tango's movement offers.

Like Vladimivsky, Hodgers explicitly uses the verb "recuperate" to describe the relationship between dance (contemporary and tango) and traumatic memory. Hodgers (2014) testified that dance generally and *María Mar* specifically served to "recuperar mi cuerpo" (recuperate my body) following her experiences in the 1970s. For Hodgers, the practice of dancing and choreographing allowed her to work through and live with traumatic experiences that can never be fully known. Her journey to Buenos Aires in *Juntos* emphasizes the inability to assemble clear narratives of the past; conversations with ex-PRT-ERP members about shared experiences in particular reveal the instability and mutability of memory across time. As mentioned earlier, she also confronted the limited information available about her partner's death. Hodgers knows that Fernández Baños most likely died in a death flight between May and December 1976; however, his bones are not among those that have been recovered from the Río de la Plata (Aellig Régnier and Wiedmer 2001). The *mar,* or ocean, of the *María Mar* title suggests Fernández Baños's most probable final resting place. While Hodgers's experiences as a political prisoner motivated the creation of *María Mar,* like *El nombre,* the piece also mourns the absences left by forced disappearance. When describing a rolling motion during a rehearsal, Hodgers states, "It's as though one of the Marías wants to slip into the ocean, while the other holds her back a bit" (Aellig Régnier and Wiedmer 2001). *María Mar* choreographically probes the sensations that bodies on death flights experienced and imagines, if only briefly, the macabre possibility of a reencounter in the depths of the sea.

For both Vladimivsky and Hodgers, contemporary dance in conversation with the tango provides the literal steps for moving through trauma's returns. Vladimivsky's work draws explicitly on tango's national particularities; that is, *Alma doble* and *El nombre* rehearse tango's turn-of-the-century roots. At the same time, they situate tango music and movements as culturally specific palimpsests that activate and accrue individual and collective struggle and loss across time. Tango still inevitably marks the national in *Juntos* and *María Mar,* but both works emphasize the political possibilities of the act of dancing tango both in Buenos Aires *milongas* and on one's stomach. In the first instance in *Juntos,* the *milonga* facilitated a chance encounter with another body that had differently experienced political violence. Onstage, the stomach tango questions how these historically charged movements might aid in a conscious recovery of the body's agency in the wake of torture and sexual assault. However, for both Vladimivsky and Hodgers, tango functions as a privileged corporeal repertoire for moving into, dwelling in, and sifting through the pieces of the past. As a gesture toward the futures of dance studies, these cases nuance a lively discussion on tango's many lives—on the concert stage and off. They also powerfully evidence contemporary dance's response on the concert stage to the individual and collective trauma of the last military dictatorship and, most critically, the possibilities of memory and mourning in motion.

Notes

A longer version of this chapter first appeared in *Moving Otherwise: Dance, Violence, and Memory in Buenos Aires* (New York: Oxford University Press, 2019). All translations are by the author unless indicated otherwise.

1. Influential choreographer Ana Itelman's 1955 *Esta ciudad de Buenos Aires* (This city of Buenos Aires) was the first among many works to blend tango with modern and contemporary dance vocabularies.

2. The left-wing Peronist administration of Néstor Kirchner (2003–7) reopened a national conversation around memory of the last military dictatorship, including restarting trials of war criminals. Studies of postdictatorship activism and cultural production are numerous; for a thorough book-length study on theater and performance, see Werth (2010).

3. Notable pieces include Susana Tambutti's *La puñalada* (The stab, 1985), a solo that cites early tango culture to critique political violence. For an analysis, see Fortuna (2011). Tambutti's company Nucleodanza (codirected with Margarita Bali) also appeared in Fernando Solanas's 1985 film *Tangos: El exilio de Gardel* (Tangos: The exile of Gardel). The film depicts a group of Argentine exiles living in Paris who decide to stage a *tanguedia* (tango + *tragedia* [tragedy] + *comedia* [comedy]). Susanna Zimmermann's *Dolentango* (1999) and Alejandro Cervera's *Tangos golpeados* (Coup tangos, 2008) also express the memory of state violence through hybrid tango and contemporary dance vocabularies.

4. An impressive Spanish- and English-language literature has documented and analyzed the form's transnational past and present. In addition to Savigliano's work, notable texts in English include J. Taylor (1998), Chasteen (2004), and Thompson (2006). For a consideration of recent trends in the Buenos Aires tango dance scene, see Merritt (2012).

5. Argentina's institutionalized concert dance history began with the foundation of the Colón Theater Ballet in 1925. However, influential artists and thinkers had championed national investment in ballet since the late 1800s. For a discussion of early Argentine ballet culture, see Destaville (2008). Modern first dance took root in the 1940s; for a historical overview, see Tambutti (2000).

6. For a volume that critically engages this dichotomy, see Foster (2009).

7. Gottschild (1996) demonstrates the Africanist influences in US concert dance, and S. Manning (2006) explores the racialized dynamics that constructed modern dance as white and Negro dance as other at midcentury. Srinivasan (2011) traces the crossings of Indian classical dance and modern dance in the twentieth century. For considerations of the transnational development of modern dance, see also Purkayastha (2014) and Giersdorf (2013).

8. Chatterjea (2013) clearly outlines the political stakes of negotiating the "traditional" and the "contemporary" on the global concert stage, and Reynoso (2015) addresses the Latin American context specifically.

9. For a study of the relationship between contemporary dance and histories of political and economic violence in Buenos Aires from the mid-1960s to the mid-2010s, see Fortuna (2019).

10. The translation is based on the English subtitles in the documentary.

11. In her reading of tango as a kind of ruin, Olivera-Williams also invokes Benjamin's concept of the past's ability to "flash up" in the present (2009, 98).

12. Savigliano makes a similar observation (1995, 12), as does Varela (2016, 187–99).

13. My descriptions of the Italian and Buenos Aires productions are based on video documentation from Vladimivsky's private collection.

14. Thank you to Jennifer Schaefer for this insight.

15. For a discussion of the role that dancing played in the attempted escape, see Fortuna (2019).

16. Unfortunately, neither Hodgers nor Aellig Régnier has retained complete video of the work.

17. Thank you to Elliot Leffler for this insight.

Works Cited

Aellig Régnier, Raphaëlle, and Norbert Wiedmer. 2001. *Juntos: Un Retour en Argentine.* Geneva: RaR Film and Biograph Film. https://www.artfilm.ch/juntos-un-retour-en-argentine.

Benjamin, Walter. 2003. "On the Concept of History." In *Selected Writings Volume 4, 1938–1940,* translated by Harry Zohn, edited by Howard Eiland and Michael W. Jennings, 389–400. Cambridge, MA: Belknap Press of Harvard University Press.

Bosso, Ivana, and Francesca Gentile. 2007. *Alma doble.* Turin: La Sarraz Pictures. DVD.

Caruth, Cathy. 1996. *Unclaimed Experience: Trauma, Narrative, and History.* Baltimore, MD: Johns Hopkins University Press.

Chasteen, John Charles. 2004. *National Rhythms, African Roots: The Deep History of Latin American Popular Dance.* Albuquerque: University of New Mexico Press.

Chatterjea, Ananya. 2013. "On the Value of Mistranslations and Contaminations: The Category of 'Contemporary Choreography' in Asian Dance." *Dance Research Journal* 45 (1): 4–21.

Del Priore, Oscar, and Irene Amuchástegui. 2011. *Cien tangos fundamentales.* Buenos Aires: Aguilar. E-book.

Destaville, Enrique Honorio. 2008. "Mirada sobre el siglo XIX y el siglo XX en sus primeros años." In *Historia general de la danza en la Argentina,* edited by Beatriz Durante, 13–49. Buenos Aires: Fondo Nacional de las Artes.

Fortuna, Victoria. 2011. "A Dance of Many Bodies: Moving Trauma in Susana Tambutti's *La puñalada.*" *Performance Research* 16 (1): 43–51.

———. 2019. *Moving Otherwise: Dance, Violence, and Memory in Buenos Aires.* New York: Oxford University Press.

Foster, Susan Leigh, ed. 2009. *Worlding Dance.* New York: Palgrave Macmillan.

Giersdorf, Jens Richard. 2013. *The Body of the People: East German Dance since 1945.* Madison: University of Wisconsin Press.

Gottschild, Brenda Dixon. 1996. *Digging the Africanist Presence in American Performance: Dance and Other Contexts.* Westport, CT: Greenwood Press.

Hodgers, Silvia. 2014. Skype interview with the author, Geneva, Switzerland, and Oberlin, Ohio, August 9.

Juntos. 2016. SWISS FILMS Foundation. Accessed May 1, 2016. http://www.swissfilms.ch/en/information_publications/festival_search/festivaldetails/-/id_film/-1499420850.

Lifschitz, Laura. 2010. "Silvia Hodgers: La danza y la militancia política." *Tiempo Argentino*, October 24. Accessed September 9, 2011. http://tiempo.elargentino.com/notas/danza-y-militancia-politica (site discontinued).

Manning, Erin. 2007. *Politics of Touch: Sense, Movement, Sovereignty*. Minneapolis: University of Minnesota Press.

Manning, Susan. 2006. *Modern Dance, Negro Dance: Race in Motion*. Minneapolis: University of Minnesota Press.

Merritt, Carolyn. 2012. *Tango Nuevo*. Gainesville: University of Florida Press.

Olivera-Williams, María Rosa. 2009. "The Twentieth Century as Ruin: Tango and Historical Memory." In *Telling Ruins in Latin America*, edited by Michael J. Lazzara and Vicky Unruh, 95–106. New York: Palgrave Macmillan.

Purkayastha, Prarthana. 2014. *Indian Modern Dance, Feminism and Transnationalism*. New York: Palgrave Macmillan.

Reynoso, Jose Luis. 2015. "Racialized Dance Modernisms in Lusophone and Spanish-Speaking Latin America." In *The Modernist World*, edited by Stephen Ross and Allana C. Lindgren, 392–400. New York: Routledge.

Salessi, Jorge. 1997. "Medics, Crooks and Tango Queens: The National Appropriation of a Gay Tango." In *Everynight Life: Culture and Dance in Latin/o America*, translated by Celeste Fraser Delgado, edited by Celeste Fraser Delgado and José Esteban Muñoz, 141–74. Durham, NC: Duke University Press.

Savigliano, Marta. 1995. *Tango and the Political Economy of Passion*. Boulder, CO: Westview Press.

Srinivasan, Priya. 2011. *Sweating Saris: Indian Dance as Transnational Labor*. Philadelphia: Temple University Press.

Tambutti, Susana. 2000. "100 años de danza en Buenos Aires." *Funámbulos: Revista Bimestral de Teatro y Danza Alternativos* 13 (1): 23–32.

Taylor, Diana. 1997. *Disappearing Acts: Spectacles of Gender and Nationalism in Argentina's "Dirty War."* Durham, NC: Duke University Press.

———. 2003. *The Archive and the Repertoire*. Durham, NC: Duke University Press.

Taylor, Julie. 1998. *Paper Tangos*. Durham, NC: Duke University Press.

Thompson, Robert Farris. 2006. *Tango: The Art History of Love*. New York: Vintage Books.

Varela, Gustavo. 2016. *Tango y política: Sexo, moral burguesa y revolución en Argentina*. Buenos Aires: Ariel.

Vladimivsky, Silvia. 2009. Interview with the author, Buenos Aires, Argentina, July 7.

Werth, Brenda. 2010. *Theatre, Performance, and Memory Politics in Argentina*. New York: Palgrave Macmillan.

Economics

Of all the keywords structuring *Futures of Dance Studies*, economics is the approach least explored in the field. How have the economics of neoliberalism altered the dance scene in Europe, Great Britain, and the United States? What constitutes "infrastructure" for dance performance—government subvention, nonprofit institutions, the un- or undercompensated labors of dancers and other workers? How can quantitative methods familiar from the social sciences complement the qualitative methods of (auto)ethnography, movement description, and performance analysis to probe the intersection of dance and economics?

In "Breaking Point? Flexibility, Pain, and the Calculus of Risk in Neoliberal Multiculturalism," Anusha Kedhar calls attention to the dancers' labor that creates and sustains contemporary South Asian dance in Great Britain. In particular, she examines "pain and injury as an embodied condition that tracks with problematic labor conditions, namely, the increasingly risky and flexible labor conditions of neoliberal capitalism." Acknowledging that dancers in many genres deal with pain and injury as part of their profession, she nonetheless argues that dancers in contemporary South Asian dance in Britain encounter precariousness in an acute form, since the British dance market demands that they acquire the speed and physical risk-taking that connote Western-style innovation while also demonstrating a thorough mastery of culturally specific techniques. Thus performing the "ideal assimilated British South Asian subject," the dancer stretches herself to the breaking point. Yet Kedhar's ethnographic study also reveals that dancers use their arsenal of "corporeal tactics to manage life and pain under neoliberalism" through self-care and care for others. In this way, her study builds on the work of Randy Martin, among others, to rethink questions of agency and bodily labor in late capitalism.

Like Kedhar, Sarah Wilbur moves away from the focus on the choreographer to attend to the labors of other makers in the dance field. In "Who *Makes* a Dance? Studying Infrastructure through a Dance Lens," Wilbur defines "dance maker" in the broadest possible terms "to include artists, administrators, production personnel, funders, and audience members." Through an ethnographic study of Dance Place, a center for dance training and production in Washington, DC, founded in 1978 by Carla Perlo, Wilbur understands infrastructure as embodied through the students, interns, volunteers, and staff who "expose 'kinesthetic indebtedness,' a weighted and shared sense of social belonging that compels people to labor on behalf of an organization despite any promise of economic gain." Initially located in Adams Morgan, Dance Place lost its lease when the neighborhood gentrified, and this led Perlo to purchase the building in Brookland where the center is currently located. Thus property becomes another dimension of embodied infrastructure, as Wilbur describes the many activities and interpersonal encounters in Dance Place's studios, offices, and corridors. In one of the more polemical essays in *Futures of Dance Studies*, she notes that "at its worst, disciplinary silence around infrastructural issues renders the project of critical dance studies complicit with the isolationist discourses of modernist autonomy (of art) or of capitalist alienation (of artists), or both."

In contrast to the ethnographic approaches of Kedhar and Wilbur, Lizzie Leopold looks for quantitative measures on how the dance world values choreography. In "The Choreographic Commodity: Assigning and Policing Value for Nite Moves and William Forsythe," Leopold recounts how closely the dance world guards financial data. Consequently, she turned to copyright cases, publicly available tax forms, and new insurance instruments, among other sources, to define the choreographic commodity, a form of value that results from an elite tier of choreographers licensing dance works to companies around the globe and even selling their works to museum collections. Following Susan Foster, Leopold traces the choreographic commodity to the era of court ballet and, following Anthea Kraut, to the emergence of choreography as a protected category in US copyright law. Yet she argues that the choreographic commodity has taken on a new importance in an era of neoliberalism, as is evident in the career of William Forsythe, whose dance works are licensed globally and whose recent relocation to the United States caused the German government to assess the financial value of his dances. Leopold further demonstrates the raced and classed dimensions of choreography through reference to a recent tax case in New York State that levied taxes on the club Nite Moves, as a commercial rather than a cultural venue, because its dance entertainment did not conform to the judge's understanding of choreography as an elitist art form deploying "wholly planned bodily movements that are learned in professional and prolonged educational settings and that are performed in specific clothing and in designated locations." As neoliberal economics have created an increasing gap between the rich and the poor, so the choreographic commodity has accrued financial capital at the same time as other dance arenas have faced increasingly scarce resources.

Natalie Zervou documents one of these arenas in her essay, "Walking Backward: Choreographing the Greek Crisis." In 2011, two years after Greece faced a major financial crisis, the state slashed spending in many programs and eliminated governmental support for dance altogether. In response, choreographers joined other artists in creating their own spaces for production and pooling their limited resources. Works such as Artemis Lampiri's *META* (2014–15), Syndram Dance Company's *Fragile Nothing* (2014), and Amalgama Dance Company's *On the Seesaw* (2014) register the disorientation of the economic crisis and "promote embodied agency at a time when bodies are devalued, disenfranchised, and ignored by the state." Their works demonstrate a "forward-backwardness," a corporeal quality that Zervou also sees in the 2016 protest staged by members of the Union for Workers in the Field of Dance in front of Greece's Ministry of Employment: holding hands, they walked backward to enact their demands. It is a move, Zervou believes, that "could be an act of solidarity or of resistance or an urgent call to action. Or it could be all three, combined in one step."

Research into dance and economics has taken its own complex first steps, and the chapters in this section raise questions about the relations of dance, labor, precariousness, property, infrastructure, embodiment, value, and finance, all of which demand further inquiry.

Breaking Point?

Flexibility, Pain, and the Calculus of
Risk in Neoliberal Multiculturalism

ANUSHA KEDHAR

In 2009 I auditioned for a contemporary South Asian dance company in Britain to work on a new ensemble work.[1] The audition was grueling. It tested my ability to pick up movement quickly; perform difficult movements with speed, precision, and attack; and repeat those movements over and over again. The choreographer told me she liked the way I moved but was worried about my ability to keep up. "It's going to be hard on your joints," she cautioned. "You'll need to strengthen your legs and feet." She told me I did not stamp hard enough or lift the arches of my feet high enough when I did *kudichumettu* [in *bharata natyam*, a hopping step with raised heels]. This new work, she warned, would be very rigorous and fast-paced. I didn't get the job. Instead, my audition was extended. The company offered me a provisional contract for two weeks to develop the full-length work. Extension of my contract was conditional on how well I could keep up in rehearsal. Because I was unemployed, I was hesitant to turn down the offer, even though I was unsure if I wanted to subject myself to the physical pain and sense of insecurity I knew it would engender. After weighing up my options, I decided taking the job would be too risky, both financially, and physically.

Contemporary South Asian choreographers in Britain have created their signature daring and dynamic choreography by stretching and pushing the physical limits of classical Indian dance forms through experimentation and risk-taking. In doing so, they have challenged racialized readings of South Asian dance as static, traditional, and exotic, actively decolonizing notions of South Asianness that situate Indian dance forms within a fixed and unchanging past (Jeyasingh 1998, 46). These changes to technique and aesthetics have also enabled choreographers to gain access to limited funding streams, attract mainstream audiences, and present their work on prestigious national and international stages. In this regard, contemporary South Asian choreographers have transformed the British dance landscape both aesthetically and politically. While their contributions to South Asian dance in Britain are widely recognized, the important labor of dancers in generating these contemporary South Asian dance aesthetics has been overlooked. This essay seeks to redress this gap.

In particular, this essay foregrounds the labor of dancers by making pain and injury visible to the scholarly eye. Due to their seemingly banal, normalized, and sometimes even celebrated existence in the dance industry, pain and injury are undertheorized in dance studies scholarship. While much has been written about injury in the field of dance medicine and dance science, those studies tend to highlight the physiological, psychological, or phenomenological aspects of dancers' pain and injury (Mainwaring, Krasinow, and Kerr 2001; Deighan 2005; Wainwright and Turner 2005; Aalten 2007; Tarr and Thomas 2011). In contrast, and drawing specifically on the experiences of contemporary South Asian dancers in Britain, I analyze pain and injury as an embodied condition that tracks with a labor condition, namely, the increasingly risky and flexible labor conditions of neoliberal capitalism.

The beginnings of neoliberalism in the 1970s are marked by a significant shift in capital's relationship to risk, from risk aversion to risk seeking.[2] Whereas economic policies prior to the 1970s were largely concerned with stability and how to reduce or remove risk, since the 1970s financial discourse has centered more on how to manage and price risk and even how to profit from volatility and fluctuations in the market, such as derivatives (Harvey 2007; Martin 2013). According to dance scholar Randy Martin (2013), this maximizing and rewarding of financial risk, which began in the late 1970s, parallels the rise of risk-based dance and movement practices such as skateboarding and b-boying. The lack of social safety nets, government regulations, and economic stability gave way to a new sense of precariousness that encouraged taking risks not just at the financial level but also at the bodily level. Such risk-taking among dancers was/is often racialized (DeFrantz 2015).

Risk-taking in dance, however, has a different function than it does in finance and economics. In neoliberalism, economic risk is encouraged even as social safety nets are withdrawn and failure (e.g., injury, illness, poverty) is blamed on the risk-taker rather than the lack of social safety nets (O'Shea 2018, 89). These are risks taken under compromised conditions of constraint and precarity. In dance and other movement practices, on the other hand, "skill-building requires risk-taking of some kind," as dance scholar Janet O'Shea notes in her research on risk, failure, and play in martial arts training (95). Injuries in this context are the result of a fundamental aspect of training. However, risk-taking is only ethical, she argues, when it is taken on willingly and when exposure to risk occurs in controlled situations (92). Only then can risk be a source of pleasure, which I will come back to at the end of this essay. In a dance company where dancers are often evaluated on their ability to take risks, it is not always clear if risks are taken on "willingly." That is, risk-taking is often influenced by other considerations, including financial concerns, desires for visibility on stage, and the likelihood of being rehired.

The emergence of contemporary South Asian dance in Britain in the 1980s roughly aligns with the late twentieth-century rise in risk-taking I discussed above. The shift from more traditional South Asian performance aesthetics to more contemporary South Asian choreography can be similarly characterized by an increase in South Asian dancers' interest in, as well as British audiences' appetite for, daring work. When contemporary South Asian dance was first emerging, a number of choreographers experimented with the rhythms, symmetry, and spatial geometry of Indian classical dance forms. Over the years, contemporary South Asian dance aesthetics have incorporated different movement techniques such as ballet, release-based contemporary dance, capoeira, *kalaripayattu*, hip hop, and partner work. Choreographers have also pushed the limits of classical Indian dance forms in terms of speed and flexibility. Today, contemporary South Asian dance work in Britain is by and large fast, virtuosic, dynamic, and athletic. Physicality and speed have become the hallmark of excellence. As South Asian dance in Britain has evolved beyond its traditional aesthetics, the risk of injury has increased.

Though the link between dance, risk, flexibility, and pain may seem obvious and commonplace (Doesn't *all* dance involve pain? Don't *all* dancers take risks? Don't *all* dancers have to be flexible?), this essay argues that risk, flexibility, and pain take on a particular valence when viewed through the twin lenses of neoliberalism and race. In particular, I show how neoliberal demands for risk and flexibility echo and intersect with British multiculturalism's expectations of South Asian dancers to display virtuosity, speed, and versatility. Together, they create conditions of physical pain and economic precariousness for racialized dancing bodies.

Marxian scholar David Harvey argues that capital shapes bodies to its own requirements: "The exigencies of capitalist production push the limits of the working body—its capacities and possibilities—in a variety of different and often fundamentally contradictory directions," noting that while healthy laboring bodies may be required, "deformities, pathologies, sickness are often produced" (2000, 115; 103). Jasbir Puar's notion of "debility," a system of disablement in which entire populations are living in a state of precarity, and Lauren Berlant's theory of "slow death" are also useful here (2009). For Puar, the relentless pursuit of profit creates debility through the slow depletion of marginalized populations. Similarly, for Berlant, slow death describes "the phenomenon of mass physical attenuation" under regimes of capitalist subordination (2007, 754). The destructiveness of capital results in the destruction of the very thing that fuels the further accumulation of capital: the worker. This is one of the fundamental contradictions at the heart of capitalism. Examining dancing bodies lays bare this contradiction. Sprains, tears, and chronic pain, as I have argued elsewhere, are the bodily traces of neoliberalism's debilitating effects (Kedhar 2014).

While many dancers navigate precarious working conditions and demands for risky and flexible labor (short-term contracts, lack of benefits, longer working hours, job security), South Asian dancers must also make their work legible and valuable to dance audiences unfamiliar with South Asian dance. This often means displaying greater physical risks, technical virtuosity, spectacular choreography, and cultural authenticity. Thus, for contemporary British South Asian dancers, pain and injury are induced not just through neoliberal working conditions in the studio but also through multicultural expectations for assimilation and legibility outside it. Critical race theorist Jodi Melamed calls this new form of racial capitalism "neoliberal multiculturalism," in which multiculturalism perpetuates racial capitalism while simultaneously "mask[ing] the centrality of race and racism to neoliberalism" (2006, 1).

I suggest that an ethnographic approach to the study of injury (rather than a scientific one) is especially important if we want to understand how the microexperiences of pain relate to the macropolitics of race and capitalism. Through an ethnography of contemporary South Asian dancers' bodily memories and experiences of pain and injury, I seek to show how British multiculturalism and neoliberal dance economies have stretched contemporary South Asian dancing bodies to their breaking point, marking both the limits of flexibility and the costs of risk.[3]

Contemporary South Asian dancers' bodies, however, are not merely inscribed by neoliberalism and multiculturalism. Dancers use choreographic tools and other bodily tactics (what Harvey calls "the transformative and creative capacities of the laborer" [2000, 177]) to gain creative control over their bodily labor and continue to circulate within a competitive British dance economy in ways that are safe and pleasurable. While the logic of capital inevitably results in the squeezing of labor, dance makes legible how laborers can also manipulate, exploit, and accumulate capital for political and economic gain. In this essay, I will draw on anthropologist Talal Asad's notion of "pain as action" to show that contemporary British South Asian dancers intentionally and strategically respond to labor demands for risk-taking and flexibility through small, seemingly insignificant corporeal tactics, such as enduring pain, reinterpreting choreographic tasks, and practicing care of self and care of others (2000, 4). Like anthropologist Elizabeth Povinelli, who writes about endurance in late liberalism, I am interested in the "ordinary, chronic, and cruddy rather than [the] catastrophic, crisis-laden, and sublime" (2011, 13). Focusing on the ordinary efforts of dancers to endure, manage, work through, and avoid pain can illuminate the ways in which dancers do not necessarily confront hegemony head-on but instead "aggregate life *diagonal* to hegemonic ways of life" (20). Asad's theory of pain as action and Povinelli's concept of moving diagonally offer alternative ways of rethinking agency beyond the dyads of complicity/resistance, victim/agent. Like the slash between these binary terms, the trajectory of the diagonal moves away from hegemonic norms, but not necessarily in an oppositional direction. Similarly, contemporary British South Asian dancers use their experience of pain to move through multicultural dance markets rather than quitting dance or refusing to participate altogether. In this way, they offer an important case study for understanding bodily labor and rethinking conventional notions of agency under neoliberalism.

In order to capture the ordinary and often invisible aspects of pain and pain management, I take a decentered, diagonal approach to dance studies. I do this in four ways. First, I examine the material conditions of dance production, namely, choreographic processes and training regimes, rather than the performance of any single work. Second, I focus on the perspectives of dancers rather than choreographers, drawing on a wealth of material gathered from interviews I conducted with contemporary South Asian dancers in Britain between 2014 and 2017, as well as my own experiences as a dancer in London between 2004 and 2011.[4] Third, I privilege spaces offstage, such as the studio, the bathroom, and the massage table. Finally, I bring attention to the most invisible and intangible aspects of dance: pain and injury. I show that an attention to pain and injury illustrates the bodily limits of flexibility and the costs of risk-taking, as well as their continued possibilities for navigating neoliberal, multicultural dance markets. In the first half of this essay I look at pain as a marker of the limits of flexible labor. I then turn my attention in the second half to the idea of pain as bodily action.

Pain as Limit

I ask Padma to tell me about any injuries she has sustained. "That are only dance related?" she inquires. "Yeah." "And specific to any form?" she asks for clarification. "Yeah," I say. "You can elaborate too." Silence. She pauses and then laughs. "Okay, this could be a while." After recounting a few other injuries, she says:

> The hardest season I had was 2009, February, no, um, I wasn't with Rajesh [her
> boyfriend] then. It was the beginning of 2010. And it was just a horrible time
> in my life. I was living with seven people after being homeless for six months.
> And in a new part of London. . . . I injured myself within the first two weeks.
> It was a strange one. I rolled over my foot. It was just getting worse and worse.
> And then it sort of traveled up my body, because it does that, you know. Injuries,
> they sort of go to your right knee and your left hip and then your right scapula.

Before starting her contract, Padma had been homeless for six months,
couch surfing and relying on the generosity of friends. Though she had been
trying to branch out and expand her employment prospects outside the contemporary South Asian dance sector, she couldn't find other paid dance work.
Padma was driven not just by financial necessity but also by her curiosity
about the new work. Still, the physically challenging nature of the creative
process and her precarious emotional and economic situation resulted in
Padma injuring herself within the first two weeks. She continued to dance
despite knowing the injury was getting worse and affecting other parts of
her body. Though the choreographer expressed concern about her health and
well-being, Padma didn't feel she could afford to stop. Nor did she want to. By
this time, she was also invested in the project, and her desire to see it through
pushed her to continue despite the pain.

While injuries require dancers to slow down, short-term contract work
and tightly packed rehearsal and performance schedules do not accommodate
such reductions in speed; instead, they pressure dancers to speed up. This
contradiction within capitalism—the demand for speed and the resulting slow
breakdown of the body over time—leads to drawn-out experiences of pain,
creating a particularly precarious existence for dancers. Because they lack the
long-term security and health benefits that come with being a company dancer,
for contract dancers a day off from work means a day without pay (Tarr and
Thomas 2011, 148). Injury signals not only present but also future income loss
(since injuries flare up), as well as the loss of valuable job experience, which
could make a dancer more competitive in the dance market. Thus, the anxiety
that injuries cause in the present also engenders an uncertainty about the
future. This uncertainty, according to Nicholas Ridout and Rebecca Schneider, is the very definition of precarity (2012, 5). Padma continues describing
that time: "Psychologically I was fucked. All my points of safety, reference, and
sanctuary were unstable. It was a cold winter, and I was injured. The piece was
coming together in a way that was like mining. The choreographer was *mining*
for movement possibilities. And it was just really difficult work. I was gripping
the movement but also tense trying to protect my injuries. Every morning I

went in and wrapped myself up like a mummy, all my different injuries. It was like that through the entire season."

Following Karl Marx's (1976) theory of alienation, the laborer sells her labor power (that which is extracted from the body of the laborer as a commodity) to the capitalist, who then extracts the maximum amount of surplus value from the worker. For dancers, their commodity labor power is their physical strength, flexibility, and versatility, as well as their creativity in processes that ask for their input in generating choreographic material. Through choreographic tasks, choreographers extract dancers' physical and imaginative capacities and incorporate them into the final dance product, which is then sold to funders, theaters, and audiences. In that sense, their bodies and creativity are mined for movement material, which is then shaped and turned into a commodity.

As Padma recounts this period of injury to me with great detail and emotion, it is clear from the heavy tone of her voice and the strained expression on her face that the physical pain and mental exhaustion of dancing with an injury were still palpable to her. This particular project required "a lot of repetition of really difficult stuff—and a lot of it was very fast." She recalls that they had to work in a cold space, and her muscles would get hot and cold throughout the day. In addition, the work required prolonged periods of gripping and the repetition of movements at fast speeds. While traditional *bharata natyam* training is based on repetition of the basic steps or units of movement called *adavus*, it is not necessarily with the expectation of ever-increasing speed. Capital, however, privileges acceleration for its ability to maximize surplus value (Berardi 2009). Padma described not just the expectation of speed but also the expectation to repeat "really difficult stuff." The movement sequences in contemporary South Asian dance works often do not adhere to the conventional aesthetics of *bharata natyam* sequences, in which there is a sense of balance and symmetry, with repetitions done on both the right and left sides, and in which one movement flows into the other. While traditional *bharata natyam* privileges symmetry, alignment, linearity, and an adherence to the geometry of the body, contemporary South Asian dance is about challenging those conventions. One knee may be turned in, while the other one is turned out; an elbow might twist to turn a hand gesture upside down; or the upper and lower body might extend in different directions. In contemporary works, *bharata natyam* steps are intentionally fragmented, twisted, chopped up, and put back together in unexpected and unconventional ways that can be difficult to execute.

Another dancer, Lakshmi, describes the aesthetics of one contemporary South Asian choreographer in this way:

LAKSHMI: Oddly shaped stuff. Stuff that would hyperextend—what's that word—starts with a *c*. For instance, this. [She twists her arms behind her back.] Five different things popped in my body just now!

AUTHOR: You mean "contorted"?

L: Yeah, thank you! Contortion! Superhuman kind of stuff. You know. It's all about tension. The most interesting tensed shape possible. Or—unnatural. I think [the choreographer] liked the unnatural tension between you and what you were doing.

She recounts to me how the choreographer asked the dancers to stamp, jump, and land neither with the heels lifted in *swastikam* (one foot crossed behind the other) nor with both feet flat on the floor. Instead, she wanted them to land with just a small space between their heels and the floor. Lakshmi winces as she tells me the story, recalling how she could feel the ligaments pulling on her knees.

While some contemporary South Asian dance work requires hyperextension and contortions, other works ask dancers to be versatile in multiple techniques. As mentioned earlier, contemporary South Asian dance companies today incorporate a range of dance forms, including ballet, *bharata natyam*, *kathak*, release technique, *kalaripayattu*, yoga, acrobatics, and capoeira. Though most contemporary dancers cross-train in multiple movement forms, for South Asian dancers the expectation to be fluent in a range of dance techniques is relatively new. For one dancer, Anita, this was a source of pain: "[We were] willfully subjecting the body to very opposing ways of dealing with the body. Contemporary would relax my body, and *bharata natyam* stressed the hell out of it; the tautness had to be everywhere. And in release technique you had to release everything. I didn't know how to put them together." According to Anita, the mark of a good dancer depended on how willing and capable she was to subject her body to these contradictory ways of moving. "You were being a better dancer if you were able to *that that that* like a military officer and then just roll like water," she laughed, demonstrating for me the extreme contrast in her body. Her rapid-fire "*that that that*" mimicked the sound of foot stamping in *bharata natyam*, but when she mentioned water she rolled onto the floor as if performing release technique.

The physical incorporation of ballet and contemporary dance into the South Asian dancing body also points to the racial dimensions of flexibility. Hyperextension, long lines, floor work, and pointed feet index whiteness and innovation. The incorporation of these aesthetics legitimizes South Asian choreographers as artists rather than merely skilled practitioners of a cultural tradition. It also expands the range of movement possibilities choreographers have at their disposal to create new material. According to a 2016 article in a South Asian dance magazine, bringing together these disparate forms "has demanded a new physicality" and "a greater range of movement and flexibility" from contemporary South Asian dancers in Britain (Farmer and Jorge-Chopra 2016, 17). Though versatility is an asset for many different kinds of dancers, the expectation put on South Asian dancers to be versatile in multiple, often opposing movement forms echoes expectations and pressures put on contemporary South Asian choreographers to demonstrate both diversity and innovation in their work (Kedhar 2014). *Bharata natyam* gestures, *kathak* turns, rhythmic footwork, and *kalaripayattu* kicks, for example, signal the work's cultural rootedness in authentic South Asian movement traditions, while the incorporation of partner lifts, floor work, and ballet arabesques index a "modern" and flexible South Asian body able to adapt to Western dance aesthetics and, by extension, Western culture and society. The performance of their smooth integration is what marks the ideal assimilated British South Asian subject. Integrating disparate movement aesthetics into one's body, however, often requires painful bodily labor that, layered with the demands of the British dance industry, extends a racialized phenomenon of risk that undergirds neoliberalism.

"So was everyone pushing themselves more than normal?" I ask Anita. "Yes, ab-so-lutely," she replies emphatically. Those who were not trained in *bharata natyam* were pushing themselves to look more like the *bharata natyam* dancers, while those who were not trained in contemporary dance were pushing themselves to look more like the contemporary dancers. "So if my full split is less than hers, I have to push myself; if she can do *thatta adavu* [a basic foot-stamping exercise in *bharata natyam*] in five speeds, I have to do it in seven speeds." Over the years, classical Indian dance forms have become less central to the work of some, though not all, contemporary South Asian choreographers. This has meant fewer professional opportunities for South Asian dancers within an already limited labor market. Fewer dance companies means greater competition among dancers and greater expectations to be versatile, virtuosic, and flexible. Moreover, in the absence of audiences familiar with the nuances of classical Indian dance, dance that is seen as risky, fast, athletic, and virtuosic stands in as a marker of good dancing. As a result, subtlety is often sacrificed for spectacle and virtuosity. Contemporary British South Asian dance privileges the dynamic, spectacular aspects of Indian dance forms over the subtler, more nuanced aspects, such as facial expressions, emotions, and narrative. British audiences delight in seeing South Asian dancing bodies that are fast, flexible, versatile, and virtuosic. As Ariel Osterweis has noted convincingly, virtuosity is often distinctly racialized, as white audiences expect to see black (and brown) dancing bodies move ever more spectacularly (2013, 55).

If virtuosity is a way to be legible to contemporary dance audiences, then legibility is a mark of assimilation. South Asian dancers who are able to speak the language of Western dance aesthetics through convincing displays of hybridity and versatility are read as more able and willing to integrate into mainstream British culture. However, under neoliberal multiculturalism, South Asian dancers in Britain must also convincingly embody culturally specific signifiers of South Asianness (e.g., hand gestures, deep knee bends, complex rhythmic footwork) in order to stay eligible for funding streams earmarked for South Asian dance. Those dancers who display such flexibility are rewarded with greater recognition and funding, while those who are deemed either too South Asian (i.e., too traditional) or not recognizably South Asian enough (i.e., too contemporary) fear they will fall through the funding cracks. Contemporary British South Asian dancers must therefore make work that is accessible to audiences unfamiliar with Indian dance, on the one hand, while still remaining recognizably ethnic, on the other. In this regard, risk and flexibility are not just universal neoliberal economic ideologies; in the British context, they are also racialized.

Pain as Action

How do contemporary South Asian dancers in Britain respond to the precarious and risky demands of dance work? How do they dance through pain and injury, finding pleasure and aesthetic freedom within the constraints of neoliberal multiculturalism? In this section, I outline the creative ways dancers move through pain and injury to continue circulating within a multicultural dance economy. I suggest that risk and flexibility are not just post-Fordist tools to exploit labor and increase surplus value; they are also skills in a dancer's arsenal that can be mobilized as corporeal tactics to manage life and pain under neoliberalism.

If pain marks the limits of flexible labor, it also reveals the failure of racial capitalism to completely destroy the body. I understand pain not just as something that happens to the body, or the physical manifestation of something that is done to bodies, but as a site of negotiation and agency. As mentioned earlier, for Asad, "pain is not simply a cause of action, but often itself a kind of action" (2000, 31). Pain as action challenges the assumption that agency is ultimately about emancipation or liberation. To suffer, we assume, is to be in a passive state—an object, not a subject. However, as Asad suggests, "the body's ability to suffer, to use pain, makes it active" (49). Workers might submit to capital at one moment in order to enhance their powers at another (Harvey 2000, 117). Taking up these texts, we must ask, How can dancing through pain be read as a form of action rather than simply the body's passive acquiescence as raw creative material for capital gain?

Janani tells me about an injury she sustained on the first night of a run at a prestigious theater in central London. Just before the first performance, she sprained her neck and couldn't turn her head. "I pulled it out at the end of the day. We had four more nights. I was praying my way through it." She tells me she "worked through the pain." Sometimes this meant giving herself massages or applying anti-inflammatory medicines before and after performance. Sometimes it meant spending more time warming up the injury. In performance, concentrating on executing the choreography would also help distract her from the pain. Povinelli theorizes endurance as "the ability to suffer yet persist" (2011, 32). She argues for an "anthropology of ordinary suffering" in which we pay attention to the "quasi events" of endurance—everyday events that "neither happen nor not happen"—rather than the eventfulness of crisis (13–14). While many might not consider Janani's choice to endure pain and continue dancing as a form of action, a dancer's agency can also manifest "in her ability to disempower [herself] for the sake of another" (Asad 2000, 35). The notion of agency as self-empowerment parallels neoliberal fantasies of choice, autonomy, and freedom. Instead, the idea of pain as action, according to Asad, allows us "to think about agency in other than triumphalist terms" (29). Janani's ability to temporarily overcome or disguise her pain is certainly not a triumph of labor over capital; dancing on an injury can risk further damage to the body. However, it highlights her ability to subvert her threshold of pain, as well as the mental and physical effort required to perform through pain. Resistance, as Falu Bakrania reminds us through Michel Foucault, "is often tethered to the conditions of constraint" (2013, 15). Under conditions of economic precarity, dancers cannot always refuse to dance or quit. Instead, they move diagonally, carefully sidestepping injury while enduring pain.

Self-care is another way in which dancers prevent reaching a definitive breaking point. Suffering knee and shoulder pain from repetitive and fast-paced *bharata natyam* movements, Vidya posted this as her Facebook status in 2013: "Ok Dancers . . . My nightly after-all-day-rehearsal Equation: (Hot Shower + Cold Bath) × 2 = Blasting Lactic Acid + Keeping Body Whole til End of Season . . . Am I onto something or is this sheer stupidity?" "Hot shower. Cold bath. Hot shower. Cold bath," she recalls as we speak about that time. Every night after eight hours of rehearsal, she engaged in a regime of self-care in order to keep her body able to perform. As per her contract, the company paid for a limited number of physiotherapy sessions. Nevertheless, without adequate time off from dancing, Vidya had to find ways to accelerate her recovery. While this kind of self-care may seem aligned with neoliberal values, Vidya used her experience of pain to help her negotiate benefits with the company later that year. When she was subsequently asked to tour the

same work she was able to convince the company to include biweekly massages in her contract. She used her labor power as a dancer who was prized for
her willingness to take risks and be flexible to secure healthier working conditions. As a result of her efforts, the company decided to change its policy and
offer biweekly massages to every dancer.

Berlant urges us "to think about agency and personhood not only in normative terms but also within spaces of ordinariness" (2007, 758). Vidya's actions
in the most ordinary of spaces and encounters index a form of agency that we
might find hard to recognize immediately as empowering or meaningful. In
the context of "slow death" and the exploitation of bodies by capital, however,
"agency can be an activity of maintenance, not making" (759). Vidya's nightly
bath routine and biweekly massages were an ordinary activity of maintenance,
a way of "keeping [her] body whole" that allowed her to continue dancing
despite the relentless demands on her body.

Contemporary British South Asian dancers also deploy other, subtler tactics to prevent pain and injury. Instead of refusing to dance with certain choreographers or to do certain kinds of work, which would entail financial loss and
a greater risk of precarity, dancers use their creative capacities to reinterpret
choreographic tasks in ways that feel safe and ethical. Like many contemporary choreographers, contemporary South Asian choreographers often rely on
dancers to generate the raw movement material for the work through a series
of creative tasks. Anita, usually the most virtuosic dancer and the one most
willing to take risks, recounted to me that eventually she learned not to make
movements during creative tasks that put too much strain on her body, since
she knew the choreographer was probably going to like those the best. She
knew she would not only have to repeat the movement phrase again and again
but also have to inflict that motif onto someone else's body, since movement
material was shared among the dancers. Thus, dancers learn to avoid creating
material that would be damaging or induce too much pain because they don't
want to inflict that kind of pain either on their own bodies or on other dancers' bodies. Such intentional caretaking and concern for the other dancers
subverts neoliberal imperatives that perpetuate and celebrate competition over
cooperation, collaboration, and empathy. Choreographic tasks allow dancers
to assume greater authoritative agency over the work, regain creative control
over their bodily labor, and thus reduce the likelihood of pain and injury. In
these small but significant acts of restorative care and redirection, contemporary British South Asian dancers have found a space of agency and an ethical
practice within the strictures of choreographic authority.

If the experience of pain is debilitating, overcoming it can be exhilarat-
ing. Lakshmi returned after a season of being injured to tour with the same

company. She felt vindicated because she was able to do the work with a healthy body this time. Like Padma, she attributed many of her previous injuries to a lack of financial and emotional stability in her personal life. By linking her social and economic situation with a greater vulnerability to injury, Lakshmi indicated importantly how financial and physical precarity are intertwined. She also noted, "It was the creation that made a massive difference." The pain she felt before came from creating movements that were fast and tense, as well as from the repetition that came from trying out new things to see what worked. Once the choreography was set, she could find ways to approach and embody it, allowing her to perform the work without the same level of pain. Returning several months later to tour, she found pleasure in conquering her injuries, a sense of vindication that she could find enjoyment in overcoming the pain she experienced during the creation phase.

Without romanticizing pain and injury, I suggest they constitute a bodily archive that enables dancers to remember and relish a rich and varied dance career. Kamala Devam (2017), the only dancer who allowed me to use her real name, notes how each of her injuries correlates to distinct moments in her dance career working with distinct choreographers and vocabularies. With one company, it was "stuck pain" from static, rapid, and twisted *bharata natyam*–based movements; with another, it was knee pain from sitting for prolonged periods in *araimandi*; in her own work, it's upper back pain from inversions, as well as all the time she spends on the computer now that she runs her own dance company, Kamala Devam Company. Each injury triggers memories both pleasurable and painful and forms a history of pain, but also of strength and resilience, that she carries with her to this day.

For many South Asian dancers, this history of pain has meant making difficult career choices. Anita chose to take an extended break from dancing because she was "not prepared to do very extreme things again." However, rather than leave the world of performance altogether, she worked with theater artists and photographers to create interdisciplinary work in which "the stress of a performance was distributed between body, text, and images." Others, such as Janani, have chosen to work for companies that are less physically demanding. Kamala chose to start her own dance company, despite the financial risks. She admitted during our interview in 2017 that in the past she pushed herself too hard. Focusing now on her own choreography, Kamala feels she has more control over how her body moves.

Given Kamala's past experiences of pain and injury, I was surprised to see that her work as a choreographer is even more athletic and dangerous than her work as a dancer. Incorporating dynamic, acrobatic jumps, leaps, and lifts, her work includes some of the most high risk contemporary South Asian choreography

I have seen. Not surprisingly, she has injured herself in entirely new and unexpected ways. In her most recent work, *Ankusha* (2016), her neck was so tense from trying to flip out of headstands that she was restricting the blood to her brain and experiencing dizziness. Interestingly, though, she doesn't equate the pain of her own work with the pain she experienced dancing for other companies, in part because she has redefined risk as pleasurable. She explained in 2016 that she is interested in work that "takes risks physically, that is fierce, sexy, and, at times, funny"; it is also really important to her "to really have fun, to have as much fun onstage as possible." Thus, for some contemporary South Asian dancers, risk, and the pain and injury that inevitably accompany it, is not incompatible with pleasure. After all, as Martin reminds us, risk-taking is "at the heart of creativity" in dance (2013). Her pain is also more bearable because she has more control over the means of production as artistic director and choreographer. In 2017 she explained, "I have more freedom to choose inside of my experience of choreographing my own work. And I think that *that* kind of pain is easier to take because I'm inflicting it on myself."

When I asked Kamala in 2016 about her dancers, she told me confidently that "they're all hard core. They like to push it . . . in the right way, with an understanding of the calculated risk involved for themselves and others." Mindful of the risks she's asking them to take, Kamala pays her dancers over the Equity minimum in order for them to have a living wage: "I'm asking them to do crazy things. So they're worth that." She also provides dancers with adequate breaks, warm studios, and time to stretch out. Striking a balance between risk-taking and care, both she and her dancers have found pleasure and fulfillment in taking risks and pushing their bodies "in the right way."

Perhaps, as dance scholar Susan Foster notes, this is what unalienated labor looks like, when "the creation of an object, in this case the dance, is not separated from the maker and placed into circulation under conditions beyond the maker's control" (2016, 21). While contemporary South Asian dancers' physical abilities and creativity are often mined for movement material, Kamala's notion of pushing in the right way connotes an understanding of and a respect for her and her dancers' bodily limits. Though economically things are still very precarious for Kamala and her company, she has found a way to circulate within the competitive British contemporary dance market while ensuring longevity through an ethics of care and a renewed, embodied pleasure in risk-taking.

Conclusion

The title of this essay began with a question about the breaking point. Has the push to take ever-greater risks driven dancers to their bodily limits? Do pain and injury constitute flexibility's breaking point under neoliberalism? The online Merriam-Webster dictionary defines the breaking point as "the moment of greatest strain at which someone or something gives way," "the point at which a situation becomes critical," and "the point at which something loses force or validity" (www.merriam-webster.com). I would argue that while neoliberalism might accelerate the body's breaking point, the moment of greatest strain might also give way to something else. In other words, a breaking point can signal both a loss of force and a redirection of that force. Flexibility, speed, and versatility are economic tools to increase a dancer's value; however, they are also important bodily tools in the dancer's arsenal. Given that, as dancers, our labor power resides not only within our bodies but *as* bodies, we have the capacity to stretch ourselves or shorten our reach, take risks or hold back, slow down or speed up. In other words, we can "leverage our own [movement] capacities to take risks" (Martin 2013). Paying attention to the body in pain reveals dancers' abilities to both submit to and struggle against pressures to perform in increasingly risky and flexible ways. In addition to resistance and empowerment, agency can also look like enduring pain, reinterpreting tasks, finding pleasure in risk, and caring for both self and others. Resistance to neoliberalism's hold lies in these ordinary ways of moving and surviving. Dancers make legible these movements and movement choices.

In this essay, I have outlined the complex and vexed intersections between risk, pain, pleasure, and agency. Dancers depend on and operate within neoliberal, multicultural dance markets that demand versatility, flexibility, athleticism, speed, and virtuosity from racialized dancing bodies. The dancers I have focused on here are often caught in a double bind in which they must weigh up the pleasures of taking risks (e.g., recognition, money, satisfaction, and career opportunities) against the possible pain and injury that may result. This is the calculus of risk: the complex equation contemporary South Asian dancers calculate with their bodies in order to move through postcolonial, multicultural, neoliberal Britain in ways that are both pleasurable and painful, challenging and safe. By focusing on dancers' pain and injuries we can see more clearly both the bodily limits of flexible labor and dancers' abilities to overcome, sidestep, and stretch those limits by moving, as Povinelli writes, "diagonal to hegemonic ways of life" (2011, 20).

Notes

1. The term "contemporary South Asian dance" encompasses a wide range of movement aesthetics, choreographic approaches, and staging choices. In this essay, it refers to work that experiments with South Asian movement practices and combines South Asian dance forms with other techniques and/or choreographic approaches. By and large, it includes South Asian artists who have been mobilized by strategic public

funding initiatives (e.g., through the Arts Council) since the 1980s to diversify the British arts sector.

2. Randy Martin defines risk under neoliberalism as "the measurable anticipation of an unexpected gain" (2013).

3. Contemporary South Asian dancers in Britain are a heterogeneous group encompassing migrant dancers from the Indian subcontinent and Southeast Asia; diasporic South Asian dancers; male and female dancers; and non–South Asian dancers from the United States, United Kingdom, and Europe who have trained in Indian dance forms.

4. The interviews for this essay were conducted in person in London or on Skype between 2014 and 2017. In order to protect the identities of my interlocutors, I have changed the names of all the dancers and choreographers in this essay unless otherwise indicated. I have also deployed a number of other ethnographic writing strategies, including creating composite and deconstructed subjects, altering identifying details, and excluding names altogether. Unless otherwise indicated, I have not included specific citations that indicate where and when I conducted the interviews, as this would undo my efforts to protect my interlocutors.

Works Cited

Aalten, Anna. 2007. "Listening to the Dancer's Body." *Sociological Review* 55 (1): 109–25.

Asad, Talal. 2000. "Agency and Pain: An Exploration." *Culture and Religion* 1 (1): 29–60.

Bakrania, Falu. 2013. *Bhangra and Asian Underground: South Asian Music and the Politics of Belonging in Britain.* Durham, NC: Duke University Press.

Berardi, Franco. 2009. *The Soul at Work: From Alienation to Autonomy.* Los Angeles: Semiotext(e).

Berlant, Lauren. 2007. "Slow Death (Sovereignty, Obesity, Lateral Agency)." *Critical Inquiry* 33 (4): 754–80.

DeFrantz, Thomas. 2015. "Bone Breaking: Black Flexibility and Danced Oppositionality." Paper presented at Duke University, September 12. http://vimow.com/us/watch/x36n3oz_Thomas+F.+DeFrantz%3A+%22BoneBreaking%3A+Black+Flexibility+and+Danced+Oppositionality%22.

Deighan, Martine. 2005. "Flexibility in Dance." *Journal of Dance Medicine and Science* 9 (1): 13–17.

Devam, Kamala. 2016. Interview with the author. February 12.

———. 2017. Interview with the author. February 19.

Farmer, Claire, and Seema De Jorge-Chopra. 2016. "Fitness: What Does It Have to Do with Performance in South Asian Dance Forms?" *Pulse*, Winter, 18–19.

Foster, Susan. 2016. "Why Is There Always Energy for Dancing?" *Dance Research Journal* 48 (3): 12–26.

Harvey, David. 2000. *Spaces of Hope.* Berkeley: University of California Press.

———. 2007. *A Brief History of Neoliberalism.* Oxford: Oxford University Press.

Jeyasingh, Shobana. 1998. "Imaginary Homelands: Creating a New Dance." In *The Routledge Dance Studies Reader*, edited by Alexandra Carter, 46–53. London: Routledge.

Kedhar, Anusha. 2014. "Flexibility and Its Bodily Limits: Transnational South Asian Dancers in an Age of Neoliberalism." *Dance Research Journal* 46 (1): 23–40.

Mainwaring, Lynda, Donna Krasinow, and Gretchen Kerr. 2001. "And the Dance Goes On: Psychological Impact of Injury." *Journal of Dance Medicine & Science* 5 (4): 105–15.

Martin, Randy. 2013. "Dance and Finance: Social Kinesthetics and Derivative Logics." Paper presented at EMPAC, New York, October 9. https://vimeo.com/95306125.

Marx, Karl. 1976. *Capital: Volume One.* London: Penguin Books.

Melamed, Jodi. 2006. "The Spirit of Neoliberalism from Racial Liberalism to Neoliberal Multiculturalism." *Social Text* 24 (4): 1–24.

O'Shea, Janet. 2018. *Risk, Failure, Play: What Dance Reveals about Martial Arts Training.* Oxford: Oxford University Press.

Osterweis, Ariel. 2013. "The Muse of Virtuosity: Desmond Richardson, Race, and Choreographic Falsetto." *Dance Research Journal* 45 (3): 53–74.

Povinelli, Elizabeth A. 2011. *Economies of Abandonment: Social Belonging and Endurance in Late Liberalism.* Durham, NC: Duke University Press.

Puar, Jasbir K. 2009. "Prognosis Time: Towards a Geopolitics of Affect, Debility and Capacity." *Women & Performance: A Journal of Feminist Theory* 19 (2): 161–72.

Ridout, Nicholas, and Rebecca Schneider. 2012. "Precarity and Performance: An Introduction." *Drama Review* 56 (4): 5–9.

Tarr, Jenn, and Helen Thomas. 2011. "Mapping Embodiment: Methodologies for Representing Pain and Injury." *Qualitative Research* 11 (2): 141–57.

Wainwright, Steven P., and Bryan S. Turner. 2005. "Fractured Identities: Injury and the Balletic Body." *Health*, January 9, 49–66.

Who *Makes* a Dance?

Studying Infrastructure through a Dance Lens

SARAH WILBUR

I am in the lobby of Dance Place waiting for its founder, Carla Perlo, to come down for a tour and an interview. Through the closed theater doors I can hear a rehearsal for the August Energizers summer camp youth performance. A lot of drumming, stepping, stomping, and shouting is going on. Suddenly, the action stops and the double doors burst open. A pair of twentysomething counselors exit, walking at a relaxed pace, one without his shirt on, and a flood of roughly twenty youth rush past them, some singing, all running toward the basketball hoop and picnic table outside between the campus's two main buildings, Brookland Arts Loft and the Dance Place Studio Theatre. Inside the theater, a few campers stay behind to practice a more sophisticated stomp sequence under the watchful eye of another youth camp leader. In the lobby, two ponytailed girls, likely in their late teens or early twenties, are perform-ing various work-study duties behind a desk. They answer phones, hand out brochures, and give directions to people who stroll in. There are probably ten other people in the area who are enjoying staying put in the air conditioning on this sweltering August weekday. At a small cabaret table nearby, Dance Place's production and education managers are meeting with potential renters who want to book the theater for a performance. The guests are asking questions about community classes and other ways to use the space. One of the front desk workers hands a plastic garbage bag to a parent who has been waiting in the lobby for one of the campers. The parent uses the bag to clean up after her toddler. Outside, Carla's partner, Steve Bloom, is laying bricks to create a slab of sidewalk on the north side of the building (figure 36). Each brick is stamped with the name of a donor who gave between $250 and $500 to the organization in exchange for a personalized piece of Dance Place's real estate.

Surrounded by these interactions, I start to sense how this compendium of activities produces an anchoring effect on this nonprofit dance organization,

FIGURE 36. Dance Place bricks. (Photo by the author.)

which Carla and her conspirators relocated to Brookland in 1986 from a previously rented space in the now-bustling Washington, DC, neighborhood of Adams Morgan. As I stand in the lobby, struggling to keep track of all the bodies that are responsible for keeping this dynamic "place" in operation, Carla taps me on the shoulder. I turn. She welcomes me with a generous hug and says in her ironic and unforgettable monotone, "Thanks for coming."

Theorizing Infrastructure as a Collectively Embodied Exercise

Who *makes* a dance? More specifically, how do armies of people cooperatively authorize and sustain enabling environments for dance in local US communities? While dance researchers have gained significant academic traction through critical analysis of dancing bodies, dance's "offstage" labor and cooperation have received minimal attention in dance research. And while no method of studying dance's variable cultures of support can possibly include all the people and interactions that make a dance possible, this prospectively oriented collection offers a key opportunity for dance researchers to expand our commitment to analyzing embodied particulars beyond the realm of artistic practices to include infrastructural ones, complex choreographies in their own right.

The term "infrastructure" is frequently invoked by researchers in the social sciences and the humanities to suggest hidden or taken-for-granted entities that sustain forms of life. Scholars from the fields of economics, information science, and urban planning tend to study infrastructure by way of its objects, from roads and sewage systems, to libraries and museum archives, to various technological media (Bowker et al. 2009). My project trades this object-oriented view of infrastructure for a subject-oriented one by examining the committed enactments of people who sustain daily operations at a local dance nonprofit. Viewed through a dance and ethnographic lens, infrastructure emerges less as a *thing* that makes other things *run* (Star 2002) and more as a *thing done* by people with variable power and diverse commitments to the practice and production of dance.

In what follows, I offer an ethnographically informed analysis of the previously hidden people, policies, and practices that undergird operations at Dance Place, a nonprofit dance organization based in Washington, DC. When I suggest that the supportive enactments of these local organizers have been "hidden," I do not mean to imply that people who work at Dance Place are somehow oblivious to the work that they do daily. Rather, I invoke the term "infrastructure" polemically in order to challenge dance scholars to notice broader "lines of activity" that sustain dance operations at a local dance hub (Jackson 2011). I attend to supportive people and practices that authorize dance that are, too often, inadvertently relegated to the wings in dance studies due to narrow ways of looking. The "infrastructuralist" approach that I privilege here credits the discursive dimensions (power-filled, in the Foucauldian sense) of dance organization by analyzing nondance labor practices at close range. This emphasis on dance's hidden labor and laborers challenges methodological biases in dance and arts research that individualize dance production or inscribe false distances between artists and the many people who organize on their behalf.[1] With certain exceptions, dance scholars have sidestepped consideration of infrastructure as an embodied *doing* by casting artists either as strictly aesthetic laborers or as uniquely dealienated agents of cultural production.[2] Following Janet Wolff's (1981) insistence that arts researchers remember that Karl Marx himself did not distinguish or partition artistic activity as a unique domain of creative labor, I insist here that the social movement required to sustain an enabling environment for dance is worthy of study as collective labor that operates both for and against capital gains.[3] At its worst, disciplinary silence around infrastructural issues renders the project of critical dance studies complicit with the isolationist discourses of modernist autonomy (of art) or capitalist alienation (of artists), or both.

In focusing critical attention on the embodied politics of dance work within the neoliberalized project of twenty-first-century global capitalism, dance scholars have, in different ways, theorized the corporeal contours of dance production using terms like "risk" (Martin 2012), "sweat" (Srinivasan 2011), and "flexibility" (Kedhar 2014). They have done this by integrating embodied descriptions into structural critiques to extend and complicate strictly economic understandings of dance labor. But where most scholars in our field cast dancers as their principal research protagonists, I define dance "makers" more broadly to include artists, administrators, production personnel, funders, and audience members whose energies buttress dance practice and production. My inquiry adds the word "debt" to the mix, focusing on the term's tripartite function as an economic liability for dance organizers, a necessary ingredient for capital, and a kinesthetic affordance that the interactions of Dance Place organizers make uniquely visible.

To illuminate the wanted and unwanted debts that keep dance in this particular "place," this essay draws together arts policy and philanthropic data on the organization's history and ethnographic observation and interviews conducted during site visits to Dance Place in 2014, 2016, and 2017. Additionally, I situate my personal investment in this topic by interjecting occasional insights gained from my over twenty-year experience as a nonprofit dance organizer. Unfolding in two parts, my "infrastructuralist" perspective highlights how political economic conditions steer the comportment of dance organizers and also credits the practical ways that different dance "makers" negotiate instabilities in the field. I argue that the dedicated energies of Dance Place's many supporters reveals a hidden "kinesthetic indebtedness," a term that I invoke to describe the weighted sense of shared belonging that compels people to labor on behalf of dance despite any promise of economic gain. I also maintain that these desirable corporeal debts, held in the bodies of local dance organizers, productively complicate understandings of debt as negative freight—a strictly isolationist burden—such that prevails in political economic discourse (Lazzarato 2012, 2015). Weighing economic and embodied debts together at close ethnographic range reveals how dance's many "makers"[4] depend on and make demands upon the forces that surround them, even the forces that hold them down.

The Case of Dance Place

Early on in her career as an artist-presenter, dance artist Carla Perlo decided to split her abundant energies between producing her own choreography and producing the dances of other artists by developing an in-house space for performance and an ambitious annual production calendar. The institutional by-product of her efforts and the efforts of armies of energetic supporters is Dance Place (est. 1978), a studio, theater, and community arts nonprofit that embraces dance traditions including modern dance, hip hop, salsa, jazz, and West African dance and cultural practices such as drumming, visual arts, craft making, and even gardening as rigorously embodied pursuits. These activities are principally housed at its large arts campus, located in the now-burgeoning cultural district of Brookland's 8th Street corridor and also exported to area schools where Dance Place resident artists teach and perform. Among the organization's crowning achievements is its ambitious dance-presenting schedule, which features weekend performances by resident professional dance ensembles, youth performers from its educational programs, and rental productions mounted by local, national, and international artists at all stages of the career continuum. The Dance Place Theatre is a 144-seat venue that generates artistic demand and dedicated audiences an incredible forty-four weeks of the year.[5] A sought-after hub for dance creation, education, and performance, Dance Place has received regular institutional recognition from nonprofit arts funders due, in large part, to its organizational embrace of cross-cultural traditions in dance and to the multigenerational and multifaceted ways that local dance organizers deliver on this complex mission. What's impressive about this funder recognition, in addition to its sheer regularity, is how Carla and the Dance Place team have consistently realigned organizational goals with federal funding architectures that have changed radically over the past three decades. A brief glimpse at one example bolsters this point.

One of Dance Place's more enduring institutional partners over the years has been the National Endowment for the Arts (NEA), the lone philanthropic arm of the US federal government. Starting in 1981, Dance Place began receiving yearly grants for dance presenting at a time when NEA dance funders steered resourcing toward the promotion and preservation of dance on concert stages as their primary philanthropic priority. Since the mid-1990s, overlapping demographic shifts, controversies over the NEA's censorship of artists whose work engaged counterhegemonic themes, and the neoliberal streamlining of the federal bureaucracy writ large have conditioned a structural reengineering of federal arts support. NEA funding instruments, post-millennium, increasingly reward grants to dance organizers who can effectively tool art toward non-art economic deliverables (Wilbur 2017, 2018). Whereas Dance Place principally won NEA recognition in the 1980s and 1990s as a dance presenter, today the organization is one of very few dance entities to be awarded funds from the NEA's *Our Town* grant program (est. 2010), a program that mandates its grantees partner with municipal and non-arts economic investors to produce various economic and human capital gains as part of its criteria for support. In contrast to its early years safeguarding EuroAmerican "fine art" dance productions across regional proscenium stages, the NEA's current approach privileges arts organizers who can tool "creativity" in ways that generate economic impacts in non-art policy areas like transportation, economic development, education, housing, and health and human services.[6] In a philanthropic market that today privileges arts organizers who control their own real estate, Dance Place's ownership of their campus facilities could not be more significant.

In 2012 Dance Place received a $150,000 grant from the NEA to develop an outdoor plaza to further attract residents and tourists to the neighborhood. This initial expansion has since led the organization to attract additional six-figure donations from "place-based" philanthropic foundations like ArtPlace and the Kresge Foundation.[7] While these accolades commemorate Dance Place's capacity to inspire widespread belonging, they also obfuscate the organization's struggle to anchor its physical location in the early years amid major economic developments in the Washington, DC, area. Dance Place's checkered history of touring, squatting, and staying put is worth briefly rehearsing lest we lose sight of artists' labor as a critical engine of twenty-first-century community cultural development.

Carla and her partner, Steve Bloom, officially incorporated DC Wheel Productions, Inc./Dance Place in 1980 while working as teaching artists at a nonprofit run by local dance organizer Jan Van Dyke. Van Dyke's relocation to New York City that same year motivated them to take over the lease of the built-out studio on the first and second floors at 2424 18th Street NW. A former automotive warehouse and comparatively inexpensive rental, the couple's cheap lease had endured, in Carla's view, because the building was difficult for customers to find due to its back entrance, which forced visitors to traverse what she termed to be a "really horrible, rat infested alley" (Perlo 2014). Such adverse conditions did not stop leagues of people from showing up to support weekly classes and performances by local and touring dance artists over the next five years in the neighborhood. Organizational loyalty grew strong as funders, artists, students, spectators, and strangers came to depend on the organization's 120-seat theater and its "umbrella" attitude toward dance as a cross-cultural and intergenerational exercise. Changes were afoot, and the surrounding neighborhood in Adams Morgan was officially on the rise.

What forced Carla and company to ultimately reconsider her residency status in Adams Morgan was not the rats in the alley, but the thirty-day kick-out clause attached to her lease. In 1985, a classic gentrification scenario played out in Adams Morgan as property values began to skyrocket and the ownership of the building changed hands. A new owner served the organizers with notice of an immediate rent increase of four times the initial amount, from $1,500 to $6,000 per month. The landlord gave them one month to either pay the increase or exit the premises. Busy raising their then two-year-old son, Carla and Steve were threatened with the prospect of losing their work space, jobs, and income in one fell swoop. Improvising under duress, they negotiated a shaky compromise with the new owner, who agreed to let them squat for a compromised rate of $3,000 per month for six months while they searched for a new location. To cover the double rent increase, they beefed up class offerings and space rentals, two more dependable areas of earned income in dance that were entirely dependent on physical space. Another vital strategy to assuage economic costs was their mobilization of Dance Place's many loyal followers, who lent both material and physical support to the relocation effort.

Structurally, it is easy to align the dispossession and subsequent triage efforts of Dance Place's organizers with what arts policy critics have termed the "artist colonization process," in which artists, who are a cheap labor force generally known to do more with less, consent to rent suboptimal spaces and serve as veritable "place holders" to stimulate economic capital within infrastructurally compromised neighborhoods (Moss 2012). In such scenarios, landlords initially advertise lower rents to secure artist tenants; their presence is thought to reverse negative perceptions of a neighborhood. The lure of affordable space is enough to initially attract many artists to consider taking up shop, despite the escalating cost of living that transpires when more aggressive economic development schemes follow. Artists who opt in to such shaky residency terms do not produce immediate financial gains for developers, but they do offer cultural credit—symbolic subsidy that generates interest among middle- and upper-class visitors who are inclined to spend their money and time in areas deemed "hip," "up and coming," or "on the rise."

Critics of artists' participation in urban economic development schemes supported by philanthropic programs like Creative Placemaking have gone as far as to suggest that twenty-first-century gentrification runs on the sweat equity of artists (Shkuda 2012). The artist colonization process, in their view, installs an unwanted kind of debt hierarchy between incoming artists and low-income legacy residents, one that casts artists as a worthier investment. Remembering that the generation of surplus capital for real estate developers is the ultimate goal, artists are viewed as a "good" kind of poor resident, one whose occupancy stands a better chance of producing economic returns in the long haul. In contrast, poor residents who lack visible cultural or economic capital—frequently nonwhite and immigrant populations in US cities—are viewed by planners as a drain on the neighborhood brand. For these critics, artists' acceptance of suboptimal residency clauses (Carla and Steve's acceptance of the Adams Morgan kick-out clause, for example) risks contributing to the ongoing dispossession of already disadvantaged community members.

While Carla described Dance Place's sudden exodus from Adams Morgan to me as a cross-county "tour" that befell the organization by force of circumstance, the organization's effort to secure a permanent space evidences a more complex exchange of values and neighborhood relations than the above critiques of "place-based" cultural development tend to suggest (Perlo 2014). Lacking any immediate income of their own to spend, Carla and her then codirector, Deborah Riley, rode the DC Metro line, toured adjacent neighborhoods and ultimately landed at the Brookland/CUA stop to look for an appropriate harbor for Dance Place. A neighborhood designated as "Little Rome" by municipal leaders, Brookland is home to over sixty Catholic historic sites, including the Catholic University of America (CUA), and has historically been a successful site of black-white racial integration and political organizing. Residents successfully fought from 1970 to 1977 to prevent interstate developments that would have destroyed homes between the area and the Metro (Kresge Foundation 2017, 3). Spying a warehouse at 3225 8th Street NE, an empty space lit by the sun on two sides, Carla, Steve, and Deborah were, quite literally, sold on the neighborhood. Securing a temporary economic boost from Carla's father, Hyman Perlo, they cosigned the $210,000 sale of the warehouse and surrounding land. To this date, Dance Place remains one of the few US nonprofit dance organizations to fiscally and physically control their own facilities. The campus today includes studios, theaters, galleries, lobbies, offices, and housing units for interns and touring artists, located just across the street.

Dance Place's organizational arrival in Brookland required a dizzying array of administrative acts: filling out zoning permits, attending construction meetings, and conducting fund development exercises all served to enable armies of dance organizers to stay put in Brookland for the next thirty-five-plus years. A 2017 report from the Kresge Foundation (which awarded Dance Place $500,000 in 2014 to develop the 8th Street Art Park) details the vigilant work done by Dance Place organizers to spotlight the creative expression of the area's low-income residents and engage long-standing neighbors in particular (70 percent African American, many senior and retired) in conversations about the battery of development schemes currently underway in the Brookland-Edgewood neighborhood. As the neighborhood continues to experience economic and cultural resurgence, and Dance Place organizers and neighbors sit together on boards with the District of Columbia Office of Planning (DCOP), a municipal entity charged with long-term economic development, Dance Place organizers have also brokered relationships between long-term area artists and residents and for-profit developers at Bozzuto Development, the firm that built and now manages the Monroe Street Market, a mixed-use space aligned with the Brookland/CUA Metro station. Physical displacement has not yet become a problem at the time of this writing, since the market took over a vacant property. But displacement remains on the Dance Place radar due both to its own history of dispossession and to the community conversations that the organization now fosters between residents, developers, and newcomers (Kresge Foundation 2017).

When I asked her to reflect on Dance Place's enduring success seeking and securing support for material expansion, Carla interestingly spoke not of dance activities or community conversations but of her ability to secure material ownership of land and physical infrastructure as the organization's most valuable leverage point: "Dancers do not regularly participate in culture of ownership. They are faced with the problem of terminal rentals, always leasing, holding down temporary residencies and touring, sometimes even performing in insufficient spaces—these are all commonly understood as field norms. Pipelines exist, but flows of support are always temporary. . . . So yes, the idea of Creative Placemaking works as a concept. But you better own it" (Perlo 2014). Carla characterized the territory of nonprofit dance production as a tumultuous landscape dotted with rentals, time-stamped opportunities, and rusted-out career pipelines. She also worried about dance artists' vulnerabilities to politically asymmetrical contracts that favor funders or developers who hold surplus capital and access to space. Such unwanted economic debts remain a problem that can only be circumvented through individual proprietorship of dance's material infrastructure. Her promotion of economic proprietorship ("you better own it") evidences Carla's panicked memory of dispossession from Adams Morgan and her ambivalence about funder-instituted paternalisms at once. Speaking with refreshing frankness, Carla recounted the organization's financial challenges to build awareness of the paradoxes of twenty-first-century dance organizing in the hopes that I might recount these puzzles for a broader audience here, in print.

As a researcher invested in studying institutions as embodied infrastructures, I view Carla's coalitional advocacy and economic mobilization as vital forms of dance organizational activism. Still, I struggle to take her strictly at her word in the paragraph above. Her ideas about weak wages in dance are not unfounded; they echo recent census findings that flag dance as among the least sustainable career trajectories in the US artist workforce.[8] Yet despite dance's wobbly contracts and economic contradictions, her suggestion that dance artists do not "regularly participate in a culture of ownership" seems to me to betray her broader commitment to casting every person who enters the building as collaborative co-organizer, not a customer, client, or consumer. So as a gesture of acknowledgment of my own (wanted) ethnographic indebtedness to Carla as my activist-informant, I want to return now to our stroll through the Dance Place campus in the summer of 2014 (see Figure 37). Walking with Carla revealed micropractical evidence that dance in this particular "place" runs on much more than funds. While there may never be enough money to go around at Dance Place, and despite Carla's commentary, there is a palpable sense of co-ownership.

Ethnographic Sidesteps: Walking with Carla

Let's return now to my August 2014 visit to Brookland. After introductory hugs, smiles, and head nods, Carla suggested that we stay inside and take a tour of the main building. Neither of us wanted to return to the heat of the street on this sticky summer afternoon. The testimony I share below derives from the ambulatory interview that I carried out with Carla during our tour of the facility. We started our itinerary by venturing toward the Dance Place Theater. As we walked down the backstage hallway, Carla murmured something about the construction dust that had settled on the theater stairwell and on the steps between the dressing rooms and the stage door. Spying a ten-year-old camper named Paris, she introduced us and then asked Paris: "Hey, can you do me a favor? Can you get a broom and sweep up the basement stairs? Get someone else to help you do it. Thank you."

Paris nodded and ran down the stairs, and we parted ways. Carla and I next climbed to the second-floor offices, which wrap around the windowed side of the building and include a long row of tables where interns and staff were typing feverishly at computers. None of them interrupted Carla, but she frequently halted our conversation in order to interrupt the staff in fits and starts. These dialogues were almost familial in that they lacked any contextualizing sentences, so Carla offered me clarifying information via whispered asides. These conversations and her intimate translations revealed to me a shared politics of redistributive authority, creativity, labor, and debt weathered together through the cooperative exercise of nonprofit management. During our walk, my role expanded from that of an indebted ethnographer and visitor to that of an institutional insider. This transformation was not incidental, it was strategic. Carla was using our interview as an occasion to expose me (and a prospective readership) to the organization's energized social infrastructure.

We breezed past an intern running house management that summer, and Carla interjected: "Hey, Michelle! The carpet looks *good*! Thank you!" Michelle responded: "Oh, *good*!" Carla continued: "The thing works pretty good. I mean it's not perfect, that's what you said on Sunday, it's not perfect, but it's a

FIGURE 37. The intersection of 8th and Kearny in Washington, DC's Brookland neighborhood, home of Dance Place. (Photo by the author)

lot better, isn't it? It looks so much better! Thanks!" Michelle smiled and shook her head, and we continued walking past the door to a small interior office that was occupied by a former studio dancer and another intern. Carla peeked her head in and asked: "Judy, are you alright? This is Sarah. I'm giving her twenty minutes. Are you alright? Hanging in there?" Judy responded: "I'm okay. We're getting there!" "Anything good in the mail?" Carla looks quickly through a stack of papers handed to her by Judy. "Capezio rejection. Hmph. Fifteen hundred dollars from Verizon. That's pretty good." As we left, Carla leaned closer to me and explained that Judy was a former Dance Place student who then became an intern and is now an arts administration graduate and full-time staffer. She murmured: "She's fabulous. Director of grants. Came for twenty hours a week right out of college. Been here now for four years."

We veered over to an empty corner table to continue our chat, and Carla stopped suddenly and bent down, spying a piece of garbage on the floor. Picking up the trash and talking halfway to herself, she muttered: "Could be money in here." She opened the crumpled piece of white paper, and her instincts were confirmed. It was a quarter. She put it in her pocket and gestured with her right hand toward the table ahead. Somewhat uncannily, our conversation turned toward the organization's struggles with depleted funding and undercapitalization. She continued: "Today we're not at risk of being pushed out. Our biggest risk is replacing funds. There are just zero operating funds. Multiyear funds are lacking in the nonprofit arts world. This is a real problem for us."

As I listened to her explain Dance Place's struggle with securing support for daily operations, my mind drifted to my own similar struggle as a nonprofit dance organizer, a factor that motivated me to study cultures of support and to learn more about Dance Place operations in particular. As I had explained in my initial email request to Carla for a visit, I had worked for a decade as a nonprofit dance organizer at a similarly configured "umbrella" dance organization in the Midwest (1997–2007) prior to returning to academia. For me, this infrastructural "pre-fieldwork" offered a preparatory trade school of sorts,[9] a firsthand introduction to the practice Carla described of stitching together piecemeal operating funds. Where I'm from, we used to sarcastically call this "Frankensteining" funds. When Carla went on to lament the burdensome written reporting and communications that were involved in twenty-first-century grant seeking, I blurted out "Hamster-wheeling!" to signal my familiarity with the cyclical barrage of prospective, midterm, and final reporting that I know that this process entails. As I enthusiastically affirmed her frustrations with the emotional and physical labor of this "paper exercise," Carla nodded and moved on to a new topic.[10] She knew that I knew what she was talking about.

Carla next shifted the conversation to the highly sophisticated tiered system of employment, exchange, and volunteerism that Dance Place has cultivated over the years. This social infrastructure, I want to suggest, is what enables dancing returns in the absence of economic ones. When Carla mentioned that "basically almost everyone here has received on-the-job training," I asked her to walk me through the staff structure. She explained how Dance Place's nineteen full-time paid staff members came up through the organization's administrative and artistic pipelines. While she was talking, Carla's eyes wandered past my shoulder and into the distance. She shouted abruptly to the technical director, seated at a cubicle in the distance: "Hey, Benjamin, do we have any shellac in the basement?" Benjamin, typing and not looking up, responded: "I'd have to look." Carla continued: "Not really? Don't worry about it. The basement's looking good. I want you to get one of these kids to sweep that hallway going down there. That has to be a regular thing for some of the junior staff who are going to be working for you." Benjamin, still facing his computer screen, said: "Okay." "Thanks."

Carla continued to explain the institutional engineering of the Dance Place internship program. Senior staff review and accept twelve college-age interns (aged nineteen to twenty-seven) each year for administrative or production positions. Accepted applicants hail from colleges across the country, receive academic credit, are housed in the Dance Place apartments, and get access to performances, classes, and on-the-job training in exchange for a six- or nine-month service contract. While these contracts are designed to expire, Carla wanted me to understand that a large number of interns return to Dance Place to eventually join the ranks as artists, volunteers, or part- or full-time staff: "We give very few jobs to people who haven't been an intern here, primarily because the interns are already trained; they know the mission and core values; they know the people; they know everything. It also helps that we have room to house nine interns twelve months of the year, and then we turn our housing into visiting artist housing. We really need help to pick up the slack."

To help pick up the slack, Dance Place also enlists up to forty student leaders from its local youth dance and drumming programs to serve as junior staffers who assist staff (like Benjamin) and who help with other programs in exchange for free or discounted classes. Junior staffers like Paris, whom we met on the stairwell, are singled out for their natural leadership skills and tasked with assisting daily operations in addition to their dancing duties. Carla pressed the point: "The kids really help me. I've always counted on the kids in the Energizer program—we call it that because it keeps going and going. You start at six, now they're fifteen, now they're nineteen, and they're still here. . . . They are the next generation. We call all of the kids' programs 'Next Generation.'"

To say that Dance Place has sustained generations of dance supporters over its thirty-five-year history is an understatement. Within a given summer, up to five hundred Energizer Summer campers (age six to twelve) attend camp for seven weeks to learn dance, drumming, visual art, and an array of "life skills" (*Energizers Summer Camp* 2012). During the academic year, the organization also enlists student leaders to support after-school arts camps by escorting youth traveling to 8th Street from local schools, supervising snacks and homework, and coteaching dance, creative arts, and academically oriented programs. As Carla explained this intricate intergenerational exercise, Paris, the junior staffer previously charged with sweeping the theater stairs, walked past us. Carla flagged her down once more: "Paris, thank you for taking care of that." Paris responded: "You're welcome." Carla continued: "Grab a couple of people and get them to help you if you don't want to do it by yourself. But go from the top of the house all the way down. Thanks."

Paris is listening. She is also glistening, having just returned from practicing a group hip hop routine in the theater. Her sweat, in this instance, commemorates what performance scholar Michael Shane Boyle has called the exceptional labor of theater making (2017, 19). In an effort to unpack the complicity of noncommercial theatrical laborers in capitalist production for performance scholars, Boyle argues that supporters of live theatrical performance operate as both consumers and producers, at once. By this logic, Paris's dancing and sweeping together reinforce her unstable role as a dance "maker." Her many gestures impress themselves outwardly in that they sustain the material operations of the organization and also inwardly in that they generate meaning held privately within her own body as a producer-worker-consumer.[11] In other words, Paris's work is both *indirectly productive* for capital—she sweeps the stairs and makes a workspace for revenue-generating art activity—and *directly unproductive*, in that her dancing generates noneconomic values within the collective bodies of the dancing ensembles of which she is a part. At a biological level, Paris's sweat also evidences her body's deeply intelligent, material capacity to release pent-up heat and cool itself. Her sweat, thus, commemorates kinesthetic and social energy spent maintaining both an inner and outer "place" for dance. While it is possible to argue that Paris's dance work participates in the social reproduction of capital, she is no *virtuoso*, to borrow the individualized creative labor concept advanced by post-*operaismos* like Paolo Virno (2014); Paris's labor both *depends* on and *produces* a lasting sense of collectivity that endures beyond the moment of its performance. An ethnographically informed account of the multifaceted participation of Dance Place organizers reveals how the committed enactments at play in dance organizing cannot be fully contained by the logics of capitalist production, nor can they be considered a total break from those logics. The enduring efforts of supporters like Paris expose the competing ways that dance makers dedicate energies toward satisfying personal desires, serving others, and contributing to the social reproduction of capital together, in practice.[12]

Throughout our walk and talk, Carla repeatedly stressed the desirable social returns involved in dance organizing as the hidden engine of the Dance Place support system. While speaking, she spied another dancer and reached both arms out: "Janae, come here for a second." Janae walked up to our table and met Carla with a double-arm embrace. "Janae is a wonderful modern dancer, and she's also a percussive dancer. When did you first join Dance Place?" Janae responded: "Age six." "She's beautiful." They squeezed each other once more, and Janae walked away. "Now some of them leave and then come back. Janae left for college, but now she's back, which tells you she had a good experience here when she was young. Same with Delante." Delante was one of the counselors bursting through the lobby doors when I first entered. He now serves as youth program director for the organization. "I lost him in his teen years, but then I got him back" (figure 38).

I'm not sure what these hugs amount to in terms of economic gain. But that so many supporters arrive and continue to return to Dance Place over time suggests the possibility that the *kinesthetic* debts incurred through the cooperative

FIGURE 38. Carla Perlo and Delante White, youth director at Dance Place. (Photo courtesy Carla Perlo, Dance Place)

act of dance "making" function as desirable weighted exchanges between people who affirm each other's humanity and take pride in protecting a physical space that sets such affirmation in motion. This ethos of coauthorization and co-ownership has remained central to Dance Place codirectors Carla Perlo and Deborah Riley, who have recently engineered a leadership transition. On May 17, 2017, Carla and Deborah announced their intention to step down from their leadership roles within Dance Place with the hiring of Christopher K. Morgan as new artistic and executive director. Morgan is a choreographer and long-standing beneficiary of Dance Place opportunities; his entrance and the cofounders' exits will test whether and how Dance Place's social infrastructure adheres into the future. Morgan's return to Dance Place, like Delante's and Janae's and so many others', evidences the collective gravitational pull of dance "making," as a force that stalls the lonely logics of neoliberal entrepreneurship. Morgan may be a choreographer, but he is hardly a lone agent of production.

As I concluded my interview with Carla, the stakes of this leadership transition were not yet in play. When I asked her to reflect long-term on the project of instilling in new arrivals this ethos of mutual responsibility, her response disclosed a level of fatigue: "I'm not going to ask you to do all of the dirty work, the dirty work that I have to do, but you have to help me here. I beg and ask them all again, How do you get people to move?" The ironies of that last sentiment notwithstanding, the project of supporting a material "place" to dance in Washington, DC, has moved hundreds of energized dance makers through Dance Place's support system throughout its long history. Dance's living infrastructures are not static, nor do they promise to last. But something intangible endures beyond the broom handles, alongside the dust pans, and beneath the names of donors etched into the brick-and-mortar surface of the organization's material infrastructure: a desire to attend to dance as a vital midpoint in human connection. The kinesthetic contours of dance's collective attendance demand closer scrutiny on regionally and culturally contingent grounds. To quote Randy Martin, "If you get deeply enough into how dance works, it will compel you to write differently about how social life works" (quoted in Kowal, Siegmund, and Martin 2017, 2).

Conclusion

What would dance scholarship look like if we approached the study of dance and arts infrastructures under the assumption that only *verbs* count? Can studying infrastructure as an embodied *doing* critique structural inequities while also crediting non-arts labor and laborers? How can attention to body-level adjustments to economic undercapitalization highlight discursive movements that swerve around these estrangements? The ethnographic sidesteps

I've attempted here acknowledge funder-allocated pitfalls and highlight acts of cooperation that default on strictly economic goals. Dance histories are made through layered footfalls and collective gestures beyond the footlights. These backstage exercises suggest a need for greater regional and local attention to histories of dance production as a sweaty, collective exercise. There is far more work to be done.

I want to end by challenging dance researchers to embrace the study of dance infrastructures with a choreographic spirit. Let's keep mixing our methods in ways that credit the critical cooperation that keeps people returning to dance and that keeps dance's diverse traditions in constant circulation. Let's keep messing with how knowledge of dance is structured in order to collapse forever the vertical ladder that elevates artistic enactments above the compendium of supportive acts that see a dance through. Local dance organizers are primary sources for this inquiry. Let's cast them as the infrastructural experts that they are. Let's leverage our institutional privilege as academics to critique structural inequities while noticing how dance makers swerve around institutionally imposed landmines in practice. As scholars, let's not hide our own debts in the footnotes. Let's acknowledge debt within the body of the text. Dance scholars are not strangers to institutional belonging. Let's share ideas with unlikely partners in arts administration and policy studies, partners presently estranged from dance discourse. And, above all, let's commit to the radical possibility that *we are* elemental aspects of the dance infrastructure. Tools in our hands, our methods are already in motion.

Notes

1. For a current investigation of arts "organizers" that defines the term pluralistically, cross-culturally, and with an eye for performance, see Paul Bonin-Rodriguez (2014).

2. Exceptions that do not focus exclusively on infrastructural practices but that have influenced my approach include Naima Prevots (1998), Lynn Garafola (1999), Linda Tomko (1999), Mark Franko (2002), Julia Foulkes (2002), Anthea Kraut (2008), Rebekah Kowal (2010), and Clare Croft (2015). Randy Martin's (1998) efforts to theorize dance mobilization as de-alienated social labor leaves infrastructural acts largely unattended. His later work (2010) on administration recuperates this effort for higher education. I am extending Martin's notion of "mobilization" toward the complex social labor of dance organizing.

3. In *The Social Production of Art* (1981) Wolff rehearses Marx's famous bee and the architect analogy (vol. 1 of *Capital*) to delineate Marx's view that preindustrial labor was a creative impulse central to man's [sic] essence as a *species being*. Marx defined desirable labor as a willed impulse to "make" and take care of another species being while preserving one's sense of self, and he upheld creative labor as an attribute of any

and all forms of work. Creative work as a willing impulse was precisely what Marx saw as under siege in industrial capitalism.

4. The question "Who *makes* a dance?" in my chapter title and my invocation of the term "maker" here are indebted to choreographer Liz Lerman, whose intergenerational approach to dance production seeks to expand the number of achieved standpoints that contribute to danced expression to include dance participants whose bodily authority and experiences have been hidden or subordinated.

5. Carla and her fellow codirector Deborah Riley have suggested that, early on, Dance Place met a major demand for a dedicated performance venue due to the scarcity of affordable production space in the DC area, the lack of venues for artists producing work in the city at a smaller scale, and Dance Place's proximity to dance's self-proclaimed (and arguable) epicenter, New York City. For a list of current performances, see http://www.danceplace.org/performances/.

6. For more on the NEA's *Our Town* grant program, see https://www.arts.gov/grants-organizations/our-town/introduction.

7. For more on ArtPlace America, see http://www.artplaceamerica.org. For more on Kresge, see http://kresge.org/creative-placemaking-case-studies.

8. Recent Bureau of Labor statistics evidencing the low wages and short employment prospects for US dancers and choreographers are viewable here: https://www.bls.gov/oes/current/oes272031.htm (dancers) and https://www.bls.gov/oes/current/oes272032.htm (choreographers). For an alternative census that defines an artist as a worker with an art degree and that is introduced by a collective of artists, designers, technologists, organizers, and educators who work in the intersection of art, technology, and political economy, see BFAMFAPHD: http://censusreport.bfamfaphd.com/artistclasses.

9. Here I invoke the term "pre-fieldwork" following Karen Ho's (2009) apt depiction of her prior status as an investment trader and institutional insider as a critically embodied resource for her later ethnography of Wall Street banks.

10. Sarah Ahmed's (2012) ethnographic work on institutionally imposed documentation and reporting brilliantly theorizes the *non*performative force of paper pushing as a strategy to condition a sense of political immobilization on the part of its harshest critics.

11. Here I extend Sally Ann Ness's (2008) suggestion of inward migrations of meaning in dancing toward nondanced enactments that sustain dance production.

12. For more on how structural economic change looks and feels to arts organizers in late capitalism, see Judith Hamera (2017).

Works Cited

Ahmed, Sara. 2012. *On Being Included: Racism and Diversity in Institutional Life*. Durham, NC: Duke University Press.

Bonin-Rodriguez, Paul. 2014. *Performing Policy: How Contemporary Politics and Cultural Programs Redefined U.S. Artists for the Twenty-First Century*. New York: Palgrave Macmillan.

Bowker, Geoffrey C., Karen Baker, Florence Millerand, and David Ribes. 2009. "Toward Information Infrastructure Studies: Ways of Knowing in a Networked

Environment." In *International Handbook of Internet Research*, edited by J. Hunsinger et al., 97–117. Dordrecht: Springer.

Boyle, Michael Shane. 2017. "Performance and Value: The Work of Theatre in Karl Marx's Critique of Political Economy." *Theatre Survey* 58 (1): 3–23.

Croft, Clare. 2015. *Dancers as Diplomats: American Choreography in Cultural Exchange.* New York: Oxford University Press.

DeFrantz, Thomas F. 2004. *Dancing Revelations: Alvin Ailey's Embodiment of African American Culture.* New York: Oxford University Press.

Energizers Summer Camp. 2012. Dance Place. YouTube, August 9. https://www.you tube.com/watch?v=iyw8°vayBy8.

Foulkes, Julia. 2002. *Modern Bodies: Dance and American Modernism from Martha Graham to Alvin Ailey.* Chapel Hill: University of North Carolina Press.

Franko, Mark, 2002. *The Work of Dance: Labor, Movement, and Identity in the 1930s.* Middletown: Wesleyan University Press.

Garafola, Lynn. 1989. *Diaghilev's Ballets Russes.* New York: Oxford University Press.

Hamera, Judith. 2017. *Unfinished Business: Michael Jackson, Detroit, and the Figural Economy of American Deindustrialization.* New York: Oxford University Press.

Ho, Karen. 2009. *Liquidated: an Ethnography of Wall Street.* Durham: Duke University Press.

Jackson, Shannon. 2011. *Lines of Activity: Performance, Historiography, Hull-House Domesticity.* Ann Arbor: University of Michigan Press.

Kedhar, Anusha. 2014. "Flexibility and Its Bodily Limits: Transnational South Asian Dancers in an Age of Neoliberalism." *Dance Research Journal* 46 (1): 23–40.

Kowal, Rebekah. 2010. *How to Do Things with Dance: Performing Change in Postwar America.* Middletown: Wesleyan University Press.

Kowal, Rebekah J., Gerald Siegmund, and Randy Martin, eds. 2017. *The Oxford Handbook of Dance and Politics.* Oxford: Oxford University Press.

Kraut, Anthea. 2008. *Choreographing the Folk: The Dance Stagings of Zora Neale Hurston.* Minneapolis: University of Minnesota Press.

Kresge Foundation. 2017. "Creative Placemaking Case Studies." Accessed February 26, 2018. https://kresge.org/creative-placemaking-case-studies.

Lazzarato, Maurizio. 2012. *The Making of the Indebted Man: An Essay on the Neoliberal Condition.* Translated by Joshua David Jordan. New York: Semiotext(e).

———. 2015. *Governing by Debt.* Translated by Joshua David Jordan. Los Angeles: Semiotext(e).

Markusen, Ann, and Ann Gadwa. 2010. *Creative Placemaking.* Washington, DC: National Endowment for the Arts.

Martin, Randy. 1998. *Critical Moves: Dance Studies in Theory and Practice.* Durham, NC: Duke University Press.

———. 2010. "Dialogues: The State of the Body; Toward a Decentered Social Kinesthetic." *Dance Research Journal* 42 (1): 77–80.

———. 2012. "A Precarious Dance, a Derivative Sociality." *TDR / The Drama Review* 56 (4): 62–77.

Moss, Ian David. 2012. "Creative Placemaking Has an Outcomes Problem." *Createquity.* http://createquity.com/2012/05/creative-placemaking-has-an-outcomes-problem/.

Ness, Sally Ann. 2008. "The Inscription of Gesture: Inward Migrations in Dance." In *Migrations of Gesture*, edited by Carrie Noland and Sally Ann Ness, 1–30. Minneapolis: University of Minnesota Press.

Perlo, Carla. 2014. Interview with the author. Brookland, Washington, DC, August 13.

Prevots, Naima. 2012. *Dance for Export: Cultural Diplomacy and the Cold War.* Middletown: Wesleyan University Press.

Shkuda, Aaron. 2012. "The Art Market, Arts Funding, and Sweat Equity: The Origins of Gentrified Retail." *Journal of Urban History* 39 (4): 601–19.

Srinivasan, Priya. 2011. *Sweating Saris: Indian Dance as Transnational Labor.* Philadelphia: Temple University Press.

Star, Susan Leigh. 2002. "Infrastructure and Ethnographic Practice: Working on the Fringes." *Scandinavian Journal of Information Systems* 14 (2): 107–22.

Tomko, Linda. 1999. *Dancing Class: Gender, Ethnicity, and Social Divides in American Dance, 1890–1920.* Bloomington: Indiana University Press.

Virno, Paolo. 2014. *A Grammar of the Multitude.* Los Angeles: Semiotext(e).

Wilbur, Sarah. 2017. "Does the NEA Need Saving?" In *TDR/The Drama Review* 61 (4): 96–106.

———. 2018. "Endangered Strangers: Tracking Competition in Federal Dance Funding." In *The Oxford Handbook on Dance and Competition*, edited by Sherril Dodds, 87–110. New York: Oxford University Press.

Wolff, Janet. 1981. *The Social Production of Art.* London: Macmillan.

The Choreographic Commodity

Assigning and Policing Value for Nite Moves and William Forsythe

LIZZIE LEOPOLD

What is a dance worth?

This may seem like a simple question, but the inquiry signals the complexity in the inextricable intertwining of financial and cultural value that both lays the foundation for the field of concert dance and burdens the field with offering a historical account of the vexed integration of the arts into capitalist structures. To this end, this essay uses a 2012 New York State tax case and a 2014 proposed German expatriation tax in order to explain the monetary valuation of choreography as it relates to and reflects concepts of cultural value in the larger neoliberal landscape of twenty-first-century American concert dance. With increased commercialization across all creative industries, what I am calling a "choreographic commodity" has emerged, in both theory and practice, as an elite tier of choreographers license works to dance companies across the globe and enter permanent museum collections. While scarce monetary data is available on concert dance specifically, a result of both the market's youth and the privacy of its transactions, other sources of evidence (copyright cases, publicly available tax forms, new insurance instruments, interviews, and journalistic reports), along with data and methods from adjacent artistic fields, provide indirect clues as to how choreography is being valued, by whom, and with what innate ideologies in tow. A close reading of a 2012 tax audit against Nite Moves strip club in New York and the 2014 repatriation of choreographer William Forsythe from Germany to the United States provide preliminary examples and quantitative data to populate this important yet often veiled archive of dance and valuation. Through these case studies, the choreographic commodity illuminates the ways in which twenty-first-century choreographic commercialization perpetuates the raced and classed implications carried by earlier generations of choreographers and other artists and exaggerates the gross financial inequities between choreographic ideation and the labor of its embodied realization.[1]

We can define the choreographic commodity as organized movement ideas that are realized in bodies and prepared for commercialization not just in a singular moment of monetary exchange but as a tenet of choreographic production. Following Marxian theories of the commodity and value and Pierre Bourdieu's theories of cultural capital, the choreographic commodity appears innately contradictory—a choreographic object outside the body whose value and ontology nevertheless derive from corporeal labor. Questions of living labor are doubled, as choreography or the choreographic object is produced through the physical labor of bodies, congealed into "-graphy," and then reconstituted by those or other laboring bodies. In this way, the labor of production is continuous; choreography is in a constant state of (re)production. Or, as Rebecca Schneider says in her comparison of theater and capitalism with deadness, "what preserves value is the ongoing extraction of the labor of the live" (2012, 156). Proposing a choreographic commodity is, in this sense, a reinvestment in the live dancer's body and not a cold, detached expression of quantitative data. Schneider continues, "In this schema, commodities and laborers alike become like little packets of isolated temporal duration, frozen liveness, congealed as potential, posed as *tableaux vivant*—the packed duration of the live labor of the laborer. Reanimation is then another word for work, or for exchange" (156). And "performance" is another word for "reanimation." While the choreographic commodity can exist in "frozen liveness," it cannot express a monetary worth in this state. Its participation and exchange in the marketplace necessitate movement—moving bodies onstage and in studios, movement between people as it circulates and is viewed, and movement disseminated across borders through licensing. As evidenced by the tax cases that follow, it is the quality and understanding of this movement both within and between bodies that begets or negates value.

Karl Marx's foundational theorization of the commodity as "an external object, a thing which through its qualities satisfies human needs of whatever kind," was complicated immediately by Marx himself (1976, 125). He too was invested in the corporeal, focusing on the relationship between the commodity value and the labor of its construction: "As exchange-values, all commodities are merely definite quantities of congealed labour-time" (130). Marx is referring to cost of production when he explains that the productiveness of labor has an inverse relationship to value; the labor-time required for creation is an expense "crystallized" into the commodity's value and price (Baumol and Bowen 1968). Critics of Marx have faulted his labor theory of value for its inability to account for commodities not produced by labor (such as land) and for the exception of artworks, whose exchange value appears to be independent of labor time determinable by structures of wage labor (Heinrich 2004).

But performance and theater scholars have recently reengaged Marxian theory to argue for the deep interrelation of artistic labor and (economic) value (Boyle 2017; Lubin-Levy and Shvarts 2016; Jackson 2012; Martin 2002; Schneider 2012). This growing body of literature suggests that the choreographic commodity can be linked to larger cultural shifts in neoliberal capitalism that respond to financialized affect, increased commercialization, and increasing discord about the place of the performing arts in regard to the economization of artistic production. Shannon Jackson notes a long-term link between the immaterial turn, a result of twenty-first-century post-Fordist labor politics, and "the domain of performance" (2012, 16). Yet, citing Schneider, she reminds us that theatrical labor is not newly immaterial:

> Once again, dance and theatre workers had already inhabited the "unproductive" realm for quite some time by virtue of the fact that their products did not last, at least not in the ways that the market, the museum, or the archive understood the idea of lasting. But if, after Marx, such performance labor produced a product that "is not separate from the act of producing," the labor was not so much "dematerialized" as different material. The inseparability of such forms from the body of the laborer in fact made them feel hypermaterial, requiring feats of gestural, often repetitive, and kinesthetic effort to bring them continually into being. (Jackson 2012, 19)

The contradiction between immateriality and corporeal materiality, along with a repetitive, kinesthetic effort, is what keeps the choreographic commodity both a commodity object par excellence of the post-Fordist economy and a challenge to capitalist structures that valorize an ease of circulation and distribution that accompanies the intangible, disembodied good.

A 2013 decision by the US Bureau of Economic Analysis and the National Endowment for the Arts (NEA) to count creative industry profitability toward the gross domestic product (GDP) makes a significant statement about neoliberal governmental agendas concerning economization of the arts, recently complicated further by the Trump administration's threatened defunding of the NEA (Cohen 2014). The integration of creative industries into GDP calculations signals an investment in cultural *monetary* value at the federal level. Thus, it has become necessary for artists to assert the financial value of their congealed or living labor time in order to survive economically. In order to explore this new mandate, I examine the case studies of the 2012 New York State tax court ruling against Nite Moves strip club and adult juice bar and the proposed expatriation tax against choreographer William Forsythe. These examples illuminate how conclusions regarding choreographic value are derived, showing how quantitative calculations and cultural belief systems drive these highly subjective calculations within a profit-driven economy.

Cultural Capital and Neoliberal Capitalism

While the relationship of choreography to commerce is not new, the choreographic commodity has gradually emerged as a particular entity because of a shift in the concert dance field from choreographer-centered companies to repertoire models. This shift began in earnest after the founding of both the NEA and the Ford Foundation corporate granting program in the late 1960s and 1970s, which seeded the field with regional companies not founded around a singular artistic voice. Before this, a founding generation of American modern and ballet choreographers, including Martha Graham, George Balanchine, and Merce Cunningham, among others, created dance companies that served each choreographer's individual output.

Alternatively, works by many contemporary choreographers, including William Forsythe, Ohad Naharin, Jiri Kylian, and Twyla Tharp, were available for licensing much earlier in each choreographer's career. In this way, the licensing of dance works is now used as a commercial, money-generating mechanism and not primarily as a mode of performance preservation. This shift toward the constant licensing of dance repertoire has not only changed possibilities and necessities for touring but also mandated the monetary valuation of choreography as an everyday contractual obligation. A company and a choreographer, or choreographic estate, cannot enter into a licensing agreement until they agree on the cost, price, and worth of the choreography. Thus, the shift from a choreographer-centered company to a repertoire model, along with an increasing interest in museum acquisition of performances, has conjured the choreographic commodity as a twenty-first-century circulating market entity.

Just as Lawrence Levine chronicles in his book *Highbrow/Lowbrow: The Emergence of Cultural Hierarchy in America*, scholar of nonprofit organizations Paul DiMaggio describes America's early twentieth-century cultural capitalists, newly rich industrialist magnates like Andrew Mellon and John D. Rockefeller, institutionalizing elite European art forms (visual arts, opera, orchestra) in order to protect them from the demands and influences of the commercial marketplace. DiMaggio writes that a class distinction "emerged between 1850 and 1900 out of the efforts of urban elites to build organizational forms that, first, isolated high culture and, second, differentiated it from popular culture" (1986, 41). By establishing artistic spaces outside the consumerist grasp of the marketplace, these American patrons could align themselves with the elitist high-culture

ethos of imperial European art forms, separate these art forms (and themselves) from the low-brow entertainments of the burgeoning vaudeville stages,
and appear to construct a forced division between high art forms and lowly
economic influence. To claim this division as forced is to say that the cultural
capitalists did not succeed in wholly separating art from the commercial,
popular marketplace; rather, they set the stage for another, parallel, although
increasingly intertwined, market for art and artists. This is all to say that with
the nonprofit corporate structure as container, concert dance does not and
never has operated outside of financial pressures to generate capital. Thus,
the idea of a choreographic value expressed monetarily is neither threatening
nor demeaning to the art; rather, it is a central condition of making art within
capitalism.

Neoliberal principles do not favor the nonprofit sector (Brown 2015; Harvey
2005). The nonprofit sector generally argues for art as *public good* and champions ideas that would place art outside (or above) the demands of the free
market. In twenty-first-century neoliberal capitalism, the state aims to let the
market regulate itself through pricing. For concert dance and many other subsidized arts, this is a particularly difficult mandate. In the post–World War II
nonprofit organizational structure, concert dance has not primarily been subject to the supply-and-demand cycle of a free market; rather, only a portion
of the nonprofit's annual operating budget comes from earned income (ticket
sales), with donations and grants making up a significant portion of this income deficit (Kaiser 2015). The National Center for Charitable Statistics reports
that in 2012, the largest source of revenue for arts was individual giving, at 42
percent of total revenue for the cultural sector (National Endowment for the
Arts 2012). Yet as Wendy Brown writes, neoliberalism "wages war on public
good," subjecting all domains to the free market (2015, 39). These logics have
encouraged emergent repertoire and museum markets for choreography and
demanded a financial valuation of an asset that has enjoyed more than a half-
century of exemptions from this level of explicit commerciality. The phrase
"choreographic commodity" describes an explicit expression of commerciality
that, though always present, had been subdued.

Despite the failure of the 1976 federal copyright law to assert a stable definition for "choreography," dance scholar Susan Leigh Foster has offered an incredibly rich description. In *Choreographing Empathy: Kinesthesia in Performance,*
Foster unpacks the word's Greek etymology (*choreia*, the synthesis of dance,
rhythm, and vocal harmony manifest in the Greek chorus; and *graph*, the act
of writing), lists the *Oxford English Dictionary* definitions, and proceeds to
track the term from its inception to its current usage with a particular focus
on the term's connection to writing (as in *graph*) (2011, 16).[2] The history of

sixteenth- and seventeenth-century dancing masters is, as Foster tells it, particularly relevant to the questions examined in this research: "Sometime in the 1670s, Louis XIV ordered principal Dancing Master Pierre Beauchamps to 'discover the means of making the art of dance comprehensible on paper'" (18). The collections of notated dances that emerged from the king's mandate, along with three distinct dance notation systems, can be seen as precursors to the circulation of dance repertoire, as well as a precursor to the development of the choreographic commodity. Foster chronicles how these dances traveled across countries and continents as colonizing forces, choreographing distant populations into courtly movements, controlled bodies, and imperialist ideologies (16–31).

This deeply historical and ideological connection between concert dance and its notation undergirds the emergence of a global dance repertoire marketplace. The contemporary concert dance landscape is still impacted by the colonizing ideologies embedded in this early choreographic circulation. Foster connects the definition of choreography to its mandate for circulation, reminding us that this dissemination was never ideologically neutral. Rather, as a precursor to today's global and commercial concert dance marketplace, these early imperial choreographic networks were politically motivated, and they propagated colonial ideologies through the body and through dance. Acknowledging this lineage means understanding the commerce of a twenty-first-century concert dance marketplace as one born of colonial ideologies and therefore predicated on class distinctions and racial inequities.

The choreographic commodity is a luxury good, carrying prestige and cultural cachet to artists and audiences. Bourdieu's writings on artistic value provide us with a theoretical groundwork for exploring the integration of financial and cultural value, defining *cultural capital* as measurements of symbolic status bestowed upon individuals as markers of classed tastes (1993, 24). According to Bourdieu, because fields of cultural production can only function if "they succeed in simultaneously producing products and the need for those products through practices which are the denial of the ordinary practices of the 'economy,' the struggles which take place within them are ultimate conflicts involving the whole relation to the 'economy'" (1993, 82). Louis XIV's dancing master disseminated ballet as a product of the imperial court, and inextricable from this circulation was the circulation of European cultural hierarchies and economic models that imbued this dance with value and prestige. Similarly, a concert dance repertoire network simultaneously produces dance repertoire and a cultural demand for that repertoire—the fields of cultural production reinscribe the colonialist logics that circulate concurrently with the dance repertoire they produce. These are significant points to consider while working to understand *how* and *for whom* choreography's current financial valuation occurs. As Arjun Appadurai asserts, a "commodity is not a certain kind of thing, but things in a certain situation" (1986, 13). Commodification is temporal, social, and cultural, and the case studies that follow define the situations of choreographic commodification as much as the commodity itself.

The Choreographic Commodity in Use

In contemporary creative industries, there are many entities already broadly participating in the monetary valuation of choreography. Major museums, including New York City's Museum of Modern Art (MoMA) and London's Tate Modern, have instituted whole departments dedicated to the valuation and acquisition of durational artworks or time-based media such as choreography, performance art, and conceptual art installations. In response to the increased circulation of these properties, AIG, a multinational insurance company, in conjunction with boutique insurance firm Crystal and Company, introduced an insurance product in the fall of 2015 for their private clientele to cover conceptual artworks. This insurance product recognizes artistic expression as central to the work's value, as opposed to the form and material of the "object" (*Insurance Journal* 2015). Additionally, artistic estate planning continues to be inextricably tied to the task of valuation, as mandated by federal law. Similarly, choreographic licensing is tied to questions of financial valuation, with licensing fees understood as an income stream contributing to an overall appraisal of the work. Tax cases from Nite Moves and Forsythe offer some concrete examples of choreographic appraisal in practice. Here, I illustrate the innate complications and contradictions in current valuation practices and how these practices reinforce highly classed categories of moving bodies using monetary power as a threat and a promise to choreographic value, both cultural and financial.

Nite Moves

In 2005 Nite Moves was audited by the New York Division of Taxation because the state believed it was owed back taxes for "both the door admission charges allowing patrons to see dancers on stage, and the sales of private dances" (Weiss 2012). These taxes were to be collected under New York State Tax Law 1105, "charges for admission to places of entertainment, amusement, or sport," with an exemption for "live dramatic, choreographic, or musical arts performances."[3] Thus, it became the work of Nite Moves to prove that its services were tax-exempt as "live dramatic, choreographic, or musical arts performance." The various court rulings and appeals, as well as the accompanying transcripts, offer a legal definition of "choreographic" as it relates to the term's taxability or, more broadly understood, its relationship to American conceptions of *public good.* Therefore, the 2012 New York State tax case against Nite Moves provides a contemporary definition and understanding of choreography as a financially empowered (or, conversely, disenfranchised), market-integrated, and government-regulated commodity property.

This case included the initial audit (and declaration of $124,921 owed), an appeal by Nite Moves to exempt their services as "dramatic or musical arts" (ruled in favor of the club), a subsequent (and successful) Tax Appeals Tribunal to overturn this initial appeal, and a final failed challenge from Nite Moves against the tribunal's ruling (Witt 2013). The Tax Appeals Tribunal predicated its case on the idea that Nite Moves did not prove, beyond reasonable doubt, that these dances constituted choreography. On October 23, 2012, the New York Court of Appeals ruled against Nite Moves, ordering it to pay sales tax on all pole and lap dances and defining choreography (and its antithesis) in the process. The implications of this ruling for the choreographic commodity, both defined and financially valued, are wide and far-reaching.

Expert witness and dance scholar Dr. Judith Hanna relied upon her years of anthropological research, both in and outside the strip club, to offer a definition of choreography: the composition and arrangement of dances. Cataloging approximately sixty-one distinct moves from a Nite Moves promotional video, she noted variations, patterns, repetition, locomotion, gesture, and pole, mirror, and floor work at variable levels in response to music (Weiss 2012). The tribunal dismissed her interpretation as "sweeping" and ruled that she failed to establish the movements of performers at Nite Moves as choreographic. The tribunal further argued that Hanna did not use any specialized language to describe the pole or jazz dancing (jazz dancing, as a genre, falls into the court transcripts rather abruptly, with no explanation). The training of the Nite Moves performers was also attacked; the tribunal asserted that a dancer's pedagogical past is directly related to her ability to invoke the choreographic and its subsequent public good or monetary value. An excerpt from the court transcript on this topic reads:

JUDGE PIGOTT: Well, how about if they don't train—if the owner himself says we don't require any dance training whatsoever, and they pay us to come to our establishment. He doesn't hire these people to be dancers. He hire—they hire him so they can come in and do whatever they do. He gets paid by them, and he gets paid by them for the rooms.
MR. MCCULLOUGH [Nite Moves' attorney]: He provides—he's the one who's provided the training by way—
JUDGE PIGOTT: No, he's not.
MR. MCCULLOUGH: —in some cases it's video. In some cases it's—

JUDGE PIGOTT: No he's not. He's just giving them a pole and a stage and saying give me twenty-five bucks and you can go do what you're doing.

MR. MCCULLOUGH: He said in his testimony that he provided other dancers
to help and also videos to help, and that it takes a period of time to learn. If
you saw—and it's part of the record—if you saw what these dancers do, you
would be saying, no, it's not the Bolshoi, but it's good. And I would point
out, Your Honor, that pole dancing is under serious consideration as an
Olympic sport. And there are people—

JUDGE PIGOTT: Are you comparing it to dressage now?

MR. MCCULLOUGH: You know, I don't make those decisions either.

JUDGE PIGOTT: Well, then why make the argument?

MR. MCCULLOUGH: But if it's under consideration as an Olympic sport, these
girls, certainly the ones that you would see on these videos, would be in
standing to make the team. They're that good.[4]

This disjointed discussion is illustrative of how the New York Court of Appeals
understands specialized dance training as an integral component of choreographic possibility, defining the term in relation to modes of learning whose
value is refracted through hierarchies of economic class. Learning from video-
tape and/or on-the-job experience is not a sufficient education to label the
movement as choreographic.

The Tax Appeals Tribunal further attacked a perceived lack of rhetorical
distinction between the terms "dance" and "choreography" in the defense's
case. This discussion devolved into a pitting of "choreography" and its accompanying tax exemption against "improvisation" as supposed unplanned movement and therefore falling into a gray area of taxability.

MR. GOLDFARB [attorney for the respondent]: The tribunal applied a commonly understood dictionary definition of choreography, meaning a dance
where the steps and the moves are all planned, arranged, and composed in
advance and then it's performed in that way. And the record just simply does
not bear this out.

JUDGE SMITH: So you are saying that an improvised dance is taxable?

MR. GOLDFARB: I think that's correct, Your Honor. Well, not the dance itself,
but admission fees. . . . [T]he statute uses the term "choreographic." It doesn't
use the term "dance." . . . What the record reflects is simply that there are
some commonly used moves in stripping. The women would perform what
they called various pole tricks, some of which are very difficult to perform,
but that doesn't make the entire performance a choreographed one.[5]

This definition of choreography is restrictively narrow. To expect the choreographic commodity to be absolutely fixed and unchanging is unrealistic and oppressive for a thing that depends so totally on its ability to move and morph. But despite this fact, the 2012 New York State tax ruling aligns its definition of choreography with that of the 1976 Copyright Act, dependent upon the commodity's fixity (Kraut 2016). And while fixity has a direct relationship to reproduction and thus commerciality, the choreographic commodity depends upon an ontological unfixity that accompanies liveness in order to imbue its commodity state with the auratic singularity that begets cultural and financial capital.

The costuming of the Nite Moves performers also became a point of interest for the courts. "I would submit, if the women kept their clothes on, no one would be coming to this bar for the dance performance," remarked respondent attorney Goldfarb in argument for the nature and purpose of the venue's programming.[6] Through this discussion, he hoped to prove that Nite Moves was a place patrons visited not for a choreographic performance but rather for libations and sexualized bodies during which any choreography that occurred was merely incidental. This separation of body from choreography is impossibly forced. The court seems to be asserting that the nude body negates, or at least opposes, the choreographic. Much like the "culture wars" of the 1990s, the tax audit of Nite Moves is an example of the government leveraging capital (and its regulation) in order to influence cultural production.

With all this discussion, this legal definition of choreography is primarily concerned with policing economic class and its subsequent relationship to tax exemption and public good, the primary requirement for exemption. The court transcripts reveal a pointed debate about the responsibility of the courts and their ability to police these boundaries. Chief Judge Lippman asked, "Is there a difference between the ballet dancer and these pole dancers in terms of their artistic value or their benefit to the world? And could that be the basis for what the tribunal found, or does it have nothing to do with that?"[7] Tax exemption is predicated on the idea of public good; therefore, the court asked whether or not the pole dancer offers a benefit to the world worthy of this exemption. Synthesizing all these statements, the Tax Appeals Tribunal of the State of New York defined "choreography" as wholly planned bodily movements that are learned in professional and prolonged educational settings and that are performed in specific clothing and in designated locations. This definition highlights the elitist, high-culture ideologies innate to choreographic valuation and perpetuated by choreographic commodification and circulation.

William Forsythe's *In the Middle, Somewhat Elevated*

Throughout his more than forty-year career, the dances of choreographer William Forsythe, in contrast to the dances at Nite Moves, have fallen squarely into a tax-exempt sector. These dances are a mixture of set dance steps and improvisation. They are costumed with varying levels of bodily exposure. And Forsythe has even used nontrained movers in some of his later conceptual art installations. Yet no government court has argued against his right to claim *public good*. In fact, a recent and more anecdotal tax case reveals the way in which the choreographic commodity is strategically policed to simultaneously leverage maximum profit and reassert the cultural value systems put into place by the early twentieth-century cultural capitalists, as mentioned earlier in reference to the work of Paul DiMaggio on the nonprofit sector.

In 2014, after nearly three decades of work in Germany as artistic director and choreographer of the government-funded Ballett Frankfurt and Forsythe Company, Forsythe announced his successor and relocated to the United States. While not publicly announced by either Forsythe or the German government, his current tax situation leaves him with an expensive proposition. The German government has threatened to charge the artist an expatriation tax toward the sum of $35 million; having invested an estimated $100 million in his choreographic output over thirty years, the government feels entitled to future earnings from his dances, those already premiered and those yet to be conceived (Forsythe 2014). This unexpected hiccup in his repatriation plan has forced Forsythe to establish a foundation and have his dances appraised.

Forsythe Productions, established in late 2013, is based in Germany, allowing Forsythe to relocate to the United States but leave his dances behind, avoiding some of the exit taxation. This does not mean that his works won't be performed across the globe; rather, it means that they legally reside in Germany. The geographical fixity of these supposedly ephemeral objects is another legal characteristic of the choreographic commodity. Defining a home locale is both a part of asserting ownership and asserting or avoiding taxation. Because choreographies exist in multiples, unlike the singularity of much visual artwork, the seminal dance works of William Forsythe can be simultaneously housed in Frankfurt and performed in Seattle. This also makes them particularly difficult taxable assets to police, as transnational circulation (and the border crossings implicit in this movement) is a primary tool for taxation.

In our conversation in May 2014 at the Houston Ballet, Forsythe explained his current dilemma with candor and excitement. An exit tax, or an expatriation tax, is a capital gains taxation against unrealized gain attributed to the period in which the taxpayer was a tax resident of the country in question.

Forsythe expressed a sort of simultaneous delight and terror at the idea. He explained that he had begun to have his dances appraised, like fine art. Richard Branson's tax attorney, who acted as appraiser, valued Forsythe's iconic 1987 ballet, *In the Middle, Somewhat Elevated*, at $10 million. While the tax attorney's appraisal methods were not entirely clear, he had used YouTube view counts as a primary metric; that is, the number of clicks a YouTube excerpt of *In the Middle* generated was related to the market valuation of the dance.

Of course, there is an innate conflict of interest in using YouTube views to calculate value, as Forsythe and his foundation police the online presence of his choreography in video and photographs (not to mention the fact that the photographic record of the dance is not necessarily the dance itself). Licensing contracts, the primary income stream for his ballets, stipulate the maximum length of a public video clip used for promotional purposes in order to protect the choreography from theft (Scott 2014). Ensuring the relative scarcity of *In the Middle*'s video circulation contributes to a demand for the live performance through licensed productions, driving up income revenue for the invested parties. Thus, YouTube's catalog of *In the Middle* includes approximately 11,200 clips related to the ballet, including authorized promotional materials and performance highlights, illegal performance documentation, high school dance troupes' rechoreographies of Dutch composer Thom Willem's score or the Forsythe material, an Australian television show's repurposing of the ballet's title for an episode arc, audition videos with multiple ballet variations included, and more.[8] This digital archive unearths questions about transnational labor in the digital space; the global circulation of choreographic ideas, sequences, and steps; and the complicated economics that accompany the legalities of regulating this flow. It does not, however, offer a neutral reading of the ballet's circulation, popularity, reception, or monetary value.

While concert dance choreography can easily be accused of an ephemerality and an intangibility that keep it outside capitalist concerns and economic scholarship, the ubiquity of Forsythe's *In the Middle, Somewhat Elevated* concretizes the choreographic commodity in visceral, sweating bodies and physical, corporeal, commodified labor.[9] The premiere of *In the Middle* at the Paris Opéra was, in fact, a watershed moment for contemporary ballet. Forsythe dared to distort the codified ballet vocabulary, exaggerating positions and stretching shapes beyond recognizability. The author of the opening night review lauded the work as "the most exciting I have seen in years. . . . The eye and the mind are ravished by the urgency, intricacy and authority of the movement" (Percival 1987). The work is a plotless series of virtuosic solos and duets, almost always witnessed by a less prominent dancer standing casually in the shadows. Forsythe also costumed the piece simply in practice leotards and tights, stripping away

the elaborate decor that had for centuries characterized Paris Opéra productions. Two golden cherries are the only set piece, hung—as the title suggests—
in the middle, somewhat elevated.

During our conversation, Forsythe explained that he would try to sell the
ballet and others of similarly high value to an investor to pay off the German
government's imposed exit tax. The rich intellect and curiosity that have fueled
his illustrious choreographic career seemed to bait him into this unknown
terrain. Our discussion evolved into musings about artistic control versus legal
ownership, the taboo relationship between concert dance and commerce, dance
in the museum, and appraisal processes. However, because my efforts to follow up on this conversation with Alexandra Scott, Forsythe Productions executive director, have been harshly shut down, I am left waiting with the rest of
the dance world for this precedent-setting transaction to take place. If *In the
Middle* is sold for the appraised price, then it would, much like the Nite Moves
case, reinscribe systems that valorize certain choreographic genres (and artists)
and imbue these genres with the financial capital that begets cultural capital,
and vice versa. The high-price sale of Forsythe's work validates its worth within
a neoliberal logic that holds profit as the best measure of merit.

Whether or not the tax is levied or the sale takes place, the proliferation
of choreographic estates and foundations continues to press ideas of repertoire
value. The Merce Cunningham Trust's groundbreaking Legacy Plan includes
the disbanding of the dance company in favor of protecting and preserving the
dances themselves in "capsule" form. These capsules are "digital packages comprised of the array of creative elements that make up a specific Cunningham
work" ("The Legacy Plan" 2012). Designed for the purposes of both restaging
and scholarly research, these materials include performance videos, Cunningham's notes, sound recordings, lighting plots, decor images, costume designs,
and production notes from rehearsals and performances and are stored in an
online format with password-protected access. At the launch of the trust, eighty-
six of Cunningham's more than two hundred works had been encapsulated
("The Legacy Plan" 2012). Reading the trust's Form 990 (2013, 2014 tax returns)
reveals that the Dance Capsules are not understood as assets, nor are they in-
sured against loss. The more than $9 million in assets listed on the 2013 form are
categorized as corporate stocks, corporate bonds, security deposits, land, buildings, and equipment, among others. This is not through any fault of the trust,
as the IRS form offers no place for listing these complicated choreographic commodities. The form alone suggests that the Merce Cunningham Trust, having
spent millions of dollars to create the Dance Capsules, sees no monetary value
in their existence.

There are, of course, large economic advantages to choreography's outsider status in this realm. Paying taxes on dances as assets would create huge new expenses for artists and organizations already burdened by financial insolvency. Yet in an age of the rampant privatization of neoliberal capitalism, a denial of dance's monetary possibility is tantamount to pitting it against the public good, as the Nite Moves example makes clear. This denial thus seems to me to be a more damaging suggestion. Is it possible that a recognized dance asset could also empower the financially unstable nonprofit industry? Like the sale of William Forsythe's ballets, the sustained success of the Cunningham Dance Capsules will additionally clarify the role and necessity of choreographic valuation through estate and foundation planning and the accompanying taxation and insurance concerns.

Conclusion

Extracorporeal technologies of choreographic fixity—legal, written, and videographic—beget its circulation. Choreographic circulation begets repetition, and within the neoliberal logics of the twenty-first-century creative industries, repetition invites commodification. And while the purpose of capitalist production is the valorization of capital, the extraction of resources, and the exploitation of labor for profit, the possibility for choreographic repetition is a mechanism for dance's market participation and commodification, as well as the subsequent economic support of dancers and dance makers. The choreographic commodity persists through repetition, continually realized in performance and production rather than enduring in an inactive, static state. As many others have before him, Noah Horowitz calls performance itself a "mode of circulation," an assertion that holds true for the choreography in question (2011, 113). Concert dance choreography has largely followed this linear progression, by which the fixing of a dance is followed by its circulation as (live) commodity.

The commercial drive for the ubiquitous circulation of a product as a mode of profit seeking creates homogenization across the field, both in bodies and on stages. The body and the body politic of the nonprofit are similarly produced. The more than twenty productions of William Forsythe's *In the Middle, Somewhat Elevated* over the last five years are just one example of how choreographic fixity, circulation, and commodification create conditions for the homogenization of the field of concert dance. The same choreography is circulated and performed constantly because a combination of previous critical success and portability (small size of cast, costumes, set, recorded music, etc.) makes it more easily commodified (i.e., more readied for market participants).

Furthermore, a legal misrepresentation of the relationship of choreography to improvisation (as exemplified in the Nite Moves case study and written into choreographic copyright law) demands that the choreographic commodity achieve a level of stasis and sameness that, while imbuing the asset with a level of financial possibility, counters the auratic singularity of live performance.

Through these examples, the choreographic commodity emerges not just as a theoretical concept but as a highly complex, circulating, and financially complicated free-market entity. A merger of theory and pragmatism helps to define the choreographic commodity as a temporally based, culturally conservative, embodied expression of spatially concerned ideas as it realizes monetary value and participates in free-market circulation. Furthermore, the choreographic commodity most often refers to classed understandings of movement possibility, dance pedagogy, performance venues, and the body itself, institutionalized by the 501(c)3 tax code in the mid-twentieth century and reinforced by the 1976 copyright ruling. Its value is derived from relationships to elitist European art forms patronized by early twentieth-century cultural capitalists and adopted by a pioneering generation of American modern dancers. The actions of private sector and government agencies implicitly police the possibility for choreographic value and imbue the choreographic commodity with classed ideologies that perpetuate the failing divide between the nonprofit sector and the commercial marketplace.

Notes

1. Writing for web publication *Culturebot*, Andy Horwitz (2014) reports that, on average, dancers working with an early career choreographer can expect to make $100 to $500 over a three-month rehearsal process; with only nominally better compensation from midcareer choreographers, dancers in this demographic average $15 per hour. And dancers working for established choreographers, albeit nonunion contracts, can make as little as $5,000 per year, with more for touring ($500–$700 per week). For more, see "Expense Report" (2017).

2. "The *Oxford English Dictionary* offers two definitions for the word 'choreography': the first, a simple assertion, informs us that choreography is the 'art of dancing'; the second, marked as an obsolete usage, refers to choreography as 'the art of writing dances on paper'" (Foster 2011, 16).

3. New York State Tax 1105 (f)(1), Tax Bulletin ST-8.

4. Court of Appeals State of New York, Matter of 677 New Loudon Corporation, Appellant against Tax Appeals Tribunal of the State of New York, Respondent, September 5, 2012, pp. 30–32. http://www.nycourts.gov/ctapps/arguments/2012/Sep12/Transcripts/090512-157.pdf.

5. Ibid., 22–23.

6. Ibid., 17.

7. Ibid., 25.

8. This number was generated by using the search words "in the middle somewhat elevated." Search completed on March 4, 2017.

9. Recent restagings and premieres of *In the Middle, Somewhat Elevated* over the last five years include 2017: Astana Ballet (Kazakhstan), Boston Ballet (five-year Forsythe partnership); 2016: Washington Ballet, Australian Ballet, Oregon Ballet Theatre, Royal New Zealand Ballet; 2015: English National Ballet, Pacific Northwest Ballet (Seattle), Ballet West (Utah), Pittsburgh Ballet Theatre, Zurich Ballet, Dresden Semperoper Ballett (*Impressing the Czar*); 2014: Houston Ballet, Pennsylvania Ballet, Tulsa Ballet, Balet Narodni Divadlo (Czech Republic), Universal Ballet Korea, Sofia National Opera and Ballet (Bulgaria); 2013: Mariinsky Theatre (Russia), Ballet Nacional del Sodre (Uruguay); 2012: Paris Opéra Ballet, Joffrey Ballet of Chicago.

Works Cited

Appadurai, Arjun. 1986. *The Social Life of Things: Commodities in Cultural Perspective.* New York: Cambridge University Press.

Baumol, William, and William Bowen. 1968. *Performing Arts: The Economic Dilemma.* New York: Twentieth Century Fund.

Bourdieu, Pierre. 1993. *The Field of Cultural Production.* Cambridge: Polity Press.

Boyle, Michael Shane. 2017. "Performance and Value: The Work of Theater in Karl Marx's *Critique of Political Economy*." *Theatre Survey* 58 (1): 3–23.

Brown, Wendy. 2015. *Undoing the Demos: Neoliberalism's Stealth Revolution.* New York: Zone Books.

Cohen, Randy. 2014. "BEA's Arts in the GDP Study: How You Can Help Make It Great." *Americans for the Arts.* January 28. http://blog.americansforthearts.org/2014/01/28/bea%E2%80%99s-arts-in-the-gdp-study-how-you-can-help-make-it-great.

DiMaggio, Paul. 1986. *Nonprofit Enterprise in the Arts: Studies in Mission and Constraint.* New York: Oxford University Press.

"Expense Report." 2017. National Center for Arts Research at Southern Methodist University. March 2. http://mcs.smu.edu/artsresearch2014/reports/expenses/how-much-operation-revenue-directly-invested-programs-first-considering-all-direct#/averages/arts-sector.

Forsythe, William. 2014. Interview with the author. Houston, May 20.

Foster, Susan Leigh. 2011. *Choreographing Empathy: Kinesthesia in Performance.* New York: Routledge.

Harvey, David. 2005. *A Brief History of Neoliberalism.* New York: Oxford University Press.

Heinrich, Michael. 2004. *An Introduction to the Three Volumes of Karl Marx's "Capital."* New York: Monthly Press Review.

Horwitz, Andy. 2014. "The Untenable Economics of Dancing." *Culturebot: Maximum Performance.* March 27. http://www.culturebot.org/2014/03/21361/the-untenable economics-of-dancing/.

Horowitz, Noah. 2011. *Art of the Deal: Contemporary Art in the Global Financial Market.* Princeton, NJ: Princeton University Press.

Insurance Journal. 2015. "Crystal, AIG Offer Conceptual Art Insurance for Private Clients." March 31. http://www.insurancejournal.com/news/national/2015/03/31/362 698.htm.

Jackson, Shannon. 2012. "Just-in-Time: Performance and the Aesthetics of Precarity." *Drama Review* 56 (4): 10–31.

Kaiser, Michael M. 2015. *Curtains? The Future of the Arts in America.* Waltham, MA: Brandeis University Press.

Kraut, Anthea. 2016. *Choreographing Copyright: Race, Gender, and Intellectual Property Rights in American Dance.* New York: Oxford University Press.

"The Legacy Plan: A Case Study." 2012. Cunningham Dance Foundation, Inc. https:// www.mercecunningham.org/themes/default/db_images/documents/Merce_Leg acy_Plan.pdf.

Levine, Lawrence. *Highbrow/Lowbrow: The Emergence of Cultural Hierarchy in America.* Cambridge, MA: Harvard University Press, 1990.

Lubin-Levey, Joshua, and Aliza Shvarts. 2016. "Living Labor: Marxism and Performance Studies." *Women and Performance: A Journal of Feminist Theory* 26 (2–3): 115–21.

Martin, Randy. 2002. *The Financialization of Daily Life.* Philadelphia: Temple University Press.

Marx, Karl. 1976. *Capital.* New York: Penguin Books.

National Endowment for the Arts. 2012. "How the United States Funds the Arts." https://www.arts.gov/sites/default/files/how-the-us-funds-the-arts.pdf.

Percival, John. 1987. "Ballet with a Power to Thrill: Review of 'In the Middle, Somewhat Elevated' at Opera, Paris." *Times,* June 27.

Schneider, Rebecca. 2011. *Performing Remains: Art and War in Times of Theatrical Reenactment.* London: Routledge.

———. 2012. "It Seems as if . . . I Am Dead: Zombie Capitalism and Theatrical Labor." *Drama Review* 56 (4): 150–62.

Scott, Alexandra. 2014. Phone interview with the author. February 4.

Weiss, Marie-Andree. 2012. "Pole Dancing Not an Artistic Performance under New York Law." *Entertainment, Arts and Sports Law Blog.* November 2. http://nysbar.com/blogs/EASL/2012/11/pole_dancing_not_an_artistic_p.html.

Witt, Jim. 2013. "'TAX' Sales—Lap Dance Fees." *Lawletter* 38 (4). http://www.nlrg.com/legal-content/the-lawletter/bid/93355/TAX-Sales-Lap-Dance-Fees.

Walking Backward

Choreographing the Greek Crisis

NATALIE ZERVOU

On Tuesday, March 8, 2016, a very unusual and highly performative protest took place in the heart of Athens. Members of the Union for Workers in the Field of Dance (UWFD) (Σωματείο Εργαζομένων στο Χώρο του Χορού, or Σ.Ε.ΧΩ.ΧΟ) gathered in front of the Ministry of Employment to protest the current state of infrastructural support for dance and labor conditions for dancers in Greece. They formed a human chain by holding hands as they made their way to the Ministry of Culture, walking backward. Each protestor had pinned to their shirt a piece of paper asking "So You Think We Can Dance until 67?" The question was a reference to the homonymous *So You Think You Can Dance* TV show and simultaneously hinted at one of the main demands of the UWFD members concerning review of their pension age. Their other demands included the establishment of a public university for studying dance with subsidization and financial support for performance work and for research in the field of dance.[1]

The literal "backwardness" of the protest was a deliberate choice that could be perceived as an analogy to the backwardness of the current policies on dance's role in public education, as well as a tactic to draw attention to the field of dance and distinguish this protest from others that were happening around the same time. As the list of demands of the UWFD protest evidences, dance is still not recognized as an academic discipline in Greece, and professional dance degrees are not considered equivalent to other university degrees, even though they are recognized by the Ministry of Culture. The urgency to have dance be recognized as an academic field of study has been increasingly highlighted during the crisis years (2009–17 and ongoing) following the extensive budget cuts imposed by the state, which since 2011 had ceased to provide any governmental support for dance. In part as a result of protest activism by dancers and others, subsidies were finally reinstated in 2017 for the 2017–18 season, but as of this writing the situation remains precarious, and workers in the field of dance feel that precariousness quite acutely.

Dancers' need to have dance recognized and supported as an autonomous profession and the increased demand that dance be acknowledged as an academic discipline are tied to the devaluation of bodies, particularly of dancers' bodies, by the state. The need to attend to this devaluation was heightened during the crisis due to extensive budget cuts, which impacted dance production subsidies and, subsequently, the working conditions for choreographers and performers. Taking a cue from the protestors' response to their own precariousness by choosing to walk backward, this essay utilizes this metaphor of the motion of *forward-backwardness* to capture and unpack a pivotal moment in the development of dance in Greece in the midst of the crisis. At a moment when the chronic devaluation of dance reached its peak, artists decided to actively reclaim embodied agency both through engaging in activism on the streets and through their choreographies on the stage. The artists' creative endeavors simultaneously exposed the devaluation of bodies observed at the height of the crisis (backwardness) and made an attempt to challenge the established order of things (aspiration to move forward).

The metaphor of forward-backwardness alludes to an image of an oscillating body—a body that has a purpose yet repeatedly fails to achieve it or arrive at its final destination. It is this disoriented body that I invite you to follow in the next few pages as she navigates the emergence of a new social and financial order in Athens during the crisis.[2] Sometimes this body is mine as the author of this text: the eager ethnographer, the outside observer, and the audience member. At other times the body takes on multiple subjectivities and fluctuates between different identities: she is the dance graduate who struggles to find work, the performer who has difficulty making ends meet, or the choreographer who becomes an activist on the streets stepping backward, as well as onstage attempting a forward motion.

Our trajectory starts in the streets of downtown Athens. We are holding hands tightly and carefully extending one leg back. When you do this, your toes reach the ground first, and then the rest of your foot follows until you transfer your weight fully onto that leg. We have taken our first step backward.

Narrative Loss: The Disoriented Greek Subject

Our first step backward has been an exercise not only in space but also in time. The financial crisis broke out in Greece in 2009. Beyond its devastating financial impact, including increasing unemployment, corporations declaring bankruptcy, and the rise of the national debt, it also brought about a rupture of social values and shook the core ideas of Greek national identity, particularly in relation to its European counterparts.

The primary way that the financial crisis also became a crisis of identity was through the prevailing experience of being at a loss that provoked a sense of disorientation as individuals slowly came to terms with the austerity measures imposed on them and adapted their lives to the shifting sociopolitical land-scape.[3] The gradual changes in the country's financial and political spheres, which ranged from a rise in taxation and shifts in individual spending habits to shifts in the public health insurance system, contributed to creating a sense of disorientation as far as the social life of individuals was concerned. Beyond individual sociality, however, the disorientation provoked a crisis of national identity concerned primarily with Greece's position in the European Union.

The fact that the European Union needed to provide financial support to Greece so that it could avoid default rendered the country the scapegoat of Europe and reignited national anxieties about the othering of the country (Herzfeld 1986; Gourgouris 1996). These anxieties were heightened by international media representations that painted Greece as backward and violent in coverage of numerous protests that were organized in resistance to the enforcement of austerity measures. General anxiety about Greece's international image further contributed to the initial sense of disorientation at the beginning of the crisis in a process akin to what Naomi Klein has described in her book *The Shock Doctrine* (2007). In an article published in the newspaper *Eleftherotypia*, she discussed the Greek example:

> Greeks have this particular fear that's being exploited, around the fear of becoming a developing country, becoming a third world country. And I think in Greece there's always been this sense of hanging on to Europe by a thread. And the threat is having that thread cut. . . . The state of shock that is so easy to exploit is a state of confusion. It's the panic that sets in when things are changing very, very quickly, when the story is lost. And those are the moments when we need our media, as a collective way to "renarrativise" ourselves. (Klein 2013)

The anxiety about Greece's potential primitivization motivated some groups to attempt to reclaim what they perceived to be a lost sense of the Greek subject. The most striking example of renarrativization was the gradual rise of ethnocentric nationalism in the 2012 national elections, observable primarily through the popularization of the extremist right-wing party Golden Dawn. Much of Golden Dawn's rhetoric focuses on Greece's past glories and seeks to revive Hellenic ideals, which the extremist group perceives as the cornerstone of Greek national identity. Perhaps in response to this alarming rise of ethno-centrism and in an attempt to counter it, a new thematic trend emerged in the arts that focused on rendering the significant differences and inconsistencies between the Hellenic past and the neoliberal present visible for critique. The new trend draws attention to more recent histories and has been evidenced in both dance and literature (often, in literature, through the lens of immigra-tion) (Gotsi 2012, 155).

The shift of focus to the more recent (post-1940s) past is a departure from the majority of the narratives that were presented in contemporary dance pro-ductions in Athens before the crisis. In previous decades, particularly in the so-called golden decade of dance in Greece (1990s–2000s), there was a plethora of dance productions that revived narratives from the ancient past and based works on ancient Greek tragedies and comedies or on mythology (Fessa-Emannouil 2004; Grigoriou and Mirayias 2004; Rigos 2010). The effort to grapple with the crisis has inspired a thematic shift toward the recent past as artists attempt to contextualize the contemporary moment and trace the trajectory of twentieth- and twenty-first-century events that led to the crisis. Such new themes relate directly to political activism as observed primarily on Athenian stages between 2013 and 2015. Many of the works produced in those two years critiqued the current political moment or constructed and proposed theoretical frameworks through which to perceive, analyze, and understand the sociopolitical crisis experienced in parallel to the financial one. We will return to explore exam-ples of such productions in the last section of this essay, but first we should ask the question, Why these two years? Drawing from archival research on national and cultural economies in Greece and my fieldwork in Athens (2013–16), I trace the shift in thematic orientation to the second half of the crisis years (after 2013). The reason that the time frame of this study is limited to the years between 2013 and 2015 is because when the crisis started (2009–11) there were no significant changes in the mode of artistic production, and sub-sidies for dance were still available. It wasn't until 2011, when the subsidies from the Ministry of Culture ceased, that previously funded dance artists realized that they had to find alternative means to support their creative endeavors.

While at first the lack of financial support seemed to bring about artistic stagnation among dance artists, soon certain groups surpassed it and began find-ing different ways to either fund their work (such as through EU subsidies) or create work with limited funds. Some examples of such alternative approaches include the emergence of some so-called self-organized spaces, which offered free workshops, classes, and performances or operated on a pay-what-you-want/what-you-can basis (Zervou 2017). The most outstanding instance is EMBROS

(Onward), an abandoned theater that was occupied by artists in 2011. The building has been operating under occupation to this day, in spite of numerous governmental attempts to shut it down. Another instance is the Kypseli Market, a building that used to host a local market that was similarly occupied by artists and activists. It has been turned into a communal space offering Greek-language classes to immigrants and refugees, hosting movie nights, and providing alternative spaces for performances. Both of these examples attest to another shift, namely toward communal initiatives and collaborations, simultaneously seen in the emergent performance trend toward fostering collaborations during the crisis (Tsintziloni and Panagiotara 2015). Integral to the rise of communal initiatives has also been the rise of communal forums. Such forums manifest either as seminars or as "talk backs," where people can become educated about the performances they are attending. These events foster open discussion on socially critical topics and on the role of the arts in previously marginalized communities, such as the queer community in Greece, the homeless, or the immigrants and political refugees who make their way to the European Union by way of Greek shores.

Before we take our second step in this exploration, it is important to contextualize the observations made thus far as being in strong opposition to the common narrative, often circulated about crises, that economic hardship offers opportunity for the avant-garde arts to flourish. Instead, I would like our next step to work to expose the devaluation of bodies, the hardship imposed upon bodies, and the lack of regard for the art of dance, which required dancers and choreographers to take urgent action. Delving into this exploration, the forward-backwardness of the protest action begins to appear as more than a choreographic allegory for the state of dance in Greece. Rather, the backward walking becomes representative of the often futile attempts of people working in dance to move forward. That is, protest actions seem to either go nowhere or land dancers right back where they started.

Devalued Bodies: The State of Dance Education in Greece

The perceived backwardness characteristic of the state of dance in Greece, which was partially summed up in the demands of the UWFD protest, can be further supported by considering the position of dance in the hierarchy of Greek education. At this moment of writing (2019), dance is still not recognized as a university-level discipline; instead, postsecondary school training is offered primarily in private conservatories and in one public institution sponsored by the state.

In order to become a professional dancer and/or dance teacher, a student applies either to the National School of Dance in Athens (the most prestigious public school for higher education in dance in Greece) or to a privately owned dance school. All students participate in entry and certification exams, validated by the Ministry of Culture; these exams are judged by a ministry-appointed committee of practitioners and scholars. The dance scholars serving in these committees have usually obtained terminal degrees abroad (MFAs or PhDs). The degree awarded at the end of the three years of study at one of the professional dance schools is not equivalent to a BA or BFA degree but is instead considered a professional diploma. This immediately creates an issue for practitioners, as many of them choose to further their studies and gain advanced degrees abroad. After dancers return to Greece, however, their degrees are not recognized, because graduate degrees cannot be awarded to people who do not hold a university-level diploma. This results in overqualified workers whose expertise is not reflected in their wage range.

The conditions of employment for laborers in the field of dance in Greece have always been characterized by low wages and professional precariousness, but during the crisis the conditions worsened incomparably. A choreographer and teacher of contemporary dance who holds an MFA degree and has worked both in professional dance schools and as a dance teacher in public high schools spoke with me in confidence about her experience.[4] In one of the high schools, she could not be appointed as regular faculty because her degree in dance was not recognized as a "higher education degree," so she was asked to reapply for the job every year. In 2013, when she reapplied for the coming academic year, the school informed her that due to budgetary cuts she would now have to be paid by the hour at the rate of three euros per hour. Based on the exchange rate at the time, this amount roughly equaled four US dollars. There was no additional coverage provided on top of the hourly rate, not even for transportation expenses.

At the height of the crisis, dance studios faced a similar situation, as did some professional dance schools. Wages for dance teachers were always rather low, averaging ten to fifteen euros per hour (roughly thirteen to twenty dollars), but during the crisis they dropped even lower or were rendered conditional, based on the studio's monthly income and enrollment rosters. The budget cuts also impacted the Ministry of Culture's exam committees and for a while threatened the cancellation of entry and certification exams, which would jeopardize the already precarious career paths of hundreds of young dancers.

Conditional pay has also been a reality for some dancers working as performers. As another dancer confided to me, some choreographers did not pay their dancers, nor did they cover insurance for them, yet they still expected them to be available around the clock to attend rehearsals. These choreographers were intolerant of the fact that, in order to survive, dancers had other job commitments on the side. According to my informant, some of his peers took on two or even three additional jobs to cover their living expenses. There has always been a need for additional jobs in the Greek dance scene (most dancers and choreographers are also dance teachers), which is a common situation in the United States and in many countries in Europe. However, the extremely low wage range during the crisis pushed dancers to additional jobs often not related to their profession, which resulted in more strain on their bodies and thus makes them more prone to injuries.

All these examples attest to the institutionally perceived dispensability of dance in Greece but contrast, interestingly, with the observed rise in physical exercise and dancing that has been noted by some Greek dance scholars during the crisis. Indicatively, dance scholar Ioanna Tzartzani noted a shift in physical engagement offstage. As she argues, there has been a rise of people becoming more and more involved in physical activities such as cycling and running, a trend that has emerged during the crisis years: "As a low-budget and easy to practice sport, running is probably the most popular activity. Indicatively, more than 10 different popular rallies have been launched during the 'crisis years.' . . . Besides the apparent antidepressant role of exercise, at the hormonal level, taking action and regaining control over one's body also appears as a (semi-)conscious reaction to the surrounding chaotic reality" (Tzartzani 2014, 43). This embodied reaction to the chaotic economic reality seems to contrast with the institutional disregard for bodies evident in the disenfranchisement of dance and demonstrates a wider interest in reclaiming embodied agency by the general population. Nondancers similarly have been forced to take on multiple jobs, have had to deal with changes in public health insurance policies, and often have been faced with increased incidents of violence (either as the result of uprisings and lootings or in confrontations with extremist groups such as the Golden Dawn), all of which have a direct impact on one's body. It is not just dancers who advocate for bodily agency and support; other people have also decided to care for their bodies after realizing that their bodies are their only stable referent in the constantly fluctuating landscape of the crisis.

There is an indisputable resonance between the heightened investment in physical activity as a means by which individuals choose to try and cope with the crisis and subsequent imposed austerity, and the protests themselves, which have primarily been composed of embodied actions. Thus, circling back to the protest that opened this essay, dancers' investment in making public the act of walking backward becomes all the more symbolic as it actively calls for the visibilization of the undervaluation of bodies not just of dancers but of the general public more broadly.

From the Streets to the Stage:
Strategies for Choreographing the Crisis

Having discussed the working conditions that the crisis has created for artists
and the devaluation of bodies that ensued as a result of the imposed budget cuts
offstage, I now consider how these topics have been explored in performances
onstage in Athens. Between 2013 and 2015 there were many works concerned
with the aftermath of the crisis and its effect on human relations. Three of the
works that stood out were Artemis Lampiri's *META* (AFTER, 2014, 2015),
Syndram Dance Company's *Fragile Nothing* (2014), and Amalgama Dance
Company's *On the Seesaw* (2014). All three of these works explore the disorientation brought about by the crisis. By briefly looking at excerpts from each
of these productions, I question how the choreographic approaches employed
in each work suggest strategies for navigating forward-backwardness and promote embodied agency at a time when bodies are devalued, disenfranchised,
and ignored by the state.

META is a piece for two to four dancers, all female. (In some stagings it
was presented with two performers, whereas the full version of the piece
was created for four.) In the staging that I attended at the Arc for Dance 6 //
NETWORKing Festival (May 2014), there were two performers. They started
at the back of an otherwise empty stage. One performer is lying on her side
with her knees close to her chest, feet flexed. Her hands are shaped into tight
fists with her knuckles facing the audience, arms bent ninety degrees at the
elbow. She appears frozen in a sideways seated position. Her coperformer is
standing next to her with one leg placed slightly forward, as if she has just
taken a step. She also appears frozen. After a few moments of stillness the
dancer on the floor slowly straightens one leg and directs one of her elbows to
the floor so that her arm now supports her head. The other responds to this
change by taking another slow step forward.

The piece progresses at a similar slow pace at first, but then the dancers
gradually transition to poses that involve some weight sharing. For instance,
they lock their wrists to create a hold so they can help each other transition
from the floor to a standing position or have one dancer become the basis for
the other to climb on the first dancer's back. Throughout all these sequences
their hands remain in tight fists and their faces are expressionless. Even at
moments when they perform sequences with one another, they seem to gaze
past each other, thus not allowing the audience to attach any relational meaning to their partnering.

The reason for this choreographic choice is to communicate an overarching
sense of numbness and shock, which lay at the core of the piece's narrative. As

FIGURE 39. The promotional flyer for *META* handed out at the Arc for Dance 6 // NETWORKing Festival, 2014. (Personal archive of the author)

the program notes describe it: "META is a dance piece that deals with the state of being, straight after a shocking experience, a big fight, when we realize that life goes on without us and redefine ourselves. META is a moving picture of two women, of two of the survivors, with the tension of no intention of moving forward" (Lampiri 2014). While there is no direct connection to the crisis in this description, the condition of shock and attempted recovery is a very familiar crisis scenario, as discussed above by Klein (2007, 2013). The choreographic strategy employed in this piece to achieve the reference to shock revolves around a unique movement vocabulary, as the dancers maintain their tight fists and flexed feet for the majority of the performance. This posturing communicates an uncomfortable sense of stiffness that renders the performers unrelatable and at times almost alien.

An alternative approach to the embodiment of alienation in human relations was taken by Syndram Dance Company and choreographer Chrysiis Liatziviry in the work *Fragile Nothing*. In this work, alienation is paired with isolation, as the piece primarily focuses on the lack of meaningful relationships during the crisis. In this piece, created for four performers (three female and one male), there are no set characters, and no relationships form between any of the dancers. The scenes appear deliberately fragmentary in order to obscure the possibility of working out a linear narrative that encompasses the performance from beginning to end. Some of the most striking imagery of this performance comes from the opening of the piece.

The stage is set as a house on the move. Boxes are scattered around the stage. The four performers start at different parts of the stage. Their focus is inward; they are not looking around them. They maintain an internal focus, almost as if they do not want to be seen. Some of them utilize a stack of boxes, curling beside it and hiding from the audience's view. They deliberately remain in the dark parts of the stage, avoiding the light. A woman laughs in a corner. A man struggles as if fighting an invisible opponent. Another dancer drops to the floor. A figure at the back pushes a stack of boxes; she is pushing and going nowhere. She pauses; the laughter persists. Each performer is in his or her own world, not facing each other, battling their own demons, each engaging in their own neurosis. Trying to stand, they repeatedly fall down. The laughter turns maniacal and escalates to crying. The other dancers stare into the void, speechless, engaging in the same routine over and over again, like four shadows of Sisyphus. Their lips move and shape voiceless words. The silence builds into indignation until one dancer yells, "Stop!" Everyone ignores her and keeps going. In the corner, another dancer hits her palm maniacally, her breath clearly audible from the exhaustion of countless repetitions.

The piece continues in a similar tone as the dancers come together momentarily in group sequences only to break apart again and highlight individuality and a sense of isolation. Even though four performers share the stage, they continually seem absorbed in their individual worries, almost unaware of what else is happening around them. They are in a constant state of motion that gradually results in physical exhaustion and becomes visible through the expanding sweat stains on their clothes and their loud panting, which increases in tempo as the performance progresses. Sporadically throughout the performance they pause to express their indignation by morphing their faces into silent screams of agony.

The choreographic strategy employed in *Fragile Nothing* presents the dancers' bodily tension and indignation as volatile suppressed energy. The viewer constantly expects that energy to blow up, yet it never does. We see the performers morphing their faces into screams, yet we hear no sound. As an audience member, I found this to be an extremely effective, albeit frustrating, strategy, as I felt the tension constantly building without any satisfactory release. In a 2014 interview with Liatziviry, I commented on how I perceived the piece as a chaotic environment that deliberately highlights a state of constant nonarrival. She confirmed that this was indeed a deliberate choice: "We decided to frame

FIGURE 40. A still image from *Fragile Nothing*, 2014. Dancers (*left to right*) Sophia Kyriazidou, Eleni Lagadinou, and Yannis Polyzos. (Photograph by Elpida Tempou)

the performance as a house on the move not because we are moving out but to indicate this state of being in flux" (Liatziviry 2014, translated by the author). She remarked that people who experience this sense of flux either seclude themselves or react soundlessly, which was mirrored in the choreography. The sense of soundless aggression, agony, self-harm, and depression present in the choreography was the result of observational research conducted by Liatziviry and the performers in public spaces and offices. Thus, the performance was an embodied culmination of their research findings, which produced a framework for contextualizing the sociopolitical landscape during the crisis.

The third example, which provides a different approach to choreographing the crisis and theorizing alienation, is *On the Seesaw*, a work by Amalgama Dance Company, directed by choreographer Maria Gorgia. From 2011 to 2014 Gorgia created a trilogy of works that explored Greek subjectivity, focusing both on national identity and gender identity, from the establishment of the independent Greek state (1830) until the present. *On the Seesaw*, a duet for a man and a woman, was the third piece of the trilogy and could be thought of as a continuation of the two solo pieces that preceded it.[5]

Contrary to the two examples discussed thus far, which each presented a creative exploration of alienation and the impact of the crisis on human relations, *On the Seesaw* is presented first and foremost as an embodied exploration of political theory and of discourses of precariousness and devaluation, thus proposing a theoretical framework for contextualizing the crisis. The program describes the dance as follows:

> A man and a woman act and coexist in a space where the protagonists are a series of computer hardware equipment. They are "precariats." Insecurity, anxiety, fear, anger, resentment, short-term thinking, information overload, and online addiction have taken over them completely. . . . Even though the primary web [of the work] stems from the book *Declaration* by Hardt and Negri, and the second sources are *The Precariat: The New Dangerous Class* by Guy Standing and *Precarious Life* by Judith Butler, the new work *On the Seesaw* focuses primarily on highlighting the issue and leaving open a window for suggestions on how to resolve it. (Gorgia 2014, translated by the author)

In this instance, the choreographic approach is closely informed by political theory, and the performers become characters who navigate the range of shifting subjectivities theorized by Michael Hardt and Antonio Negri in *Declaration*:

> The triumph of neoliberalism and its crisis have shifted the terms of economic and political life, but they have also operated a social anthropological transformation fabricating new figures of subjectivity. The hegemony of finance and the banks has produced the *indebted*. Control over information and communication has created the *mediatized*. The security regime and the generalized state of exception have constructed a figure prey to fear and yearning for protection—the *securitized*. And the corruption of democracy has forged a strange depoliticized figure, the *represented*. These subjective figures constitute the social terrain on which—and against which—movements of resistance and rebellion must act. (2012, 9)

The four different types of subjectivities introduced in *Declaration*—the mediatized, the indebted, the securitized, and the represented—are enacted in Gorgia's *On the Seesaw*. Each becomes an actual person and their defining characteristics are danced in exaggerated form in order to make these subjectivities legible and open to critical interpretation.

The stage is full of old computer hardware equipment, which the dancers manipulate to create furniture (such as a recliner made out of laptops and old printers), a seesaw (made out of a circuit board), and even an imaginary dog named Jack (a monitor "taken on a walk" by its dangling cable). The presence of computer hardware as the primary props in this performance puts emphasis on the subjectivity of the mediatized and highlights the subsequent alienation that the constant use of social media brings about for users. As the performance progresses, the dancers' movements become more and more cyborgian and robot-like—a transformation that hints at the subjectivities of the securitized and the indebted, who are driven by fear and doubt. Fear lies at the core of the embodiment of the represented, which is portrayed as a transaction between the female performer, who becomes Red Riding Hood, and the male performer, who becomes the Wolf—Red Riding Hood fearfully feeds votes to the Wolf.

Weaving these subjectivities together, the dance makes direct references to images commonly encountered during the crisis. Instances of conflict are generated between the performers, who are repeatedly seen fighting and yelling vulgar swear words at one another. In fact, the performance begins with the dancers verbally directing their indignation toward the audience while they are lounging on computer hardware equipment, which they periodically reposition into new shapes. Gradually they turn against one another, which eventually becomes a recurring trope in the performance and ultimately the way that the piece ends. The dancers are balancing one another on a seesaw, and the balance is disrupted by loud yelling, during which the person on the higher end of the seesaw takes a turn blaming the person on the lower end and vice versa, up and down, until the lights go out.

As was true with the previous examples, the dancers in *On the Seesaw* do not follow a narrative plot, nor is their relationship fixed with any labels. Instead, everything is constantly in flux. This flux relates to the alienation resonant in the other works as well; however, the form that alienation takes here is varied and manifold. In *On the Seesaw,* disorientation manifests either as a possible lack of trust in the system of representation or as hypnotization by the media, which prevents physical contact. Other potential manifestations include the indignation that leads to repetitive fights and the fear that leads to recalcitrant isolation. In fact, the emotional and financial stresses that are the result of the crisis and subsequent austerity measures manifest in isolation because people do not have the financial means to engage in extracurricular activities anymore— possibly even including dance. So the embodiment of states of isolation on-stage is profoundly moving for the profession as a whole.

The affective dimensions of the representational responses to austerity theorized in these three performance examples together highlight isolation, indignation, anger, and fear as the primary traits that have emerged during the crisis. All three pieces engage with disoriented subjects who are in flux. Each also manifests a state of nonarrival. The choreographic and dramaturgical strategies employed, such as participant observation or the embodiment of political theory, ground dance as a site of embodied agency and simultaneously challenge its current disavowal in the hierarchy of Greek education.

Reviewing the choreographic strategies encountered in these three pieces in light of the overall state of dance in Greece, I would argue that these works manage to challenge dance's devaluation through laying bare the effects that the crisis has had not just on the emotional aspects of human relations but also on the corporeal dimensions of those relations. By highlighting isolation, alienation, the potential of a cyborgian transformation of the mediatized, and what happens behind closed doors (such as the violence and self-harm suggested in *Fragile Nothing*), these works emit a loud cry for action.

Conclusion: Facing Forward

These are our final steps together. During our brief walk through the Athenian streets and across Athenian stages we followed dancing and nondancing bodies and focused on some of the struggles that subjects in crisis encounter. As we are taking our last few steps, I invite you to follow me again, this time in my capacity as a dance scholar.

Writing about bodies in crisis and the crisis of devalued bodies can itself have an alienating effect similar to the one problematized by the choreographers in the three pieces discussed. As a reader, you may encounter the experiences of research subjects and informants in a country that may seem remote. In the tight time frame of the two years between 2013 and 2015 that I investigated in this essay, the dancers and audience members whom I discuss here experienced disorientation and devaluation, and some of them consequently experienced alienation as their friends withdrew and isolated themselves. The one stable referent and common ground for all of them, however, was their bodies, which they engaged overtly during the crisis through techniques of self-care and through concerted efforts at physical activity.

The dancers' activism on the Athenian streets and the transfer of social critique to the Athenian stages became the means by which individuals tried to navigate the social landscape and question their relationships to sociopolitical forces. Thus, performances have been reclaiming embodied agency by actively shaping an affective discourse and educating audiences while at the same time calling on those audiences to problematize and question the devaluation of dance and of bodies more broadly. In doing so, such performances on the street and the stage open up critical space for inquiry that had not been previously available, in part due to the lack of respect for dance in higher education and resultant lack of academic discourse on dance in Greece. Through making these case studies available for analysis, I hope to shed light on a previously marginalized area of research in dance scholarship, that of the Greek contemporary dance scene, but also to propose a framework for analyzing the impact of austerity not just on dance practices but also on a very real, corporeal, and material bodily level.

Let us now take the final step backward. I invite you to momentarily put down this book or turn away from your computer screen and fully focus on the act of taking this step. It is a slow and meticulous process. You cannot rely on your vision, so this step requires a heightened state of awareness of yourself in relation to your surroundings or in relation to others who share the space with you. For a moment you may also feel disoriented as you experience space differently. Your agency, based on your position in the world at the moment when you are completing this action, is shaped accordingly. This step could be an act of solidarity or of resistance or an urgent call to action. Or it could be all three, combined in one step. Take it.

Notes

1. The complete list of demands is as follows: "(1) social insurance for dancers, taking into account the nature of the profession; (2) incorporation of dance in seasonal professions; (3) acknowledgment of the professional studies of dance as a higher-education degree equivalent to a university degree; (4) inclusion of dance classes in elementary and secondary education; (5) financial subsidization for the production of artistic work, research, and educational work in dance; (6) founding of an institution for dance; and (7) founding of a public dance university" (Kemmos 2016, translated by the author).

2. I undertook the majority of my ethnographic research in Athens between 2013 and 2016. As the capital of Greece, Athens is the main site of artistic activity in the nation, and most contemporary dance companies are based there, arguably shaping broader trends and movements in Greece as a whole.

3. Greece was the first country to receive a bailout agreement from the International Monetary Fund (IMF), the Eurogroup, and the European Central Bank, in 2010. This agreement was conditional on a memorandum that introduced the first round of austerity measures in 2010, with two more to follow in 2012 and 2015.

4. Names have deliberately been omitted here to maintain the anonymity of the source. No citations are provided for the same reason.

5. The first work in the trilogy, titled *The Mattress* (*Το Στρώμα*), explored masculinity in parallel with the history of the Greek state from its establishment in the mid-1800s to 2011, when the piece premiered. It was a solo for a male dancer, who performed with a mattress as a metaphor for the spatial confines of both the nation-state and the home. The second piece, titled *Hidden in the Olive Groves* (*Κρυμμένη στους Ελαιώνες*), premiered in 2012 (restaged in 2014) and revolved around a female solo protagonist, who engaged primarily with the history of enfranchisement of Greek women.

Works Cited

Fessa-Emmanouel, Eleni, ed. 2004. *Χορός και Θέατρο* [Dance and theater]. Athens: Efessos.

Gorgia, Maria. 2014. Program notes for *On the Seesaw (Στη Τραμπάλα)*. Amalgama Dance Company, Rabbithole Theater, Athens, February 8.

Gotsi, Georgia. 2012. "Beyond 'Home Identity'? Immigrant Voices in Contemporary Greek Fiction." *Journal of Modern Greek Studies* 30 (2): 155–89.

Gourgouris, Stathis. 1996. *Dream Nation: Enlightenment, Colonization and the Institution of Modern Greece.* Palo Alto, CA: Stanford University Press.

Grigoriou, Maro, and Angelos Mirayias. 2004. *Χορός* / Dance. Athens: KOAN Books, Greek Choreographers Association.

Hardt, Michael, and Antonio Negri. 2012. *Declaration.* Argo Navis.

Herzfeld, Michael. 1986. *Ours Once More: Folklore, Ideology and the Making of Modern Greece.* New York: Pella Publishing.

Kemmos, Yannis. 2016. *Οπισθοπορεία διαμαρτυρίας από χορευτές στο κέντρο της Αθήνας* [Backward protest from dancers in the center of Athens]. March 8. http://www.news beast.gr/greece/arthro/2162921/opisthoporia-diamartirias-apo-choreftes-sto-kentro -tis-athinas.

Klein, Naomi. 2007. *The Shock Doctrine.* London: Penguin Books.

———. 2013. "Is Greece in Shock?" *Eleftherotypia.* April 26. Accessed July 11, 2014. http://www.enetenglish.gr/?i=news.en.article&id=766.

Lampiri, Artemis. 2014. "Arc for Dance 6 // NETWORKing." Program notes for *META.* MAN Dance Company, Syghrono Theatro, Athens, May 3.

Liatziviry, Chrysiis. 2014. Interview with the author. March 5.

Rigos, Konstantinos. 2010. *Dance Theatre Oktana—10 Years.* Athens: Kastaniotis.

Tsintziloni, Steriani, and Betina Panagiotara. 2015. "A Shifting Landscape: Contemporary Greek Dance and Conditions of Crisis." *Journal of Greek Media & Culture* 1 (1): 29–45.

Tzartzani, Ioanna. 2014. "Embodying the Crisis: The Body as a Site of Resistance in Post-bailout Greece." *Choros International Journal* 3 (Spring): 40–49.

Zervou, Natalie. 2017. "Rethinking Fragile Landscapes during the Greek Crisis: Precarious Aesthetics and Methodologies in Athenian Dance Performances." *Research in Drama Education: The Journal of Applied Theatre and Performance* 22 (1): 104–15.

Virtuosities

Virtuosity is typically understood as a performance quality that exceeds the norm for trained dancers in a style or genre. The two essays in this section syncopate the rhythm of the keywords that organize *Futures of Dance Studies* and deploy the idea of virtuosity to riff on keywords titling other sections, especially desires and economics. How might the virtuosic technique of Romantic ballet embody raced and gendered norms linked to the imperial capitalism of nineteenth-century France? How might contemporary choreographers expose and explode the ideal of virtuosity?

Echoing Daniel Callahan's query, Rebecca Chaleff opens her essay with the statement that "ballet has a new problem that's actually very old." In "Dance of the Undead: The Wilis' Imperial Legacy," Chaleff defines the problem as the intertwined racism and sexism of the form. Building on Susan Foster's research, she interrogates "the innovations of ballet technique during the Romantic era as a reflection and protraction of imperial politics in order to analyze how ballet works through the body to craft durable yet flexible performances of whiteness that morph over time." In Chaleff's reading of *Giselle* (1842), France's conquest of Algiers in 1830 and Théophile Gautier's reference to Myrtha, the leader of the Wilis, as queen of a *petit empire* align the Wilis with colonized subjects, eroticized and racialized others. The Wilis' otherness signifies on multiple levels, for they also are linked to the sexual availability of the prostitute and the queerness of the vampire (the linguistic source for their name). Paradoxically both powerful and powerless, the Wilis haunt the ballet stage, "marking the atemporal ruptures of performance."

If the virtuosity of the Romantic ballet is taken for granted, that is not the case in contemporary choreography. In "Disavowing Virtuosity, Performing Aspiration: Choreographies of Anticlimax in the Work of Yve Laris Cohen, Narcissister, and John Jasperse," Ariel Osterweis profiles three artists who share an aesthetic and an ethic, although each rejects virtuosity in a different way. Trans choreographer Laris Cohen works with objects and tasks in alternative theaters, as well as in gallery and museum spaces. In several works, Laris Cohen performs movements from *Giselle*. For example, in *Duke* (2010) Laris Cohen quotes a passage from the Romantic ballet after moving planks and other performers around the stage, demonstrating that "the same amount of care is given to lifting wooden planks as is given to lifting fleshly humans." Like Laris Cohen, Narcissister performs in galleries and clubs, as well as in experimental dance venues. Always masked, her performances deconstruct the hypervisibility and hypersexuality of the black woman by staging radical, even perverse acts of self-care. In *Every Woman* (2010) she begins nearly nude, then removes articles of clothing from her mouth, vagina, and anus to dress herself. John Jasperse, a more established choreographer than Laris Cohen and Narcissister, developed strategies strikingly parallel to their works in *Within between* (2014). Deconstructing ballet and black vernacular forms, Jasperse joins Laris Cohen and Narcissister "in referencing culturally specific dance techniques within wider experimental, queer choreographic contexts that critique capitalist exploitation."

In one sense, the works described by Osterweis enact a critique of theatrical dance similar to that articulated by Chaleff. Artists and scholars often work in parallel, evident not only in this section but also in the essays by Laura Karreman, Giulia Vittori, VK Preston, and Natalie Zervou. The essays collected in *Futures of Dance Studies* resonate with one another in myriad ways: none can be subsumed under only one keyword.

Dance of the Undead

The Wilis' Imperial Legacy

REBECCA CHALEFF

Ballet has a new problem that's actually very old. Questions of race and gender have been raised repeatedly among ballet's lovers and critics over the past decade. In 2007 Gia Kourlas's now infamous article, "Where Are All the Black Swans?," shook the dance world by highlighting the remarkable lack of black dancers in internationally renowned ballet companies. The noticeable absence of female ballet choreographers has also become a popular topic of debate. In 2017 there was heated discussion surrounding Alexei Ratmansky's problematic assertion that the male domination of the field is simply not a worthwhile concern (Sulcas 2017). It would be unfair to say that ballet companies have not sought remedies to these systemic problems. Some feature programs with works exclusively by female choreographers. And dancers of color, such as Misty Copeland, have continued to rise through the ranks. But these instances are often perceived, and rightly so, as the exception rather than the rule; the celebration of Copeland's exceptionalism speaks to the persistent exclusion rather than the inclusion of dancers of color. As Sara Ahmed (2007) has argued, such emphases on certain forms of "diversity" ultimately reinforce the centrality of whiteness in the field.

These systemic problems are deeply engrained in ballet's historical relationship with power. In *Choreographing Empathy: Kinesthesia in Performance*, Susan Leigh Foster argues that ballet's form, notation, and global dissemination are intrinsically linked with the imperatives of European colonialism. Notation positioned the body of the ballet master as the central point of an abstract space that extended outward and introduced "the world's dancers to the finest accomplishments of a colonial power" (Foster 2011, 32). Foster's explanation of how structure, notation, and technique in ballet conditioned a dancer's physical and psychological orientation to the colonies is fundamental to my approach. Dance notation initiated a phenomenological becoming by, in Ahmed's words,

415

"making whiteness worldly" so that whiteness becomes "the very 'what' that cues the world" (2007, 150). This essay considers the dissemination of imperial legacies, including whiteness, through performances that exceed the bounds of visual and temporal fixity. I interrogate the innovations of ballet technique during the Romantic era as a reflection and protraction of imperial politics in order to analyze how ballet works through the body to craft durable yet flexible performances of whiteness that morph over time.

The critical move I propose here is to include France's colonial history within our understanding of the ballerina's complex and seemingly paradoxical performance of race and gender. While France embarked on its second colonial empire, initiated with the conquest of Algiers in 1830, the Romantic ballets portrayed racialized otherness and the sanctity of white womanhood through the singular body of the ballerina and the collective body of the corps de ballet. But within the history of the ballet blanc, the name of which emphasizes the centrality of whiteness, this move is difficult to make. How can whiteness double as racialized otherness? Once the ballerinas powder their already pale skin to portray an ethereal sylph or ghostly Wili, they appear even whiter. Perhaps it is in response to their performance of otherness that they literally lay their whiteness on so thick; the ballerina's "too white" appearance indicates that she is, in Homi Bhabha's words, "almost the same, but not white" ([1994] 2004, 128). The ballerina's entangled choreography of race, gender, and sexuality enfolds conventional representations of otherness within her dancing such that her performance mobilizes abjection to secure the unmarked status of whiteness as an "imperial enterprise" (Dyer 1997, 22). Robin Bernstein argues that whiteness is characterized by "the ability to retain racial meanings but hide them under claims of holy obliviousness," and I agree (2011, 8). Here I consider racial meaning deployed across the ballerina's blanched flesh to expose abjection within carefully choreographed performances of whiteness.

Focusing on the historical convergence of imperial economies with cultural conventions embedded within ballet technique and choreography, this essay examines the intersectional geneses of ballet's racism and sexism. Balletic conventions conflate race, gender, and sexuality with categorical abjection; by the nature of their embeddedness, these conventions move across time, circulating prolifically through the medium of performance. Social and political economic relations of imperial capitalism were thus perpetuated by the bodies that rehearsed the ideologies of imperial enterprise through their perfection of technique. Reading ballet against its own grain for what it hides and gives away simultaneously, I analyze the Wilis of the ballet *Giselle* (1842), the story of a young girl with a weak heart who loves to dance. Giselle is deceived by Prince Albrecht, and her despair proves too much to bear; in what appears to be a fit of madness, hysteria, or syphilitic psychosis, Giselle dances until she collapses in death. The ballet follows Giselle to her afterlife, where she is transformed into a Wili and ruled beyond the grave by Myrtha, the queen of a cadaverous caste of women.

I am interested in the Wilis as disembodied specters of dance history that become reembodied *as* disembodied each time they are danced. Recalling the original title and exploring the "or" of *Giselle, ou les Wilis*, we might consider the lasting impact of the undead women who haunt the canon through their dual performances of power and powerlessness. In many ways, the Wilis represent the idealized Romantic ballerina—not unlike the mysterious, ephemeral, and ethereal sylphs who preceded them both in live performance and in widely circulated lithographs. Yet the Wilis also diverge wildly from the norms of the period to perform a sexualized gender deviance that indicates the racialization of their coven. The Wilis' dancing illustrates how the movements of history become inscribed on the very bodies that are situated simultaneously within and outside linear time through their haunting performance and their performance of haunting. The choreopolitics of capital and colonialism are refracted through the Wilis, who both perform and perpetuate the violence of the institution that produced them. As undead mutations of the prima ballerina, the Wilis are positioned outside the bounds of history—structurally reproduced effigies that body forth both imperial capitalism's forceful dissemination and the deviants that threatened its supremacy (Roach 1996, 36). Positioned within the ballet as moving independently of history and time, these undead ballerinas nevertheless irrupt into it, thereby marking the atemporal ruptures of performance.

How White Ballerinas Became Black

Within the field of dance history, French Romanticism is frequently interpreted as a prime example of ballet's bond with a capitalist economy. The Romantic era marked a transformation in ballet dancing and choreography due in large part to the changing culture of the Paris Opéra and its school. Although the great ballerinas continued to "emerge from the theatrical clans that had survived from the eighteenth century" (Garafola 1985–86, 36), beginning in 1821 the Opéra's School of Dance admitted up to sixty children annually, many from impoverished families who hoped for financial profit and class mobility for their children supported by the artistic institution (Guest 1966, 23). These pupils earned the nickname *petits rats* for the way they rushed about backstage, working for the lowest wages until they assumed the title of artist. Their excessive abundance allowed the School of Dance to produce large pools of young dancers. The language of excess works on two correlating levels: within

Marxian discourse, as characteristic of the mass-produced commodity; and within feminist discourse, as representative of sexualized and racialized bodies.

The excess of ballerinas, in both senses of the term, precipitated competition within the ranks of the company and spurred the development of their technique and virtuosity, both of which underscored their reproducibility and commodification. The introduction of codified technique in the dancer's training in the early to mid-nineteenth century sculpted dancers into artists who were both skillful and replicable. Dancers were no longer taught ballet technique in individual and personal lessons but fit within large classes that taught standardized forms of training. As Foster explains, the drawings of correct placement by Italian dancing master Carlo Blasis in *An Elementary Treatise upon the Theory and Practice of the Art of Dancing* align the dancers' limbs with geometric axes. These lines became "internalized, embedded within the flesh, with the musculature wrapping around it," so that ballet notation could be both absorbed and reproduced by the body and its movements (Foster 2011, 40). Technique provided physically embedded templates that ensured the ballerina's marketability for public consumption.

But the inscription of technique on and in the body also signaled a corporeal synchronization of liberal and imperial capitalisms. Ballet's geometries could also be utilized to "docilize the foreign forms" that fascinated European choreographers, "giving them intrigue and novelty while assimilating them into a standardized style of execution" (Foster 2011, 42). Exotic settings, peoples, and customs (Gypsy, Native American, Caribbean, etc.) were reduced to pastiche and assimilated within ballet's codified positions. Technique thus served as a choreographic proxy that "imbued each ballet with local color while simultaneously displaying the ballet's mastery over all forms" (42). In this description, a paradox emerges: the dancer was required to perform the role of the exotic other while simultaneously embodying the mastery of the European technique that facilitated her control over a foreign form. The effects of a capitalist economy that commodified the dancer also supported an imperial economy premised on European supremacy. The dancer's association with exoticism was also premised on her presumptive sexual availability. Marxian dance historians have argued that the dancer's commodification was precipitated by her prostitution. Under the directorship of Dr. Louis-Désiré Véron (1831–35), the Paris Opéra transitioned from being a state-sponsored enterprise to one that relied predominantly on private sources of funding and support. This shift in structure placed the subscribers and spectators in an unprecedented position of power and influence (Garafola 1985–86, 35). As a result, the Opéra produced work that catered to the desires of its patrons and critics. Dr. Véron created the Foyer de la Danse, an exclusive backstage salon where patrons were invited to mingle with the female dancers before or after a performance. The Foyer de la Danse quickly evolved into an informal system of prostitution that conflated spectatorship with sexual patronage. "Nowhere," Lynn Garafola writes, "was the clash . . . between the idealized femininity of balletic ideology and the reality of female exploitation so striking as in the Opéra's backstage corridors" (1985–86, 36).

Specifically within the context of mid-nineteenth-century Paris, the ballerina's prostitution bound her with racialized abjection—an association that, I argue, is foundational to the politics of her performance at the same time that her whiteness appears to overpower her persona. As Sander L. Gilman (1985) argues in "Black Bodies, White Bodies: Toward an Iconography of Female Sexuality in Late Nineteenth-Century Art, Medicine, and Literature," the conflation of female prostitution and racialized alterity became increasingly conventional throughout the nineteenth century. Gilman claims that the association of race and prostitution was exacerbated by Western Europe's fascination with the genitalia of Khoikhoi women, who were called Hottentots by European colonizers.[1] This fascination coalesced intensely on Sarah Baartman, who arrived in Paris in 1814. Gilman interrogates the biases of those who examined and displayed the Khoikhoi "ethnographic subject" to substantiate the popular presumption that African women were hypersexual because their buttocks and genitals were deemed excessive. By the middle of the century, the association between blackness, excess, and sexuality became commonplace, even common sense; it extended from African women to any woman rendered abject due to class and/or sexuality. Per the conventions of the time, examiners and observers also described prostitutes according to markers of blackness, which they identified in the shape of the buttocks, genitalia, and facial features. Their descriptions drew an especially strong correlation between prostitutes' sexuality and deviant gender. In his critical 1837 publication, *On Prostitution in the City of Paris*, A. J. B. Parent-Duchatelet asserts that French prostitutes who appeared superficially attractive were merely deceptive, for their masculine qualities became apparent over time. As prostitutes age, he argues, their "strong jaws and cheek-bones, and their masculine aspect . . . stand out, and the face grows virile, uglier than a man's; . . . the countenance, once attractive, exhibits the full degenerate type which early grace had concealed" (quoted in Gilman 1985, 226).

Parent-Duchatelet's explication of how the prostitute's masculinity renders her abject strengthens the relationship we are charting between the European prostitute and the ballerinas of the Paris Opéra. In the new economy of Dr. Véron's Opéra, dancers sought techniques for distinction that required both the development and the concealment of characteristically masculine strength.

For the European dancers who received the same training at the School of Dance, accomplishing virtuosic skill meant meeting the standards for deceptive femininity set by famous ballerinas such as Marie Taglioni. Although Taglioni was renowned for "weaving the use of the *pointes* into the fabric of dance technique" to give the ballerina "a fairy-like quality," her performance of effortlessness was dependent on strengthening exercises that required extensive repetition (Guest 1966, 18). As Jennifer Homans describes, Taglioni's father, Filippo, committed to training his daughter all day, every day: "two hours in the morning dedicated to a series of arduous exercises, repeated many times on both legs, and two hours in the afternoon on adagio movements" (2010, 139). Before bed, Taglioni worked for another two hours exclusively on jumps. These exercises made Taglioni's body extremely muscular—even "heavy," according to Homans (140). The purpose of ballet training therefore became all the more important; having developed this impressive strength, Taglioni utilized her technique to conceal it. Ballerinas' efforts toward prestige also led them to master steps previously performed only by danseurs. Many dancers, including Taglioni, sought to distinguish themselves by emulating their male colleagues—especially Auguste Vestris—despite the fact that at this time the pirouettes and jumps performed by men were excluded from the ballerina's vocabulary.

Practically speaking, the ballerina fulfilled the image of flight through the Opéra's use of technical apparatuses. In 1822 candles were replaced by gas lighting, which produced a mellow light that could be intensified or dimmed to complement the ballerina's "delicate" visage (Beaumont 1946, xxiv). With the invention of a wooden, seesaw-like contraption, ballerinas could hover from offstage to appear as though solely supported by the fairy wings fashioned on their backs. Indeed, the seesaw is an apt metaphor for the ballerina's counterbalance of strength and effortlessness. Both the ballerina's technique and the stage technologies were premised on and emphasized the binary forces of Newtonian physics and the dialectical relation of equal and oppositional reactions. The ballerina's lightness and grace are produced through the unseen operations of offstage weightedness and force not only of the stage hand in the wings but of the ballerina's daily practice in the studio.

In addition to the ballerina's development of conventionally masculine strength, she was also detached from the sanctity of European domesticity through the choreographic conventions of the ballet blanc. The ballet blanc is defined by its second act, which is populated by otherworldly creatures—hyphenated women (half woman and half sylph or something haunting) dressed in white who occupy a space separate from the city. Lithographs from ballets of this period illustrate how the ballerina "haunted" the era that she symbolized (Garafola 1997, 2). With gauzy skirts and slender feet that scarcely touch the ground, the Romantic ballerina is depicted as inhabiting a world apart from that in which humans dwell. She is often posed by a lake or within a glen, "an exotic dwelling on the periphery of European civilization" (2). The ballerina perches on the cusp of society, perpetually beyond the reach of those who desire her: a delicate yet dangerous threat to the sanctity of Parisian society.

Situated beyond the bounds of civilization, the ballerina's moonlit glade reproduces a form of what Anne McClintock (1995) terms an "anachronistic space" of primitive time. McClintock builds on anthropologist Johannes Fabian's (1983) argument that discursive constructions of primitivity articulate a hierarchical and oppositional relationship between white Europeans and their "others." Discourses of the primitive constitute this binary by scripting the placement of the subject within time—the so-called primitives are situated as constitutively backward in time, even though they are coeval with the anthropologist or European spectator. The role of temporal discourse in categorizations of the colonial subject is crucial to McClintock's description of anachronistic space, which refers to a conflation of space and time through discourses of primitiveness that position the Other in binary opposition to modernity. Imperial progress, she writes, was "figured as a journey backward in time to an anachronistic moment of prehistory. . . . Geographic difference across *space* [was] figured as a historical difference across *time*" (1995, 40). The colonies were thus deciphered "not as socially or geographically different from Europe and thus equally valid, but as *temporally* different and thus irrevocably superannuated by history" (40). Women and members of the working class were also projected onto anachronistic space through discursive and cultural associations with temporal displacement and backwardness. In this spatiotemporal field, working women and colonial subjects alike were primed as primitive, potentially excessive, and abject. Transgressive women, McClintock explains, "stigmatized specimens of *racial* regression" and represented "the prototypes of anachronistic humans, existing in a permanently anterior time with modernity" (42). This is to say that the setting that makes a ballet a ballet blanc also establishes the implicit racialization of the blanc ballerinas through an association with primitivity. As Rebecca Schneider writes, "Because the 'primitive' is scripted according to hierarchies of race," women are historically "wrapped up in racist paradigms of symbolic displacement," and white women are "caught in an effort to control, contain, defy, or manipulate an inherent primitivism" (1997, 28). Schneider foregrounds the relationship between gender, sexuality, and race by drawing attention to the pressure on women to deny their "inherent primitivism." Most importantly, she asserts that the "primitive" is the overwriting script positioning women in gendered hierarchies (the economy of the Opéra) within racist paradigms (the economy of imperialism). Ballerinas also fall within this paradigm: the dominating sexuality of their roles implicates them in a racialized relationship with primitivity.

In nineteenth-century France, the ballerina / prostitute / *petit rat* occupied an anachronistic space within Parisian culture. This specific conflation of temporal and spatial dislocation is projected onto her performance in ballets like *Giselle*. As I will explain in the next section, it is the very proximity of the Wilis' temporally distant landscape to France's cultural center that renders their anachronistic realm dangerous; the Wilis perform the threat of the colonized other close to home. In *Giselle* the male heroes travel only as far as a graveyard to encounter the deadly Wilis. Although graveyards were built on the outskirts of Paris in the 1800s after mass graves were moved into the Catacombs, they nevertheless occupied a space directly adjacent to the city itself. The presence of Giselle's tombstone onstage in act 2 reminds the viewers that this enchanted and terrifying scene takes place in close proximity to the main metropole. The graveyard setting also ties the Wilis' deathly status to the free-floating fear of disease and contagion associated with abjection. Indeed, graveyards were constructed on the outskirts of the city precisely because Parisians, aware of the fact that dead bodies carrying disease were also toxic to the living, were afraid. Already associated with the physical and social contagion of prostitutes and racialized subjects, the deathly toxicity of the Wilis (and the *petits rats* who embodied them) was made literal and even more palpable through their association with death and resultant ghostly status. Their unique performance of feminine ethereality, therefore, signified not only the Wilis' inhabitance of a strange and enigmatic place but also their threat to the sanctity and whiteness of the domestic sphere.

How the Wilis Became White Again (and Again)

In addition to my theoretical speculation on the racialization of the ballerina in the nineteenth century, there are explicit examples from both the libretto and the choreography for *Giselle* that mark the Wilis as colonized subjects. In his own journals, librettist Théophile Gautier describes Myrtha, the leader of the Wilis, as queen of a *petit empire*. As dance historian Peter Stoneley writes, "Myrtha's ritualistic dances seem designed to establish the forest glade as *her* 'petit empire'" (2007, 31). While this narrative explicitly delegates Myrtha as warden of the colony, it also implicitly depicts the Wilis as the colonized. Stoneley also explains that Gautier's original concept of *Giselle* specified that the Wilis "feature deceased maidens from a variety of races and nations, so that a young man's encounter with them becomes a sort of murderous sexual world tour" (31). This interest in exotic maidens locates *Giselle* within the trend outlined by Foster in her description of ballet technique's mastery over foreign forms. Furthermore, this passage connects the Wilis' status as colonized subjects with the ballerina's sexual objectification. Although Gautier's collaborator, Vernoy de Saint-Georges, dissuaded him from this idea, it is productive to consider how this seed may have grown within the choreographic coding of the Wilis. To Gautier, it seems, an encounter with women from a variety of races and nations leads to sexual encounters, as though one follows naturally from the other.

As explained earlier, *Giselle* tells the story of a young girl who dances herself to death. Act 2 picks up in Giselle's afterlife as a Wili, ruled beyond the grave by Myrtha. Onstage, Myrtha and the Wilis signify a substantial shift in the ballerina's comportment. More than any other characters of this period, the Wilis exposed the masculine strength that the ballerina had concealed through the control of her technique. As female specters of intrigue and enchantment, the Wilis are sylph-like in their unearthly qualities, not to mention the wings that spring from their backs the moment their veils are removed. Dressed purely in white, lofted across the stage on wires or skimming over the ground *en pointe*, the Wilis appear to occupy two worlds at once: the worldly and the otherworldly, the living and the dead. Yet unlike the soft and dewy sylphs who preceded them, the Wilis are dangerously cryptic and unforgiving in their strength and stature. The Wilis thus perform a duality of womanhood that encompasses both danger and vulnerability. Whereas other sylphs soften their arms and wrists to appear light and waif-like, the Wilis' dances incorporate jagged gestures, deeper pliés, and repetitions that usher a trance-inducing command of the stage. This style etches the Wilis' presence onto their nocturnal terrain as clearly as their skimming motions set them aloft. As otherworldly, nonhuman, and deathly women, the Wilis haunt the stories and ballets in which they appear with a vampire-like presence that is both threatening and hypersexual. Indeed, the Wilis derive their name from the Slavic word *vila*, which translates as "vampire"; the plural, *viles*, became the Germanic spelling *wilis*, which replaces the letter *v* with a *w*. Although the Wilis are reminiscent of the sylphs often portrayed in Romantic ballets, their derivation communicates a unique violence—these ballerinas have fangs.

The Wilis originated from a Slavic legend related by German writer Heinrich Heine in his 1835 collection of essays and stories, *De l'Allemagne*. Heine's text characterizes the Wilis as affianced young maidens who died before their wedding days. More than their liminal position between allegiance to a father and allegiance to a husband, these maidens are made Wilis in death because in life they loved to dance (Beaumont 1988, 19). Dressed in bridal clothes, garlands, and sparkling jewelry, Heine's Wilis rise from the earth each night to dance feverishly in the moonlight before descending once again into their icy

graves. The terrible threat of the Wilis is enacted through their custom of kill-
ing the men who cross their paths by enchanting them into an exhausting
dance that drives them to their deaths. It is from this spell-like enchantment
that Giselle saves Albrecht, who stumbles into the Wilis' realm when he visits
her grave. As dance historian and theorist Sally Banes writes, the fact that the
Wilis "all died from 'dancing too much' hints that, while they may have died
with their virginity intact, nevertheless, they perished from excess lust" (1998,
33). The Wilis' love of dancing marks them as sexually excessive, libidinous,
and predatory. More so than the average ballerina, then, this characterization
associated the Wilis with prostitutes and—as described earlier—racialized and
gendered deviance. In the context of the mid-nineteenth century, the Wilis'
sexuality also likened them to groups of single women from working- and
middle-class backgrounds who were "beginning to cause a number of social
anxieties, including those about prostitution" (32). These anxieties developed
in response to an increasing number of unattached young women who circulated freely through both street life and bourgeois society. Even if they were not
prostitutes, such women were associated with sexual activity and disease transmission. Indeed, Giselle's madness scene is interpreted by Felicia McCarren
(1998) as the consequence of syphilis. Stoneley connects the bold sexuality of
the Wilis to their potential queerness, which "also finds an echo in the public
perceptions of dancers": "Myrtha seems also to embody a masculine fantasy of
the older woman's desire for predominance over the incoherent or undecided
young woman. . . . Perhaps Myrtha provokes the desires of the male viewer by
challenging his right to all the young women" (2007, 27, 31).

Women released from the domestic sphere held the dangerous potential to
destabilize heteronormative domesticity and the fundamental stability it provided for political and cultural control over the reproduction of the capital-
colonial relation. Indeed, as Silvia Federici explains in her reconsideration of
the Marxian concept of "primitive accumulation," the precapitalist development of commodity production introduced several significant changes in the
social position of women and the production of labor power. These changes
included the subjugation of "women's labor and women's reproductive function to the reproduction of the work force," the construction of a patriarchal
order "based upon the exclusion of women from waged-work," and the transformation of women "into a machine for the production of new workers"
(Federici 2004, 12). Women (and witches) thus posed a considerable threat to
production by partaking in wage labor and refusing their reproductive role
in the workforce. Women like the Wilis, who expressed excessive pleasure in
sexual activity and whose anachronistic setting facilitated a cross-temporal
stretch between periods of precapitalism and capitalism, were thus perceived

as dangerous to both the sanctity of female domesticity and the means of production that such civility facilitated.

The Wilis' entangled expressions of strength and (homo)sexual pleasure thus recall the transition from feudalism to capitalism by describing a structural condition of accumulation that "survives into the present" (Federici 2004, 12). It is precisely this temporal slipperiness between different periods of linear, economic progress that produces the anxiety surrounding the Wilis' haunting. As Lynda Hart argues in *Fatal Women: Lesbian Sexuality and the Mark of Aggression*, depictions of violent women facilitate the seclusion of sexual deviance to the margins of discourse and performance. "The shadow of the lesbian," Hart explains, "is laminated to the representation of women's violence. . . . [I]ndeed it is the lesbian's absent presence that both permits women's aggression to enter the specular field and defuses the full force of its threat" (1994, x). Hart's description of the relationship between lesbianism and haunting suggests that the Wilis' sexuality is also bound to their spectral status. The Wilis' deathliness thus calls attention not only to their abjection but also to their resonance within a cultural haunting that shadows the Western canon. In other words, the Wilis' queerness signifies not only their boundedness to alterity but also the boundlessness of their ghostly legacy. The contagion that the Wilis both present and absent from the stage may cohere around their status as deathly figures, but it also spreads from their performance of sexually deviant women to a more pronounced threat to the white male subject: the racialized colonial subject. Like queerness, the performance of race in *Giselle* is at once both violently apparent and violently concealed within complex conflations of variant alterities. The Wilis' sexuality and gender deviance not only contribute to their conventional association with colonial subjectivity but also conceal the complexity of their abjectness within the ambiguity of cultural convention.

The paradoxical display of alterity and normativity is bodied forth through the complex temporalities of the Wilis' movement motif, the arabesque. The arabesque was one of the most important technical developments of nineteenth-century dance, as well as one of the steps that most clearly showcased the ballerina's grounded strength. In the shape of the arabesque, one leg supports the dancer while the other leg extends in a straight line behind the body. According to Foster, the arabesque has an innately temporal quality. As a position that registers "a moment of stillness at the highest possible elevation without jumping," the arabesque contributes to the ballerina's sylph-like hovering (Foster 1998, 204). Within the pause of the arabesque reverberated a "dynamic energy generated by the suspenseful balance and the motion-filled shape of the pose" (204). This pause "allowed a moment of reflection . . . while at the same time demonstrating the compelling need to move forward" (204). The arabesque exemplifies how the ballerina's technique enabled her to convey a temporal complexity within the concrete physicality of the work of art. The arabesque also produces a useful analogy for the ballerina as a future-oriented figure. Always exceeding the present tense, the ballerina lends herself to an imperial orientation directed toward determining futurity. As an emblematic position of the Wilis, the arabesque might be interpreted as a position of mastery over new horizons, even as the Wilis are, structurally, a threatening revenant of the past. Certainly, this step orients the ballerina toward her own future within ballet history as a symbol of whiteness. The strength required to execute this position itself signifies the progress of the ballerina's technique up to this moment while pointing forward in an imperial gesture toward the future of the ballerina's legacy on a globalized stage. As we have already seen, however, the Wilis are as much revenant of a sexualized and racialized undead as they might be poised in arabesque toward an imperial future for whiteness to come. How can this paradox be sustained? As we will see, the Wilis' arabesque is slightly different from the norm, and in this minor difference lies the Wilis' precarious balance, always on the verge of threat.

Although the ballerina's use of the arabesque *en pointe* usually connotes a hovering, gliding quality, in *Giselle* the Wilis also move through arabesques in deep pliés (with their standing legs bent) that appear to skim across the stage. This step, the *arabesque voyage*, both embodies the steady forward pace of progress and exemplifies the strength of the ballerina's technique. In one scene of act 2, the corps de ballet forms phalanxes that approach and cross one another from opposite sides of the stage, locomoted by the *arabesque voyage* through a weaving pattern. The Wilis perform control over the stage through the repetition of this single movement, which appears to simultaneously stall and progress the momentum of the ballet. Although in this scene the *arabesque voyage* exemplifies the ballerina's mastery over her own body, elsewhere the plié arabesque implies the opposite. In Giselle's first dance as a Wili under Myrtha's spell, she circles maddeningly in a plié arabesque, on the verge of spiraling out of control. Whereas the *arabesque voyage* is a step that highlights a ballerina's technical control, Giselle's turns signify the character's loss of control and Myrtha's gain.[2]

These choreographies exemplify the Wilis' precarious balance between the mastery of their technique and the requirement that the body be mastered. The question might be posed as follows: Is the ballerina the master over her body, or is her body mastered by ballet? Through an imperial metaphor, this duality places dancers simultaneously in the position of the colonizer (the queens of the *petit empire*) and the colonized (as implied through their association with racialized abjection). Although, on the one hand, as the undead inhabitants of an anachronistic space the Wilis perform the role of the racialized other, they simultaneously assert a commanding performance of white, even hyperwhite, womanhood and European supremacy through their technical control. The physical rigors of technique that enabled the ballerinas of the Paris Opéra to dance beyond the parameters previously prescribed to female dancers, there-fore, also reinforced the need to regulate those bodies that threaten to slip toward abjection.

This central paradox of the Wilis' performance of power and powerless-ness may also be interpreted as a product of the Paris Opéra's sexual economy, which was cultivated through a culture of voyeurism. From this perspective, the Wilis' performance of power through acts of technical strength and threat-ening violence reproduces the violence of the fetishistic economy that produced them. This larger-scale performance of danger aligns the Wilis with the aes-thetic category of "cuteness" as defined by Sianne Ngai. Ngai describes cute-ness as "commodity fetishism, but with an extra twist" (2012, 64). Despite the fact that the Wilis precede the avant-garde (Ngai's historical focus) by nearly a century, they enact a similar cuteness through their position as commodified objects whose visage of powerlessness enables their performance of power. Ngai reminds her readers that the term "cute" itself contains a significant dual-ity. "Cute" derives from "acute" through the process of aphaeresis, "the process by which words lose initial understressed syllables to generate shorter and 'cuter' versions of themselves" (87). More than merely containing its opposite, cuteness creates an encounter with "a perceived difference in the power of the subject and object" that affectively entangles violence within intimacy (87). The cute object stimulates an acute (violent) response, mimicking the subject by foregrounding the violence of its own production. As Ngai explains, the subject feels intimate with the cute object because she or he cannot establish the other as truly other. This failure is "endemic to an aesthetic of powerless-ness" that "seems to give rise to a fantasy about the cute object's power, one epitomized by the boomeranging of the aggressive affect projected onto the object back outwards and toward the subject" (98). Eliciting violence precisely where intimacy is felt, the (a)cute reflects the spectator's sense of mastery and surrender through its dialectical performance.

Describing the Wilis within this aesthetic category helps to explain the last-ing effects of their paradoxical performance. The institutional misogyny of the Paris Opéra is embodied by the Wilis' performance of violence toward men and boomeranged (to borrow Ngai's phrase) to and from the audience through the affective residues of gendered voyeurism. This enactment of the mimetic relationship of the (a)cute within the Opéra's patriarchal culture stresses the

importance of the Wilis' gender deviance. The ballerina's employment of masculine strength in her own dancing and technique is refracted within the ballet through the Wilis' (a)cute leitmotifs, which mark them as both covertly
similar to and overtly different from the male voyeur. Onstage, the ballerina
performs a power play that uses the gendered dynamics of the institution to
subvert them. Although the Wilis' (a)cute aesthetics reveal the ballerina's potential power within commodity capitalism, they do not account for the many
associations with difference that alienate ballerinas from Parisian culture. Interpreting the Wilis solely within a mimetic, subject-object relationship as enactors
of gendered agency does not fully account for their performance of conventional conflations between gendered, sexualized, and racialized differences. The
Wilis' violence exceeds the aesthetic of the (a)cute in two important ways. First,
it contributes to the popular interpretation of the Wilis (and other groups of
cloistered women) as a homophobic representation of lesbianism. Second, it
feeds a cultural paranoia of contagion that extends through metaphors of disease from sexually aberrant to racialized bodies. These conventional markers
of otherness are disguised within the realm of suggestion to simultaneously
make visible and erase depictions of difference within dance history. Thus,
figures such as the Wilis not only carry forward the sexist and racist ideologies
that produced their characterization but also conceal those ideologies within
the cultural legacies of the Romantic ballet. The Wilis slip from century to
century through a cultural memory that lapses with conflation. Their pronounced physical performances incite embedded ideological violence.

The Wilis' temporal slipperiness does not divorce them from history or time,
as their anachronistic setting might imply, but enables them to act as critical
reminders of violent histories of dispossession and feminization. Through the
motif of the arabesque, in particular, the Wilis perform a seemingly paradoxical relationship to time and power that nevertheless remains grounded in their
historical moment. At the dawn of France's burgeoning imperial economy, the
Wilis appear as revenants of a precapitalist moment of "primitive accumulation" that bound expropriation and enslavement to the subjugation of women
through the reproduction of the workforce and the extermination of witches
in the sixteenth and seventeenth centuries (Federici 2004, 63). The Wilis perform the violence of the histories, economies, and institutions that produced
them through the menace and allure of their unconventional strength and
uncontainable sexuality. Yet while they seem to access a critique of their own
sociopolitical production, they simultaneously reproduce the conventions of
colonial-capital relations by gesturing toward the future of the ballerina as
an emblem of capitalist progress. Disguised within layers of conflations, the
Wilis' otherness and whiteness circulate, unmarked, to pose a resurgent conflict

between mastery and surrender, power and powerlessness. From this realm, they rise again. Disinterred, perhaps by the critical excavations of dance studies if not also by reperformance, they might continue to touch and embolden our contemporary conflicts within the ballet institution as we wrestle with the legacies of racialization, sexualization, imperialism, and capitalist exploitation. Ballet's old, new problem is in the archive, the repertoire, the bodies, and the ghosts, paradoxically moving with and against the grain of imperial history—the problem is, like the Wilis, haunting the stage.

Notes

1. Although Gilman's 1985 article analyzes an important association between racialized and sexualized abjection, his writing slips between racialized markers and historical periods to make generalizations that use Khoikhoi women to represent all African women in the European imagination. After the "discovery" of the Khoikhoi, the skin tone of the "Hottentot" was described not as black but as a yellowish brown. Because most racial thinking at the time was based on categories of complexion and geography, the Hottentot posed a problem for Western Europeans: even though she was from southern Africa, she could not necessarily be categorized as black. The slipperiness of Gilman's writing on associations between blackness and prostitution reinforces a conventional conflation between colonized subjects, despite differences in color, and a broad alterity that encompassed sexual abjection. For more on the distinction between black and Khoikhoi women, who were portrayed as savage, barbaric, and therefore in direct opposition to white Europeans, see Strother (1999), Merians (2001), and Hoxworth (2017).

2. My interpretation of the choreography for *Giselle* is based primarily on written accounts of the original version that attest to the significance and novelty of the arabesque in the original choreography. However, my understanding of the choreography has also been influenced by the version of *Giselle* that continues to be performed today, which survived in Russia while it was dropped from the repertoire in France. This version was edited and amended by Marius Petipa, who was renowned for the complex and challenging choreography he created for the corps de ballet. It is possible that the accentuation of the arabesque in their dances was emphasized in Petipa's revisions.

Works Cited

Ahmed, Sara. 2007. "A Phenomenology of Whiteness." *Feminist Theory* 8 (2): 149–68.

Banes, Sally. 1998. *Dancing Women: Female Bodies on Stage*. New York: Routledge.

Beaumont, Cyril W. 1946. *Ballet Design: Past & Present*. New York: Studio Publications Inc.

———. 1988. *The Ballet Called "Giselle."* London: Dance Books Ltd.

Bernstein, Robin. 2011. *Racial Innocence: Performing American Childhood from Slavery to Civil Rights*. New York: New York University Press.

Bhabha, Homi K. (1994) 2004. *The Location of Culture*. New York: Routledge.

Dyer, Richard. *White*. 1997. New York: Routledge.

Fabian, Johannes. 1983. *Time and the Other: How Anthropology Makes Its Objects*. New York: Columbia University Press.

Federici, Silvia. 2004. *Caliban and the Witch: Women, the Body and Primitive Accumulation*. New York: Autonomedia.

Foster, Susan Leigh. 1998. *Choreography and Narrative: Ballet's Staging of Story and Desire*. Bloomington: Indiana University Press.

———. 2011. *Choreographing Empathy: Kinesthesia in Performance*. New York: Routledge.

Garafola, Lynn. 1985–86. "The Travesty Dancer in Nineteenth-Century Ballet." *Dance Research Journal* 17 (2) / 18 (1): 35–40.

———. 1997. *Rethinking the Sylph: New Perspectives on Romantic Ballet*. Middletown, CT: Wesleyan University Press.

Gilman, Sander L. 1985. "Black Bodies, White Bodies: Toward an Iconography of Female Sexuality in Late Nineteenth-Century Art, Medicine, and Literature." *Critical Inquiry* 12 (1): 204–42.

Guest, Ivor. 1966. *The Romantic Ballet in Paris*. London: Sir Isaac Pitman and Sons, Ltd.

Hart, Lynda. 1994. *Fatal Women: Lesbian Sexuality and the Mark of Aggression*. Princeton, NJ: Princeton University Press.

Homans, Jennifer. 2010. *Apollo's Angels: A History of Ballet*. New York: Random House.

Hoxworth, Kellen. 2017. "The Many Racial Effigies of Sara Baartman." *Theatre Survey* 58 (3): 275–90.

Kourlas, Gia. 2007. "Where Are All the Black Swans?" *New York Times*, May 6.

McCarren, Felicia. 1998. *Dance Pathologies: Performance, Poetics, Medicine*. Stanford, CA: Stanford University Press.

McClintock, Anne. 1995. *Imperial Leather: Race, Gender and Sexuality in the Colonial Contest*. New York: Routledge.

Merians, Linda E. 2001. *Envisioning the Worst: Representations of "Hottentots" in Early-Modern England*. Newark: University of Delaware Press.

Ngai, Sianne. 2012. *Our Aesthetic Categories: Zany, Cute, Interesting*. Cambridge, MA: Harvard University Press.

Parent-Duchatelet, A. J. B. 1840. *On Prostitution in the City of Paris*. 2nd ed. London: T. Burgess.

Roach, Joseph. 1996. *Cities of the Dead: Circum-Atlantic Performance*. New York: Columbia University Press.

Schneider, Rebecca. 1997. *The Explicit Body in Performance*. New York: Routledge.

Stoneley, Peter. 2007. *A Queer History of the Ballet*. New York: Routledge.

Strother, Z. S. 1999. "Display of the Body Hottentot." In *Africans on Stage: Studies in Ethnological Show Business*, edited by Bernth Lindfors, 1–61. Bloomington: Indiana University Press.

Sulcas, Roslyn. 2017. "A Conversation with 3 Choreographers Who Reinvigorated Ballet." *New York Times*, April 20.

Disavowing Virtuosity, Performing Aspiration

Choreographies of Anticlimax in the Work of Yve Laris Cohen, Narcissister, and John Jasperse

ARIEL OSTERWEIS

You are angling for a peek, standing up from your seat to try to see if he is actually doing it. Your view is partially obstructed by a four-foot wall that the artist has just spent a quarter of an hour constructing. It seems he is giving a man from the audience a hand job. As part of his performance, *Call Home* (2011), Yve Laris Cohen has painstakingly built a stage set that mirrors the structure of the venue, the Judson Memorial Church, the historic home of the 1960s Judson Dance Theater. Depending on where you are situated on the raked seating, you might see a penis struggling to stay hard; no "happy ending" ensues. This act comprises one half of an exchange between Laris Cohen and the anonymous man; earlier, you saw this man give cash to Laris Cohen. When you are standing, you can see the performers' gestures and above-the-belt actions over the top edge of the wall. Thus, you and the rest of the audience witness Laris Cohen return the cash to the man after the sex act, which appears to have remained aspirational, not fully realized to climax. After returning the cash, Laris Cohen takes center stage behind the wall to perform a series of men's ballet chugs (repeated turns *à la seconde*), the type you would encounter in the coda of a full-length classical story ballet. By building a wall and exchanging cash for sex work and, subsequently, cash for dance, Laris Cohen brings attention to the status of labor in various unexpectedly overlapping contexts—construction, sex, and dance.

In one sense or another (one more literal than the rest), all of these "jobs" qualify as types of manual labor. However, according to the transactions taking place, you are led to believe that the task of dance is not as valuable as that of sex, because Laris Cohen returns the cash to the anonymous man just before

431

executing his turn sequence, in effect paying the man to watch him dance. Might that be because Laris Cohen stumbles out of his turns? Regardless, all too often dancers dance for free or incur out-of-pocket expenses. Staging labor through task-based performance, Laris Cohen compels us to consider the value of human output in a live visual field that brings to mind, yet exceeds, Karl Marx's formulations of concealed labor in commodity fetishism. A familiar point of reference for dance studies, Mark Franko (2002), after Hannah Arendt, suggests that labor, like dance itself, is the force behind work and refers more to effort than any final (capitalist) product. In *Call Home*, physical labor is alternatingly concealed and revealed; we find that not all dance "work" exposes its labor. The turns *à la seconde* are framed through repetition, duration, and error as Laris Cohen interrupts a potentially climactic series with falls, stopping and starting again whenever he loses his balance. Because Laris Cohen has taken the action farther upstage, we catch glimpses of this teetering, as well as his extended leg, also known in ballet as one's "working leg" (always at the mercy of the stability or lack thereof of one's "standing leg"). His exposed chest reveals evidence of top surgery, and we become privy to markers of trans identity. During ballet training, a girl would not be taught these turns; they lie outside the scope of expectations for women in ballet. Gendered according to standards unconventional to classical ballet, Laris Cohen's turn passage, like the entirety of *Call Home*, is accompanied by a short excerpt from the climax to the score of the film *E.T.*—on loop. To perform these turns as a trans man, barefoot, inconsistently, and in the home of Judson Dance is to perform a sense of aspiration without the fulfillment of climax. Who is the extraterrestrial in this piece? Faced with the task of executing difficult turns, Laris Cohen, unlike *E.T.* and his young friend Elliott, never ascends into the sky via bicycle, spaceship, or any other apparatus. On loop and clumsily interrupted, the pursuit of climax is thus rendered banal, surging incessantly without resolution. What of this continuous, melancholic withholding of release?

Walls function in numerous ways—as barriers, structural supports, and partitions. They can be indoors, outdoors, or both at once. They only fully enclose space with the addition of ceilings and are most often secured to the ground. Walls are material and architectural, but "wall" can also refer to an impediment or obstruction, psychic or social. In this essay, I locate in the work of three contemporary artists—Yve Laris Cohen, Narcissister, and John Jasperse—a shared interest in an aesthetics of concealment in the face of work that seems otherwise explicit and revealing. Through different means, these artists engage in a dialectics of concealing and revealing and deliberately aestheticize a kind of partial access. They invest in making art that addresses societal walls built to delineate identities and adjudicate degrees of excellence; moreover, such walls are evoked through actual material constructions, as well as through choreographic processes of concealing through movement. Laris Cohen works with the materiality of wall and floor constructions to mine the status of embodied labor, Narcissister covers her face in a mask at all times to bring attention to bodily excess in hypersexual depictions of black femininity, and Jasperse folds black popular dances into (and within) formal choreographies that stage the evacuation of affect and the indiscernibility of appropriation.

All three artists disavow dance-based virtuosity through performances of aspiration—almost virtuosic but not quite. In the proper use of the term, "virtuosity" indicates something in excess of exceptional technical mastery that has been accumulated over time. In other words, as anthropologist Anya Peterson Royce (2004) has indicated, "artistry" refers to the fulfillment of a composition, while "virtuosity" refers to that affectively felt yet difficult-to-describe quality that exceeds the call of the composition. Additionally, virtuosity cannot be theorized in the absence of technique. Conceptualizing skill in degrees is important to an understanding of virtuosity: ability is inherent/latent, skill (and thus technique) points to ability plus training, and virtuosity is ability plus skill and that unnamable excess (which is identifiable with the help of charisma). Instead of presenting audiences with climactic resolution, slick mastery, and the excess inherent to virtuosity, Laris Cohen, Narcissister, and Jasperse expose the fraying, chafing, and awkwardly embodied exertion of effort. In their works, efforts conventionally directed toward virtuosity have been redirected from goal to process, from capitalist "success" to queer experiments with "failure." However, they do not situate failure as loss or even escape from convention. Rather, they perform aspiration and shift our experience from one of spectating feats of virtuosity to confronting the uneven repetition and potential violence of its pursuit. Their aspirational performances labor through modes of questioning that offer glimpses into dance training, eventually detouring away from such conventional regimes of discipline. Rather than displaying unfettered excellence in any one medium or technique, Laris Cohen, Narcissister, and Jasperse all insist on bringing otherwise disparate forms and contexts into proximity with one another. As they all aspire to virtuosity rather than achieve it, their work makes clear that the pursuit of virtuosity requires the exclusion of alternative possibilities. Because they do not achieve the virtuosity they aspire to, the drive to exclude those other possibilities remains legible in their work and is marked, very often, as culturally heterogeneous. Such aspirationally excluded bits provoke a rub or a tension in their work that is palpable to the audience.

Formal heterogeneity in the work brings attention to the challenge of human coexistence, which requires relationality. Relationality is built on degrees of care between people, but virtuosic performance, having achieved a degree of exclusion, eclipses the appearance of care—care both of the self and of the other. Even if one must care in order to achieve virtuosity, the kind of care at play when acquiring, mastering, and then exceeding technique is care about form and composition (as in training passionately and committedly) more than care about generating and maintaining holistic (bodily, emotional, social) well-being. After all, virtuosity is characterized by nonchalance in the face of overachievement. Virtuosos conceal the effort that goes into their performance and appear *as if* their work were effortless and often *as if* they had not worked at all. On the other hand, artists who adopt the kind of aspirational aesthetic I interrogate here uncover such labor while simultaneously withholding other aspects of performance. They do this in part to emphasize dynamics of care. The aspirational, even obsessive focus of Laris Cohen's, Narcissister's, and Jasperse's work suggests that stripping away virtuosity's excess excellence reveals the unevenness of processual labor. Taking care of one's self or one's peers is not typical in the training rhetorics of Western dance practices. A dancer in training commonly hears tropes of admonishment and advice borrowed both from athletics and from religion: "Toughen up," "No pain, no gain," "Sacrifice yourself," and "Be responsible toward your God-given 'gift' of talent."

Laris Cohen, Narcissister, and Jasperse all locate their work in the aspirational phase of training, one that imagines but never fulfills a virtuosic future. Thus, they work within a peculiar sense of spatiotemporality, somewhere between "queer failure" (Halberstam 2011) and "queer futurity" (Muñoz 2009), neither lamenting defeat nor untethering themselves from the present. If Jack Halberstam frames queer failure spatially as an "escape" (2011, 1, 3), José Muñoz imagines queer futurity temporally—queer as "not yet here" (2009, 29). The temporality of aspirational performance aesthetics I posit here is thus simultaneously one of past and present. Artists working in this mode are retrieving and slogging through once-held aspirational disciplines and practices without the resolution of arriving at the goal that should have been or was meant to be predetermined by the training. Their destination is arrived at instead by a burrowing within. Erstwhile goals (but not processes of attaining them) may have been abandoned in the face of difficulties of a technical or institutional sort—a lack of skill acquisition in dance technique or rejection at the hands of institutional curatorial structures. All three artists rummage through the muck of trial and error that is typically effaced from virtuosic concert performance. When bravura is dispensed with in favor of exposing dance labor, inevitable displays of erring make available the possibility of care, addressing minor failures, and tending to the well-being of those performing. As such, their aspirational aesthetics enliven a foundational motif that runs through so much contemporary performance theory—the celebration of "repetition with a difference," with the difference being the reinclusion of that which virtuosity conventionally excludes. There is a paradox in this celebration, however. The displays of care in these works emerge out of a need to respond to coinciding displays of struggle or violence, from physical exhaustion in Laris Cohen's work, to bodily self-objectification in Narcissister's work, to the violence of invisibilized appropriation in that of Jasperse. In the work of Laris Cohen, Narcissister, and Jasperse, walls—material and otherwise—delineate and aestheticize limits of inclusion and exclusion of regimes of corporeal discipline.

Yve Laris Cohen

"Between" is not the sort of transitional zone that compels me. The transitions I'm invested in are among, within, and elsewhere.

—YVE LARIS COHEN (Jaskey 2014, 198)

In task-based performances troubling the institutions of the proscenium and the white cube (of the gallery and museum), Laris Cohen lays bare the labor required of dancers, sex workers, and carpenters alike. Through repetition and duration, otherwise climactic tour jetés become a site of exhaustive return,

FIGURE 41. Yve Laris Cohen and Michael Mahalchick in *Duke*, December 8, 2010, performance view, Dance Theater Workshop, New York. (Photo by Yi-Chun Wu)

and buoyancy becomes chore instead of freedom. In a recent interview, Laris Cohen stated, "I benefit from this renewed interest in dance and visual art performance, but I'm not wild about some of the institutional modifications to the 'white cube' made in an effort to accommodate dance. Accommodation is the wrong strategy. I respond more to barriers and constraints than I do to gestures of inclusion. Often, new spaces in museums specially designed for performance have no use for me" (quoted in Jaskey 2014, 198). Instead of capitulating to gestures of accommodation made by museums and galleries in order to neatly package reskilling, Laris Cohen constructs his own floors and dismantles preexisting walls, building and tearing down architectural and figurative barriers that other performers might find untenable. While Laris Cohen actively disavows ballet-based virtuosity in his work, he also disavows the discourse of "deskilling" and "reskilling" that we find most recently taken up by Claire Bishop (2011). Ever one to cite labor disparities in his pieces, Laris Cohen intervenes in virtuosity's formulation. If, as described above, ability is inherent or latent, skill points to ability plus training, and virtuosity is ability plus skill and that unnamable excess, then Laris Cohen purposefully lingers in the middle category of skill, performing both excellent training and aspirational imperfection (as we find in the turn sequence of *Call Home*). And by most often positioning himself in relation to other bodies and players—usually untrained, everyday people whose body types or ages lie outside expected parameters of concert dance performance—Laris Cohen rarely appears in the virtuoso's domain as a soloist juxtaposed with a group. He suggests that the profane, relational body places pressure on the cult of the seemingly sacred, gifted individual typically championed through much of dance's conventional thrall to virtuosity.

The reason Laris Cohen distances himself from tropes of deskilling and reskilling in contemporary art-world parlance is that he is skilled (and highly trained) in both dance and visual art, and he does not "deskill" to perform his work. In addition to childhood ballet training that included American Ballet Theatre summer programs, Laris Cohen studied art, dance, and performance studies at the University of California, Berkeley, before earning his MFA in art from Columbia University. Nevertheless, reskilling is not an entirely inaccurate description. According to Bishop (2011), reskilling can occur when an art form moves from its own conventional space of presentation to another. Thus, concert dance presented in the museum would require, inherently, a kind of reskilling. More resonant with Laris Cohen's project, however, is the idea of "transing" as movement not only between genders but also between genres. Susan Stryker, a scholar of gender studies, reminds us that "*transing* [is] a practice that takes place within, as well as across or between, gendered spaces . . . a practice that assembles gender into contingent structures of association with other attributes of bodily being, and allows for their reassembly" (quoted in Stryker, Currah, and Moore 2008, 13). As the epigraph to this section makes clear, Laris Cohen prefers the transitions *among*, *within*, and *elsewhere* to the liminality suggested by *between*.

Through a commitment to a mode of transing that insists on remaining *within*—as opposed to *between*—Laris Cohen is almost obsessively invested in rehearsing particular moments from the famed Romantic ballet *Giselle*, which is based on a tale of madness, unrequited love, exhaustion, and dancing one-self to death. (See Rebecca Chaleff's chapter in this volume.) One moment in particular that preoccupies Laris Cohen is the scene in act 2 when Giselle hovers over Albrecht after Myrtha and the Wilis have forced Albrecht to dance into a state of collapse. In *Duke* (2010) a shirtless Laris Cohen in football pants and padding positions himself as Giselle in a deep lunge with arms spread and suspended over his fellow player, seemingly untrained in ballet and also shirtless. This Giselle allusion arrives after a laborious series of chores—moving planks and other performers around the stage. Task, support, exhaustion, and gestures of care come to the fore. Laris Cohen has cast new light on both task and ballet, rendering contrasting types of support equal to one another: in ballet, men are typically charged with lifting, and in *Duke*, the same amount of care is given to lifting wooden planks as is given to lifting fleshly humans. With exhaustion, though, comes emotion, and new forms of care emerge throughout the piece.

The theme of *Giselle* is repeated in *al Coda, from D.S.*, a performance that actually did involve a sense of between as Laris Cohen removed and transported a section of the wall of the original Whitney Museum of American Art downtown to the new Whitney building construction site as part of the 2014 Whitney Biennial. Creatively working within limitations unexpectedly placed on the performance by site managers, Laris Cohen had a section of the performance narrated in the absence of mobile propane heaters, which were meant to comprise a *corps de ballet* of sorts. A performer in the piece explained to hard hat–wearing audience members that the heaters were to have been positioned in the unfinished space in a formation that evoked the Wilis' choreography in *Giselle*'s act 2.

Laris Cohen's performances, in placing people and objects on an equal, relational plane, show us that care cannot be static and must be actively rehearsed. Even so, such repetitive, compulsive, or obsessive actions never quite seem resolved. Halberstam writes,

> If success requires so much effort, then maybe failure is easier in the long run and offers different rewards. . . . Perhaps most obviously failure allows us to

escape the punishing norms that discipline behavior and manage human development with the goal of delivering us from unruly childhoods to orderly and
predictable adulthoods. . . . And while failure certainly comes accompanied by a
host of negative affects such as disappointment, disillusionment, and despair, it
also provides the opportunity to use these negative affects to poke holes in the
toxic positivity of contemporary life. (2011, 3)

Laris Cohen's repeated efforts, though rife with a sense of trial and error, refuse
queer failure, privileging an almost masochistic commitment to discipline.
Nevertheless, he, like Halberstam, rejects the "positivity" of capitalist paradigms of success and looks back toward childhood, especially his childhood
training as a girl in classical ballet. Thus, while Halberstam and Laris Cohen
may share a disdain for neoliberalism's hyperprivatized individualism and celebrate the temporality of a backward glance, Laris Cohen's work offers anything
but escape. Similarly, Laris Cohen works against what Muñoz (2009) refers to
as the utopic potential of "waiting." In witnessing this slogging-through (this
aspirational burrowing into time and space), we become privy to the potential
of agency, of choice over chance.

Narcissister

When I was training as a dancer, I loved the feeling of dance in my body and
I loved moving my body to music. . . . It was very private for me, and I wanted
to dance with my eyes closed.

—NARCISSISTER (2012)

Like the airline steward who tells you that you must put your oxygen mask on
first before helping others, Michel Foucault writes that care of the self is ontologically prior to care of others (1997, 287). While the airplane adage has taken
on metaphorical status, it is in fact a matter of life or death in the event of
an emergency landing or loss of cabin pressure. But how does this supposed
ontological truth hold up in the context of those who are not or have not been
taken care of to begin with? Performance artist Narcissister, who only ever
appears in a mask, exposes the reality that black women's experiences often lie
outside of Foucault's chronological demand that care of the self takes place
ontologically prior to that of others. How often do we encounter representations of black women being cared for (by themselves or by others) *first*? Performing most often as a soloist or among a community of other people also
masked as Narcissisters, Narcissister stages images of self-care. Appearing narcis-
sistic and even autoexploitative, her performances are masturbatory inasmuch
as they are about survival. Whereas Laris Cohen presents the manual labor of

FIGURE 42. Narcissister, *Upside Down*, 2010, studio view. (Courtesy of Narcissister)

a hand job through the framework of an exchange or transaction, Narcissister's hands are directed toward herself as she rubs the clit of a handmade soft sculpture vagina costume she wears in *AssVag* (2008). The anonymity of her mask is met with the privacy of her "parts," and she uses her hands to insert and remove objects into and out of her vagina, mirroring the audience's own fetishization, its oscillating, dildo-like acceptance and rejection of the foreign other, the object.

In 2010 I was reintroduced to Narcissister over email by dance maker Trajal Harrell, who recommended my services as a performance dramaturge; as it turned out, we had trained together at the Ailey School and shared the privilege and burden of being mixed-race. Narcissister's artwork is informed by the liminality that has shaped her life. Between races and between genres, she performs at the intersection of multiple styles, finding audiences at burlesque clubs and experimental dance venues, as well as in galleries and on mainstream television. Thus, she works through feeling both *between* and *within*, doing so through a dynamic of nudity and shrouding, baring and covering her skin while making reference to black dance and performance traditions. She trained formally in modern dance at Ailey after graduating from Brown University and moving to New York City, and though her Ailey-inspired dance passages may appear as haphazard citation, they are instead a form of critical homage. This inversion, or undecidability, between criticality and homage runs through her work on many levels. For instance, she performs striptease and its reversal. In her video and live performance *Every Woman* (2010), danced to the 1978 Chaka Khan song, Narcissister begins almost nude; she is in a mask, a merkin, and an Afro wig. One by one, she removes items of clothing from her bodily orifices—mouth, vagina, and anus. After she dons one piece of clothing at a time, her final outfit consists of tights, gloves, a tube top, and a skirt; a purse and pumps emerge from her wig. Khan sings "I'll do it naturally" as Narcissister covers her body in artifice. Narcissister takes on roles such as Angela Davis, Marie Antoinette, Josephine Baker, Whitney Houston, a mammy, and a trucker, fluidly slipping between iconicity and stereotype, celebration and degradation. In her live theatrical shows, on video, and in her performances in public spaces she engages in a disavowal of the majoritarian modes of performance (especially dance-based virtuosity) expected of black women. Narcissister's aesthetic of dramaturgical disavowal ultimately performs an alternate imaginary for the body racialized and gendered as "American."

Foucault suggests that proper care of the self necessitates avoiding abuses of power (1997, 287). Narcissister's exploitative images of self-care move toward perversion and could be labeled hyper-self-care. While her performances involve passages of sexual (and aesthetically formal) climax, such climax is taken to the extreme—too objectifying, too long, and too pleasurable. Because these passages follow explorations into virtuosic dance, yoga, and burlesque routines, they arrive after Narcissister has generated an expectation for resolution. Instead, she displaces virtuosity's technical excess onto her masturbatory sexuality. This is to say that if a virtuoso dancer derives pleasure from performing in excess of technique, Narcissister's performances suggest a desperation in the pursuit of pleasuring oneself—a metaphor for the struggle of minoritarian self-care. Like Laris Cohen, performances of the self that exercise agency and effort that is not beholden to an outside authority do not necessarily amount to freedom. Potentially the most intimate of bodily spaces, her vagina becomes the site of a penetrability that is nothing more known than a universal sign of (self-)pleasure: to observe Narcissister inserting her hands into or extracting objects from her vagina is not to gain access to her subjectivity or sense of self. We couldn't be further from the trope of the body as a temple. Narcissister repeatedly slaps her masked face against a large brown dildo dangling from above the stationary bike's handlebars in *The Workout* (2007) while riding a butt plug that she has attached to the bike seat. Such moments of hyper-self-care are especially poignant in reference to popular culture's inability to render images of black women being cared for, but they reek of an internalization of cultural imagery that objectifies.

Theorists of blackness, modernism, and "cool" in the humanities have repeatedly turned to the mask (Thompson 1983), and Narcissister's performances—in their refusal to reveal her face—inherently question assumptions of diasporic representation and racialized performance. In "Racial Kitsch and Black Performance," Tavia Nyong'o (2002) expands Clement Greenberg's proposition that kitsch is failed seriousness to include the idea that racist kitsch, from historical ceramic figurines of black children to the self-conscious curating of such imagery in the Spike Lee film *Bamboozled*, generates shame in the African American and antiracist viewer and promotes oppositional spectatorship. Nyong'o suggests a mode of spectatorship that seeks to locate a way to transform the shame of feeling less than human that comes with rac*ist* kitsch's oppositional spectatorship into an experience of rac*ial* kitsch that escapes scapegoating and instead engenders self-recognition. He wonders if there is a way for the African American spectator to regain innocence without the bloodletting of—and identification with—the scapegoat in black performance. Narcissister calls upon the objecthood of racist kitsch and then complicates it with the performance of the moving body. By donning hard masks and inserting doll heads into various bodily orifices, as in her topsy-turvy performance of *The Dollhouse*, Narcissister places the brittle surface of the racist kitsch object (such as that of Nyong'o's figurine) onto—and into—the mutable muscular surface of a live fleshly body. Her performances in masks and merkins are costumed (and uncostumed) in a way that questions the fluctuating status of objecthood and subjectivity in performances that cite racialized and gendered figures from history.

Whether draped in dozens of dresses or clothed in nothing more than her own sinewy musculature, her particular engagement with dance and virtuosity ultimately functions as disavowal or displacement, as fragmentary quotation that leaves us wanting more. For example, in *Hand Dance* (2012), performed at the Box NYC, Narcissister performs in a larger-than-life wedding-banded hand costume that covers her face and body. She inserts a series of turns from the Horton technique into the performance, the kind in which the dancer extends her arms in a vertical overhead parallel position, tracing a circular right-back-left-front pattern. Ailey choreographed a series of these very turns in his piece *Memoria* (1979), an homage to Horton dancer Joyce Trisler. To reference such a turn sequence is to comment on expectations and imperatives for popular black performance to be presentational, outwardly directed, and deliberately kinetic.

Narcissister displays how *dis*avowal, too, can take on dramaturgical qualities. If avowal is a promise but not a contract, then disavowal—as performed by Narcissister—functions as a promise of an alternative, an acknowledgment of normative visual regimes followed by movements that escape their hold. Material articles do not always remain on her body, and her body communicates in the absence of utterance. Narcissister's disciplined transgressions perform an inexhaustible mutability that refuses to commit to the binding performances of race and gender scripted by mainstream culture.

John Jasperse

I am working on disorienting myself.

—JOHN JASPERSE (2013)

At first, choreographer John Jasperse wanted to frame the stage of his 2014 dance *Within between* with bracket-shaped side walls, thus removing the wings of the theater. "Square brackets," according to the *OED*, "are mainly used to enclose words added by someone other than the original writer or speaker, typically in order to clarify the situation." If parenthetical commentary is meant to reveal a writer's own subcutaneous thought, then brackets are installed by a writer when making an addition or inserting a comment into another's quoted words. They are also used when erasing or omitting words when quoting another

FIGURE 43. Maggie Cloud, Stuart Singer, Simon Courchel, and Burr Johnson in John Jasperse's *Within between*, 2014. (Photo by Yi-Chun Wu)

person's words. Isn't quotation a form of appropriation at its most basic level? And the original author has no control over what someone else will [clarify] in brackets. Perhaps it is no accident, then, that Jasperse initially imagined his stage bounded by enormous brackets, as if to clarify that his dance occurs within the dance of another.

After training at Sarah Lawrence College, Jasperse danced professionally in Brussels with Rosas, Anne Teresa De Keersmaeker's company. He is also influenced by the work of Trisha Brown, among others. In *Within between*, Jasperse formally deconstructs ballet and black vernacular dance forms to the extent that they appear as something other; stripping ballet, stepping, and twerking of their accompanying affect, Jasperse aestheticizes the way cultural and artistic appropriation can go undetected. We find here the coalescence of Laris Cohen's commentary on classical ballet and labor and Narcissister's reappropriation of black dance forms and focus on objecthood. Radically distinct from one another in their approaches, Laris Cohen, Narcissister, and Jasperse share a common interest in referencing culturally specific dance techniques within wider experimental, queer choreographic contexts that critique capitalist exploitation.

In 2013–14 I worked as a dramaturge with Jasperse during the creation of *Within between*. The process of working on the piece was often laden with a sense of occlusion, which I found difficult initially, but ultimately occlusion fit the piece's eventual aesthetic. Given that *Within between* was to explore black vernacular dance forms such as twerking and stepping, I had some initial trepidation about entering into a dramaturgical relationship with a white choreographer with this interest. Yet what attracted me to Jasperse was that I detected in him a dual uncompromising formalism and a self-doubting vulnerability that was more about the integrity of the work than about egocentric self-deprecation. Early in the rehearsal process I wrote to him:

> Why stepping? Why the MLK speech excerpts? What I find in these sections . . . is a generic "America." And the way I see these symbolic glimpses into "America" functioning is through an acceptance of the view that America is inherently Africanist, that black performance is already an aspect of America's whitenesses, blacknesses, Asiannesses, hispanicnesses. . . . Moreover, moments that call upon collegiate marching band–derived dances and performances stage questions more than they provide definitive answers. The more time I spend in rehearsal with you and the dancers, the less I feel that we can demarcate a true shift between a "Jasperse style" and a "post-Jasperse style." Trying things on seems to be how you've arrived at your idiosyncratic and highly explored movement style, and no matter how "foreign" a trope might be—whether a collegiate dance form

like stepping or a theoretical concept like perception. If we consider Deleuze and Guattari's concept of "minor literature" (which refers to Kafka's writing), we might ask ourselves if these moments in your new piece generate a minoritarian choreography . . . or, if they point to minoritarian culture within a choreography that is already (differently) minoritarian in its queerness, its careful embrace of a rigorous vulnerability. Would it be too crude to ask, how does choreography that emanates from a white gay masculine consciousness inform and ingest black performance (oration, music, dance)? Alternatively, the collective effervescence of university sports arenas (the occasion for marching bands and their accompanying cheers and dances) is hardly a comfortable context for the queer kid, the experimental choreographer, or the contemporary dancer. While I think it would be overwrought to claim a "post-Jasperse style," I want to leave a question out in space (a queer space?): how is your new choreography racializing and gendering its "America"? Does a generic America exist? Or is the US only ever a personal, particular amalgamation of disparate cultural, historical, and symbolic images, experiences, and commodities?

Jasperse was interested in working from a place of difference, not affinity. In a mode similar to choreographer Ralph Lemon (especially his piece *How Can You Stay in the House All Day and Not Go Anywhere?* [2010]), Jasperse wanted to challenge both his preexisting movement vocabulary and his conceptual vantage point. Initially, he gave me the task of analyzing and describing his earlier work in an effort to assist him in initiating a pivot away from his previous aesthetic habits. What had stood out to me from his previous work was a consistent engagement with objects that moved—*things* with agency. Recalling players such as jeans, leaf blowers, sculptures, penises, mattresses, emptied water bottles, and inflated pool rafts, I was continually struck by the way Jasperse was able to create choreographically political ecologies. Without disregarding the formal precision of a nuanced tilt of the head or the spiraling energetics of a connected trio moving across the stage at twenty miles per hour, he maintained an undertone of sociocultural critique. In *Misuse liable to prosecution* (2007), Jasperse brought to our attention the desperate financial mechanics of putting together a dance performance, commenting on the scarcity of resources for artists working within a commodity culture of waste, investigating capitalist materiality through corporeal materiality (money through the body).

But in rehearsals for *Within between*, I thought, where did the objects go? No rafts, hangers, orange cones, or boxes! While some work in the humanities has recently taken a turn from cultural to ecological framings, I noted an inverse shift in Jasperse's work from the ecological to the cultural. Whereas Jasperse's stages were once littered with animated things, they had been stripped down to bodies—just people. He told me he wanted to try on culturally foreign movement styles.

As opposed to mimicking a new dance style, Jasperse wanted to translate dialogue about such styles into movement, which is a type of abstracted praxis, a "doing" of theory (and he does this differently from Trajal Harrell, who uses voguing as a "theoretical praxis" in his long-term project, *Twenty Looks or Paris Is Burning at the Judson Church*). Such abstraction skirts around embodiment. Rather, it means to embody an idea about a dance form instead of embodying a dance form itself, privileging the affect of translation over the integrity of precise replication. What I find in this method is a commitment to form and structure. Jasperse was ever willing to admit his failures and displeasures, but there is always a return to structure.

In a section of *Within between* that is the result of the twerking experiments, we find a great distancing from the original referent. Engaged in a duet, Simon Courchel and Burr Johnson receive each other's jiggling body parts—a buttocks on the shoulder, a leg in the hand—amounting to a humorous yet tender exploration of teasing and support. The movement feels comfortably queer, but the faint echo of a marching band in the background conjures questions of the US preoccupation with gays in the military. How do we as audience members perceive movement passages that allude to cultural experiments with the likes of twerking (if we perceive them at all)? Jasperse could be commenting on Eurocentric classicism, race, modernist abstraction, high and low culture, or the idea of "America." At the level of choreography, what qualifies as "American"?

All four dancers (Courchel, Johnson, Maggie Cloud, and Stuart Singer) perform a repeated stepping passage from upstage to downstage in a minimalist vein and with very low affect. The first time through, the dancers are costumed in black and white, and the second time they are in brightly colored printed costumes. Are they tourists along a journey of cultural dress-up? We encounter stepping in black colleges; both entertainment and competition, it is a performance of aspiration. Jasperse contrasts and integrates culturally disparate dance techniques and evacuates them of their aspirational qualities. The audience is made aware of aspiration through its absence, the sense that some quality is missing from the dancers' delivery of the movement. For example, in one section, the four ballet- and contemporary-trained dancers execute the kinds of methodical tendus and port de bras you might find at the beginning of the center section of ballet class—fifth position, croisé, and so on. There is a creepy nonchalance to this sequence of movements, a restraint you wouldn't find in a ballet class in a classical ballet academy, but the kind you might find in a "ballet-for-modern-dancers" class, like a rejection of épaulement's reach, its aspiration. More specifically, if virtuosity includes a curious brew of technique and charisma (in perfect excess), we find in the example of Jasperse that the dancers perform a basic level of skill without the expected degree of charisma.

In other words, Jasperse, Narcissister, and Laris Cohen alike play not only with approximations of virtuosity but also with the presence and absence of qualities that comprise aspiration—skill and charisma. Jasperse challenges us with such ambivalence in a collegiate section with allusions to cheerleading in which the dancers barely crack a smile, a far cry from the plastered patriotic glee of televised cheerleaders or effervescent frat boys. Is this Jasperse's way of rejecting "America" or of refiguring its commoditized affects and rendering them banal? Who owns these images? How are they felt in our bodies? Distortion is introduced into the ballet section, contaminating—or freeing—the dance.

Jasperse has stated that he still believes in skill amid a terrain of postdramatic choreographers such as Jerome Bel and Xavier Le Roy, who present choreographies of deskilling and nondance. William Forsythe comes to mind as a contemporary of Jasperse who also holds onto skill. Nevertheless, Forsythe's is a choreography that embraces classicism and certainly a relationship to ballet (whether enlivened, dissected, distorted, or displaced). It would be remiss, however, to mistake Jasperse's ever-footy articulations with something balletic. They are decisively not. The balletic foot is pointed; it is pointed by discipline. The Jasperse foot is undisciplin*ing* and redisciplin*ing*, adhering to something more modern or postmodern. The Jasperse foot is both highly articulated and unapologetically pedestrian, gritty even—a great oxymoron in terms of concert dance. A seemingly minor issue, the foot indicates something more profound about Jasperse's work.

Toward the end of the rehearsal period, a thing re-entered the studio. *Within between* began to feature a pole dance of sorts. This pole appears only at the beginning of the hour-long piece. Instead of the transparent, light-catching attributes of clear plastic bottles and blow-up pillows (of *Misuse*), *Within between* begins with a nudge. A pole threatens to penetrate the audience. Contact? A probe? A rifle taking aim? Initially weaponized by a dancer, the pole becomes a structure of support, and two dancers lean on it while somehow keeping it suspended atop their toes and shoulders. As the dancers embark on the ballet section, they kick away the pole with their feet, as if to reject a fallen ballet barre. Not merely an allusion to moving from barre to center in a ballet class, this gesture of kicking away the barre indicates a rejection of classical modes of artistic support, a movement away from the institutional.

Jasperse reintroduced his penchant for the ecological to the otherwise cultural landscape of *Within between*, creating a meeting point between political things and social people. We might ask, then, where does identity reside in this work—in the dancers, in Jasperse, in the pole, in the idea of "America," or in the choreography itself? It has been said that movement is fleeting, but what, then, of the way we attach ourselves to a dance? In a tender duet, Courchel and Singer begin by facing each other and giving each other movement directions. This section culminates *Within between* and is the only one that includes speaking. From rehearsals, I had remembered commands given in the second person (such as "You kneel"), but these had shifted in performance to first-person statements (such as "I get up" or "I sit") that functioned as dual first-person descriptions of movement in real time, as well as second-person directives. As opposed to coming to climactic conclusion, the piece ends in a moment of aspiration as Courchel and Singer try to fulfill each other's descriptions with their eyes closed, devoid of visual cues. Isn't it with our eyes closed that we listen most closely? Courchel and Singer develop a quiet intimacy, then one of them utters, "I leave." Both dancers walk offstage. The audience is silent, unsure if the next moment calls for applause or attention. Incrementally, a few claps are joined by more, and the applause surges.

Through an uneven dialectic of concealing and revealing the dancer's labor, Laris Cohen's, Narcissister's, and Jasperse's work draws and drags us into ambivalent loops of aspiration, recurrently citing the nearly impossible climaxes of virtuosity's promise. Laris Cohen painstakingly builds and disassembles physical walls to suggest societal barriers while repeating and reappropriating gestures of care that emerge from heteronormative ballet narratives. As such, by creating an unexpected spectacle of the mundane working body while simultaneously rendering the romantic balletic gesture banal, Laris Cohen creates space for us to reimagine—and trans—hierarchies of the physical. In the work of all three artists, we find pointed vacillation between physical bodies and physical objects. Narcissister preempts the audience's knee-jerk tendency to objectify the black female body by presenting herself as an object. The uncanny animation of her doll-like presence and techniques of self-exploitation render care obscene, ultimately pointing to the absurdity of society's racialized, gendered, and classed standards of feminine beauty in and around dance and popular culture. Jasperse's performances of incomplete embodiment—skill in the absence of charisma—subtly stage the banal violence of appropriation. By surveying and distorting aspirational dance traditions, he traces the pedagogical process of technical acquisition in a culturally confused "America." Faint, sonic snippets of marching bands and Asian tones evoke the clashing of the militaristic and the spiritual inherent to any nationalist project and its embodied practices. The work of all three artists is comprised of alternating moments of violence and care strung together by effort and error. Their disavowal of virtuosity and subsequent performances of aspiration ultimately urge us to question how we will carry on within spaces that may not readily embrace our practices.

Works Cited

Bishop, Claire. 2011. "UNHAPPY DAYS IN THE ART WORLD? De-skilling Theater, Re-skilling Performance." *Brooklyn Rail,* December 10. https://brooklynrail.org/2011/12/art/unhappy-days-in-the-art-worldde-skilling-theater-re-skilling-performance.

Foucault, Michel. 1997. *Ethics—Subjectivity and Truth.* Vol. 1 of *The Essential Works of Michel Foucault 1954–1984,* edited by Paul Rabinow. Translated by Robert Hurley and others. London: Penguin Press.

Franko. Mark. 2002. *The Work of Dance: Labor, Movement, and Identity in the 1930s.* Middletown, CT: Wesleyan University Press.

Jasperse, John. 2013. Phone interview. August 8.

Halberstam, Jack. 2011. *The Queer Art of Failure.* Durham, NC: Duke University Press.

Jaskey, Jenny. 2014. "Among, Within, and Elsewhere: Yve Laris Cohen." *Mousse Magazine* 42. http://moussemagazine.it/yve-laris-cohen-jenny-jaskey-2014/.

Muñoz, José. 2009. *Cruising Utopia: The Then and There of Queer Futurity.* New York: New York University Press.

Narcissister. 2012. Interview with the author. Brooklyn, New York, July 30.

Nyong'o, Tavia. 2002. "Racial Kitsch and Black Performance." *Yale Journal of Criticism* 15 (2): 371–91.

Royce, Anya Peterson. 2004. *Anthropology of the Performing Arts: Artistry, Virtuosity, and Interpretation in a Cross-Cultural Perspective.* New York: Altamira Press.

Stryker, Susan, Paisley Currah, Lisa Jean Moore. 2008. "Introduction: Trans-, Trans, or Transgender?" *WSQ: Women's Studies Quarterly* 36 (3–4): 11–22.

Thompson, Robert Farris. 1983. *Flash of the Spirit.* New York: Vintage Books, Random House.

Circulations

Essays in this final section of *Futures of Dance Studies* emphasize the circulation of dance practices—and the practice of dance studies—across national borders. Thus these essays continue the work of decentering dance studies away from the US and European axis noted in the section on politics. Whereas the essays in that section detail rich and complex dance worlds in Canada, Cuba, and Argentina, the essays in this section trace dancers and ideas across the territories defined by nation-states. Misunderstandings abound in these case studies, but so too does the potential for mapping a truly global account of bodies in motion.

In "Do Iranian Dancers Need Saving? Savior Spectatorship and the Production of Iranian Dancing Bodies as 'Objects of Rescue'" Heather Rastovac-Akbarzadeh compares the emigration of dancer Afshin Ghaffarian from Iran to France with a fictionalized film based on his life, *Desert Dancer* (2014). The directorial debut by British filmmaker Richard Raymond, *Desert Dancer* features choreography by Akram Khan, a well-established British South Asian artist. Rastovac-Akbarzadeh compares the transnational reception of the film to media accounts of Ghaffarian's emigration in 2009, seeing both as examples of savior spectatorship, whereby "audiences project empathetically charged responses upon Ghaffarian's life and choreographic work to understand him as an object of rescue and themselves as compassionate saviors." This mode of spectatorship elides not only the realities of dance in contemporary Iran but also the role of "Euro-American collaborations in [Iranian] oppression, historically and today." Moreover, the reception of Ghaffarian's choreography and his fictionalized portrayal in *Desert Dancer* reveal the paradox of French citizenship, a citizenship that is defined in terms of "difference-blind republican equality" yet is still based on "gendered and racial exclusions." Thus the transnational reception of Ghaffarian onstage and onscreen reinforces the unequal power relations of the global War on Terror.

Like Rastovac-Akbarzadeh, Royona Mitra addresses the (mis)understandings of dancers and citizens of non-European descent in European nation-states. In "Costuming Brownnesses in British South Asian Dance," Mitra recalls Anusha Kedhar in her examination of how British South Asian artists negotiate the symbolically white scene of British dance and society. Borrowing African American theorizations of blackness by Thomas F. DeFrantz, Anita Gonzalez, and E. Patrick Johnson, Mitra proposes that the term "British brownnesses" more clearly describes her own experience—and the experience of her subjects—than does the term "British South Asian." From this perspective, she investigates the costuming of a *kathak* dancer, differentiating between what she calls "annotative costuming," or "traditional clothing [that] authenticates the dancer's brown heritage," and "choreographic costuming," or costuming that "becomes an extension of her choreography" and is "closer to her twenty-first-century hybrid reality." Focusing on dancers Sonia Sabri and Aakash Odedra, Mitra concludes that female dancers like Sabri face more pressure to don annotative costuming than do male dancers like Odedra. The next challenge, she believes, is "a further troubling of these gender-normative costuming practices such that British South Asian dancers can also represent androgyny, transgenderism, and transsexuality as equally representative constituents of British brownnesses."

Hentyle Yapp continues the investigation of how dancers of color are (mis)understood across national borders. In "Intimating Race: Tao Ye's *4* and Methods for World Dance," Yapp probes the reception of *4*, a 2012 work for four dancers that "catapulted the Chinese company [Tao Dance Theatre] into circulation across Asia, the United States, and Europe." The dancers' faces are covered with black cloth, and their bodies are clothed in loose gray shirts and black culottes, so their gender and racial identities are obscured. This costuming accents their abstract choreography, which starts in a "hyperkinetic mood" and then modulates into a slower and heavier mode before ending with only the dancers' shadows. In contrast to Ananya Chatterjea, who considers such abstract works by Asian choreographers derivative of Western postmodernism, Yapp believes that Tao's method is an "*intimation* of race" that gestures toward "histories of violence . . . without permitting them to continue to dominate as the only available narrative." To make this argument, Yapp first opposes what he considers two main approaches to dance studies—a Foucaultian analysis of representation that attends to questions of Eurocentrism and colonialism versus a Deleuzian analysis of affect that attends to questions of difference and relationality. Yapp then proposes to combine both approaches with a phenomenological approach indebted to Frantz Fanon that promises to achieve "a simultaneous sense of openness (affect) and grounded history (representation)."

It is only in this way, Yapp suggests, that dance studies can adequately account for the circulation of companies like Tao Dance Theatre.

Whereas Yapp assesses the relevance of present-day European and US dance studies to contemporary Chinese dance, Emily Wilcox assesses the relevance of dance studies to the circulation of Asian dance on global stages in the mid-twentieth century. In "Locating Performance: Choe Seung-hui's East Asian Modernism and the Case for Area Knowledge in Dance Studies," Wilcox examines the career of Choe Seung-hui, who was born in Korea and trained with Ishii Baku in Tokyo before touring as a soloist in North America, Europe, and Latin America from 1938 to 1940. During the Second World War Choe performed in China; in 1946 she moved to North Korea and then returned to China in 1950 for an extended stay. Wilcox focuses on her career after 1945, a period overlooked in English-language scholarship during the years of the Cold War. Using Chinese-language sources, Wilcox demonstrates how Choe's oeuvre took on new meaning as a model for how Chinese artists could research and transform "indigenous performance practices into movement forms that could exist independently from their traditional cultural contexts and become abstracted vocabularies used to train dancers and create new dance works." This approach was influential not only in the People's Republic of China but also in other socialist nations in East Asia. For Wilcox, Choe's career demonstrates the need for area studies approaches to dance, where knowledge of non-Western languages and regions reveals the significance of circulation within Asia and, by extension, the Global South and demonstrates the ethnocentrism of European- and English-language scholarship that cannot recognize alternate modernisms. As she concludes, "Area studies helps us to locate dance in multiple histories that move in different ways."

Jose L. Reynoso also calls for a "broader cartography" for dance studies in his essay, "Toward a Critical Globalized Humanities: Dance Research in Mexico City at the CENIDID." The research center CENIDID (Centro Nacional de Investigación, Documentación e Información de la Danza José Limón) was founded in 1983 and named after the Mexican American choreographer José Limón, whose career exemplifies what Reynoso calls "transnational nationalism," the formation of the nation-state in response to transnational ideas and practices. In twentieth-century Mexico the confluence of the local and the global led to the creation of "embodied mestizo modernisms," "the combination of European and Mesoamerican bodies and cultures, with the tacit exclusion of Mexican populations of Asian and African descent." In a process similar to what Wilcox describes in China, dancers researched indigenous traditions and then integrated these traditions with Western dance styles to create distinctively Mexican modernisms. Publications by CENIDID have documented the history of Mexican modernisms in multiple languages while also applying multiple theoretical perspectives to this history. In the end, Reynoso calls for scholars "to unsettle the Europe / United States dyad" and to "decenter the underlying colonial logic of forward and backward modernities between the Global North and the Global South."

Like Wilcox, Reynoso underscores the limitations of English as the lingua franca for dance studies. Like Yapp, Reynoso undertakes a critical history of dance studies in order to open space for a more globalized approach. In a myriad of ways, the authors featured in this volume critically examine the past of the field in order to script the futures of dance studies.

Do Iranian Dancers Need Saving?

Savior Spectatorship and the Production of Iranian Dancing Bodies as "Objects of Rescue"

HEATHER RASTOVAC-AKBARZADEH

> When you save someone, you imply that you are saving her from something.
> You are also saving her *to* something. What violences are entailed in this
> transformation? What presumptions are being made about the superiority of
> that to which you are saving her?
>
> —LILA ABU-LUGHOD, *Do Muslim Women Need Saving?*

Interwoven with stunning dance scenes choreographed by British South Asian choreographer Akram Khan, the biographical drama *Desert Dancer* (dir. Richard Raymond, United States, 2014) paints a dark story of Iran as an oppressive society where "dance is forbidden" and where a dancer has been jailed by the Islamic regime. In this fictionalized portrayal of real-life Iranian dancer Afshin Ghaffarian, played by British actor Reese Ritchie, the film character Afshin has no option but to flee his homeland in order to shed the chains of despotism and save his life through liberation in the West. France, in turn, embodies quintessential benevolence through affording Afshin asylum and the freedoms that he had been deprived in Iran, namely, his human right to dance.[1] Similar to the narratives of liberation enacted in *Desert Dancer*, mainstream French media has established Ghaffarian as a liberal subject who has been granted the freedom to dance after acquiring political asylum in France in 2009. Ghaffarian's contemporary dance aesthetics are replete with images of a physically struggling body, which for him gesture toward a universal resistant body. However, French media reads Ghaffarian's choreographies as in-the-flesh evidence authenticating the persistent discourses that frame the Islamic Republic of Iran as wholly oppressive. I argue that, in distinct yet interrelated ways, the representations of Ghaffarian in French media and in *Desert Dancer* construct

him—and, by extension, Iranian dancers—as an "object of rescue." For Inderpal Grewal, universal human rights frameworks produce the subject position
of an "object of rescue" as a result of how the militaristic First World "is rarely
present in [the] visual evidence of human rights violations, [and how its]
absence constructs the authoritative and objective viewer and rescuer" (1998,
502). I extend Grewal's theorization to propose that viewing and rescuing are
intertwining practices in the reception and conflation of Ghaffarian's biography
and choreography: audiences project empathetically charged responses upon
Ghaffarian's life and choreographic work to understand him as an object of
rescue and themselves as compassionate saviors.

Building on transnational feminist analyses of Euro-American (neo)imperial-
ist "saving" enterprises, I draw critical parallels between militaristic and moralistic missions to save female and LGBT Muslim / Middle Eastern subjects and
the tropes of freedom employed in discourses surrounding Iranian dancers
in and outside of the Islamic Republic of Iran. Increasingly since the events
of 9/11, scholars and activists have critiqued racialized modes of scrutiny in
which Islam's treatment of women and homosexuals becomes a barometer
with which to measure modernity and freedom, highlighting how the colonial
"white wo/man's burden" has become reconfigured into Islamophobic, (neo)
liberal state intervention (Massad 2007; Puar 2007; Abu-Lughod 2013). Arguing that acts of protection are a gendered enterprise, Minoo Moallem insists,
"The barbaric other is there to legitimize and give meaning to the masculinist
militarism of the 'civilized' and his constant need to 'protect'" (2002, 298).
While Ghaffarian's subject position as an Iranian male might construct him
within contemporary Euro-American geopolitical paradigms as a prototypical
terrorist threat, his position as a dancer—working in a medium often understood as a quintessentially human, yet gendered, endeavor—prompts liberal
human rights frameworks to establish Ghaffarian, like Muslim women and
LGBT individuals, as an object of rescue.

Because of Iranian state-enforced regulations of public dance performance,
effective since Iran's 1979 Islamic Revolution, many dancers, audiences, and
media construct diasporic Euro-American spaces as offering Iranian dancers
the unconditional freedom to fully realize themselves as artists. This narrative
suggests that Iranian dancers gain subjecthood *as* dancers only through non-
Iranian spaces, thus positioning them as in need of saving from the "oppressive"
Iranian state or family, which forbids dance, a restriction that is often associated
with Islam.[2] French audiences of Ghaffarian's live performances and the transnational audiences of Ghaffarian's fictionalized biography in *Desert Dancer*—as
subjects living in contemporary postcolonial and War on Terror contexts—
participate in and enact a certain set of "racialized looking practices" (Barber

2015) that I term "savior spectatorship." These savior spectatorship practices, enacted across sites of Ghaffarian's live and cinematically depicted performances, entail the incorporation of prereceived transmedia images and discourses into the interpretations of his Iranian dancing body as an object of rescue. While "spectatorship" often implies a passive, uncritical consumption of cultural products, Jacques Rancière (2009) insists that spectators are inherently active in their interpretations and coproduction of meaning. My theorization of savior spectatorship goes further to interrogate the prevalent assumption that *active* spectatorship is inherently *critical* or politically progressive. Put simply, active spectatorship does not by definition intervene into relations of power; as this essay argues, it also has the capacity to actively sustain and produce its own forms of power relations.

Furthermore, savior spectatorship practices surrounding Ghaffarian's performances are enhanced by kinesthetic empathetic responses to the corporeal enactments of physical distress that Ghaffarian performs in his choreographic work and that Ghaffarian's fictionalized character ("Afshin") experiences in *Desert Dancer*. Kinesthetic empathy—theorized across dance studies and cognitive science—is loosely defined as the sensations one feels in one's body upon watching other bodies move.[3] Deidre Sklar suggests that ocular perception of other bodies has the tendency to construct them as distanced objects, whereas "empathetic kinesthetic perception implies a bridging between subjectivities" (2001, 32). Sklar nonetheless acknowledges that this bridging does not produce an easy or complete merger; instead, it emphasizes a "perception of differences" (32). Susan Foster's (2011) study on kinesthetic empathy goes further to situate sympathy/empathy within histories of colonization as practices that construct(ed) categories of difference and provided rationalization for power and control. Thus, considering the power relations that empathy practices enact, as Foster and others highlight, kinesthetic empathy does not, by definition, necessarily evade constructing other bodies as objects, as Sklar implies. In savior spectatorship, I argue, images, discourses, and kinesthetic empathy collude to construct objects of rescue out of particular dancing bodies like Ghaffarian's.

In what follows, I first provide context to Ghaffarian's trajectory as a dancer through an overview of dance in contemporary Iran. I then briefly turn to France, where the media construction of Ghaffarian as an "Iranian artist in exile" and the reception of his choreographic work provide insight into practices of savior spectatorship within France's moralistic frameworks of asylum. Finally, I close with a reading of *Desert Dancer* to explicate how savior spectatorship reveals political limits and paradoxes of spectatorship and kinesthetic empathy. My intention is not to situate Ghaffarian as a representative for all

Iranian dancers; indeed, there are distinct histories and aesthetics among them. However, I have recurrently observed similar conditions of savior spectatorship across the reception of many diasporic Iranian dancers, musicians, and visual artists over the past two decades. Dance, in particular, lends itself to savior spectatorship for the distinctive ways it genders and racializes bodies even while it is simultaneously considered a universal human experience. Neither does my theorization of savior spectatorship assume a singular spectator in the viewing of Ghaffarian's performances and *Desert Dancer*. As Susan Manning emphasizes, "Spectators from different social locations may view the same performance event differently" (2004, xvi). Accordingly, spectators certainly engage with and interpret Ghaffarian's choreographic work and the film differently. Rather, what savior spectatorship enacts is a multimodal *practice* that is produced and sustained through historical and contemporary sociopolitical power relations and longer trajectories of Euro-American saving enterprises. As neoliberal geopolitical subjects in the era of the global War on Terror, spectators' affective and kinesthetic empathetic responses to performances of Iranian dancers' corporeal struggle and liberation become entangled in acts of savior spectatorship.

Dance in Contemporary Iran

Iran's 1979 Revolution overthrew the secularist Pahlavi monarchy and ultimately installed the Islamic Republic of Iran, a government based on rule by Islamist jurists. Associating dance with moral corruption, the new government enforced stringent restrictions on dance performance and practice (though there is no constitutional law against dancing), with a wide range of penalties for transgressing these prohibitions. The enforcement of restrictions shifts with internal politics and depends on interpretations of what is considered "dance" (*raqs*). In fact, many dance performances occur in Iran within both official and unofficial (underground) spheres, albeit under regulated conditions and under names other than "dance" and "dancer." For instance, the Iranian government often commissions the theatrical movement form *harakat-i mawzun* (rhythmic movements) for performances that convey religious and revolutionary themes.[4]

Like other artistic productions in Iran, movement-based artists must receive permission from the Ministry of Culture and Guidance in order to present public performances. Permission is contingent upon adhering to governing laws and moral codes, particularly those related to the mandatory head covering for women and physical interactions between members of the opposite sex. Those involved in presenting performances without governmental permission or performances that transgress governing laws and moral codes are subject to penalties ranging from monetary fines to arrest. International headlines in

2014, for instance, covered the plight of "Iran's 'Happy' dancers." Seven young men and women were arrested for obscenity charges and "ignoring Islamic norms" of public chastity after publishing a YouTube video featuring themselves lip synching and dancing to American pop singer Pharrell Williams's hit single, "Happy" (Rofugaran quoted in Neuman 2014).[5] Williams himself responded to the headlines, insisting that "Iranians should be free to dance," and the hashtag #FreeHappyIranians began to circulate across social media. In response to the American media coverage of this event and to the media's selective focus on certain human rights issues over others, journalist Sana Saeed expressed on *Mic.com*: "We are uncomfortably selective . . . in which human rights stories from Iran get our attention. . . . The issues and stories that indict us of any complacency and wrongdoing are ignored or justified. When Iranians are denied the apparent basic human right to make a Pharrell video, we are maddened and disappointed. When Iranians are unable to access basic medical supplies as a result of our sanctions, we don't even know" (2014). Iranians and non-Iranians often formulate the Iranian dancing body as a symbol of resistance against the Islamic Republic of Iran. However, in Laudan Nooshin's examination of the rhetoric surrounding the *Happy in Tehran* video, Nooshin insists that fetishizing resistance "rests on a somewhat reductionist view of a unified oppressive regime acting upon a similarly unified resistant population, something that is far from the reality" (2017, 176). In conjunction, uncritically linking dance and resistance in/of Iran has the problematic potential to frame the West as a liberating benefactor without regard for Euro-American enactments of, and collaborations in, oppression both historically and today. This is not to undermine the potential of dance as a viable intervention into power; indeed, Iranian dancers in and outside Iran do enact such interventions. Nonetheless, I am apprehensive about romanticizing resistance, since, as Saba Mahmood argues, (neo)liberal notions of resistance and agency "impose a teleology of progressive politics on the analytics of power" (2005, 9).

Although Iran's 1979 Revolution is a critical point of rupture for dance in Iran, it is important to emphasize that, despite regulations, dance and other movement-based performances continue to develop in Iran. Dance historian Ida Meftahi explains, "Within the three decades after the [Islamic] revolution, the dance scene has grown enormously" (2016, 10). Many officially approved female dance performances occur for all-female audiences, and public performances of men's folk dance for mixed-sex audiences have recently become sanctioned (Shay 2014). Additionally, dance classes of many genres (such as "Iranian," ballet, modern, tango, and breakdancing) are popular in affluent parts of urban centers. While most dance classes remain same-sex, occur in private, or have names that reference benign exercise, Meftahi explains that many classes are advertised in the community press, and male-instructed dance videos are becoming more available for store purchase. There is also a thriving contemporary theater scene in Iran, much of which is government-sponsored, such as the annual international Fardj theater festival, in which theater makers from around the world participate. Many of these theater performances incorporate stylized movements that function under diverse names such as physical theater and rhythmic movements. Nonetheless, dance remains highly regulated and, in some cases, prohibited. Female dancers and those performing styles that involve movements the moral police consider provocative face particular challenges in presenting performances. Thus, a significant amount of dance in Iran takes place in private spaces or in so-called underground scenes without official permission instead of occurring in the official public sphere. Furthermore, many individuals who wish to pursue professional dance training and careers choose to leave Iran for Europe or North America.

"Iranian Dancer in Exile": The Savior Spectatorship of Compassionate French Publics

It was through Ghaffarian's involvement in Tehran's official and unofficial theater scenes that he began his trajectory as a dancer-choreographer. Ghaffarian explained to me, "I participated in a style of theater in Iran we call 'physical theater,' because we're not allowed to present 'dance.' But it was dance for me. The problem is just this title. We are not allowed to call it 'dance,' but we *can* dance. That's why in Iran they invented a new term, *harakat-i mawzun*" (Ghaffarian 2012). In October following the 2009 Iranian presidential elections, Roberto Ciulli, the theater director of the Theater an der Ruhr, which sponsors an exchange program between Mülheim, Germany and Iran, invited Ghaffarian and his performance partner to Germany to present their original theater work, *Strange but True*. Toward the end of that performance, without giving notice to his partner, Ghaffarian broke from the choreography, exhibited a green bracelet around his wrist, and raised two fingers into a V. Through this gesture, Ghaffarian signified his solidarity with the millions of Iranian Green Movement protestors who utilized this same gesture to mean "victory" as they rallied against what they considered a stolen election by incumbent president Mahmood Ahmadinejad. Although this performance took place three months after Iran's elections, the Green Movement remained particularly sensitive for the Iranian government. Ghaffarian explained to me that the governmental officials who chaperoned his trip warned him after the performance that he would be punished for his political statements once he was back in Iran. While it may seem inconsequential, it is important to distinguish that this threat of punishment resulted from Ghaffarian's political statement, not because of the vehicle through which he made it (dance), contrary to what the narratives I describe in this essay would like us to believe. Ghaffarian had previously been arrested and beaten in Iran for filming the Green Movement protests after the Iranian election; thus, the chaperones' threats of punishment prompted Ghaffarian, with the help of another Iranian dancer in Paris, to file for political asylum in France, which he was soon thereafter granted.[6] Shortly after Ghaffarian's arrival in Paris, he became an artist-in-residence at the Centre National de la Danse (CND, or National Dance Center), an institution sponsored by the French Ministry of Culture, and during his residency he founded the interdisciplinary performance ensemble Reformances Company.

As part of his 2010–11 CND residency, Ghaffarian performed his first choreographic work in France, *The Piercing Shout* (2010). This work garnered a significant amount of attention from the French media, which saw the performance as emblematic of Ghaffarian's newfound freedom in France and which lauded the CND for offering residency to an amateur Iranian dancer in exile. Furthermore, because the choreographic content involves physical enactment of struggle and suffering, the work was received as an embodied testimony of an oppressed artist in Iran. In this performance, Ghaffarian walks slowly through a darkened space into a circle of scattered light cast upon a dirt-covered floor by a single hanging light bulb. Clothed only in shorts and covered in red and brown dust, he appears fatigued, as if he has been confined in a cramped, dark chamber. He falls and quickly lifts himself to standing again, ultimately conceding to his precarious balance. As if acquiescing to forceful blows, he resumes a fetal position, clutches his arched body, and unleashes loud cries. Pain seems to be afflicted upon him from an unspecified source external to the boundaries of his own flesh, but it is difficult to ascertain whether the torment is inflicted externally or internally—the suffering subject remains alone in the performance space. Eventually, after a climactic sequence of vertical turns that suggest transcendence from this suffering, Ghaffarian brings himself to a microphone. His mouth stretches wide open, screaming without sound. Silence fills the room until he whispers a single Persian word, *azadi* (freedom).

Ghaffarian (2012) explained that *The Piercing Shout* explores universal themes of the four elements; the "original birth of humanity"; and humans' acquisition of language, particularly of the word "no," which Ghaffarian utters in multiple languages throughout the performance. Yet the CND and other online sources frame the performance exclusively within the context of Ghaffarian's immigration story, not a universal journey that transcends time and space. For Paris-based dramaturge Leyli Daryoush, for instance, *The Piercing Shout* becomes a proclamation of Ghaffarian's freedom to dance, which, inferred by her rhetoric, is enabled only through exile in France: "Afshin Ghaffarian is an Iranian choreographer. It sounds simple, but it is not. Look at his career: protests, prison, torture, exile. He was exiled in France since 2009 following his position against the Iranian regime. . . . For his first creation in France, *The Piercing Shout*, [he] wanted to create a dance around the four elements, but it is also the announcement of exile, coming to the free world in which he can finally dance" (2011). By reading *The Piercing Shout* as an "announcement of exile," Daryoush projects her empathetically charged interpretations onto Ghaffarian's performance of physical struggle. While Ghaffarian describes his work as representing universal human themes, Daryoush claims instead that it is representative of his liberation in the "free world" and constructs Ghaffarian as an object of rescue who "can finally dance."

Despite the universalist themes prevalent in Ghaffarian's choreographic work and much of his own self-definition, mainstream French media, state-funded dance institutions, and art-dance circles remain largely invested in fixing Ghaffarian's personal and artistic identity as the particular subject of an "Iranian dancer in exile." Ghaffarian explained to me in 2012: "There are a lot of people in France who prefer to keep me in the strict category as an Iranian exile artist, that France hosted this. They think, 'We don't want to accept Afshin as a professional dancer. Afshin is just this exiled artist.' But that is what I try to avoid. I am not identifying myself as an 'Iranian exile' in France. I identify myself as an artist, a doer. Apart from being Iranian or Muslim or neither, to express myself and defend my human existence is most important for me." As Ghaffarian implies and as Daryoush's aforementioned quote illustrates, the French discourse surrounding Ghaffarian consistently narrates his biography within the terms of a struggle for artistic expression rather than the forms his artistic expression takes. That is, far more prevalent than commentary on the formal components of Ghaffarian's choreographic works is a focus on the illegality of dance in Iran, Ghaffarian's "escape" and "rescue," and the "newfound" freedom afforded to him in France. For instance, articles about Ghaffarian (translated from French) are entitled "Iranian in Exile: The Dance Is His Freedom" (*Ouest France*, 2013), "Being a Dancer in the Land of the Ayatollahs" (*Les inrocks*, 2009), and "In Iran, the Body Is a Sin" (*Le Monde*, 2010). In the eighteen French web news sources I surveyed (published between 2009 and 2014), the following words surfaced: free or freedom (forty times); exile(d) (nineteen); banned, illegal, prohibited, or forbidden (seventeen); refugee or asylum (nine); torture or beating (eight); protest (eight); fled/escaped (five). The overdetermined discourses of freedom that are mobilized through these sources must be placed within the historical legacy of French colonial constructions of race and religion. Despite French claims to difference-blindness, Joan Wallach Scott (2007) and others argue that colonial practices employed racial categories as a means through which France began to establish itself as a benevolent entity on a "civilizing mission." If, as Foster explains, kinesthetic exchanges between dancers and viewers are constructed "by common and prevailing senses of the body and of subjectivity" in a given sociohistorical moment (2011, 2), then postcolonial conditions of racialized looking practices together with the discourses surrounding Ghaffarian create ideological conditions for savior spectatorship and, in advance, determine the frames through which audiences will view his work.[7]

While identity categories are a persistent frame through which many non-Euro-American and other racialized artists are represented and valued within multicultural Anglo-American art markets, these identity politics do not apply in the sociopolitical context of France. The French national body claims and asserts a difference-blind republican equality that requires its citizens to identify with an abstract national community rather than the communalism of racial, ethnic, or religious belonging. Postcolonial feminists have interrogated the terms of abstract citizenship to which French republicanism claims to adhere, insisting that these claims obscure the gendered and racial exclusions inherent to and constitutive of French citizenship. The framing of Ghaffarian as an "Iranian dancer in exile" is a salient example of these paradoxes of universalism as they relate to race and ethnicity. Considering the framework of universalism integral to French citizenship, we must ask why narratives about Ghaffarian remain fixed to this particular subject formation. As Ghaffarian describes, his self- and artistic associations do not directly or intentionally revolve around an overdetermined sense of "being Iranian," nor do his choreographies focus on Iran or his immigration experience. In fact, Ghaffarian's discourse and choreographies align more with the universal, humanistic tenets of French republicanism, as *The Piercing Shout* and his personal claim to "humanness" illustrate.

Emine Fisek's (2010) research on theatrical aid work in France provides salient insight into the contradiction between abstract French citizenship and the insistence on immigrant particularity that Ghaffarian's case highlights. Fisek shows that theatrical aid performances—community theater programming through which immigrants and asylum seekers performatively and legally to access French citizenship—emphasize communitarian particularities only as part of immigrant performers' narratives of arrival, disavowal of communal allegiances, and desire to become abstract French citizens. Projected onto the stage is "an irresolvable yearning to have these 'individuals' both transform radically into 'integrated' citizens and yet remain 'other' for the duration of that transformation, most crucially at moments when the transformation is to be shared with an appreciative, compassionate public" (Fisek 2010, 72). Ultimately, then, fostering a space for these particularities to be highlighted allows French audiences to collectively imagine themselves as inclusive, compassionate citizen-spectators. Furthermore, Fisek explains that an emphasis on immigrant suffering is central to this exchange: "Compassion, as well as its object, another's suffering, appears at the heart of how abstract individuality is to be secured in the non-abstract citizen" (100). While Ghaffarian did not participate in theatrical aid programs, the moralistic frameworks that Fisek describes provide insight into French responses to Ghaffarian and his choreographic work. Within these frameworks, French audiences are apt to read and empathize with Ghaffarian's *The Piercing Shout* not as an exploration of universal themes but as an embodied testimony of particularist suffering, specifically at the hands of Iran's Islamic regime. In doing so, French audiences actively participate in and enact kinesthetic empathy and racialized looking practices as modes of savior spectatorship, establishing themselves as compassionate and humane. As evidence for the virtue of abstract citizenship, French superiority is secured through extending refugee status to—and enthusiastic applause for—an "Iranian dancer in exile."

Transnational Circulations of
Savior Spectatorship in *Desert Dancer*

These affective and kinesthetic audience relations of savior spectatorship are enacted transnationally through the fictionalized biographical drama *Desert Dancer*. In a 2012 interview with *Digital Spy*, the film's female lead, Indian actress Freida Pinto, describes *Desert Dancer* as "a very human story born out of feeling restricted and fighting to break free and express yourself in a very human way. . . . I had taken dance for granted my whole life, freedom of speech, freedom of movement. And then to see someone in another country who was my age, who looked like me but had all these obstacles that are imposed by the regime, . . . was mind-blowing" (quoted in Joshi 2012). Pinto's statement, "someone who looked *like me*," illustrates the "bridging of subjectivities" that Sklar suggests kinesthetic empathic relations with dancing bodies can conjure. Surely, the intensive dance training that Pinto underwent with the film's choreographer, Akram Khan, which did not involve consultation with Ghaffarian but likely involved online viewing of his choreographic work, helped contribute toward Pinto's connection with Ghaffarian's plight.[8] Yet, rather than an unmediated "natural or spontaneous connection between the dancing body and the viewer's body" (Foster 2011, 2), Pinto's conflation of resistance, dance, and freedom is in fact emblematic of our particular historical moment within which these very tropes constructing Middle Eastern and Muslim subjects continue to gain currency in the American-led global War on Terror.

If dance uniquely conjures kinesthetic empathy, then how are we kinesthetically and ideologically seduced as spectators of Iranian dancing bodies within the film's choreographed framing? Sherril Dodds explains that "the presentation of a 'live body' is unavoidably transformed when it becomes a 'screen body,'" and she references the loss of kinesthetic empathy that may occur in this transformation (2001, 29). However, while kinesthetic empathy has primarily been theorized in relation to live performance, many scholars theorize film spectatorship as embodied and mimetic, observing that various filmic devices kinesthetically engage viewers of filmic bodies (Marks 2000; D'Aloia 2011). Dee Reynolds explains that film can intensify "the spectator's own kinesthetic sensations as they internally 'imitate' the movement of the camera as well as the character" (2011, 88). As a film text, *Desert Dancer* kinesthetically interpellates its viewers into a heightened practice of savior spectatorship through the strategic use of camera angles and framing, such as close-ups of the protagonist's dancing body in choreographic and quotidian depictions of violence, pain, struggle, and liberation. In *Desert Dancer*'s portrayal of dance in Iran, the discursive and visual depictions of Iranian dancing bodies struggling for freedom to dance vis-à-vis the stereotypical images of stern-faced, weapon-wielding Islamic militia contribute to the construction of Iranian dancers as objects of rescue.

Desert Dancer begins with white text on a black screen: "Iran—The birthplace of great poetry. And the first charter of human rights. Yet today the regime denies freedom of expression. Now on the streets and behind closed doors, the youth are defiant. Bar ehsas yek dastan-e vaqaei [in Persian script]. Based on a true story." The film then cuts to its opening scene. It is nighttime, and a car's headlights provide the only light. Shown from the waist up, college-aged Afshin is lying on the ground with his face planted in the dirt and his hands tied together at the wrists. Suddenly, a man's leg shown from behind kicks Afshin's face and then his stomach. From the start, the film implicates its viewers as savior spectators through this close-up of Afshin's body while being beaten by a member of the *basij*, the quasi-official voluntary militia that often enacts and represents state violence. The filmic technique of the close-up amplifies kinesthetic empathy through which spectators are encouraged to inhabit Afshin's subjectivity and glean visceral insight into Afshin's predicament.

A voice-over speaks first in Persian and then in English, all while the *basiji* relentlessly kicks Afshin. "Man Afshin-e Ghaffarian hastam. My name is Afshin Ghaffarian. Moqueam-e Iran. I am a citizen of Iran. Va yek raqqaas hastam. And I'm a dancer." Although Persian language is seldom employed throughout the film except as novel backdrop, employing spoken Persian in this initial scene works to establish the film's authenticity and authority for the viewer.

Juxtaposing this declaration—"I am a citizen of Iran"—with images of the *basiji* beating Afshin helps the film conflate the violence the character is experiencing with the state in which he holds citizenship and interpellates the Iranian state as the perpetrator of violence rather than the protector of its citizenry. Thus, an implicit human rights framing tied to this specific act of violence sets the tone for the remainder of the film. This introductory scene closes with Afshin's most significant defiant declaration, "And I'm a dancer," establishing Afshin as the defiant youth to which the film's opening quote refers. The conjunction "and" implies a paradox: being a citizen of Iran *and* being a dancer are in tension or in contradiction with each other, and the linking of Afshin's beating with the declaration conflates the punishment with the statement.

Following this opening scene, the plot recounts Afshin's childhood dream to become a dancer, and we learn through his mother's warning that "dance is forbidden" in Iran. The film then jumps ahead to Afshin entering college in Tehran, where he starts an underground dance company, meets his primary dance partner and love interest, Elaheh (played by Freida Pinto), and performs a secret performance in the desert for a small audience of college-aged friends. The threat of the *basij* permeates the film both as visual backdrop and as characters whom Afshin and his friends must consistently dodge. After a near encounter with the *basij* during Afshin's secret performance in the desert, the film then turns to Afshin's arrest for filming the presidential election protests. After returning to the film's opening scene enacting Afshin's beating, Afshin ultimately escapes from the *basij*, spends a night wounded in the desert, and makes his way to a friend's house. Convinced that the *basij* will kill Afshin, Afshin's friend offers him the opportunity to use the friend's passport and take his place in his theater group's upcoming performance of Shakespeare's *The Tempest* in Paris ("Take my passport and never come back!"), an offer that Afshin eventually accepts.

After modifying the passport and bidding a tearful good-bye to Elaheh, Afshin nervously but successfully boards the plane with the theater group and makes his way to Paris, marking his (almost too easy) escape from Iran. This depiction of Afshin's escape is significant for how it distorts the facts about Ghaffarian's original departure from Iran, which, as I described, occurred through the invitation to perform in Germany through the Mülheim-Iran theater exchange program. More importantly, however, the emotional and kinesthetic empathy that this scene conjures—the tearful good-bye, the tense boarding of the airplane—gives the film viewer visceral relief when the plane successfully takes off and makes the film character Afshin's arrival in France—and, by extension, France itself—seem all the more extraordinary.

Once in Paris and while performing in *The Tempest,* Afshin breaks from the play's script, unbeknownst to the remainder of the cast, and begins to enact a performance of his own. This particular filmic moment draws from the actual aforementioned performance in Germany when Ghaffarian broke from his performance partner; however, the film fabricates the details to more force-fully produce the savior spectatorship of the audience *in* the film and for the audience *of* the film. The opening scene depicting Afshin's beating conjures in the film viewer a kinesthetic identification with Afshin's subjectivity. How-ever, much of this final scene marking Afshin's defection from Iran directs the film viewer's identification toward the subjectivity of the Parisian audience member watching Afshin's performance. Afshin breaks the fourth wall of *The Tempest* performance and addresses the diegetic audience with his gaze and his performative utterance: "My name is Afshin Ghaffarian. I'm a citizen of Iran. I'm a dancer. And my government won't let its people be free. In my country, even dance is forbidden. I want my rights. I want my freedom." He pauses for a moment and declares once again, this time shouting, "My name is Afshin Ghaffarian!" Afshin looks at his open hand; he then forcefully covers his mouth, gripping his face. With his other hand, he peels away the gripping hand. As the hand reluctantly releases, he declares once again, "My name is Afshin Ghaf-farian, and I'm a dan—" His hand again quickly covers his mouth, interrupt-ing his declaration. The faces of the audience convey increasing confusion over this break from *The Tempest* performance. The two official chaperones accompanying the theater group's trip from Iran grow irritable as they observe Afshin's performance from the stage wings.

After Afshin releases his grip, his movements become percussive, angular, and forceful, presumably expressing his frustration with and defiance of his censored position as an artist in Iran. Afshin then traces buoyant circles with his arms before propelling his body into a progression of stationary spins. A smile comes to his face as he seems to forget that the audience is there at all. Afshin's fast spins show up as a blur on the film, which depicts him from behind, inviting the film viewer to embody Afshin's momentary transcendence and freedom. Finally, Afshin brings the film full circle as he begins his reenact-ment of its violent opening scene. Again, the film viewer is encouraged to iden-tify with the diegetic audience through long frontal shots of Afshin's dancing body that interpellate both audiences of and in the film as savior spectators. Afshin's buoyant arms seem to have become caught at the wrists, and he abruptly cycles through falling and standing. As if trying to escape from someone, Afshin crawls on the ground, contracting as if being kicked, begging, "Please!" The film then inserts a flashback to its opening scene; Afshin is shown once again on the dusty ground being kicked by the *basiji.* Through montage alternating between these two temporal moments, the film produces a strong association. In the Parisian performance, Afshin grips the front of his shirt and pulls himself up to his feet. The chaperones attempt to stop the performance from the wings; they shout "Shut it down!" and demand the technician to shut the curtains. With Afshin now behind closed curtains, the chaperones rush over to restrain him. The audience grows increasingly concerned upon hearing the commotion. Afshin frees himself from the chaperones' restraint and falls onto the ground downstage of the curtains in full view of the spectators. Accepting defeat, the chaperones abruptly leave.

This scene lucidly represents spectators as saviors: the presence of the diegetic audience literally saves Afshin from an unknown but presumably dire fate. Simultaneously confused and exhilarated by this spectacle, the audience begins to applaud. Afshin looks up from his place on the floor; the camera pans from behind him so that the film spectator can see the same faces that Afshin sees. The audience is nodding and smiling, encouraging and compassionate. Afshin is finally receiving what he had allegedly always dreamed of, validation from a "real" audience. He brings himself to his feet, pulls a green scarf from his pocket, wraps it around his palm, and raises two fingers into a V. One by one, members of the French audience stand up to also perform the V gesture.

In this final scene, both the diegetic and film audience witness Afshin's liberatory performance: liberatory in that it frees him from having to return to "oppressive" Iran, and liberatory in that it marks the inaugural moment when he becomes an authentic dancer-subject, enabled by the presence and validation of the compassionate savior spectators. The film spectators are called to engage in what Manning refers to as "cross-viewing" (2004). Their kinesthetic empathy shifts from Afshin's dancing body to the bodies of the savior spectators in the film, who move to their feet, perform Afshin's hand gesture of victory, and nod in acceptance as if to convey, "You're now one of us. Welcome to the civilized world!"

Conclusion

Savior spectatorship operates through a network of media affiliations and representations, a transmedia environment wherein discourses and images (static and moving) cooperate to coordinate ideological messages about Iranian dancing bodies. The framework of savior spectatorship troubles notions that presume that an active spectator is inherently one who critically identifies and interrogates ideologies embedded in any given performance. While narratives of suffering and scenes of rescue position savior spectators surrounding Ghaffarian as affectively and kinesthetically moved and engaged in a performance of compassion, these narratives and the spectators' performative consumption of Ghaffarian's story work to validate hegemonic political structures rather than question or dismantle them. As a kinesthetically charged spectatorship, the identification of the suffering dancing body as "similar to us" affects how viewers decide whose lives are and are not worth saving, or, in Judith Butler's (2004) terms, who is and is not a "grievable life."

In my critique of representations that frame Iranian dancers as objects of rescue, I do not wish to minimize the experiences of Iranians who have been impacted by various forms of Iranian state restriction and punishment or of those who have actively struggled to develop a sustained dance practice within Iran. As I have described, there are indeed vast restrictions on dance in Iran. However, I wish to draw attention to the ways Iranian dancers' experiences can become appropriated for what Ghaffarian himself during our interview called "political agendas cloaked as advocacy," which can advance Islamophobic views and become potential alibis for racist domestic and foreign policies.[9] The representations of Ghaffarian's asylum in France support a mentality of savior spectatorship whereby Western spectatorship of Iranian dancers constructs a model of Iranianness that fits neatly within political discourses of Iran as backward and premodern. Particularly with US president Trump's preoccupation with war on Iran and his 2017 ban on travelers from Muslim-majority countries, including Iran, we are called upon to imagine new practices and frameworks that reveal and undo the uneven power relations produced through savior spectatorship and (neo)liberal notions of freedom.

Notes

All translations are mine.

1. To avoid confusion between the fictionalized Afshin Ghaffarian in *Desert Dancer* and Ghaffarian's real-life biography and choreography, I refer to the film character as "Afshin" and to the real-life figure as "Ghaffarian."

2. In putting "oppressive" in scare quotes, I do not mean to imply that oppression does not occur in Iran. Rather, I wish to draw attention to how, in political and popular Euro-American discourse, "oppression" becomes an automatic and unquestioned moralistic qualifier affixed to the construction of the Islamic Republic.

3. Dance scholars grapple with the promises and limits of kinesthetic empathy as a framework for examining the relationship between dancers' and viewers' bodies. Insisting upon the inherent incompleteness of kinesthetic empathy, critics interrogate the presumed "universal" body—a white, male, middle-class, abled body—that feels with and for other bodies and emphasize how race, gender, sexuality, class, and (dis)ability shape power relations within kinesthetic exchanges (Manning 2004; Foster 2011).

4. I thank scholar Ida Meftahi for our discussions about the legal status of dance in Iran. For more on dance and other movement-based theater in contemporary Iran, see Meftahi (2016).

5. Presumably, the offenses against public chastity were based on the fact that the women in the video were not wearing the mandatory headscarf and that the inter-actions between the men and women exceeded proper moral conduct. The director and the six actors were released from jail after one day with suspended sentences with the stipulation that they not reoffend.

6. Ghaffarian's website states that Ghaffarian renounced his refugee status in 2014. At the time of writing, he resides in Paris as a student of political science at the Sorbonne.

7. Ghaffarian's Iranian identity situates him differently within France from Arab Middle Eastern / North African postcolonial subjects, who make up the largest demo-graphic of Muslims in France and who tend to be the primary targets of exclusionary discourse and policy.

8. In online interviews, Ghaffarian expresses ambivalence about *Desert Dancer* and explains that the film took great liberties in the representation of his life and dance in Iran. Aside from an interview with the film's director before the making of the film, Ghaffarian did not contribute toward the actors' dance training or the film's choreo-graphic content. Neither was he consulted during the making of the film. I have no evidence that Khan viewed Ghaffarian's work online; however, Khan stated in the online French media *CCCdanse* that he "adapted certain movements of the real Afshin in the style of the film" (Anna 2015). I see similar movement vocabularies in the film's and Ghaffarian's choreographies, such as the cycling of falling and supine contractions I have described from *The Piercing Shout*, leading me to believe that Khan viewed and drew from Ghaffarian's choreographic content available online.

9. Showings of the film *Desert Dancer* have included UCLA's Burkle Center for International Relations Human Rights Film Festival and Washington, DC's Newseum Institute, whose website describes its mission as exploring the "challenges confronting freedom around the world." Furthermore, Newseum's marketing materials assert that *Desert Dancer* demonstrates "the current connection between arts, foreign policy, and the fight for freedom." These showings hosted influential attendees, including foreign correspondents, scholars, and celebrities. While there is no evidence that this film or the discourse surrounding it have directly influenced policy, it is telling that showings of this fictionalized biographical drama have been sponsored by centers related to international relations, human rights, and journalism.

Works Cited

Abu-Lughod, Lila. 2013. *Do Muslim Women Need Saving?* Cambridge, MA: Harvard University Press.

Alexandre, Xavier. 2013. "Iranien en exil: La danse est sa liberté." *Ouest France,* Septem-ber 27. https://www.ouest-france.fr/iranien-en-exil-la-danse-est-sa-liberte-580869.

Anna. 2015. "Film 'Desert Dancer': La danse comme acte politique." *CCCdanse,* December 30. https://cccdanse.com/actus/film-desert-dancer-la-danse-comme-acte-politique/.

Arvers, Fabienne. 2009. "Être danseur au pays des ayatollahs." *Les in rocks,* December 19. http://www.lesinrocks.com/2009/12/19/actualite/societe/etre-danseur-au-pays-des-ayatollahs-1135202/.

Barber, Tiffany E. 2015. "*Ghostcatching* and *After Ghostcatching*: Dances in the Dark." *Dance Research Journal* 47 (1): 44–67.

Butler, Judith. 2004. *Precarious Life: The Powers of Mourning and Violence*. New York: Verso.

D'Aloia, Adriano. 2011. "Cinematic Empathy: Spectator Involvement in the Film Experience." In *Kinesthetic Empathy in Creative and Cultural Practices*, edited by Dee Reynolds and Matthew Reason, 91–107. Bristol: Intellect Books.

Daryoush, Leyli. 2011. "The Persian Scream, Afshin Ghaffarian." Modified June 6, 2015. Translated from French. http://liveweb.arte.tv/fr/video/Le_Cri_Persan/.

Desert Dancer. 2014. Directed by Richard Raymond. Relativity Media.

Dodds, Sherril. 2001. *Dance on Screen: Genres and Media from Hollywood to Experimental Art*. London: Palgrave Macmillan.

Fisek, Emine. 2010. "Incorporating Immigrants: Theatrical Aid Work and the Politics of Witnessing in France." PhD diss., University of California, Berkeley.

Foster, Susan Leigh. 2011. *Choreographing Empathy: Kinesthesia in Performance*. New York: Routledge.

Ghaffarian, Afshin. 2012. Interview with the author. Paris, July 19.

Grewal, Inderpal. 1998. "On the New Global Feminism and the Family of Nations: Dilemmas of Transnational Feminist Practice." In *Talking Visions: Multicultural Feminism in a Transnational Age*, edited by Ella Shohat, 501–30. Cambridge, MA: MIT Press.

Joshi, Priya. 2012. "Freida Pinto: 'Dance Training for Desert Dancer Was Daunting.'" *Digital Spy*, October 12. http://www.digitalspy.com/bollywood/news/a430306/freida -pinto-dance-training-for-desert-dancer-was-daunting/.

Mahmood, Saba. 2005. *Politics of Piety: The Islamic Revival and the Feminist Subject*. Princeton, NJ: Princeton University Press.

Manning, Susan. 2004. *Modern Dance, Negro Dance: Race in Motion*. Minneapolis: University of Minnesota Press.

Marks, Laura U. 2000. *The Skin of the Film: Intercultural Cinema, Embodiment, and the Senses*. Durham, NC: Duke University Press.

Massad, Joseph A. 2007. *Desiring Arabs*. Chicago: University of Chicago Press.

Meftahi, Ida. 2016. *Gender and Dance in Modern Iran: Biopolitics on Stage*. New York: Routledge.

Moallem, Minoo. 2002. "Whose Fundamentalism?" *Meridians: Feminism, Race, Transnationalism* 2 (2): 298–301.

Neuman, Scott. 2014. "Iran's 'Happy' Dancers Receive Suspended Sentences." *NPR*, September 19. https://www.npr.org/sections/thetwo-way/2014/09/19/349842310/irans -happy-dancers-receive-suspended-sentences.

Nooshin, Laudan. 2017. "Whose Liberation? Iranian Popular Music and the Fetishization of Resistance." *Popular Communication* 15 (3): 163–91.

Puar, Jasbir. 2007. *Terrorist Assemblages: Homonationalism in Queer Times*. Durham, NC: Duke University Press.

Quillard, Marion. 2010. "En Iran, le corps est un péché." *Le Monde*, modified February 2. http://www.lemonde.fr/culture/article/2010/01/28/afshin-ghaffarian-en-iran-le -corps-est-un-peche_1298069_3246.html#Q5ztgU63MY6jxBgq.99.

Rancière, Jacques. 2009. *The Emancipated Spectator*. New York: Verso.

Reynolds, Dee. 2011. Introduction to *Kinesthetic Empathy in Creative and Cultural Practices*, edited by Dee Reynolds and Matthew Reason, 87–89. Bristol: Intellect Books.

Saeed, Sana. 2014. "The West Loves the Story of Iran's Jailed 'Happy' Dancers for All the Wrong Reasons." *Mic.com*, May 22. Accessed December 12, 2015. http://mic.com/articles/89827/the-west-loves-the-story-of-iran-s-jailed-happy-dancers-for-all-the-wrong-reasons#.vGvb5UIaz.

Scott, Joan Wallach. 2007. *The Politics of the Veil*. Princeton, NJ: Princeton University Press.

Shay, Anthony. 2014. "Reviving the Reluctant Art of Iranian Dance in Iran and in the American Diaspora." In *The Oxford Handbook of Music Revival*, edited by Caroline Bithell and Juniper Hill, 618–43. Oxford: Oxford University Press.

Sklar, Deidre. 2001. "Five Premises for a Culturally Sensitive Approach to Dance." In *Moving History / Dancing Cultures: A Dance History Reader*, edited by Ann Dils and Ann Cooper Albright, 30–32. Middletown, CT: Wesleyan University Press.

Costuming Brownnesses in British South Asian Dance

ROYONA MITRA

This chapter examines the role of costuming in the dance experiments of Sonia Sabri and Aakash Odedra, leading British South Asian dancers, in order to demonstrate how costuming negotiates the performance of British brownnesses at the intersections of race and gender within British South Asian dance. In dialogue with African American theorizations of blackness (Johnson 2003; DeFrantz and Gonzalez 2014), the chapter further conceptualizes British brownnesses as a consciously racialized identification that champions the multidimensional lived realities of British people with lineages in South Asian nations in order to critique the geopolitical label "South Asian" and its evasion of race politics in categorizing these diasporic groups. Sabri's and Odedra's distinct aesthetic endeavors are catalyzed by their second-generation British Indiannesses as a woman and a man, respectively, and their training in the north Indian classical dance style of *kathak*. In their artistic projects the role of costuming is vital in its commentary on how their gender and race intersect to represent their British brownnesses, but it has yet to receive scholarly scrutiny.[1]

Drawing on theater scholar Aoife Monks's distinction between the noun "costume," the articles of clothing worn by performers, and the verb "costuming," the process of deploying costumes in order to engineer how audiences read the bodies wearing them (2010, 3), this chapter considers the repercussions of costuming British South Asian dance from double perspectives: the dancer who engages in costuming as an act of self-representation, and the audience who encounters this costuming as a mediating site between the dancer and the dance. My methodology draws on costume studies, critical race theory, costuming analysis in selected performance events, and the voices of the artists discussed here via interviews I conducted. While I focus predominantly on costuming in Sabri's and Odedra's works, my interview with Aditi Mangaldas, the internationally renowned Indian *kathak* exponent, provides a wider global

context for examining costuming in contemporaneous *kathak* choreographies
in India and the British South Asian diaspora.

Theorizing Costuming as Annotative and/or
Choreographic Practices

I propose that costuming in British South Asian dance operates along a spectrum between two possibilities: annotative costuming and choreographic costuming. These two artistic potentials are not mutually exclusive binaries; rather,
they are creative possibilities that coexist along the same spectrum. My conceptualization is derived from marrying Monks's notion of costuming with
dance scholar Prarthana Purkayastha's concept of annotative practice: an aesthetic process of culturally inscribing already racially marked skin, for example,
through the application of henna on the body of the conceptual artist Hetain
Patel (2015, 114). On the annotative end of the spectrum, I argue, exists the practice of costuming a racially and culturally marked diasporic body in vernacular-
coded attire, making the dancer stand out within a predominantly white and
Western environment. Here, traditional clothing authenticates the dancer's
brown, South Asian heritage, leading to an ironically concealed yet extrane-
ously ornamentalized "hyper-visualisation and hyper-orientalizing of the skin"
beneath (114). On the choreographic end of the spectrum exists the practice
of costuming a brown, South Asian diasporic body in urban clothing that is
closer to her twenty-first-century hybrid reality, that does not mark her in any
culturally specific way, and that becomes an extension of her choreography itself.
Through choreographic costuming, the dancer's body, movement, and clothing enter into a lived, pliable, and mutually affective dialogue as they breathe
life into each other.

 This conceptualization of costuming British South Asian dance as a spectrum
of possibilities that lie between the annotative and the choreographic is my
contribution to the burgeoning field of critical costume studies. While Donatella Barbieri (2017), Aoife Monks (2010), and Rachel Hann and Sidsel Bech
(2014) have added to this field in important ways, scholarship on the politics
of costuming diasporic dancers of color, as signaled by Yutian Wong (2010),
begs more critical attention. In addition, while I owe much of my thinking to
Monks, I recognize that costuming for actors and dancers differs on practical,
aesthetic, and political levels. In traditional text-based theater, costuming for
actors visually contextualizes their characters' spatialities, temporalities, histories, classes, genders, sexualities, ethnicities, and races, among other biographical information. These contexts are then aurally reinforced (or contradicted)
by text spoken by the characters, which enables the audience to navigate
meaning making between what they see and what they hear. It is the power of

the spoken word and its relationship to embodied gestures that brings the actor's costumes to life. In dance performances that rely predominantly, though not exclusively, on nontextual means of communication, costuming can, on the surface, lend similar visual contexts to performers' danced realities. However, in the absence of the spoken word, these contexts remain ambiguous, enabling the dancer to play with, even undermine, audience perceptions about whom and what they are watching. Therefore, beyond its material presence to lend visual depth and enhance or constrict movement, costuming in dance becomes a choreographic language through which the dancer speaks, deliberately generating ambiguities and ruptures between her moving body and the clothes she inhabits.

So far I have engaged with predominantly Western concepts of costuming dance. In order to take a decolonial approach into this discourse, I wish to complicate these discussions through the concept of *aharya*, the principles of costuming and makeup as laid down in the Natyashastra, an ancient Indian dramaturgical treatise.[2] According to the Natyashastra, dancers train to perform *abhinaya*, a codified language that narrates stories, conjures characterizations, and evokes emotional states through gestures and facial expressions (*angika*), textual delivery (*vachika*), and costumes and makeup (*aharya*). Here too, then, *aharya* functions not as mere surface ornamentation of the dancer but as an inseparable part of the choreography and its signification processes. It is crucial to remember, though, that despite being interpreted by many as a prescriptive edict on all aspects of *Indian* performing arts, the Natyashastra clearly calls for its artistic principles to evolve beyond this cultural specificity (Nair 2015). Yet the practice of *aharya* has been perceived as specifically Indian, incapable of change or transgression. In British South Asian dance experiments, the use of this fixed notion of *aharya*, or what I argue as annotative costuming, can become an authenticating trope. While on the one hand it signals one's cultural heritage/s, on the other it generates an ambiguity between the ostentatious surface of the dancers' costumes, which hark back to an imagined, pure link to the Natyashastra's Indianness, and the dancers' multiethnic, twenty-first-century diasporic and urban realities. Such ambiguity can both empower and reinforce the silence embodied by a mute/d dancer. When British South Asian dancers engage in annotative costuming, they risk their audiences simply engaging with the costume as an ornamental extraneous surface that accentuates the dancers' brown exoticism, as often demonstrated in Orientalist readings of these dance practices. This can create an irreconcilable disjuncture between a dancer's costume and her art, and can further prevent the audience from being able to look beyond the surface in order to engage with costuming as a process of "critically interrogating the body" within it (Hann and Bech

2014, 4). In my theorization of costuming British South Asian dance along the choreographic end of the spectrum, I emphasize the practice as not fixed but evolving, such that it mirrors the principle of *aharya* as an "active component of choreography" itself (Bugg 2014, 69). *Aharya's* manifestations as an extension of choreographic practice, regardless of cultural specificities, has the potential to dislodge costuming from problematic discourses that celebrate authenticity as fixed, pure, rooted, and immutable. Instead, choreographic costuming as *aharya* and *aharya* as choreographic costuming, can reframe authenticity as the condition of being always responsive to one's fluid, evolving, multifarious, and shifting affiliations to diasporic and multiethnic embodiments of British brownnesses.

British Brownnesses

At the heart of costuming British South Asian dance lies its myriad representations of British brownnesses. The plural *brownnesses* is important, as it represents an identification category for people with lineages predominantly in India, Pakistan, and Bangladesh and to a lesser extent in Sri Lanka, Nepal, and Bhutan. Some of them immigrated to the United Kingdom in the 1950s as part of the postwar "migration of labour" (Hesse and Sayyid 2006, 15), others sought higher educational opportunities, and still others arrived as economic migrants through the late twentieth and early twenty-first centuries and have settled in the UK. These British brown people, distinguishable from each other on many grounds, such as language, religion, class, and ethnicity, have been homogenized in the UK through the geopolitical label "South Asian." I contend that under the guise of championing multiethnicities over brownness and therefore evading the issue of race politics, which fundamentally frames the identities and experiences of these diasporic groups, the label "South Asian" ignores their racialization while simultaneously being an implicitly racialized category.

According to British South Asian sociologists Sarita Malik and Anamik Saha, this euphemized representation of brownness as South Asianness has become punctuated by three kinds of reductive manifestations in white British consciousness. South Asians are either exoticized through a "'positive' commodification of a globalized, Bollywood-influenced South Asian popular culture" (Malik 2008, 352), sanitized to create a diluted and palatable form of non-threatening difference (Saha 2012, 431), or sensationalized as violent and uncivilized people through a "'negative' preoccupation with Islam" in a post-9/11 and 7/7 landscape (Malik 2008, 352). Thus, despite inherent differences, all British brown people continue to be Orientalized, homogenized, imagined, and mediated through a predominantly white British lens. It would seem, then, that the

promise of the unmarkedness of the label "South Asian" is but a fallacy. Theater scholar Dimple Godiwala signals such implicit racialization of black and
South Asian identity in the UK in the messy collapse that pervades British
discourses on race and ethnicity. She argues that British people of color are
"generally perceived as being located in a difference from, and not within the
constructed ethnic identity (Englishness) of the mainstream" (Godiwala 2006,
4), implying a relational, value-laden identification process of people of color
vis-à-vis white natives.

    In critiquing this problematic label, "South Asian," I enter into dialogue with
African American theorizations of blackness (Johnson 2003; DeFrantz and
Gonzalez 2014) and propose a theorization of British brownnesses, an explicitly
racialized categorization of British people with lineages in South Asian nations.
My concept of British brownnesses recognizes four things. First, that despite and
because of prevalent discourses surrounding the constructed nature of race,
British brownnesses' inherent and powerful impact on the marginalization of
people of color as Others in the UK, especially in the current post-Brexit landscape, is undeniable. Second, British brownnesses champion plurality, acknowledging the myriad differences between British brown people on the basis of
not only their multiple histories, home nation affiliations, and ethnic heritages
but also their genders, sexualities, classes, and ableisms. Third, the plurality of
British brownnesses makes them unfixable and slippery, like E. Patrick Johnson's conceptualization of blackness, "ever beyond the reach of one's grasp,
[although] its elusiveness does not preclude one from trying to fix it, to pin it
down" (2003, 2). Finally, British brownnesses signal, through such plurality, a
simultaneous commonality of experience that arises from being, and being
perceived as, brown in the UK—those deemed responsible for complicating
the native white British landscape, thereby irrevocably decentering old colonial power relations. The label "British brownnesses," therefore, acknowledges
the plurality of its manifestations, rejects the fixity of these people of color as
static and primitive (Madsen 2011, 108), and exposes the complex lived realities of British brown people with South Asian lineages.

    British brownnesses are therefore as much a response to nation-specific histo-
ries and aesthetics as they are to the evolution and mobility of identities within
one's transethnic diasporic temporality. Here I evoke African American performance studies scholars Thomas F. DeFrantz and Anita Gonzalez's dialogic
theorizations of black. For DeFrantz, "black is the manifestation of Africanist
aesthetics" as "action: action engaged to enlarge capacity, confirm presence, to
dare" (DeFrantz and Gonzalez 2014, 5). DeFrantz's notion of black as action is
rooted in Gonzalez's concept of black as dialogic imagination: "I understand
black as a response to histories that extend beyond Africa and its aesthetics.

Black performance expands, synthesizes, comments and responds to imaginations about black identity as much as to its own inherent expressions. . . . I view black as a dialogic imagination" (6). Gonzalez's "dialogic imagination," I contend, manifests as DeFrantz's "action." It is with this spirit that I theorize British brownnesses as a dialogic imagination that is generated between living, experiencing, perceiving, and imagining British brownnesses.

Sabri and Odedra both represent distinct dialogic and activist embodiments of British brownnesses in their respective dance experiments. Their works become the fulcrum through which they politically and aesthetically comment on audience perceptions of their brownnesses through deploying costuming choices along the spectrum between the annotative and the choreographic. My understanding of their costuming as politically discerning choices derives from an embodied space of intellectual enquiry as I try to make sense of the annotative nature of costuming that I have been subjected to over the years as a first-generation brown female dance studies scholar in the UK.

Annotative Costuming of Self as Other

In 2001 I started my first academic job as lecturer in drama at a UK university and inherited a module called World Theatres. The module was designed as a weekly whistle-stop tour through non-European performance traditions around the world, providing touristic glimpses of Japanese Noh theater, Chinese Peking opera, Indonesian shadow puppetry, Indian classical dance forms, and African masked performances. While I was troubled by the neocolonial gaze implicit in the module design and worried how I could possibly speak with authority on all these living traditions, my colleague who had written the module clearly felt that as the first academic of color in the department, I would be ideal to deliver the content. Moreover, I was encouraged to deliver the session on Indian classical dance in a *sari*.[3] This is when it hit home. It was not enough that I was a classically trained *kathak* dancer and therefore able to speak from an embodied place, regardless of how I dressed for that session. Unless I adorned visual signifiers of my Indianness in the form of a *sari*, my embodied knowledge would mean little.

But something else troubled me more: the assumption that female *kathak* dancers wear *saris* when in fact they predominantly wear either a *ghagra-choli* (a long skirt and a fitted blouse) or a *churidar-angarakha* (fitted trousers and a long, flowing tunic) depending on the dancer's Hindu or Muslim *gharana*, or "lineage," respectively. This is accompanied by a *dupatta*, a long scarf that has been traditionally used to cover the upper torso of female *kathak* dancers in order to conceal the outline of their breasts as an act of modesty. Finally, a dancer wears *ghungroos*, a set of ankle bells, on both feet; the bells are designed to musically enter into conversation with the characteristic hollow sound produced by the barefoot rhythmic stamping of *kathak*'s intricate footwork. I realized in those moments that while I knew that wearing a *sari* to deliver a performance/lecture on *kathak* was in some ways a misrepresentation of the form that I had grown up with, it would in fact make hypervisible my Indian brownness and would be the very thing that would authenticate me as an Indian classical dancer to the Western eye.

The political power with which we people of color are viewed when in annotative costumes is undeniable. Both the costumes and the gaze not only locate us as the Other but also fix us as such, rendering us incapable of growth, let alone transgression. However, this is not just true of a white (neo)colonial gaze in the diaspora. Strict costuming codes of indigenous performance traditions are policed just as restrictively by nationalist gazes. These costumes (or the lack of them) can become the sites in and through which particularly female artists find their very artistic practices being judged and challenged. This is exactly what the eminent Indian *kathak* artist Aditi Mangaldas discovered in the recent past.

"Has the Dupatta Become a Noose?"[4]

The *dupatta* has become a prescriptive component of classical *kathak*'s repertoire and the fulcrum of recent debates on the tensions between tradition and change that frame *kathak*'s past, present, and future. Mangaldas, inspired by her guru Kumudini Lakhia's forgoing of the *dupatta* and other ostentatious costuming styles and jewelry in order to emphasize the clear lines and complex bodily articulations of dancers' upper torsos, has entered into minimalist and provocative explorations with the *dupatta* herself. In her ensemble piece *Within* (2016), Mangaldas turns the *dupatta* into a shroud, accentuating the facelessness of the dancing bodies while drawing attention to their bodily presence, muscular density, and physical virtuosity.

Mangaldas's experimentations with *kathak*'s traditionalist *aharya* has come under national scrutiny. In January 2013 she turned down the Sangeet Natak Akademi Award, a prestigious national recognition of artistry, claiming that her work had been wrongly categorized under "Creative and Experimental Dance." Instead, she asserted that she had dedicated her career to advancing the classical field of *kathak* (Mangaldas 2013). Although Mangaldas did not state that it is her experimentations with *kathak* costume that was responsible for classifying her art not as "Kathak" but as "Creative and Experimental Dance," she cited an incident at the Kathak Kendra, India's National Institute of Kathak Dance, that insinuated a connection. Her letter to the Kathak Kendra became the fulcrum of an ensuing debate on *kathak*, classicism, tradition, and the role of costuming in navigating preservation and changes to the art form: "Recently, the Kathak Kendra . . . held a festival in which a young dancer was made to change her publicity material as her photograph portrayed her without a *dupatta*. The letter issued to her, stressed that she abide by a certain form of 'Vesh—bhusha.' We need to beware of such authoritarian decrees. Wearing of a dupatta is not an essential hallmark of Kathak but a question of aesthetics, relevance and context, which the artists themselves must have the prerogative to choose" (Mangaldas 2013). In the response that followed from a collective of senior dancers at Kathak Kendra, Mangaldas's questioning of "authoritarian decrees" vis-à-vis *kathak*'s costuming was very clearly cited as a reason why her art could not be considered under the "Kathak" category. The senior dancers cited five key points to support their rationale:

> As senior dancers we say that Kathak dance has a classical dress code like all other dance forms. . . . You identify any dance form through the costume first and that is the essential part of it, classically called "Aaharya." . . . Kathak Kendra is an institution to teach the tradition of the age old Kathak form and costume also is a part of it, which all the students have to learn. . . . Last but not the least we feel surprised that you want yourself to be considered in the category of Kathak awardees but on the other hand you are refusing the basic traditional attire of it. (Gurus of Kathak Kendra 2013)

Mangaldas replied that in her training, the "*aaharya* of *kathak* is and has always been flexible while it has maintained the overall sensibility of the style." She concluded with the provocation: "What is basic traditional attire is the debate, and who decides that?" (Mangaldas 2013). She elaborated on further details of the debate in an interview with me, stating that those defending the *dupatta* as integral to the traditional *kathak* aesthetic argue that it enables the *kathak* dancer to deliver a third and desirable dimension of the art, which is inaccessible without it. Mangaldas cited this rationale as fundamentally sexist, questioning that such a premise suggests that male *kathak* dancers are born with this third dimension, since they are not required to use a *dupatta* in this policed way (Mangaldas 2016).

Never shy of openly challenging such "authoritarian decrees," Mangaldas (2016) deploys costuming not as an annotative surface ornamentation but as an embodied extension of her choreographic concepts themselves, shaped by "context, relevance and aesthetic." Even when sourcing culturally specific clothing, she advocates using styles that speak to twenty-first-century Indian realities, such as her use of the simple and contemporary kurta-pyjama/churidar (long and fitted tunic with fitted trousers). In order to accentuate the muscular densities and physical lines of tensions and releases in the female *kathak* dancer's back, Mangaldas has used the Rajasthani *choli*, a backless and fitted blouse that has been transformed, through the use of boning, into a secure bustier to provide security to the dancer while accentuating her physical form. For Mangaldas, the *kathak* dancer has to evolve with the times, constantly adapting to her age, her circumstances, her physicality, and her audience. And this means that her costuming processes must evolve too—never stagnant but always responsive to the need for change.

Costuming British Brownnesses at the Intersections of Race and Gender

If the *dupatta* discourse around the performance of *kathak* within India pertains to the policing, preservation, and performance of a national identity, costuming British diasporic *kathak* dancers, whose ethnicities and national and cultural heritages cut across India, Pakistan, Bangladesh, and other South Asian countries, also becomes about representations of race, in particular, British brownnesses. However, we cannot ignore the ways in which gender politics shape this discourse. To understand how brownnesses manifest through the artistic visions of Sabri and Odedra, an intersectional analysis of these representations is vital. I therefore conduct my comparative analyses of Sabri's and Odedra's costuming of brownnesses, mindful that Sabri's role as a female diasporic *kathak* dancer is distinct from that of her male brown colleague, Odedra. And these gender differences impact how these artists represent their British brownnesses, consequently influencing how they are read by their predominantly white Western audiences.

Echoing the Indian nationalist trope of the woman as the bastion of a chaste national identity (John and Nair 1998), women in the British South Asian diaspora have borne the responsibility for the preservation and transmission of home cultural values, and the learning of South Asian dance forms has been central to this project (Werbner 2004, 905). Therefore, as Andree Grau notes in her influential report, "South Asian Dance in Britain," South Asian dance in the UK has become a predominantly female domain in which Sabri is a norm while Odedra an exception (2002, 8). So while Sabri may not have had to face the odds that would have been set against Odedra as a brown man who wanted to pursue dance professionally, the judgments reserved for her contemporization of *kathak*, both in how it is danced and in how it is costumed, are indeed disproportionately gendered. Sabri notes that a certain kind of annotative costuming-desiring criticism prevails among both tradition-bound British South Asian audiences and white Arts Council representatives. The latter, in a recent artistic assessment of Sabri's performance of *Salaam* (2016) (figure 44), questioned why Sabri had not worn traditional *kathak* costume, mistaking her fitted *churidar* as leggings and critiquing Sabri's artistic choices to opt for less ostentatious clothing. In our 2016 interview Sabri explained that it is the fear of being subjected to this kind of ill-informed aesthetic judgment that prevents many up-and-coming female dancers working in the UK from challenging prescriptive and annotative costuming norms.

Odedra echoed Sabri's assertion in my 2016 interview with him, commenting on the gendered costuming expectations placed on British *kathak* dancers: "I think there is a difference between what male and female *kathak* dancers are expected to wear during classical recitals. There is greater pressure and expectation on women *kathak* dancers to preserve the iconic and traditional image

FIGURE 44. Sonia Sabri in *Salaam*, 2016. (Photo by Simon Richardson)

of the art form itself, especially outside of India." He pondered whether because male *kathak* costumes have traditionally always been more minimalist in the form of *churidar-kurta*, that diasporic male *kathak* artists can and do get away with breaking costuming norms.

Sabri's performance of her classical *kathak* repertoire with her company of brown and white dancers at the British Conservative Party's annual conference in 2010 in Birmingham, which marked the party's return to power in coalition with the Liberal Democrats after a hiatus of thirteen years, becomes a fascinating case study to examine how race, gender, and nation play out intersectionally in both Sabri's performance of, and the event's framing of, British brownnesses. Sabri was not fully cognizant of the significance of this invitation at the time. During our interview she described her conversation with party representatives: "They wanted some work that would represent the diversity of the multiethnic communities we live in in Birmingham. And I said, 'Are you sure? Do you just want to see some brown faces, or do you want to see what brown faces can do, or do you want to see where brown faces derive from?' To this they replied simply, 'We just want it to be spectacular.'" While it would seem that the Conservative Party representatives did not rise to Sabri's racialized interrogation of their request to perform the regional diversity of the city of Birmingham, they did not deny it either. Instead, their association of diversity with spectacle laid the path for Sabri to strategically choose to perform her classical over her contemporary *kathak* repertoire. She clarified her rationale: "Why did I choose to perform the classical idiom-based strand of my work in this context? Because I thought I had a responsibility to represent all constituent British Asians in my community, the globalized and integrated ones, the more tradition-bound ones, and the many others who fall in spaces in between. And in this instance I wanted to show the Conservative Party that some of Birmingham's Asian communities could be tradition-bound and British at the same time. So that's how we went in." Costuming herself and her company in brightly colored traditional *angarakha*, *churidars*, and *dupattas*, in this instance Sabri chose annotative modalities of the spectrum that accentuated brownnesses onstage, making them hypervisible within the British landscape. In the case of her English company dancer, Ursula Chamberlain, the annotative costuming complicated Chamberlain's whiteness via "browning up" through traditional costumes, sanctioned by Sabri's choreographic choices. In making these choices, Sabri reappropriated historical practices of browning up not with makeup but with clothing instead, using it to signify a removable layer of skin. While dance scholar Priya Srinivasan (2012) has rightly critiqued brownfacing as an imperialistic practice in the Orientalist works of the early twentieth-century white American modern dancer Ruth St. Denis, Chamberlain's browning up through clothing created instead a schism between her whiteness beneath and her annotated costumed brownness. Chamberlain, unlike St. Denis, did not pretend to inhabit the condition of brownness itself through faking the pigmentation of her skin.

Risking a potentially exoticized reading of both her repertoire and *kathak* itself but committed to embodying South Asian traditions as living, evolving, and inclusive of twenty-first-century British conditions, Sabri encountered a dilemma. Prior to their ten-minute performance, Jeremy Hunt, the government's cultural secretary at the time, came backstage to meet Sabri and her dancers. Sabri recalls his exoticizing comments about the brown women, who were dressed in their traditional attire, as beautiful. Hunt (2010) echoed these Orientalist thoughts in his introductory speech before the company's performance: "Now just before I came to speak to you this afternoon, I had a slightly surreal experience walking down from the green room, flanked not by members of the shadow cabinet. . . . I was flanked by three beautifully dressed dancers who are going to be part of our first performance." Hearing Hunt's reductive exclamations, which only referred to the surface of the dancers, convinced Sabri that she had to counter such colonizing mindsets by speaking out before their performance, despite a strictly controlled sequence of events in which, originally, she was not scheduled to have a voice. During our 2016 interview she explained: "A spur-of-the-moment decision made me decide to do an introductory speech. All the personnel and camera were thinking 'what the hell is she doing?' Because it's a live program, you only have a predesignated slot, and you have to stick to schedule. But I thought, I cannot lose this opportunity to speak. . . . It was vital that the gorgeous doll had a voice." As per Sabri's articulated intentions, she not only introduced *kathak* itself but also took the opportunity to politicize her company's participation at the event by urging the Conservative Party to support the role of the arts toward sociocultural progress, despite rumors of the party's plans to implement significant cuts to arts funding. The company then went on to perform their pieces to thunderous applause, and Hunt returned to the green room after the show to assure Sabri that the Conservative Party would indeed continue to support the arts. However, it is also vital to consider here that Sabri's decision to leverage the opportunity to speak out *precisely* in her manifestation as a gorgeous doll was a strategic one. She played into the exoticism expected of her and afforded by her annotative costume in order to further her financial appeals to the Conservative Party.

It is clear that Sabri is aware of the potential pitfalls of annotative costuming of British brownnesses through the use of traditional *kathak* attire within a predominantly white environment. She agreed that it is "undeniable that audiences can be potentially alienated by traditional costume as exotic and are therefore unable to see beyond the surface and consider the experimentations and the enquiry into the art itself" (Sabri 2016). However, she maintains that it is her artistic right to strategize costuming in ways that can enhance the visibility of a tradition-bound manifestation of British brownnesses. By undercutting the ornamented brownness of her traditional costume with her twenty-first-century, diasporic, and politically charged introduction, Sabri used annotative costuming to challenge white British perception of a British brown woman in traditional attire as desirable and submissive and as a muted object who cannot speak English before carefully "blowing these misconceptions apart" (Sabri 2016).

Sabri's strategic deployment of costuming cuts across the spectrum between annotative and choreographic modes and is driven by an innate desire to consider costuming not as extraneous but as another integral choreographic partner that shapes her art. She says that while at times her classical idiom-based performances like *Salaam* (2016) are costumed in traditional *kathak* attire and her more contemporary experimentations like *Kathakbox* (2011) and *Hatke* (2008) deploy more urban clothing such as T-shirts and leggings, she is not afraid to blur these stylistic choices either. In a recent dance-film called *Nu Body* (2016), which takes *kathak* to an outdoor and gritty location, Sabri (2016) wears "sexy leather boots with stiletto heels and looks grotty" while performing classical *kathak*. She is committed to this kind of experimentation to witness how her classical *kathak* footwork evolves and is reinvented because of her urban costuming choices of performing *tatkar*, *kathak*'s signature intricate, fast, and mathematically precise footwork, in high-heeled boots. Like Mangaldas, then, for Sabri, her changing *kathak* language and its evolving relationship to costuming are mutually responsive and open-ended components of her choreographic enquiries, oscillating between annotative and choreographic modalities that are dependent on context.

When we shift our focus to the codes of annotative traditional male *kathak* attire, it is clear that the male attire codes are undeniably less restrictive in comparison to those imposed upon Sabri as a female *kathak* dancer. Where Sabri must wear ostentatious *ghagra-cholis* or *churidar-angarakhas*, always covering her upper body with a *dupatta*, Odedra can wear minimalist *churidar-kurtas* without the need for the scarf. Consequently, Odedra's costuming navigates between annotative and choreographic modalities with more ease, as demonstrated in his debut performance of *Rising* (2011). *Rising* is comprised of four solos ("Nritta," "In the Shadow of Man," "Cut," and "Constellation"), which were choreographed by Odedra, Akram Khan, Russell Maliphant, and Sidi Larbi Cherkaoui, respectively, and which conjure an austere, sparse, solitary, and fragmented man's world visualized by men in and through a brown male body. The male, muscular, and fragile brownnesses of Odedra's form find myriad manifestations through a cyclical journey through the solos, from the annotative to the choreographic, and back again. In "Nritta," a pure technique-driven *kathak* recital, Odedra stands in a shaft of austere gray light dressed in a black *churidar-kurta* but without the signature *ghungroos*, the ankle bells. His brownness beneath is shrouded by his black clothing, and the dark lighting of the stage obscures his presence, making him nearly invisible at times. The dance is possibly a commentary on the experienced invisibility of people of color in white Western societies, but Odedra does not choose to challenge such invisibility by countering it through Sabri's hypervisible presence making. Instead, in a space that only he occupies, Odedra allows its vacuum to suck him in, making him an apparition in the darkness. His hands, face, and feet are the only glimpses of brown that intermittently appear and disappear repeatedly within the dark void.

The theme of obscured visibility in "Nritta" continues into "In the Shadow of Man" (figure 45). The piece starts with a shaft of tightly focused warm light on Odedra's bare and writhing brown muscular back, which is glistening with sweat and contorting to articulate his presence. As we encounter a mostly faceless Odedra, whether because the choreography keeps his back to the audience or lowers his face toward the ground, his bare brown upper torso becomes both visible and isolated by this lighting. But where Odedra works with the presence of brownness, Sabri makes it hypervisible. While his manifests through the revelation of his brown skin, hers manifests through its concealment. In his most embodied bare-torsoed stance, inviting a voyeuristic gaze upon his faceless, barebacked state, Odedra evokes a vulnerable, insecure, fragile, even sensualized male British brownness, while Sabri's annotative adorning of traditional attire hides her skin in order to emphasize its brownness through extraneous cultural signifiers. But both representations are symbolic of British brownnesses, which are gendered, sexualized, and racialized simultaneously.

The emphasis of Odedra's brown skin finds a fragmented form in "Cut," where with a close choreographic collaboration with lighting designer Michael Hulls, Odedra's sharp and agitated moving hands, limbs, elbow, arms, and fingers are lit in complete isolation, such that we never see his whole body, let alone what it is clothed in, but only his fragmented body parts. His brownness is not whole but a patchwork of multiple and fragmented affiliations and allegiances to multiple histories and heritages. And it is costumed in tightly framed knife-like slivers of white light that cut through his skin, constantly altering our perception of his brownnesses. The stark white light makes his fragmented body parts appear paler, almost whiter, than in the previous solo, evocatively signaling postcolonial theorist Homi Bhabha's concept of the post/colonial

FIGURE 45. Aakash Odedra in "In the Shadow of Man," *Rising*, 2011. (Photo by Pippa Samaya)

object's desire for mimicry, where some British brownnesses' desire to emulate the nuances of the predominant whiteness around them in order to blend in results in a manifestation that is "almost the same but not white" (1994, 128).

Finally, moving from the dark and austere landscapes to "Constellation," Odedra's brownness as colonial mimicry of whiteness takes on a clearer visual form. Dressed in a white *churidar-kurta*, he walks around the stage under white light bulbs, which hang at different heights in the space and provide different amounts of light. "Constellation" brings together Odedra's constituent and fragmented body parts from the previous solos into an organic and omnipresent whole that plays with the interdiction between his concealed brownness beneath and his white clothing on the surface. His annotative *churidar-kurta* conceals his brown skin in order to highlight his brownness through the clothing itself, signaling that brownnesses are symbolic of more than just one's epidermal reality. At the same time, his clothing's white hue reminds us that just like attempts to emulate whiteness, clothing too is an impermanent and unstable performance of racialized identity and can be removed at any point.

Odedra's deployment of annotative costuming in *churidar-kurta* signals a visual link to his Indian heritage without emphasizing its hyperpresence. There isn't the same desire or strategy to be hypervisible in his wearing of traditional *kathak* costumes as there is in Sabri's annotative costume. In fact, where Odedra works with and within visual tropes and signifiers of invisibility/ obscuring of brownness, Sabri works toward its hypervisibility. And even when Odedra's brownness is made present through his bare-chested and barebacked solo, the fragmented presentation of his body counters its hypervisibility.

Conclusions

Through my endeavor to theorize the costuming of British brownnesses in the works of Sonia Sabri and Aakash Odedra, what has become apparent are the ways in which gender politics inform and complicate British brownnesses' performance and reception. Imbued more heavily with the responsibilities of cultural heritage transmission, female *kathak* dancers in the diaspora resort to more annotative modes of costuming, hiding their skin beneath layers of traditional attire that, through their visual and culturally loaded significations, ironically accentuate the brownnesses within. Here, the vernacular-coded costumes conceal actual brown skin to make the conceptual condition of brownnesses hypervisible and hyper-Orientalized. When these women choose to opt for more choreographic costuming modalities in culturally nonspecific or urban attires that are closer to their diasporic realities, their very commitment to the classical origins of *kathak* is often queried, as we see in the case of Mangaldas in India and Sabri in the UK. Consequently, in these contested moments, these female artists' professional careers are called into question. In contrast, male *kathak* dancers start out with a different set of challenges to overcome and expectations to meet vis-à-vis being male dancers within a predominantly female domain in the British South Asian diaspora. Since the codes of male *kathak* costuming are less ostentatious and prescriptive in the first place, dancers like Odedra can experiment with simple traditional *churidar-kurtas* in blocks of muted colors or extend this minimalism by stripping down to reveal brown skin through bare-torsoed costuming. Here brownnesses receive varied treatments of being obscured, emphasized, fragmented, sensualized, and even paled down through the use of intense lighting, representing the multidimensional manifestations of British brownnesses in the British South Asian diaspora. But the sheer presence of the barebacked male muscularities signals the more open choreographic costuming possibilities available to men, as well as the simultaneous sexualization of these brown male bodies. Together, Sabri's and Odedra's distinct approaches to costuming complicate and stretch representations of brownnesses and their myriad hues in the British landscape, signaling an innately gendered depth to this discourse and blowing apart its perceived homogeneity and unidimensionality. What remains to be seen, in perhaps more substantial ways than Odedra's bare-bodied costuming signals, is a further troubling of these gender-normative costuming practices such that British

South Asian dancers can also represent androgyny, transgenderism, and trans-sexuality as equally representative constituents of British brownnesses.

Notes

1. See Prickett (2012, 2013) and Mitra (2010) for analyses of Sabri's works at the intersections of postcoloniality, contemporization of *kathak*, and British multiculturalism. Odedra's works, though, are yet to receive substantial scholarly scrutiny.

2. It remains unclear who authored the Natyashastra, and while it has been commonly attributed to the historical-mythical figure Bharata, it is debated whether this name is in fact a pseudonym for one individual or a writers' collective. What is accepted, however, is that the contents of the book were originally generated as part of an oral tradition that acquired its written form between 200 BC and AD 200.

3. A *sari* is a type of Indian female clothing that is made up of a long piece of fabric, usually between five and nine yards long and between two and four feet wide. It is draped in a variety of ways that are determined by regionally specific ethnic groups and their class. See Miller (2010) on cultural theorizations of the *sari*.

4. I derive this subheading from the dance scholar and choreographer Pallabi Chakrovorty's (2013) comments on the role of the *dupatta* in costuming *kathak*.

Works Cited

Barbieri, Donatella. 2017. *Costume in Performance: Materiality, Culture and the Body*. London: Bloomsbury Academic Press.

Bhabha, Homi K. 1994. *The Location of Culture*. London: Routledge.

Bugg, Jessica. 2014. "Dancing Dress: Experiencing and Perceiving Dress in Movement." *Scene* 2 (1–2): 67–80.

Chakrovorty, Pallabi. 2013. "Comments to Rose and Thorns: Turning Down the Sangeet Natak Akademi Award." *Narthaki*. http://www.narthaki.com/info/rt/rt53.html.

DeFrantz, Thomas F., and Anita Gonzalez. 2014. "Introduction: From 'Negro Expression' to 'Black Performance.'" In *Black Performance Theory*, edited by Thomas F. DeFrantz and Anita Gonzales, 1–15. Durham, NC: Duke University Press.

Godiwala, Dimple. 2006. "Alternatives within the Mainstream: British Black and Asian Theatres. An Introduction." In *Alternatives within the Mainstream British Black and Asian Theatres*, edited by Dimple Godiwala, 3–19. Newcastle: Cambridge Scholars Press.

Grau, Andrée. 2002. "South Asian Dance in Britain: Negotiating Cultural Identity through Dance (SADiB)." Leverhulme Trust Report (1999–2001): 1–85.

Gurus of Kathak Kendra. 2013. "Rose and Thorns: Turning Down the Sangeet Natak Akademi Award." *Narthaki*. http://www.narthaki.com/info/rt/rt53.html.

Hann, Rachel, and Sidsel Bech. 2014. "Critical Costume." *Scene* 2 (1–2): 3–8.

Hesse, Barnor, and S. Sayyid. 2006. "Narrating the Postcolonial Political and the Immigrant Imaginary." In *A Postcolonial People: South Asians in Britain*, edited by N. Ali, V. S. Kalra, and S. Sayyid, 13–31. London: Hurst.

Hunt, Jeremy. 2010. "Sonia Sabri at Conservative Party Conference 2010." YouTube. https://www.youtube.com/watch?v=sAgnh6eo_3g. Accessed 12 May 2016.

John, Mary E., and Janaki Nair. 1998. "A Question of Silence? An Introduction." In *A Question of Silence: The Sexual Economies of Modern India*, edited by Mary E. John and Janaki Nair, 1–51. New Delhi: Kali for Women.

Johnson, E. Patrick. 2003. *Appropriating Blackness: Performance and the Politics of Authenticity*. Durham, NC: Duke University Press.

Madsen, Deborah L. 2011. "Authenticity." In *The Routledge Companion to Race and Ethnicity*, edited by Stephen M. Caliendo and Charlton D. McIlwain, 108–9. Abingdon: Routledge.

Malik, Sarita. 2008. "Keeping It Real: The Politics of Channel 4's Multiculturalism Mainstreaming and Mandates." *Screen* 49 (3): 343–53.

Mangaldas, Aditi. 2013. "Rose and Thorns: Turning Down the Sangeet Natak Akademi Award." *Narthaki*. http://www.narthaki.com/info/rt/rt53.html.

————. 2016. Interview with the author. May 8.

Miller, Damien. 2010. *Stuff*. Cambridge: Polity Press.

Mitra, Royona. 2010. "Performing Cultural Heritage in 'Weaving Paths' by Sonia Sabri Dance Company." In *Performing Heritage: Research, Practice and Innovation in Museum and Live Interpretation*, edited by Anthony Jackson and Jennifer Kidd, 144–57. Manchester: Manchester University Press.

Monks, Aoife. 2010. *The Actor in Costume*. Basingstoke: Palgrave Macmillan.

Nair, Sreenath, ed. 2015. *The "Natyashastra" and the Body in Performance: Essays on Indian Theories of Dance and Drama*. Jefferson, NC: McFarland.

Odedra, Aakash. 2016. Interview with the author. April 22.

Prickett, Stacey. 2012. "Defying Britain's Tick-Box Culture: Kathak in Dialogue with Hip-Hop." *Dance Research: The Journal of the Society for Dance Research* 30 (2): 169–85.

————. 2013. *Embodied Politics: Dance, Protest and Identities*. Binsted: Dance Books.

Purkayastha, Prarthana. 2015. "The Annotation of Skin." *Performance Research Journal* 20 (6): 114–21.

Sabri, Sonia. 2016. Interview with the author. April 21.

Saha, Anamik. 2012. "Bears, Scarves, Halal Meat, Terrorists, Forced Marriage: Television Industries and the Production of 'Race.'" *Media, Culture & Society* 34 (4): 424–38.

Srinivasan, Priya. 2012. *Sweating Saris: Indian Dance as Transnational Labour*. Philadelphia: Temple University Press.

Werbner, Pnina. 2004. "Theorising Complex Diasporas: Purity and Hybridity in the South Asian Public Sphere in Britain." *Journal of Ethnic and Migration Studies* 30 (5): 895–911.

Wong, Yutian. 2010. *Choreographing Asian America*. Middletown, CT: Wesleyan University Press.

Intimating Race

Tao Ye's 4 and Methods for World Dance

HENTYLE YAPP

Tao Dance Theatre emerged on the world dance market in 2008. The choreographer Tao Ye's 2012 dance titled *4* is the main work that catapulted the Chinese company into circulation across Asia, the United States, and Europe. Performed in thirty minutes, the piece is fast-paced, as four dancers kinetically ricochet their bodies with minimized muscular engagement. Their faces are covered in black cloth. They wear voluminous gray and black shirts and pants that puff around the body. Their movement infuses release technique with a weighted direction, propelling their bodies as vectors. They dance abstractly, with little references to concrete symbols. In addition, their clothes and masks function to cover physical references to gender and bodily contours, further amplifying a presumably formalist aesthetic. The sound, by composer Xiao He, is similarly abstract and draws from rhythmic bells and voices, singing and speaking. The noise score pulses with a hyperkinetic mood that syncopates a consistent beat at double the rate of a resting heart.[1]

Tao Ye's *4* is emblematic of the limits placed on the reception of what has come to be known as world dance or contemporary global dance, a genre that indexes choreographic projects understood simply as projects not made within the West. I utilize the term "world dance" to refer to works that are produced by artists *perceived* to be from outside the West—even when they are making work within the United States or Europe. World dance directs us to the process of racialization, which presumes that an artist's aesthetic inheritance is knowable based upon her or her parents' origin of birth. Since Tao was educated in Chongqing and worked with Jin Xing Dance Theatre and Beijing Modern Dance Company, many journalists have situated the artist primarily within the context of China. However, his use of movement, sound, and costume operates within aesthetic formalism, leading many reviewers to compare the choreographer to US and European luminaries like Lucinda Childs and

489

Anne Teresa De Keersmaeker. This formalist approach often serves as either an all-consuming frame by which to understand Tao's choreography or an incompatible aesthetic with his Chineseness.

A key paradox thus surrounds world dance, whereby non-Western artists must explore an aesthetic beyond a simplistic depiction of what some presume to be traditional dance practices, yet those who do so by employing formalist or avant-garde tools are said to be mimicking the West. Many artists operating within the genre encounter this mixed range of reactions. On the one hand, a racialized artist working in a formalist mode generally coded as a white or European aesthetic piques interest. On the other, this mix of aesthetics and non-Western status draws disapproval, since the artist could be understood as mimicking Western formalist standards or as not referencing legible Chinese traditions. We can approach Tao's work and reception as a case study to understand the possibilities and limits placed on those located under the banner of world or global dance. How do we begin to situate the use of abstraction by an artist whose work circulates in the category of global dance? What methods are available to theorize these aesthetics alongside an account of the transnational?

The wide range of reactions to world dance conditions the reception of non-Western choreographers across the global arts scene, where a universalizing discourse renders the particularities of their contexts and aims opaque. Non-Western artists who engage with formalism tend to be dismissed as inauthentic, given that the universal aesthetic is tacitly coded white. To contend with this problem, I take stock of the methods that have informed the field of dance studies, particularly as they relate to analyses of race and movement. I do so to understand how representational analysis, phenomenology, and affect provide divergent yet critical approaches to race and the body. Rather than privileging one over another, I argue that the tensions and limits of each approach must be situated together. Ultimately, I show how contending with all three allows us to better understand Tao and other world dance artists' use of abstraction as an *intimation* of race. Rather than overtly critiquing how racialization structures the paradox of formalism for non-Western artists, Tao's piece intimates, hints at, or gesturally implies race. Intimating rather than fully representing race directs us to how *4* opens ways to produce possibilities for discourses around the universal that are often foreclosed for global artists. Tao produces a method that renders race open while holding onto its historical link to colonization and violence. Through delicate intimations of race, intimacies across space and time are opened up in his work to shift the universal away from being a dominant measure by which to compare the particularized, nonwhite other. I thus illustrate this aesthetic of intimation in Tao's work to reexamine the paradox that situates the reception of world dance.

To read the ways in which dances intimate race even in the context of abstraction, a scholar must contend with the approaches mentioned above, as each produces different methodological possibilities for dance studies. In this essay, I examine the tensions and limits between two dominant approaches: representation-based analysis, which broadly critiques racism and colonization, and affect-based analysis, which generally focuses on a universalized sense of aesthetics and relationality. Rather than privileging one approach, I argue that together representation and affect assist in contending with phenomenology, which has had a complicated relationship to the field of dance studies. I thus offer the intimation of race as a way of mediating these three dominant strains. On the one hand, phenomenology renders loose representation's commitment to an explicit political critique against racism by emphasizing the minutiae and gestural details of the body. On the other, phenomenology works against the universalizing tendencies of affect-based analysis by connecting affect to embodied and grounded experience. Therefore, through phenomenological engagements, affect and representation commingle in ways that produce the intimation of race, which I argue is necessary to grapple with the paradoxes of world dance. To do so, I first examine how Tao's choreography intimates a sense of race. I then turn to the popular reception of *4* by offering the remark as a way to analyze racist and problematic responses to Tao's piece. Lastly, I examine the theoretical bases that inform the intimation of race and the remark.

Intimation, Intimacies, and the Universal

4 begins with light, fast-paced movement. However, an external pressure accumulates onto the dancers' bodies as the piece develops. The first third accelerates rapidly as performers explore the full expanse of the stage. At the beginning, four dancers are crouched in an open second position with their backs to the audience. The starting momentum is initiated when the dancers move their torsos side to side, which ultimately propels their bodies upward. Their constant movement intimates poses but never holds them. The four performers move in unison for the majority of the piece. Internally, dynamic exchanges from bone to bone propel the dancers as sequential directions ricochet throughout their bodies. The movement primarily exists in internal circular momentums centered on the shoulders, head, and hips. From there, the sequence carries through the limbs and extends through space. The body's energy manifests in traversing the proscenium stage as internal potential energy translates into kinetic energy. However, beginning in the second third, the mood shifts as dancers take on heavier and slower movement.

The *4* dancers' mobile trajectories eventually become constrained by an outside force. Tao decelerates the performance as the audience's gaze accumulates

on the performers' bodies; he is playing with an audience's expectations surrounding world dance. Tao is aware that his moves are not easily legible as what
some may consider traditionally Chinese. His aesthetic of intimation arises
through movements that are not immediately indexed as traditional. This interplay across artist intent and audience reception structures the intimation of
race that results. In particular, the choreographer understands that his work is
bound by the paradox delimiting other world dance artists: racialization limits
the reception of his choreography. However, rather than rejecting this condition, Tao contends with it by intimating the history of racialization through
his abstractionist aesthetics. Specifically, the bodies that initially move with
abandon in his dances eventually contend with the weight of an outside gaze.

To intimate race means to create slack in otherwise overdetermined definitions of race and the body, key terms for understanding power. To create slack
and to gesturally imply without definitively stating are modes of affective engagement that enable us to attend to race and the body differently. The intimation of race gestures to racialization without rendering our critical vocabulary
for understanding power fully stable. Although the concept of intimacy has
picked up traction in the academy to analyze power in terms of relationality
across time and space (Berlant 1998; Lowe 2015), I turn to intimation to contend specifically with colonization and its lingering histories across many
communities. When one *intimates* race, one relies on open affective relational
methods that hold onto histories of violence, gesturing toward such histories
without permitting them to continue to dominate as the only available narrative. To intimate race means to ground race in its long history and trace its
contours over time; however, to intimate also requires us to not be faithful to
this grounding and not be beholden to the contours we trace.

Tao intimates race to produce connections across different communities
that have been affected by state violence. In this way, he uses intimation as a
way to reformulate an understanding of the universal through this condition
of mass violence. Tao has framed 4 as universal through the use of minimalist
abstraction. In response to critics comparing Tao to formalist dance luminaries, Tao states that "art transcends geographical or cultural boundaries" and
that he is not "an Eastern or a Chinese choreographer" (quoted in Kourlas
2013). Standard art historical treatments of form as universal have often been
critiqued for ignoring the particularities of identity, location, and historical
context (Jones 2012). However, Tao frequently situates his work purposefully
within such frames. Rather than dismissing his attempt to explore a universal
movement vocabulary as ideologically backward, is there a way to take such
affective connections to the universal as concerned with the political? What
constitutes the universal and particular is debatable, and debates about world

art often founder on these points even as the categories continue to shape discourse around global art (Elkins 2007; Harris 2011). Rather than arguing for or against the universal, Tao directs us to the function of the universal as a standard. By displacing the universal as a predetermined category, Tao reveals how the category itself produces global difference that undergirds the paradoxes surrounding world dance.

Tao privileges the universal in both his written and spoken statements, along with his choreography. By minimizing the body's legibility as gendered and racialized through face covers and costumes, Tao highlights the racialized condition relative to which he works: that a non-Western artist must obscure physical markers of difference to be taken for the standard, or universal, that still grounds formalism and abstraction. Through this simple gesture of cloaking, his attempt to enter the universal can be read as intimating a critique of whiteness as the protouniversal norm. Tao literalizes what Frantz Fanon (2008) calls a racial bodily schema by bringing to the fore the continual need of contending with bodily difference to register as a universalizable body. This act of marking the existence of the racial schema reveals how the universal is not simply natural; rather, it is upheld through norms. Tao's gesture of covering the surface of his dancers' bodies highlights how the universal predetermines the legibility of otherness, or racial particularity. Rather than overtly representing his Chinese difference or dismissing the universal as problematic, Tao aesthetically intimates and brings to the fore the overdetermined nature of the universal. The unremarkable gesture of covering parts of the body literalizes the act of intimation, whereby one gently hints at the limits of the universal. This minimization of bodily difference allows us to track how the universal is produced, whereby the universal becomes a process rather than a predetermined standard.

However, what is the political purpose of destabilizing the universal? To intimate race is to gesture to its conditions in producing the very terms of existence for non-Western, minoritarian, and global artists. Through this intimation of race, Tao reworks the universal to destabilize it as a standard, rendering it as a process. When intimating race, Tao formulates a political mode that creates intimacies across space and time. In other words, Tao does not represent Chineseness as an insular identity. Rather, he intimates and gestures to his own conditions of racialization to form relations and intimacies with those who have similarly experienced such modes of vulnerability. He tries to find others like him.

Abstraction and formalism are coded as universal. This aesthetic is generally characterized as precise, depending on the choreographer. In addition, the feel or mood of most formal works emphasizes the mobility of the body as released, weighted without attachments. Tao, however, develops a melancholic and heavy mood to his formalist aesthetic. *4*'s emotional landscape affectively accumulates weight. As described earlier, the arc of the work shifts from hyperkinetic to heavy. The piece begins with light movement. However, as the mood changes, the music takes a slower pace through long strums on a cello. The lighting shifts from a brightly lit stage to a focused spot in the middle. The four dancers then plant their feet at the peripheries of the lit center as movement slowly ripples from sacrum to head. Dancers move as if they are syrup on a tilted plate, thick and dripping.

Tao takes the conventions of formal, universalized dance aesthetics and adds weight. This heavier aesthetic alters the codes of abstraction by emphasizing the addition of another layer or schema. Akin to Fanon's racial schema, Tao's weighted abstractionism amplifies how racialized beings must contend with an external force. Tao's formalist aesthetic uses universalism to intimate the corporeal effects of racialization, producing a relationality with those who similarly contend with such schemas and layers.

Through a weighted formalism, Tao intimates a shared minoritarian state based on the phenomenologically informed racial schema. He aestheticizes this schema as a way to produce intimacies across differently racialized populations. In other words, the racial schema becomes an additional way to understand a larger condition that structures the universal, since many racialized populations (the majority of the world) must contend with such a schema. This turn to intimacies and shared empathy has been critical in rendering the universal into a structuring problem rather than a standard. In particular, Lisa Lowe's (2015) invocation of finding *intimacies* across continents marks the differential yet related modes of survival that connect populations across space and time. Marta Savigliano similarly proposes that we focus on how world dance is constructed to connect differently racialized people as "neighbors" (2009, 184–87).

Tao does not try to properly represent Chinese existence. Rather, he takes his experiences and history as a point of departure to then intimate, gesture, and produce relations of shared vulnerabilities across space and time. The universal is located at the moment of vulnerability, opening up the possibility for empathic relations and making us feel less alone in this world. Rather than relying on autobiographical realism to represent himself or his nation, he uses abstraction and formalism to intimate and generalize his own existence to connect with racialized others.

Remarking on World Dance

Beyond Tao's relation to his choreography, the critical reception of *4* directs us to additional ways of intimating race. Varied responses to the work range from dismissive to laudatory and should be understood as *mere remarks* rather than definitive statements of value regarding good or bad politics. Shifting to remarks rather than declarations offers an intimating engagement with *4*. By taking a broad account of the divergent responses to Tao's abstractionism, we schematically locate phenomenal engagements with Tao without seeking to argue for the best or proper way to represent racialized subjects. Oftentimes, in bids to work against the continued dehumanization of racialized subjects, some critics offer representations of such individuals as fully and properly human— as a means to be considered a full part of a modern, liberal, and humanist order. Rather than replicate such a project, the remark takes pause to provide space for other discursive moves. In particular, offering remarks rather than expert denunciations or distanced judgments creates slack and provides a way to hold onto race or speak from or about a racialized position without letting that position predetermine an engagement with an artwork. Rather than framing comments about Tao's work as racist, I ask us to take pause and engage such statements affectively or, in the words of Eve Kosofsky Sedgwick, "reparatively" (2003, 127). Doing so highlights how world dance is constructed within a racialized condition while simultaneously creating moves for reimagination. A remark can produce criticism but not monolithic claims, such as statements about misrepresentations of the other. Rather, the intimating logics of the remark contend with the way that the project of worlding dance is always already racialized. Such an approach amplifies Savigliano's call for world dance to not only think about good or bad representation but also contend with the multiple affective ties that produce interest in world dance. The remark allows us to intimate race rather than trying to properly or definitively represent it in what some might want to perceive to be the more proper and humanizing fashion.

The pure movement in *4* leaves a viewer little room for rest. Some critics have noted their own and other audience members' fatigue when watching it (Scherr 2012). While Apollinaire Scherr highlights audience members walking out midway through the performance, other critics have celebrated the hypnotic allure of *4* (Seidman 2015). In fact, viewers' affective responses range from exhaustion to excitement. Often the word that arises in the context of world dance is that the work is "interesting." Sianne Ngai develops "interesting" as an aesthetic category that tracks this wavering range of reactions. According to her, interest is "a particularizing attachment to an object (one that endows it with empirical qualities); yet the feeling seems to have no qualities of its own" (2014, 129). She highlights how an affective relationship involves a range of feelings. "Interesting" thus operates in a lower register, where it does not exist within "the once-and-for-allness of our experience of, say, the sublime"; instead, interest requires an object that "we tend to come back to, as if to verify that it is *still* interesting" (Ngai 2008, 786). "Interesting" creates an affective engagement of return for a viewer—a way to remark and come back.

Akin to Ngai, Savigliano produces a model of engagement that returns to the world dance object to understand its construction. The ability to offer remarks regarding the affective aesthetic of "interesting" follows Savigliano's call for a mode that first asks *how* as opposed to delving into denunciation. She shifts away from a predominantly representational politics and directs us to the contextual formation of the category of world dance to ask: "What is legitimating this object [world dance], and the ends (justifications) inscribed in it? What is arranging this desire to learn, and learn about world dance?" (Savigliano 2009, 178). Savigliano is less invested in defining world dance than she is in asking questions about it—asking how and why the genre garners notice. Questioning and remarking upon what is interesting in these practices allow us some access to return, in this case, to trace the racialized conditions that structure the divergent reactions to world dance. Rather than making declaratory judgments about the genre as symptomatic of racist ideologies (even when it is) or dismissing world dance's popularization as multicultural (even though this may be the case), I ask that we deflate such tendencies toward declaration in order to reparatively approach our objects with "interest" and to produce additional narratives that contend with the fullness and complexities, intimacies and paradoxes, of world dance.

Attending to the range of affective registers allows us to understand *4* as interesting—a word that is often accompanied by the word "mere" as if something could be merely interesting (even while recommending return). Certainly, *4* forces some viewers to stop and remark on the object and then return to it. In other words, the piece is remark-able. In this way, the moniker "interesting" may be less remarkable in a grand sense and more remark-able in a minor way, even a mere way, where one takes notice but without affective intensity. The virtuosity of flexible limbs in some Chinese performance forms maintains a viewer's attention, while the repetitive formal structure of Tao's work might leave some audiences disappointed that the piece registers as not Chinese enough. Regardless of the intensity of one's reaction, one will remark or take notice. *4* does not inspire the grand passions of "remarkable!" Rather, the goal of the work is to force one to remark, to take note, rather than to chiefly excite (although this might occur within the range of responses). Tao's *4* produces the remark, compelling audiences to ask questions rather than proclaim pronouncements. The political and theoretical possibilities embedded in the low affective act of intimating provide the space to ask questions and make remarks rather than ascribing full meaning.

To better understand the role of the category of "interesting" for Tao, let us consider an additional response to *4*. Tao deploys the rules of release technique that rely on sequentially based movement, by which the momentum created by a lift of the leg articulates through the spine and into the rolling of the skull. Alastair Macaulay of the *New York Times* Orientalizes *4* while simultaneously situating it within this larger (white) postmodern legacy: "In '4' especially the movement combines the characteristics of Asian martial arts forms (tai chi not least) with the physicality of American postmodern dance or early Twyla Tharp choreography. (Those tics of the head and shoulder!) Human individuality is not the point. In each work the movement seems both involuntary and visceral: a powerful drive, like a collective unconscious onstage" (2012). Tao is described in predictable ways, whereby most Asian and Asian American choreographers are always understood as related to what some consider an ancient tradition like Taichi, butoh, and martial arts. These types of narratives about Eiko and Koma and Shen Wei, among other choreographers, have long been a part of modern and contemporary dance discourse. One could certainly declaim and dismiss these comments as Orientalist. However, by solely focusing on direct critique, we ignore what lies in excess of such dismissals and miss the opportunity to remark. The remark enables us to take such statements as indexical of how race is always intimated in both Western dance traditions and world dance. Akin to Savigliano's call, we must not simply create counternarratives against racist depictions of world dance, which often privilege a certain method of proper analysis that forecloses other ways of reading. Rather, by remarking interest, we situate Tao as intimating the racial in the universal.

Intimation and Remarking:
Representation, Affect, and Phenomenology

Intimation and the remark draw from three central approaches for dance analysis: representation-based, affect-based, and phenomenological approaches. In this section, I first examine how *4* can be understood through representation-based analysis and then affect-based analysis. I finally introduce phenomenology as a supplementary approach to assist in remarking the intimation of race. By doing so, I track how all three overlap and diverge, particularly in light of intellectual figures and pairings that bring to the fore methodological tendencies for (world) dance studies: Michel Foucault for representation, Gilles Deleuze and Félix Guattari for affect, and Frantz Fanon for phenomenology. World dance amplifies the stakes in employing these methodologies in that transnational work can problematize some of the universalizing tendencies in standard approaches to dance. In particular, Savigliano warns that identity and representation have limits: "Identity politics has turned from a source of organization and mobilization for those disempowered into a dangerous ideological device in the hands of Empire" (2009, 183). By demarcating the limits of a representation-based approach, Savigliano calls for a more dynamic analysis for world dance that does not deploy difference for the consumptive pleasures of multicultural viewership.

The two main methods that have dominated both Western theatrical and world dance studies have been representation-based analysis and affect-based analysis. Although this bifurcation is meant to be schematic, these two approaches are often imagined as distinct. Representation is the better-known model by which, simply, an image or other form of expression is given to stand in as a surrogate for that which it renders. Historically, representation has been informed by readings of symbols and semiotics—an approach that generally attends to how a body is coded or situated (Barthes 1975; Foster 1986). Meanwhile, affect-based work generates intensities of feeling or a physical state rather than redoublings as images or surrogates, as in representation (Foster 2010). Mark Franko locates an affect-based analysis that is informed by scholars in the lineage of Baruch Spinoza, such as Gilles Deleuze and Félix Guattari, and tied to what Franko calls "states of the body." This affect-based analysis is placed "in tension with representation" (Franko 2010, 2). Also aligned with affect-based analysis, Derek McCormack juxtaposes affect theory against representation, arguing that efforts to *represent* culture often limit a full account of space: "While [representation] offers a great deal of critical purchase on the cultural geographies of bodies, this approach clearly leaves something out: a concern with the experiential—and more precisely the affective—dimensions of geographies that are excessive of a practice of cultural-critical reading that attends to the codification of corporeality" (2014, x). Although affect and representation certainly overlap, I amplify here their separation, particularly as representation is more often deployed as the better method for world dance. I parse these two apart to remark upon the theoretical tendencies and citational figures that undergird this separation.

The distinction between affect and representation can be traced through two lines of thought: Deleuze and Guattari for affect and Foucault for representation. For dance, the body has historically been the site of primary analysis. Representation-based analysis often uses history and the body's materiality to make arguments about power. In this vein, Foucault's work, as noted by Franko (2011), has become central to this particular analytic. In distinction, affect-based analysis does not presume to engage the body as finite, as its extensions and states are emphasized over its full knowability. From this perspective, Deleuze and Guattari are often heavily invoked. The underlying tension across these two theoretical methods, which we might call Foucaultian and Deleuzo-Guattarian, informs dance studies. Although these intellectual figures have a complex relationship, it is necessary to parse out not only what theoretical tendencies emerge from the separation between these approaches but also why phenomenology comes to be left out of both accounts of the body.

First, many world dance scholars privilege a representation-based method to explore issues related to Eurocentrism, mimicry, race, and colonization. The renowned artist-scholar Ananya Chatterjea questions contemporary dance from Asia, challenging what she sees as the mimicry of Western codes of avant-gardism. Exemplifying the standard disapproval of artists like Tao, Chatterjea writes, "What seems to be increasingly popular in the sphere of Asian 'contemporary' dance is a kind of ventriloquism, where contemporary Asia finds its voice through the signifiers of Euro-American modern/postmodern, the latter passing once again as the neutral universal, which is able to contain all difference" (2013, 11). Here, Asia represents itself through indexes of Euro-American formalism. Chatterjea is well aware of the problems surrounding notions of tradition and artistic freedom. Thus, her critiques rely upon the way that "choices are political, [and] that bodies come with visual histories and contracts" (12). In this way, her method of analysis connects to established protocols in the field.

If we read 4 as representational, then we might see Tao's choices around costume, music, and movement as mimicry of Western conventions. On the one hand, his use of formalist codes is partly responsible for his success. After all, his use of formalism has created access to global circulation, particularly as many European reviewers herald his work as "mesmerizing and hypnotic" (Monahan 2014), as well as "minimalist" and "magnetizing and deeply disturbing" (Seidman 2015). On the other hand, his formalism has been framed as "underwhelming" to the point that his work "won't add up to much" (Levene 2014). Looked at as representational, Tao's use of formalism is embraced or dismissed as either innovative or boring. I focus on these divergent opinions of Tao's work to emphasize how 4 does not garner a political or theoretical valence when read by critics as representational.

Representation-based analysis can be situated relative to dance studies' own shifting deployment of ethnographic methods. Earlier anthropological accounts mobilized a colonial gaze at dance to catalog non-Western dances according to Western frames of reference. However, ethnographic tools have been used to produce counterrepresentations that work against negative depictions of the non-West. Joann Kealiinohomoku's (1983) key essay was and continues to be central in ongoing efforts to thwart the exoticizing tendencies of the anthropological gaze. She "provincializes," in the words of Dipesh Chakrabarty (2007), the Western gaze by rendering ballet an ethnic form of dance. Representation often takes codes and symbols to be indexical of specific identities and cultural forms. Thus, work in dance studies that performs analyses through a representation-based approach often usefully mobilizes Foucault. Indeed, as Franko notes, Foucault is a "pivotal figure in the transition from traditional dance history to dance studies that transpired in the 1980s" (2011, 2).

In the late 1990s and 2000s, a second approach to dance began to emerge employing affect-based analysis. Though attention to affect in dance bears a long history, dance scholars began to use the critical theory associated with Deleuze and Guattari to amplify modes of attending to affect. Affect-based analysis is useful for Tao's choreography as it taps into registers that open up questions of relationality and intimacies. Thinking about trajectories of affect instead of positions of identity (more common in representation-based analysis) invites us to reroute any apparently universalizing aesthetic through the affective tracks of difference and relationality. Through the pulsing and intense sonic landscape, along with the similarly rhythmic movement, Tao and sound artist Xiao He produce *4* to exist within what Deleuze and Guattari (2009) might call a "plane of intensity." The dancers add texture to Tao's minimalist aesthetic through ticks of the head and flicks of their arms. Repetition cultivates an affective sense of space, time, and being. Within this plane of intensity, multiple affects and reactions are evoked rather than represented, and they range from interest to boredom.

4 benefits from an affect-based analysis with an emphasis on the relational, emotive, and gestural. Although it might be tempting to singularly situate Tao's affects within a contemporary moment, it is important to recall that affect-based analysis bears a long historical relation to dance studies. In fact, well before the "affective turn" (Clough 2007), affect can be related to the long-standing dance studies preoccupation with describing movement. Frameworks like kinesthesia, empathy, proprioception, and corporeality have been theorized to create a language not only for bodily movement but also for that movement's relation to others and/in space (Noland 2009; Foster 2010). Recently, some scholars have emphasized affect as a way to produce different, emergent claims for dance. For example, André Lepecki (2010) frames the contemporary trend around reperforming archived works as not about good or bad representations of or memories about those pieces. Instead, he privileges a choreographer's affective connection to the past to open up theoretical insights.

In distinguishing between representation-based and affect-based analyses, I do not want to privilege one over the other. Rather, the now frequent pitting of affect against representation might direct us to other methods that could be critical in helping us escape the trap of an oversimplified and binarizing standoff. Such a method might be phenomenology. Interestingly, proponents of both representation and affect have often distanced themselves from phenomenology. Franko notes how the dominant influence of Foucault often relies on analytics that "worked against the phenomenological model" (2011, 2). Sally Ness (2011) has offered the most in-depth exploration of this dynamic, noting that Foucault's influence on dance studies is shaped by his critiques of phenomenology. Both representation-based and affect-based approaches have distanced themselves from phenomenology, as its analytics are often centered around an ableist reliance on visuality, presumptions of a holistic sense of perception, the universalization of a subject and experience, and an overreliance on intention (May 2014; Peden 2014). Accounts from European intellectual history have revealed that the recent shift toward affect, with the increased reliance on Spinoza, Deleuze and Guattari, historically emerged as a move away from phenomenology. Thus, an invitation to reengage with phenomenology might seem counterintuitive to or incompatible with dance studies' primary engagements of methods that privilege representation or affect. However, rather than replicating this divide, I have developed the notion of intimating race as informed by phenomena to weave these approaches together.

In particular, the materialist concerns informed by representational analysis ground the openness of affect and phenomena. When all three approaches are engaged together, we begin to not overly rely on a stable sense of the body; in other words, we intimate race and the body. Franko notes how phenomenology connects a performer's own kinesthetic sensation to an audience's perception, what he eloquently calls "an anthropology with an aesthetics" (2011, 1). In this tempered recuperation of phenomenology, Franko compels us to renegotiate phenomena and perception. Dance studies' development of phenomenology by Maxine Sheets-Johnstone (2015), Anna Pakes (2011), and Susan Kozel (2008) often relies on a set of figures: Iris Marion-Young, Jean-Paul Sartre, Edmund Husserl, Martin Heidegger, and Maurice Merleau-Ponty. Here I would like to open consideration to the decolonial phenomenologist and psychoanalyst Frantz Fanon, who engages phenomena in ways that complicate notions of the body *and* centralize questions surrounding materiality, race, and colonization. In other words, a figure who intimates race. As Jeremy Weate has argued, Fanon develops a "new humanism" by which community is an incomplete, affectively open ideal that requires approaching the other by "recognising both their capacity and our own for suffering" (2001, 19). Such a recognition requires *both* affect-based and representation-based analyses. That is, such a recognition requires both attention to the historical drag of the material force of representational practices and attention to the ways historical identities have affective resonance or reverberation.

Fanon's phenomenology achieves a simultaneous sense of openness (affect) and grounded history (representation). In particular, he revises Merleau-Ponty's corporeal schema, which is meant to produce connections between agency, subject, structure, and history. Fanon's historicoracial bodily schema *remarks upon* (and does not reject) Merleau-Ponty's universalizing frame, as Fanon critiques how whiteness predetermines all existence and being. As such, phenomena mediate affect alongside representation by placing an expanded sense of the body within a materialized and grounded notion of the world and social structuration. This balance across open theorization and historicomaterial concerns produces an alternative universalism, one that is premised upon shared vulnerability *in difference*. Rather than representing the specificity of Fanon's phenomenal experience, he intimates how he has been racialized. He performs this intimation to create relations and intimacies with those who have been similarly colonized. The act of intimating rather than representing race produces intimacies and relations across continents and histories. When race becomes so particularized, we begin to lose the possibility of producing shared states of vulnerability and, by extension, of rendering the universal unstable. However, rather than turning race into an ahistorical category or standard (whereby we all have a race or there's only one race, the human race), we must simultaneously hold onto the material effects and affects that compose both the history of colonization and ongoing efforts toward decolonization. Gesturing and grasping such histories without letting them predetermine our analyses direct us to not only intimate race but also ethically engage, by way of the remark, how people phenomenally respond to art.

In light of these multiple approaches for thinking through world dance and acknowledging the French and Francophone theoretical traditions that inform these approaches, what about China? Fanon's development of phenomena in relation to worlding, race, and colonization offers intellectual purchase beyond the black diaspora for recombining affective and representational theories that have contended with the transnational. The condition of Western colonization continues to herald what has become known as the long "racial century" (Eng 2016, 2), providing a critical model of globality for world dance. Further, literary scholar Shu-mei Shih attributes the occlusion of situating China, France, and the Americas together as a result of disciplinary limits, precluding us from producing a "creolization of theory" (2012, 32). Akin to Shih, my aim in this essay has been to offer a sense of the world that can contend with multiple fields and areas. Further, the stances of intimation and the remark extend beyond dance studies to deal with the disciplinary tendencies that dictate how we analyze art, the world, and art in the world.

From the grand scale of the world to the movement details in *4*, multiple approaches are required to grapple with the demands of world dance. At the end of *4*, the music turns silent. Dancers slowly move limbs in ways that direct them away from the bright white pool of light illuminating the lower stage. Four dancers recede one by one away from the remaining body of light. In this moment, physical bodies are replaced by a single light, in which only the dancers' shadows periodically intimate against the lit floor. At the end of *4*, the shadow predominates and extends from the material body, translating into phenomena that abstract and represent the moving body. During this moment, Tao highlights the shadow, which becomes an intimation that emerges from the body as symbolic representation *and* affective entity—a phenomenal intimation that entwines both understandings of the body together.

Note
1. My observations on this piece come from video footage of the full work shared by the company manager, along with a live viewing of the work in 2012 at the Lincoln Center.

Works Cited

Barthes, Roland. 1975. *S/Z.* Translated by Richard Miller. New York: Hill and Wang.

Berlant, Lauren. 1998. "Intimacy: A Special Issue." *Critical Inquiry* 24 (2): 281–88.

Chakrabarty, Dipesh. 2007. *Provincializing Europe.* Princeton, NJ: Princeton University Press.

Chatterjea, Ananya. 2013. "On the Value of Mistranslations and Contaminations." *Dance Research Journal* 45 (1): 4–21.

Clough, Patricia. 2007. *The Affective Turn.* Durham, NC: Duke University Press.

Deleuze, Gilles, and Felix Guattari. 1996. *What Is Philosophy?* Translated by Graham Burchell. New York: Columbia University Press.

———. 2009. *Anti-Oedipus.* New York: Penguin Classics.

Elkins, James. 2007. *Is Art History Global?* London: Tailor and Francis.

Eng, David. 2016. "Colonial Object Relations." *Social Text* 34 (1): 1–19.

Fanon, Frantz. 2008. *Black Skin, White Masks.* Translated by Richard Philcox. New York: Grove.

Foster, Susan Leigh. 1986. *Reading Dancing.* Berkeley: University of California Press.

———. 2010. *Choreographing Empathy: Kinesthesia in Performance.* New York: Routledge.

Franko, Mark. 2010. "States of the Body." *Dance Research Journal* 42 (1): v–viii.

———. 2011. "What Is Dead and What Is Alive in Dance Phenomenology?" *Dance Research Journal* 43 (2): 1–4.

Harris, Jonathan. 2011. *Globalization and Contemporary Art.* London: Wiley-Blackwell.

Jones, Amelia. 2012. *Seeing Differently.* New York: Routledge.

Kealiinohomoku, Joann. 1983. "An Anthropologist Looks at Ballet as Form of Ethnic Dance." In *What Is Dance*, edited by Roger Copeland and Marshall Cohen, 533–49. Oxford: Oxford University Press.

Kourlas, Gia. 2013. "Interview with Tao Ye." *TimeOut New York,* July 19. https://www.timeout.com/newyork/dance/tao-yi-talks-about-tao-dance-theater.

Kozel, Susan. 2008. *Closer*. Cambridge, MA: MIT Press.

Lepecki, André. 2010. "The Body as Archive: Will to Re-enact and the Afterlives of Dance." *Dance Research Journal* 42 (1): 28–48.

Levene, Louise. 2014. "Tao Dance Theatre, Sadler's Wells." *Financial Times*, October 22. https://next.ft.com/content/1f14b78e-5906-11e4-9546-00144feab7de.

Lowe, Lisa. 2015. *The Intimacies of Four Continents*. Durham, NC: Duke University Press.

Macaulay, Alistair. 2012. "The Strength of (Small) Numbers)." *New York Times,* July 26. http://www.nytimes.com/2012/07/27/arts/dance/tao-dance-theater-at-alice-tully-hall.html.

May, Todd. 2014. *The End of Phenomenology*. Edinburgh: University of Edinburgh Press.

McCormack, Derek. 2014. *Refrains for Moving Bodies*. Durham, NC: Duke University Press.

Monahan, Mark. 2014. "Tao Dance Theatre." *Telegraph*, October 21. http://www.telegraph.co.uk/culture/theatre/dance/11176901/Tao-Dance-Theatre-Dance-Umbrella-Sadlers-Wells-review.html.

Ness, Sally. 2011. "Foucault's Turn from Phenomenology." *Dance Research Journal* 43 (2): 19–32.

Ngai, Sianne. 2014. *Our Aesthetic Categories*. Cambridge, MA: Harvard University Press.

———. 2008. "Merely Interesting." *Critical Inquiry* 34 (4): 777–817.

Noland, Carrie. 2009. *Agency and Embodiment*. Cambridge, MA: Harvard University Press.

Pakes, Anna. 2011. "Phenomenology and Dance." *Dance Research Journal* 43 (2): 33–49.

Peden, Knox. 2014. *Spinoza contra Phenomenology*. Stanford, CA: Stanford University Press.

Savigliano, Marta. 2009. "Worlding Dance and Dancing Out There in the World." In *Worlding Dance*, edited by Susan Leigh Foster, 163–90. New York: Palgrave.

Scherr, Apollinaire. 2012. "Tao Dance Theatre." *Financial Times,* July 26. https://www.ft.com/content/9b49ab72-d70b-11e1-8e7d-00144feabdco.

Sedgwick, Eve Kosofsky. 2003. *Touching Feeling: Affect, Pedagogy, Performativity*. Durham, NC: Duke University Press.

Seidman, Carrie. 2015. "Review: Tao Dance Theatre." *Sarasota Herald-Tribune*, October 17. http://ticket.heraldtribune.com/2015/10/17/riaf-review-tao-dance-theatre-weight-x-x-3/.

Sheets-Johnstone, Maxine. 2015. *The Phenomenology of Dance*. Philadelphia: Temple University Press.

Shih, Shu-mei. 2012. "Is the Post- in Postsocialism the Post- in Posthumanism?" *Social Text* 30 (1): 27–50.

Weate, Jeremy. 2001. "Fanon, Merleau-Ponty, and the Difference of Phenomenology." In *Race*, edited by R. Bernasconi, 169–83. Oxford: Blackwell.

Locating Performance

Choe Seung-hui's East Asian Modernism
and the Case for Area Knowledge in Dance Studies

EMILY E. WILCOX

In Seoul, the capital of South Korea, rare film footage of Korean dance history can be found on display at the National Theater of Korea Museum of Performing Arts, a relatively new museum that opened its first permanent exhibit in December 2009.[1] Following the museum's chronology, the first moving images the viewer encounters are those of Choe Seung-hui 최 승희 / 崔承喜 (aka Ch'oe Sŭng-hŭi / Choi Seunghee / Sai Shōki, 1911–69), a Korean dancer, choreographer, pedagogue, and dance theorist whose international career spanned the 1920s through the 1960s. The display features short clips from several of Choe's most well known solo choreographies from the late 1930s and early 1940s. In one, *Seokguram Wall Carvings*, Choe stands still, feet together and body squarely forward, as she moves her arms in deliberately slow, symmetrical patterns framing her chest and head (Takashima and Chong 1994, 118). She begins with her arms out to the side, palms facing forward at head height and elbows at ninety-degree angles in line with her shoulders. Breathing out from her nose, she pulls her arms down from the elbows, keeping her palms high and forward. When her hands reach waist height, she circles them forward until her middle fingertips meet at abdomen level. Then, with a breath in, she raises her wrists upward and brings her hands slowly up to her chest. In another, *Hourglass Drum Dance*, Choe walks in small, slightly bouncing steps backward and forward as she plays a large hourglass-shaped drum that is suspended on the front of her body from a shoulder strap (Takashima and Chong 1994, 96). As she walks, Choe leans her upper body back at a near forty-five-degree angle to counterbalance the drum's weight while she curves her head forward, keeping her face level. Using a stick in her right hand and the fingers of her left hand, she beats out complex rhythms, alternating on the drum's two faces. Between beats, she floats her arms out to the side and up above her shoulders and at times adds spins,

all creating a feeling of lightness in the upper body typical of dance vocabularies known today as "Korean dance" (Van Zile 2001). At the end of the clip,
Choe faces the audience and walks forward with both arms extended straight
out to the sides at shoulder level. By placing each foot slightly across the other,
she causes the drum to sway very slightly from side to side, which produces a
subtle counterbalancing action in her torso and shoulders. On each step, her
opposite wrist bobs forward, creating a stylized walk that matches the pulsing
rhythm of the drum beat.

The two dances described above belong to the historical category of *shinmuyong*, literally, "new dance," an innovative genre developed by Korean dancers
and choreographers during the Japanese colonial era in Korea (1910–45). After
being exposed to early Western modern dance via Japanese teachers, *shinmuyong* practitioners used these new choreographic approaches to reinterpret indigenous material, with Choe being among the most successful (Lee et al. 1997,
95–102). The museum summarizes this complex history in the video caption
as follows: "Choe Seung-hui was a pioneer of Korean modern dance who incorporated Western modern dance techniques into native traditions. She began
her career while learning modern dance, which at that point had recently been
introduced to Japan, but she gradually focused on creatively reinventing Korean
traditional dances. As an accomplished choreographer and educator, she performed in numerous venues around the world. She even formulated her own
doctrine of Oriental dance, and her work is remembered not just in Korea
but also in Japan and China."[2] The types of indigenous materials that Choe
invoked in her choreography were quite diverse. In *Seokguram Wall Carvings*,
Choe borrowed the imagery of guardian figures carved into the walls in an
eighth-century Korean Buddhist cave temple, Seokguram (Gu Yewen 1951, 101).
The costuming in this piece visually resembles the clothing of the carved figures, giving the impression of a largely exposed upper body with loose fabric
draped over the arms and wrapped around the legs. Photographic documentation suggests that this dance also included a series of poses modeled after those
displayed in the carvings. In *Hourglass Drum Dance*, by contrast, she took
inspiration from the performances of *kisaeng*, traditional Korean courtesan-
entertainers (Gu Yewen 1951, 93). The drum used in this dance, known as the
changgo, is a standard percussion instrument in all forms of Korean indigenous
music (Lee et al. 1997, 221). When played in this way, fastened to the dancer's
body as she walks, it is linked to traditional farmers' dance and music, giving it
a folkloric quality (Van Zile 2001, 194). Although both dances reference indigenous material, what makes them exemplary of *shinmuyong* is their creative reinterpretation of these sources. In other words, these are not traditional dances
aimed at reproducing actually existing dance forms. Rather, they are modern

FIGURE 46. Choe Seung-hui's *Hourglass Drum Dance*. (Reproduced with permission from the private collection of Siqintariha and the Pioneers of Chinese Dance Digital Archive, Asia Library, University of Michigan)

dances, in the sense that they emphasize the creative voice of the individual artist and adapt to the changing social conditions of modern life. As Judy Van Zile has argued regarding Choe's *shinmuyong* works, "She tried to create a kind of dance that was both distinctively Korean *and* modern" (2013, 136). Through *shinmuyong* choreographies such as *Seokguram Wall Carvings* and *Hourglass Drum Dance,* Choe thus laid the foundation for a new kind of modern dance, one that diverged from both Western modern dance and Korean traditional dance yet took inspiration from both.

As the museum caption cited above acknowledges, Choe's dance innovations had a lasting impact not just in South Korea but also across much of East Asia, a region today comprising the political entities of China (including Taiwan), Japan, North Korea, and South Korea. Despite a recent explosion of new research on Choe's work, however, this transnational component of her legacy is still not well understood. One reason for this is that scholarship on Choe has long been limited by political factors. Research on Choe was censored in South Korea until the early 1990s because of her status as a "communist defector" after 1946, when she immigrated to Pyongyang, now the capital of North Korea.[3] Since the ban on Choe-related research was lifted, however, the South Korean dance community has recognized her as a pioneering figure in their field, as demonstrated by the national museum exhibit described above. South Korean recognition of Choe led to a corresponding rise in Anglophone scholarship. However, limited access to North Korean sources has caused this work to remain limited primarily to Choe's development of *shinmuyong* during the Japanese colonial era, prior to 1945 (Lee et al. 1997; Van Zile 2001,

FIGURE 47. Choe Seung-hui's *Seokguram Wall Carvings.* (Reproduced with permission from the private collection of Cui Yuzhu and the Pioneers of Chinese Dance Digital Archive, Asia Library, University of Michigan)

2013; Park 2004; Kim Young-Hoon 2006; Atkins 2010; Kleeman 2014; Romero Castilla 2017).[4] Nevertheless, it was during the under-researched post-1945 period of her career, I argue, that Choe's transnational impact on East Asian dance modernism was most evident. After her move to North Korea, Choe's new role as an icon of socialist internationalism allowed her to develop the choreographic approaches she had originally devised for the creation of *shin-muyong* into a generalizable method for the proliferation of new forms of modern dance across East Asia.

To tell the story of Choe's post-1945 career and her role as an architect of East Asian dance modernism during this period, I employ Chinese-language sources that have previously been overlooked by Anglophone scholars. The original documentation of Choe's visits to China between 1941 and 1952 offers abundant insights into not only Choe's activities in China but also her own theoretical conceptualization of the new dance forms she was creating at the time. From as early as 1943, Chinese dance critics and scholars have been generating their own interpretations of Choe and her work, and they offer different perspectives from those available in either the South Korean or Anglophone literatures.[5] By turning to these previously unexamined Chinese-language sources, it is possible to gain new insights into Choe's work and to better understand her impact on the development of dance in East Asia. Methodologically, such an approach demonstrates the need for deeper engagements between Asian studies and dance studies, as well as a shift from "East–West" models of globalization to consider circuits of artistic exchange across political and linguistic boundaries within Asia.

Patriot and Visionary:
Chinese Views on Choe Seung-hui

On June 1, 1951, Shanghai-based dance editor Gu Yewen published the first Chinese-language book on Choe Seung-hui, less than two years after the founding of the People's Republic of China and while Choe was temporarily living in Beijing as a Korean War refugee.[6] In contrast to predominant South Korean perceptions of Choe at the time as a pro-Japanese collaborator, Gu presented her as a heroic figure who safeguarded Korean culture in the face of Japanese colonial suppression:

> [At Ishii Baku's school] she spent many years studying and researching Western dance. . . . Once she had fully mastered the techniques of modern dance, this patriotic daughter, ever faithful to her compatriots, threw herself committedly into her future path to become a performer of national dance art.[7] As an artist in a colonized country, however, this was impossible. The Japanese fascists not only

suppressed the Korean people politically and economically, their cultural policies also obliterated and exterminated national culture and art. As a girl of fourteen or fifteen, she may not have realized her mission, namely, that in a country
under the bondage of Japan, she dedicated herself to researching national dance.
But whether she realized it or not, she did the work of rescuing her country's
national culture and art. Moreover, she finally completed it. (Gu Yewen 1951, 4–5)

Like the South Korean condemnation of Choe, Gu's praise was motivated at
least in part by Cold War politics. As socialist neighbors fighting on the same
side of the Korean War, China and North Korea were allies, and this alliance
called for a positive view of North Korea and its cultural representatives. Much
like the Soviet ballet experts who would arrive in China a few years later, Choe
was an honored guest whose artistry was to be both admired and studied by
her Chinese counterparts. Gu thus interpreted her commitment to Korean-
themed choreography during the colonial era as a patriotic stance against the
suppression of Korean culture rather than a capitulation to imperialist desires.

Cold War alliances were not the only factor shaping Chinese views of Choe's
art. Since her first tours to China during the colonial era in the early 1940s,
Chinese critics had praised Choe as a cultural visionary whose performances
would pave the way for dance developments in China. In a detailed review of
Choe's 1943 performances in Shanghai, for example, Chinese critic Liu Junsheng
wrote that Choe's creativity, especially her skillful manipulation of rhythm,
had effectively launched her own school or "sect" of interpretive dance, which
Liu compared to those of Duncan, Wigman, the Russian ballet, and Negro
dance (1943, 26). Liu asserted that while interpretive dancers had performed in
Shanghai before, their audiences had mainly been foreigners, whereas Choe
attracted more local viewers. With her public performances, Liu argued, she
thus became "the first to open up an atmosphere [for art dance] in China,"
meaning that she set an example for dance as a serious stage art, in contrast to
the entertainment-oriented productions then dominating Shanghai stages (29).
Finally, Liu praised Choe's theoretical sophistication. Referring to a symposium held in Shanghai in which Choe had articulated her ideas on dance creation, Liu equated her views with "the highest principles of modern art" and
wrote enthusiastically of her intentions to help promote "pure art dance" in
China (30).

Given that Shanghai was under Japanese occupation in 1943 and Choe was
then touring as a representative of Japan, Liu's enthusiasm for Choe may have
reflected local political conditions, namely, the impact of Japanese occupation
on Shanghai's media. Choe's interactions with Chinese performing artists, however, suggest the existence of a genuine artistic connection that transcended

these political circumstances. Choe gave her first two performance tours in China in 1941 and 1942, shortly after she returned to Japan from her world tour. According to Korean Chinese dance scholar Li Aishun, these performances attracted positive attention from leading figures in the Chinese theater community, and Choe began to develop a strong interest in Chinese performance forms (2005, 17). During her third tour to China in 1943, Chinese media reports indicate that, in addition to Korean-themed works such as *Seokguram Wall Carvings* and *Hourglass Drum Dance,* Choe was also performing new choreography using Chinese themes, some of which were inspired by her experiences in China ("Cui Chengxi wudao" 1943; "Chongyi zhe meili" 1943). Between 1944 and 1945 Choe made extended visits to Beijing and Shanghai, both major centers for Chinese opera forms such as Peking opera and Kun opera. During this time, the Chinese media documented Choe's meetings with Mei Lanfang and other leading Chinese opera actors, as well as Choe's study of Chinese opera and her founding of a research institute in Beijing devoted to the creation of a new dance genre she called "Eastern Dance" or "Oriental Dance" (Ao 1944; Gu Xue 1944; "Haiwai tongxin" 1944; "Zuji san dazhou" 1944; "Cui Chengxi yi ge" 1945; Luo 1945; "Cui Chengxi nicong" 1945; "Riben wuyongjia" 1945; "Cui Chengxi nüshi" 1945; see also Wilcox 2018b). During the Japanese occupation of Shanghai, Mei famously refused to perform for the occupation government, growing a mustache as a form of protest. Meanwhile, Mei publicly praised Choe's artistic work, calling her "a great artist . . . [who] respects past Eastern art traditions and gives them new life" and lamenting that there were not more great dancer-choreographers like her in China (quoted in Luo 1945, 85–86). Mei personally taught Choe segments of his stage repertoire, and he even offered to perform for her privately in costume in his home (85; "Cui Chengxi zuo" 1946; Yu 1946).

When Choe returned to China for her second extended stay in late 1950, she renewed relationships with artists such as Mei and continued her previous work of researching Chinese opera movement to create new dance forms (Bai 1950; "Guonei wenyi" 1951; Ming 1951). In an essay published just before Choe's arrival, Chen Jinqing (1950), then a leading figure in the Chinese dance field, praised Choe as a model for the future development of "new dance art" (*xin wudao yishu,* 新舞蹈藝術) in China. During the previous years, the main challenges that had been facing Chinese dancers, Chen explained, were how to create new works that successfully adapted folk and traditional dance forms for the modern stage and how to create new pedagogical systems appropriate to train professional dancers for these new repertoires. According to Chen, Choe had already found ways to resolve both problems and thus offered a model for Chinese dance workers. Regarding the problem of choreography,

Chen cited specific works from Choe's repertoire and explained how in each one Choe had dealt especially deftly with traditional and folk material. She wrote, "These works all directly absorb folk styles and rhythms, then polish them and make them more beautiful. . . . [T]hese precedents are very worthy of our study" (1950, 21). Choe's system for professional Korean dance training, which she had demonstrated during a tour to China in late 1949, had also greatly impressed Chen: "We have seen a set of Choe's basic training methods; she established it by using dance movements from her own national traditions and following the life movements of the Korean people, then absorbing western scientific methods. This set of basic training is completely in a Korean national style. . . . [It] is [also] very worthy of our study, because we currently need to create our own basic training system" (22).[8]

With the support of admirers in China such as Mei, Chen, and others, Choe received an invitation from the Chinese Ministry of Culture in early 1951 to establish her own course at the Central Academy of Drama in Beijing, where she developed and implemented a dance curriculum based on Chinese opera movement ("Guonei yishu" 1951; "Zhengli Zhongguo" 1951; Fang 1951).[9] As Chinese dance scholars such as Su Ya (2004) have documented, this course

FIGURE 48. Choe Seung-hui teaching at the Central Academy of Drama in Beijing in 1951. (Reproduced with permission from the private collection of Siqintariha and the Pioneers of Chinese Dance Digital Archive, Asia Library, University of Michigan)

had a tremendous influence on the development of dance in China, especially on what became known as Chinese classical dance (*Zhongguo gudianwu* 中國 古典舞). An essay that Choe published in China's leading newspaper in 1951 in which she outlined her methodology for developing this course also remains a key theoretical text in the historiography of Chinese classical dance in China (Choe 1951; Li Zhengyi et al. 2004).

Abstracting Culture: Choe's East Asian Modernism

The period spanning the mid-1940s to the mid-1950s marked an important turning point in Choe's career. During the 1930s and early 1940s, Choe had developed a Korean dance repertoire that had brought her success among both Japanese and Western audiences, at least in part because they resonated with Orientalist, primitivist, and pan-Asian discourses about Korean culture that predominated in these communities at the time due to cultural structures of colonialism and imperialism. *Seokguram Wall Carvings* and *Hourglass Drum Dance* are both representative of this repertoire, which at the time helped construct Japanese and Western notions of Korea as exotic, backward, or familiar, depending on the situation. With the end of the Pacific War in 1945 and Korea's independence from Japan, however, a new political space opened up in which Choe's dances took on new meaning as the patriotic protection of Korean culture in the face of Japanese and later also Western imperialism. It was in part because of Cold War knowledge politics that these dances were long underexplored in Anglophone scholarship. Choe's work developed these new meanings mainly in the Soviet-allied countries of North Korea and the People's Republic of China, not in US-allied countries such as South Korea and Japan. This contributed to Anglophone scholars' tendency to locate Choe exclusively in the pre-1945 Japanese colonial period rather than in the sphere of socialist nation building.

Chinese sources are especially helpful for understanding the post-1945 period in Choe's career because they demonstrate the fundamental flexibility of her earlier repertoire to take on different meanings for different audiences, a flexibility that anticipated their translatability from the political sphere of Japanese colonialism to that of socialist nation building. During her tours in the early 1940s, what struck Chinese audiences most about Choe's performances was their demonstration of dance as a serious modern art form, something that in China was quite new and relatively unfamiliar at the time. Choe's creative adaptations of traditional dance resonated with ongoing activities of artists such as Mei, who himself had been long engaged with experiments in the modernization of Chinese theater and dance with the goal of creating new spaces for Chinese traditional performance both in China and on international stages (Goldstein 2007; Yeh 2016). For Mei and others like him in early 1940s China, Choe's performances inspired new ideas about how to analyze and reconstruct conventional movement, as well as new ways of staging the body as an artistic medium independent from singing and speaking. Rather than interpreting Choe's works through the desires of her Japanese and Western audiences, Mei and others saw in her dances reflections of their own desires: hope for Chinese performing arts to take on new forms that would please new audiences, a desire for cultural modernity in the expression of new artistic ideas and tastes, and a desire for East Asian artists to maintain independent cultural identities at a time when such identities were under threat by both the Japanese Empire and Western cultural hegemony. Choe's repertoire fulfilled the localized desires of her Chinese audiences just as it had fulfilled those of her Japanese and Western audiences. By viewing Choe's work through the lens of Chinese sources, therefore, it is possible to recognize and appreciate how different audiences viewed her repertoire in diverse ways.

Although her activities during the 1930s and early 1940s offered the foundation for her later accomplishments, Choe's contributions to the development of East Asian dance modernism were realized most fully during the socialist period of her career, with her activities in early 1950s China offering the most useful illustration. The crux of Choe's modernism was her transformation of contextualized indigenous performance practices into movement forms that could exist independently from their traditional cultural contexts and become abstracted vocabularies used to train dancers and create new dance works. Abstraction has often been considered anathema to socialist dance creation; however, it played an important role in the construction of socialist Chinese and Korean dance form as developed by Choe (S. Kim 2017; Wilcox 2018b, 2019).

In this context, "abstraction" refers to the process by which movement vocabularies that were originally derived from existing sources were given new meanings and deployed in new arrangements for new choreographic purposes. In the context of dances derived from Peking opera, for example, Choe extracted movements that had specific theatrical meanings in the context of opera performance and redeployed them as purely formal movement sequences to train dancers. When these movements were used in new choreography, they conveyed a broad sense of cultural association, such as "Korean" or "Chinese," "popular" or "elite," or "rural" or "urban." However, their specific theatrical meanings were not necessarily maintained.[10] Rather than seeking a real adherence to traditional practice, therefore, Choe mined traditional performances for their visual images, aesthetic qualities, and movement vocabularies, which she then revised, recombined, and redeployed for new purposes. In *Seokguram Wall Carvings*, we can see Choe's modernism at work in her borrowing of postures and imagery from the Buddhist stone reliefs, producing a movement vocabulary that maintains an aesthetic connection to these cultural artifacts while allowing for a large amount of abstraction and recomposition disconnected from the original context of a Buddhist temple. Similarly, in *Hourglass Drum Dance*, we can see Choe's modernism in her adaptation of aspects of *kisaeng* dances and farmers' music and dance, such as specific walking techniques and arm, hand, and head movements, rhythmic patterns and ways of engaging with the drum, and, of course, the materiality of the *changgo* drum itself as a stage property. In this new form, however, the dance is separated from the social identity of the *kisaeng* or the context of farmers' music and dance; instead, it becomes an expressive medium of the individual choreographer.

Choe's construction of a new Chinese dance vocabulary based on the movements of Chinese opera represented a culmination of her modernist practice because it showed the transferability and applicability of her approach as a generalizable mechanism for new dance innovation across East Asia and potentially beyond. In her 1951 essay outlining her creative method, Choe highlighted the difference between her curriculum of Chinese dance movements and their operatic sources. First, she explained that the vocabulary that appeared in her curriculum represented only a selection of the full spectrum of Chinese opera movements, those that she felt were appropriate for the aesthetic and expressive goals of dance as she understood them. Movements that did not suit the needs of dance were actively weeded out and discarded. Second, she made clear that movements were analyzed and organized into a new system of categories that allowed them to be recombined in new ways. Whereas previously, operatic movements were organized in sequences according to story lines and characters, in Choe's system they were organized into sequences according to movement qualities and their usefulness as exercises to train dancers' bodily abilities. Third, she clarified that movements were expanded in scale so that they would be able to maximize the expressiveness of bodily movement as an artistic medium independent from song and speech. Through these changes, Choe argued, Chinese opera movement could retain its aesthetic cultural properties while being extracted from its embeddedness in theater and expanded to produce a new independent dance language and system for training dancers. Choe reasoned that because the creative source was still Chinese opera movement, the system would possess national distinctiveness while at the same time being a medium for new creation (Choe 1951).

Interviews with Choe published in Chinese newspapers and magazines during the 1940s suggest that she did not view the relationship between tradition and modernity in absolute terms but instead took a progressive view of cultural heritage that saw it as inherently dynamic. In a conversation between

Choe and Mei documented in a Chinese magazine in 1945, for example, Mei asked Choe whether her works were all new creations, to which she responded:

> My dances, such as past examples in the style of *Bodhisattva, Scattered Tunes*, and *Subtle Cleanliness*, portray Eastern atmosphere. However, I do not completely follow inherited dances that previous people have passed down. Some say new creation is destructive to tradition. I rather believe that new creation has always been the normal development of tradition. In the past, our ancestors' artistic creations were passed down and became today's art traditions. The new creations of today's artists will also become the traditions of future generations. I think Mr. Mei's creations will certainly become the classical legends of the future! (Luo 1945, 86)

This understanding of tradition as renewable rather than fixed gave the national dance forms that grew out of Choe's East Asian dance modernism a different quality from those in other places where the supposedly pure and unchanging nature of national culture was more emphasized (Wilcox 2018a). The two most obvious examples of this approach in practice appear in the new forms of Korean and Chinese dance developed under Choe's guidance in socialist contexts after 1945, specifically in North Korea and the People's Republic of China. One reason Choe's approaches were so welcomed in socialist societies is their resonance with the socialist dream of devising a new form of modernity that could compete with Western capitalist models and be grounded in folk culture. Insofar as much of Choe's choreography achieved these qualities, she became the ideal architect of a new form of dance modernity for East Asian socialism.

Conclusion: Bringing Back the Area

Choe Seung-hui offers a rich case for exploring the potential of area studies for stimulating new research and approaches in dance studies. At the linguistic level, Choe's case demonstrates the need for area studies approaches because her career left traces in multiple languages. With the exception of reviews from her 1938–40 world tour, the majority of primary source materials on Choe's life exist only in Korean, Japanese, and Chinese, making knowledge of at least one East Asian language a prerequisite for in-depth primary source research on her life and work. On another dimension, because Choe is a transnational figure who mainly traversed borders within Asia, her case necessitates a shift from East–West to East–East relationships when conceptualizing and historicizing transnational phenomena such as colonialism, imperialism, diaspora, and intercultural exchange in the context of her work. Additionally, Choe's life and career highlight the role of the Cold War in shaping historical memory, a topic that too often goes unacknowledged in US- or Anglo-centered disciplinary research, which tends to focus on and normalize historical phenomena and experiences in the capitalist world (Wilcox 2017). Choe's artistic legacy demonstrates the importance of taking seriously cultural and artistic production in socialist countries and the alternatives that production poses to capitalist modernity, especially during the twentieth century. This is particularly important in the dance field, since many dance forms and genres that exist today were developed or institutionalized in socialist contexts. Because most current and formerly socialist countries are in places that fall into the rubrics of area studies regions (the Cold War was itself a prominent factor in determining these regions in the first place), area studies training is often necessary for in-depth research on dance in socialist or formerly socialist societies.

As a dance studies scholar based in an area studies department, I have a personal investment in the power of area studies to innovate dance research. While area studies has been rightly criticized for its sectioning off of the world into nations and regions, the reverse impulse to focus on globalization and diaspora also generates its own problems (Dirlik 2010). The fields of area studies were created to support in-depth, interdisciplinary research on regions of the world outside the United States, Canada, and Western Europe. By emphasizing linguistic knowledge and expertise in local history, politics, and culture, area studies (especially in its humanistic forms) aims at forming deeply contextualized readings of culture and art outside Anglophone and Western European spaces. Area studies offers a counterpoint to the historical Eurocentrism of the disciplines by challenging historical periodizations, theoretical concepts, and social or cultural categories developed on the basis of US or European models but too often deemed to be universal. As one authority on area studies explains, the goal of area studies since the 1950s has been "to historicize and contextualize—in effect, to de-naturalize—the formulations and universalizing tendencies of the US social science and humanities disciplines which continue to draw largely on US and European experience" (Szanton 2004, 2). Whereas ethnic studies aims at something similar by focusing on the experiences of people of color residing as minorities or diasporas within predominantly white communities, area studies accomplishes this by focusing on parts of the world where people of color are the majority. While borders are important for area studies, movements across borders have also always been important. The goal of area studies, however, is to ensure that studies of border-crossing movements do not retrench Eurocentric knowledge, whether through a linguistic emphasis on sources in English or other Western European languages or through a geographic emphasis on activities taking place in the United States and Western Europe. Too often, this has been the unintended result when a focus on diaspora studies and interculturalism becomes a substitute for area studies research.

Like many subjects in area studies, Choe's case challenges basic historical and theoretical paradigms often taken for granted or universalized in Eurocentric disciplinary narratives. John Martin, a foundational figure in the early development of theoretical and historical paradigms in US-based dance studies, included a photograph of Choe's *Hourglass Drum Dance* in his 1947 book *The Dance*. Unsurprisingly, however, he placed it in the category of "basic dance," along with almost all other dances he associated with non-Western culture, rather than in the category of modern dance (Martin 1947, 22). Dance studies today is deeply critical of Eurocentrism, racism, and other vestiges of the field's past that are reflected in Martin's outdated categorization scheme. Nevertheless, there is still work to be done in gaining a global perspective that fully realizes this critique by replacing old paradigms with new categories, ideas, and historical narratives. In the case of Choe Seung-hui, her career moved in the reverse of the developmental narrative Martin visualized in his book. The earliest dance photographs of Choe look like what we often envision today as "modern dance." Dressed in form-fitting leotards and short tunics with legs and arms exposed and expressions of seriousness or ecstasy, Choe leaps through the air, shows off her muscular and flexible body, and articulates through extended lines, pointed feet, and angular planes. For Choe, however, these dances ultimately came to represent imitation and convention rather than innovation and creativity. Whereas these dances followed in the styles of others and worked in their voices, it was in formulating dances like *Seokguram Wall Carvings* and *Hourglass Drum Dance* that Choe invented her own forms and established something new that would be imitated by others. In this sense, what looks like modern dance from a US or European perspective for Choe and her Chinese collaborators was less modern than the Korean-style modern choreographies that she started to develop in the 1930s and spent the remainder of her career expanding, implementing, and theorizing. It was in these latter forms that Choe made her mark as a modernist choreographer, dancer, theorist, and pedagogue. In Choe's case, area studies knowledge makes it possible to see the modern and the new in what, from a conventional US or European perspective, does not fit existing understandings or expectations for dance modernism. In this way, area studies helps us to locate dance in multiple histories that move in different ways.

Notes

Research for this essay was funded by grants from the Social Science Research Council Inter-Asia Program and the University of Michigan Lieberthal-Rogel Center for Chinese Studies. I am grateful for feedback from Janice Ross, Judy Van Zile, Jongsung Yang, and Engseng Ho. All translations from Chinese are my own.

1. Museum display observed on June 29, 2017.

2. The full caption appeared in Korean, with a shorter summary in English. This is a transcription of the English portion.

3. On Choe's career in North Korea, see Suzy Kim (2017). On South Korean censorship, see Kim Young-Hoon (2006).

4. This research begins with her childhood in Japanese-occupied Korea. It then traces her move to Tokyo in 1926 and her work with Japanese modern dancer Ishii Baku. It culminates with her mid-1930s rise to stardom in Japan; her 1938–40 world tour of North America, Europe, and Latin America; and her activities supporting Japanese military expansion during the height of the Pacific War mobilization in 1941–44.

5. I do not speak or read Korean. My understanding of the South Korean literature is based on commissioned English translations of recent Korean-language writings published in South Korea, English-language publications by South Korean scholars, and conference panels I attended in Seoul in 2017.

6. According to a Chinese newspaper report, Choe's school in Pyongyang had been destroyed by US bombs, and two of her students had been killed (Bai 1950).

7. "National" is a translation of *minzu* 民族. Here it refers to Korea.

8. On the 1949 performances, see Chen Ji (1949) and Li Yang (1950). Chen had also studied in Choe's school in Pyongyang around 1948 (Dong and Long 2008, 731).

9. For a detailed account of this program, including testimonials from dancers who participated, see Tian and Li (2005).

10. This does not mean that the resulting new choreographies were completely "abstract" in the sense of being absolutely nonreferential. This is an area that requires further exploration, however, since formalist choreography was sometimes used to develop new dance vocabularies.

Works Cited

Ao Jianqing 敖劍青. 1944. "Cui Chengxi, Mei Lanfang huijian ji" 崔承喜，梅蘭芳會見記 [Record of meeting between Choe Seung-hui and Mei Lanfang]. *Taipingyang zhoubao* 太平洋周報 1 (93): 2102–3.

Atkins, E. Taylor. 2010. *Primitive Selves: Koreana in the Japanese Colonial Gaze, 1910–1945.* Berkeley: University of California Press.

Bai Sheng 柏生. 1950. "Zhong Chao renmin zhandou de youyi" 中朝人民戰鬥的友誼 [Wartime friendship between China and North Korea]. *Renmin ribao* 人民日報, December 11.

Chen Ji 陳跡. 1949. "Chaoxian funü daibiaotuan fangwen ji" 朝鮮婦女代表團訪問記 [Interview with the North Korean women's representatives]. *Renmin ribao* 人民日報, December 17.

Chen Jinqing 陳錦清. 1950. "Guanyu xin wudao yishu" 關於新舞蹈藝術 [On new dance art]. *Wenyi bao* 文藝報 (2): 20–23.

Choe Seung-hui 崔承喜. 1951. "Zhongguo wudao yishu de jianglai" 中國舞蹈藝術的 將來 [The future of Chinese dance art]. *Renmin ribao* 人民日報, February 18.

"Chongyi zhe meili de wuji Cui Chengxi" 充溢著魅力的舞姬崔承喜 [Choe Seung-hui, a dancing girl overflowing with charm]. 1943. *Taipingyang zhoubao* 太平洋周 報 1 (84): 1853.

"Cui Chengxi nicong Shang Xiaoyun xue Yubei ting huabu" 崔承喜擬從尚小雲學御 碑亭滑步 [Choe Seung-hui follows Shang Xiaoyun to study the sliding step from *Yubei Pavilion*]. 1945. *Liyan huakan* 立言畫刊 (328): 9.

"Cui Chengxi nüshi yu xiao mingdan Zhang Junqiu zhi heying" 崔承喜女士與小名 旦張君秋之合影 [Photograph of Choe Seung-hui with famous female-role actor Zhang Junqiu]. 1945. *San liu jiu huabao* 三六九畫報 31 (2): 14.

"Cui Chengxi wudao zuotanhui" 崔承喜舞蹈座談會 [A roundtable discussion of Choe Seung-hui's dance]. 1943. *Zazhi* 雜志 12 (2): 33–38.

"Cui Chengxi yi ge you tiancai er huanxi chuangzao de wuyongjia" 崔承喜一個有天 才而歡喜創造的舞踊家 [Choe Seung-hui, a dance artist who is talented and likes to create]. 1945. *Xin shiji* 新世紀 1 (2): 29–30.

"Cui Chengxi zuo jipu nülang" 崔承喜做吉普女郎 [Choe Seung-hui becomes a Jeep girl]. 1946. *Hai tao* 海濤 (4): cover.

Dirlik, Arif. 2010. "Asia Pacific Studies in an Age of Global Modernity." In *Remaking Area Studies: Teaching and Learning across Asia and the Pacific*, edited by Terence Wesley-Smith and Jon Goss, 5–23. Honolulu: University of Hawai'i Press.

Dong Xijiu 董錫玖 and Long Yinpei 隆蔭培, eds. 2008. *Xin Zhongguo wudao de dian-jishi* 新中國舞蹈的奠基石 [Cornerstones of new Chinese dance]. Hong Kong: Tianma chubanshe.

Fang Ming 方明. 1951. "Peiyang Zhong Chao wudao gongzuo ganbu Cui Chengxi wudo yanjiuban chengli" 培養中朝舞蹈工作幹部崔承喜舞蹈研究班成立 [Choe Seung-hui dance research class established to cultivate Chinese and North Korean dance work cadres]. *Guangming ribao* 光明日報, March 20.

Goldstein, Joshua. 2007. *Drama Kings: Players and Publics in the Re-creation of Peking Opera, 1870–1937*. Berkeley: University of California Press.

"Guonei wenyi dongtai" 國內文藝动态 [The domestic literary and arts scene]. 1951. *Renmin ribao* 人民日報, February 11.

Gu Xue 孤血. 1944. "Si zhe ban kexi niang han ceng jian Cui Chengxi zhi yinxiang gaitan" 似這般可喜娘罕曾見崔承喜之印象概談 [A rare woman: Impressions of Choe Seung-hui]. *Li yan huakan* 立言畫刊 (326): 2–3.

Gu Yewen 顧也文, ed. 1951. *Chaoxian wudaojia Cui Chengxi* 朝鮮舞蹈家崔承喜 [Korean dance artist Choe Seung-hui]. Shanghai: Wenlian chubanshe.

"Haiwai tongxin liu Ri qingnian zuojia Chen Lingxiu ban Cui Chengxi yan Zhong-guo guzhuangwu" 海外通信留日青年作家陳靈秀伴崔承喜演中国古裝舞 [News from abroad: Japan-based Chinese youth writer Chen Lingxiu accompanies Choe Seung-hui in performing Chinese ancient costume dance]. 1944. *San liu jiu huabao* 三六九畫報 28 (2): 51.

Kim, Suzy. 2017. "Choe Seung-hui between Ballet and Folk: Aesthetics of National Form and Socialist Content in North Korea." Paper presented at the University of Michigan "Dancing East Asia" conference, April 7–8.

Kim Young-Hoon. 2006. "Border Crossing: Choe Seung-hui's Life and the Modern Experience." *Korea Journal* 46 (1) (Spring): 170–97.

Kleeman, Faye Yuan. 2014. *In Transit: The Formation of the Colonial East Asian Cultural Sphere.* Honolulu: University of Hawai'i Press.

Lee Duhyun et al. 1997. *Korean Performing Arts: Drama, Dance & Music Theater.* Seoul, Korea: Jipmoondang Publishing Co.

Li Aishun 李爱順. 2005. "Cui Chengxi yu Zhongguo wudao" 崔承喜與中國舞蹈 [Choe Seung-hui and Chinese dance]. *Beijing wudao xueyuan xuebao* 北京舞蹈學院學報 (4): 16–22.

Li Yang 力揚. 1950. "Guoji de you'ai" 國際的友愛 [International friendship]. *Renmin ribao* 人民日報, January 22.

Li Zhengyi 李正一 et al. 2004. *Zhongguo gudianwu jiaoxue tixi chuangjian fazhan shi* 中國古典舞教學體系創建發展史 [History of the development of the teaching system of Chinese classical dance]. Shanghai: Shanghai yinyue chubanshe.

Liu Junsheng 劉俊生. 1943. "Lun Cui Chengxi de wudao" 論崔承喜的舞蹈 [On Choe Seung-hui's dance]. *Zazhi* 雜志 12 (2): 26–30.

Luo Chuan 洛川. 1945. "Cui Chengxi er ci lai Hu ji" 崔承喜二次來滬記 [Notes on Choe Seung-hui's second visit to Shanghai]. *Zazhi* 杂志 15 (2): 84–88.

Martin, John. 1947. *The Dance: The Story of Dance Told in Pictures and Text.* New York: Tudor Publishing Company.

Ming 明. 1951. "Dai Ailian biaoyan 'tuobei de xiaoma' Cui Chengxi zhengli Zhongguo jiuju wudao" 戴愛蓮表演‘駝背的小馬’崔承喜整理中國舊劇舞蹈 [Dai Ailian performs 'Hump-backed horse'; Choe Seung-hui organizes old drama dance]. *Guangming ribao* 光明日報, February 21.

Park, Sang Mi. 2004. "The Making of a Cultural Icon for the Japanese Empire: Choe Seung-hui's U.S. Dance Tours and 'New Asian Culture' in the 1930s and 1940s." *positions: asia critique* 14 (3): 597–632.

"Riben wuyongjia Cui Chengxi yu ming xiaosheng Ye Chenglan heying qibianhui juzhao" 日本舞踊家崔承喜與名小生葉盛蘭合攝奇雙會劇照 [Photographs from joint photography event between famous Japanese dancer Choe Seung-hui and famous young male-role actor Ye Shenglan]. 1945. *San liu jiu huabao* 三六九畫報 31 (2): cover.

Romero Castilla, Alfredo. 2017. "Choi Seunghee (Sai Shoki): The Dancing Princess from the Peninsula in Mexico." *Journal of Society for Dance Documentation and History* 44 (March): 81–96.

Su Ya 蘇婭. 2004. *Qiusuo xinzhi: Zhongguo gudianwu xuexi biji* 求索新知—中國古典舞學習筆記 [In search of new knowledge: Notes on studying Chinese classical dance]. Beijing: Zhongguo xiju chubanshe.

Szanton, David. 2004. "The Origin, Nature, and Challenges of Area Studies in the United States." In *The Politics of Knowledge: Area Studies and the Disciplines*, edited by David Szanton, 1–33. Berkeley: University of California Press.

Takashima Yusaburo 高嶋雄三郎 and Chong Pyong-ho 鄭昞浩. 1994. *Seiki no bijin buyoka Sai Shoki* 世紀の美人舞踊家崔承喜 [One of the most beautiful dancers of the century, Choe Seung-hui]. Tokyo, Japan: MT Publishing Company.

Tian Jing 田靜 and Li Baicheng 李百成, eds. 2005. *Xin Zhongguo wudao yishujia de yaolan* 新中國舞蹈藝術家的搖籃 [New China's cradle of dance artists]. Beijing: Zhongguo wenlian chubanshe.

Van Zile, Judy. 2001. *Perspectives on Korean Dance*. Middletown, CT: Wesleyan University Press.

———. 2013. "Performing Modernity in Korea: The Dance of Ch'oe Sung-hui." *Korean Studies* 37 (1): 124–49.

Wilcox, Emily. 2017. "When Place Matters: Provincializing the 'Global.'" In *Rethinking Dance History*, edited by Larraine Nicholas and Geraldine Morris, 160–72. 2nd ed. New York: Routledge.

———. 2018a. "Dynamic Inheritance: Representative Works and the Authoring of Tradition in Chinese Dance." *Journal of Folklore Research* 55 (1): 77–112.

———. 2018b. "Crossing Over: Choe Seung-hui's Pan-Asianism in Revolutionary Time." *Journal of Society for Dance Documentation and History* 51 (December): 65–97.

———. 2019. *Revolutionary Bodies: Chinese Dance and the Socialist Legacy*. Oakland, CA: University of California Press.

Yeh, Catherine. 2016. "Experimenting with Dance Drama: Peking Opera Modernity, Kabuki Theater Reform and the Denishawn's Tour of the Far East." *Journal of Global Theatre History* 1 (2): 28–37.

Yu Si 于思. 1946. "Yitan yi ye jiu shi: Cui Chengxi tinong Mei Lanfang" 藝壇上一頁舊事崔承喜捉弄梅蘭芳 [An old story from the arts world: Choe Seung-hui tricks Mei Lanfang]. *Haichao zhoubao* 海潮周報 (34): 10.

"Zhengli Zhongguo wudao yishu peizhi zhuanye wudao ganbu" 整理中國舞蹈藝術培植專業舞蹈幹部 [Organize Chinese dance art, train professional dance cadres]. 1951. *Guangming ribao* 光明日報, February 14.

"Zuji san dazhou, guanzhong erbaiwan" 足跡三大洲, 觀眾二百萬 [Footprints on three continents, over two million audiences]. 1944. *Zhonghua zhoubao* 中華周報 1 (13): 21.

Toward a Critical Globalized Humanities

Dance Research in Mexico City at the CENIDID

JOSE L. REYNOSO

In this essay I advocate for expanding dance studies' international map, delineated primarily by Europe and the United States, as I reflect on possibilities toward a broader cartography. My discussion highlights the role dance studies, as an international field of critical inquiry, plays in conceptualizing what I call "critical globalized humanities." I argue that sustained interactions among distinctive dance research initiatives around the world, like the Centro Nacional de Investigación, Documentación e Información de la Danza José Limón (CENIDID) in Mexico City, is a necessary condition to the formation of critical globalized humanities as praxis of decolonial relational ethics. "Critical" signals epistemological and methodological approaches employed to reframe neocolonial impulses in "globalization" as a rhetoric that unevenly fulfills its alleged promises of different forms of prosperity and development. "Humanities" points to an academic tradition as a discursive site where cultural assumptions reflective of Eurocentric intellectual genealogies are reproduced and contested by diverse ways of thinking and being.

This is not an attempt to create autonomous spaces or imagine institutional entities where scholars exist perpetually and exclusively, resisting legacies of European neocolonization (i.e., since the arrival of Europeans in the Americas in the fifteenth century) and/or US expansionist imperialism (i.e., the annexation of Mexican territory by the United States in 1848). To different extents and levels of success, some governments and individuals actively resist while adapting aspects of those historical forces. Resistive and strategic adaptation efforts have been contextualized by the fact that Mexican postcolonial history, as well as the configuration of Latin America as a geographical region and as an idea, has been impacted by European and US influences. The CENIDID represents a case where these transnational influences *fuse* with the legacies of revolutionary nationalism that have shaped the dance research center's more than thirty-year history.[1]

I propose the concept of "transnational nationalism" to account for the international forces that directly or indirectly coalesce with local cultural specificities, economic interests, and political ideologies to influence the development of nationalist movements, the institutions that implement forms of governmentality, and resistive alternatives to them. In other words, the local is a necessary but not sufficient condition to the construction of nation-states and/or nationalist movements that align with or resist "external" forces. As an analytical tool, transnational nationalism calls for attending to histories of domination and resistance within formulations of the national/local and in relation to the transnational/global. This approach implies that putting histories of dance studies around the world in conversation, physically and by other means, can provide opportunities for undoing neocolonial and imperialist legacies that shape (academic) transnational relations while also reimagining fixed notions of the concept of "nation."

From this perspective, I imagine two English-reading audiences for this chapter.[2] One audience in Latin American countries such as Mexico who might not be as familiar with developments of dance studies in Europe and the United States, which has constituted my own academic formation. Also, I address an audience who might be familiar with these histories but not with dance studies initiatives in places such as Mexico and other countries outside the Europe / United States dyad. I hope this essay joins efforts that foreground the heterogeneity of the world vis-à-vis Eurocentric epistemological paradigms, including the rhetoric of (Western) modernity, in order to account—through the study of dance—for constructions of the posthuman as a shifting entity, experience, and concept in relation to other species and the environment (Braidotti and Gilroy 2016). Thus, by expanding dance studies' international map, inclusive of more expansive transnational histories of the discipline, *we* can imagine the possibility of a more egalitarian critical globalized humanities. First, I trace a genealogy of the field within the Global North. Then I discuss the case of the CENIDID's development within its historical and cultural context. Finally, I conclude by examining some implications involved in expanding dance studies' international cartography.

Tracing an Epistemological and International Map of Dance Studies: The Europe / United States Dyad

In the early twentieth-century United States, systems of support inside and outside universities set precedents for dance studies to constitute itself as an academic formation.[3] The inclusion of modern dance in colleges from the 1920s onward, as well as other supportive infrastructures in subsequent decades, enabled the production and circulation of knowledge about dance history and theory across the country (Ross 2000; Manning 2004). Critics wrote what dance was and meant within their specific historical and cultural contexts. Dance scholars developed their own research methodologies while integrating approaches from established disciplines. Although dance artists and writers of color were active during these decades, their histories were often sublimated components of mainstream (modern) dance history, representative primarily of work by white dance artists and writers.[4] During the 1980s, the influence of poststructuralist theory in the US academy shifted the epistemological orientations with which a new cadre of dance scholars, many of whom were dancers and/or choreographers, approached the study of dance (Desmond 1997). Rather than seeing dance in terms of evolutionary theory, placing emphasis on dancers' biographies, or rehearsing tropes of artistic genius, dance became a site for the critical study of the functions of power and ideology in relation to dance practices and the formation of social identities (Desmond 1997). These analytical approaches were being reflected in publications such as Susan Leigh Foster's *Reading Dancing* (1986), Mark Franko's *The Dancing Body in Renaissance Choreography (c. 1416–1589)* (1986), Cynthia Novack's *Sharing the Dance* (1990), and Susan Manning's *Ecstasy and the Demon* (1993).

During the 1990s, dance studies as an academic formation experienced a surge in debates about interdisciplinarity in relation to film and art theory, literary and feminist studies, and other approaches associated with cultural studies (Bryson 1997; Desmond 1997; Koritz 1996). Randy Martin contextualized the interdisciplinarity of dance studies in relation to the "reflexivity of difference" and thus advocated for a "critical" multiculturalism. In this epistemological context, he argued, "critical" dance studies could emerge as a discipline capable of "mobiliz[ing] in writing the conceptual challenges that dance offers to conventional ways of understanding politics and the world" (1998, 183). Employing this interdisciplinary approach for the critical analysis of difference and power in national and transnational arenas, emerging dance scholarship in the 1990s set the basis for the new millennium when publications focused on revising and recuperating dance histories, challenging the rhetoric of modernity, and accounting for histories of de/colonization. Some of these efforts were published in works such as Marta Savigliano's *Tango and the Political Economy of Passion* (1995), Thomas F. DeFrantz's *Dancing Revelations* (2004), Jacqueline Shea Murphy's *The People Have Never Stopped Dancing* (2007), and Priya Srinivasan's *Sweating Saris* (2011). The critical multiculturalism of the 1990s propelled the field of dance studies into the twenty-first century with new theoretical frameworks and interdisciplinary methodologies. Publications and pedagogical approaches in university programs centered dance as the primary analytical lens to study the vital role that dancing bodies played in the production of culture, the circulation of power, and the articulation of individual and collective subjectivities.

In the new millennium, scholars interested in dance continued discussing the relevance and direction of dance studies as part of ongoing endeavors to carve a space for the field as a legitimate and relevant (inter)discipline within the academy. While tracing intellectual genealogies between cultural studies and dance studies, Gay Morris suggested for the latter a way to avoid the "crisis" that cultural studies experienced at the dawn of the twenty-first century. Highlighting interdisciplinarity, Morris advocated for "reaching out beyond the confines of the academy to connect with others" and urged scholars interested in dance research to embrace the key aim of cultural studies: "to make a difference in the world" (2009, 97). Her proposition resonated with how Martin (1998) situated dance studies within a broader epistemological context, critical multiculturalism, as part of academia and the discipline's direct engagement with mobilizing politics and impacting the world. Morris's call to action also resonated with Manning's (2008) suggestion that the public humanities could be one of the directions dance studies could take, in this case, to reach to populations outside academia.

In addition to the public humanities, Manning identified the digital humanities and the globalized humanities as fertile arenas where the study of dance could continue to thrive into the twenty-first century. She thus implied the field's potential to make a difference in the world. However, she noted that the greatest challenge facing the field was how to create an infrastructure to expand dance research that would be produced not only by scholars associated with dance-related departments and institutions in the United States but also "across languages and nation-states" (Manning 2008, 7). In 2010 Janet O'Shea historicized the intellectual "roots" and "routes" of the field. She acknowledged that dance studies initiatives were "developing in exciting ways in [other] languages and places" but that for the purposes of her study, she would focus on some works produced in the United States, the UK, and former US and British colonies (O'Shea 2010, 2). On a similar international map, Jens Richard Giersdorf (2009) traced developments of dance studies as a disciplinary formation in East Germany, the UK, and the United States. More recently, Manning suggested that for dance studies, a "move toward the global" represented a force "incredibly powerful at the [current historical] moment" (quoted in Clayton et al. 2013, 22). Rebecca Schneider concurred by stating that "obviously building/initiating within the *North* American academy is only one wing. We need the Global South in the room(s)" (22–23, emphasis in the original). It is at this historical juncture that in order to remain relevant, dance studies—the individual and institutional bodies that constitute it—should mobilize forces and resources toward an expansive redrawing of the field's international map and thus create a more inclusive and critical globalized humanities. To make a difference in the world would imply a proactive relational ethics to face the neocolonial and imperial histories that mediate relations within as well as between the Global North and the Global South, including transnational histories of dance studies.

The Production and Documentation of
Mexican Dance *and/as* Nation: Setting the Stage for the CENIDID

The history of the CENIDID as a dance research center is intricately intertwined with Mexico's history of institutional nationalism.[5] In 1910, only two months after the state-sponsored celebrations for the centennial of Mexico's independence from Spain, an armed insurrection broke out seeking to remedy what some saw as the unfulfilled promises of the independence movement. Efforts to revolutionize the country's sociopolitical, economic, and cultural life mandated a revalorization of indigenous and popular cultures as official discourse in forging the emergent revolutionary nation. The combination of European and Mesoamerican bodies and cultures, with the tacit exclusion of Mexican populations of Asian and African descent, constituted a manufactured mestizo racial identity that has dominated cultural discourse and policy for most of the twentieth century and beyond.[6] The means of cultural production—the infrastructure for the formation of artists and artisans, the spaces for showcasing their art and crafts—were funded and managed by the government as part of forming a mestizo nation-state.

"Art" and "crafts" as practices and discursive categories served specific bourgeois and populist ideological purposes for the Mexican state and for individual artists and artisans in the development of different embodied mestizo subjectivities. On the one hand, art (literature, painting, muralism, music, etc.) served as a referent for cultural sophistication that for many enabled claims for inclusion within the rhetoric of "modernity." On the other hand, the craft of the artisan served as a marker of cultural uniqueness associated with the "traditional," an artifact valorized for its representational value but fixated in a colonized timeline that lagged behind modernity. In the realm of dance, I problematize the discursive polarity between cultural production associated with "modernity" and "tradition." I propose the concept of embodied mestizo modernisms in order to analyze the politics corporealized in combinations of ballet and modern dance with various forms of indigenous and popular expressive cultures.[7] In response to shifting national and international sociopolitical and economic contingencies, these collisions and fusions among disparate dance forms constituted powerful embodiments that the state attempted to employ in forging a national identity while individuals aligned with and/or resisted those official efforts.

Mestizaje as the foundational discourse for an emerging revolutionary country with modernizing aspirations found its fullest expression in the early 1920s during José Vasconcelos's influential short tenures, first as the rector of the National University (1920–21) and later as the minister of education (1921–24). Under his guidance, cultural production as instrument to construct a national identity became integral to Mexico's system of formal education. Vasconcelos's nationalist pedagogical agenda included a program of cultural missions that sent experts from agriculture, literacy, hygiene, and physical education across the country to rural and indigenous communities with the mandate to help improve daily conditions among Mexico's diverse ethnic groups. At the same time, cultural missionaries researched indigenous and popular expressive practices in order to create cultural repertoires that could be selectively integrated in the fabrication of mestizo nationalism, a project embraced in different ways by some writers, musicians, and muralists during the 1920s. I suggest that these cultural missions satisfied the revolutionary impetus for inclusivity motivated by modes of governmentality that attempted to revalorize the "traditional" indigenous while implementing the rhetorical project of modernization.

Reservoirs of diverse ways of knowing and being, resulting from ethnographic research done as part of cultural missions, informed the first institutional efforts in the professionalization of Mexican dancers and subsequent establishment of art and dance research centers such as the CENIDID. This nationalist impetus for knowledge production propelled the search for a genuinely Mexican dance form that could reflect the mestizo nature of the nation, local in character and ostensibly universal in its appeal. State-sponsored dance schools in Mexico City served as primary centers for the application of what was learned in regions throughout the country as dance artists produced embodied research through new mestizo dance practices. Hipólito Zybin, a Russian ballet dancer, led the first official effort in 1931 at the Escuela de Plástica Dinámica (School of Dynamic Plastic Art), where he proposed to combine the "traditional" and the "modern" (Ramos Villalobos 2009). Although variations of ballet technique had been around for centuries, it was thought of as an embodied technology for modernizing "ethnic" dance forms, and thus it was instituted as the foundational training regimen for dancers to perform Mexican-themed ballets. In a context of fervent nationalism, the extent to which one dance form was emphasized over the other by different people was often a source of tension. Starting in the late 1910s, government officials and artists debated to what extent overt Mexican cultural markers should be included or not in artistic productions in order to constitute legitimate modern art and thus to not compromise art's ostensible universal potential. That was certainly the case when Anna Pavlova danced Mexican folkloric dances using principles of ballet vocabulary and performing these dances *en pointe* during her first visit to Mexico City in 1919 (Reynoso 2014). After Zybin's short-lived school, the Escuela de Danza (School of Dance) was founded in 1932, and as dance research continued, so did the debates.

The School of Dance, later the Escuela Nacional de Danza (National School of Dance), continued these discussions while designing and implementing a variety of dance curricula and research initiatives.[8] When Nellie Campobello became the director of the school in 1937, she kept ballet as the foundational training regimen while valorizing popular and indigenous dance traditions as sources for composing choreographic works. In line with the cultural missions, Nellie and her sister Gloria, who taught classical ballet technique, conducted dance research in rural and indigenous communities. They published their findings in 1940 in a book titled *Ritmos indígenas de México* (Mexico's indigenous rhythms). In 1947 the founding of the state-sponsored Academia de la Danza Mexicana (Academy of Mexican Dance) provided a new space for reconfiguring embodied mestizo modernisms as a result of the advent of modern dance in Mexico in the early 1940s. Mexican dance artists who had studied and performed with Anna Sokolow and Waldeen Falkenstein, two modern dance choreographers from the United States who helped develop modern dance in Mexico, became directors and teachers of the academy, which promoted dance research first as a dance company and then as a school. For years to come, dance artists, critics, and government officials continued debating the relationship between folkloric, ballet, and modern dance techniques, as well as choreographic approaches in relation to ideologies of nationalism, universalism, and modernity.

Dance research in Mexico during the first half of the twentieth century focused primarily on knowledge production for purposes of training dance educators and dancers, as well as for the creation of cultural repertoires that served as sources for choreographic works. It would take a few more decades for this emphasis to shift as Mexico's official institutions created an infrastructure that supported research in the arts, including dance.

Institutional Mechanisms in the Production of a
National Culture: The CENIDID's First Dancing Steps

Complex networks of ideological state apparatuses mediated the production
and functions of ethnographic, embodied, and written knowledge about the
arts in general and dance in particular. As Mexican institutions worked to con-
solidate a manufactured mestizo national identity, an ideology of *indigenismo*
(indigenism) that idealized indigenous populations as "traditional" served as a
subtext while the nation dealt with the so-called Indian problem—how to
include the "noble savage" in a mestizo national imaginary with modern aspirations. This seemingly benevolent ideology continued to imagine and treat
indigenous populations as possessing essential traits that rendered them culturally unique but implicitly lagging behind on a Darwinian evolutionary continuum (Knight 1990). As a revolutionary nationalist project, the discursive
revalorization of the indigenous and popular cultures in the national imaginary, even as they were economically marginalized, led to the reconstitution of
prerevolution cultural institutions that had privileged European culture under
Porfirio Díaz's dictatorial regime (1876–1911).

The major arts organizing institution in the country, the Instituto Nacional
de Bellas Artes (INBA; National Institute of the Fine Arts), was founded in
1946. Its official mandate stipulated guidelines based on a conceptualization of
the arts as "the most sincere and vigorous expression of the national spirit. . . .
Art, in all its forms, is capable of the consolidation of Mexicanness" (Ley
Orgánica [Organic Law], quoted in Tortajada Quiroz 2008b, 183). These new
initiatives led to the creation of the Academy of Mexican Dance in 1947 and
culminated in 1952 with what became known as the golden age of Mexican
dance, a time when dancers and choreographers such as José Limón contributed to attempts at consolidating a modernized Mexican dance form that
sought to integrate the European American, the mestizo, and the indigenous.

After World War II, government institutions attempted to integrate, direct,
and often contain emerging artistic approaches that deviated from aesthetic
premises foundational to established creative practices, including those espoused
by artists associated with the state. Like others in various countries around the
world during the postwar era, many artists, intellectuals, and popular sectors
in Mexico rebelled against the dictates of official nationalism. In the early 1950s,
painters such as Rufino Tamayo and his main advocate, poet and art critic,
Octavio Paz, among others, challenged the Mexican muralist school as a pivotal
instrument associated with official nationalist discourse (Coffey 2012). Thus
Tamayo became a leading figure for a generation of artists who moved from
the didactical concerns some people saw as integral to the muralist movement

to more formalist experimentations. Echoing similar efforts in earlier decades, collectives such as Los Interioristas, later known as Nueva Presencia, during the early 1960s (Goldman 1981) advocated for a new art conceptualized against the "cactus curtain" (José Luis Cuevas, quoted in Tortajada Quiroz 2008b, 187).[9]

In attempts to restructure a more expansive postwar Mexican nationalism, President Adolfo López Mateos (1958–64) instituted the Subsecretaría de Asuntos Culturales (Subsecretariat of Cultural Affairs) as part of the Secretaría de Educación Pública (Secretariat of Public Education) in 1958. The new agency would organize the production, research, and documentation of cultural activities by various institutions. In the words of president López Mateos, these efforts aimed at the "invigoration of our most elevated culture in all its manifestations" (quoted in Tortajada Quiroz 2008b, 187). This integrative rhetoric was meant to include the postwar internationalist, the mestizo, and the indigenous. While the latter continued to represent a source of nationalist pride, indigenous cultural practices were taken as "raw" cultural material to be "refined" by artists using different approaches to articulating embodied mestizo modernisms. As repositories of "raw" cultural resources, state-sponsored music and theater research centers focused on organizing international events related to folkloric cultures, including the music Seminar of Folkloric Research, as the Subsecretariat of Cultural Affairs emphasized the recollection and documentation of popular and indigenous dances (Tortajada Quiroz 2008b, 188).

The discursively selective interest in indigenous and popular cultures as the "soul" of the Mexican (mestizo) revolutionary nation was also a source for continuous national renewal in times of conflict. The new middle classes of intellectuals, artists, and college students that arose in the 1960s represented a new active dissident force in Mexico City. On October 2, 1968, clashes between the Mexican military and college students, professors, and other sectors of the population culminated with the mass murder of primarily college students at the Plaza de las Tres Culturas (Plaza of the Three Cultures) in Tlatelolco, just ten days before the opening of the Olympic Games in the city. Two years later, Luis Echeverría Álvarez became Mexico's president (1970–76). He had been part of his predecessor Gustavo Díaz Ordaz's cabinet (1964–70), and not until years later was he accused and persecuted for his participation in the organization of the Tlatelolco massacre. President Echeverría strategically implemented a series of policies, including generous subsidies for universities, as part of the process to reconcile the nation and its "return to normalcy" (Aguilar Camín and Meyer 1993, 187). He also directed his attention to indigenous communities and popular sectors, I suggest, as one attempt among others to heal the national wound that Tlatelolco had left open and that he had helped inflict. In 1972 Echeverría instituted the Fondo Nacional para el Desarrollo de la Danza Popular Mexicana (FONADAN; National Fund for the Development of Mexican Popular Dance) at the Academy of Mexican Dance. Among the initiative's primary goals were the creation of a dance atlas that documented dance practices in regions across the country as well a calendar of festivities and ceremonies for which dance was a central component. This new endeavor also sought to promote choreographic and ethnographic research in order to expand existing archives that could be accessible to people interested in dance re-creation and academic publishing (Tortajada Quiroz 2008b, 188–89).

During the rest of the decade and into the presidency of José López Portillo (1976–82), other research centers for music and the visual arts were created. Toward the end of López Portillo's presidency in 1982, Mexico's external debt amounted to $80 billion. A concurrent decline in the oil market forced his administration to devalue its currency by 70 percent and to declare its inability to pay the debt as the government nationalized Mexico's banking system (Aguilar Camín and Meyer 1993). As it had in the past, even in the midst of political and economic crises, the Mexican state instituted projects to convey not only a sense of stability that included the co-optation of dissident factions but also displayed the country's continuous progression toward modernity. In this context of precariousness and the pursuit of progress, members of the dance community who had kept *juntando papeles* (gathering papers, i.e., legal documents, newspapers, personal letters, etc.) and any other materials they could archive and use as sources to historicize dance in Mexico and abroad, continued advocating for dance research (Tortajada Quiroz 2017). Their persistent commitment led president Miguel de la Madrid Hurtado to institute the Centro de Investigación y Documentación de la Danza (CIDD; Center for Dance Research and Documentation) upon taking office in 1983. After a series of transformations, including a period of integration with the Centro de Investigación Choreográfica (CICO; Center for Choreographic Research), the center for dance research became the CENIDID. The new institution became part of a group of four art research centers and four art schools located on the same grounds under the name Centro Nacional de las Artes (CENART; National Center for the Arts) in 1995.

In the midst of historical sociopolitical and economic upheavals Mexican governmental institutions attempted to support ongoing processes of cultural modernization. Within this tumultuous history of nation building and rhetoric of modernity, dance research in Mexico, its goals, and its methodologies, have developed as government administrators, dance artists, teachers, and scholars have debated divergent approaches to reimagining the production of official national culture in an increasingly globalized world.

Over Three Decades of Dance Research: The CENIDID's Reconfigurations of a Transnational Nationalist Context

Previous efforts to professionalize dance research in Mexico City culminated with the institutionalization of the Centro Nacional de Investigación, Documentación e Información de la Danza José Limón. It is a long name indeed. Each part of its name signals what the CENIDID does and how it does it. "Investigación" refers to the various research methods (i.e., ethnographic, archival, and choreographic) employed in the production of knowledge about dance. "Documentación" denotes primarily methods (physical and digital) for archiving and publishing knowledge and materials recuperated from the past or recently produced. "Información" reflects one of the major tenets of the democratizing impetus promulgated by the Mexican Revolution: to actively make information accessible to the widest audience possible, especially to those parties serving a pedagogical mandate throughout the country and abroad. Three departments, each devoted exclusively to research, archives, and diffusion of information, operate to accomplish the goals implied in the institution's name.

The selection of José Limón to personify the CENIDID undoubtedly honors the indelible influence that the famous Mexican American dancer-choreographer had in the development of the golden age of Mexican dance during his visit to Mexico City in the early 1950s. Also, within a nationalist imaginary, he could be seen as a heroic Mexican who crossed the border to a perceived and/or real imperial center and became there, against many odds, a sort of artistic Mexican reconqueror. In 1915, escaping the turbulence of the Mexican Revolution, Limón's family immigrated to the United States when he was seven years old. His return to Mexico as a consolidated modern dance artist gained him the status of honorary (readopted) Mexican in the field of dance. As Margarita Tortajada Quiroz asserts, "Limón is still the pride and joy of Mexican dance" (2008a, 148). His name certainly embodies the decades-old national project of cultivating a mestizo national dance form that could be culturally distinctive and universal in its appeal, a dance form that the CENIDID has endeavored to understand, document, and share. I would add that perhaps Limón secured such an iconic status in Mexico, for he represented the transnational embodiment of contemporary mestizo modernity: the combination of the Indigenous, the mestizo, and the Estadounidense (US national). It is precisely this transnational mestizo embodiment, what it enables and what it complicates, that characterizes the crisscrossing, collisions, and fusions of dance studies histories as its institutional and individual bodies move on a more expansive transnational map.

Since its inception, including in its founding directorship, the CENIDID's efforts have been constituted directly and indirectly by a generative transnationalism. Initially, dancers and choreographers conducted embodied research as they kept "gathering papers" and were eventually joined by scholars with academic training in various disciplines in the humanities and the social sciences. The center's roster of researchers, currently thirty, has always included scholars and dance artists who have migrated from and/or have received academic education and/or dance training in the United States, Canada, and countries in Latin America and Europe. I would suggest that the CENIDID reflects diverse transnational genealogies that have always coalesced to constitute Mexican history, from colonization to the independence movement, from the Mexican Revolution to today. The history of Mexican nationalism—including the role dance forms such as ballet, modern dance, folkloric dance, and popular dance have played in its construction—has been shaped by networks of interconnectivity, flows of people and ideas from various countries around the globe as well as the collaborative and contentious exchanges such encounters inspire.

From the beginning, this transnational nationalism represented the adaptation of multiple influences to the specificity of approaches CENIDID researchers employ within the geopolitical localities and positionalities they inhabit. Archivization, the center's initial emphasis, was complemented by the production of publications that employed distinctive methodologies and theories to address a variety of interests. During the 1980s, publications began to historicize various dance forms in the country. In 1984 a fifty-three-page book written in Spanish, English, and French contextualized the development of concert dance from 1934 to 1959. In 1986 two volumes recorded fifty years of national and international dance at the Palace of Fine Arts in Mexico City. The 1990s saw more biographies of key figures in the development of Mexican dance both in books and in a series of *cuadernos* (booklets) that started in the mid-1980s.

Transitioning from the 1990s to the new millennium, CENIDID monographs also included structuralist and poststructuralist theoretical frameworks. Some works analyzed and theorized about dance and its relation to the production of culture, power, and identities. Amparo Sevilla (1990) employed concepts on hegemony and subalternity to examine the relationship between various Mexican dance forms and social classes. Hilda Islas (1995) looked at how dance training related to constructions of the body and different forms of power. Tortajada Quiroz (1995) historicized relationships between dance and institutional power during the first fifty years of postrevolutionary Mexican history.

Others have approached the study of dance from literary perspectives (Bidault de la Calle 2003; Ponce 2010) and philosophy (Bastien van der Meer 2015). The diversity of approaches and interests characteristic of the CENIDID researchers has reflected their own academic and/or artistic trajectories in various disciplines and dance forms inside and outside Mexico.

The CENIDID has continuously produced either by itself or in collaboration with other national and international organizations conferences related to dance production, research, and pedagogy. In 1987 two volumes, one in Spanish and one in English, compiled presentations made as part of the center's International Conference on Dance Research. The CENIDID's organization of dance scholarship exchanges has also included the practice of different dance forms. Recently, the center hosted the festival-conference Urban Dance Generation Hip Hop 2016. The event brought together hip hop artists and scholars from across Mexico, Latin America, the United States, and Korea. It was, in fact, in response to one of these transnational collaborations, Diálogos México: Encuentro Latinoamericano de Creadores de Danza Contemporánea (Mexico Dialogues: Gathering of Latin American Contemporary Dance Creators), co-organized by the CENIDID and other international institutions in 2008 that the idea for the Center's master's degree came into being.

In order to systematize the professionalization of dance researchers in the country, the CENIDID inaugurated in 2011 the *maestría en investigación de la danza*, the first master's degree program in dance studies in Latin America. It is a two-year, low-residency program where students take online courses and meet for intensive workshops on three occasions. The program admits between fifteen and twenty-five students who have completed a bachelor's degree in any discipline in the social sciences, the humanities, dance performance, choreography, or education. Students are selected based on a proposed project for which they receive theoretical and analytical tools and the support of a thesis committee in order to develop their final research project. Depending on their interests, student can concentrate in one of four areas: (1) theories and strategies for research in dance pedagogy; (2) modes and processes for dance making and production; (3) social science and humanities dance research employing epistemological and methodological perspectives from cultural studies, philosophy, sociology, anthropology, semiotics, and hermeneutics; or (4) dance criticism, memory, history, and historicity. Each year, a small group of dance scholars from across Mexico, the United States, Latin America, and Europe are invited to lecture.[10] Most faculty members at the CENIDID speak and/or read English. An advanced level of proficiency in this language is required for admission to the master's degree program, which has admitted students from countries in Latin America and Europe.[11]

In its composition, history, and mission, the CENIDID embodies a transnational nationalism that reflects how Mexican projects of modernization have been constituted at different moments in the country's history. The research center also demonstrates an active willingness to reach out and establish transnational relationships in order to promote the flow and exchange of bodies and ideas.[12]

Conclusion

With all that it enables through national and transnational efforts, the CENIDID is an official organ of an institutional national body. As such, the center's constitution, diverse operations, goals, and methods are mediated by nationalist mandates, institutional bureaucracy, and internal quarrels. As part of a state apparatus, the research institution participates, at times explicitly and at times tacitly, in official processes of governmentality. However, if one can think of this indirect participation in modes of governance as a form of nationalist colonization, I would argue that institutions like the CENIDID also enable resistances to historical forms of transnational colonization and imperialism. In other words, while the nation-state, nationalism, and the institutions that constitute them might be thought of as "anachronistic," they are certainly not "dead" in the era of neoliberal transnationalism. In fact, the nation-state and nationalist movements seem to be alive and well, perhaps as alive as the nuclear threat many thought had totally died with the so-called end of the Cold War. Perhaps the question is not whether the nation-state and nationalist movements have died or not but rather how they reconstitute themselves at different moments in history as colonizing forces and, in some circumstances, as anti-colonial or decolonizing strategies. How can we account for the tension between the nation-state's biopolitical mechanisms of population control on the one hand, and on the other hand the nation-state's potential to either restrain or unleash the exploitative violence by neoliberal transnational corporations that will neither naturally regulate themselves nor fulfill the promise of trickling down their profitability, as we have seen in recent history? I suggest that the concept of transnational nationalism might enable the analysis of the simultaneity of these de/colonizing processes. It can help us realize and analyze how the workings of totalizing and resistive forms of power constitute individual subjects, as well as the collective imaginaries that align and/or clash with attempts to produce subordinate regions and populations, nationally and transnationally.

"Who needs whom?" is the question my colonized-colonizing subjectivity begs me to ask while imagining more expansive transnational exchanges if the field of dance studies is to remain relevant and make a difference in the world. Who should make the initial effort? Who should reach out? Who should make the investment of time and resources? What would be gained by the different parties involved? Our specific positionalities within histories of international unequal power relations might lead some of us to seemingly obvious responses to these questions. However, not engaging in the process of finding answers through actual encounters, with all the tensions and failures these efforts might entail, would continue perpetuating those colonized-colonizing histories and their dominant epistemological, geopolitical, and geographical cartographies.

As I have discussed above, the CENIDID's sustained efforts embody its own struggles to negotiate the nationalist legacies under which it was conceived during the twentieth century, as well as the desire to be a catalyst in the transnational flow and exchange of bodies and ideas shaping the center's existence in the twenty-first century. Proactive attempts to understand the emergence of dance studies within a variety of transnational nationalist contexts can enable an epistemological reimagining of countries such as Mexico not as "culturally backward" nation-states fixated within rigid geographical areas but as porously dynamic interconnected geopolitical spaces with their own histories of alternative modernities. Active willingness to create opportunities for face-to-face encounters and exchanges of ideas and resources (human and material) may help us decolonize our histories of international relations in order to decenter the underlying colonial logic of forward and backward modernities between the Global North and the Global South. I hope this essay contributes to ongoing conversations that can lead us to cultivate the willingness necessary to unsettle the Europe/United States dyad and thus redraw a more expansive international map reflective of ongoing transnational histories of the field.

The decolonizing relational ethics of these efforts may demand accepting the fact that the interconnected globalized world (of dance studies) does not exist exclusively in English and in universities. Thus *we* might need to fracture the hegemony of English as the lingua franca and the university as the legitimizing entity. For those working in university settings, qualified personnel should be assigned to review merit and tenure files that include productivity in languages other than English as the legitimate result of collaborations with international researchers and other populations inside and outside institutions of higher education. The broadening of a transnational map for dance studies may require relocating events, promoting alternative collaborative exchanges, and revalorizing a more diverse repertoire of epistemological and methodological paradigms. Perhaps only then can dance studies as an expansive transnational field make a difference by moving us toward a critical globalized humanities that can reconstitute the ever-changing and often divisive geographical, geopolitical, and academic worlds in which we thrive and relate to one another as individuals and collectives.

Notes

All translations from Spanish are my own.

1. Since 2009 I have participated in multiple events and developed professional relationships with scholars at the CENIDID, where I recently completed a MEXUS-CONACYT one-year research residency. For additional critical feedback for this chapter, I am grateful to CENIDID dance historians, Dolores Ponce and Margarita Tortajada Quiroz.

2. I will eventually translate this text into Spanish.

3. This brief historical genealogy intends to signal some key shifts in the development of dance studies in Europe and the United States. It is also strategically selective in its function of constructing my argument. For more detailed historical accounts, see the works cited section.

4. For an account of African American dance artists' and writers' work during the first half of the twentieth century, see Manning (2004).

5. For a survey of dance research activities during the center's first decade, see Stark and Tortajada Quiroz (1994).

6. For analyses of the relationship between dance and Afro-Mexicans in the context of nation formation in Mexico, see Gonzalez (2010).

7. "Embodied mestizo modernisms" is a concept I develop more fully in my book project.

8. For a detailed description and analysis of curriculum development and implementation in various educational settings in Mexico City between 1919 and 1945, see Ramos Villalobos (2009).

9. In this phrase, "cactus" alludes to a stereotypical form of nationalism that evokes the legend of the Aztecs' arrival to Tenochtitlan, where they found the sign that prompted them to build the city that later became Mexico City: an eagle resting on a cactus while devouring a snake. This same symbol is displayed on the current Mexican flag.

10. From the United States, for instance, Randy Martin lectured for the first cohort. Susan Foster has participated via Skype at least once.

11. For more details about the CENIDID's master's degree program, see http://www.cenididanza.bellasartes.gob.mx/.

12. In a subsequent work, I will address relatively independent initiatives that are currently decentralizing the CENIDID as the primary national center for dance research in Mexico.

Works Cited

Aguilar Camín, Héctor, and Lorenzo Meyer. 1993. *In the Shadow of the Mexican Revolution: Contemporary Mexican History, 1910–1989*. Translated by Luis Alberto Fierro. Austin: University of Texas Press.

Bastien van der Meer, Kena. 2015. *Filosofía y danza*. Mexico City: CENIDID Danza / INBA / Conaculta.

Bidault de la Calle, Sophie. 2003. *Nellie Campobello: Una escritura salida del cuerpo*. Mexico City: CENIDID Danza / INBA / Conaculta.

Braidotti, Rosi, and Paul Gilroy. 2016. Introduction to *Conflicting Humanities*, edited by Rosi Braidotti and Paul Gilroy, 1–8. London: Bloomsbury Academic.

Bryson, Norman. 1997. "Cultural Studies and Dance History." In *Meaning in Motion: New Cultural Studies of Dance*, edited by Jane C. Desmond, 55–57. Durham, NC: Duke University Press.

Clayton, Michelle, Mark Franko, Nadine George-Graves, André Lepecki, Susan Manning, Janice Rose, and Rebecca Schneider. 2013. "Inside/Beside Dance Studies: A Conversation, Mellon Dance Studies in/and the Humanities." Edited by Noémie Bernier-Solomon. Transcribed by Stefanie Miller. *Dance Research Journal* 45 (3): 5–28.

Coffey, Mary K. 2012. *How a Revolutionary Art Became Official Culture: Murals, Museums, and the Mexican State*. Durham, NC: Duke University Press.

DeFrantz, Thomas. 2004. *Dancing Revelations: Alvin Ailey's Embodiment of African American Culture*. New York: Oxford University Press.

Desmond, Jane C. 1997. "Embodying Difference: Issues in Dance and Cultural Studies." In *Meaning in Motion: New Cultural Studies of Dance*, edited by Jane C. Desmond, 29–54. Durham, NC: Duke University Press.

Foster, Susan Leigh. 1986. *Reading Dancing: Bodies and Subjects in Contemporary American Dance*. Berkeley: University of California Press.

Franko, Mark. 1986. *The Dancing Body in Renaissance Choreography (c. 1416–1589)*. Birmingham: Summa Publications.

Giersdorf, Jens Richard. 2009. "Dance Studies in the International Academy: Genealogy of a Disciplinary Formation." *Dance Research Journal* 41 (1): 23–44.

Goldman, Shifra. 1981. *Contemporary Mexican Painting in a Time of Change*. Austin: University of Texas Press.

Gonzalez, Anita. 2010. *Afro-Mexico: Dancing between Myth and Reality*. Austin: University of Texas Press.

Islas, Hilda. 1995. *Tecnologías corporales: Danza, cuerpo e historia*. Mexico City: CENIDID Danza / INBA / Conaculta.

Knight, Alan. 1990. "Racism, Revolution, and Indigenismo." In *The Idea of Race in the Latin America, 1870–1940*, edited by Richard Graham, 71–114. Austin: University of Texas Press.

Koritz, Amy. 1996. "Re/Moving Boundaries: From Dance History to Cultural Studies." In *Moving Words, Re-writing Dance*, edited by Gay Morris, 88–103. London: Routledge.

Manning, Susan. 1993. *Ecstasy and the Demon: Feminism and Nationalism in the Dances of Mary Wigman*. Berkeley: University of California Press.

———. 2004. *Modern Dance, Negro Dance: Race in Motion*. Minneapolis: University of Minnesota Press.

———. 2008. "Looking Back Moving Forward." In *Looking Back/Moving Forward: International Symposium on Dance Research. Proceedings*, 1–9. Society of Dance History Scholars Conference: Skidmore College.

Martin, Randy. 1998. *Critical Moves: Dance Studies in Theory and Politics*. Durham, NC: Duke University Press.

Morris, Gay. 2009. "Dance Studies / Cultural Studies." *Dance Research Journal* 41 (1): 82–100.

Novack, Cynthia J. 1990. *Sharing the Dance: Contact Improvisation and American Culture*. Madison: University of Wisconsin Press.

O'Shea, Janet. 2010. "Roots/Routes of Dance Studies." In *The Routledge Dance Studies Reader*, edited by Alexandra Carter and Janet O'Shea, 1–15. 2nd ed. London: Routledge, Taylor & Francis Group.

Ponce, Dolores. 2010. *Danza y literatura, ¿que relación?* Mexico City: CENIDID Danza / INBA / Conaculta.

Ramos Villalobos, Roxana Guadalupe. 2009. *Una mirada a la formación dancística mexicana (ca. 1919–1945)*. Mexico City: INBA / Centro de Investigación, Documentación e Información de la Danza José Limón.

Reynoso, Jose L. 2014. "Choreographing Modern Mexico: Anna Pavlova in Mexico City (1919)." *Modernist Cultures* 9 (1): 80–98.

Ross, Janice. 2000. *Moving Lessons: Margaret H'Doubler and the Beginnings of Dance in American Education*. Madison: University of Wisconsin Press.

Savigliano, Marta. 1995. *Tango and the Political Economy of Passion*. Boulder, CO: Westview Press.

Sevilla, Amparo. 1990. *Danza, cultura y classes sociales*. Mexico City: CENIDID Danza / INBA / Conaculta.

Shea Murphy, Jacqueline. 2007. *The People Have Never Stopped Dancing: Native American Modern Dance Histories*. Minneapolis: University of Minnesota Press.

Srinivasan, Priya. 2012. *Sweating Saris: Indian Dance as Transnational Labor*. Philadelphia: Temple University Press.

Stark, Alan, and Margarita Tortajada Quiroz. 1994. "Dance Research in Mexico." *Research in Dance Journal* 26 (2): 73–78.

Tortajada Quiroz, Margarita. 1995. *Danza y poder*. Mexico City: CENIDID Danza / INBA / Conaculta.

———. 2008a. "José Limón and La Malinche in Mexico: A Chicano Artist Returns Home." In *José Limón and La Malinche: The Dancer and the Dance*, edited by Patricia Seed, 119–53. Austin: University of Texas Press.

———. 2008b. "La investigación artística mexicana en el siglo XX: La experiencia oficial del Departamento de Bellas Artes y del Instituto Nacional de Bellas Artes." *Cultura y Representaciones Sociales, Contribuciones: El INBA en México* 2 (4): 169–96.

———. 2017. Interview with the author. Mexico City, June 5.

Contributors

DANIEL CALLAHAN is an assistant professor of music at Boston College. His first book project, "The Dancer from the Music," explores the use of music in American modern dance. His article on John Cage and Merce Cunningham, "The Gay Divorce of Music and Dance," appears in the *Journal of the American Musicological Society*. He previously taught at Columbia University, where he received his PhD, and the University of Chicago, where he was a Mellon Postdoctoral Fellow. He will work on his second book project, *Conducting Oneself*, exploring the choreographies and identities of orchestra conductors who challenge the maestro stereotype as a 2019–20 fellow at the Radcliffe Institute of Advanced Study at Harvard University.

RACHEL CARRICO'S research explores the aesthetic, political, and social histories of second lining, an improvisational dance form rooted in New Orleans's African diaspora parading traditions. She holds a PhD in critical dance studies from the University of California, Riverside, and an MA in performance studies from NYU. In 2015–16 she was the Mellon Postdoctoral Fellow in Dance Studies in/and the Humanities at Stanford University's Department of Theater and Performance Studies and has taught in dance and anthropology departments at Colorado College, Reed College, and the University of Oregon.

REBECCA CHALEFF is a dance scholar, performer, and dramaturge. Her research mobilizes dance studies, queer theory, and critical race theory to examine how choreographies are transmitted between and across bodies. Her book manuscript de-idealizes reperformance to explore the dual possibilities of exposure and occlusion in reconstructive projects that craft durable

histories of dance. Rebecca is an assistant professor in the Department of
Theatre and Dance at the University of California, San Diego.

CLARE CROFT is a dance historian, theorist, and sometime dramaturge and
curator. She is the author of *Dancers as Diplomats: American Choreography in
Cultural Exchange* (2015) and the editor and curator of *Queer Dance:
Meanings and Makings* (2017). She is an associate professor at the University
of Michigan.

JOANNA DEE DAS is an assistant professor of dance at Washington
University in St. Louis and the author of *Katherine Dunham: Dance and the
African Diaspora* (2017), which won the 2018 de la Torre Bueno First Book
Award from the Dance Studies Association. She is also the recipient of a
2019–20 ACLS Fellowship. Her research interests include dance in the
African diaspora, the politics of performance, and musical theater.

KATHRYN DICKASON is a postdoctoral fellow at the University of Southern
California. She received her PhD in religious studies from Stanford
University and lectured for the Theatre and Dance Department at Santa
Clara University. Her research explores medieval Christianity in Western
Europe. Her past and forthcoming publications examine ritual, performance,
dance, gender, and literature of the Middle Ages. Currently she is preparing a
book manuscript entitled "Ringleaders of Redemption: How Medieval
Dance Became Sacred."

VICTORIA FORTUNA is an assistant professor of dance at Reed College in
Portland, Oregon. Her research interests include Latin American concert
dance, dance as a mode of political and community organization, and
cultural histories of dance in transnational perspective. Her book, *Moving
Otherwise: Dance, Violence, and Memory in Buenos Aires* (2019), examines the
relationship between contemporary dance practices and histories of political
and economic violence in Buenos Aires from the mid-1960s to the mid-
2010s. Victoria holds a BA from Brown University and a PhD in
performance studies from Northwestern University.

ALANA GERECKE is a settler dance artist and Banting Postdoctoral Fellow
(Department of Theatre, York University) whose academic and artistic
research practices cohere around embodied assembly. She recently coedited a
special issue of *Canadian Theatre Review* exploring "Choreographies of
Assembly" (2018) and coedited a dance studies special issue of *Performance*

Matters that explores the productive possibilities of backspace (2019). Her book project, *Moving Publics: Dance, Public Space, and Orientation*, examines the social and spatial lives of both subtle and virtuosic choreographies set in public spaces in Canada.

AMANDA JANE GRAHAM is associate director of engagement at Carolina Performing Arts, University of North Carolina at Chapel Hill. She is a former visiting professor of media and society at Hobart and William Smith Colleges and an Andrew Mellon Postdoctoral Fellow in Dance Studies at Northwestern University. Her scholarly articles on dance, art, and media have appeared in *Art Journal, Dance Chronicle*, and *ASAP/J*. Graham's current book project investigates dance's ambivalent history with art museums from 1930 to the present.

JASMINE ELIZABETH JOHNSON is an assistant professor of Africana Studies at the University of Pennsylvania. A Ford Foundation Diversity Pre- and Post-Doctoral Fellow, she earned her PhD in African diaspora studies at the University of California, Berkeley. She writes about dance, performance, gender, and diaspora.

ADANNA KAI JONES is an assistant professor of dance and critical dance studies in the Theater and Dance Department at Bowdoin College. Jones is a dancer/choreographer/scholar whose general research focuses on Caribbean dance and identity politics within the diaspora. Her current book project uses multi-sited, transnational ethnography to track the ways in which Caribbean choreographers and dancers complicate US-based constructions of black identity.

LAURA KARREMAN is an assistant professor in the Department of Media and Culture Studies at Utrecht University, the Netherlands, where she teaches in the MA program Contemporary Theatre, Dance and Dramaturgy and the BA program Media and Culture. She researches the role of embodied knowledge in dance transmission practices. Her PhD dissertation, "The Motion Capture Imaginary: Digital Renderings of Dance Knowledge" (2017), examines how dancing bodies are reimagined through emerging practices and applications involving motion capture and other digital capturing technologies.

ANUSHA KEDHAR is an assistant professor of critical dance studies at the University of California, Riverside. Her research interests include dance, labor, and global political economy; yoga in India and the Indian diaspora;

and the performance of eroticism and sexuality in Indian dance. Her current book project, *Flexible Bodies: British South Asian Dancers in the Age of Neoliberalism*, examines South Asian dance and dancers in Britain at the nexus of neoliberalism and postcoloniality. Kedhar's scholarly writing has been published in *Dance Research Journal, The Feminist Wire*, and *The New York Times*. Kedhar is also an established *bharata natyam* dancer and choreographer and has performed and collaborated with various dance companies and choreographers in the US, UK, and Europe. Her choreography has been presented in London, Malta, Los Angeles, Colorado, and New York.

HANNAH KOSSTRIN is a dance historian whose work engages dance, Jewish, and gender studies, and modes of movement analysis. At The Ohio State University she is an associate professor in the Department of Dance and affiliated with the Melton Center for Jewish Studies and the Center for Slavic and East European Studies. She is the author of *Honest Bodies: Revolutionary Modernism in the Dances of Anna Sokolow* (2017), which was awarded Finalist (second place) for the Jordan Schnitzer Book Award from the Association for Jewish Studies.

LIZZIE LEOPOLD is an independent scholar and executive director of the Dance Studies Association, currently a lecturer at the University of Chicago and working on the film archives of midcentury modern dance pioneer Sybil Shearer. She received an interdisciplinary PhD in theater and drama from Northwestern University. Her research focuses on the political economy of choreographic production and circulation, asking questions about the intersection of cultural and financial value. Her essays have been published in *Perspectives on American Dance* and *Oxford Handbook to Shakespeare and Dance*. Leopold is also a choreographer and the director of Chicago-based modern dance company the Leopold Group.

GILLIAN LIPTON is a writer of dance history and theory as well as a performer. With Ford Foundation support, she worked on a multiyear initiative with Arthur Mitchell to develop his archive and related performance projects. A lecturer in critical dance studies at Yale University, and previously at Barnard and Queens College (CUNY), Lipton holds a PhD in performance studies from New York University. She is the recipient of a research fellowship from the Center for Ballet and the Arts (NYU). As a performer, she has collaborated on several exhibitions with the Museum of Modern Art in New York.

SUSAN MANNING is Herman and Beulah Pearce Miller Research Professor in English, Theatre, and Performance Studies at Northwestern University. She is the author of *Ecstasy and the Demon: The Dances of Mary Wigman* (1993, 2nd ed. 2006) and *Modern Dance, Negro Dance: Race in Motion* (2003), curator of *Danses noires/blanche Amèrique* (2008), dramaturge of Reggie Wilson's 2013 work *Moses(es)*, and coeditor of *New German Dance Studies* (2012) and *Routledge Encyclopedia of Modernist Dance* (2020).

ROYONA MITRA is a reader in dance and performance cultures at Brunel University London and the author of *Akram Khan: Dancing New Interculturalism* (2015), which was awarded the 2017 de la Torre Bueno First Book Award by the Dance Studies Association. Her research addresses intersectionalities between bodies, race, gender, sexuality, and postcoloniality in performance, and she contributes to the fields of intercultural performance, diaspora and dance, contemporary South Asian dance, and dance theater.

ARIEL OSTERWEIS earned her PhD in performance studies at the University of California, Berkeley, and is on faculty at the Sharon Disney Lund School of Dance at CalArts. Her book, *Body Impossible: Desmond Richardson and the Politics of Virtuosity*, is forthcoming. She is developing her next monograph, *Prophylactic Aesthetics: Latex, Spandex, and Sexual Anxieties Performed*, as well as a book of interviews called *Disavowing Virtuosity, Performing Aspiration: Dance and Performance Interviews*. Her publications appear in *Dance Research Journal, TDR / The Drama Review, Women and Performance, e-misférica, Theatre Survey, The Oxford Handbook of Dance and the Popular Screen* (2014), and *Choreographies of 21st Century Wars* (2016). Osterweis has danced with Complexions Contemporary Ballet, Mia Michaels R.A.W., and Heidi Latsky, has choreographed, and has served as dramaturge for John Jasperse and Narcissister.

VK PRESTON is an assistant professor at the Centre for Drama, Theatre and Performance Studies and member of the executive at the Institute for Dance Studies at the University of Toronto. She holds a PhD from Stanford University's Department of Theater and Performance Studies and writes on both early modern and contemporary dance theory and historiography. Her work appears in *TDR / The Drama Review, The Oxford Handbook of Dance and Reenactment, The Oxford Handbook of Dance and Theatre, Performance Research, Theatre Journal*, and *Imagined Theatres: Writing for a Theoretical Stage*.

HEATHER RASTOVAC-AKBARZADEH is a scholar-practitioner who researches the racialized and gendered economies of Iranian performance in transnational art markets and among diasporic audiences in North America and Western Europe. She analyzes how diasporic Iranian performance impacts and is impacted by Euro-American (neo)liberal discourses on freedom, immigration, citizenship, and the global "War on Terror." Rastovac-Akbarzadeh earned her PhD in performance studies from the University of California, Berkeley, with a designated emphasis in women, gender, and sexuality. She was the 2016–18 Mellon Postdoctoral Fellow in Dance Studies in/and the Humanities at Stanford University and a 2018–20 University of California Chancellor's Postdoctoral Fellow at the University of California, Davis.

JOSE L. REYNOSO, dance scholar, choreographer, and performer, is an assistant professor of critical dance studies at the University of California, Riverside. His research emphasizes the role corporeality in general and dance in particular play in the development of racial and social formations as they intersect with gender and sexual expressions. He examines how these factors relate to ideological aspects in the production of artistic discourse and subjectivities within contexts of colonial legacies and decolonial possibilities. He employs these approaches in his book project, *Mestizo and Other Modernities: Dance and Politics in the Construction of Modern Mexico(s)*, an analysis of the ways Mexican dance forms, combined with ballet and modern dance idioms, aligned with and resisted the state's rhetoric of modernity and nationalism before and after the 1910 Mexican Revolution.

JANICE ROSS is a professor in the Theatre and Performance Studies Department at Stanford University. She is the author of four books: *Like A Bomb Going Off: Leonid Yakobson and Ballet as Resistance in Soviet Russia* (2015), *San Francisco Ballet at 75* (2007), *Anna Halprin: Experience as Dance* (2007), and *Moving Lessons: Margaret H'Doubler and The Beginning of Dance in American Education* (2000).

REBECCA SCHNEIDER is a professor of performance studies in the Department of Theatre Arts and Performance Studies at Brown University. She is the author of *The Explicit Body in Performance* (1997), *Performing Remains: Art and War in Times of Theatrical Reenactment* (2011), *Theatre & History* (2014), *Remain* (with Jussi Parikka, 2019), and more than fifty essays in the field. She began her career as a dancer in New York. She has also collaborated as a "performing theorist" with dancers and choreographers such as Xavier Leroy, Marten Spangberg, Alice Chaucat, Jerome Bel, and Tino Seghal at such sites as the British Museum in London, the Mobile Academy in Berlin, the Tanzquartier in Vienna, and the Gulbenkian in Lisbon.

ELIZABETH SCHWALL earned her PhD in history from Columbia University and has taught at the University of California, Berkeley, and Stanford University. She has been a Mellon Postdoctoral Fellow in Dance Studies in/and the Humanities at Northwestern University and a fellow at the Center for Ballet and the Arts at New York University. Her current book project examines Cuban dance and politics from 1930 to 1990. Her research has appeared in the journals *Hispanic American Historical Review*, *Dance Chronicle*, *Cuban Studies*, and *Studies in Musical Theatre*, as well as in the edited volume *The Revolution from Within: Cuba, 1959–1980* (2019).

MELISSA TEMPLETON is a lecturer of dance at the University of Nebraska–Lincoln. Her research combines critical race theory and Canadian dance studies to examine African diaspora dance practices in Montreal. She completed her PhD at the University of California, Riverside, and was the recipient of a Social Sciences and Humanities Research Council Doctoral Fellowship. Her writing has appeared in *Los Angeles Review of Books* and *Dance Research Journal*.

GIULIA VITTORI is an artist-scholar who completed her PhD in theater and performance studies from Stanford University and earned her bachelor's and master's degrees in theater history at Università Ca' Foscari, Venice. She studies the embodiment of the image in contemporary Western dance and theater using interdisciplinary approaches from the visual arts and philosophy. She has presented her work at PSI, Mellon Dance Studies, and Dance Studies Association and has published in American and Italian academic journals. With "A Meditation on Stillness: Ann Carlson's *Picture Jasper Ridge*," she won the TDR 2015 Student Essay Contest. Vittori directs and choreographs experimental performance.

SARAH WILBUR is a cross-sector choreographer and Assistant Professor of the Practice of Dance at Duke University, where she is collaboratively engaged in developing a new dance MFA that takes checkered patterns of arts recognition and resourcing strongly into account. Sarah's artistic and scholarly research seeks parity between dances that are performed and aspects of dance making that are suppressed or ignored. Her current book looks at how US federal dance funding criteria makes artists move and organize their work. From 2016 to 2018 Sarah was the Mellon Postdoctoral Fellow in Dance Studies in/and the Humanities at Brown University.

EMILY E. WILCOX is an associate professor of modern Chinese studies in the Department of Asian Languages and Cultures at the University of Michigan. She specializes in Asian performance, focusing on intersections among movement, aesthetics, and politics. Her first book, *Revolutionary Bodies: Chinese Dance and the Socialist Legacy*, was published in 2018.

HENTYLE YAPP is an assistant professor at New York University in the Department of Art and Public Policy and is also affiliated with Performance Studies, Comparative Literature, the Disability Council, and Asian/Pacific/ American Institute. He has published articles in *American Quarterly*, *GLQ: A Journal of Lesbian and Gay Studies*, *Journal of Visual Culture*, and *Verge: Studies in Global Asias*.

NATALIE ZERVOU is an assistant professor in the Dance Department at the University of Wisconsin–Madison. She holds a PhD in critical dance studies from the University of California, Riverside, and her research focuses on contemporary dance in Greece during the sociopolitical and economic crisis, with an emphasis on the ways that dancing bodies negotiate national identity construction in this fluctuating landscape. She has published articles in *CHOROS*, *RiDE: Research in Drama Education*, *TDR / The Drama Review*, *Dancer Citizen*, and *Dance Research Journal*.

Index

Page numbers in *italics* indicate illustrations.

549

STUDIES IN DANCE HISTORY

Published under the auspices of the Dance Studies Association